W9-BNI-330

lonely planet

British Columbia

Julie Fanselow
Debra Miller

LONELY PLANET PUBLICATIONS
Melbourne • Oakland • London • Paris

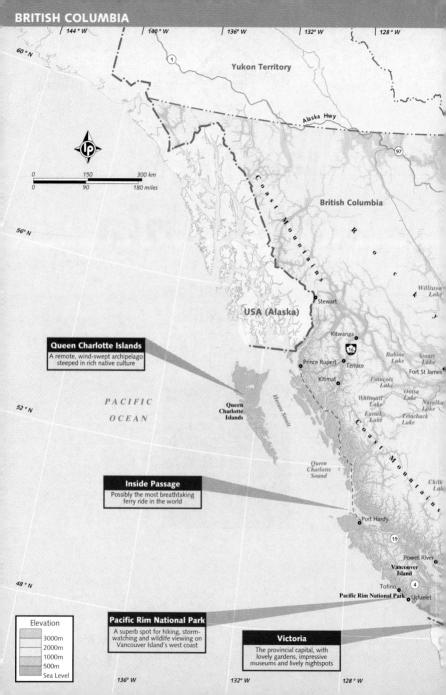

BRITISH COLUMBIA

60° N

144° W 140° W 136° W 132° W 128° W

Yukon Territory

Alaska Hwy

97

British Columbia

0   150   300 km
0   90   180 miles

Coast Mountains

R

o

c

Williston
Lake

Stewart

56° N

USA (Alaska)

Kitwanga

16

Queen Charlotte Islands
A remote, wind-swept archipelago
steeped in rich native culture

Prince Rupert   Terrace

Babine
Lake

Stuart
Lake

Fort St James

Kitimat

François
Lake

PACIFIC

OCEAN

Hecate Strait

Queen
Charlotte
Islands

Whitesail
Lake

Ootsa
Lake

Natalku
Lake

Eutsuk
Lake

Tetachuck
Lake

52° N

Queen
Charlotte
Sound

Coast Mountains

Chilk
Lak

Inside Passage
Possibly the most breathtaking
ferry ride in the world

Port Hardy

19

Powell River

48° N

**Vancouver
Island**

Tofino

4

Pacific Rim National Park

Ucluelet

Elevation	
	3000m
	2000m
	1000m
	500m
	Sea Level

Pacific Rim National Park
A superb spot for hiking, storm-
watching and wildlife viewing on
Vancouver Island's west coast

Victoria
The provincial capital, with
lovely gardens, impressive
museums and lively nightspots

136° W 132° W 128° W

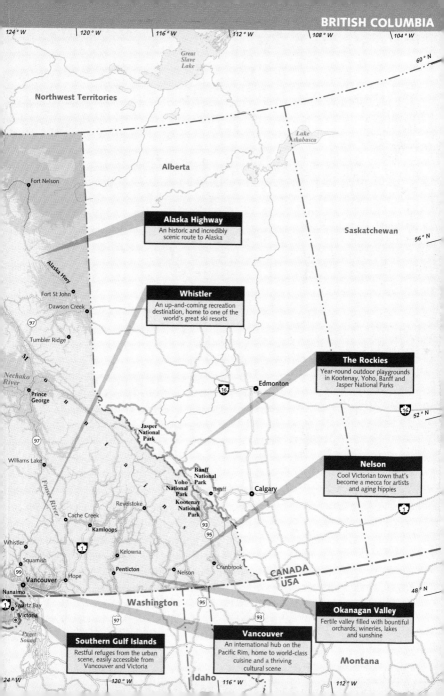

124° W   120° W   116° W   112° W   108° W   104° W

60° N

Great
Slave
Lake

Northwest Territories

Lake
Athabasca

Alberta

Fort Nelson

56° N

Saskatchewan

Alaska Highway
An historic and incredibly
scenic route to Alaska

Alaska Hwy

Fort St John

Dawson Creek

97

Whistler
An up-and-coming recreation
destination, home to one of the
world's great ski resorts

Tumbler Ridge

Nechako
River

The Rockies
Year-round outdoor playgrounds
in Kootenay, Yoho, Banff and
Jasper National Parks

Prince
George

16   Edmonton

97

16   52° N

Jasper
National
Park

Williams Lake

Banff
National
Park

Nelson
Cool Victorian town that's
become a mecca for artists
and aging hippies

Fraser River

Yoho
National
Park   Banff   Calgary

Revelstoke

Kootenay
National
Park

1

Cache Creek

Kamloops   93

95

Whistler

Kelowna

1

99

Squamish

Penticton   Nelson   Cranbrook

Vancouver   Hope

Nanaimo

CANADA
USA

48° N

Swartz Bay

1

Victoria

Washington   95

Okanagan Valley
Fertile valley filled with bountiful
orchards, wineries, lakes
and sunshine

Paget
Sound

97   93

Southern Gulf Islands
Restful refuges from the urban
scene, easily accessible from
Vancouver and Victoria

Vancouver
An international hub on the
Pacific Rim, home to world-class
cuisine and a thriving
cultural scene

Montana

24° W   120° W   Idaho   116° W   112° W

British Columbia
1st edition – April 2001

Published by
Lonely Planet Publications Pty Ltd ABN 36 005 607 983
90 Maribyrnong St, Footscray, Victoria 3011, Australia

Lonely Planet Offices
Australia Locked Bag 1, Footscray, Victoria 3011
USA 150 Linden St, Oakland, CA 94607
UK 10a Spring Place, London NW5 3BH
France 1 rue du Dahomey, 75011 Paris

Photographs
Many of the images in this guide are available for licensing from
Lonely Planet Images.
email: lpi@lonelyplanet.com.au

Front cover photograph
Paddling on Emerald Lake (Mark Lightbody)

ISBN 1 86450 220 7

text & maps © Lonely Planet 2001
photos © photographers as indicated 2001

Printed by SNP Offset Sdn Bhd
Printed in Malaysia

2   Contents

WHISTLER & THE SUNSHINE COAST   153

VANCOUVER ISLAND   177

SOUTHERN GULF ISLANDS   234

FRASER VALLEY   249

Contents

THOMPSON-OKANAGAN 259

THE KOOTENAYS 296

THE ROCKIES 336

CARIBOO-CHILCOTIN 371

THE NORTH 385

INDEX 432

BRITISH COLUMBIA MAP LEGEND 440

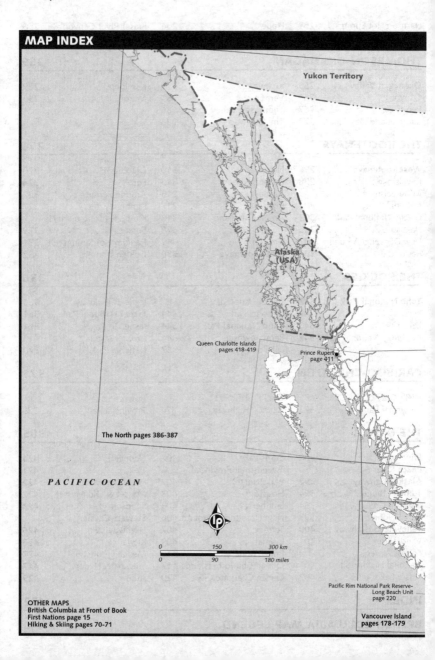

MAP INDEX

Yukon Territory

Alaska
(USA)

Queen Charlotte Islands
pages 418-419

Prince Rupert
page 411

The North pages 386-387

PACIFIC OCEAN

0   150   300 km
0   90   180 miles

Pacific Rim National Park Reserve-
Long Beach Unit
page 220

Vancouver Island
pages 178-179

OTHER MAPS
British Columbia at Front of Book
First Nations page 15
Hiking & Skiing pages 70-71

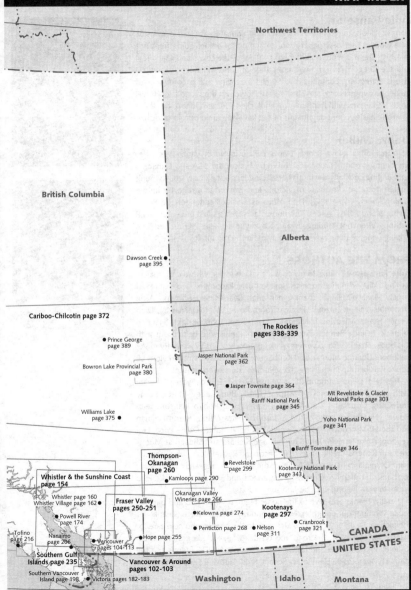

MAP INDEX

Northwest Territories

British Columbia

Alberta

Dawson Creek
page 395

Cariboo-Chilcotin page 372

The Rockies
pages 338-339

Jasper National Park
page 362

Prince George
page 389

Jasper Townsite page 364

Bowron Lake Provincial Park
page 380

Banff National Park
page 345

Mt Revelstoke & Glacier
National Parks page 303

Williams Lake
page 375

Yoho National Park
page 341

Banff Townsite page 346

Thompson-
Okanagan
page 260

Revelstoke
page 299

Kootenay National Park
page 343

Whistler & the Sunshine Coast
page 154

Kamloops page 290

Okanagan Valley
Wineries page 266

Whistler page 160
Whistler Village page 162

Fraser Valley
pages 250-251

Kootenays
page 297

Powell River
page 174

Kelowna page 274

Tofino
page 216

Nanaimo
page 206

Vancouver
pages 104-113

Penticton page 268

Nelson
page 311

Cranbrook
page 321

Hope page 255

CANADA

Southern Gulf
Islands page 235

UNITED STATES

Southern Vancouver
Island page 198

Victoria pages 182-183

Vancouver & Around
pages 102-103

Washington

Idaho

Montana

The Authors

Julie Fanselow

Born in Illinois, raised in Pennsylvania and educated at Ohio University, Julie worked as a newspaper reporter and editor before going freelance in 1991. She has written guidebooks to Idaho, the Lewis and Clark Trail and the Oregon Trail and was co-author of Lonely Planet's *Texas*. Julie also is a frequent contributor to *Sunset* magazine and a cofounder of guidebookwriters.com, a Web site that showcases the world's top travel writers. She lives with her family in landlocked southern Idaho, but these days she has frequent daydreams of sea kayaking amid purple starfish.

Debra Miller

Born in Halifax, Nova Scotia, Deb grew up in North Vancouver. After wandering around Europe and through Mexico, the USA and Canada – and slinging cocktails at various bartending gigs – she finally got a writing degree from the University of Victoria and worked as a reporter before joining Lonely Planet's Oakland office as a senior editor for the Pisces Diving & Snorkeling guides. This book marks Debra's first project as an LP author. When not tapping away at a keyboard, she spends her time sipping wine, reading novels and playing in the mountains.

FROM THE AUTHORS

Julie Fanselow Thanks to my co-author Deb Miller, whose enthusiasm, writing skill and native expertise made our collaboration a pleasure. At Lonely Planet-Oakland, thanks to Mariah Bear, Kate Hoffman, Maria Donohoe, Valerie Sinzdak, Tracey Croom Power, Matt DeMartini, Dion Good, Henia Miedzinski, Margaret Livingston, John Spriggs, Hannah Reineck, Belinda Bennett-Gow and everyone else who helped out with this book. Thanks also to writers Mark Lightbody, Chris Wyness, Ryan Ver Berkmoes, Joanne Morgan and Kent Spencer, whose work on previous LP books was helpful in charting this volume's course and content.

Plenty of people around BC gave me a hand. Especially helpful were Catherine Adams, Patrick Armstrong, Cindy Burr, Peggy Chute, Kathy and Craig Copeland, Carolyn Gray, Larry Hall, Robyn Hanson, Jean Howell, Heather Jeliazkov, Ron Johnson, Sheliza Mitha, Aaron Naiman and the HI-Vancouver Downtown staff, Cheryl Noble, Diane Price, Lisa Reynon, Anke Smeele, John Threlfall, and Richard and Shaeah at Mooncradle in Roberts Creek. Hugs to Rebecca and Rachel Hom, who came up from Olympia to have some fun near the end of my research. I'd also like to thank the many readers of LP's Canada and Vancouver books who wrote in with helpful updates and suggestions.

Finally, thanks and love to the home team: my husband and partner, Bruce Whiting; our daughter, Natalie; and my father, Byron. (Thanks for the picture, Dad.) My gratitude also goes to the people who help care for Natalie when I'm on the road and on deadline, including Sara Gulick, Katie Blair, the Barlow and Neiwirth families, our UUFTF friends and the staffs at Morningside Elementary School, Kids' Club and Sage Gymnastics.

Debra Miller So many people came together to give me advice and support on this book. My friends and fellow LPers Susan Charles, Carolyn Hubbard, Jacqueline Volin and Roslyn Bullas graciously bestowed early encouragement and enthusiasm. In San Francisco, thanks to Brendan Annett and Brian Wood for their inspiring outdoor spirit. To Tilly Woods and Fiona Mayhill, thanks for planting the seed (so long ago!) and sharing your love for this incredible province.

I could not have pumped out all the pages without the love and generosity of my family. Big thanks to Barb and Elko Kroon, who selflessly gave up their North Vancouver dining room so I could sprawl out with my books and files. To my muse Maggi, who kept me company and whose furry ears melt my heart. Thanks to Bill and Morgan Miller for their support and upkeep of my California life while I was on the road. To Marny Van Camp and Karen and Alan Magelund, thanks for the love that oozes from you guys no matter where I am. And a special thanks to Samantha Nicole, whose birth in the middle of this project was truly inspirational.

Thanks also go to Robert Landau, whose understanding, phone calls, haiku poems and bear hugs kept me sane and grounded throughout this entire project. Big love to you, dude. And, of course, to Hoagy.

I met so many people on the road who happily shared their local knowledge, be it in passing, or over coffees and pints of beer. Your stories and opinions added uniqueness and energy to this book. Very special thanks to Shirene Salamatian and Jason Mercier for welcoming me into their Vernon home and to Doris and Paul Toovey for the yummy wine and excellent steaks. Niomi Mio, thanks for dinner in Loops and the scoop on Smithers. Rivers of gratitude to Rob Silver in Banff for the awesome hospitality, dinners and hikes. In Vancouver, a giant hug to Randy Scott for welcoming me into his house and to Jennifer Young and Sandy Fleischer for continually sharing their home. Sandy, a big thanks also for the lowdown on Vancouver's Ultimate Frisbee scene. Thanks to the Murphys for the heart-thumping raft trip on the Kicking Horse, and, for her giant welcome and invaluable information, I send a big thanks to Mary Kellie at Queen Charlotte Adventures. Thanks also to Steve Palfy for the unforgettable boat trip through Louise Narrows at Gwaii Haanas.

Tourism British Columbia offered invaluable logistical and informational support. Thanks especially to Cindy Burr, Linda Trudeau at Thompson-Okanagan, Marilyn Quilley and Suzanne Shears in the North, Dan Wall in the Cariboo-Chilcotin and Chris Andrews at BC Rockies.

It's been a joy to work with senior editor Maria Donohoe and senior cartographer Tracey Croom Power. Huge kudos to Valerie Sinzdak for her professionalism and editorial prowess and to Matt DeMartini for carefully creating the maps. Thanks also to the LP design team.

Thanks to Ryan ver Berkmoes for laying excellent groundwork in LP's *Canada* guide and for the pre-trip beers and advice. A final burst of gratitude to my co-author Julie Fanselow, whose guidance, support and collaborative spirit inspired me every step of the way. Hey, Julie, when are we doing the West Coast Trail?

This Book

Julie Fanselow and Debra Miller co-authored this 1st edition of British Columbia. Julie served as coordinating author and wrote the introductory chapters, as well as Vancouver & Around, Whistler & the Sunshine Coast, Vancouver Island, Southern Gulf Islands and the Fraser Valley. Debra covered the Thompson-Okanagan, Kootenays, Rockies, Cariboo-Chilcotin and the North and contributed to the introductory chapters. Portions of this book originally came from Lonely Planet's *Vancouver*, written by Chris Wyness, and the British Columbia chapter of LP's *Canada*. Ryan ver Berkmoes covered the province for that guidebook.

FROM THE PUBLISHER

A whole lot of people in Lonely Planet's Oakland office helped make this book happen. Valerie Sinzdak edited the book, with invaluable assistance from fellow editor Elaine Merrill and senior editor Maria Donohoe. Paul Sheridan, Rachel Bernstein, Tullan Spitz, Vivek Wagle and Gabi Knight chipped in at the crucial proofreading and layout review stages.

Senior cartographer Tracey Croom Power and lead cartographer Matt DeMartini coordinated the heroic efforts of the cartography department, helped out by Dion Good, Ed Turley, Andrew Rebold, Eric Thomsen, Kat Smith, Patrick Huerta, Sara Nelson, Tessa Rottiers, Annette Olson, Chris Gillis, Stephanie Sims, Patrick Bock and Naoko Ogawa. Bart Wright, Ivy Feibelman and Tim Lohnes also lent a hand, and cartography manager Alex Guilbert oversaw the whole process.

Despite the tight deadlines, designer Henia Miedzinski demonstrated great grace under pressure and laid out the pages in record time. Margaret Livingston brought her keen eye to the design of the cover and the colorwraps. Beca Lafore headed up the illustrious illustration team, which included Trudi Canavan, Hugh D'Andrade, Shelley Firth, Hayden Foell, Beca Lafore, Justin Marler, Henia Miedzinski, Jennifer Steffey, Jim Swanson and Tamsin Wilson. Justin Marler penned some fun new drawings for this guide. Design manager Susan Rimerman provided plenty of assistance along the way. The inimitable Ken DellaPenta indexed the book. Finally, thanks too to the authors themselves, for their conscientiousness, patience, flexibility and sense of humor through it all.

Foreword

ABOUT LONELY PLANET GUIDEBOOKS

The story begins with a classic travel adventure: Tony and Maureen Wheeler's 1972 journey across Europe and Asia to Australia. Useful information about the overland trail did not exist at that time, so Tony and Maureen published the first Lonely Planet guidebook to meet a growing need.

From a kitchen table, then from a tiny office in Melbourne (Australia), Lonely Planet has become the largest independent travel publisher in the world, an international company with offices in Melbourne, Oakland (USA), London (UK) and Paris (France).

Today Lonely Planet guidebooks cover the globe. There is an ever-growing list of books, and there's information in a variety of forms and media. Some things haven't changed. The main aim is still to help make it possible for adventurous travelers to get out there – to explore and better understand the world.

At Lonely Planet we believe travelers can make a positive contribution to the countries they visit – if they respect their host communities and spend their money wisely. Since 1986 a percentage of the income from each book has been donated to aid projects and human-rights campaigns.

Updates Lonely Planet thoroughly updates each guidebook as often as possible. This usually means there are around two years between editions, although for more unusual or more stable destinations the gap can be longer. Check the imprint page (following the color map at the beginning of the book) for publication dates.

Between editions, up-to-date information is available in two free newsletters – the paper *Planet Talk* and email *Comet* (to subscribe, contact any Lonely Planet office) – and on our Web site at www.lonelyplanet.com. The *Upgrades* section of the Web site covers a number of important and volatile destinations and is regularly updated by Lonely Planet authors. *Scoop* covers news and current affairs relevant to travelers. And, lastly, the *Thorn Tree* bulletin board and *Postcards* section of the site carry unverified, but fascinating, reports from travelers.

Correspondence The process of creating new editions begins with the letters, postcards and emails received from travelers. This correspondence often includes suggestions, criticisms and comments about the current editions. Interesting excerpts are immediately passed on via newsletters and the Web site, and everything goes to our authors to be verified when they're researching on the road. We're keen to get more feedback from organizations or individuals who represent communities visited by travelers.

Lonely Planet gathers information for everyone who's curious about the planet – and especially for those who explore it firsthand. Through guidebooks, phrasebooks, activity guides, maps, literature, newsletters, image library, TV series and website, we act as an information exchange for a worldwide community of travelers.

Research Authors aim to gather sufficient practical information to enable travelers to make informed choices and to make the mechanics of a journey run smoothly. They also research historical and cultural background to help enrich the travel experience and allow travelers to understand and respond appropriately to cultural and environmental issues.

Authors don't stay in every hotel because that would mean spending a couple of months in each medium-size city and, no, they don't eat at every restaurant because that would mean stretching belts beyond capacity. They do visit hotels and restaurants to check standards and prices, but feedback based on readers' direct experiences can be very helpful.

Many of our authors work undercover; others aren't so secretive. None of them accept freebies in exchange for positive write-ups. And none of our guidebooks contain any advertising.

Production Authors submit their raw manuscripts and maps to offices in Australia, the USA, the UK or France. Editors and cartographers – all experienced travelers themselves – then begin the process of assembling the pieces. When the book finally hits the shops, some things are already out of date, we start getting feedback from readers and the process begins again....

WARNING & REQUEST

Things change – prices go up, schedules change, good places go bad and bad places go bankrupt – nothing stays the same. So, if you find things better or worse, recently opened or long since closed, please tell us and help make the next edition even more accurate and useful. We genuinely value all the feedback we receive. Julie Young coordinates a well-traveled team that reads and acknowledges every letter, postcard and email and ensures that every morsel of information finds its way to the appropriate authors, editors and cartographers for verification.

Everyone who writes to us will find their name in the next edition of the appropriate guidebook. They will also receive the latest issue of *Planet Talk*, our quarterly printed newsletter, or *Comet*, our monthly email newsletter. Subscriptions to both newsletters are free. The very best contributions will be rewarded with a free guidebook.

Excerpts from your correspondence may appear in new editions of Lonely Planet guidebooks, the Lonely Planet Web site, *Planet Talk* or *Comet*, so please let us know if you *don't* want your letter published or your name acknowledged.

Send all correspondence to the Lonely Planet office closest to you:

Australia: Locked Bag 1, Footscray, Victoria 3011
USA: 150 Linden St, Oakland, CA 94607
UK: 10A Spring Place, London NW5 3BH
France: 1 rue du Dahomey, 75011 Paris

Or email us at: talk2us@lonelyplanet.com.au

For news, views and updates, see our Web site: www.lonelyplanet.com

HOW TO USE A LONELY PLANET GUIDEBOOK

The best way to use a Lonely Planet guidebook is any way you choose. At Lonely Planet, we believe the most memorable travel experiences are often those that are unexpected, and the finest discoveries are those you make yourself. Guidebooks are not intended to be used as if they provided a detailed set of infallible instructions!

Contents All Lonely Planet guidebooks follow the same format. The Facts about the Country chapters or sections give background information ranging from history to weather. Facts for the Visitor gives practical information on issues like visas and health. Getting There & Away gives a brief starting point for researching travel to and from the destination. Getting Around gives an overview of the transport options available when you arrive.

The peculiar demands of each destination determine how subsequent chapters are broken up, but some things remain constant. We always start with background, then proceed to sights, places to stay, places to eat, entertainment, getting there and away, and getting around information – in that order.

Heading Hierarchy Lonely Planet headings are used in a strict hierarchical structure that can be visualized as a set of Russian dolls. Each heading (and its following text) is encompassed by any preceding heading that is higher on the hierarchical ladder.

Entry Points We do not assume guidebooks will be read from beginning to end, but that people will dip into them. The traditional entry points are the list of contents and the index. In addition, however, some books have a complete list of maps and an index map illustrating map coverage.

There may also be a color map that shows highlights. These highlights are dealt with in greater detail later in the book, along with planning questions. Each chapter covering a geographical region usually begins with a locator map and another list of highlights. Once you find something of interest in a list of highlights, turn to the index.

Maps Maps play a crucial role in Lonely Planet guidebooks and include a huge amount of information. A legend is printed on the back page. We seek to have complete consistency between maps and text, and to have every important place in the text captured on a map. Map key numbers usually start in the top left corner.

Although inclusion in a guidebook usually implies a recommendation, we cannot list every good place. Exclusion does not necessarily imply criticism. In fact, there are a number of reasons why we might exclude a place – sometimes it is simply inappropriate to encourage an influx of travelers.

Introduction

This is the first Lonely Planet guidebook to single out one of Canada's provinces. What is it about British Columbia that merits this milestone?

British Columbia, usually called BC, is not Canada's largest province nor its most populous. But there's a dynamic at work in BC that makes it unique not just in Canada but possibly the world. It has to do with the almost mystical allure of BC's physical environment. For years, the Pacific province's tourism slogan has been 'Super, Natural British Columbia,' and rarely has a marketing campaign so aptly captured the soul of a land.

BC is a place where you can stand dwarfed by trees that are among the tallest in Canada. It's a place where the air is so saturated with moisture that rainbows split apart to reveal extra layers of color. Whether you're standing amid the grandeur of the Rockies or on the wind-swept West Coast, you will feel nature's power here in a way you've probably never experienced it before. And there are endless opportunities to enjoy it, from short strolls through ancient forests to multi-day backpack treks, from an afternoon in a sea kayak to a week paddling around far-flung archipelagos.

As you might expect, the people drawn to and nurtured by such a place are intensely attuned to the natural world. At their restaurants, the region's chefs serve meals infused with the bounty of the land and of the sea so close at hand. In their artwork, the First Nations peoples of BC pay homage to the Earth that has sustained

them for thousands of years. Although there are ecological travesties happening here, including some of the worst forest clear-cutting on the planet, it says something about BC's consciousness that the province is home to some of the world's most vocal, effective environmental organizations.

BC is a work in progress, not just physically but demographically. Waves of new immigrants have arrived in recent decades, most settling in the Lower Mainland area. The Vancouver region is growing explosively yet retains (and tenaciously preserves) most of what has long made it one of North America's most livable cities: abundant parkland, accessible beaches, walkable streets and a lively cultural scene. Vancouver is a dynamic place, full of cosmopolitan, tolerant people. You'll definitely want to spend some time in its embrace.

BC's other regions are just as enticing. The pretty provincial capital of Victoria is the most British spot on BC's map, but it's also the staging area for incredible outdoor adventures on Vancouver Island, the largest island off the coast of the Americas. The Southern Gulf Islands are favorite playgrounds for BC residents and visitors alike. The Fraser Valley, to Vancouver's east, abounds in history and offers hair-raising white-water adventure. The Sea to Sky Hwy north of Vancouver leads to the winter wonderland of Whistler, while a ferry ride to the Sunshine Coast transports travelers to a little-known maritime paradise.

The sun-soaked Thompson-Okanagan region of south-central BC belies the rumor that the province is perennially awash in rain (yet the region's many lakes and ski resorts show that it's not all desert). The Kootenays of southeastern BC are filled with mountains, rivers and hip small towns like Nelson and New Denver. The BC Rockies boast alpine vistas, hot springs and great recreation. The Cariboo-Chilcotin is BC's version of the Wild West, with open spaces and guest ranches galore, yet it's also home to remote coastal villages and the awesome Great Bear Rainforest. And then there's the North, an expansive region rich in Native culture, natural wonders and human achievements.

BC has lately become known for its prodigious production of marijuana, which (unofficially, of course) is one of the province's top cash crops. But rest assured, you won't need any chemical help getting high in BC. From the riotously colored wildflowers in mountain meadows to the iridescence of an ocean sunset, BC is a mind-blowing feast for the senses. No matter where you go, no matter how long you stay, the memories you will make are sure to be the ones that you'll savor for years to come.

Facts about British Columbia

HISTORY
Early Inhabitants
The ancestors of BC's modern First Nations peoples showed up in North America at least 10,000 years ago. It's likely that, after the last Ice Age, they crossed to Alaska on a land bridge over what is now the Bering Strait. Some settled along the Pacific coast, while others found their way to the interior.

The Pacific coast Native Indians included the Nuxalk (Bella Coola), Cowichan, Gitksan, Haida, Kwakwaka'wakw, Nisga'a, Nuu-chah-nulth (Nootka), Salish, Sechelt and Tsimshian groups. With plenty of animal, marine and plant life available, they were able to evolve a highly sophisticated, structured culture and an intricate trade network. Coastal peoples dwelled as extended families in large, single-roofed cedar

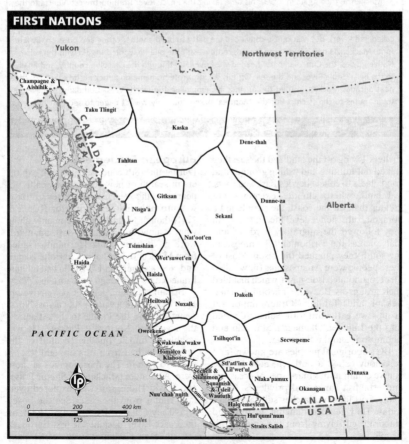

FIRST NATIONS

Yukon

Northwest Territories

Champagne & Aishihik

Taku Tlingit

Kaska

Dene-thah

Tahltan

Gitksan

Dunne-za

Alberta

Nisga'a

Sekani

Nat'oot'en

Tsimshian

Wet'suwet'en

Haida

Haisla

Heiltsuk

Dakelh

Nuxalk

PACIFIC OCEAN

Oweekeno

Kwakwaka'wakw

Tsilhqot'in

Secwepemc

Homalco & Klahoose

Sechelt & Shishalh

Stl'atl'imx & Lil'wet'ul

Ktunaxa

Squamish & Tsleil Waututh

Nlaka'pamux

Okanagan

Nuu'chah'nulth

Comox

Haig'emeylem

Hul'qumi'num

Straits Salish

CANADA USA

0   200   400 km
0   125   250 miles

They Charted BC

When history buffs reflect on the exploration of the North American West, they usually think first of Meriwether Lewis and William Clark, whose 1804-1806 expedition at the behest of US President Thomas Jefferson paved the way for commerce and settlement in the region. But Lewis and Clark were not the first people of European descent to cross North America by land. Alexander Mackenzie beat them by a dozen years, reaching the mouth of BC's Bella Coola River in the summer of 1793, seven weeks after Captain George Vancouver had arrived at the same point by sea.

A Scotsman who emigrated to the New World as a boy, Mackenzie made his first attempt at finding the Pacific Ocean in 1789, when he and a group of French voyagers set off from Lake Athabasca, on what is now the border of northernmost Alberta and Saskatchewan. They found salt water 2500km downstream, but it was the Arctic Ocean. Mackenzie named the waterway they had followed the River of Disappointment. Today, it bears his name.

Mackenzie tried again in 1793, this time taking the Peace River from northwest Alberta to the Parsnip River. With the help of a Sekani Indian map, he and his party successfully portaged to a tributary of the Fraser River. Their canoe was destroyed in the rapids of James Creek (which they called Bad River), but Mackenzie convinced the party to build another canoe and press on. By late June, Mackenzie had decided the Fraser's route wasn't the one he wanted. Again with the help of Native guides, the Canadian party headed west overland through the Chicoltin country, and finally to the Bella Coola River and the sea. On July 22, he wrote his name on a rock at the coast. For the next decade, Mackenzie tried to convince his employer, the North West Company, to develop trade routes to the Pacific. But the Montreal-based company wasn't eager to see that happen,

shelters. Living off the land and the sea, they staked out hunting and fishing grounds and good places to collect berries, bark and roots.

Inland, where climate extremes are greater than on the coast, the people led a nomadic, subsistence-level life. In the north they followed the migratory herds of animals such as the caribou and the moose; in the south they pursued the bison. Most of these people were Athapaskans (now called Dene, pronounced 'de-nay'), which included such groups as Beaver, Chilcotin, Carrier, Sekani and Tahltan. Other important groups were the Interior Salish (divided into the Lillooet, Okanagan, Shuswap and Thompson) and the Kootenay.

BC's aboriginal peoples are known for a ceremony called a potlatch, held to help Native communities mark special occasions and establish ranks and privileges. Often many days long, potlatches still take place today. They feature dancing, fasting and elaborate gift-giving from the chief to his people.

European Settlement

During the 18th century, European explorers in search of new sources of wealth appeared off the West Coast. Alexsey Chirikov was probably first, exploring for Russia in 1741, though his travels were mainly along what is now the Alaskan coast. Spaniards were next: Juan Pérez Hernández sailed from Mexico to the Queen Charlotte Islands and Nootka Sound in 1774, followed by Juan Francisco de la Bodega y Quadra in 1775.

Britain's Captain James Cook arrived in 1778, looking for a water route across North America from the Pacific to the Atlantic – the legendary Northwest Passage. He was unable to find it, but his account of the riches to be had from furs brought traders eager to cash in. The most famous of these were Alexander Mackenzie, Simon Fraser and David Thompson, who explored overland routes from the east. (See the boxed text 'They Charted BC.') Fort St. John, on the Peace River, became the first European settlement in 1794; in its wake came many

They Charted BC

since it would boost the fortunes of the rival Hudson's Bay Company and diminish Montreal's importance as a trade center. Mackenzie finally returned to Britain in frustration in 1805.

By that same year, however, the North West Company had seen the light and sent a group led by Simon Fraser to establish trading posts west of the Rockies. Fraser founded Rocky Mountain Portage House at the Peace River Canyon, Fort McLeod at McLeod Lake, Fort St James at Stuart Lake, Fort Fraser (which Fraser called Fort Caledonia after his mother's home in Scotland) and Fort George. But by the spring of 1808, he craved another adventure: exploring a river he wrongly believed, as had Mackenzie, to be the Columbia. Fraser's trip down the river that now bears his name is one of Canada's great adventure stories, particularly his party's late-June passage through the Fraser River Canyon. 'We had to pass where no human being should venture,' he wrote at the area now known as Hell's Gate. The going was much easier past the gorge, and Fraser reached the mouth of the river on July 2, 1808.

David Thompson was another explorer whose name and achievements made the map of BC what it is today. As a young man stationed on the Saskatchewan River with the Hudson's Bay Company in the late 1780s, Thompson met Philip Turnor, who taught him surveying and mathematics. By 1797, Thompson joined the North West Company. He surveyed the 49th parallel, detouring south to visit the Mandan Indians (with whom Lewis and Clark would winter in 1804-1805) and nearly finding the source of the Mississippi River. He continued to travel and survey widely, making repeated trips across the Rockies and an 1811 trek down the Columbia to its mouth. He, like Fraser, is memorialized by the name of a great BC river.

more trading posts which, by the 1820s, went under the control of the Hudson's Bay Company. (The HBC, known as The Bay, remains one of Canada's largest department stores.)

In the meantime, initially to counter the Spanish presence, Captain George Vancouver had circumnavigated and claimed Vancouver Island for Britain from 1792 to 1794. 'The serenity of the climate, the innumerable pleasing landscapes and the abundant fertility that unassisted nature puts forth requires only to be enriched by man to render it the most lovely country that can be imagined,' Vancouver observed in 1792. (The comment has long been a source of ire to First Nations people, who resent Vancouver's implication that there was no one around when he arrived.) Vancouver also explored far up BC's north coast. By the 1840s, the Hudson's Bay Company was warily watching the US make an increasingly indisputable claim to the Oregon country anchored by HBC's Fort Vancouver

on the Columbia River near present-day Portland. In 1843, the HBC dispatched James Douglas to Vancouver Island, where he established Fort Victoria. Vancouver Island became a crown colony in 1849.

The discovery of gold along the Fraser River in 1858 brought a flood of people seeking their fortunes and led to mainland BC also being declared a crown colony, with New Westminster its capital. A second wave of fortune hunters arrived when gold was discovered farther north in the Cariboo region. Although the gold rush only lasted a few years, many of those who came in the wake of the miners remained behind to form more permanent settlements. A downside to the gold rush was soaring debt created by massive infrastructure projects like the Cariboo Rd (which cost about $300,000).

Mainland BC and Vancouver Island were united in 1866, with Victoria named capital in 1868. Meanwhile, in 1867, the British government passed the British North American

Act, creating the Dominion of Canada, a confederation that maintained British ties but conferred many powers to a central Canadian government and individual provinces. The eastern provinces of Canada united under the confederation, and BC decided to join in 1871 on the condition that a transcontinental railroad be extended to the West Coast. This was finally achieved in 1885; the settlement of the prairies around this same time created demand for the BC's resources, particularly timber.

The late 19th century proved a difficult time for BC's First Nations people. The gold rush era brought displacement from their traditional lands to many bands, leading to violence among both Natives and whites. Moreover, the Canadian government, heeding complaints from missionaries and others about pagan Native practices, outlawed potlatches in the 1880s with legislation, which was not repealed until 1951.

The Early 20th Century

The building of the Panama Canal, which was completed in 1914, meant easier access for BC to markets in Europe and along North America's east coast. The province's interior profited, too, with the completion of the Grand Trunk Railway from Edmonton, Alberta, to Prince Rupert. As big business grew, so did big unions. Workers in great numbers organized into labor unions in the 1910s, protesting working conditions and pay rates. A number of strikes targeted key industries like lumber mills and shipping, and in several instances BC saw armed confrontations between union members and soldiers. However, one issue where the unions, the government and business were in accord was with nonwhite workers – both felt the growing Chinese and Japanese population was a problem that only punitive legislation and violence could solve.

Large numbers of Chinese had moved to the province, and were instrumental in building the Canadian Pacific Railway. Japanese settlers came slightly later, establishing truck farms and becoming the area's principal commercial fishermen. That these were hard working people seeking opportunity,

like the Europeans who were also flooding the province, seemingly didn't matter to whites. On several occasions in the province's early history, Vancouver's Chinatown and Little Tokyo were the scene of white mob violence.

Following WWI, Canada experienced an economic downturn that led to industrial unrest and unemployment. After a brief recovery, the Wall St crash of 1929 brought severe depression and hardship. Prosperity only returned with the advent of WWII and was sustained after the war with the discovery of new resources and the development of a manufacturing base.

The war years were hard times for immigrants. During WWI, anti-German riots took hold of the streets of Vancouver, and many German-owned businesses were burned. In 1941, Japanese Canadians were removed from their land and their fishing boats, and were interned by the government on farms and work camps in inland BC and Alberta, Saskatchewan and Manitoba.

First Nations people remained under siege, too. In 1921, Kwakwaka'wakw chief Dan Cranmer defied the ban on potlatches by staging what may have been the largest gathering of that type ever. Chiefs gathered at Alert Bay to celebrate and exchange gifts, but local whites called the authorities to report the then-illegal activity. Chiefs who agreed to surrender their potlatch possessions were freed, but those who refused – including Cranmer – were sent to jail. Many of the potlatch artifacts wound up at the National Museum of Canada in Ottawa, which finally agreed to return them to the Natives in the 1980s. They now can be seen at museums at Alert Bay and on Quadra Island.

Post-War Prosperity

BC's natural resources-based economy enjoyed periods of great prosperity in the mid-20th century, following WWII, as transportation networks extended farther into the resource-rich interior. Forestry led the way, as BC's mills worked to meet ever-growing demands for pulp, paper and plywood. At the time, small operations dominated logging, but this is no longer true; today, a handful of companies dominate the industry.

Throughout the 20th century, BC's population growth continued, with many people from elsewhere in Canada moving west to call the province home. At the beginning of the 1990s, BC experienced another economic upsurge, led by Vancouver, which enjoyed its links to then-booming Asia. The area also experienced a large influx of moneyed immigrants fleeing Hong Kong ahead of the handover to China. However, what goes up must come down, and these economic ties to Asia were both a blessing and a curse. The crash of the Asian economies in the late 1990s sent a chill through the province. This, coupled with the collapse of fishing stocks, resulted in a recession stretching from the metropolitan southwest to the rural towns of the far north. But BC seemed to be on the rebound at the start of the 21st century, its economy buoyed by a national economic growth spurt, a healthier Asian economy, leaping gains in high technology and surging tourism.

GEOGRAPHY

BC is Canada's most westerly province and its third-largest, after Quebec and Ontario. Its 948,596 sq km make up about 9.5% of Canada's surface area. BC is bordered to the north by the Yukon and the Northwest Territories; to the east by Alberta; to the south by the three US states of Montana, Idaho and Washington; to the northwest by Alaska; and to the west by the Pacific Ocean. With its many inlets, the West Coast is more than 7000km long; alongside it are hundreds of islands ranging from large (Vancouver Island, the Queen Charlotte Islands) to tiny.

Victoria, BC's provincial capital, is at the southern tip of Vancouver Island, which lies southwest of the mainland. Vancouver, the province's business center and by far its largest city, sits alongside the ocean near the mouth of the Fraser River.

The bulk of BC lies within the Canadian Cordillera, a system of mountain ranges running roughly northwest to southeast.

Within the cordillera are several major mountain ranges – the Rocky Mountains to the east; the Cassiar Mountains in the north (including the Stikine, Kechia, Finlay and Ominica ranges); and the Columbia Mountains in the south (which include the Selkirk, Purcell, Monashee and Cariboo ranges). The glaciated Coast Mountains loom over the Pacific almost to water's edge from Vancouver north to the Alaskan panhandle. The province's high point is 4663m Mt Fairweather, part of the St Elias Range on the BC-Alaska border. The low point, of course, is sea level.

The province has scores of freshwater lakes and fast-flowing rivers. The Fraser River is BC's longest, stretching from the Rocky Mountains to the Pacific Ocean near Vancouver. Roughly 60% of BC is covered by forest, mainly coniferous trees. There's a small desert in the southern interior near Osoyoos, while the lush Pacific coastal area has countless inlets and islands. The Peace River region in northeast BC is the only really flat area. More than 90% of BC's landmass is 'Crown Land,' that is, it's owned by the provincial government.

GEOLOGY

An Ice Age starting about a million years ago was the primary force shaping BC's geology. Huge ice sheets repeatedly scraped over the province's lofty mountain ranges, wearing them down to bedrock and creating great valleys between the peaks. This continued until about 7000 years ago, when the last ice melted, giving rise to the province's lakes and rivers (which remain fed by annual snowmelt today). Since the end of the Pleistocene epoch, glacial, wind and water erosion have continued to alter BC's landscape in more subtle ways.

BC's mineral wealth spurred Europeans to settle here in the 19th century, and the industry remains important today. Major mineral deposits include coal on the coastal islands and the eastern slopes of the Rocky Mountains; gold in the Coast Mountains; copper, lead, silver and zinc in the Kootenays; and natural gas-containing sandstone and shale in the Peace River region. Jade is the official mineral of British Columbia, widely used in jewelry and sculptures.

CLIMATE

British Columbia has a varied climate, influenced by latitude, mountainous terrain and distance from the moderating effects of the Pacific Ocean. On the coast it is mild, with warm, mostly dry summers (June through September) and cool, very wet winters (December through March). The interior is much drier, particularly in the south along the Okanagan Valley, which gets less than 347mm of rain each year (compared to 6550mm at Henderson Lake on Vancouver Island's Barkley Sound); summers are hot and winters are cold. In the mountains, summers are short, with warm days and cool nights. Winter snowfalls are heavy.

Unless you're coming for winter activities like skiing, the best time to visit is from early June to early October. During this period there is less rain, temperatures are warm, daylight hours are long, and the transport routes are open. But even if you come in a colder, wetter season, take a cue from BC residents, who rarely seem to let the weather keep them inside or get their spirits down. With good rain gear and an umbrella, you too can have a good time no matter what the skies have in store. Note, however, that when the sun shines, people's spirits visibly lift. (You may see people walking about in T-shirts in 10-degree temperatures, as long as the sun is shining.) It's these periods of sublime weather that help British Columbians endure the long spells of gray skies.

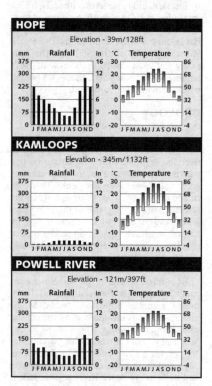

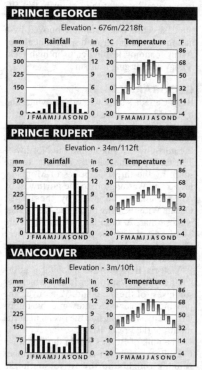

ECOLOGY & ENVIRONMENT

British Columbia is a schizophrenic place when it comes to the environment. Most Lower Mainlanders see the province's vast wild lands and coastal environments as places to protect and enjoy, while people living in geographically far-flung, resource-dependent regions tend to view the environment as their meal ticket. Then there are areas like Tofino on Vancouver Island's West Coast where a sometimes uneasy truce holds between people employed by extractive industries and those sworn to defend the planet from plunder.

In any case, BC has a long history of environmental activism, and even casual visitors are likely to encounter debates and perhaps protests over such issues as forestry practices and large-scale fish farming. Key groups include Greenpeace (founded in Vancouver more than 20 years ago – see the boxed text); the Western Canada Wilderness Committee; the Tofino-based Friends of Clayoquot Sound; the Raincoast Conservation Society (which spearheaded recognition of the Great Bear Rainforest on BC's central coast as the largest contiguous tract of coastal temperate rain forest left on Earth) and the New Denver–based Valhalla Wilderness Society, whose efforts to protect wildlife habitat have moved far beyond its Kootenays base.

Making Waves

The modern Canadian environmental movement can be traced to a Vancouver living room, where a group of concerned people met in 1969 to discuss a one-megaton nuclear bomb dropped as easily and quietly as a raindrop on Amchitka, an ecologically diverse island near the tip of Alaska's Aleutians. It was the first bomb in a series of US atmospheric nuclear tests, which were scheduled to continue intermittently over the following few years.

The meeting marked the birth of the Don't Make a Wave Committee, which came up with a plan to sail north and disrupt US atomic activity before the next bomb fell on Amchitka. Bad weather thwarted their efforts, but the group pressed on, soon taking the name Greenpeace and continuing to raise public awareness. The strategy worked. By 1972, all atomic testing on Amchitka ceased.

In the three decades since, Greenpeace has remained a leader in the international environmental movement. From confronting Russian whalers to convincing the *New York Times* to cancel all contracts with logging giant MacMillan Bloedel, Greenpeace has combined creative protest with dedication to attracting high-profile media and focusing public attention on environmental issues surrounding hydroelectric industries, forestry, commercial fishing and nuclear and chemical testing.

Greenpeace opponents have argued that the organization's renegade environmentalism and impromptu confrontations cause more harm than good. Like a pesky mosquito that just won't go away, Greenpeace has emitted an incessant, irritating buzz in the ear of many corporations, creating sleepless nights and public relations nightmares.

However annoying and aggressive, the buzz has made a difference: By forcing companies to wake up to global environmental problems and potential catastrophes, Greenpeace's eco-warfare has raised the standard for corporate accountability, or at least brought environmental concerns out of the cold and into the boardroom. Greenpeace's success has inspired a generation of activists.

In 1979, national Greenpeace organizations in Australia, Canada, France, the Netherlands, New Zealand, the UK and the US formed Greenpeace International, now headquartered in Amsterdam. There are organizations in more than 30 countries worldwide.

From its humble beginning in a Vancouver home, Greenpeace has gone on to protect rain forests, whales and drinking water, among many other things. As for Amchitka, the island is now a flourishing bird sanctuary.

The provincial government has taken some action, too. In the 1990s, encouraged by the United Nations, BC Parks adopted a plan aimed at protecting 12% of the province as parklands – about double the 1993 amount. By 2000, BC Parks had added or expanded several hundred areas and was nearing the 12% goal. Key additions during the 1990s included the Stein Valley Nlaka'pamux Heritage Park, the Khutzeymateen Grizzly Bear Sanctuary and Tatshenshini-Alsek Provincial Park which, together with adjacent parks in Alaska and the Yukon, forms the largest World Heritage Site. Yet the legacy strategy has drawn criticism from environmentalists, who say the plan leaves too many critical areas unprotected. BC's Ministry of Forests controls most of the province's public, or Crown, lands (a total of 59 million hectares). The forest industry, many environmentalists believe, remains the ministry's first master. Activists continue to fight logging in such pristine areas as the Elaho Valley and Stoltmann Wilderness near Whistler, Salt Spring Island, the Great Bear Rainforest along BC's southwest coast, the Nass Valley near Terrace and the Queen Charlotte Islands.

FLORA & FAUNA

With all its geographical and climatic diversity, it's no surprise BC has a wide range of plants and animals. With 14 distinct ecological zones, nature flourishes everywhere, from the large urban parks of Vancouver and Victoria to the tops of the Rockies to tiny coastal tide pools. For a selection of field guides to the province's natural history, see Books in the Facts for the Visitor chapter.

Flora

British Columbia has always been a lush place, with species varying widely depending on location, climate and human impacts. The province's official symbol is the white flower of the Pacific Dogwood, a tree known for springtime blossoms and red berries in autumn. BC's summertime wildflower displays are among the best in North America, with showy blooms of every hue scattered along trails and roadways. But BC is probably best known for its trees, which rank among the world's tallest and most majestic.

Western red cedar, Sitka spruce, hemlock and Douglas fir are prevalent trees in the moist coastal regions. Red cedar, the official provincial tree, was of special importance to indigenous coastal peoples, who used it to make everything from canoes and clothing to totem poles and medicines. The tallest tree in Canada, a Sitka spruce known as the Carmanah Giant, stands 95m in the Carmanah Valley of western Vancouver Island.

Coastal BC is well known for the arbutus (are-**byoo**-tus) tree, a distinctive species with twisted branches, reddish peeling bark and shiny dark green leaves. The only broadleafed evergreen tree in Canada, it's similar to the madrona trees found elsewhere in North America. Southern Vancouver Island and the Gulf Islands also are home to Garry oak, though unfortunately, many of these once-prolific, low-growing trees have been wiped out by human development.

Ponderosa pine, Englemann and white spruce, Douglas fir, birch, aspen, cottonwood and larch trees are among the species growing along the river valleys and mountains of BC's interior. Closer to the Continental Divide, along the slopes of the Columbia and Rocky Mountains, rain-forest species such as hemlock and red cedar once again predominate. Northern landscapes are characterized by such scrappy trees as white and black spruce, tamarack and the subalpine fir.

Western hemlock

Fauna

BC provides habitat for 143 mammal species, 467 bird species, 453 fish species, 18 reptile species and 20 types of amphibians. About 100 species (including the burrowing owl and Vancouver Island marmot) are on the province's endangered species list; another 100 or so are considered at risk. Ecosystems are at their most diverse in southern BC, but that's also where threats from human pressures are at their strongest.

The province has more mountain goats than anywhere else in North America; in fact, 60% of all the world's mountain goats live here. Bears are another prominent mammal, with an estimated 150,000 black bears and an unknown but much smaller number of grizzlies. Kermode bears, sometimes called spirit bears, are whitish in color. Unique to BC, they're found mostly along the lower Skeena River Valley near Prince Rupert and Terrace. Another unusual species, the Columbia black-tailed deer, is a small subspecies native to Vancouver Island and BC's West Coast. Other large mammals include bighorn sheep, mountain lions (also called cougars), moose, Roosevelt elk, Dall and Stone sheep, mule deer, white-tailed deer, coyotes and wolves.

Whales are among the best-known and most beloved of BC's mammal species. About 20,000 Pacific gray whales migrate along BC's coast twice each year: southbound to Mexico October through December and northbound to the Bering and Chukchi seas February through May. Less numerous and even more striking are the black-and-white orca, or killer whales. Some groups (called pods) of orca live permanently off the coast of southern Vancouver Island; others range more widely in waters to the north, but reliably spend late summer near the Robson Bight Ecological Reserve in Johnstone Strait near Port McNeill on northern Vancouver Island. Other commonly sighted sea mammals include porpoises, dolphins, sea lions, seals and otters.

Salmon rank among the most important fish in BC. Sacred to many First Nations bands, and a mainstay of the province's fishing industry, salmon come in five species: chinook (also called king), coho, chum, sockeye and pink. Salmon life cycles are among the most amazing in the animal world: At adulthood, they leave the ocean to swim upriver to the same spawning grounds where they were born. Once there, they take their turns at reproducing, and then they die. (See the boxed text 'Saluting the Sockeye in the Thompson-Okanagan chapter.) Other fascinating BC sea life include the world's largest species of octopus, playful wolf eels and colorful sea stars (also called starfish), easily seen clinging to rocks and dock pilings all along the coast.

Of the province's nearly 500 bird species, the black-and-blue Steller's jay is among the most famous; it was named the province's official bird after a government-sponsored contest. Prominent birds of prey include bald eagles, golden eagles, great horned owls and peregrine falcons. A variety of seabirds and waterfowl nest on the shores of BC's coastal areas; others migrate through the province, including Canada and snow geese, trumpeter swans, harlequin ducks, sandhill cranes, brant and sandpipers. Blue herons are abundant in riparian areas. Tiny hummingbirds are seen all over southern BC, endlessly flitting to welcoming feeders in many backyards and even at a BC Ferries dock or two.

NATIONAL PARKS

British Columbia contains a number of world-famous parks, including the Canadian National Parks UNESCO World Heritage Site, which encompasses Kootenay and Yoho National Parks, as well as neighboring Alberta's Banff and Jasper National Parks and Hamber Provincial Park (see the Rockies chapter for more information).

You have to buy a park pass upon entry into any national park, no matter how you arrive, be it by car, bicycle or on foot. Passes are sold at all park gates and information centers. Day passes are $5/4/2.50 for adults/seniors/children, and they're valid in any of the parks until 4 pm the following day. If you are planning on spending more than a week in the national parks, your best bet is to buy a Great Western Annual Pass (sometimes also called the Western Canada Annual Pass), which gives you unlimited admission to all 11 national parks in western Canada for a year. With it you get a book of coupons that will save you money at campgrounds, hot springs and other park attractions. The pass costs $35/27/18 for adults/seniors/children. If you've already bought a day pass, you can upgrade to an annual pass at anytime. To find out more about fees or to purchase an annual pass ahead of time, call ☎ 800-748-7275.

If you're planning on overnight treks in the backcountry, you need to buy a Wilderness Pass, which allows you to use any of the backcountry campsites. The fee is $6 per night, with a maximum charge of $30. Note that some quota systems are in effect; there may be a limit on the number of backcountry passes issued in some of the more popular areas. Passes are available from Parks Canada at all the information centers.

GOVERNMENT & POLITICS

British Columbia has a parliamentary government, with a 75-member unicameral legislature that convenes in Victoria. The lieutenant governor is the formal head of state, but real power goes to the premier, who is usually the head of the majority party. Premier Ujjal Dosanjh of the New Democrat Party (NDP), who assumed his post in 2000 after predecessor Glen Clark resigned, is the very first BC leader of non-European descent.

BC also sends representatives to the national House of Commons and Senate in Ottawa. But, since Canadian power is concentrated on the provincial level, most people in BC pay little heed to what's happening in the national capital. The Social Credit Party (Socreds), ostensibly the party of small business, came to power in BC in the 1950s and governed into the 1970s. During the 1960s the NDP emerged, advocating a form of limited socialism. Beset by scandals, the Socreds fell out of favor by 1990. The NDP has been in power since then, but it also has had its share of scandal. There is usually viable opposition from the

Liberals (who, despite their name, actually take mostly right-wing to moderate stands) and, more recently, from the Alliance Party, formed in 2000 by merging the Reform Party, which advocates minimal government involvement and conservative morals, and some factions of the Conservative party.

Not that much of this matters to average BC residents, most of whom feel they have little power to change anything through the political process. Most BC voters are happy to have Canada's strong social services (including universal health care and welfare and an excellent public transportation network), but they're disgusted with scandal and bureaucracy, and fed up that pervasive and unpredictable government regulations seem to affect almost every area of their lives. When people get involved, it tends to be on the local level, often through nongovernmental, community-based activism aimed at bringing about societal or environmental change.

The ongoing effort to resolve aboriginal land claims is a major issue in BC politics. In 1993, the provincial government established the BC Treaty Commission, intended to establish a framework by which land claims can be worked out, but little headway has been made since then. In 2000, the province and federal government reached the first modern-day treaty agreement, a pact which would give the Nisga'a Nation in northwestern BC's Nass River valley extensive self-rule rights and about $190 million in cash. But the treaty was immediately challenged in court by Liberal party leadership, who called it unconstitutional; meanwhile, many of the 100 or so other treaty negotiations have broken down due to various disagreements between the government and aboriginal bands.

It's also worth noting that the various regions of British Columbia aren't always in agreement on policy issues. In particular, people who live east of the Rockies in the province's northeastern Peace River region often feel aligned with the more conservative politics of Alberta. (Peace River region residents are particularly irked by BC's 7% provincial sales tax, which they say drives business away to Alberta, where there is no such tax.)

ECONOMY

Perhaps more so than the rest of Canada, BC's economy is driven by factors outside its control. The province's fortunes are closely tied to Asian economies, for example – when the East prospers, BC's timber and forestry exports boom. Also, the Lower Mainland sits in the shadow of nearby Seattle, the headquarters of such thriving companies as Microsoft and Amazon.com and one of the principal areas driving the US-based high-technology boom. Finally, due to its location on the main north-south transportation corridors of western North America, BC was strongly affected by implementation of the North American Free Trade Act (NAFTA), which liberalized trade among Canada, the US and Mexico.

When NAFTA took effect, many Canadians feared a loss of sovereignty to the US. Certainly, US business interests wasted no time in beefing up their Canadian presence (witness GM Place in Vancouver). Today, 85% of Canada's exports go to the US, prompting many to worry that Canada is now too reliant on the its southern neighbor for trade. Others voice concerns that, although the US has invested heavily in Canada, most profits flow to shareholders and corporate headquarters in the States.

Canada's weak dollar has also meant mixed blessings for BC. The Canadian dollar has consistently been worth only about two-thirds the value of the US dollar, which has spurred great increases in tourism from the US (up 12% in 1999) and investment. But prices and taxes in BC tend to be high, and BC residents saw an average 10% drop in real income during the 1990s. Though most BC residents would rather stay in Canada, increasing numbers head south to the US in search of greater opportunities and earnings. Those who remain in Canada are often reluctant to change jobs or take entrepreneurial risks because, as one Canadian put it, 'they fear they can't get any better than what they've already got.'

BC's Booming Pot Industry

It's possibly the third-leading industry in British Columbia, after forestry and tourism. Marijuana is big business in BC, fueled by spotty drug law enforcement and a seemingly insatiable demand for the high-potency 'BC Bud' produced by an estimated 10,000 'grow ops,' most located in the Lower Mainland and the Kootenays. Although it's obviously difficult to track the value of the illegal crops, sources estimate that BC's marijuana crop is worth between $3 billion and $3.5 billion annually.

British Columbia residents – and Canadians in general – definitely have a laissez-faire attitude toward weed. A 2000 Gallup Poll showed 33% of BC residents believed pot possession should be entirely decriminalized, with most of the rest favoring only a small fine. Not everyone in BC is a stoner, but nearly half the province's teens report trying pot at least once. It's certainly not uncommon to smell wafting pot smoke on the street. The Marijuana Party frequently fields candidates in local, provincial and federal elections. Gibsons, BC, on the Sunshine Coast, is home to Marc Emery, among the world's best-known pot activists and founder of the all-dope, all-the-time Web site (www.pot-tv.net).

That's not to say marijuana is an entirely benign matter in BC. The US, which has far tougher drug laws, is serious about intercepting as much marijuana as it can at the Canadian border. Seizures have soared in recent years; in July 2000 alone, US officials confiscated 150kg of pot on the US-Canada border, much of it at BC crossings. Moreover, some grow-ops are tied to organized crime and street gangs, and others are targeted by robbers, making active participation in pot commerce a dicey proposition. In many people's minds, that's another argument for decriminalization, as are marijuana's medicinal usefulness and the huge tax revenues the government stands to get if pot goes legit. Underground or not, marijuana cultivation will likely continue to be a key part of the modern BC economy.

POPULATION & PEOPLE

British Columbia's population was estimated in 1999 at just fewer than 4 million people, about 12% of the entire population of Canada. Nearly 2 million people live in Greater Vancouver, and another half-million reside on Vancouver Island, most in the Victoria area. About 80% of the population live in areas defined as urban. About 170,000 people are members of First Nations bands.

BC was built by wave upon wave of immigrants, and the province has many people of British, Irish, German, Italian, Japanese, Chinese, Russian and East Indian descent. Immigration isn't a phenomenon of the past, either; during the 1990s, more than a quarter-million people immigrated to BC. Many came from Asia, especially Hong Kong; most settled in the Vancouver area, though pockets of immigrants can be found province-wide. There is, for example, a thriving East Indian community near Duncan on Vancouver Island, while many Japanese-Canadians live in the Slocan Valley, where their forebears were interned during WWII.

EDUCATION

The Hudson's Bay Company started the first schools in what is now BC in the 1850s on Vancouver Island. The Public School Act of 1872 provided the framework for the present-day school system. Today, about 2000 elementary and secondary schools educate more than 600,000 students. In the urban areas especially, English is a second language for many students.

BC children typically attend school through Grade 12 (age 18); most then go on to technical-school training or university. Major universities include the University of British Columbia in Vancouver, Simon Fraser University in Burnaby (a suburb of Vancouver), the University of Victoria and the University of Northern British Columbia in Prince George.

ARTS

British Columbia has a strong arts community that bravely forges ahead despite government funding cuts and the always heavy-handed influence of the nearby US. The following sections mention a mere sampling of BC-based artists, musicians, filmmakers, writers and others who make the province a vibrant arena for creativity.

Music

Vancouver and Victoria have strong music scenes that have produced many major talents known far beyond BC. The province's biggest pop success stories belong to Bryan Adams and Sarah McLachlan. Adams had a string of hits in the 1980s and early 1990s, including 'Cuts Like a Knife,' 'Summer of '69' and 'Everything I Do (I Do It For You).' Ontario-born, he settled in North Vancouver with his family in 1974, shortly before he started waking up the neighborhood with his catchy guitar-driven rock. Sarah McLachlan is among the most successful Canadian singer-songwriters of recent years; her hits include 'Sweet Surrender,' 'I Will Remember You' and 'Building A Mystery.' She's also well known as founder of the Lilith Fair tours that showcased women musicians during the mid- to late 1990s. At the time of writing, the Matthew Good Band ranked among BC's biggest stars. The Vancouver-based group has been selling out concerts across Canada and seems poised to gain wider recognition. Burnaby-born singer Michael Buble is another rising talent to watch.

Alternative rock has always done well in BC, even before the Seattle scene gave the world grunge and riot grrrls. Notable BC alternative acts from the 1980s and 1990s include Skinny Puppy, a major industrial rock act through the mid-1990s; Bif Naked (sometimes called Canada's answer to Courtney Love); Nomeansno, a Victoria-based outfit whose music blends punk, funk and jazz; Vancouver's 54-40, compared favorably with REM; and Spirit of the West, which combined Celtic music with rock 'n' roll. Vancouver-based headbangers Superconductor found fame by having as many as nine guitarists. Neko Case is a major alt-country figure on the Northwest scene.

Groups that helped put BC on the map in the '70s include Doug and the Slugs,

Bryan Adams

Chilliwack, Loverboy, Terry Jacks and the Poppy Family (most notably for 'Seasons in the Sun'), Bachman-Turner Overdrive (BTO), Heart (although originally from Seattle) and punk rockers DOA.

Pianist-vocalist Diana Krall, who grew up in Nanaimo, is a major jazz star known for her sophisticated renderings of such standards as 'Peel Me a Grape' and 'I've Got You Under My Skin.' In Vancouver, key jazz figures include Tony Wilson, who pieces together quintets, sextets, septets and other ensembles from among the city's hottest jazz musicians. Wilson, a guitarist, tends to lean toward the post-bop and avant-garde stylings of musicians such as John Coltrane and Ornette Coleman. Blues guitarist Colin James, a Saskatchewan native, found fame after moving to Vancouver, though he is still better known in Canada than elsewhere.

Literature

British Columbia's ever-active literary scene has cultivated a wide range of literary talent, from fringe 'zine publishers to best-selling authors who were either born here or decided later in life to call the province

home. This is a land of readers, too: In the five years after the Vancouver Public Library opened its new downtown facility in 1995, patrons checked out nearly 10 million items. Readers and writers alike devour the quarterly publication *BC Bookworld*, widely available at bookstores or by writing to 3516 W 13th Ave, Vancouver, BC V6R 2S3. The Association of Book Publishers of British Columbia maintains a Web site at www.books.bc.ca.

BC writers have a knack for coining terms that become part of the culture. West Vancouver native Douglas Coupland did it in 1992 with his popular novel *Generation X*, and North Carolina transplant William Gibson introduced the word 'cyberspace' way back in 1984's *Neuromancer*. Both continue to write important works that mirror and frequently anticipate modern culture; see Coupland's *Microserfs* or Gibson's *Idoru*.

Both an illustrator and author, Nick Bantock ranks among BC's most adventurous figures. Bantock, originally from England, first drew acclaim with his *Griffin & Sabine* trilogy from the early 1990s. More recent works include his autobiographical *The Artful Dodger: Images & Reflections* and *The Museum at Purgatory*. Lynn Johnston, whose cartoon strip *For Better or For Worse* is published in 1400 newspapers worldwide, grew up and studied art in BC's Vancouver.

Hard-drinking Malcolm Lowry, best known for *Under the Volcano*, was a profoundly influential BC writer. Gordon Bowker's *Pursued by Furies: A Life of Malcolm Lowry* is a fine biography of the enigmatic writer. Roderick Haig-Brown (*The Seasons of a Fisherman*) was an avid angler devoted to conservation, especially of the Adams River sockeye salmon. A provincial park is named in his honor.

A two-time recipient of the Governor-General's Award for poetry and fiction, George Bowering has more than 40 titles to his name, including the novels *Burning Water*, about Captain George Vancouver, and *Caprice*. Alberta native WP Kinsella has long lived in BC; he's best known for his novel *Shoeless Joe*, which was adapted for the film *Field of Dreams*. Denise Chong is author of *The Girl in the Picture: The Story of Kim Phuc, the Photographer and the Vietnam War* and *The Concubine's Children*. Joy Kogawa has written two novels about the internment of Japanese Canadians: *Obasan* and *Itsuka*.

William Deverell *(Kill all the Lawyers)* and Christopher Hyde *(A Gathering of Saints)* are well-known BC-based writers of thrillers. Lee Maracle writes about the struggles of Native Indians, particularly from a woman's perspective, in such books as *Ravensong*. Another Native author, Eden Robinson is a Haisla woman who has gained notice for her short stories *(Traplines)* and novel *(Monkey Beach)*. Vancouver writer Lynn Coady has gained notice for her novel *Strange Heaven* and short-story collection *Play the Monster Blind*.

The author of about 150 books, and one of BC's most respected authors, George Woodcock was, among other things, a poet *(Tolstoy at Yasnaya Polyana* and *The Cherry Tree on Cherry Street)*, a historian, a literary scholar, a biographer and a travel writer. Another influential BC poet, Al Purdy, died in 2000 after a long and colorful career. Susan Musgrave, a *Vancouver Sun* writer and poet, is still going strong with such collections as *Things That Keep and Do Not Change*. Victoria poet Lorna Crozier has written a fistful of poetry books, most notably *Inventing the Hawk* and *Everything Arrives at the Light*. Patrick Lane, also from Victoria, is well represented in his collection *Too Spare, Too Fierce*. Other writers who have spent time in BC include Evelyn Lau, Margaret Atwood, Simon Gray, Alice Munro and Margaret Laurence.

Cinema

Vancouver is North America's third-largest film and TV production center, ranking behind only Los Angeles and New York, but filmmaking happens all over the province. Recent movies and TV series shot in BC include *The X-Files* (now relocated to Cali-

fornia), *Stargate SG-1*, *The Outer Limits*, *The Pledge*, the remake of *Get Carter*, *Scary Movie*, *The Guilty*, *Mission to Mars*, *Millennium* and *The New Addams Family*.

BC was discovered as a film location in the early 1970s, when Robert Altman directed Warren Beatty and Julie Christie in *McCabe and Mrs Miller*, shot in Vancouver. The 1980s brought two BC film classics: *First Blood*, filmed in and around Hope and best known for Sylvester Stallone's first appearance as the character John Rambo, and the delightful *Cyrano de Bergerac* update, *Roxanne*, set in Nelson and starring Steve Martin and Daryl Hannah. Today, the BC film industry generates a billion dollars in annual economic activity.

Many film productions are US-based projects that have headed north of the border to take advantage of lower production costs and BC's wide array of scenic locales. (The Vancouver area has stood in for everything from Tibet in Martin Scorsese's *Kundun* to New York City in Jackie Chan's *Rumble in the Bronx*.) But the province also has a home-grown film industry rich in directing, acting and technical talent. BC-based directors include Lynne Stopkewich *(Suspicious River)*, Anne Wheeler *(Bye Bye Blues)*, Mina Shum *(Double Happiness)* and Bruce Sweeney *(Hard Core Logo)*. Notable BC-bred actors include Hayden Christensen (who will star as the future Darth Vader in episodes two and three of George Lucas' *Star Wars* films), Michael J Fox *(Spin City, Back to the Future)*, Jason Priestly *(Beverly Hills 90210)*, Cynthia Stevenson *(The Player)*, Bruce Greenwood *(St Elsewhere)*, Fairuza Balk *(Gas Food Lodging)* and Joshua Jackson *(The Mighty Ducks)*.

The BC Film Commission supports and promotes the province's film industry. Its Web site is at www.bcfilmcommission.com. British Columbia Film is a nonprofit society established by the provincial government to expand and diversify independent film and video production in BC; its Web site is at www.bcfilm.bc.ca.

Reel West (www.reelwest.com) is an excellent source for what's going on in BC's film scene, including contact information for upcoming productions.

Vancouver Film School, established in 1997, has 750 full-time and 2000 part-time students training for a variety of careers in the film industry. For information, contact Vancouver Film School (☎ 604-685-5808, 800-661-4101), 400 W Hastings St, Vancouver BC V6B 1L2, or see the school's Web site at www.vfs.com.

Visual Arts

The best-known artist in BC history is Emily Carr, beloved for her vibrant visions of the West Coast and its Native people. (See the boxed text 'The Life and Work of Emily Carr.') Frederick Horsman Varley and Laren Harris were two members of the Group of Seven, Canadians who most strongly influenced the nation's early 20th-century art scene. WP Weston did for the mountains in his paintings what Carr had done for the coastal forests in hers. A commercial artist and landscape painter, Paul Rand was interested in making painting accessible to everyone, while Charles H Scott was more interested in finding new ways of depicting the landscape. Charles Marega is best known for his public sculptures, including the lions on the south side of Lions Gate Bridge.

British Columbia produced two Native Indian carvers who preserved the past while contributing to a new generation of Native artists. Charles Edenshaw, the first professional Haida artist, worked in argillite, gold and silver. Mungo Martin was a Kwakiutl master carver of totem poles. Martin passed on his skills to Bill Reid, the outstanding Haida artist of his generation and the first Haida artist to have a retrospective exhibition at the Vancouver Art Gallery.

Charles Edenshaw's great-grandson Robert Davidson explored innovative ways to transform Haida art, while his great-great-grandson Jim Hart is best known for his large carvings, including a newly erected totem in front of the University of British Columbia Museum of Anthropology in Vancouver. Both artists apprenticed under Bill Reid. Another family connection comes by way of Henry Hunt and his son Tony Hunt, the son-in-law and the grandson of Mungo Martin, who continued the carving tradition and the totem preservation work at the Royal British Columbia Museum in Victoria. Roy Henry Vickers is another Native artist who has found new ways to express traditional themes, often through wildlife paintings. Susan Point, a Coast Salish artist, has combined a distinctive personal style with traditional themes in a variety of mediums. See the regional chapter The North for more information on aboriginal art.

Jack Shadbolt is one of the better-known artists in Vancouver whose experimental work is often abstract, as are the paintings of Gordon Smith. Toni Onley has a distinctive style that imparts the feeling of the West Coast landscape through abstract elements, while EJ Hughes paints more realistic landscapes. Julie Duschenes paints still lifes and landscapes using abstract forms, while the landscapes, cityscapes and still lifes of Vicki Marshall are more traditional. Robin Ward is an illustrator whose drawings focus on Vancouver's heritage buildings.

Richard Prince is a sculptor who specializes in machines that often move with the wind, while Alan Storey also likes to create moving machines, such as *Pendulum* in the Hongkong Bank building on W Georgia St in Vancouver. Video art is best represented by the works of Paul Wong. Chilliwack-based painter Chris Woods recently made the *Macleans* magazine list of '100 Young Canadians to Watch.'

SOCIETY & CONDUCT

Canadians from the eastern and prairie provinces sometimes refer to British Columbia as 'Lotus Land' or 'the California of Canada.' But BC, more than twice as big as California, cannot be so easily contained.

The southwestern parts of the province – Vancouver, Victoria, the southern part of Vancouver Island as well as the Lower Mainland – do share many traits with the US West Coast. People, fashion standards and schedules are all generally more casual than in Eastern Canada. Technological advances have had the same impact here as

The Life & Work of Emily Carr

When Emily Carr died in 1945, only 50 mourners attended her funeral. These days, hundreds of people view her art each week at museums in Vancouver and Victoria – fitting vindication for a talent that was just barely recognized during her lifetime in British Columbia.

Carr was born in Victoria in 1871; both her parents died by the time she was 17. She yearned to attend art school in San Francisco, but instead became a teacher in early adulthood. It wasn't until 1899, when she accompanied a churchman to his mission at Ucluelet on Vancouver Island, that she found her spark as an artist. The Native Indian villages had a profound effect on Carr and, inspired by what she saw, she began using both the landscape and the Natives as subject matter. She soon realized, however, that she needed to learn technique, so she went to London to study landscape painting.

In 1906, after traveling to Europe, Toronto and the Cariboo region of BC, Carr moved to Vancouver to paint and teach art. She returned to Europe in 1910 for more study in Paris. It was during this time that Carr developed a unique style that combined the use of dark colors, undulating broad brush strokes and the subject matter of British Columbia's coastal forests and Native culture.

Returning to Vancouver in 1912, Carr rented a studio at 1465 W Broadway to exhibit her French paintings; she had another exhibit of 200 paintings in 1913. But her work wasn't taken seriously; some of her paintings were even deemed offensive, resulting in the withdrawal of students from her art classes. A social outcast at 42, she returned to Victoria, living on family property and working as a landlady to make ends meet.

It wasn't until the late 1920s that her scorned 1912 paintings were shown in eastern Canada and finally discovered. She then met the members of the increasingly well-known and influential school of painters called the Group of Seven, and with renewed energy and confidence continued to develop as an artist. Over the next 10 years she revisited many of her cherished Indian locales and painted some of her most acclaimed art. She also succeeded in capturing the changing face of BC's forests. *Scorched as Timber, Beloved of the Sky* (1935) shows a few solitary trees amid stumps against a billowing background of clouds. *Logger's Culls* from the same year shows a field of stumps, but the eye is drawn mainly to the rippling blue sky and lofty clouds.

As Carr's health failed and she became bedridden, she took to writing. Her book *Klee Wyck*, meaning 'laughing one,' the name given to her by the Kwakiutl people, is a collection of stories recalling her life among the Native Indians. *The Book of Small* chronicles her childhood in Victoria and *The House of All Sorts* describes her years as a landlady.

Her house in Victoria, the Carr House, is open to the public, and her paintings can be viewed at the Vancouver Art Gallery and the Art Gallery of Greater Victoria, as well as at other major museums across Canada.

they've had elsewhere; everyone in Vancouver and Victoria seems to have a cell phone and email address. Yet one senses that these things don't define their users here. Instead, people place higher priority on time to play outdoors, enjoy the arts and simply relax with friends and family. It's a trait that makes even the most urbanized areas in BC feel friendly to both frequent and first-time visitors.

Americans especially sometimes wonder if Canadians are cold, or perhaps shy. Most BC residents simply aren't as gregarious as their American counterparts, but if asked for directions or information, British Columbians are typically more than happy to help. Politeness goes a long way in laid-back BC, where people don't take kindly to loud, boorish behavior.

Farther afield in BC, the atmosphere gets even more relaxed, and it is possible sometimes to feel thoroughly removed from modern life. Bank machines, telephone service (beyond radio phones) and traffic signals are rarities in many northern towns, and a few communities even lack electricity. People in BC's smaller towns and rural areas revel in their self-sufficiency. There's certainly a strong sense of community in these rural areas, although their insular cohesiveness can sometimes make it harder for travelers to blend in than in BC's more populated areas.

First Nations culture also is more pronounced in such far-flung areas as the Queen Charlotte Islands and Prince Rupert, where aboriginal peoples aren't as badly outnumbered as they are on the Lower Mainland. But throughout BC, the First Nations influence can be felt in one important way: widespread – though not universal – respect for the environment and its riches.

RELIGION

Protestant denominations are prevalent in BC, with about 39% of the population as adherents. A quarter of the population claims no religious affiliation. Other major identifications include Catholic, Sikh, Buddhist, Muslim and Jewish.

First Nations spirituality has impacted religion and life in BC. Most aboriginal peoples believe animals and even inanimate objects possess powerful spirits, and these spirits are invoked for everything from seeking a good salmon catch to paying homage to the dead.

LANGUAGE

British Columbia, like the rest of Canada, has two official languages, English and French. English is far and away the language of the majority, though most BC residents speak at least a bit of French, and all government literature and signs use both. But many other tongues are routinely spoken in BC, especially in the Lower Mainland, where Chinese has unquestionably surpassed French as a primary language.

BC's aboriginal people are noted for their linguistic diversity. Scholars estimate that when the Europeans arrived, the region's Natives were speaking as many as 30 dialects of seven different languages. Today's First Nations bands do what they can to keep this linguistic heritage alive, although English is now the predominant language spoken among BC's Native people.

The one expression you're sure to hear in BC is 'eh?' Canadians use 'eh?' much the way Americans employ 'huh?' – as a friendly interjection that means 'Don't you agree?' or 'What do you think?' Not everyone in BC says it, but enough do that, if you spend more than a week or so here, you're likely to start using it yourself.

Facts for the Visitor

SUGGESTED ITINERARIES

Your route through BC will depend on how much time you have, what you most want to see and the activities you most enjoy. If you have only a week or two and favor outdoor pursuits, you may want to focus on exploring and savoring a small area of the province in depth. Yet urban holidays can also include plenty of recreation; Vancouver and Victoria are renowned for having abundant outdoor activities close to town, as are BC's smaller cities.

If you like road trips and want to take in as much of the province as possible, see the scenic loop-drives outlined in the annual *British Columbia Vacation Planner* published by the province. The itineraries run from three to 14 days, and many routes can be linked together. British Columbia has six tourism regions: Northern British Columbia; Victoria and the Islands; Vancouver, Coast and Mountains; Cariboo Chilcotin Coast; Thompson Okanagan; and BC Rockies. Literature outlining possible regional loop tours can be obtained for all of them. For a vacation planner or more information, call ☎ 800-435-5622 or see the Web site at www.hellobc.com.

PLANNING
When to Go

British Columbia attracts visitors year-round, though summer (June through late September) is the busiest season. Snowsports enthusiasts will probably want to come in winter (December through March), yet it's possible to ski in BC (on the slopes of Blackcomb Glacier, for example) nearly every month. Likewise, although the famous West Coast Trail on Vancouver Island and many beautiful alpine trails are accessible only in summer, many other trails are open year-round.

If you enjoy the arts and urban attractions, consider visiting Vancouver and Victoria in spring (March through May) or autumn (late September through November).

The weather is generally pleasant, and prices for accommodations are far lower than in summer. Outdoors-oriented regions like the Okanagan and Gulf Islands also are nice in spring and autumn. Accommodations and activities are usually available year-round throughout BC, but call ahead, since some places are only open summers, and others have limited schedules.

Maps

The maps in this book are sufficient to get you from place to place and around the larger towns. Free local and regional maps also are available from Visitor Info Centres throughout the province (see Tourist Offices later in this section).

Members of the Canadian Automobile Association or American Automobile Association (CAA/AAA) or affiliated clubs can get free maps before leaving home or from offices in BC. (See BCAA in the Getting Around chapter for a list.) Bookstores, gas stations and convenience stores usually sell a wide variety of maps, ranging from regional overviews to detailed street atlases. MapArt produces many sheet maps and atlas books covering BC. See them in shops or online at www.mapart.com.

What to Bring

People who need special medications should bring a supply from home or stock up before leaving the larger towns. Generally, BC stores will carry just about anything else you might need. Other standard travel gear includes an extra pair of prescription glasses or contact lenses (and an eyeglasses retainer to secure glasses if you plan outdoor activities); a small travel alarm clock; flashlight with extra bulb and batteries; and a day pack for extra layers of clothes. People planning to stay in hostels should pack a toiletries kit and small padlock or combination lock. Many hostels require a sleep sheet; if you have one, bring it, otherwise you can usually rent one at the hostel.

Dress is casual everywhere in British Columbia. The key consideration, especially for outdoors, is layering: You'll want to put on and take off clothing as needed and as the weather changes. Rain gear and an umbrella (or hooded raincoat) are essential almost everywhere. Lightweight fleece clothing works well as a layer for warmth without bulk. Hiking boots, athletic shoes and Birkenstock-type sandals are standard footwear. Visitors to Vancouver and Victoria may want to include a dressier outfit for special nights out. Pack warmer clothing (gloves, hats, a parka) for trips to mountainous areas in winter.

People planning outdoor activities needn't necessarily bring their gear with them. Outdoor equipment rental is widely available, with bicycles, in-line skates, kayaks and skis especially easy to find. People in the market for outdoor clothing and gear can bear in mind that, with the weak Canadian dollar, it may make sense to buy in BC. The selection is excellent, the quality is high and prices are reasonable.

Drivers who plan long-distance road trips should be sure their vehicle has a good spare tire, flashlight, first-aid kit and detailed maps. Bring along an extra container of gas when traveling in the north or on remote logging roads, where gas stations are few and far between. A spare blanket, some extra food and water and a cellular telephone are other good ideas for far-flung travel (though cell phones may not work in the most remote areas; if that's the case and you must stay in touch, a satellite phone may come in handy). Cell and satellite phones are now widely available for rent in BC; try your auto rental agency or Rent Express (☎ 604-713-7368 or 888-622-7368) on the Arrivals Level of the International Terminal at Vancouver International Airport.

RESPONSIBLE TOURISM

British Columbia is environmentally conscious, with widespread recycling and strict laws against littering. Do your part to help keep the province clean and green by properly disposing of your trash and recycling whenever possible. Recycling bins can be hard to find because curbside recycling is so common, but an inquiry at your accommodations should point you in the right direction. Most hostels have bins, and retail stores usually take back bottles and cans. If you camp or hike, be sure to pack out whatever you pack in.

British Columbia has many First Nations reserves. Be aware that the Native community may have different rules and regulations from the rest of the province; speed limits can vary, for example, or you may need special permission or licenses to fish, hike or hunt. Some areas sacred to the tribe may be off-limits to outsiders. Watch for posted signs, or check with the local Indian band office.

TOURIST OFFICES

Run by the government, Tourism British Columbia can assist with reservations, itinerary planning and more. Call ☎ 800-435-5622, 604-435-5622 within Greater Vancouver; or 250-387-1642 outside North America. Information is also available at the Web site www.hellobc.com or by writing to Tourism British Columbia, PO Box 9830, Stn Prov Govt, Victoria, BC, V8W 9W5, Canada.

British Columbia has a superb system of Visitor Info Centres, which can be found in more than 100 towns; all sport a distinctive green, blue and yellow logo. Typically staffed by well-trained local volunteers, the VICs offer helpful advice, maps and brochures. Many can help you secure reservations for local accommodations. Most centers operate year-round, though some keep limited schedules in the off-season. See the Information heading under each town in this book for the address of the local Visitor Info Centre.

Tourism British Columbia also has an office at 3 Regent St, London, SW1Y 4NS, England.

VISAS & DOCUMENTS
Passports & Visas

The most current information on visas can be found at Citizenship and Immigration Canada's Web site at www.cic.gc.ca. Visitors from major western countries (including

Mexico, Australia, Great Britain, New Zealand, Ireland, Japan, Germany, France and the Netherlands) need only a valid passport, and not a visa. But tourists from more than 130 nations, including most in Africa, the Caribbean, Central America, South America, Eastern Europe and the former Soviet Union, will need a visa. A complete list of Canadian embassies and consulates around the world is available at www.cic.gc.ca/english/info/emission.

Visitor visas cost $75 (or the equivalent in the currency of the country where the visa is obtained) and are good for six months. Visa requirements change frequently, and since visas must be obtained before arrival in Canada, check well before you travel. A separate visa is required for visitors intending to work or go to school in Canada.

Visitors from the USA, Greenland (Denmark) and Saint Pierre and Miquelon (France) do not need passports if they are entering from their homelands, but they do need to carry valid identification such as a driver's license, birth certificate or a certificate of citizenship or naturalization. US citizens arriving in Canada from somewhere other than the USA should carry a passport.

A passport and/or visa does not guarantee entry. Admission and duration of permitted stay is at the discretion of the immigration officer at the point of entry. If you are refused entry but have a visa, you have the right of appeal at the Immigration Appeal Board at the point of entry.

Parents of minors under 18 who are subject to a custody order must have proof of custody and a letter signifying the other parent's consent. Minors traveling alone or with only one parent also will be asked to show a letter of consent from the nonaccompanying parent or parents.

Visa Extensions An application for a visa extension must be submitted at least three weeks before the current visa expires. The fee for an extension is $75. The length of the extension is at the discretion of the particular immigration officer who is handling your application. Extensions must be applied for at a Canada Immigration Centre office. Because the office does not provide a walk-in service, call ☎ 604-666-2171 to get information on how to proceed with your application.

Travel Insurance

Residents of BC are covered by the provincial health-care system. Visitors to the province, however, are not, so it's smart to take out travel insurance before leaving home. Not only does it cover you for medical expenses (see the Health section later in this chapter) and luggage theft or loss, but also for cancellations or delays in your travel arrangements under certain circumstances, such as becoming seriously ill the day before your scheduled departure. Before obtaining special travel insurance, check what's already covered by your other insurance policies or credit card; you might find that you won't need to take out a separate policy. However, in most cases this secondary type of coverage is very limited with lots of tricky small print. For peace of mind and guaranteed security, take out a separate insurance policy at the highest affordable level. Buy travel insurance as early as possible so that you are covered if, for example, your plans are delayed due to strikes or industrial action.

Driver's License & Insurance

A valid driver's license from another country is good in Canada for up to six months, depending on where it was issued. An International Driving Permit, available in your home country through your local automobile association, is cheap, and good for one year almost anywhere in the world, although it must be shown in conjunction with your original license.

You can't drive in Canada without auto insurance. US citizens planning a trip to Canada may want to investigate the Canadian Non-Resident Interprovince Motor Vehicle Liability Insurance Card, which is only available in the USA. Visitors with US or British passports are allowed to bring their vehicles into Canada for up to six months. If you have rented a car, trailer or any other vehicle in the USA and intend to drive it into Canada, be sure to have a copy of the rental agreement with you to avoid problems at the border. The rental agreement should stipulate that taking the vehicle to Canada is permitted; in some cases, for example, cars rented in Seattle cannot be taken beyond the Vancouver/Victoria area. Also check for restrictions if you've rented a car in Canada and plan to drive into the USA.

Useful Cards

A Hostelling International (HI) card is useful at official youth hostels – nonmembers are welcome but pay between $4 to $7 more per night. If you don't get a card from HI before leaving home, you can buy one at youth hostels in BC. Many non-HI hostels also honor the HI cards for discounts.

An International Student Identity Card (ISIC) will get you admission discounts at museums, galleries and other attractions. If you are a student and don't have an ISIC card, be sure to have a valid student card from your school so you can prove you are eligible for the student admission fee.

Photocopies

All important documents (passport data page and visa page, credit cards, travel insurance policy, travel tickets, driver's license, etc) should be photocopied before you leave on your trip. Leave one copy with someone at home and keep another one with you, separate from the originals.

It's also a good idea to store details of your vital travel documents in Lonely Planet's free online Travel Vault, in case you lose the photocopies or can't be bothered with them. Your password-protected Travel Vault is accessible online anywhere in the world – create it at the Web site www.ekno.lonelyplanet.com.

EMBASSIES & CONSULATES
Canadian Embassies, High Commissions & Consulates

For embassies and consulates not on the following list, consult the Department of Foreign Affairs and International Trade. Web site: www.dfait-maeci.gc.ca/english/missions/menu.htm.

Australia
High Commission: (☎ 02-6273-3844), Commonwealth Ave, Canberra ACT 2600, www.canada.org.au
Consulate: (☎ 02-9364-3000; Visa Immigration Office ☎ 02-9364-3050), 111 Harrington St, Level 5, Quay West, Sydney, NSW 2000
Consulate: (☎ 03-9811-9999), 123 Camberwell Rd, Hawthorn East, Melbourne, Vic 3123
Consulate: (☎ 08-9322-7930), 267 St George's Terrace, Perth, WA 6000

Denmark
Embassy: (☎ 33-48-32-00), Kr Bernikowsgade 1, 1105 Copenhagen K, www.canada.dk

France
Embassy: (☎ 01-44 43-29-00), 35, Ave Montaigne, 75008 Paris, www.amb-canada.fr
Consulate: (☎ 04-72-77-64-07), 21, rue Bourgelat, 69002 Lyon

Germany
Embassy: (☎ 30 20 31 20), 12th Floor, Friedrichstrasse 95, 10117 Berlin, www.dfait-maeci.gc.ca/~bonn

Ireland
Embassy: (☎ 01-478-1988; after hours 01-478-1476), Canada House, 65/68 St Stephen's Green, Dublin 2

Japan
Embassy: (☎ 03-5412-6200), 3-38 Akasaka 7-chome, Minato-ku, Tokyo 107-5803, www.dfait-maeci.gc.ca/ni-ka

Netherlands
Embassy: (☎ 070-311-1600), Sophialaan 7, 2500 GV, The Hague, www.ocanada.nl

New Zealand
High Commission: (☎ 04-473-9577), 61 Molesworth St, 3rd Floor, Thorndon, Wellington, www.dfait-maeci.gc.ca/newzealand

UK
High Commission: (☎ 020-258-6600), Canada House, Consular Services, Trafalgar Square, London SW1Y 5BJ, www.canada.org.uk
Immigration Information: (☎ 09068-616644), 38 Grosvenor Street, London W1X 0AA
Consulate: (☎ 0131-220-4333), Standard Life House, 30 Lothian Road, Edinburgh, EH1 2DH Scotland
Consulate: (☎ 0131-220-4333), 378 Strandmillis Road, Belfast, BT9 5BL Northern Ireland

USA
Embassy: (☎ 202-682-1740), 501 Pennsylvania Ave NW, Washington, DC 20001, www.canadianembassy.org
Consulate General: (☎ 617-262-3760), 3 Copley Place, Suite 400, Boston, MA 02116

Consulate General: (☎ 312-616-1860), Two Prudential Plaza, 180 N Stetson Ave, Suite 2400, Chicago, IL 60601

Consulate General: (☎ 212-596-1600), 1251 Ave of the Americas, Concourse Level, New York, NY 10020-1175

Many other US cities have Canadian Consulate Generals; see www.dfait-maeci.gc.ca/english/missions/menu.htm.

Consulates in British Columbia

In Vancouver there are several dozen consulates (but no embassies), which are located in Ottawa, Ontario, the capital of Canada. For consulates not listed here, check the Yellow Pages under 'Consulates & Other Foreign Government Representatives.' Key consulates include the following:

Australia
 (☎ 604-684-1177), Suite 1225, 888 Dunsmuir St
Denmark
 (☎ 604-684-5171), Suite 755, 777 Hornby St
France
 (☎ 604-681-2301), Suite 1201, 736 Granville St
Germany
 (☎ 604-684-8377), Suite 704, 999 Canada Place
Ireland
 (☎ 604-683-9233), Suite 401, 1385 W 5th St
Italy
 (☎ 604-684-7288), Suite 1100, 510 W Hastings St
Japan
 (☎ 604-684-5868), Suite 900, 1177 W Hastings St
Netherlands
 (☎ 604-684-6448), Suite 821, 475 Howe St
New Zealand
 (☎ 604-684-7388), Suite 1200, 888 Dunsmuir St
UK
 (☎ 604-683-4421), Suite 800, 1111 Melville St
USA
 (☎ 604-685-4311, fax 685-7175), 1095 W Pender St

Your Own Embassy

It's important to realize what your own embassy – the embassy of the country of which you are a citizen – can and can't do to help you if you get into trouble. Generally speaking, it won't be much help in emergencies if the trouble you're in is remotely your own fault. Remember: You are bound by the laws of the country you are in. Your embassy will not be sympathetic if you end up in jail after committing a crime locally, even if such actions are legal in your own country.

In genuine emergencies, you might get some assistance, but only if other channels have been exhausted. If you need to get home urgently, a free ticket home is exceedingly unlikely – the embassy would expect you to have insurance. If all your money and documents are stolen, it might assist you with getting a new passport, but a loan for onward travel is out of the question.

Some embassies used to keep letters for travelers or have a small reading room with home newspapers, but these days most of the mail-holding services have been stopped and even newspapers tend to be out of date.

CUSTOMS

Along with your personal possessions, you are allowed to bring into Canada a duty-free allowance of 1.14L (40oz) of liquor, 1.5L or two 750mL bottles of wine, or 8.5L of beer or ale, as well as up to 200 cigarettes, 50 cigars or 200g of tobacco. Only those at least 19 years old, the age of adulthood in BC, can bring in alcohol and tobacco products. You are allowed to bring in gifts up to a total value of $60. Gifts with a value higher than $60 are subject to duty and taxes on the over-limit value.

Sporting goods, including cameras, film and two days' worth of food can be brought into the country. It's probably worthwhile to register excessive or expensive sporting goods and cameras with customs, as this will save you time and trouble when leaving, especially if you plan on crossing the Canadian-US border a number of times.

If you are bringing a dog or cat into the country you will need proof that it has had a rabies shot in the past 36 months. For US citizens this is usually easy enough, but for residents of other countries there may well be more involved procedures. To avoid problems check with the Canadian Food Inspection Agency, which also handles plant and animal health, at ☎ 888-732-6222 before leaving home.

Pleasure boats may enter Canada either on the trailer or in the water and stay up to one year. An entry permit is required and is obtainable from the customs office at or near the point of entry. All boats powered by motors over 10hp must be licensed.

Pistols, fully automatic weapons, any firearms less than 66cm (26 inches) in length and self-defense sprays (like pepper or mace) are not permitted into the country.

MONEY
Currency
The Canadian dollar ($) is divided into 100 cents (¢). Coins are 1¢ (penny), 5¢ (nickel), 10¢ (dime), 25¢ (quarter), $1 (loonie) and $2 (toonie) pieces. The 50¢ coin is seldom seen. Notes come in $5, $10, $20, $50 and $100 denominations. Bills in larger denominations are produced but rarely used, and even the $50 and $100 bills can prove difficult to cash. Canadian bills are all the same size but vary in their colors and images. Some denominations have two styles as older versions in good condition continue to circulate.

All prices in this book are in Canadian dollars unless otherwise noted. Some BC companies – capitalizing on the weak Canadian dollar – now quote their prices in US dollars in advertisements and brochures, so read the fine print if the prices seem too good to be true.

Exchange Rates
At press time, exchange rates were:

country	unit		Canadian dollar
Australia	A$1	=	$0.85
euro	€1	=	$1.33
France	1FF	=	$0.20
Germany	DM1	=	$0.68
Hong Kong	HK$10	=	$1.90
India	R10	=	$0.33
Japan	¥100	=	$1.40
New Zealand	NZ$1	=	$0.64
UK	£1	=	$2.17
USA	US$1	=	$1.49

Exchanging Money
Although some businesses in British Columbia, especially along the US border, accept a variety of currencies, it's best to exchange your money soon after arriving in the province. There are several 24-hour currency exchange machines placed throughout Vancouver International Airport, as well as several full-service Royal Bank branches within the terminals. Currency exchange offices are abundant in Vancouver and Victoria, as well as other larger towns throughout the province. Note, however, that most charge a commission fee and give less favorable exchange rates.

Traveler's Checks Traveler's checks offer protection from theft or loss. American Express, Thomas Cook and Visa are widely accepted and have efficient replacement policies. Keep a record of the check numbers and the checks you have used, and safeguard this record in a separate place from the checks. You will save yourself trouble and expense if you buy traveler's checks in Canadian dollars.

Banks & ATMs Major banks in British Columbia include Scotiabank, Canadian Imperial Bank of Commerce (CIBC), Royal Bank, and Toronto Dominion (TDBank). Most branches have automatic teller machines (ATMs), usually referred to as 'bank machines' in Canada. Banks are generally open weekdays from 9:30 am to 4 pm, and many offer 24-hour access to their ATMs.

You can get Canadian currency by withdrawing money from your home bank account at any ATM that carries the same network symbol (Pulse, Cirrus, Interlink etc) as your ATM card. Typically, these will automatically give you the current official exchange rate. Fees are usually lower at bank ATMs than at machines found in restaurants, bars and stores.

Credit & Debit Cards North America is a credit-card oriented market, and major credit cards are accepted everywhere. Indeed, car rental agencies, travel agents and most hotels prefer them to cash. The most commonly accepted cards are Visa, MasterCard (which are both affiliated with European Access Cards) and American Express. Diners Club-enRoute cards are also accepted by many businesses. Banks that issue Visa and MasterCard also offer debit cards that deduct payment directly from your savings or checking account. These are very popular and widely accepted in Canada.

If you lose your credit cards or they get stolen, contact the company immediately by calling one of the following 24-hour numbers:

American Express	☎ 336-393-1111
	(call collect)
Diners Club-enRoute	☎ 800-363-3333
MasterCard	☎ 800-826-2181
Visa	☎ 800-336-8472

International Transfers Although this method seems somewhat obsolete in these days of ATMs and debit cards, you can instruct your bank at home to send you money. Specify the city, bank and branch to which you want your money directed, or ask your home bank to tell you where a suitable one is, and make sure you get the details right. The procedure is easier if you've authorized someone at home to access your account.

Money sent by telegraphic transfer should reach you within a week; by mail allow two weeks. When it arrives it will most likely be converted into local currency – you can either take it as is or buy traveler's checks.

You can also transfer money by American Express, Thomas Cook or Western Union, though the latter has fewer international offices.

Costs

Urban and resort-oriented British Columbia are not bargain-travel destinations. Vancouver, Victoria and Whistler rank among the most expensive places in North America to visit. However, if you are prepared to stay in a hostel, cook many of your own meals and seek free or inexpensive entertainment,

you could get by on $45 to $50 a day. Staying in a very cheap hotel (or a bit nicer one, if you share costs), eating in inexpensive restaurants and allowing yourself a bit more latitude with your entertainment dollar will cost you about $100 a day. Prices are lower in the off-season (winter for most of BC; spring, summer and fall for the ski resorts).

Travel can be expensive beyond the cities, too, for different reasons. Transportation costs are high, which leads to inflated prices for everything else. There are almost no hostels in the Cariboo-Chilcotin and the North; restaurants, groceries and gas are more expensive, and Greyhound buses and rental cars are pricey because of the great distances between cities.

Tipping

Tipping is expected by restaurant and bar servers, as well as by taxi drivers, hairdressers, barbers and baggage carriers. Remember that in restaurants, bars and clubs the staff is paid minimum wage and relies on tips to make a reasonable living. Never tip less than 10% of the pre-tax bill; leave 15% if the service was fine, up to 20% if it was exceptional. Some restaurants impose a service charge on the bill, in which case no tip should be given. You needn't tip in fastfood, take-out or buffet-style restaurants where you serve yourself.

Taxi drivers, hairdressers, barbers and tour guides get 15% if their service is satisfactory. Baggage carriers (in airports or hotels) receive $1 for the first bag and 50¢ for each additional bag. Don't forget to leave a few dollars for the motel or hotel housekeeping staff if you stay more than one night.

Taxes & Refunds

The Goods & Services Tax (GST), often derided by Canadians as the Gouge & Screw Tax, adds 7% to just about every product, service and transaction, with groceries being one of the few exceptions. BC's provincial sales tax (PST) adds another 7% to the bill and is applied to most items except groceries, books and magazines. Always remember to add 14% to prices so you won't be surprised when you are handed the bill.

Some guesthouses and B&Bs don't charge GST for rooms, and foreign visitors can try asking for an exemption from the GST on their hotel bill when making payment. If paid, however, the GST added to all accommodations is refundable. The provincial sales tax is nonrefundable; however, items shipped out of BC directly by the seller are exempt.

In addition to a refund on accommodations GST, foreign visitors also get a GST refund on nonconsumable goods bought for use outside Canada, provided the goods are removed from the country within 60 days. Tax paid on services or transportation is not refundable nor is the tax paid on consumable items such as restaurant meals, gas and tobacco. The value of the goods and accommodations taxed must be at least $200 (and each individual receipt for goods must total at least $50 before taxes) and you must have original receipts; credit-card slips and photocopies are not accepted as proof of purchase. Receipts for goods must either be validated at the border if you leave by private vehicle, or accompanied by your boarding pass or tickets as proof of when you left the country by plane, bus, train or boat. Receipts for accommodations do not need to be validated, but they must be originals.

Get a copy of the *Tax Refund for Visitors to Canada* brochure (G152), which explains all the regulations and includes a rebate form. Brochures are widely available in BC, or you can write to Visitor Rebate Program, Summerside Tax Centre, Revenue Canada, 275 Pope Rd, Suite 104 Summerside, PE C1N 6C6, Canada. You can also get information by calling the Visitor Rebate Enquiries Line at ☎ 800-668-4748 within Canada or ☎ 902-432-5608 outside Canada, or online at www.rc.gc.ca.

Be wary of refund services described in brochures distributed by private companies, which charge a fee that you need not pay if you go direct through Revenue Canada. Expect to wait four to six weeks for your refund check, which is paid in Canadian dollars. Your receipts will not be returned.

Travelers driving to the USA can claim an immediate cash rebate on Canadian goods and/or accommodations at duty-free shops on the border at Abbotsford, Aldergrove, Kingsgate, Osoyoos and Surrey. Be sure to have the original receipts and proof of residence (picture identification such as a passport or driver's license).

POST & COMMUNICATIONS
Post
Canada Post is the national postal service. There are offices throughout British Columbia, as well as outlets at many pharmacies, gift shops and convenience stores (look for the Canada Post sign in the front window); many outlets are open seven days a week. Hotel gift shops or front desks often stock stamps, too.

Mail is delivered locally on weekdays. All letter or postcard mail, whether it's going to a local or an international destination, can be dropped into the red mailboxes that are found on the streets of the province's cities and small towns, often on street corners. It's best to take even small parcels to the post office if you're sending them out of Canada, because you may need to fill out a customs declaration.

A standard 1st-class airmail letter is limited to a maximum of 50g to North American destinations but up to 500g to other international destinations. First-class letters or postcards within Canada are 46¢ for up to 30g, while 1st-class letters or postcards to the USA are 55¢ for up to 30g. To all other destinations, 1st-class letters or postcards are 95¢ for up to 20g.

To the USA, heavier mail can go either by surface or, more expensively, by air in small packet mail. Anything over 1kg goes by surface parcel post. To other international destinations, letter packages up to 2kg can be sent by air. Small packet mail up to the same weight can go by either surface or air. Packages over 2kg are sent by parcel post, and different rates apply. For full details, go to a post office and pick up a pamphlet that explains all the options, categories, requirements and prices – or see the Web site at www.canadapost.ca.

Telephone

Telus (formerly BC Tel) operates the local phone system in BC; many companies offer long-distance services. Phone numbers within Canada consist of a three-digit area code followed by a seven-digit local number. If you're calling from overseas, the international country code for Canada is 1.

As of November 2001, the Greater Vancouver area will have two area codes: the old 604 and the new 778 area code. This means if you're calling locally in Greater Vancouver (including the suburbs as far east as Abbotsford and Mission), you'll need to dial ten digits: the area code plus the seven-digit number. The 778 code is an overlay assigned to newer numbers, so you may find businesses on the same street with two different area codes.

The 604 code also continues to cover the Fraser Valley (as far north as Boston Bar), Sunshine Coast and Whistler/Squamish regions. The rest of the province, including Vancouver Island, has the 250 area code.

Toll-free numbers begin with an 800, 888 or 877 area code. Note that some toll-free numbers are good for anywhere in North America, others may be within Canada only, while still others may cover just the province. Sometimes you won't know until you try the number.

Calls made from a private phone within the local calling area are free. Local calls made from a coin or pay phone cost 25¢. For cellular calls, Telus has the most extensive wireless network in BC and Alberta, and it's allied with Verizon, the largest cellular network in the US.

Hotels, motels and guesthouses often add a service charge of up to $1 for every call made from a room phone; they also have hefty surcharges for long-distance calls. To cut costs, use a public phone, which can be found in most hotel lobbies, public buildings, shopping malls, and on the streets. You can pump in quarters; use a calling card or prepaid phone card (see the section on Calling Cards & Phone Cards below for more information); or make collect calls from pay phones.

Long-distance calls to anywhere in the world can be made from any phone, but the rate varies depending on how it's done and when. It's free to dial an operator (☎ 0) to get information about rates or services, but don't ask the operator to put your call through because operator-assisted calls are much more expensive than direct-dial calls. A call made without the assistance of an operator (which can be done if you know the area code as well as the number) is not only cheaper but faster.

To make an international call direct, dial ☎ 011 + the country code + the area code + the phone number. To find a country code, look in the front of the White Pages or call the operator (☎ 0). International rates vary depending on the time of day, the destination and the telephone provider used. Call the operator or your calling card network for information.

There is no charge from a public phone for dialing local directory assistance at ☎ 411. Or you can just look in the local phone book, which usually has three parts: residential listings in the white pages, government listings in the blue pages and businesses in the Yellow Pages (which are capitalized by custom). To obtain telephone numbers for other locations in BC, Canada or the USA dial ☎ 1 + the area code + 555-1212. To find out if a business has a toll-free number call ☎ 800-555-1212. You can also look up phone numbers online at www.mybc.com.

Calling Cards & Phone Cards These wallet-sized cards can help you manage and sometimes cut your phone expenses. Your home long-distance carrier usually provides calling cards. To use them, you typically dial a toll-free number, enter a code, then enter the number you're calling. (You may need a separate toll-free access number inside Canada; call your card's customer-service number for information.) The charges for calling-card calls appear on your home phone bill.

Phone cards, by contrast, are pre-paid. You buy a card worth $10, $20 or more, and the cost of your call is deducted from the face value after you make each call. (Typically, you'll be told how much monetary value or how many minutes you have remaining before each call.) Local and international phone cards are available at just about every convenience store, grocery store, post office and pharmacy; you'll also see phone card vending machines in many ferry terminals, bus and train depots and airports.

Lonely Planet's eKno Communication is aimed specifically at independent travelers and provides budget international calls, a range of messaging services, free email and travel information. You can join online at www.ekno.lonelyplanet.com or by phone from British Columbia by dialing ☎ 800-294-3676. To use eKno's services from British Columbia once you have joined, dial ☎ 800-808-5773.

Check the eKno Web site for joining and access numbers from other countries and updates on super budget local access numbers and new features. At the time of writing, eKno rates in Western Canada tended to be higher than those for Eastern Canada (meaning, for example, it is cheaper to call Vancouver from Montreal than from Kamloops). You may be better off buying a local phone card, but be sure to compare prices and surcharges; lots of carriers quote cheap rates but add extra fees and have higher minimums/increments. (eKno calls are billed for a minimum of 30 seconds duration and then charged in increments of 15 seconds with no connection fee or surcharges.)

Fax, Telegraph & Internet Access

Faxes can be sent and received through the front desk of most hotels. Business centers such as Kinko's and Mail Boxes Etc offer reasonably priced faxing as well as computer and photocopying services.

Telegrams can be sent anywhere in Canada or overseas through AT&T Canada (☎ 888-353-4726).

Email access is available everywhere in BC. Many hostel, motel and hotel lobbies have coin or credit-card operated terminals, with access priced from 10¢ to 25¢ cents a minute, usually with a 10-minute minimum. Internet cafés charge similar rates. Some

BC libraries allow visitors to access email for free, as long as they sign a release form first agreeing to abide by the library's rules (which generally forbid accessing porn sites and the like).

INTERNET RESOURCES

The World Wide Web is a rich resource for travelers. You can research your trip, seek bargain airfares, book hotels, check on weather conditions and chat with locals and other travelers about the best places to visit (or avoid).

There's no better place to start your Web explorations than the Lonely Planet Web site (www.lonelyplanet.com). Here you'll find succinct summaries on traveling to most places on earth, postcards from other travelers and the Thorn Tree bulletin board, where you can ask questions before you go or dispense advice when you get back. You can also find travel news and updates for many of our most popular guidebooks, and the subWWWay section links you to the most useful travel resources elsewhere on the Web.

Good British Columbia–specific Web sites include:

www.hellobc.com Tourism British Columbia's official site list trip ideas, accommodations and activities

www.discoverbc.com Discover British Columbia's site is heavily commercial, but lots of useful links

www.travel.bc.ca Travel British Columbia Tourism industry site

BOOKS

The titles below offer only a sampling of the array of books written about British Columbia. Most books are published in different editions by different publishers in different countries. So a book might be a hardcover rarity in one country but readily available in paperback in another. Fortunately, searches can be done by title or author, so your local bookstore or library is best placed to check on the availability of the following recommendations.

Look at the Literature section in the Facts About British Columbia chapter for more books and writers. In addition, see the regional and activities chapters for books that focus on specific outdoor attractions and pursuits.

Lonely Planet

Although this book covers the city in some depth, Lonely Planet's *Vancouver* has even more information, especially on lodging, dining, entertainment and shopping. Other useful LP titles on the region include *Canada*, *Alaska*, *Seattle* and *Pacific Northwest*.

Guidebooks

British Columbia bookshelves are loaded with many special-interest and region-specific guides. Vancouver journalist Jack Christie is the author of several titles including *Inside Out British Columbia: A Best Places Guide to the Outdoors*. *Kids' Vancouver: Things to Do and Things to See for Kids of Every Age!* by Victoria Bushnell covers family activities throughout the metro area, with some information on Victoria, too. *A Traveller's Guide to Aboriginal BC* by Cheryl Coull is a complete guide to Native Indian sites, history and culture and includes a full range of touring options.

Vancouver: Secrets of the City by Shawn Blore and the editors of *Vancouver* magazine is an entertaining read offering lots of inside information about BC's biggest city. A similar book on Victoria (from the editors of the city's *Monday Magazine)* should be available from the same publisher by the time you read this.

Other good regional guides include *British Columbia's Gulf Islands Afoot & Afloat* by Marge & Ted Mueller; *The Gulf Island Guide: A Guide to Salt Spring, Galiano, North and South Pender, Mayne, and Saturna* by Irene Rinn; and *Sunshine & Salt Air: The Sunshine Coast Visitor's Guide*.

History & Reference

Most British Columbia history books focus on Vancouver and Victoria, but *Beyond the City Limits: Rural History in British Columbia* casts a wider net to paint a vivid picture of the frontier province. *The West Beyond the West* by Jean Barman offers a thick and

comprehensive overview of BC's infrastructural and cultural development. Ted Stone's *British Columbia History Along the Highways & Waterways* is filled with quirky stories about BC's past.

The *Historical Atlas of British Columbia and the Pacific Northwest* by Derek Hayes includes more than 300 historical maps from early expeditions to the region. *In the Path of the Explorers* by Steve Short and Rosemary Neering has a concise, readable text overview of the area's early expeditions, accompanied by beautiful photos. *The First Nations of British Columbia* by Robert J. Muckle is a good modern and historical look at the province's Native people. *Native Sites in Western Canada* by Pat Kramer provides another good overview of the province's Native sites and communities.

Published in 2000, *The Encyclopedia of British Columbia* is probably the definitive work on the province, with more than 4000 entries, 600 photographs and an accompanying CD-ROM. Also, the *Raincoast Chronicles* series details the history and culture of BC's coastal regions. These annual anthologies are now available in several bound volumes. *The Greater Vancouver Book – An Urban Encyclopaedia* edited by Chuck Davis is a hefty resource book on anything and everything to do with the city.

Natural History & the Environment

British Columbia: A Natural History by Sydney Cannings and Richard Cannings offers a comprehensive look at the province's physical and natural environments, along with analyses of global warming, forestry practices and other environmental issues.

In the Bight: The BC Forest Industry Today by Ken Drushka is a thorough and recent look at the economics and politics of BC logging. *The Great Bear Rainforest: Canada's Forgotten Coast* by Ian McAllister, Karen McAllister and Cameron Young is a beautifully photographed, readable book that details grizzly bear ecology and forestry impacts along BC's north coast.

Birds of Coastal British Columbia: A Field Guide to Common Birds of the Pacific Northwest Coast covers the islands as well as coastal mainland BC. For information on plant life, turn to *Field Guide to Old-Growth Forests: Explore the Ancient Forest of California, Oregon, Washington and British Columbia* by Larry Eifert or *Mountain Plants of the Pacific Northwest: A Field Guide to Washington, Western British Columbia, & Southeastern Alaska*, which covers 450 species of wildflowers, ferns, grasses and shrubs.

Hilary Stewart is one of Canada's best-known writers on Native Indian cultures and natural history, with books including *Stone, Bone, Antler & Shell: Artifacts of the Northwest Coast* and *On Island Time*. The latter, a delightful look at modern homesteading on Quadra Island, features numerous sketches of BC flora and fauna. The excellent *Understanding Northwest Coastal Art,* by Cheryl Shearar, is an easy-to-use guide explaining symbols in First Nations art such as totems, carvings and paintings.

General

For a nice coffee-table book, look for *British Columbia*, part of Whitecap Books' photographic series on Canadian provinces, or David Leighton's *British Columbia*. Andrew Scott's *Secret Coastline: Journeys and Discoveries Along BC's Shores* blends essays and photographs to depict the most remote stretches of BC's coast. *Bush Telegraph: Discovering the Pacific Province* is a collection of essays by *Vancouver Sun* writer Stephen Hume about the people and places of British Columbia, focusing on its small towns.

FILMS

Most of the many films made in British Columbia have stories set somewhere else, but there are exceptions. Noted Canadian director Atom Egoyan first drew wide notice with *The Sweet Hereafter*, which won the Grand Jury prize at the 1997 Cannes Film Festival for its portrayal of a fictional BC town torn apart by a school bus crash (although the Russell Banks novel that in-

spired the film actually took place in New England). *My American Cousin*, an intelligent coming-of-age comedy-drama, depicts the rocky friendship between a 12-year-old small-town BC girl and her 17-year-old relative, who is the epitome of California cool. Other films set in BC include *Far From Home: The Adventures of Yellow Dog, Once a Thief, Magic in the Water* and *The War Between Us*.

NEWSPAPERS & MAGAZINES

The two Vancouver newspapers, *The Vancouver Sun* and *The Province*, circulate widely throughout BC. *The Sun* is a fairly conservative paper, but with thoughtful coverage and some willingness to address touchy issues. Its weekly 'Mix' section on Saturdays has interesting social commentary and good writing on Canadian arts. The tabloid-style *Province* is more sensational, but it occasionally breaks important investigative stories.

The *Globe & Mail* newspaper, sometimes termed Canada's newspaper, is published daily in Toronto but is available across the country and provides a well-written record of national affairs from politics to the arts. The *National Post* is another quality national paper with an emphasis on business.

Although based in Vancouver, the weekly *Georgia Strait* is devoured throughout the Lower Mainland for its entertainment and events coverage. *Maclean's Magazine* is Canada's weekly news journal. *Beautiful British Columbia* is a handsome quarterly magazine with good photography and a broad mix of articles on travel, human and natural history, geography and other assorted 'Columbiana.' Other magazines to look for include *Outpost*, an adventure-oriented travel magazine that's published in Toronto, and *Geist*, a BC-based magazine with a great blend of fiction and nonfiction plus detailed, often hilarious maps like the 'National Beer Map of Canada.'

RADIO & TV

The Canadian Broadcasting Corporation (CBC) is heard in Vancouver at 690 AM and in Victoria at 90.5 FM. Elsewhere in the province, watch for signs on the outskirts of town telling you where CBC and local stations are on the dial. Most people consider the CBC, with its lively mix of arts, news and commentary, a national treasure.

Major towns throughout BC have a good blend of stations featuring different genres of music, news and talk. But remote areas can be 'dead zones,' where radio signals are scarce. You might want to pick up a few cassette tapes or compact discs for your car or your portable personal player.

British Columbia, especially the Lower Mainland, has a large selection of television stations, but not every TV will tune in every station. It depends on whether the set you're watching has cable and, if so, what provider serves the community. Many motels place current TV listings, or at least channel guides, in each room; if not, check the local newspaper or click around the stations to find a channel devoted to listings.

The Canadian Broadcasting Corporation is on TV, too; its Vancouver stations are CBUT (3) and CBUFT in French (7). The Canadian Television Network (CTV), the country's commercial station, is on BCTV (11) in Vancouver and CHEK (6) in Victoria. Other stations that might be of interest (check the cable guide for numbers) include the Weather Network, CBC Newsworld, the Women's Television Network and Much-Music. The major US-based broadcast and cable networks are also carried on many cable systems in BC, especially in the Lower Mainland.

PHOTOGRAPHY & VIDEO

Print film is available at supermarkets and discount drugstores (both of which offer the best prices). Slide film is a bit more difficult to find; you may need to go to a camera store. Carry an extra battery for your built-in light meter or compact camera.

Pharmacies and grocery stores are good places for cheap film processing. If you drop off film by 11 am or noon, you can usually pick it up the next day. If you want your pictures right away you can find one-hour processing outlets throughout British Co-

lumbia, but be prepared to pay up to double the overnight cost.

For videos, Canada uses NTSC color TV standard, which (unless it is converted) is not compatible with other standards (PAL or SECAM) used in Africa, Asia, Australia and Europe. If you are visiting from anywhere outside the Americas or Japan, keep in mind that if you buy a pre-recorded video tape here it might not be playable at home. Shops may stock PAL versions, but very few have tapes in SECAM.

TIME

Most of BC is on Pacific Standard Time, which is eight hours behind Greenwich Mean Time; four hours behind Atlantic Standard Time (encompassing the Maritime Provinces apart from Newfoundland which is 4½ hours behind); three hours behind Eastern Standard Time (including Montreal, Ottawa and Toronto); two hours behind Central Standard Time (including Winnipeg and Regina); and one hour behind Mountain Standard Time (including Edmonton and Calgary). But the eastern part of the province (including Cranbrook, Fernie, Golden, Dawson Creek and Fort St John) observes Mountain Time.

The province generally observes daylight saving time; clocks go forward one hour on the first Sunday in April and are turned back one hour on the last Sunday in October.

ELECTRICITY

Canada uses 110 volts and 60 cycles, and plugs have two or three pins (two flat pins often with a round 'grounding pin'). Plugs with three pins don't fit into a two-hole socket, but adapters are available at Radio Shack, other electronic stores and hardware stores.

WEIGHTS & MEASURES

Canada officially changed from imperial measurement to the metric system in the 1970s, but even today, you'll find both systems remain for many day-to-day uses. The old system can never be eliminated completely as long as the USA, Canada's largest trading partner, still uses its version of imperial measure.

All speed-limit signs are metric – so don't go 100mph! Gasoline is sold in liters, but items such as ground beef and potatoes often are sold by the pound. Radio stations usually give temperatures in Celsius.

For help in converting between the two systems, see the chart on the inside back cover of this book. Note that the US system, basically the same as the imperial, differs in liquid measurement, most significantly (for drivers) in the size of gallons.

LAUNDRY

British Columbia has an abundance of coin-operated laundries and dry cleaners. Some coin laundries offer a drop-off service where you leave your clothes for the day and they will wash, dry and fold your laundry for about $1 a pound. Self-service washing machines generally cost $1.25 to $1.50 for a 25-minute cycle, while it will take another dollar or two to get your clothes dry. Most also have coin-op vending machines for laundry supplies.

Many hotels, especially the more upscale ones, offer laundry services but charge very high prices. Many lower-priced motels, hostels and campgrounds have guest laundries on the premises. Or you can check the regional chapters in this book or the Yellow Pages under 'Laundries' to find one close to you.

TOILETS

Public toilets, more commonly referred to as washrooms or restrooms, are free to use, easy to find and are located in shopping malls, department stores, most restaurants, bars and service stations. You may have to ask for a key, but as long as you look reasonably well presented, or especially desperate, you shouldn't have a problem. You will also find toilets at highway rest areas and in many public parks. Most are clean, but some (especially in parks) can be hangouts for drug users, which means that you'll have to keep an eye out for discarded needles. Always accompany small children into public restrooms.

HEALTH

You don't need any special vaccinations to visit Canada and you are unlikely to encounter any serious threat to your health. Up-to-date tetanus, polio and diphtheria immunizations are always recommended no matter where you are traveling.

You are well advised to take out travel insurance before leaving home, since a visit to a hospital or a dentist could wipe out your budget. The standard rate for a bed in a city hospital is at least $500 a day and up to $2000 a day for nonresidents. The largest seller of hospital and medical insurance to visitors to Canada is Ingle Life & Health, which offers hospital medical care (HMC) policies for a minimum of seven days to a maximum of one year, with possible renewal of one additional year. The 30-day basic coverage costs $90 for an adult under the age of 55, $110 for ages 55 to 64 and $126 above that. Family rates are available. Coverage includes the hospital rate, doctor's fees, extended health care and other features. Visitors to Canada are not covered for conditions they had prior to arrival. If you are planning a side trip to the USA be sure to inquire about coverage details. Ingle also offers insurance policies (at reduced rates) for foreign students and to those visiting Canada on working visas. For more information call ☎ 604-684-0668, or look in the Yellow Pages for a local agent.

In Vancouver, try Customplan Financial Services (☎ 604-687-7773) 1440 – 1055 W Hastings St. Customplan pamphlets are available in about 15 languages and can be found at post offices, pharmacies, doctor's offices and some shopping centers. Read the information carefully, as there are exclusions and conditions that should be clearly understood. Also, check the maximum amounts payable, as different policies allow for different payments.

For nonemergency health concerns, many BC towns have no-appointment-necessary clinics, usually with extended evening hours. You might also visit a pharmacy and talk with the pharmacist.

Look in the Yellow Pages for HIV/AIDS information and testing in major BC towns.

WOMEN TRAVELERS

British Columbia is generally a safe place for women traveling alone, although the usual precautions apply. In Vancouver, the Main and Hastings Sts area is best avoided, and it's probably not a good idea to go for a walk in Stanley Park on your own after dark. In more remote parts of the province, particularly the North, women traveling alone will find themselves a distinct minority.

It's a bad idea to accept a drink from strangers. The use of such 'date rape' drugs as Rohypnol and Clonazepam isn't unheard of in BC; these drugs, usually slipped surreptitiously into alcoholic beverages, quickly render the drinker unconscious and vulnerable to rape or other attack. If you're alone in a bar or restaurant and face an unwanted advance, politely and firmly say 'no' and you'll usually be left alone.

On a cheerier note, the more populated and frequently visited parts of BC are great for women travelers. Hostels usually have formal or informal group outings to pubs and local attractions, and many outfitters, ski areas and the like offer trips and classes geared to women. With these opportunities, BC is an excellent place to experiment with new recreational activities and meet many like-minded women and men who enjoy adventure and active travel.

GAY & LESBIAN TRAVELERS

In BC, there is a vast gulf between the urban attitude toward gays and lesbians and the sensibilities you'll encounter in the hinterlands. In Vancouver and the Lower Mainland, gay and lesbian couples are numerous and welcome, and few people look askance at public displays of affection. (The gay rights movement in Canada began in Vancouver when, in 1964, a group of feminists and academics started the Association for Social Knowledge, the first gay and lesbian discussion group in the country.) In places like Victoria, Nanaimo, the Okanagan and Nelson, gay life is a bit more underground, but still visible to anyone who's interested. But in farther-flung towns, any gay or lesbian communities that exist are hard to find, and people are advised to keep their orientation to themselves to avoid harassment or, at the minimum, discomforting stares.

In Vancouver, the weekly newspaper *Xtra West* is the best source of information on local gay and lesbian events, entertainment and services. The Vancouver Gay and Lesbian Business Directory is online at www.glba.org. On Vancouver Island, look for copies of the *Vancouver Island Region Pink Pages*, also available online at www.gayvictoria.com/pinkpages. Both directories list some businesses outside the metro areas as well; try searching online by city name.

DISABLED TRAVELERS

British Columbia is generally an easy place for disabled travelers to get around. Vancouver was the first city in Canada to provide scheduled bus service for people with disabilities, and BC Transit runs lift-equipped buses on many of its local systems throughout the province. Most municipal systems also have HandyDART, a custom door-to-door service that can be booked up to four days in advance. Call the local transit systems listed throughout this book for more information. Greyhound Lines of Canada (☎ 604-661-8747) also has lift-equipped buses, and the major airlines all offer special services to physically challenged passengers.

Vancouver Taxi (☎ 604-255-5111) runs 30 wheelchair-accessible cabs in BC's largest city, and many other companies throughout the province have similar services. Public and private parking lots have designated spaces for disabled drivers. Many motels and other accommodations have rooms designed for people with mobility problems.

The BC Coalition of People with Disabilities (☎ 604-872-1278) has an advocacy service and can help find answers to questions on disability issues in the province. Other helpful information sources include the Sport and Fitness Council for the Disabled (☎ 604-737-3039) and *We're Accessible*, a newsletter for disabled travelers (☎ 604-588-3731).

Headquartered in the USA, the Society for the Advancement of Travel for the Handicapped (SATH; ☎ 212-447-7284), 347 Fifth Ave No 610, New York, NY 10016, has information sheets on a wide range of destinations around the world, or it can research your specific requirements. Membership is $45 a year ($30 for seniors and students); the information charge for nonmembers is $5, which covers costs. Information also is available online at www.sath.org. Mobility International USA (☎/TTY 541-343-1284), PO Box 10767, Eugene, OR 97440, offers disability-related international exchanges and a free information and referral service for study, work, research or volunteering abroad.

SENIOR TRAVELERS

Much of southern BC is a retirement haven. The Okanagan Valley (Penticton, Kelowna, Vernon), with mild weather and a gazillion golf courses, is especially popular; Victoria (and much of southern Vancouver Island), Vancouver and the Gulf Islands have many retirees, too. Canadian retirees like BC because the exchange rate isn't as favorable in US retirement areas like Florida and Arizona; US retirees are heading north because their money, by contrast, goes far against the weak Canadian dollar.

Seniors are generally considered to be those over the age of 60, although discounts may apply as early as 50 or as late as 65. You might be asked to show proof of age, so carry your passport or driver's license with you. Discounts are widely available at restaurants, pharmacies, banks, movies and other entertainment venues. There are special discounts for seniors on BC Transit, and the HandyDART system is also available to seniors who have difficulty walking (see Disabled Travelers for details). Travel on BC Ferries is free for seniors who are BC residents Monday to Thursday, except on public holidays. There are also seniors' discounts on BC Rail, VIA Rail and the various bus companies.

The country's main seniors' organization is the Canadian Association for the Fifty-Plus (CARP; ☎ 416-363-8748), Suite 1304, 27 Queen St E, Toronto, ON M5C 2M6. Its Web site is www.fifty-plus.net. CARP promotes and protects Canada's fifty-plus population and offers group discounts on products and services. A one-year membership for Canadian residents costs $15.95 including a subscription to *CARP News/ Fifty-Plus* magazine.

TRAVEL WITH CHILDREN

British Columbia-based Kid Friendly! Services (☎ 604-925-6063) promotes businesses and services geared toward children and families, including hotels, restaurants, attractions, stores and festivals. See its directory online at www.kidfriendlyworld.com. The local Visitor Info Centres also have good ideas on where to have fun with children of all ages.

Children are welcome in all but the fanciest restaurants. Most places have children's menus and place mats to color (though it's always a good idea to pack along your own stash of crayons and paper, as well as crackers or other finger foods for small children who can't wait to eat). Many establishments have separate dining rooms for families (since minors cannot go into the pubs, bars or lounges, even when accompanied by their parents). Families with very young children will appreciate that diaper-changing and nursing facilities are available at most restaurants, shopping centers and major attractions, as well as on larger BC Ferries boats. Most city and suburban accommodations are family friendly, though some bed-and-breakfasts and resorts – especially in more adult-oriented areas like the Gulf Islands – aren't well suited for children.

There are special events and activities aimed at children throughout the province. The biggest of these is the Vancouver International Children's Festival (☎ 604-687-7697), which is held annually in Vanier Park during the last week in May. The festival is a world of fun and entertainment for children of all ages and attracts about 200 Canadian and international acts, including musicians, actors, mimes, clowns, puppeteers, jugglers and storytellers. The Vancouver Island Festival for Young Audiences takes place in

Nanaimo about the same time of year; call ☎ 250-753-8828 or 888-734-9833 for more information.

If you want a break from the kids for a day trip or evening out, you might consider leaving them with a qualified child-care service. Some hotels offer such a service, or they can advise you on whom to contact. Generally, the better agencies use people 18 or older who have been trained in first aid and CPR, have had a security clearance through the police and are insured. There is usually a three-hour minimum, and the cost is approximately $11 an hour. Reputable agencies include Just Like Mum! (☎ 604-325-4225) and Kids Included (☎ 604-803-3337) in Vancouver. The latter specializes in outings for children ages three to 12.

The Lonely Planet book *Travel With Children,* by Maureen Wheeler, is a good place to start if you want some tips on the fundamentals of traveling with youngsters. Above all, remember that children's attention spans vary from day to day, and most kids appreciate time just to hang out. Don't try to pack too many activities into your trip, allow plenty of breaks and share their sense of discovery and fun.

DANGERS & ANNOYANCES
Urban Problems

British Columbia is generally a very safe place. Violent crime is unusual, but theft is common; Vancouver is especially plagued with car break-ins, car theft and bicycle theft. Always lock your car and take anything of value with you or secure it in the trunk. Rent a car locally, if possible, because vehicles with out-of-province plates are most vulnerable to break-ins. Parking is a major hassle in Vancouver, too; it's best not to bring a car at all, if possible. Always lock your bicycle with a sturdy U-shaped lock. No matter where you travel, always be aware of your surroundings and never leave personal belongings such as shoulder bags or backpacks in a location where you can't lock them up or watch them at all times.

Beggars work the streets of Vancouver and, to a lesser extent, Victoria. Because of southern BC's mild winter climate (at least compared to the rest of Canada), many people end up here without a job or a home, so they resort to begging in order to scratch out an existence. Drug abuse is a problem in the city, which means many panhandlers are only after enough money to pay for their next fix. They bring out all the tired old lines like 'I only need another 70¢ to make up my bus fare,' 'My wallet was stolen, can you help me?' or 'I've just lost my job and my baby son needs food.' Some beggars simply sit under a blanket in a doorway with their hand extended.

Prostitution has always been a problem on Vancouver's streets; all the authorities seem to be able to do is shift it from one neighborhood to another. A large number of streetwalkers tend to work in East Vancouver in areas that tourists aren't likely to visit unless, of course, they are looking for this particular service.

Outdoor Hazards

Bears Bear attacks, though rare, are a very real threat in BC. Black bears do not eat meat. Grizzlies, though carnivores, mostly eat rodents, not people. Bears generally avoid humans, but they're attracted by the smell of food. Bears who become conditioned to the presence of humans and food are the most likely to cause trouble.

Never approach or feed a bear. Cook and clean up well away from your sleeping area. If you're car camping, store food in airtight containers in your vehicle. Double-bag smelly garbage, and use provided refuse containers or pack it all out. In the backcountry, you'll need to use a bear cache or hang food away from your tent, and away from tree trunks, since most bears can climb. Hoist it up high enough (about 5 or 6m) and away from the trunk so a standing or climbing bear can't reach it. Never, ever keep food or even toothpaste or any other odorous material in your tent. When you're in bear country, always sleep in a tent, not under the stars.

Don't try to get close-up photographs of bears and never come between a bear and its cubs. If you see any cubs, quietly and quickly disappear. Do everything you can to reduce your chances of surprising a bear. While hiking through woods or in the mountains in bear country, some people wear a noise-maker, like a bell, but talking, singing and clapping are good, too, especially as you move around bends in the trail. It's best to hike in groups. Children hiking with you must be kept close by, in a carrier if they're small enough. Keep pets at home if possible (they're prohibited in some BC Parks), but definitely on a leash. Stay on marked trails and comply with all posted warnings.

Other potentially dangerous wild animals in BC's backcountry include mountain lions (cougars), elk, bighorn sheep, moose and wolves. Always photograph and view wildlife at a distance through telephoto lenses or binoculars. Never feed or approach wildlife, especially not mothers tending their young. Report any encounters with bears or mountain lions to park staff, forest rangers or other local authorities.

Blackflies & Mosquitoes In spring and summer, blackflies and mosquitoes can be murder in the interior and northern reaches of BC. There are tales of lost hikers going insane from the bugs. This is no joke – they can make you miserable. The effect of a bite (or sting, technically, by the mosquito) is a small itchy bump. The bite itself inflicts just a minor, passing pain and an unsightly welt and ensuing itch. The potential trouble is mainly psychological; the cumulative effects of scores of bites can keep you up at night, itchy, grumpy and paranoid that you're being eaten alive.

Though mosquitoes only average a month's lifespan, and only the females bite, there are 36 different species living in BC. June and July are generally the worst months, especially in the late afternoon in the woods. Building a fire will help, and camping in a tent with a zippered screen is a necessity. In clearings, along shorelines or anywhere there's a breeze you'll be safe, which is why Vancouver and the coast are relatively bug-free.

Darker clothes attract biting insects more than lighter ones. Perfume, too, evidently attracts the wrong kind of attention. Wherever you go, bring 'bug dope' in liquid or spray repellents. Two recommended names are Muskol and Off. Deet, an ingredient often used in repellents, will do the trick, but is harmful to the environment and should not be used on children. Avon's Skin-So-Soft cream is one of the best 'natural' bug repellents around. If you're left empty-handed with no bug spray at all, try using your deodorant (the zinc in it helps), or rub lemon or orange peel on your skin. Cover yourself up by wearing a long-sleeved shirt, long pants and a hat. Most of all, make friends with dragonflies, whose favorite food is the buzzing mosquito.

Ticks Wood ticks hop onto warm-blooded hosts from tall grasses and low shrubs throughout BC. They're most troublesome March through June. Protect your legs by wearing gaiters, or pants tucked into socks. Give yourself, your children and pets a good going over after outdoor activities. According to BC Parks literature, if you find a tick burrowing into your skin, it's most easily removed by grasping and pulling it, gently, straight up and out with a small pair of tweezers. Disinfect the bite site with rubbing alcohol. Save the tick in a small plastic or glass container if possible. That way, a doctor can inspect it if a fever develops or the area around the bite appears to be infected.

Swimmers Itch A tiny parasite in some of BC's lakes can generate this pesky rash. However, warnings are usually posted at places where it's a problem. To prevent itching, apply baby oil before you enter the water and dry off completely with a towel after getting out.

Fire Campfires should be confined to fire rings at designated campgrounds or fire pans in the backcountry. Before going to bed or leaving an area, make sure fires (including cigarettes) are completely out. Special care must be taken during the summer months, when fire danger is at its highest. Forest fires often force temporary

Bear Encounters

Bear-encounter tips continue to evolve as biologists and others study previous attacks to learn what worked and what didn't. These are good general guidelines, mostly from BC Parks:

In an encounter, you need to try and tell if it's a black bear or a grizzly. Black bears can be as dangerous as grizzlies, sometimes more so, and they definitely behave differently. Black bears can be any color. They are usually about 90cm high at the shoulder, with a straight face profile; short, curved claws; and a barely noticeable shoulder hump. Grizzlies are usually (though not always) larger, about 1m at the shoulder or 1.8 to 2m when standing. Grizzlies have a dished, or concave, face profile; curved claws; and a prominent shoulder hump.

If the bear is spotted in the distance, make a wide detour or leave the area immediately. If you are at close range, do not approach the bear. Remain calm, keep it in view. Avoid direct eye contact. Move away without running.

If the bear approaches you and is standing up, it is usually trying to identify you. Talk softly so it knows what you are. If it is snapping its jaws, lowering its head, flattening its ears, growling or making 'woofing' sounds, it is displaying aggression. Do not run unless you are very close to a secure place. Move away slowly, keeping it in view. Avoid direct eye contact. Dropping your pack or an object may distract it to give you more time.

If the bear charges, your response depends on the species and whether the bear is being defensive or offensive. Bears sometimes bluff their way out of a confrontation by charging then turning away at the last moment. Generally, the best response is to do nothing to threaten or further arouse the bear. Each incident is unique, and the following are only guidelines, offered as possible ways to deal with an unpredictable animal and complex situation:

If a grizzly attacks, play dead. Some experts advise the 'cannonball position' with your hands clasped behind neck and face buried in knees, mostly to protect your internal organs. Others advise lying face down, with your legs apart and your hands clasped behind your neck, which will

campfire bans even far from the burning areas, so obey posted signs.

Water Tap water in BC is safe to drink, but in the backcountry, you'll need to purify environmental water before drinking it. The simplest way of purifying water is to boil it – vigorous boiling for five minutes should be satisfactory even at high altitude. (Remember that water takes longer to come to a boil at high altitudes, so be patient.)

Simple filtering will not remove all dangerous organisms, so if you cannot boil water it should be treated chemically. Chlorine tablets (Puritabs, Steritabs or other brand names) will kill many pathogens, but not giardia and amoebic cysts. Iodine is very effective in purifying water and is available in tablet form (such as Potable Aqua), but

follow the directions carefully and remember, too much iodine can be harmful.

EMERGENCIES

Nearly everywhere in BC, the emergency number for police, fire department and ambulance is ☎ 911. All federal, provincial and city government offices appear in the blue pages in the telephone directory; the front of every phone book also contains a complete list of community organizations that might be useful.

The Royal Canadian Mounted Police (RCMP) has a Tourist Alert program by which the media and visitor centers team up to get urgent messages (about an illness at home, for example) to BC visitors. If you see or hear your name in such an alert, call the phone number given.

Bear Encounters

make it harder for the bear to flip you over. Do not move until the bear leaves the area, then get up and leave the area without running. If a black bear attacks, do not play dead and don't climb a tree. While fighting back usually increases the intensity of an attack, it may cause the bear to leave. Fighting back is not advised against grizzlies or against any bears with cubs.

If a grizzly or black bear attacks aggressively (including when you are sleeping), do not play dead. Try to escape to a secure place (car or building); if it's a mature grizzly, you can try to climb a tree. If you have no other option, try to intimidate the bear with deterrents or weapons such as tree branches or rocks. If a bear attacks for your food, abandon the food and leave the area.

Bear pepper sprays have helped deter some attacking bears, but only when they've been used properly. Be sure you know how to use the spray if you carry it (read the label and know which way the wind is blowing; you'll want to be upwind from the bear so the spray doesn't blow back in your face). If you pack spray, carry it in a holster where it will be easily accessible, not in your pack. Never use pepper spray as a substitute for other precautions.

If you're hiking or camping in the national parks, definitely read the pamphlet *You Are in Bear Country*, which offers advice on steering clear of bears.

LEGAL MATTERS

If you are arrested, you are allowed to remain silent. There is no legal reason to speak to a police officer; however, never walk away from an officer until given permission. If arrested you must be formally told of the charges and are allowed to make one phone call. You also have the right to an interpreter if English is not your first language. If you don't have a lawyer or someone who can help you, call your consulate. The police will give you the number upon request.

If you want legal advice or referral to a lawyer, contact the Legal Aid-Legal Services Society at ☎ 604-601-6100; this is a taped message, but if you listen long enough you will eventually find the information you need, hopefully before you're due to appear

in court. In Vancouver, you can also visit the Legal Resource Centre at 200-1140 West Pender St.

BUSINESS HOURS

Stores in downtown retail areas open around 9 or 10 am and close around 5 or 6 pm. Suburban shopping centers, discount stores and grocery stores typically stay open until 9 pm; some groceries and pharmacies are open 24 hours. On Sunday, businesses have more limited hours, with department stores and some shopping centers not opening until noon and closing at 5 pm.

PUBLIC HOLIDAYS & SPECIAL EVENTS

National public holidays are celebrated throughout Canada. Banks, schools and government offices (including post offices) are closed and transportation, museums and other services are on a Sunday schedule. Holidays falling on a weekend are usually observed the following Monday, and these long weekends (Victoria Day, Canada Day, BC Day and Labour Day) are among the busiest on BC's roads and waterways. Either plan your visit for a different time or secure accommodations far ahead for any of these long-weekends. The following is a list of the main public holidays:

January
New Year's Day (January 1)

March-April
Easter (Good Friday, Easter Monday)

May
Victoria Day (Monday preceding May 24)

July
Canada Day (July 1)

August
BC Day (first Monday of the month)

September
Labour Day (first Monday of the month)

October
Thanksgiving (second Monday of the month)

November
Remembrance Day (November 11 – banks and government offices closed)

December
Christmas Day (December 25)
Boxing Day (December 26; many retailers open, other businesses closed)

Nearly every small town in BC has an annual festival or two, and the larger cities have a steady stream of them. Festivals serve not only to attract tourists, but also to give far-flung neighbors an opportunity to come together and party. BC's festivals include food- and wine-centered events (the Okanagan spring and fall wine festivals), First Nations celebrations (pow wows in Kamloops and Squilax), arts-and-crafts shows (the Filberg Festival in Comox), music and dance events (the DuMaurier International Jazz Festival in Vancouver and the International Street Performers Festival in Nelson) and harvest-time fairs and rodeos (Williams Lake, Bella Coola, Fort St

John and more). You'll find more information on many of these in the regional chapters. The annual British Columbia Vacation Planner from Tourism British Columbia includes many listings, too.

COURSES
Many people come to Canada to learn how to speak English. The Canadian College of English Language (☎ 604-688-9366), 1477 W Pender St, Vancouver, offers intensive and super-intensive English as a Second Language classes, as well as a four-week training program for people who want to be ESL teachers. Home-stay and farm-stay accommodations can be arranged. See the college's Web site at www.canada-english.com or email ccel@direct.ca for more information.

WORK
People who aren't Canadian citizens or permanent residents need to apply for employment authorization (EA), which will be issued by an immigration officer after a Human Resources Canada Centre (HRCC) approves your job offer. You usually must apply outside Canada and allow six months for processing; there's also a $150 fee. Residents of the US, Greenland, St. Pierre and Miquelon can apply for an EA when entering Canada. To apply this way, you must produce your confirmation of offer of employment and other papers when you arrive at the port of entry. Find out what papers you will need before arriving in Canada. For complete information, see the 'Do You Want to Work Temporarily in Canada?' section of Citizenship & Immigration Canada's Web site at www.cic.gc.ca. Another section on this helpful site details opportunities for live-in caregivers; many young women from abroad work in Canada as nannies.

Of particular interest to Australian students may be the Student Work Abroad Program (SWAP), organized by the National Union of Students (NUS) and the Canadian Federation of Students (CFS). This program allows Australians between the ages of 18 and 25 to spend a year in Canada on a working holiday. This program only has space for 200 people a year, and applicants must be enrolled in a post-secondary educational institution. For details contact, in Australia, the NSU (☎ 03-9348-1777), PO Box 1130, Carlton, Victoria, 3053.

The Working Holiday Program is for all Australians between the ages of 18 and 25, and they need not be enrolled in a post-secondary educational institution. This program has an annual quota of 3000. Application forms can be obtained by contacting the Canadian Consulate General in Australia at Level 5, 111 Harrington St, Sydney NSW 2000; ☎ 02-9364-3000; fax 02-9364-3098; email sydny@dfait-maeci.gc.ca. Applications for this program take up to two months to process.

Willing Workers On Organic Farms (WWOOF) is an international organization dedicated to helping people learn organic farming techniques and to help farmers make organic production economically viable. WWOOF Canada has about 200 farm and homestead hosts throughout BC where people can volunteer in exchange for accommodations and meals. For information, write to WWOOF Canada, RR 2, S.18, C.9, Nelson, BC, Canada, VIL 5P5; call ☎ 250-354-4417; or email wwoofcan@uniserve.com. A one-year membership, which includes a descriptive booklet covering all of Canada, costs $30 plus postage.

ACCOMMODATIONS
Most areas of British Columbia have abundant accommodations, available for a wide range of prices. The North is the only exception; this far-flung region has almost nothing in the way of hostels, and its relatively few and generally spartan motel rooms are priced higher than comparable inns elsewhere.

The annual accommodations directory published by Tourism British Columbia is a helpful, highly detailed guide to what's available in all classes of lodgings. Everything listed has been inspected and approved by Tourism British Columbia. The guide is free; it's available at Visitor Info Centres or by calling ☎ 800-435-5622 (☎ 250-387-1642 outside North America).

Camping
Camping is among the most popular activities enjoyed by BC residents and visitors. There are many available places to camp, from primitive forest sites to deluxe campgrounds with resort-style amenities. Reservations are a good idea during the summer, and they're essential in the most popular places for holiday long weekends.

The annual magazine-style booklet *Super Camping Guide* is a good resource for finding private, RV-oriented campgrounds, although it also lists BC Parks sites. Look for the guide at visitor centers or online at www.camping.bc.ca. Private campground sites cost about $20 to $35 a night for two people, depending on the services (electricity, water, cable TV) your rig requires. Tent sites usually cost about $17 to $23, but most tent campers will be happier in a less-expensive, more outdoorsy BC Parks or BC Forest Service campground.

British Columbia Parks manages hundreds of campgrounds, with fees ranging from $8 per party for basic sites to $18.50 per party for the most highly developed campgrounds. About 70 parks offer reserved sites; your best bet is to get a current copy of the brochure *Reserve Your Spot in BC's Great Outdoors* published annually by the Discover Camping Campground Reservation Service and available online at www.discovercamping.ca. or at all Visitor Info Centres. Reservations numbers are ☎ 800-689-9025 or 604-689-9025 in Greater Vancouver. This service can also reserve spots at Green Point, the only Parks Canada campground within Pacific Rim National Park Reserve. It costs $6.42 per night (to a maximum of $19.26 for three or more nights), plus campsite fees.

Of course, many BC Parks campgrounds (and often some sites within the reservable campgrounds) operate on a first-come, first-served basis. Midweek or during spring and fall, you can usually just show up and pick your spot. The parks also have many backcountry sites for backpackers and boaters. Most are $5 per person.

There are a whopping 1400 BC Forest Service campgrounds; all are first-come, first-served. They used to be free, but fees now apply: $8 per night or $27 per year ($22 for seniors). Annual and nightly passes are available at sporting goods stores and some Visitor Info Centres. About 30 of the most heavily used sites charge 'enhanced' fees of $10 per night, or $5 for annual pass holders. The BC Forest Service sites are an excellent deal if you like rustic camping and plan to be in the province for more than a few nights (long enough to justify buying the $27 annual camping pass). Kathy and Craig Copeland's *Camp Free in BC* books (Voice in the Wilderness Press) are good guides to hundreds of Forest Service sites. Volume 1 covers southern BC, and Volume 2 details the province's central regions. You can also get more information on Forest Service campgrounds by visiting the Web site at www.for.gov.bc.ca; click on 'recreation' under popular topics.

Hostels

Hostels are the best bet for cheap indoor accommodations. Most have beds for about $15 to $20 per person per night. These are usually in dorm-style rooms with four to six beds, although many hostels offer private rooms for not a whole lot more money. Expect shared baths, kitchen facilities and common areas where you can meet fellow travelers. Amenities might include a variety of discounts, laundry facilities, Internet access, game rooms, bike or other sporting gear rentals and group outings to area pubs and attractions. Unlike motels and other lodgings, quoted hostel rates usually include the tax.

The 'name brand' for budget travel, Hostelling International has locations in or near Cranbrook, Fernie, Kamloops, Nelson, Pender Island, Penticton, Powell River, Revelstoke, Rossland, Salt Spring Island, Shuswap Lake, Tofino, Vancouver, Vernon, Victoria, Whistler and Yoho National Park, as well as at Banff and Japser National Parks just over the Alberta border. HI

hostels are almost always a good bet for cleanliness, comfort and good vibes. The only downside we've seen is they can be a bit institutional. You can reserve HI beds online at www.hihostels.bc.ca or by contacting the hostel direct; each HI affiliate is covered in this book's regional chapters. For more information, see the Web site; call ☎ 604-684-7111; fax 684-7181; email info@hihostels.bc.ca; or write to Hostelling International, 402-134 Abbott St, Vancouver, V6B 2K4, BC.

Dozens of independent hostels operate in BC. Many are great; others are dives. Again, look in the regional chapters for full details. The Pacific Rim Hostel Network is a loose confederation of some of the best independents. See the Network's Web site at www.pacifichostels.net. The Backpackers Hostels Canada network also has useful listings at www.backpackers.ca, though you'll need to navigate through obnoxious ads. *The Hostel Handbook*, with very brief listings of most hostels in North America, is available for C$5 (US$4) from Jim Williams, Dept: HHB, 722 St. Nicholas Ave, New York, NY 10031, USA. Its listings are also online at www.hostelhandbook.com.

B&Bs

With an estimated 3000 B&Bs in British Columbia, the choices are almost overwhelming. North American B&Bs are typically more upscale than the casual, family-style pensions found in Europe. Many (especially those catering to honeymooners and other romantic escapists) require reservations and have fairly strict policies on children, pets, smoking and so on. But there's a wide range of places, and with a bit of investigation you can find somewhere that fits your needs and price range.

Booking agencies can come in handy for finding a suitable B&B. We've listed several in the regional chapters. The Western Canada B&B Innkeepers Association (☎ 604-255-9199), PO Box 74534, Vancouver, V6K 4P4, BC, is not a booking agency, but it can provide a list of its 140 members, all of which have been inspected for cleanliness, comfort and safety. The association is also online at www.bcbandb.com.

Motels & Hotels

Motel and hotel rates listed in this book are for summer season unless otherwise specified. Prices are quoted without taxes, so prepare to add both the 7% GST and 7% PST to the bill. Ouch. On the plus side, bear in mind that rates quoted are 'rack rates.' You can often get a better deal just by asking, especially in a town glutted with motels.

Rates vary tremendously around the province. Urban and resort locations have the highest prices; plan to spend close to $100 for a basic double room with a private bath during high season in Vancouver and Victoria. (In small, nonresort towns you can usually find a motel room for half that amount.) Prices change seasonally, too; they're highest in summer for most of the province, except ski resort areas like Whistler, where they're highest in winter. Expect higher rates for holidays and special events.

Children can often stay free in the same room as their parents, but the age limits for free stays vary. Many motels (and an increasing number of suite-style hotels) offer kitchenettes. They cost a bit more than a standard room, but you can usually recoup the difference by cooking a few of your own meals. As a happy compromise, quite a few midrange motels now include a small refrigerator and microwave in their standard-room price.

If you're looking for the cheapest places in town, drive a few kilometers away from the main highway. Chain motels typically cluster around highway exits, airports and shopping areas. By driving to the other side of town, perhaps near the junction of a secondary highway, you'll usually find a cluster of 'mom-and-pop' motels where the rates run a good $20 or $30 lower than the chains.

Most of the major North American chains are represented in BC; Motel 6 is a fairly notable exception, though it too may soon be in the province. The lowest-priced chains found province-wide are Travelodge

and Econolodge, where doubles typically run from $65 to $85. The Super 8, Holiday Inn Express, Days Inn, Howard Johnson, Sandman, Best Western and Comfort Inn are a bit more, from about $80 to $120. Stay'n Save, despite its name, is usually about $120. The Coast Hotels, a BC chain, range from $85 to $140 and up. Higher-end chains include Holiday Inn, Ramada, Radisson, Hampton Inn, Sheraton/Four Points, Delta, Hyatt, Hilton, Marriott and Westin.

Reservations It's wise to book ahead for high season in BC. You can always cancel if your plans change, though note the place's cancellation policy; many won't allow you to do so as your stay date draws closer. We've listed toll-free numbers wherever possible. Chains have central toll-free numbers, too, but you'll often get better deals by calling a hotel directly. Be sure to let the hotel know if you plan to arrive after 6 pm. You may need to guarantee a room for late arrival on your credit card.

The lowest-priced motels may not accept reservations, but it's wise to call ahead from the road to see what's available. Even if they don't take reservations, they'll often hold a room for an hour or two. In shoulder season or low season, you can usually get a room without reservations.

FOOD

British Columbia is a glorious place to eat. The province's fortuitous location, with sea bounty on the coast and long growing seasons on the islands and southern interior, means a constant supply of fresh, delicious food. That said, there aren't many signature foods that are unique to BC. One of the few is the Nanaimo bar, a rich treat that has spawned many spin-offs across the province. (See the boxed text 'BC's Signature Sweet.') But other favorite foods are popular throughout the Pacific Northwest: salmon and sushi, all kinds of berries, inventive pasta dishes and some of the best vegetables you'll ever taste.

It's very easy to eat healthy in most of BC, except in the northern reaches, where fresh fruits and vegetables are hard to come

BC's Signature Sweet

No one is really sure who invented Nanaimo Bars, or how the three-layered treats came to be named for the small city on Vancouver Island. But there's no doubt these dense delicacies can be seriously addictive. You'll find them aboard the bigger BC Ferries ships and at many bakeries and restaurants (some of which create their own variations on the classic theme). Or you can whip up a batch of your own with this 'official' recipe from Tourism Nanaimo, which credits it to Joyce Hardcastle.

NANAIMO BARS

Bottom Layer

1/2 cup unsalted butter (Euro-style cultured is best)
1/4 cup sugar
5 tablespoons cocoa
1 egg, beaten
1¾ cups graham wafer crumbs
1/2 cup finely chopped almonds
1 cup coconut

Melt first three ingredients in top of a double boiler. Add egg and stir to cook and thicken. Remove from heat. Stir in crumbs, coconut and nuts. Press firmly into an ungreased 8-inch x 8-inch pan.

Second Layer

1/2 cup unsalted butter
2 tablespoons and 2 teaspoons cream
2 tablespoons vanilla custard powder
2 cups icing sugar

Cream the butter, cream, custard powder and icing sugar together well. Beat until light. Spread over bottom layer.

Third layer

4 1-oz squares semi-sweet chocolate
2 tablespoons unsalted butter

Melt chocolate and butter over low heat. Cool. When cool, but still liquid, pour over second layer and chill in refrigerator.

Chowing down on the Nanaimo Bar

by. You're never far from a vegetarian restaurant in the populous areas, and almost all restaurants have not one or two but a whole range of health-conscious choices. Be on the lookout for the many farmers' markets around the province. They're great places to get fresh, tasty produce straight from the growers.

Breakfast is usually eaten between 6 and 9 am. Many accommodations offer a continental breakfast of some sort during these hours; it might include anything from coffee and toast (accompanied by small tubs of peanut butter as well as butter and jelly) to yogurt, cereal and fruit. Most BC residents eat breakfast at home on weekdays or grab a quick bite on the run with their morning coffee. But on weekends, a much more leisurely breakfast or brunch is often enjoyed at a restaurant.

The midday meal, typically taken between 11 am and 1 pm, is usually called lunch. For travelers interested in sampling fine urban restaurants, lunch is often the time to do it: Prices are lower than for dinner, and you probably won't need reservations. But lunch can also be as simple as a snack bought from a farmers' market or food cart, or a picnic taken on your hike.

Dinner is served anytime from about 5 to 9 pm, sometimes later on weekends. It's a good idea to make reservations for dinner in resort areas, as well as on weekends. Some restaurants offer 'early-bird specials' aimed at people ready to dine by 5 pm. Another option for a cheap dinner are the hors d'oeuvres served at many urban pubs and bars, often in conjunction with happy hour drink specials aimed at the early-evening, after-work crowd.

Restaurants are all nonsmoking by provincial law. Pubs and bars have the option of allowing smoking or not. Many that forbid smoking have an outdoor patio area for smokers. Dress is casual compared to Eastern Canadian cities; you'll be fine no matter what you're wearing in most restaurants. For dressier places, a nice shirt or sweater and pants or a skirt are appropriate. Few restaurants require men to wear a jacket and tie.

The food section wouldn't be complete without any mention of White Spot, BC's most prominent regional sit-down restaurant chain, with more than 50 locations. Started by Nat Bailey in 1928, White Spot specializes in hamburgers (with Bailey's secret 'Triple-O' sauce) and creamy thick milk shakes, though its menu has plenty of other reasonably priced choices for breakfast, lunch and dinner. Some other regional chains include ABC Country Restaurants (similar to Denny's in the US); Fogg n' Suds, with something-for-everyone menus plus good beer and wine selections; and Milestone's, which serves West Coast cuisine at surprisingly affordable prices. Of course, BC also has many of the internationally known fast-food chains including A&W, Burger King, Kentucky Fried Chicken, McDonald's and Taco Bell.

DRINKS
Nonalcoholic
You'll get tap water over ice at most restaurants as soon as you sit down. Other beverages commonly available include soft drinks (sometimes called soda, pop or fountain drinks), fruit and vegetable juices, milk and bottled mineral and spring waters. But the big drink in BC is coffee, coffee and more coffee. There's a coffee shop on just about every block in commercial areas, and many drive-up kiosks in suburban zones. Chain coffee shops like Starbucks, Second Cup and Blenz specialize in such drinks as lattes and espressos, while the coffee you get at many restaurants is likely to be just plain-old coffee. Tea is widely available, too; many coffee shops stock exotic and herbal blends.

Alcoholic
The legal drinking age in BC is 19, and the legal blood-alcohol limit is .08, or the equivalent of two drinks for an 'average-sized' person. British Columbia is very serious about curbing drunk driving, and you may encounter a mandatory roadside checkpoint, especially on summer evenings or around winter holidays. At a checkpoint, an officer will ask whether you've had anything to drink. Answer honestly. Most times you just drive through and they say, 'have a good night.' But if the officer smells booze on your breath, or if you look suspicious, drunk or stoned, you will be told to pull over. You will either do a coordination test and/or take a breathalyzer (where you breathe into a straw-like tube) which immediately determines your blood-alcohol level.

British Columbia has eased its liquor regulations over the past few decades, but some unusual laws remain on the books. One is the 'intent-to-eat' law. In any establishment with a 'restaurant license,' you must order food if you're going to drink alcohol. Places with a 'liquor license' (pubs and the like) allow you to drink without ordering food. Liquor licenses are expensive, hard to come by and heavily regulated, which is why most restaurants don't have them.

The provincial government operates BC Liquor Stores, where you can buy beer, wine and spirits. If you want cold beverages, head instead to the nearest 'cold beer and wine store' – often found attached to pubs, restaurants or hotels – but be aware their prices are higher than those at the provincial stores. British Columbia Liquor Stores keep regular business hours (typically 9:30 am to 6 pm Monday through Saturday), although a few stay open to 9 pm and on Sundays and holidays. Beer and wine stores are often open daily with extended hours.

Most every major BC town now has a microbrewery or brewpub or two. Small breweries produce a variety of beer including ales, bitters, lagers, pilsners, bocks, porters, stouts and fruit beer, and even hemp ales. Names to look for, either in pubs or in cold beer stores, include Bowen Island Brewing Co (West Vancouver), Bear Brewing Co (Kamloops), Okanagan Spring Brewery (Vernon), Shaftebury Brewing Co (Delta), Whistler Brewing Co (Whistler) and Wild Horse Brewing Co (Penticton).

It's not a microbrew, but Kokanee is the closest thing BC has to an official provincial beer, and it's pretty good. It's made in Creston by the Columbia Brewing Co. Of course beers made by the big-name Canadian brewers, Molson and Labatt, are widely available.

British Columbia is becoming increasingly known for its high-quality wines, most produced in the Okanagan. See the 'Okanagan Valley Wineries' boxed text in the Thompson-Okanagan regional chapter for more information.

ENTERTAINMENT

It's not hard to find a good time in BC. You'll find extensive discussions of each city's entertainment options in the regional chapters. Although many people visit BC primarily for its great outdoors, you'll enjoy sampling at least a bit of the province's cultural flair.

Bars & Clubs

The neighborhood pub is a venerable institution throughout BC, found everywhere from small towns to big-city neighborhoods.

You'll usually find sports on the TV and a convivial yet clubby atmosphere that acknowledges newcomers and then leaves them alone.

Vancouver, Victoria and Whistler all have plenty of clubs, with live music on many nights and DJs spinning records on others. The underground rave scene is also strong on the coast; local record stores are usually the best source of information for these all-night dance parties.

Bars, pubs and lounges are open seven days a week, and generally last call is just before 1 am, although it may come earlier in smaller neighborhood-type pubs. Nightclubs stay open until 2 am. There may be a cover charge for live entertainment.

Cinema

Moviegoing is a major pastime throughout BC. The larger towns all have multiplexes with many screens. Admission prices are about $9 in the cities, slightly less in smaller towns, with discount matinees during the afternoons and, in many places, all day Tuesday. You'll find a good selection of independent and repertory cinemas in the larger cities and on college campuses.

SPECTATOR SPORTS

Vancouver fields major-league sports teams in the National Hockey League, National Basketball Association and Canadian Football League. See the Vancouver chapter for details. Hockey is the most popular spectator sport in BC, as elsewhere in Canada (see the boxed text), but collegiate, scholastic and community soccer, baseball, curling and basketball teams all have followings, too.

SHOPPING

Good BC souvenirs include artwork, hand-knit Cowichan sweaters, food-and-wine gift boxes and outdoor gear ranging from kayaks to microfleece clothing. You'll find all these items abundantly available in the larger towns and cities, and many shops will ship your purchases home. (See Taxes & Refunds in the Money section earlier in this chapter for information about getting refunds on GST paid for larger purchases.)

Hockey for Dummies

So, you think hockey just looks like a bunch of large, ugly guys with big sticks sliding around on skates trying to kill each other on ice, eh? Well, most Canadians would beg to differ. Hockey isn't just a sport in Canada – it's an institution and an inexplicable definition of culture. Besides, it's a good game (though it's not the national sport; that honor goes to lacrosse).

It's played like this: Each team has five players on the ice at a time: a goalie, two defensemen and three forwards. The aim, of course, is to use your stick to shoot the little black disk – the puck – into the opposing team's net. While you're trying to do this, it's perfectly legal for opposing players to 'hit,' 'check' (or basically slam into) the player with the puck. It is illegal to hit a player who doesn't have the puck, and when this happens the bad guy gets a penalty and is sent to the penalty box – usually for two minutes – to wallow in what he's done. This means his team is short a player, giving the other team a one-player advantage for the duration of the penalty. This is called a 'power play' and creates the best opportunity for scoring.

Hockey is a game of strategy and skill, which Canadian kids (boys, mostly) grow up playing on frozen ponds or at indoor ice rinks. In fact, it is often one of the first sports they learn. If you're in Vancouver during hockey season, head over to GM Place and watch the Canucks play – you'll no doubt get hooked.

The Metrotown shopping center in Burnaby, a Vancouver suburb, will appeal to many people; it's one of the largest malls in Canada. On the opposite end of the spectrum, be on the lookout for the many great thrift stores in BC, where you'll find bargains on all sorts of cool stuff including clothing and slightly used outdoor gear. Ask at your lodgings for directions to the best local offerings.

Activities

When it comes to outdoor adventure, BC is hard to beat. There aren't many other places on Earth where, as the cliché goes, you can ski in the morning and sail, hike or golf in the afternoon. And there are few, if any, recreational activities that BC doesn't offer in one locale or another, usually in some of the loveliest surroundings you'll ever see. You'll find all the obvious pursuits here, including some of the planet's best hiking, skiing, scuba diving and sea kayaking, as well as some lesser-known activities like storm-watching, windsurfing, Ultimate Frisbee and spelunking.

So get out and play. Listed below are a few of the best places to pursue each activity in BC. Turn to the appropriate regional chapters for lots more information on those high spots, and also see our special section on hiking and winter sports. Other helpful sources of information include local Visitor Info Centres, the BC Parks Web site (www.elp.gov.bc.ca/bcparks) and the Ministry of Forests' site (www.for.gov.bc.ca). Also see the Dangers & Annoyances section in the Facts for the Visitor chapter for pointers on dealing with bears, insects and other potential hazards in BC's great outdoors.

SEA KAYAKING

If there is one activity you have to try in coastal BC, this is it. Sea kayaks are easy to paddle, amazingly stable and lots of fun. Unlike larger boats, kayaks can hug the shoreline, offering the perfect perch for watching shore birds and other marine life. Nearly every coastal and island town has at least one outfitter ready to take you on a guided trek lasting from a few hours (for about $40 or $50) to a week. These trips are by far the best way to learn the sport; once you know the ropes, you can rent or buy gear and go paddling on your own, though you'll always want to check into local weather and traffic conditions.

It's always best to kayak with other people for safety. Someone in the group should know how to plot a course by navigational chart and compass, pilot in fog, read weather patterns, assess water hazards, interpret tide tables, handle boats in adverse conditions and perform group- and self-rescue techniques.

You can kayak just about everywhere along BC's coast, but you'll find the greatest concentration of outfitters on Vancouver Island. For multi-day trips, the best-known destination is the Broken Group Islands,

The Trans Canada Trail

At 16,000km, the Trans Canada Trail ranks as the longest recreational trail in the world. Conceived in 1992 as a way to mark Canada's 125th birthday celebration, it was officially declared open in September 2000, although some stretches remain undeveloped. As its name implies, the trail crosses the entire country, including a 1750km stretch from Victoria to the Alberta border and another 1600km spur through northeast BC. Primary activities on the route include hiking, cycling, horseback riding and cross-country skiing; some sections also permit snowmobiling.

The centerpiece of the BC route is the abandoned Kettle Valley Railway, now converted to a 600km trail. Stretching from Midway (near Grand Forks in the West Kootenays) to Hope, the Kettle Valley route features a mostly gentle grade, but you'll have to negotiate some harrowing passages over railroad trestles, especially in the Kelowna area. For more information on the trail in BC, including suggested trips, visit the Web site www.bctrail.bc.ca or the national Trans Canada Trail Web site, www.tctrail.ca.

part of Pacific Rim National Park Reserve, on the west coast of Vancouver Island. If you don't have much time, you can always rent a kayak for a few hours or take an introductory lesson in nearly any coastal town. For more information, look up these towns in the Vancouver Island chapter: Victoria, Sooke, Port Renfrew, Nanaimo, Parksville, Qualicum Beach, Bamfield, Telegraph Cove, Port Hardy and Denman, Hornby and Quadra Islands.

In the Gulf Islands, you'll find outfitters and rental shops on each major island: Salt Spring, Galiano, Mayne and North Pender (see the Southern Gulf Islands chapter). Near Vancouver, try Bowen Island (see the Vancouver & Around chapter). Farther north, popular spots include Prince Rupert's Cow Bay and Gwaii Haanas National Park Reserve in the Queen Charlotte Islands (see the North chapter).

Despite the name 'sea kayak,' you can take one of these boats out on a lake, too. For some prime paddling, try Lightning Lake at Manning Provincial Park, east of Hope (see the Fraser Valley chapter); Kootenay Lake, east of Nelson (see the Kootenays chapter); and Babine Lake, north of Burns Lake (see the North chapter).

Campsites abound on BC's many islands, but more and more people are choosing 'mothership' sea kayaking over camping. The 'mothership,' a larger boat, takes kayakers and their gear out to sea; the kayakers then spend their days paddling and nights bunked down in the big boat.

You might want to time your BC visit to coincide with the annual Vancouver Island Paddlefest, a major kayaking event held each year at Ladysmith. Dates vary; sometimes it takes place in spring, sometimes in summer. For details, see the Web site www.island.net/~pfest.

For more information on the sport, pick up a copy of *WaveLength* magazine at kayak and sporting goods shops or look for it online at www.wavelengthmagazine.com. In the magazine, you'll find lots of articles and advertisements on sea kayaking throughout the province. Also, try the Web site www.easykayaker.com, another great resource that includes launch area maps and trip information.

CANOEING

The 116km Bowron Lake canoe circuit in Bowron Lake Provincial Park (see the Cariboo-Chilcotin chapter) is one of the world's great canoe trips, covering 10 lakes with easy portages between each. For more details, visit the Web site vts.bc.ca/bowron/parkindx.html. The lesser-known – but increasingly popular – 57km Powell Forest Canoe Route connects a dozen lakes on the upper reaches of BC's Sunshine Coast near Powell River (see the Whistler & the Sunshine Coast chapter). Other good spots to paddle include Wells Gray Provincial Park (see the Cariboo-Chilcotin chapter); Slocan Lake, just west of New Denver (see the Kootenays chapter); and Okanagan Lake, easily accessed from Kelowna, Penticton or Vernon (see the Thompson-Okanagan chapter). Ocean canoeing is possible around Vancouver, the Gulf Islands and the Queen Charlotte Islands. Again, *WaveLength* magazine (mentioned under Sea Kayaking, above) can point you toward a number of paddling possibilities.

DIVING

Justly famous for its superb diving conditions, BC features two of the top-ranked dive spots on Earth: Vancouver Island and the Gulf Islands. It's best to go in winter, when the plankton has decreased and visibility often exceeds 20m. The water temperature drops to about 7°C to 10°C in winter; in summer, it reaches 15°C. At depths of more than 15m, though, visibility remains good throughout the year and temperatures rarely rise above 10°C.

The prime diving spots lie in Georgia Strait between Vancouver Island's east coast and the mainland. Dive shops abound in this region, and they're your best sources for air and gear as well as lessons, charters and tours (see the Vancouver Island chapter for details). The Queen Charlotte Islands (see the North chapter) also offer excellent diving but have no dive shops, so you have to bring everything, including air.

Maps, Charts & Tide Tables

If you plan to do much hiking, horseback riding or other land-based backcountry activities, you'll want to invest in good topographical maps. Gem Trek Publishing in Alberta offers some of the best Rocky Mountain maps in scales from 1:35,000 to 1:100,000. Check out Gem's Web site at www.gemtrek.com for available maps. Vancouver-based International Travel Maps & Books (ITMB) publishes topo maps that cover many areas of western BC. For more information, call ☎ 604-879-3621 or see the Web site www.itmb.com.

Marine charts are absolutely essential for explorations of BC's coastal waters. You can pick up charts from marine supply stores or from the Canadian Hydrographic Service, Chart Sales and Distribution (☎ 250-363-6358, fax 250-363-6841, chartsales@pac.dfo-mpo.gc.ca.), 9860 W Saanich Rd, Sidney, BC V8L 4B2.

Tide tables are widely printed in local newspapers throughout coastal BC, and they're also available at Visitor Info Centres, sporting goods stores and outfitters. You can also get tide tables online at www.lau.chs-shc.dfo-mpo.gc.ca/marees/produits/accueil.htm.

The province contains quite a few artificial reefs, created by the sinking of old ships to provide habitat for marine life. Artificial reefs include the *Chaudiere* at Sechelt on the Sunshine Coast; the *GB Church* and *Mackenzie* at Sidney; the *Columbia* at Campbell River; and the *Saskatchewan* and *Cape Breton* near Nanaimo. For more information on these and other sites, contact the Artificial Reef Society of British Columbia at the Vancouver Maritime Museum (☎ 604-220-8061) or visit the museum's Web site at www.artificialreef.bc.ca.

For a cool variation on scuba diving, try snorkeling in the Campbell River on north Vancouver Island. Paradise Found Adventure Tours guides people to see spawning salmon make their way up the lazy river

(see the Campbell River section of the Vancouver Island chapter for details). Although there obviously isn't as much diving inland, Ellison Lake Provincial Park, on the northeastern shore of Okanagan Lake, gets a bit of action (see also the Thompson-Okanagan chapter).

Diver magazine covers scuba diving activities throughout Canada; read it online at www.divermag.com. Scuba Guide Mapping (☎ 604-980-5203, 877-384-3627), based in North Vancouver, creates maps to sites like Whytecliff Marine Park near Vancouver, the *Mackenzie* artificial reef and the Gabriola Passage near Nanaimo. See its Web site at www.divemap.com for more details. For in-depth coverage of the region's diving, see *Diving & Snorkeling Pacific Northwest* from Lonely Planet's Pisces series. For help in finding lessons, dive sites and resorts, visit the Professional Association of Diving Instructors' Web site at www.padi.com.

WHITE-WATER RAFTING

Rugged topography and an abundance of snowmelt make BC's rivers great for white-water action. You don't need to be experienced to go out rafting. The provincial government regulates commercial rafting, and operators are allowed only on rivers that have been checked by experts. Guides must meet certain qualifications, and companies must provide equipment that meets government requirements. Trips can last from three hours up to a couple of weeks. Wilderness rafting averages about $200 per day for everything, while half-day trips start at about $45. Check with the local Visitor Info Centres for details about where to go and which companies to hire.

Wherever you are in BC, you're probably close to a good white-water river. The Fraser, Thompson, Chilliwack and Nahatlatch Rivers all lie within day-trip distance of Vancouver, so they're the best bets for adding adventure to your city-based holiday (see Chilliwack and Lytton in the Fraser Valley chapter for more details). Many consider the Kicking Horse River (see Golden in the Kootenays chapter) to be one of the province's best raft trips. Visitors to Jasper

National Park (see the Rockies chapter) can book trips on the Sunwwapta and Athabasca Rivers. Other prime spots include the Clearwater River near Wells Gray Provincial Park and the Chilcotin River near Williams Lake (see the Cariboo-Chilcotin chapter); the Adams River in the Shuswap region (see the Thompson-Okanagan chapter); the Bulkley and Babine Rivers near Smithers (see the North chapter); and the remote Tatshenshini and Alsek Rivers in northern BC.

SAILING & BOATING

The sheltered waters of BC's Pacific coast make sailing a popular form of recreation that's possible almost year-round, though it's best to take out a boat from mid-April to mid-October. Coastal marine parks provide safe all-weather anchorage and offer boats for hire (powerboats as well as sailboats). Some of the great places to sail include the Strait of Georgia and the Gulf Islands. Inland, sailors tend to prefer Harrison Lake (see Harrison Hot Springs in the Fraser Valley chapter); Okanagan and Skaha Lakes in the Thompson-Okanagan region; Arrow and Kootenay Lakes in the Kootenays; and Williston Lake north of Prince George (see the North chapter).

Houseboating is another popular pastime on BC's biggest lakes, including Okanagan and Shuswap Lakes in the Okanagan Valley and Powell Lake on the Sunshine Coast. It costs about $1000 to $1200 a week, depending on location and time of year, to rent a self-contained boat that sleeps about six people. See the Thompson-Okanagan and Whistler & the Sunshine Coast chapters for more details.

SURFING & WINDSURFING

The Tofino area on Vancouver Island's west coast is ground zero for BC's best surfing. Weather conditions may be far from ideal – buckets of rain and chilly temperatures – but the waves are awesome, rolling directly off the North Pacific. Be sure to wear a wetsuit. See the Vancouver Island chapter's Tofino section for details on renting gear and taking lessons.

Nitinat Lake on Vancouver Island offers some of the best windsurfing in Canada, but you can also find good places to windsurf just outside Vancouver and Victoria. Check out the Web site www.coastalbc.com for lots of information on surf sports and other outdoor activities.

FISHING

Fishing, both the saltwater and freshwater variety, is one of BC's major tourist attractions. Saltwater anglers particularly like to cast their nets and lines in the waters around Vancouver Island, where several places (Campbell River chief among them) claim the title 'salmon capital of the world,' as well as at Prince Rupert, known for its halibut, and in the Queen Charlotte Islands. You'll find good river and lake fishing in every region. Near Vancouver, anglers enjoy casting at Steveston, where the Fraser River meets the ocean, and even right off the Stanley Park seawall. For some particularly good lake fishing farther inland, try Birkenhead Lake Provincial Park (see the Whistler & the Sunshine Coast chapter) and Golden Ears Provincial Park (see the Fraser Valley chapter). In the Okanagan area, head to Okanagan Lake or the many smaller lakes in the region. The East Kootenays see some outstanding fly-fishing, especially on creek-size tributaries of the Columbia, Kicking Horse and Kootenay Rivers along and near Hwy 95. You'll also find some great fishing on the Bella Coola River (see the Cariboo-Chilcotin chapter).

The best destination of all may be northern BC, where hundreds of lakes – some reachable only by boat or plane – give anglers endless vacation options. For good river fishing up north, head to the Fraser, Nass, Skeena, Kettle, Peace and Liard Rivers (see the North chapter).

You must obtain separate licenses for saltwater/tidal fishing and freshwater fishing. The provincial Ministry of Environment, Land and Parks controls freshwater licenses. Annual licenses cost $30 for BC residents, $40 for other Canadians and $55 for nonresidents. Eight-day licenses cost $17/25/30; one-day licenses cost $8/15/15.

On top of this, you may need to buy a conservation surcharge stamp for some locations or species. For current freshwater regulations, call ☎ 250-356-7285 or visit www.gov.bc.ca/fish online.

The federal Department of Fisheries and Oceans issues licenses for saltwater/tidal fishing. An annual license costs $23/109 for residents/nonresidents. For five days, you'll pay $18/35; for three days, $12/21; and $6/8 for one day. For general saltwater sportfishing questions, call ☎ 604-666-0583 (from 8 am to 4 pm) or 666-2828 (24-hour recording); for more information, you can also go to the Web site at www.pac.dfo-mpo.gc.ca/ops/fm/sport/index.htm.

Both types of fishing licenses are widely available from sporting goods stores and fishing outfitters, where you can also get a complete copy of fishing regulations. In general, children under 16 can fish for free, but certain regulations apply.

CYCLING & MOUNTAIN BIKING
Mountain biking is huge in BC, and road cycling is popular, too. Home to some of BC's best technical trails, Rossland (see the Kootenays chapter) is often considered to be the mountain-biking capital of BC (and possibly Canada); the best-known rides include the Dewdney, Whiskey and Rubberhead Trails. Whistler also attracts lots of fat-tire riders, while Squamish to the south offers some good rides, too (see the Whistler & the Sunshine Coast chapter). Check out the Whistler Interpretive Forest, just south of town, and the Four Lakes Trail at Alice Lake Provincial Park near Squamish. At Golden in the Kootenays, the variety of terrain offers a range of options, from easy rides along the Kicking Horse River to insane descents on Mt 7.

Your best sources of information include local bike shops (see the regional chapters) and Visitor Info Centres. The British Columbia Mountain Bike Directory Web site (www.oroad.com/bcmtbdir) features trail reports, message boards, bikeshop and bike-club links and a lot

more. Another good source of information is Cycling BC (☎ 604-737-3034), with an office at 1367 W Broadway in Vancouver and a Web site at www.cycling.bc.ca. BC's governing body for mountain-bike racing, road racing and track racing, Cycling BC also offers plenty of resources for recreational and touring cyclists.

ROCK CLIMBING & MOUNTAINEERING
BC is full of great venues for rock and mountain climbing, and even ice climbing. Squamish (see the Whistler & the Sunshine Coast chapter) is home to the Stawamus Chief, a world-class granite monolith with about 200 climbing routes. But other climbers swear by the better weather at the compact gneiss rock of Skaha Bluffs near Penticton (see the Thompson-Okanagan chapter), which boast a long climbing season on more than 400 bolted routes. Also in the Okanagan region, Kalamalka Lake and Ellison Provincial Park offer some good climbing. Lessons and guided climbs are available in all these areas; see the regional chapters for details. You'll also find indoor climbing gyms in many BC towns. Ask at the local Visitor Info Centre or check the Yellow Pages.

Climbers should always look out for hazards that might prompt a fall, causing serious injury or death. Weather is always an important factor to consider, as rain

RICK GERHARTER

FRANK CARTER

FRANK CARTER

Living the good life in British Columbia

SALLY DILLON

JULIE FANSELOW

FRANK CARTER

Plenty to do on land and water: mountain biking, sea kayaking and canoeing

makes rock slippery and lightning can strike an exposed climber. Technical climbing demands an understanding of the composition of various rock types and an awareness of the hazards of the high country, as well as a familiarity with such equipment as ropes, chocks, bolts, carabiners and harnesses. Be sure to dress appropriately for the conditions in which you'll be climbing.

HORSEBACK RIDING

If you're a big fan of horseback riding, head to BC's Cariboo country, where dude ranches offer a range of activities, from trail rides to cattle drives (see the boxed text 'Saddle Sores and the Great Outdoors' in the Cariboo-Chilcotin chapter for details). You can also saddle up in Banff and Jasper National Parks (see the Rockies chapter); at Whistler and Pemberton on the Sea to Sky Hwy (see the Whistler & the Sunshine Coast chapter); on Salt Spring and Galiano Islands in the Southern Gulf Islands; and at Mt Washington, near Comox and Courtenay on Vancouver Island.

WILDLIFE-WATCHING

BC abounds with watchable critters, whales and bears among the most popular. Ask at any Visitor Info Centre for the free *British Columbia Wildlife Watch* brochure, a concise and handy guide to viewing opportunities across the province. You can also request a copy by writing to BC Environment, Wildlife Branch, 780 Blanshard St, Victoria, BC V8V 1X5. See the Web site www3.bc.sympatico .ca/driftwood/bcwwhome.htm for more information on wildlife-watching opportunities throughout BC.

Whale-Watching

Gray and killer (orca) whales inhabit the waters off BC's west coast. The orcas live here year-round, while the gray whales migrate between Baja California and Alaska, traveling north in spring and south in autumn. Whale-watching trips are popular activities at Victoria, Ucluelet, Tofino, Telegraph Cove and Alert Bay (all covered in the Vancouver Island chapter) and Prince Rupert (see the North chapter).

Most three-hour trips start at about $75. Sometimes you can even see whales from the deck of a BC Ferries vessel or from shore, especially on headlands of the Southern Gulf Islands and on Vancouver Island's west coast.

Bear-Watching

Both fearsome and fascinating, bears have become a major aspect of life in BC. Several outfitters lead guided trips to see bears close up; see the Ucluelet, Telegraph Cove and Port Hardy sections of the Vancouver Island chapter. You can also visit the Khutzeymateen Grizzly Bear Sanctuary near Prince Rupert; for details, go to the 'Grizzlies Galore' boxed text in the North chapter. Always keep your distance and use common sense when viewing wildlife.

Bird-Watching

Home to nearly 500 bird species, BC offers superb bird-watching. Some of the best spots include the Brackendale area north of Squamish, where thousands of bald eagles congregate in winter (see the boxed text 'The Eagles Have Landed' in the Whistler & the Sunshine Coast chapter, later); the Parksville/Qualicum areas on Vancouver Island, where brant geese and other migrating species flock each spring; and the Creston Valley Wildlife Management Area in the Kootenays (see the Creston section of the Kootenays chapter).

BC's extensive bird-watching community, always eager to share its knowledge with others, maintains a helpful Web site (birding.bc.ca/bc-home.htm) that includes a species list, rare bird alerts, field reports, a list of festivals and regional contacts through much of BC. Daniel Bastaja operates another good site at www.birdingfaqs.com, with all kinds of information about birding in BC and beyond.

STORM-WATCHING

Every winter, people come to Vancouver Island's west coast praying for lousy weather. Storm-watching has become a popular regional activity, and while most visitors are content to watch nature's fury from plush Tofino- and Ucluelet-area lodgings, some people want to experience the deluge firsthand, in the outdoors. Long Beach Nature Tours Company (☎ 250-726-7099) offers guided hikes to safe viewing spots; see the Vancouver Island chapter's Tofino section for details.

GOLF

You can golf nearly year-round in many parts of BC, including much of the Lower Mainland, Vancouver Island and the Okanagan Valley. The province boasts more than 250 courses. Whistler is a big golf destination, featuring three designer courses: Chateau Whistler Golf Club, Nicklaus North Golf Course and Whistler Golf Club. Other notable offerings include Sun Peaks Resort in the Okanagan Valley (see the Thompson-Okanagan chapter) and Greywolf Golf Course at the Panorama Mountain Village Resort near Invermere (see the Kootenays chapter); the latter was voted the best new Canadian course of 1999 by *Golf Digest* magazine.

At the Web site www.bcgolfguide.com, you can search for golf courses by city or region; many listings are accompanied by course layouts and photos (check out the Sheep Pasture Golf Course at Lillooet, for example).

ULTIMATE FRISBEE & DISC GOLF

Vancouver churns out many of Canada's top Ultimate Frisbee players and has become one of the world's biggest 'Ultimate' hubs. The summer league includes more than 15 coed divisions and boasts more than 1000 league members, who don't shy away from playing in the rain.

Ultimate is a field sport played with two teams of seven members and a Frisbee (or – the cooler term – 'disc'). It came to Vancouver in the mid-1980s, though it was invented in the late 1960s in New Jersey, USA. Its hippie roots are still apparent in the 'love your brother' spirit that governs the game, keeping play clean and respectful. Unlike in most team sports, the players make all calls and settle disputes on the field; even the highest caliber tournaments never have any officiating.

League games take place at more than 20 different fields throughout Vancouver, but you can usually drop in for pickup games on Sunday afternoon at Jericho Beach. The Vancouver Ultimate League (☎ 604-878-7387) maintains a most excellent Web site (www.vul.bc.ca) that lists pickup games, field locations and league teams looking for players. Between May and October, tournaments happen all over the province – in Whistler, Vancouver, Nanaimo, Vernon and Vancouver.

Disc golf isn't quite as big as Ultimate Frisbee, but it has its followers, too. Disc golf courses are laid out much like regular golf links, but players toss a disc into a basket instead of putting a ball into a hole. Many BC towns have disc golf courses, usually in a city park; ask at the local Visitor Info Centre to see if there's one available where you're traveling.

SPELUNKING

Vancouver Island features several major spelunking (or caving) destinations, including Horne Lake Provincial Park near Qualicum Beach and the Upana Caves near Gold River (see the Vancouver Island chapter). Horne Lake offers instruction during the summer months. You can take tours at Cody Caves Provincial Park, near Nelson in the Kootenays. For more information on caving throughout Canada, see the Web site www.cancaver.ca; among other things, it lists about 10 caving groups now active in BC. (Our vote for the best-named group goes to the Under Achievers Cave Exploration Group of Kelowna.)

HANG GLIDING & PARAGLIDING

BC's rugged mountains offer some of the best terrain in the world for hang gliding and paragliding. Backcountry roads take you to launch sites throughout the province. Mt 7, southeast of Golden in the Kootenays, has been the site of several world and Canadian hang-gliding records. East of Vancouver, the Aerial Adventures Tow Park (☎ 604-888-1988), 24600 River Rd in Fort Langley, has become a major destination for hang-gliding and paragliding flights, lessons, rentals and sales; for more information, visit the Web site www.aerialadventures.com.

The Web site of the West Coast Soaring Club, a group of hang-gliding and paragliding enthusiasts in the Lower Mainland, offers information on places to pursue the sport (visit www.wcsc.simplenet.com). You can also visit the Okanagan Soaring Association's site at www.junction.net/osa or look up the Vancouver Island Hanggliding/Paragliding Site Guide online at the Web site www.cabama.com/vihgc.

BUNGEE JUMPING

Nanaimo is home to the Bungy Zone, one of the only legal jump sites in North America and probably the most elaborate. You can get into the sport for about $100. See the Vancouver Island chapter's Nanaimo section for details.

ALPINE PLEASURES:
BC'S ABUNDANT TRAILS & SLOPES

Finding BC's Best Hikes

In BC, the hiking options are endless and endlessly rewarding: You could spend a lifetime hiking in the province and never trek all the trails. Hiking is probably the most popular outdoor activity in BC, simply because it's easy to do and not much equipment is required beyond sturdy hiking shoes or boots, water and a day pack to store extra layers of clothes. For anything beyond a short stroll, you should also take along energy snacks, basic first aid supplies, a Swiss Army knife, whistle, insect repellent, flashlight and extra batteries, waterproof matches, compass, maps and a trowel for digging holes for human excrement where no outhouse is handy. (For overnight treks, add a tent, sleeping bag and pad and cook stove.) A ski pole is invaluable on muddy trails. It's better than a walking stick because the basket won't sink in the mud. Dogs don't belong in the backcountry, since they increase the chance of conflict with bears and other wildlife.

Don't overestimate your abilities. Inexperienced hikers can expect to cover about 11km in a day, or perhaps 8 to 9km over rough terrain or with a backpack. If you'd prefer a short hike, you'll find easy but rewarding trails at nearly every provincial park, as well as on many urban hiking paths.

Make sure you get good information before you set out. Most park offices offer general information. You'll also need good topographic maps for extended backcountry trips; most cost about $10. The Western Canada Wilderness Committee Stores in Vancouver and Victoria (see the Vancouver and Vancouver Island chapters) carry both hiking guidebooks and maps. For BC Forest Service maps, go to the Web site www.for.gov.bc.ca and follow the links to recreation and maps.

Because of the plethora of hiking options in BC, we asked Kathy and Craig Copeland, BC-based hiking experts and authors of the *Don't Waste Your Time* and *Gotta Hike BC* guidebooks (published by Voice in the Wilderness Press) to name their picks for the province's best hikes. These are all trips that merit the top 'four-boot,' premier status in the Copelands' boldly opinionated books, which aim to help trekkers find the best trails and avoid those that aren't worth hikers' time and energy.

Garibaldi Lake/Black Tusk/Panorama Ridge This 35km trek in Garibaldi Provincial Park south of Whistler features all the touchstones of an epic Northwest hike: towering trees, waves of wildflowers, mountainside glaciers, a lovely lake and expansive views. Plan on two to four days to backpack the route, which includes a 2450m elevation gain. You can access the park from the Sea to Sky Hwy (Hwy 99).

Nearest town: Whistler (see the Whistler & the Sunshine Coast chapter)

Musical Bumps Another classic Whistler hike, this easy 19km roundtrip day hike with a 727m elevation gain begins with a summertime ride up the ski gondola on Whistler Mountain. Go on a clear day and pack along plenty of film to capture the sweeping views of mountain peaks and glaciers. Don't let the crowds discourage you, for the alpine panoramas here are among BC's best.

Nearest town: Whistler (see the Whistler & the Sunshine Coast chapter)

East Sooke Coast Trail An easy drive from Victoria on Hwy 14, the 10km East Sooke Coast trail is a worthy warm-up for (or alternative to) the better-known West Coast Trail. The Copelands say it's best for athletic hikers who don't mind some hardy exercise on a continually steep, rough trail while taking in sublime views of Juan De Fuca Strait. Keep your eyes peeled for harbor seals, schools of dolphin and humpback whales. Allow seven hours for a day hike from Pike Rd to Aylard Farm and try to arrange shuttle service with a hiking guide so you don't have to walk all the way back.

Nearest town: Sooke (see the Vancouver Island chapter)

Gibson/Kokanee/Kaslo Lakes Trail The outstanding trail network in the Selkirk Range near Nelson offers a wide array of treks. From the Gibson Lake Trailhead, you can hike past Kokanee, Keen and Garland Lakes to Kaslo Lake, a prime spot to turn around if you're only interested in a moderate 15km roundtrip day hike. If you're in for the long haul, though, you can keep going on the alpine Glory Basin circuit or head toward Kokanee Glacier.

Nearest town: Nelson (see the Kootenays chapter)

Lake of the Hanging Glacier The Copelands say this lake, on the east side of the Purcell Range, may be the most impressive in the province. Plan on a 16km roundtrip day hike, gaining 710m, to get to the lake, which rests at the bottom of sheer glacier-clad peaks; the views are spectacular. To get to the trail, proceed to the junction of Hwys 93 and 95 at Radium Hot Springs, turn left on Forsters Landing Rd and follow it for 1.4km until Horsethief Creek Forest Service Rd. Turn west and drive 50km southwest to the trailhead.

Nearest town: Radium Hot Springs (see the Kootenays chapter)

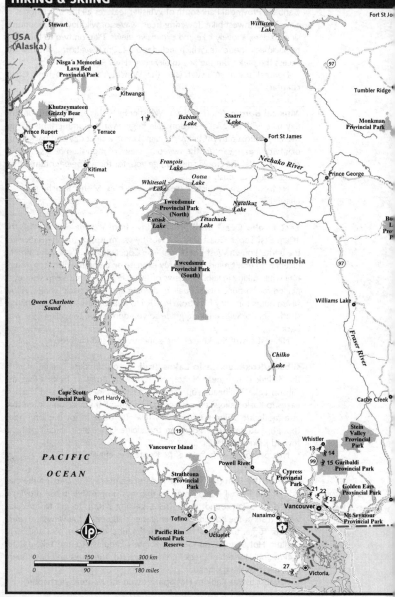

HIKING & SKIING

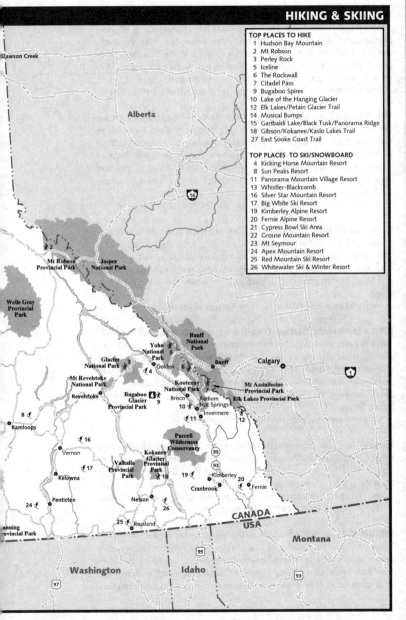

TOP PLACES TO HIKE
1 Hudson Bay Mountain
2 Mt Robson
3 Perley Rock
5 Iceline
6 The Rockwall
7 Citadel Pass
9 Bugaboo Spires
10 Lake of the Hanging Glacier
12 Elk Lakes/Petain Glacier Trail
14 Musical Bumps
15 Garibaldi Lake/Black Tusk/Panorama Ridge
18 Gibson/Kokanee/Kaslo Lakes Trail
27 East Sooke Coast Trail

TOP PLACES TO SKI/SNOWBOARD
4 Kicking Horse Mountain Resort
8 Sun Peaks Resort
11 Panorama Mountain Village Resort
13 Whistler-Blackcomb
16 Silver Star Mountain Resort
17 Big White Ski Resort
19 Kimberley Alpine Resort
20 Fernie Alpine Resort
21 Cypress Bowl Ski Area
22 Grouse Mountain Resort
23 Mt Seymour
24 Apex Mountain Resort
25 Red Mountain Ski Resort
26 Whitewater Ski & Winter Resort

Bugaboo Spires Bugaboo Glacier Provincial Park, a 1½-hour drive northwest of Radium Hot Springs, attracts lots of climbers to its giant granite spires. But day hikers can enjoy the views, too. Take the short, steep trail to Kain Hut, where you can look up at the monoliths from below. The 10km roundtrip gains 700m. To get to the park, follow Hwy 95 to Brisco and take the marked road west to the park.

Nearest town: Radium Hot Springs (see the Kootenays chapter)

The Rockwall For a challenging hike in the Canadian Rockies, consider the four-day trek between the Floe Lake and Paint Pots Trailheads in Kootenay National Park (see the Rockies chapter), on Hwy 93 north of Radium Hot Springs. En route, you'll trace the famous Rockwall, 35km of limestone cliffs along the Continental Divide. Get fit ahead of time and expect a lot of ups-and-downs, with 1490m of elevation change over the 54.8km route.

Nearest town: Radium Hot Springs (see the Kootenays chapter)

Perley Rock An 11.4km roundtrip day hike leads you from Glacier National Park's Illecillewaet Campground to Perley Rock. Best suited to athletic types, the climb is steep, with a gain of 1162m, but you'll be rewarded with staggering views of Perley Rock and Illecillewaet Glacier and Névé. Watch your step toward the top, where the going gets fairly rough.

Nearest town: Revelstoke (see the Rockies chapter)

Elk Lakes/Petain Glacier Trail The route starts out gently enough, winding past two scenic lakes and a waterfall, and it peaks at Petain Basin, with its wondrous glacier views. In the meanwhile, however, the 22km roundtrip to the basin rim involves a challenging scramble that figures heavily in the total 595m elevation gain. The road's-end trailhead at Elk Lakes Provincial Park is an hour's drive north of Elkford via the Elk River Forest Service Rd.

Nearest town: Elkford (see the Kootenays chapter)

Iceline The Copelands say Yoho National Park, although smaller than the other Canadian Rocky Mountain national parks, boasts the heaviest concentration of 'high-impact scenery.' A steep but short climb into the alpine zone starts this hike, but after that the winding trail offers plenty of places to rest and savor the scenery. The 12.8km roundtrip day hike gains 690m.

Nearest town: Field (see the Rockies chapter)

Citadel Pass A shuttle bus ride to the Sunshine Ski Area in Mt Assiniboine Provincial Park gives you a head start in reaching the high-country terrain usually only seen by helicopter-borne hikers. Sweeping meadows filled with wildflowers unfurl en route to Citadel Pass, which you can arrive at in three hours or less; the easy 18.6km roundtrip gains little elevation.

From the pass, backpackers can continue on a four- to five-day trek deep into Mt Assiniboine Provincial Park.

Nearest town: Banff (see the Rockies chapter)

Mt Robson Mt Robson looks like a beauty from the road, but getting close on a trail will leave you even more awestruck. This hike travels 39.2km roundtrip around the peak's west and north sides. Plan on four days to enjoy the views thoroughly en route to Berg Lake; the Copelands say the topography here recalls everywhere from Costa Rica to New Zealand. The trail lies within Mt Robson Provincial Park on Hwy 16.

Nearest town: Jasper (see the Rockies chapter)

Hudson Bay Mountain This trek begins from a ski area that's open for hiking in summer: the little-known Ski Smithers on Hudson Bay Mountain. Park at the end of Ski Hill Rd and begin hiking at the green T-bar. The 8.8km roundtrip day hike gains 650m, weaving through flower-filled meadows with the Coast Range as a backdrop. The hike pays off when you reach the top of Hudson Bay Mountain. Don't miss having a look at the glacier on its weathered northeast face.

Nearest town: Smithers (see the North chapter)

Exploring BC's Powdery Bliss

BC's mountains, which range from rugged alpine peaks to gradual valleys and gullies, combine with almost guaranteed snowfall to make the province ideal for winter sports. The easy-going, snow-loving locals explore anywhere the snow falls. Backcountry touring and heli-skiing get you deep into unexplored territory, but most people head to the many resorts. Whether you're a seasoned skier, veteran rider or an utter novice standing in snow for the first time in your life, the resorts and small local mountains offer options galore.

If you're interested in snowshoeing, you can generally snowshoe anywhere you can cross-country ski – and many places you can't access on Nordic skis. It's an easy sport to learn, too, with guided treks and rentals widely available. Check with the Visitor Info Centres in winter resort areas.

Cypress Bowl Ski Area Close to Vancouver, the wide, snow-filled Cypress Bowl sits in the heart of Cypress Provincial Park between Strachan and Black Mountains. Popular with intermediate downhill skiers, the mountain also features 16km of groomed cross-country runs as well as a snowboard park. In the evening, the lights come on for great night skiing and excellent views of Howe Sound.

Nearest town: West Vancouver (see the Vancouver & Around chapter)
One-day lift ticket: $36
Information: ☎ 604-926-5612, 419-7669
Web site: www.cypressbowl.com

Grouse Mountain Resort A 20-minute drive or easy local bus ride from Vancouver, Grouse Mountain is a favorite for its easy access, night skiing and cheap lift tickets (compared to Whistler). An aerial tram whisks you to the mountaintop, offering incredible views along the way. Mogul dancers head to The Peak, or explore the mountain's backside on Blueberry or Purgatory. Boarders can rip all over the half-pipe, and anyone can enjoy the views skiing or boarding down The Cut, which is visible from almost anywhere in Vancouver.

Nearest town: North Vancouver (see the Vancouver & Around chapter)
One-day lift ticket: $32
Information: ☎ 604-984-0661
Web site: www.grousemountain.com

Mt Seymour This North Shore mountain is a haven for snowboarders, who come to rip it up in Seymour's three snowboard parks – Brockton, Mystery Peak and Mushroom Junior Park. Beginner skiers and boarders find Seymour a good place to learn, and the excellent ski/board school offers good deals on lessons, including equipment.

Nearest town: North Vancouver (see the Vancouver & Around chapter)
One-day lift ticket: $29
Information: ☎ 604-986-2261
Web site: www.mountseymour.com

Whistler-Blackcomb This world-famous, dual-mountain paradise can accommodate up to 54,000 skiers and snowboarders each day, with its 1609 vertical meters and 29 sq km of bowls, glades and steeps. You could stay here for an entire season – plenty of people do – and still not explore it all. Separated by the steep Fitzsimmons Creek Valley, Whistler and Blackcomb are two distinct mountains, but the high-speed lift system allows you access to both. Four snowboard parks, more than 200 runs and university-caliber ski schools offer boundless options for all levels. Whistler's rip-roaring nightlife, abundant restaurants and wide range of accommodations offer plenty of off-mountain entertainment. If you can't afford to spend the day in the spa, spend it people-watching in the village – it'll prove just as therapeutic.

Nearest town: Whistler (see the Whistler & the Sunshine Coast chapter)
One-day lift ticket: $63
Information: ☎ 604-932-3434, 800-766-0449
Web site: www.whistler-blackcomb.com

Apex Mountain Resort If you're looking for no chairlift lines and lots of technical skiing, Apex rules. Advanced skiers love the mountain for its black-diamond mogul runs, gladed chutes and vast powdery bowls. Less ambitious (or perhaps more sane) skiers and boarders will find plenty to explore, including a snowboard park and half-pipe. Near the village, 30km of groomed trails offer excellent cross-country skiing.

Nearest town: Penticton (see the Thompson-Okanagan chapter)
One-day lift ticket: $42
Information: ☎ 250-292-8222, 877-777-2739
Web site: www.apexresort.com

Big White Ski Resort One of the highest peaks in the Monashee Mountains, Big White boasts a mild climate, more than 100 marked trails and 8 sq km of terrain. Budget-minded skiers like Big White for its two hostels, a rarity among ski resorts. Three snowboard parks, long, leisurely ski runs and 25km of groomed cross-country trails attract every level of boarder and skier. Good nightlife, restaurants and lots of snow make it a great place to hang out.

Nearest town: Kelowna (see the Thompson-Okanagan chapter)
One-day lift ticket: $44
Information: ☎ 250-765-3101, 800-663-2772
Web site: www.bigwhite.com

Silver Star Mountain Resort A recreated Klondike boomtown, the village at Silver Star is a colorful, casual place. The mountain's sunny south face, Vance Creek, features predominantly novice and intermediate runs, while Putnum Creek, the north face, mainly offers black-diamond runs boasting moguls, trees and powder. A special machine carves wicked half-pipes for snowboarders. Cross-country skiers can enjoy 37km of groomed trails.

Nearest town: Vernon (see the Thompson-Okanagan chapter)
One-day lift ticket: $48
Information: ☎ 250-542-0224, 800-663-4431
Web site: www.silverstarmtn.com

Sun Peaks Resort When there's no snow on Vancouver's mountains, head four hours northeast to Sun Peaks, where early snow falls on Tod Mountain. Historically a family-oriented resort with lots of easy cruising runs, Sun Peaks is gaining popularity by carving out more advanced routes for adventurous skiers. The 1000m-long half-pipe is one of the largest in Canada. A new hostel at the mountain makes the resort more budget-friendly.

Nearest town: Kamloops (see the Thompson-Okanagan chapter)
One-day lift ticket: $46
Information: ☎ 250-578-7842, 800-807-3257
Web site: www.sunpeaksresort.com

Fernie Alpine Resort Vast investment dollars transformed Fernie from a well-kept local secret to a fast-growing resort that could be BC's next Whistler. Surrounded by spectacular alpine peaks, the mountain features almost 100 runs, deep powdery bowls and a snowboard park. If you've got some money to invest, buy now. Fernie's going to be huge.

    Nearest town: Fernie (see the Kootenays chapter)

    One-day lift ticket: $54

    Information: ☎ 250-423-4655, 800-258-7669

    Web site: www.skifernie.com

Kicking Horse Mountain Resort Give it a few years, and this new resort on Golden's Whitetooth Mountain will start appearing in snow sports magazines as a relatively unknown but priceless jewel in BC's ever-expanding bracelet of ski hills. The mountain's protected perch between the Purcell and Rocky Mountains gives it plenty of snow and windless, almost endless tracks of powder.

    Nearest town: Golden (see the Kootenays chapter)

    One-day lift ticket: $42

    Information: ☎ 250-344-8626, 888-706-1117

    Web site: www.kickinghorseresort.com

Kimberley Alpine Resort This resort is like an actress getting her first big break in the movies. Over the next few years, investment dollars will transform her from a small, humble mountain into a flashy resort. The powdery, mostly intermediate terrain features one of North America's longest runs illuminated for nighttime skiing. A snowboard park features an exciting half-pipe. The hostel in Kimberley offers respite for bargain hunters, as everything at the resort is pricey.

    Nearest town: Kimberley (see the Kootenays chapter)

    One-day lift ticket: $43

    Information: ☎ 250-427-4881, 800-258-7669

    Web site: www.skikimberley.com

Panorama Mountain Village Resort A rather isolated resort 18km from the town of Invermere, built-up Panorama features a 1200m vertical drop, one of Canada's highest. The excellent ski school augments plenty of runs for all levels. The isolation means you're forced to spend big bucks at the pricey restaurants and bars, and there are no cheap accommodations.

    Nearest town: Invermere (see the Kootenays chapter)

    One-day lift ticket: $49

    Information: ☎ 250-342-6941, 800-663-2929

    Web site: www.panoramaresort.com

Red Mountain Ski Resort A breeding ground for Olympic skiers, 'Red' accesses two mountains – Red and Granite – and offers some of the province's best black-diamond runs. Many people come for a day and stay for a season, drawn by Rossland's low-key charm. Intermediate skiers and boarders will find lots to explore, but this is no place for novices, since the resort is known for its steep, treed terrain.

Nearest town: Rossland (see the Kootenays chapter)
One-day lift ticket: $42
Information: ☎ 250-362-7384, 800-663-0105
Web site: www.ski-red.com

Whitewater Ski & Winter Resort Filled with powdery charm, this small local mountain tends to attract skiers and boarders venturing into the backcountry. The steep terrain boasts a 400m vertical drop, and snow seems to glue itself to sheer fingers such as Ymir Peak.

Nearest town: Nelson (see the Kootenays chapter)
One-day lift ticket: $37
Information: ☎ 250-354-4944, 800-666-9420
Web site: www.skiwhitewater.com

Getting There & Away

Vancouver is Western Canada's most important transportation hub. From a distance, the province is most easily reached by air, though you can also get to BC by bus, train, boat or car.

AIR

Though many BC-bound travelers will fly into Vancouver, people who are most interested in the Rockies may want to travel instead to Calgary, Alberta, just a short distance from Banff, Yoho and Jasper National Parks and other mountain attractions.

Airports

Vancouver International Airport (YVR; ☎ 604-207-7077) is 13km south of downtown Vancouver near the suburb of Richmond. It's Canada's second-busiest airport, handling nearly 16 million passengers a year.

The main airport has two terminals, international and domestic. The newly expanded international terminal handles all flights to the USA as well as other international destinations. Arrivals are on level 2. Beyond Customs, the International Reception Lobby includes cruise ship information counters, foreign exchange and banking services, domestic airline check-in counters, ground transportation services and a Visitor Info Centre.

Departures are on level 3, and here you'll find some of the check-in counters (US check-ins are in concourse E and other international check-ins are in concourse D), US Customs and Immigration pre-clearance, a children's play area and parents' facilities and a host of shops and restaurants. In fact, there are about 60 retail outlets scattered throughout the airport. There is a tourist information counter on each level (where you can be assisted in 10 languages), as well as foreign exchange kiosks, ATMs and several Royal Bank branches. Be on the lookout for some notable BC art, including *The Spirit of Haida Gwaii, The Jade Canoe* by Bill Reid.

The domestic terminal, which is the original airport, handles arrivals on level 2 and departures on level 3, where you'll find the airline check-in counters. (The departures level is undergoing renovations through June 2002.) On level 3, in the passageway that connects the domestic and international terminals, you'll find a children's nursery and a large play area.

The smaller south airport terminal, off Inglis Drive, handles regional airlines and seaplanes. There is no regular transporta-

YVR Airport Improvement Fee

All passengers departing YVR are required to buy an Airport Improvement Fee ticket. The cost is $5 for those traveling to a destination within BC or the Yukon; $10 for passengers traveling to other North American destinations including Hawaii and Mexico; and $15 for people traveling to destinations outside North America. Children under age two and passengers with same-day connecting flights through YVR are exempt.

AIF tickets must be presented as you pass through the security checkpoint on your way to your gate. You can buy the ticket at one of the AIF ticket sales machines scattered around the terminals or at the AIF Passenger Service Booths just before the security checkpoint. Payment can be made in Canadian or US cash or major credit cards. Some travel agents sell AIF tickets, too, so they may be able to include the fee in your ticket purchase price.

tion service between this terminal and the main ones so contact your airline to have it arranged. Or take a taxi, as it's definitely too far to walk.

For information about getting to and from YVR, see the Getting Around section in the Vancouver & Around chapter. For more information on airport amenities, see the Web site www.yvr.ca.

If you're bound for Victoria, note that it's sometimes less expensive to fly there than to Vancouver, so look into direct flights. Air Canada, Canadian Airlines, Horizon Air, North Vancouver Air and WestJet Airlines serve Victoria. See Getting There & Away in the Victoria section of the Vancouver Island chapter.

For Rockies-bound travelers, Calgary International Airport has service from most major North American Airlines and several international carriers including Air Canada, Alaska Airlines/Horizon Air, American Airlines, Canadian Airlines, Continental Airlines, Delta Airlines, Lufthansa, Northwest Airlines, Scandinavian Airlines (SAS) and United Airlines.

Airlines

Air travel within Canada has seen a big shake-up with the 2000 merger of the two major airlines, Air Canada and Canadian Airlines. Many BC travelers feel the 'integration' and resulting loss of competition has led to higher fares, lost baggage, longer lines and other woes. But the airlines say all current destinations will continue to be served, though there may yet be some changes in the airlines' regional subsidiaries, Air BC (Air Canada) and Canadian Regional (Canadian Airlines).

For more information or updates, see the integrated Web site www.aircanada.ca or call ☎ 888-247-2262. Other players to watch include maverick carriers Canada 3000 and Roots Air. The latter is a venture of the Canadian clothing conglomerate; flights were slated to begin in late 2000. Both airlines are staking their reputations on providing alternatives to the Air Canada/Canadian Airlines monopoly, which is steadily taking over BC air service.

Airlines with service to Vancouver include:

Air Canada
  (☎ 888-247-2262)

Air China
  (☎ 604-685-0921)

Air New Zealand
  (☎ 604-606-0150, 800-663-5494)

Air Pacific
  (☎ 604-214-3831, 800-227-4446)

Alaska Airlines/Horizon Air
  (☎ 800-252-7522)

British Airways
  (☎ 800-247-9297)

Canada 3000 Airlines
  (☎ 604-273-0930, 800-226-3000)

Canadian Airlines
  (☎ 888-247-2262)

Cathay Pacific Airways
  (☎ 604-606-8888, 800-607-3388)

Helijet Airways
  (☎ 604-273-1414, 800-665-4354)

Japan Airlines
  (☎ 604-606-7715, 800-525-3663)

Korean Air
  (☎ 604-689-2006, 800-438-5000)

Lufthansa Airlines
  (☎ 800-563-5954)

Pacific Coastal Airlines
  (☎ 604-273-8666, 800-663-2872)

Qantas
  (☎ 800-227-4500)

Singapore Airlines
  (☎ 604-689-1223)

West Coast Air
  (☎ 604-688-9115)

WestJet
  (☎ 800-538-5696)

Buying Tickets

The plane ticket may be the single most expensive item in your budget. Do some research on the current market. Start looking early – some of the cheapest tickets and best deals must be bought months in advance, some popular flights sell out early and special offers may only be advertised in newspapers and magazines. High season in Canada is mid-June to mid-September (summer), and the week before and the week after Christmas. Consequently, the best rates for travel to and in Canada are found November through March.

Before going to your travel agent, look at the travel sections of publications like *Time Out*, *TNT* and the *Sunday Times* in the UK, or the Sunday editions of newspapers such as the *New York Times* and *Los Angeles Times* in the USA or the *Sydney Morning Herald* and *The Age* in Australia. Ads in these publications offer cheap fares, but don't be surprised if they are sold out when you contact the agents; they are usually low-season fares on obscure airlines, and come with restrictions.

Look into buying roundtrip tickets, as they are usually much cheaper than two one-way fares. Talk to recent travelers if possible – they may be able to stop you from making some of the same old mistakes. Use the Internet as another resource, either for fare-checking or to buy your tickets. There's a huge range of fares available online, and most services rate them from lowest to highest to make comparisons easier. Top online travel sites include www.expedia.com and www.travelocity.com.

Warning

The information in this chapter is particularly vulnerable to change: Prices for international travel are volatile, routes are introduced and canceled, schedules change, special deals come and go, and rules and visa requirements are amended. Airlines and governments seem to take a perverse pleasure in making price structures and regulations as complicated as possible. You should check directly with the airline or a travel agent to make sure you understand how a fare (and any ticket you may buy) works. In addition, the travel industry is highly competitive, and there are many lurks and perks.

The upshot of this is that you should get opinions, quotes and advice from as many airlines and travel agents as possible before you part with your hard-earned cash. The details given in this chapter should be regarded as pointers and are not a substitute for your own careful, up-to-date research.

Call travel agencies for bargains (airlines can supply information on routes and timetables; however, except at times of fare wars, they don't supply the cheapest tickets). Airlines often have competitive low-season, student and senior citizens' fares. Find out the fare, route, duration of the journey and any restrictions on the ticket. Fares change constantly, and sometimes fares that include accommodations may be as cheap as roundtrip (return) fares.

Outside Canada, cheap tickets are available in two distinct categories: official and unofficial. Official tickets have a variety of names, including budget, advance purchase, Apex and super-Apex. Unofficial tickets are simply discounted tickets that the airlines release through selected travel agencies (not through airline offices).

Wherever you buy your tickets, the cheapest ones are often nonrefundable and require an extra fee if you decide to change your flight (if you are allowed to change your flight at all). Many insurance policies cover the loss if you have to change your flight for emergency reasons.

You may decide to pay more than the rock-bottom fare by opting for the safety of a well-known travel agent. Established firms like Council Travel or STA Travel, which have offices internationally, or Travel CUTS in Canada, offer competitive prices to most destinations.

Travelers crossing North America may find it cheaper to go, say, from Buffalo to Seattle than from Toronto to Vancouver. If you're flying to Vancouver from Asia, it also may be cheaper to fly into US West Coast cities than into Vancouver. But check around for the best current prices, and factor in the cost of traveling from the US to Canada. (Remember, too, Vancouver has a huge car-theft problem, and vehicles with out-of-province plates are frequently the ones targeted.)

Once you have your ticket, write down its number, together with the flight number and other details, and keep the information somewhere separate from the original. If the ticket is lost or stolen, this will help you get a replacement.

Air Travel Glossary

Bucket Shops These are unbonded travel agencies specializing in discount airline tickets.

Cancellation Penalties If you have to cancel or change a discounted ticket, heavy penalties are often involved; insurance can sometimes be taken out against these penalties. Some airlines impose penalties on regular tickets as well, particularly against 'no-show' passengers.

Courier Fares Businesses often need to send urgent documents or freight securely and quickly. Courier companies hire people to accompany the package through customs and, in return, offer a discount ticket that is sometimes a phenomenal bargain. However, you may have to surrender all your baggage allowance and take only carry-on luggage.

Full Fares Airlines traditionally offer 1st-class (coded F), business-class (coded J) and economy-class (coded Y) tickets. These days, so many promotional and discounted fares are available that few passengers pay full economy fare.

Lost Tickets If you lose your airline ticket, an airline will usually treat it as a traveler's check and, after inquiries, issue you another one. Legally, however, an airline is entitled to treat it like cash: If you lose it, it's gone forever. Take good care of your tickets.

Onward Tickets An entry requirement for many countries is a ticket out of the country. If you're unsure of your next move, the easiest solution is to buy the cheapest onward ticket to a neighboring country or a ticket from a reliable airline that can later be refunded if you do not use it.

Open-Jaw Tickets These are roundtrip tickets that permit you to fly into one place but return from another. If available, these tickets can save you backtracking to your arrival point.

Overbooking Because almost every flight has some passengers who fail to show up, airlines often book more passengers than they have seats. Usually excess passengers make up for the no-shows, but occasionally somebody gets 'bumped' onto the next available flight. Guess who it is most likely to be? The passengers who check in late.

Promotional Fares These are officially discounted fares, available from travel agencies or direct from the airline.

Reconfirmation If you don't reconfirm your flight at least 72 hours prior to departure, the airline may delete your name from the passenger list. Call to find out if your airline requires reconfirmation.

Restrictions Discounted tickets often have various restrictions – for example, they may need to be paid for in advance, or altering them may incur a penalty. Other restrictions include minimum and maximum periods you must be away.

Round-the-World Tickets RTW tickets give you a limited period (usually a year) in which to circumnavigate the globe. You can go anywhere the carrying airlines go as long as you don't backtrack. The number of stopovers or total number of separate flights is decided before you set off, and these tickets usually cost a bit more than a basic roundtrip flight.

Transferred Tickets Airline tickets cannot be transferred from one person to another. Travelers sometimes try to sell the return half of a ticket, but officials can ask you to prove that you are the person named on the ticket. On an international flight, tickets are compared with passports.

Travel Periods Ticket prices vary with the time of year. There is a low (off-peak) season and a high (peak) season, and often a low-shoulder season and a high-shoulder season as well. Usually the fare depends on your outward flight – if you depart in the high season and return in the low season, you pay the high-season fare.

Travelers With Special Needs

If you have any special needs – dietary restrictions, dependence on a wheelchair, responsibility for a baby, fear of flying – let the airline know as soon as possible so that they can make arrangements. Remind them when you reconfirm your reservation (at least 72 hours before departure) and again when you check in at the airport. It may also be worth phoning several airlines before you make a reservation to find out how well each one can handle your particular needs.

Airports and airlines can be surprisingly accommodating to passengers in wheelchairs, but they do need advance warning. Most international airports provide escorts from the check-in desk to the airplane if necessary, and there should be ramps, lifts, accessible toilets and reachable phones. Toilets in the aircraft, however, are likely to present a problem; travelers should discuss this with the airline at an early stage.

Guide dogs for the blind often have to travel in a specially pressurized baggage compartment with other animals, away from their owners, though smaller guide dogs may be admitted to the cabin. Guide dogs are not subject to quarantine as long as they have proof of vaccination against rabies.

Hearing impaired travelers can ask for airport and in-flight announcements to be written down for them.

Children under two years old travel for 10% of the standard fare (or free on some airlines) as long as they don't occupy a seat (they don't get a baggage allowance either). 'Skycots' should be provided by the airline if you request them in advance; these take a child weighing up to approximately 10kg. Children between the ages of two and 12 usually occupy a seat for half to two-thirds of the full fare (though some airlines charge full fare) and they do get a baggage allowance. Strollers can often be taken on as hand luggage.

Canada

The *Vancouver Sun*, *Vancouver Province*, *Globe & Mail* and other major newspapers all produce weekly travel sections with numerous travel agencies' ads. Travel CUTS has offices in all major cities

Air travel within Canada is not cheap, certainly when compared to airfares in the USA, but there are ways to save money. There are often seat sales to take advantage of, especially if you have a friend in Canada to book the ticket for you before you arrive. Late-night flights, often referred to as redeye specials, can save you anywhere from $50 to $100.

A roundtrip ticket to Vancouver with either Canadian Airlines or Air Canada will cost you about $275 from Calgary, $400 from Winnipeg, $460 from Toronto and $480 from Montreal. Canada 3000 Airlines is a discount charter airline with flights from Vancouver to other major cities in Canada, and if you choose to fly standby, you can get to Calgary one way for around $65, or all the way to Toronto for about $160.

The USA

Council Travel (☎ 800-226-8624) and STA Travel (☎ 800-781-4040) maintain offices in major cities across the USA. The magazine *Travel Unlimited*, PO Box 1058, Allston, MA 02134, publishes details of the cheapest airfares and courier possibilities. Roundtrip flights from Seattle to Vancouver with most major carriers cost about $195 (US$130). From San Francisco, the fare is about $325 (US$215). Air Canada flies to Vancouver from Los Angeles for about $390 (US$260) and from New York for $865 (US$575).

Australia & New Zealand

In Australia and New Zealand, STA Travel (☎ 800-637-444, 1300-360-960 or 0800-007-929 in New Zealand) and Flight Centres International offer cheap airfares; check the travel agencies' ads in the Yellow Pages or visit STA's Web site www.statravel.com.au. Qantas/Canadian Airlines flies to Vancouver from Sydney, Melbourne (via Sydney or Auckland) and Cairns. Air New Zealand also offers similar flights. United Airlines flies to San Francisco and Los Angeles from Sydney. The cheapest tickets have a 14-day advance-purchase requirement, a minimum stay of seven days and a maximum stay of 60 days. Qantas/Canadian Airlines flies from Melbourne or Sydney to Vancouver for around $1800 (A$2300) in the high season, but the usual standard, advance-purchase fare runs around $1500 (A$1900) for online booking. Flying with Air New Zealand can sometimes be cheaper, and both Qantas and Air New Zealand offer tickets with longer stays or stopovers, but you pay more. Roundtrip flights from Auckland to Vancouver cost around $1250 (NZ$2100) on Qantas. Canada 3000 Airlines flies between Vancouver and Sydney or Auckland from November to April for a lower roundtrip fare of about $1100. A good place to check for cheap fares is the Web site www.travel.com.au.

Asia

Hong Kong was once the discount plane ticket capital of the region, but now Bangkok and Singapore, which have a number of bucket shops, are better places to get the cheapest fares. STA Travel has branches in Hong Kong, Tokyo, Singapore, Bangkok and Kuala Lumpur. Many flights to Canada and the USA go via Honolulu.

Japan Airlines and Northwest Airlines have direct flights from Tokyo to Vancouver, with connections to other US West Coast cities such as Seattle, San Francisco and Los Angeles; Japan Airlines also flies to Honolulu from Osaka, Nagoya, Fukuoka and Sapporo. United Airlines has flights to Honolulu from Tokyo with connections to US West Coast cities. Flying to Vancouver from Tokyo costs around $1500.

Numerous airlines fly to Canada and the USA from Southeast Asia; bucket shops in places like Bangkok and Singapore should be able to come up with the best deals. Tickets to Vancouver or US West Coast cities often allow a free stopover in Honolulu. Malaysia Airlines flies to Honolulu from Hong Kong, Bangkok, Manila, Seoul and Singapore, with connections to Vancouver and other US West Coast cities. Korean Air and Philippine Airlines also offer flights from a number of Southeast Asian cities to Honolulu, with onward connections.

The UK & Ireland

London is arguably the world's headquarters for bucket shops, which frequently place ads and can usually beat published airline fares. Unregistered bucket shops are riskier than the established vendors but sometimes cheaper. If you are traveling from the UK, you will probably find that the cheapest flights are advertised by obscure bucket shops. Many are honest and solvent, but there are a few rogues who'll take your money and disappear, only to reopen elsewhere a month or two later under a new name. If you feel suspicious, don't pay for the ticket all at once – leave a deposit of 20% or so and pay the balance on receiving the ticket. If they insist on cash in advance, go elsewhere. Once you have the ticket, phone the airline to confirm that you are booked on the flight.

Check the ads in magazines such as *Time Out* and *City Limits*, plus the Sunday papers and *Exchange & Mart*. Also check the free magazines widely available in London – start by looking outside the main railway stations. Most British travel agents are registered with the Association of British Travel Agents (ABTA). If you've paid for your flight at an ABTA-registered agent who then goes out of business, ABTA will guarantee a refund or an alternative. Two good, reliable agents for cheap tickets in the UK are Trailfinders (☎ 020-7937-5400), 194 Kensington High St, London W8 7RG, and STA Travel (☎ 020-7361-6144), 86 Old Brompton Rd, London SW7 3LQ. Another one is Travelbag (☎ 0870 737 7880) on Regent Street at Piccadilly Circus. Trailfinders produces a lavishly illustrated brochure including airfare details. The Globetrotters Club publishes a newsletter called *Globe*, which covers obscure destinations and can help you find traveling companions. You can write to the club at BCM Roving, London WC1N 3XX or see the Web site www.globetrotters.co.uk. You can fly to Vancouver from London for approximately £540, from Edinburgh for about £575 and from Dublin for about IR£460.

Continental Europe

Though London is the travel-discount capital of Europe, several other cities offer a range of good deals, especially Amsterdam and Athens. Many travel agencies in Europe have ties with STA Travel, where cheap tickets can be bought and STA Travel tickets can be altered free of charge (first change only). See www.sta-travel.com.

As usual, fares to Vancouver are significantly lower in the off-season than in summer.

Mexico & South America

Most flights from Mexico and Central and South America to Vancouver go via Miami, Houston, Los Angeles and/or San Francisco. Often the trip requires flights on two different carriers: one from Mexico or South America to the US or Canada and another one to Vancouver. In the USA, airlines such as United and American serve these destinations, as do the various countries' international carriers such as Aerolíneas Argentinas and LanChile Airlines. Continental offers flights from about 20 cities in Mexico, Central and South America, including Lima, San Jose, Guatemala City, Cancún and Mérida, most of which arrive at the Dallas-Fort Worth airport and then connection to the rest of the USA and Canada.

Round-the-World Tickets

Round-the-world (RTW) tickets that include travel within Canada are popular and can be real bargains. Prices start at about $1950, UK£900, A$2200 or US$1300. The cost, however, largely depends on the carriers you use, the seasons you are traveling in any given part of the world and the number of stops included in the ticket.

Many airlines offer RTW tickets including British Airways, Canadian Airlines, Qantas and TWA. Official RTW tickets are usually put together by a combination of two airlines and permit you to fly anywhere you want on their route systems as long as you do not backtrack. Other common restrictions are that you must book the first sector in advance, and that you are liable for normal cancellation penalties. There may be restrictions on the number of stops permitted, and tickets are usually valid up to a year. You can also see if your travel agent can create a de facto RTW pass using a combination of discounted tickets.

Although most airlines restrict the number of sectors that can be flown within Canada and the USA to four, and some airlines black out a few popular routes (like Honolulu to Tokyo), stopovers are otherwise generally unlimited. In most cases a 14-day advance purchase is required. After the ticket is purchased, dates can be changed without penalty and tickets can be rewritten to add or delete stops for about $50 each.

Circle Pacific Tickets

For Circle Pacific tickets, two airlines link up to allow stopovers along their combined Pacific Rim routes. Rather than just flying you from point A to point B, these tickets allow you to swing through much of the Pacific and eastern Asia, taking in a variety of destinations as long as you keep traveling in the same circular direction.

At the time of writing, Circle Pacific routes had essentially the same fares: around $3200 when purchased in Canada, US$2600 when purchased in the USA, A$3300 when purchased in Australia and NZ$4100 when purchased in New Zealand. Circle Pacific fares include four stopovers, with the option of additional stops for $65 each. There's a seven- to 14-day advance-purchase requirement, a 25% cancellation penalty and a maximum stay of six months.

Canadian Airlines has Circle Pacific fares from Vancouver in partnership with Qantas, Air New Zealand, Singapore Airlines, Garuda Indonesia, Cathay Pacific Airways or Malaysia Airlines. Qantas offers Circle Pacific routes in partnership with, among others, United Airlines, Delta Air Lines, Japan Airlines, Northwest Airlines and Continental Airlines. Air New Zealand offers the ticket in conjunction with, among others, Japan Airlines, Thai Airways International, Cathay Pacific and Singapore Airlines. United Airlines offers the ticket in combination with more than a dozen Pacific Rim carriers.

Itineraries can be selected from scores of potential destinations. A Canadian-United ticket, for example, could take you from Vancouver to Honolulu, on to Tokyo, south to Manila, followed by Sydney and back to Vancouver. Keep in mind that Circle Pacific fares are high and you may find better deals elsewhere. For instance, at press time Air New Zealand was offering a 'Backpacker' fare from Vancouver for about $2035 roundtrip; it allowed stopovers at two destinations, including New Zealand, Australia, Tahiti, Hawaii, Fiji, the Cook Islands, Western Samoa and Tonga, within a one-year period. Each additional stop costs an additional $165.

LAND
Border Crossings
Points of entry on the US-Canada border are open 24 hours except as noted. From west to east, they include Boundary Bay (Point Roberts); Douglas; Pacific Hwy (176 St, Surrey); Aldergrove (8 am to midnight); Huntingdon; Osoyoos; Midway (9 am to 5 pm); Cascade (8 am to midnight); Waneta (9 am to 5 pm); Nelway (8 am to midnight); Rykerts (7 am to 11 pm April through October, 8 am to midnight November through March); Kingsgate; and Roosville. There's also a 24-hour crossing at Stewart on the Alaska-BC border.

See the Visas & Documents and the Customs sections in the Facts for the Visitor chapter for information on the paperwork you'll need to have at border crossings, as well as for information on what may legally be brought into Canada.

Bus
You can travel to many places in BC from the US via Greyhound Bus Lines (☎ 800-661-8747, 604-482-8747). Sample one-way

fares from Seattle (in US$) are as follows:

destination	duration	fare
Vancouver	4-5 hours	$21
Kelowna	13 hours	$55
Kamloops	11 hours	$58
Prince George	18 hours	$72
Banff	20 hours	$92
Prince Rupert	32 hours	$122

You can save money on Greyhound tickets by buying at least seven days in advance. Greyhound also offers a Canada Coach Pass, which allows travel across Canada and to and from select US cities. Prices are $249 (10-day pass), $379 (20-day pass), $449 (40-day pass) and $599 (80-day pass).

Also, see the Vancouver chapter's Getting There & Around section for information on Quick Coach Lines and Bigfoot Adventure Shuttle service to and from Seattle.

Train
Amtrak (☎ 604-585-4848, 800-872-7245) connects Vancouver to Bellingham and Seattle with one train daily that takes four hours. In addition, Amtrak runs three buses a day from Vancouver to Seattle to connect with other main-line departures. Either way, one-way fares run between $21 and 33; earliest callers get the less-expensive seats. If you can, take the train, which leaves Seattle for Vancouver at 7:45 am, arriving at 11:40 am. The southbound train leaves Vancouver at 6 pm, arriving in Seattle at 9:55 pm.

Within Canada, VIA Rail (☎ 888-842-7245) runs the *Canadian* between Vancouver and Toronto. Stops include Kamloops, Jasper, Edmonton, Saskatoon and Winnipeg. It's a scenic trip, but it only runs three times a week, leaving Toronto at 8:45 am on Tuesday, Thursday and Saturday and departing Vancouver at 5:30 pm on Tuesday, Friday and Sunday. The one-way fare to Vancouver costs $187 from Jasper, $250 from Edmonton and $615 from Toronto. For extensive rail travel within North America, check out VIA Rail's Canrail Pass, which allows 12 days of travel throughout Canada within a 30-day period for $639 (June 1 to mid-October) or $399 the rest of the year. The North American Rail Pass ($965/675 peak/off-peak) is good for 30 days over all of VIA Rail's network and most of Amtrak's US routes. Discounts are available to students, seniors and children.

Car & Motorcycle

The US highway system connects directly with Canadian highways at many points along the BC border. (See Border Crossings earlier in this section for more information.)

Friday and Sunday are especially busy at the major border crossings. Delays can be especially bad on the holiday weekends in summer, particularly at the Douglas/Blaine crossing south of Vancouver, where you may have to wait several hours. Either avoid crossing at these times, or drive to one of the other Lower Mainland crossings such as Aldergrove or Huntingdon.

Fill your gas tank before crossing into BC. Prices are generally a bit lower in the US and Alberta.

SEA

You can get to Victoria by ferry from Seattle, Port Angeles and Anacortes, Washington. See Getting There & Away under Victoria in the Vancouver Island chapter.

Alaska Cruises

This section wouldn't be complete without a mention of what has become one of the world's most popular – and profitable – cruise destinations. In total, 25 vessels from 12 cruise lines make 335 sailings between Vancouver and Alaska every year between May and October, and Vancouver welcomes more than one million cruise passengers each season. Canada Place was designed in 1986 to handle as many as five cruise ships

at a time, with each ship averaging around 600 passengers. Due to the increased size of the new ships, averaging around 2000 passengers each, Canada Place can now service two large ships at a time. Construction of a third berth at Canada Place will be completed in time for the 2003 cruise season. Cruise ships also dock at Ballantyne Pier, a dual-purpose cargo and cruise ship terminal located in East Vancouver, which was redesigned in 1995 to service the largest modern cruise ships and their passengers. Ballantyne Pier is at the foot of Heatley St about five blocks east of Main St.

For more information about the cruises, or to make reservations, contact a travel agent or Cruise Holidays (☎ 604-737-8100, 888-702-7245). *Porthole* magazine (☎ 800-776-7678) is also a good source of information. It maintains a Web site at www.porthole.com

ORGANIZED TOURS

If money isn't a big concern, and you like the idea of traveling in a group with someone else making most of your travel arrangements, you might enjoy an organized tour. Quite a few tour companies from outside Canada offer trips to British Columbia, especially to Vancouver, Victoria and the Canadian Rockies. Maupintour (☎ 800-255-4266) has a nine-day trip that takes in Seattle, Vancouver and Victoria; a 10-day package that includes an Inside Passage cruise, train ride, and stops in Vancouver, Victoria, Prince Rupert and Prince George; and a seven-day *Rocky Mountaineer* Escape that includes time in Vancouver and Banff as well as two days on the famous scenic railroad. For more details, visit www.maupintours.com. Many companies within Canada offer similar tours. See the Getting Around chapter or the regional chapters for details.

Getting Around

AIR

Flying is a fast, convenient way to get around BC, especially if you're traveling to far-flung places on limited time. Flights are usually – though not always – pricier than a ferry, bus or car rental. But if you save a day or two getting where you want to be, the added cost may be worth it.

Most major destinations within BC can be accessed by Air Canada (☎ 888-247-2262) or its new partner, Canadian Airlines (☎ 888-247-2262) or their regional subsidiaries, Air BC and Canadian Regional. As noted in the Getting There & Away chapter, the merger of Air Canada with Canadian Airlines has changed routes and schedules, so it's best to contact the airlines or see a travel agent for the latest information.

Smaller regional airlines also serve the province. Harbour Air (☎ 604-688-1277 in Vancouver, 250-384-2215 in Victoria, 800-665-0212 elsewhere) has harbor-to-harbor seaplane service from Vancouver to Victoria, several points on the Southern Gulf Islands, Nanaimo, Prince Rupert and other destinations. Find complete information on Harbour Air's Web site www.harbour-air

.com. West Coast Air (☎ 604-606-6888, 800-347-2222) also has service between Vancouver and Victoria. Helijet Airways (☎ 604-273-1414 or 800-665-4354) has passenger helicopter service between Vancouver and Victoria; get details online at www.helijet.com. See the Getting There & Away sections of the regional chapters for more information on air service.

BUS

Greyhound covers most of BC. It may take a while (24 hours from Vancouver to Terrace, for example), and it's expensive to points distant from Vancouver, but you can pretty much get where you want to go. If you plan plenty of bus travel in Canada or North America, see the Getting There & Away chapter for details on Greyhound's Canada Coach Pass. For more information on Greyhound's routes and fares, see the Web site www.greyhound.ca or call ☎ 604-482-8747 or 800-661-8747.

Southwestern BC has a good network of regional bus carriers. Pacific Coach Lines (☎ 250-385-4411, 800-661-1725) operates buses between Vancouver and Victoria. Laidlaw Coach Lines (☎ 250-385-4411) covers Vancouver Island. Malaspina Coach Lines (☎ 604-886-7742, 877-227-8287) has service from Vancouver to the Sunshine Coast.

See the Organized Tours section later in this chapter for bus tours throughout BC, and the Ferry section for a combination bus-ferry tour of the Inside Passage.

TRAIN

Railroad service is alive and well in BC. Also see the Inside Passage heading in the Boat section, below, for a combination boat-train-bus circle tour around the province.

The national carrier, VIA Rail (☎ 888-842-7245) has only one route from Vancouver. The *Canadian* departs a paltry three times a week and makes few stops in BC. VIA Rail also runs the *Skeena* between

Calling the Airlines

The ongoing merger of Air Canada and Canadian Airlines has meant some ongoing confusion for travelers trying to book flights on one of these two airlines' subsidiaries, which include Central Mountain Air, Air BC and Canadian Regional Airlines. As of press time, these smaller carriers had discontinued their own telephone reservation lines. To book a flight with any of Air Canada's new affiliates or to obtain information about routes and fares, call Air Canada at ☎ 888-247-2262. Watch out for more changes in the future.

Prince Rupert and Jasper thrice weekly. It's a daytime-only trip with an overnight stay in Prince George and stops in Terrace, Smithers, Houston and Burns Lake. Unlike the privately run *Rocky Mountaineer* train described later in this section, passengers on the *Skeena* have a choice of service class and fare, and you book your own lodgings in Prince George.

On Vancouver Island, VIA Rail runs the Esquimalt & Nanaimo Railiner, also known as the E&N Railiner or the *Malahat*, a short, scenic trip from Victoria to Courtenay up the coast of Vancouver Island, with one train daily in each direction. See the regional chapters in this book or www.viarail.ca for more info. Also check out the Getting There & Away chapter for information on Canadian and North American rail passes available from VIA Rail.

The province's own railroad, BC Rail (☎ 604-631-3500, 800-663-8238) runs the *Cariboo Prospector* with service from North Vancouver to Squamish, Whistler, Lillooet, 100 Mile House, Williams Lake, Quesnel and Prince George. BC Rail also operates the popular Royal Hudson steam train excursion from North Vancouver to Squamish between June and September; see the Squamish section in the Whistler & Sunshine Coast chapter for details on this scenic ride.

The *Rocky Mountaineer*, a privately owned train, travels through some of Canada's most scenic landscapes from Vancouver to Banff and Calgary, a route no longer served by VIA Rail. But this isn't a service for people just trying to get from place to place; rather, it's a veritable cruise ship on land. Tickets come with accommodations (there's an obligatory overnight stay in Kamloops) and meals. One-way fares for the least-expensive trip start at about $360 in spring and $475 in summer, per person double occupancy. The trains run between mid-May and early October, with about seven trips a month in summer. For detailed information, contact a travel agent or Rocky Mountaineer Railtours (☎ 604-606-7245 or 800-665-7245) or see the Web site www.rockymountaineer.com.

CAR & MOTORCYCLE

British Columbia is a big place, and if you want to see a lot of it on your own timetable, a car or motorcycle is usually the way to go. In many ways, driving is the best way to travel in this province. You can go where and when you want, use secondary highways and roads and get off the beaten track. It's particularly good in summer when you can camp or even sleep in the car.

Canada has good, well-marked roads. The major cross-province route is the Trans-Canada Hwy (Hwy 1), which runs from Vancouver to Kamloops, Revelstoke and Golden before crossing the Alberta border to Banff, Calgary and points east. (The route also runs from Victoria part-way up the coast of Vancouver Island.) Hwy 97 is another major route, running from Osoyoos in the south through Kelowna, Kamloops, Prince George and Dawson Creek in the north, where it becomes the famous Alaska Hwy. Other major highways include Hwy 19 on Vancouver Island; the Coquihalla Hwy (Hwy 5) and Crowsnest Hwy (Hwy 3) in the Thompson-Okanagan region; Hwy 6 in the Kootenays; Hwys 93 and 95 in the Rockies; and the Yellowhead Hwy (Hwy 16) in the North.

The freedom of the open road is one thing. City driving is another. In Vancouver especially, a car is more of a nuisance than a help. If you have urban stops on your itinerary, park the car and walk or take public transportation. Cars are also unnecessary at many destinations served by BC Ferries (see the Southern Gulf Islands and Vancouver Island regional chapters for details), and you can save money by not bringing a vehicle on board.

See Driver's License & Insurance in the Facts for the Visitor chapter for information on Canada's requirements for driving.

Road Rules & Safety Precautions

North Americans drive on the right side of the road. Speed limits, which are posted in kilometers, are generally 50km/h in built-up areas and 100km/h on highways. A right turn is permitted at a red light after you have come to a complete stop, as is a left turn from one one-way street onto another one-way street. Traffic in both directions must stop when stationary school buses have their red lights flashing – this means children are getting off and on. In cities with pedestrian crosswalks, cars must stop to allow pedestrians to cross.

The use of seat belts is compulsory throughout Canada. Children under age five must be in a restraining seat. British Columbia law requires motorcyclists to drive with the lights on and for cyclists and passengers to wear helmets. Don't drive after drinking alcohol. The blood-alcohol limit when driving is 0.08%.

You may notice that the vast majority of drivers keep their headlights on throughout the day; this is not mandatory but is recommended. Newer cars have 'running' lights that turn on and off automatically with the ignition.

It's best to avoid driving in areas with heavy snow, but if you do, be sure your vehicle has snow tires or tire chains. Many Canadian cars have four-season radial tires. If you get stuck, don't stay in the car with the engine going; every year people die of carbon monoxide suffocation by doing this during big storms. A single candle burning in the car will keep it reasonably warm.

Service stations are few and far between in many parts of BC, so keep an eye on the gas gauge and try not to dip below half a tank. Make sure the vehicle you're driving is in good condition and take along some tools, spare parts, water and food.

Some additional precautions apply for off-the-beaten-track travel. Gravel logging roads tend to be particularly dangerous. Logging trucks have the right of way in every instance, and they'll often zoom past you, kicking up gravel and dust. This can take a toll on windshields, so if you're renting, sort out breakage coverage in advance. (Some rental companies prohibit customers from taking cars on gravel

Driving Distance (in kilometers)

	Cranbrook	Dawson Creek	Kamloops	Kelowna	Nanaimo	Port Hardy	Prince George	Prince Rupert	Vancouver	Victoria	Watson Lake, Yukon
Cranbrook	0										
Dawson Creek	1181	0									
Kamloops	606	931	0								
Kelowna	526	1091	163	0							
Nanaimo	853	1197	363	403	0						
Port Hardy	1240	1140	750	790	391	0					
Prince George	880	406	525	685	791	734	0				
Prince Rupert	1604	1130	1249	1409	391	10	724	0			
Vancouver	845	1184	355	395	23	410	778	1502	0		
Victoria	883	1227	393	433	113	504	821	504	69	0	
Watson Lake, Yukon	2108	985	1753	1913	1379	998	1228	988	2006	1492	0

roads.) It's best not to drive on logging roads at all during weekday working hours. Keep a good distance from the vehicle in front of you, and when you see an oncoming vehicle (or a vehicle overtaking you), slow down and keep well to the right. Carry a spare tire, fan belt and hoses.

Wild animals on the road are another potential hazard. Most run-ins with deer, moose and other critters occur at night when wildlife is active and visibility is poor. Many areas have roadside signs alerting drivers to possible animal crossings. Keep scanning both sides of the road and be prepared to stop or swerve. A vehicle's headlights often mesmerize an animal, leaving it frozen in the middle of the road. Try flashing the lights or turning them off, as well as using the horn.

Rental

Car-rental agencies are abundant in BC's population centers. The main companies include Alamo, Avis, Budget, Hertz and National but there are many more. Alamo and Budget generally have the best rates among the new-car agencies. Rent-A-Wreck is a well-known used-car rental agency and its prices are somewhat cheaper. To be certain of finding a car and to save time, it's worthwhile to make a reservation before your arrival. You will need to show a valid driver's license when renting a car.

Most companies have a daily rate of $30 to $50, or weekly rates for compact cars starting at about $130, usually including unlimited mileage. Weekend rates are often the cheapest and can include extra days; for example, if you pick up a car Friday morning and return it before midnight Monday it may be billed as just three days. Note that rates are not consistent within any company and each outlet is run independently. Downtown locations usually have better rates than rental desks at the airport.

Depending on the locations, it is possible to drop a car off at a different office than where it was picked up. In some places a fee, sometimes very high, is charged for this privilege. Check before you rent. Count on needing a credit card to rent a car in BC.

Some companies require you to be at least 21 years of age, others 26.

Beware that prices can be deceptive. The daily rate may be an enticing $25, but by the time you finish with, gasoline, GST, PST and insurance, you can be handed a pretty surprising bill. Don't automatically accept the rental company's insurance. Your home insurance company, or even the credit card on which you rent the car, may cover the rental. Call before you leave for BC to find out.

Recreational Vehicles Recreational vehicles (RVs) are hugely popular in BC, and RV rentals must be booked well before the summer travel season. In high season, mid- to large-size vehicles cost $170 to $225 a day, including 100km per day. These are good for four to seven people and include appliances. Make sure to ask for a diesel engine to save on fuel costs. One-way rentals are possible, but you'll pay a surcharge. Also budget plenty for fuel, because RVs typically get very poor gas mileage. Truck campers starting at about $125 a day and tent-trailers from $60 a day are available too, but these should be booked even earlier. For all RVs, there's usually a seven-day minimum rental.

Canada Camper RV Rentals & Sales (☎ 604-270-1833, 877-327-3003, rental@canada-camper.com), 4431 Vanguard Rd in Richmond, is close to Vancouver International Airport. See its Web site www.canada-camper.com. Go-West Campers International (☎ 604-987-5288), 1577 Lloyd St in North Vancouver, is another company with similar rates and several locations in Western Canada.

Purchase

Older cars can be bought quite cheaply in BC. Look in the local newspaper, on message boards or in one of the specialized car-sales publications available on news racks in larger towns. Private deals are nearly always the most economical way to buy a car. Used-car dealers must mark up the prices in order to make a profit. Generally, North American cars are priced lower than Japanese and European cars.

For a few months of driving, a used car can be an excellent investment, especially if there are two or more of you. You can usually sell the car for nearly what you paid for it. A fairly decent older car should be available for under $4000. Cars from BC's Lower Mainland last longer than those from Eastern Canada since the region's mild winters mean less rust-creating road salt.

You will need Canadian insurance. Bring a letter from your current company indicating your driving record. In order to get the insurance and then a plate for the vehicle, you will need an address in Canada; that of a friend or relative will suffice.

Insurance costs vary widely and can change dramatically from province to province. As a rule, the rates for women are noticeably less than for a man of comparable age and driving record. If you're planning a side trip to the USA, make sure the insurance you negotiate is valid over the border, too. Also remember that rates are linked to the age and type of car. A newer car may cost more to insure, but it may also be easier to sell when you're through with it.

Driveaways

If you are ready to leave town and know where you want to go, or, conversely don't care where you end up, you may want to check out the uniquely North American 'driveaway' system. The basic concept is that you drive someone else's car to a specific destination. Usually the car belongs to someone who has been transferred for work and has had to fly, or doesn't have the time, patience or ability to drive a long distance. Arrangements are made through a driveaway agency.

After the agency matches you up with a suitable car, you put down a deposit of $300 to $500 and are given a certain number of days to deliver the car. If you don't show up the police are notified. You are usually given a route to take and a rough kilometer guideline which translates into the most direct route from A to B.

You are not paid to deliver the car, and generally you pay for gasoline. With two or more people, this can be an especially great deal. The company will want to know who will be driving.

In summer, when demand is highest, cars may be more difficult to obtain and you could be asked for a nonrefundable administrative payment of, perhaps, $100.

Be sure to ask what happens if the car breaks down – and get the answer in writing if possible. Generally, you pay for minor car repairs of $100 or less. Keep the receipt and you will be reimbursed upon delivery. If bad luck strikes and a major repair is required, there may be hassles. The agency might get in touch with the owner and ask how to proceed. This might take time, and could involve some inconvenience. Usually the cars offered are fairly new and in good working order, or the owners wouldn't bother having them transported.

You'll need to supply good identification, a valid driver's license, the deposit and a couple of photos of yourself. Look for driveaway companies in the telephone Yellow Pages under 'Automobile & Truck Transporting,' or contact Vancouver Driveaway (☎ 604-985-8016), 1080A Marine Dr, North Vancouver.

Gasoline

At the time of this writing, gasoline (petrol, usually just called gas in BC) costs between 70¢ and 75¢ per liter. That's still low by much of the world's standards, but it's as high as it's ever been in North America.

In general, cities and large towns have better gas prices than remote places. You might also save a bit by driving a kilometer or two away from the main highway to an in-town service station.

British Columbia Automobile Association

The British Columbia Automobile Association (BCAA) has offices throughout the province, with headquarters at 4567 Canada Way in Burnaby, a suburb of Vancouver (☎ 604-268-5000; 292-2222 for 24-hour emergency road service). It provides its members, and the members of other auto clubs, with travel information, maps, travel insurance and hotel reservations. BCAA also has offices in Abbotsford, Chilliwack, Coquitlam, Courtenay, Delta, Kamloops, Kelowna, Langley, Nanaimo, Nelson, New Westminster, North Vancouver, Penticton, Prince George, Richmond, Surrey, Vancouver, Vernon, Victoria and West Vancouver.

BICYCLE

The Web site www.bccc.bc.ca is the best source of information on bicycling as transportation in BC. Bike rentals are widely available, and in the various regional chapters of this book you will find bicycle rental listings for most towns. You can take your bike on most forms of public transportation. Call ahead to the air, ferry, bus and train companies listed to see what their rates and requirements are.

HITCHHIKING

Hitchhiking is fairly common in BC, especially in rural areas, near ski resorts and on the Gulf Islands. Nevertheless, hitchhiking is never entirely safe in any country in the world, and is not recommended. Travelers who decide to hitchhike (or pick up hitchhikers) should understand that they are taking a risk. If you do choose to hitchhike, do it only in pairs. Hitching on the Trans-Canada Hwy is illegal until 40km past the Vancouver city limits.

BOAT
Ferry

The blue-and-white BC Ferries are a symbol of coastal BC as well as a mode of transportation. You'll find extensive details on BC Ferries service in the Vancouver & Around, the Vancouver Island and the Whistler & the Sunshine Coast chapters; what follows is an overview of services, plus details on the long-distance Inside Passage and Discovery Coast Passage routes, as well as the discounted Sunshine Coast CirclePac ticket.

BC Ferries Corporation (☎ 888-223-3779 in BC or 250-386-3431 in Victoria or out of province for schedules and information) operates a fleet of 40 ferries on BC's coastal waters. The two busiest routes are from

Tsawwassen (about an hour's drive south of downtown Vancouver) to Swartz Bay (a half-hour drive north of Victoria), and from Horseshoe Bay (a half-hour drive north of downtown Vancouver) to Departure Bay near Nanaimo on Vancouver Island. From Tsawwassen, ferries also go to Duke Point near Nanaimo, and to the Southern Gulf Islands (Salt Spring, Galiano, Mayne, Saturna, and the Pender Islands). From Horseshoe Bay, ferries also go to Bowen Island and the Sunshine Coast.

Other BC Ferries routes cover Gabriola Island, Thetis Island, Kuper Island, Texada Island and the Northern Gulf Islands (namely Denman, Hornby, Quadra, Cortes, Malcolm and Cormorant). There's also long-distance service between Comox on Vancouver Island and Powell River on the northern Sunshine Coast; from Port Hardy to Prince Rupert (the Inside Passage) and Bella Coola (the Discovery Coast Passage);

Ships, Big & Small

BC Ferries vessels are a diverse lot. Some of the ships hold only a few dozen vehicles and 100 or so passengers; the biggest *Spirit*-class vessels resemble floating towns, accommodating 2100 passengers and nearly 500 vehicles. Amenities on the larger ships include onboard cafeterias (some including fare from BC's beloved White Spot chain), gift shops, ATMs, game rooms, ship-to-shore telephones, private cabins and children's play areas. You won't find all these niceties on the small ferries, but there's usually at least a vending machine or two.

All the ferries are great places to load up on information about your destination. On large ships, brochure racks are stuffed with maps and literature. Even more useful and entertaining are the bulletin boards on the smaller ships. These notice boards, displaying information on special upcoming events and little-advertised guesthouses and hostels, often shed great light on the communities served by the ferry.

and from Prince Rupert to Skidegate on the Queen Charlotte Islands.

Generally, it's much cheaper to travel on BC Ferries without a motorized vehicle. You can take bicycles, canoes or kayaks onboard. See the Web site www.bcferries.com for complete information.

Vehicle reservations are recommended for weekends on the Tsawwassen-Swartz Bay, Horseshoe Bay-Departure Bay and Tsawwassen-Duke Point routes. Call Reserved Boarding (☎ 888-724-5223 in BC or 604-444-2890 out of province) for information, or reserve online at www.bcferries.com. Reservations for other routes (including the Inside Passage, Discovery Coast Passage, Queen Charlotte Islands and Tsawwassen-Southern Gulf Islands) are made through the main passenger service numbers (☎ 888-223-3779 in BC or 250-386-3431).

Inside Passage The Inside Passage route between Port Hardy and Prince Rupert is among the most scenic boat trips in the world. You'll want to check the most current schedules at www.bcferries.com, but generally the *Queen of the North* sails northbound from Port Hardy at 7:30 am on odd-numbered days in June, July and September and even-numbered days in August, arriving in Prince Rupert at 10:30 pm. (Some sailings arrive at 11:30 pm.) The southbound sailings from Prince Rupert have the opposite schedule: even-numbered days in June, July and September and odd-numbered days in August. All southbound sailings leave Prince Rupert at 7:30 am and most arrive at Port Hardy at 10:30 pm northbound, though, again, some arrive at 11:30 pm. There are sailings October through May, too; check the Web site or call ☎ 888-223-3779 in BC (or 250-386-3431 in Victoria or out of province) for dates and details. You must reserve space on Inside Passage sailings.

The one-way, peak-season (mid-June through mid-September) fare is $106 for adults, $53 for children ages five to 11 (kids under five are free) and $218 for a car. Meals can be bought à la carte or as a package ($39/21 adults/children). For some

privacy and rest, cabins with two berths, a washbasin and toilet are available for an extra $43 ($52 with a shower) for the day. Pay $94 ($117 with a shower), and you can stay onboard overnight at your destination, which works well if you're taking the same trip in reverse the next morning.

Because of the early departure times, most people stay in Port Hardy or Prince Rupert the night before their sailing. Be sure to reserve accommodations, since rooms in these towns fill up fast.

BC Ferries offers a five-day, four-night Inside Passage and Vancouver Island package starting at about $825 per person. The self-guided tour includes an overnight stay in Victoria and a bus trip up the Vancouver Island coast, followed by the Inside Passage sailing to Prince Rupert and back (with a private overnight cabin in Prince Rupert and two nights' accommodations in Port Hardy), and transportation back to Vancouver via Nanaimo.

Also available is the six-day, five-night Totem Circle Rail and Cruise Tour, which includes two rail trips between Vancouver and Prince George (on BC Rail's *Cariboo Prospector)* and Prince George and Prince Rupert (on VIA Rail's *Skeena)*; the Inside Passage sailing from Prince Rupert to Port Hardy; bus transportation from Port Hardy to Victoria for an overnight stay; and the ferry from Victoria to Vancouver through the Gulf Islands. Prices start at about $1170 per person.

Discovery Coast Passage This route covers the stretch between Port Hardy on Vancouver Island and Bella Coola on the central BC coast. It's shorter than the Inside Passage route, but just as scenic (and expensive). Ships run only from mid-June through mid-September. Reservations are necessary.

The most direct Discovery Coast northbound sailings stop only at Namu; these generally leave Port Hardy at 9:30 am Thursday and arrive in Bella Coola at 11 pm. Tuesday sailings leave Port Hardy at 9:30 am but stop at McLoughlin Bay and Shearwater and don't reach Bella Coola until 6:30 am the next day. Even longer is the Saturday-to-Monday trip that leaves Port Hardy at 9:30 pm Saturday and makes several Sunday stops (including four hours at Klemtu, a First Nations community) before finally reaching Bella Coola at 7 am Monday.

Southbound, the most direct sailings leave Bella Coola at 8 am Monday and arrive in Port Hardy at 9:30 that night. Wednesday and Friday southbound sailings have a variety of stops and arrive in Port Hardy the following morning. Check the Web site www.bcferries.com for schedules. The one-way, peak-season fare between Port Hardy and Bella Coola is $110 for adults, $55 for children ages 5 to 11 and $220 for a car.

There are no cabins on the *Queen of Chilliwack*, which sails the Discovery Coast Passage, but there are reclining lounge seats where you can sleep. Some passengers even set up their tents on deck and sleep there.

Sunshine Coast CirclePac Many BC travelers like the idea of making a circle tour from Vancouver to Vancouver Island and back without retracing their route. To accommodate them, BC Ferries offers its circular ticket, known as the Sunshine Coast CirclePac. This ticket includes all four ferries you need to make the loop at a saving of about 15 percent. For 2000, the full peak-season fare was $24.50/12.25/84.75 for adults/children/cars, and the CirclePac fare was $21/10.40/72. You can travel in either direction, and the ticket is valid for three months from the date of purchase. No reservation is necessary. Just ask for the CirclePac fare when you make your first crossing; you'll receive a receipt and tickets for each leg of the trip. If you plan to travel on Friday or Sunday, when the ferry terminals on the CirclePac routes are all quite busy, be sure to arrive early.

LOCAL TRANSPORTATION

British Columbia has excellent, widespread local public transportation. Look in the regional chapters for details on each town's offerings, or see the province-wide Web site www.transitbc.com, which features links to the local bus systems.

ORGANIZED TOURS

No matter what your travel style, you'll find organized tours to suit it in BC. Not surprisingly, many tours focus on outdoor recreation, usually in a specific area. There also are a wide variety of city tours that take in local sights. These are listed in the regional chapters.

If you're looking to cover a wide swath of the province, many options are available. Alberta-based Brewster (☎ 403-762-6700, 800-661-1152, tours-BTC@brewster.ca) has been doing bus tours in the Canadian Rockies for more than a century. Most of its excursions make a beeline from Vancouver or Calgary straight for Banff, Jasper, Lake Louise and Yoho. They're priced from about $500 to $1600, per person double occupancy, with most meals included. Find more information at www.brewster.ca.

Gray Line (☎ 604-879-3363, 800-667-0882, vancouver.info@grayline.ca) is another big player, especially in the Lower Mainland. Its many tours focus on Vancouver, Whistler and Victoria. See details at www.grayline.ca. Despite its rather staid reputation, Gray Line is moving into adventure tours in a big way, having formed a partnership with www.iamadventurous.com (☎ 604-874-0004, 800-819-6932,info@adventure-bc.com). Through the Web site that shares its name, the company offers a great selection of activity-oriented trips in everything from skiing to golf to sea kayaking.

Maverick Tours (☎ 604-940-8727, info@mavericktours.bc.ca) does organized bus tours in BC and beyond. Some of its offerings include an overnight to Salt Spring Island ($200 per person double occupancy), a four-day trip to the West Coast of Vancouver Island ($400) and a four-day trip to the Okanagan ($500). Look for more information at www.maverickcoachlines.bc.ca.

BC Rail (☎ 604-984-5246, 800-339-8752 in BC, 800-663-8238 outside BC, passinfo@bcrail.com) has a number of summer and winter vacation packages, including a four-day Barkerville Gold Rush Tour (from $750 per person double occupancy), a six-day, non-escorted Pacific Peaks and Panoramas trip including the Inside Passage ($1230) and a two-day Whistler Winter Getaway (from $282). For more information, see the Web site www.bcrail.com.

Backpacking

For fun, funky and cheap bus trips in BC and Alberta, check out Bigfoot Adventure Tours or Moose Run Adventure Tours. Bigfoot (☎ 604-278-8224, 888-244-6673, bigfoot@mdi.ca) offers eight different itineraries ranging from two-day treks between Vancouver and Banff ($99 each way) to seven-day 'Full Monty' loops ($323), which travel from Vancouver to Whistler, Kamloops, Jasper, Banff, Revelstoke and Kelowna before heading back to Vancouver. There are never more than 11 passengers in the van, and you can make extended stops at any location and catch another Bigfoot bus later. Bigfoot passengers are pre-booked into hostels along the way at an extra cost of about $15 to $20 per night. The van stops at supermarkets each day to keep food costs low. Book at your hostel, or find details at www.bigfoottours.com. Bigfoot also runs shuttle service from Vancouver to and from Whistler and Seattle. See those regional BC chapters or its Web site for details.

Moose Run (☎ 604-944-3007, 888-388-4881, info@mooserun.com) runs hop-on, hop-off summer bus tours leaving from Vancouver every Monday, Wednesday and Friday. Stops on the 'West Pass' route include Whistler, Kamloops, Jasper, Lake Louise, Banff, Kelowna, Penticton and Manning Provincial Park. Like Bigfoot, Moose Run vans stop at supermarkets to get food. Moose Run tickets are good all summer, and you can stop at any point and rejoin the tour later. Cost is $374 plus hostel accommodations; hostels are pre-booked for the nights you're on the bus. There's plenty of time for activities like hiking, rafting and rock climbing along the way, though travelers need to book and pay for these on their own. Moose Run also offers winter trips to some of the province's top skiing/snowboarding resorts. In addition, it partners with VIA Rail for a 'Canada Pass Link' to Eastern Canada. Call or see the Web site www.moosenetwork.com for details.

These trips aren't just for backpackers, but for anyone who likes to share independent, adventure-oriented travel with others. All ages are welcome, though both Bigfoot and Moose Run tend to attract people mostly in their twenties and early thirties.

Elderhostel

Run by a not-for-profit organization based in Boston, Massachusetts, Elderhostel is a great travel bargain for people 55 or older (and a traveler's spouse or any other travel partner 21 or older). Programs aim to help older adults explore interests ranging from history to science to the arts. The typical program is six days long and costs about $535, including comfortable accommodations and meals. (Elderhostelers are responsible for transportation to the site.)

In BC, programs are held at such locations as the University of British Columbia and the Lemon Creek Lodge in the West Kootenays; some go 'on the road' with bus and train trips, but these usually cost more. Programs usually feature talks and lectures in the mornings, followed by afternoon field trips and visits to related sights. For more information call Elderhostel headquarters at ☎ 877-426-8056; write to Elderhostel Canada, PO Box 4488, Station A, Toronto, Ontario, M5W 4H1; or see current course offerings and program details online at www.elderhostel.org.

Vancouver & Around

Vancouver enjoys a spectacular setting, surrounded by water on three sides and framed by the backdrop of the lofty Coast Range. Parks pop up everywhere and range from the enormous Stanley Park (which equals the size of the downtown business core) to dozens of small neighborhood green spaces. And, no matter where you are in town, you're never far from a beach.

Vancouver is a young city, both historically and demographically. Its everchanging face went through yet another transformation in the 1990s, with the arrival of tens of thousands of Hong Kong Chinese. A steady influx of young people from other parts of Canada adds spice to the cultural mix, too; although Vancouver (pop 536,000)

ranks third among Canada's major cities in population (behind Toronto and Montreal), the city has the lowest median age of any Canadian urban center, with more than a third its residents between ages 25 and 45.

Vancouver is politically progressive, environmentally conscious and readily accepting of alternative lifestyles (as proven by its large gay and lesbian population). Eastern Canadians refer to Vancouver, sometimes derisively, as the California of Canada. Yet for all its diversity and celebration of the unconventional, Vancouver retains an old-fashioned cultural refinement that reflects the city's British heritage. It's a dynamic city, full of energy and change, but it's also a city that knows, respects and preserves its past.

HISTORY

Salish Indians first inhabited the Vancouver area. Spanish explorers arrived in 1791, but the British – who followed a year later, led by Capt George Vancouver – were the first Europeans to colonize the area.

As a condition of confederation with the rest of Canada, in 1870 Ottawa promised BC that it would build a transcontinental railroad. However, if the Canadian Pacific Railway (CPR) was to link east and west, then BC would need a mainland coastal terminus, since the new province's population center and capital, Victoria, sat on an island. Railroad engineers set their sights on the sheltered Burrard Inlet and its ragtag collection of saloons, forests, lumber mills and farms. The first train arrived from Montreal in 1886, stopping at a thrown-together, brand-new settlement called Vancouver.

On June 13, 1886, a fire almost completely destroyed the city, killing 21 people. Reconstruction began immediately and by 1890, just four years after it was officially founded, Vancouver had already outpaced Victoria in population. By 1911, 120,000 people lived in Vancouver.

For West Coast Canadians, the building of the Panama Canal (completed in 1914)

Highlights

- Exploring Stanley Park, Vancouver's great green space

- People-watching on Robson St, Davie St or Commercial Dr

- Walking on air at Capilano or Lynn Canyon suspension bridges

- Strolling through the public markets at Granville Island or Lonsdale Quay

- Eating your way around the world via Vancouver's restaurants

Soaking up the sun at the Vancouver Art Gallery

Vancouver's modern public library

Skating past the skyline in Stanley Park, Vancouver

JOHN ELK III

Leisurely meal in Vancouver's Gastown

RICHARD CUMMINS

Granville Island Marina, Vancouver

JOHN ELK III

Gateway to Vancouver's bustling Chinatown

promised easier access to markets in Europe and along North America's East Coast. This triggered a boom for the BC economy and for the province's main trade center, Vancouver, until World War I and the Wall Street crash of 1929 brought severe economic depression and hardship to Canada. Vancouver, with its comparatively mild climate, became a kind of magnet for young Canadian men who were hungry, desperate and out of work. But Vancouver had no work to offer and could give no easy answers to the problems of mass unemployment. Angry demonstrators soon filled the streets of the city, occupied public buildings and rioted.

World War II catapulted the city into the modern era, and from then on it changed rapidly. The western end of downtown became the high-rise apartment center it remains today. In 1974, portions of Granville St became a pedestrians-only mall; Granville Island's redevelopment took place at about the same time. In 1986, the city hosted Expo '86, a very successful world's fair, the grounds of which are now the site of another urban renaissance.

In advance of China's takeover of Hong Kong in 1997, many wealthy Hong Kong Chinese emigrated to the Vancouver area, boosting the area's permanent Asian population by about 85%. (The area now boasts the largest Asian population in North America.) Unlike previous, poorer waves of emigrants, the new Chinese came from the Hong Kong

The Great Dividing Line

Just a 30-minute drive from Vancouver, south of Tsawwassen on Georgia Strait and across Boundary Bay from White Rock, sits a little knob of land called Point Roberts. This 12.5-sq-km peninsula is detached from Washington State by water and land, but because it is on the south side of the 49th parallel, the dividing line between Canada and the USA, it is a US possession.

Even though an exception was made for Vancouver Island in 1846, when it was decided that the border would follow the 49th parallel west to the Pacific Ocean, no such exception was made for Point Roberts. The area falls under Washington State's jurisdiction, and there is an official border crossing open 24 hours. However, the area has been utilized far more by Canadians than it has been by Americans, and over the years Canada has provided most of the services (water, gas, electricity, police, etc).

Canadians have owned summer homes here for a long time, mainly to make use of the long stretches of sandy beach and the shallow bay's warm water – the beach at Point Roberts has been ranked one of the top 15 beaches in the USA – and because property prices have remained relatively low. You'll find a marina, a small airport, shops, restaurants, two taverns and the 7-hectare Lighthouse Park, with campsites and picnic areas.

At one time, this was little more than a farming community settled by Icelandic immigrants. In time, the fishing and canning industries became the main sources of employment, along with the taverns, which for many years gave Canadians a reason to make the trip from Vancouver.

Starting in the late 1940s, Point Roberts began drawing crowds for cheap beer and music at two of the largest taverns in Washington State (The Reef and Breakers), especially on Sunday, when bars and clubs in BC were closed. In recent years, that attraction has diminished, and now most people come here for the beaches, boating, fishing and, of course, the novelty of being in the USA while still being in Canada. But the bars still do a brisk business, too, with beer gardens that seat several thousand people.

To get to Point Roberts from Vancouver, follow Hwy 99 south, turn south onto Hwy 17 (the road to the BC Ferries terminal at Tsawwassen), and at 56th St (Point Roberts Rd), turn south again.

— **Chris Wyness**

business classes. Vancouver real estate prices shot through the roof, with cost-of-living figures suddenly rivaling those of Paris, London and Tokyo. Many of the new arrivals shunned Vancouver in favor of the suburbs, especially Richmond. In the late 1990s, problems with Asian economies slowed the meteoric economic development seen earlier in the decade. But globalization and technological growth have buffered Greater Vancouver's fortunes, and the city entered the 21st century among the economic and cultural capitals of the Pacific Rim.

ORIENTATION
Greater Vancouver (Map 2) is built on a series of peninsulas bounded on the north by Burrard Inlet and on the south by Fraser River and Boundary Bay. The Coast Mountains rise directly behind the city to the north, while to the west the Georgia Strait is strewn with islands. Much of the city's recent growth has pushed suburbs far up the Fraser River to the east. All told, Greater Vancouver includes 18 municipalities that cover 2930 sq km.

Generally, the avenues in Greater Vancouver run east to west while the streets run north to south. Some of the streets in the downtown area – as well as many of the avenues in the Greater Vancouver area – are divided into east and west (eg, E Hastings St and W Hastings St). As a general rule, Main St is the dividing line in Vancouver proper. However, for address numbering purposes, the downtown east-west streets begin numbering at Carrall St near Chinatown (and with Ontario St on Vancouver's West Side). For north-south streets, the numbers begin at Waterfront Rd, along Burrard Inlet.

Downtown Vancouver lies just 40km north of the Canada-US border. Hwy 99, the continuation of I-5 from Washington State, enters the city on Oak St. But since Oak St doesn't lead directly downtown, motorists must either detour west to Granville or Burrard Sts or east to Cambie St, which have bridges. The Trans-Canada Hwy (Hwy 1) bypasses Vancouver proper to the east; Hastings St, off Hwy 1, leads downtown.

The downtown area sits on a peninsula, cut off from the rest of the city by False Creek to the south and from the northern suburbs by Burrard Inlet. Stanley Park takes up the tip of the peninsula. Pacific Centre, a three-block complex of offices, restaurants, shops and theaters, pretty much marks the center of downtown, beginning on the corner of Robson and Howe Sts. Robson St and Georgia St, one or two blocks north (depending where you are), are the two principal arteries; both cut across the city on a diagonal, from northwest to southeast. Davie St, between Burrard St and Stanley Park, is a secondary commercial street with a strong gay and lesbian vibe. Only Georgia St, which becomes the Stanley Park Causeway, continues through Stanley Park to Lions Gate Bridge. Between Stanley Park and downtown is the West End, which basically includes everything west of Burrard St and south of Robson St.

Yaletown, on Hamilton and Mainland Sts between Davie and Nelson Sts in the southeast corner of downtown, has become a hip destination, as the warehouses here have turned into bars, restaurants and loft apartments. Gastown, along Water St between Richards and Columbia Sts, is the historic center of old Vancouver, a neighborhood full of restored Victorian buildings. Chinatown is just to the southeast, in the area around Pender St between Carrall St and Gore Ave. East of Chinatown, East Vancouver revolves around Commercial Dr, which runs south from Hastings St, and passes through a developing alternative neighborhood that manages somehow to be both trendy and, well, *non*-commercial.

Most of Vancouver lies to the south of the West End and downtown, over False Creek, accessible by water taxi or via the Cambie, Granville and Burrard Bridges. You'll occasionally see or hear all or part of this area referred to as the West Side, though hardly anyone in Vancouver ever uses the phrase.

Granville Island, immediately south of downtown across False Creek, is a lively area full of shops and entertainment. Heading west after crossing Burrard Bridge or Granville Bridge, you'll enter Kitsilano, filled with students, young professionals and now-successful ex-hippies. To its west, accessible via 4th Ave and Broadway, you'll find the residential area of Point Grey, Pacific Spirit Regional Park and the University of British Columbia (UBC), at the tip of the peninsula. To Kitsilano's east are the busy commercial districts of South Granville St and Broadway. If you head farther east, you'll come to the large suburb of Burnaby; southeast of Burnaby is the city of New Westminster, once the capital of BC and now an industrial area along the Fraser River. Across the Fraser, the suburbs of Delta and Surrey sprawl; White Rock, to their south, contains the most heavily used US border crossing.

Closer to the city, immediately south of Kitsilano, are residential areas like Shaughnessy, Oakridge, Kerrisdale and Cambie. Farther south lie Vancouver International Airport, fast-growing Richmond, the timeless fishing village of Steveston and the BC Ferries terminal at Tsawwassen.

Over Lions Gate Bridge and Second Narrows Bridge, West Vancouver and North Vancouver – both essentially upper middle-class residential areas – comprise the North Shore. To the northeast, along Capilano Rd, lie Capilano Canyon, the Lions Peaks (from which the Lions Gate Bridge takes its name), Grouse Mountain and the Coast Mountains. If you continue farther west and north, you'll reach the Sea to Sky Hwy to Whistler, Horseshoe Bay (where you can catch a ferry to Nanaimo on Vancouver Island) and the Sunshine Coast (also reached by ferry from Horseshoe Bay). See the Whistler & the Sunshine Coast chapter for more information.

Maps
Tourism Vancouver distributes a nifty free map with a detailed downtown section on one side and a good metropolitan overview on the other. You'll only need to obtain a more detailed street map if you decide to venture far beyond the downtown, West End and Kitsilano areas. AAA/CAA (☎ 604-268-5000, 292-2222 for 24-hour emergency road service) produces a good street map that's free to members. For even more

detail, MapArt offers a selection of sheet maps and atlas books covering the Vancouver metro area; you can order one online at www.mapart.com.

INFORMATION
Tourist Offices
At the Visitor Info Centre, 200 Burrard St on the Plaza Level of the Waterfront Centre, the friendly staff can help with bookings for accommodation, tours, transport and activities. On busy days, you'll need to take a number, but while you wait, pick up a free copy of *Discover Vancouver on Transit*, an excellent booklet that outlines bus, SkyTrain and SeaBus routes to all area attractions, parks, recreational sites and shopping districts. Other useful publications include *The Vancouver Book*, the official visitors' guide, and the monthly mini-magazines *Where Vancouver* and *Visitor's Choice*. The Visitor Info Centre is open 8 am to 6 pm daily, late May through early September; 8:30 am to 5 pm weekdays and 9 am to 5 pm Saturday the rest of the year. For more information, call ☎ 604-683-2000, fax 682-6839 or visit the Web site www.tourismvancouver.com.

You'll also find two tourist information desks at Vancouver International Airport: one in the middle of the domestic terminal's baggage carousel area and the other in the international terminal's reception area, after you leave the Canadian Customs hall. The desks can arrange hotel and B&B bookings and answer questions about attractions throughout BC.

The Gay & Lesbian Centre (☎ 604-684-6869 for the help line or 684-5307 for programs and services), 1170 Bute St near Davie St, provides information for gay and lesbian travelers.

Money
ATM machines are widely available in the city's shopping and business districts. At the airport, you'll find three kinds of ATMs: cash machines dispensing Canadian dollars, machines dispensing US currency and foreign exchange machines that can accept 10 different currencies and issue some foreign currency.

The major national banks, including TD Canada Trust, Bank of Montreal, Royal Bank and CBIC, all have numerous branches throughout the city. Royal Bank has opened several outlets at the airport. Hours vary, but among them, they operate daily 5:30 am to 10 pm.

The Vancouver offices of Thomas Cook, which exchanges currency, include a branch in the Pan Pacific Hotel (☎ 604-641-1229) at Canada Place and another in the Pacific Centre shopping mall (☎ 604-684 3291), 777 Dunsmuir St. Money Mart (☎ 604-606-9555), 1195 Davie St, offers round-the-clock currency exchange, check-cashing and telegraph services.

Post & Communications
The main post office (☎ 604-662-5725), 349 W Georgia St between Homer and Hamilton Sts, is open 8 am to 5:30 pm weekdays. General delivery mail should be addressed to 349 W Georgia St, Vancouver, BC, Canada V6B 3P7. The many postal outlets throughout the city include the Shoppers Drug Mart (☎ 604-685-0246), 1125 Davie St; and Commercial Drug Mart (☎ 604-253-3266), 1850 Commercial Dr.

Internet-access terminals abound; access costs $5 to $8 per hour. Try the Vancouver Public Library's central branch (see Libraries, below), where the use of the public computer lab costs $5 per 55 minutes; Internet Coffee (☎ 604-682-6668), 1104 Davie St, which offers access for $5.65 per hour between 8 and 11 am and after 6 pm; Kitsilano's Cyber-Café (☎ 604-737-0595), 3514 W 4th Ave; the Mail Room (☎ 604-681-6562), 1755 Robson St, where access is always 10¢ a minute; and Kinko's (☎ 604-685-3338), 789 W Pender St.

Newspapers
The two daily newspapers are *The Province*, a tabloid, and the broadsheet *Vancouver Sun*, available on newsstands and online at Web sites www.theprovince.com and www.vancouversun.com. The *Sun* tends to be the more serious of the two, but *The Province* breaks some important stories, such as exposés of the city's filthiest restaurants.

Both publish entertainment sections on Thursday. But the city's best entertainment paper is *Georgia Straight*, a free weekly widely available all over town, as well as online at www.straight.com. The new appears each Thursday. The *WestEnder* is another entertainment-oriented weekly paper. *Xtra West* serves Vancouver's gay and lesbian community.

Radio
The CBC is at 690 AM. CKNW (980 AM) and CKWX (1130 AM) offer local news and talk, plus good information on traffic conditions. Other interesting stations include CBUF-CBC (97.7, 102.3 FM), the French station; CFRO (102.7 FM), an eclectic cooperative station; and the 'X' (104.9 FM), with alternative rock.

Travel Agencies
Travel CUTS, the student and budget travel organization, has several offices in Vancouver, including two downtown: at 567 Seymour St (☎ 604-681-9136) and at the HI hostel (☎ 604-659-2845), 1114 Burnaby St. You'll find other branches on Granville Island, at the University of British Columbia and at Simon Fraser University in Burnaby. American Express (☎ 604-669-2813), 666 Burrard St, is open 8 am to 5:50 pm Monday to Friday and from 10 am to 4 pm Saturday.

Bookstores
Vancouver's classic independent bookstore, Duthie Books (☎ 604-732-5344) has closed all of its city locations save one: 2239 W 4th Ave in Kitsilano. Blackberry Books (☎ 604-685-6188), 1663 Duranleau St on Granville Island, is another good independent shop. The Canadian mega-chain Chapters has opened several Vancouver locations, including a downtown branch at 788 Robson St (☎ 604-682-4066). The cyber café on the 3rd floor offers Internet access for $6 per hour (20-minute, $2 minimum).

For travel literature, guidebooks and maps, head to International Travel Maps & Books, at 552 Seymour St (☎ 604-687-3320) and 345 W Broadway (☎ 604-879-3621). The

Travel Bug (☎ 604-737-1122), 2667 W Broadway in Kitsilano, is a good bet for language tapes and travel accessories, as is Wanderlust (☎ 604-739-2182), 1929 W 4th Ave. For hiking guidebooks and maps, try the Western Canada Wilderness Committee Outreach store (☎ 604-687-2567), 227 Abbott St. Magpie Magazine Gallery (☎ 604-253-6666), 1319 Commercial Dr, is one of the best newsstands in town.

Book Warehouse (☎ 604-872-5711), 632 W Broadway (with branches throughout the city), offers lots of bargain-priced books. The Granville Book Company (☎ 604-687-2213), 850 Granville St, specializes in fiction, sci-fi and computer books.

If your children don't lose themselves at Kidsbooks (☎ 604-738-5335), 3083 W Broadway, you just might. Besides its fabulous collection of every kind of book imaginable for children, the store carries creative toys and games.

Banyen Books & Sound (☎ 604-732-7912), 2671 W Broadway, offers the city's best selection of New Age and metaphysical books and music. Women in Print (☎ 604-732-4128), 3566 W 4th Ave, sells books about women, for women and by women. Little Sister's Book and Art Emporium (☎ 604-669-1753), 1238 Davie St, specializes in gay literature specifically geared for women.

Libraries

Reminiscent of the Roman Coliseum, the central branch of the Vancouver Public Library (☎ 604-331-3603), 350 W Georgia St, is a destination in itself. Its airy entrance plaza features food stands, an ATM and several gift shops, most notably Bookmark, which directs its proceeds back to the library. The library is open 10 am to 8 pm Monday to Thursday and 10 am to 5 pm Friday and Saturday (as well as 1 to 5 pm Sunday, September through June). Visit the library's Web site at www.vpl.vancouver.bc.ca.

The University of British Columbia's libraries (☎ 604-822-3871), 1958 Main Mall, boast nearly 80 miles of books. In addition to the main library, there are specialty libraries, including one dedicated to one of Canada's largest collections of maps, atlases and other geographical materials.

Laundry

Convenient places include the Davie Laundromat (☎ 604-682-2717), 1061 Davie St, and the Great West Coin Laundromat (☎ 604-734-7993), 2955 W 4th Ave in Kitsilano. East Vancouver's Vicious Cycle Laundro & Leisurama (☎ 604-255-7629), 2062 Commercial Dr, includes a café that's open until midnight.

Medical Services

St Paul's Hospital (☎ 604-682-2344), 1081 Burrard St, is the closest emergency room to downtown. For non-emergencies, try the Care Point Medical Centre's walk-in clinics, open 9 am to 9 pm daily. Locations include 1175 Denman St in the West End (☎ 604-681-5338) and another at 1623 Commercial Dr (☎ 604-254-5554).

Emergency

For police, fire or ambulance, call ☎ 911.

Dangers & Annoyances

Car break-ins and bike thefts are among the most widespread crimes in Vancouver. Vehicles with out-of-province plates are often targeted. Park in a secure lot if you can, and never leave valuables in sight. Cyclists should use a U-shaped lock (not a simple chain lock) and remove a wheel if possible.

Although safer than many cities of its size, Vancouver has serious problems with drugs. The area around Hastings and Main Sts can be dodgy day and night, though Vancouverites say that if you play it smart, you'll be safe. Keep your distance from suspicious-looking people or activities. You're likely to encounter panhandlers throughout downtown, Gastown and Chinatown.

On a lighter note, one reader wrote to warn others of the 'winged thieves' of Stanley Park. Seagulls there 'have perfected the technique of swooping down and snatching the hot dog right out of your hand. It's amazing to watch, but not so much fun if it happens to you or your kid!'

[Continued on page 114]

MAP 1 VANCOUVER & AROUND

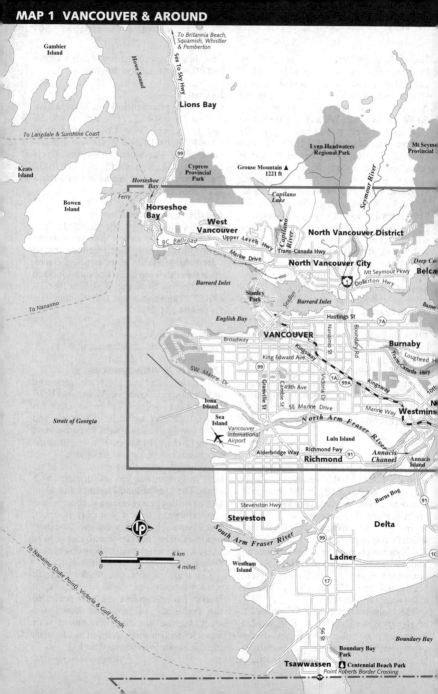

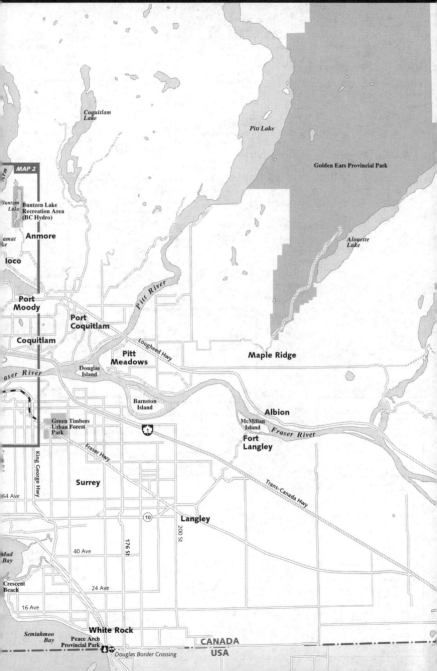

MAP 2

Coquitlam Lake

Pitt Lake

Golden Ears Provincial Park

Buntzen Lake

Buntzen Lake
Recreation Area
(BC Hydro)

amat ke

Anmore

loco

Alouette Lake

Port
Moody

Port
Coquitlam

Coquitlam

Pitt River

Lougheed Hwy

Maple Ridge

raser River

Pitt
Meadows

Douglas
Island

Barnston
Island

Albion

Green Timbers
Urban Forest
Park

McMillan
Island

Fraser River

Fort
Langley

King George Hwy

Fraser Hwy

Trans-Canada Hwy

Surrey

64 Ave

10

Langley

176 St

200 St

40 Ave

Mud Bay

24 Ave

Crescent
Beach

16 Ave

White Rock

Semiahmoo Bay

Peace Arch
Provincial Park

CANADA

USA

Douglas Border Crossing

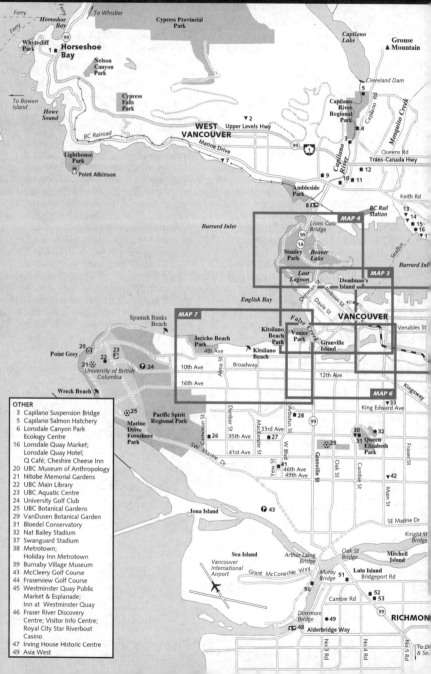

MAP 2 GREATER VANCOUVER

To Whistler

Ferry
Horseshoe Bay

Whytecliff Park

Horseshoe Bay

Nelson Canyon Park

Cypress Provincial Park

To Bowen Island

Howe Sound

Cypress Falls Park

BC Railroad

WEST VANCOUVER

Upper Levels Hwy

Marine Drive

Capilano Lake

Grouse ▲ Mountain

Cleveland Dam

5

Capilano River Regional Park

Mosquito Creek

4

3

Queens Rd

Trans-Canada Hwy

BC Rail Station

Keith Rd

13
14
15
16

Lighthouse Park

Point Atkinson

7

Ambleside Park

8

9

10 11

12

Burrard Inlet

Lions Gate Bridge

MAP 4

SeaBus

Burrard Inl

Stanley Park

Beaver Lake

Lost Lagoon

Deadman's Island

MAP 3

VANCOUVER

Venables St

English Bay

Spanish Banks Beach

Point Grey

20
21
22
23
24

University of British Columbia

Wreck Beach

MAP 7

Jericho Beach Park

4th Ave

10th Ave

16th Ave

Kitsilano Beach Park

Kitsilano Beach

Vanier Park

Granville Island

Broadway

12th Ave

MAP 6

King Edward Ave

False Creek

25

Pacific Spirit Regional Park

Marine Drive Foreshore Park

26

35th Ave

41st Ave

SW Marine Dr

Iona Island

43

33

28

33rd Ave

27

29

30
31

32

Queen Elizabeth Park

42

46th Ave
49th Ave

SE Marine Dr

Knight St Bridge

Mitchell Island

Sea Island

Vancouver International Airport

Arthur Laing Bridge

Grant McConachie Way

Oak St Bridge

Moray Bridge

51

Lulu Island

Bridgeport Rd

50

Cambie Rd

52
53

Dinsmore Bridge

49

48 Alderbridge Way

RICHMON

To D & Se

Kingsway

OTHER

3 Capilano Suspension Bridge
5 Capilano Salmon Hatchery
6 Lonsdale Canyon Park Ecology Centre
16 Lonsdale Quay Market; Lonsdale Quay Hotel; Q Café; Cheshire Cheese Inn
20 UBC Museum of Anthropology
21 Nitobe Memorial Gardens
22 UBC Main Library
23 UBC Aquatic Centre
24 University Golf Club
25 UBC Botanical Gardens
29 VanDusen Botanical Garden
31 Bloedel Conservatory
37 Swanguard Stadium
37 Nat Bailey Stadium
38 Metrotown; Holiday Inn Metrotown
39 Burnaby Village Museum
43 McCleery Golf Course
44 Fraserview Golf Course
45 Westminster Quay Public Market & Esplanade; Inn at Westminster Quay
46 Fraser River Discovery Centre; Visitor Info Centre; Royal City Star Riverboat Casino
47 Irving House Historic Centre
49 Asia West

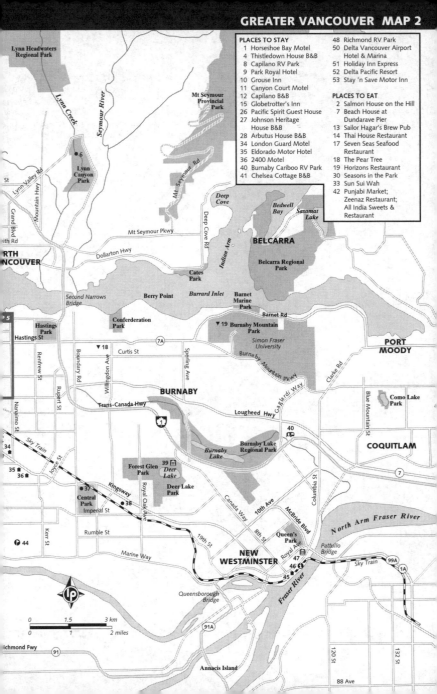

PLACES TO STAY
1 Horseshoe Bay Motel
4 Thistledown House B&B
8 Capilano RV Park
9 Park Royal Hotel
10 Grouse Inn
11 Canyon Court Motel
12 Capilano B&B
15 Globetrotter's Inn
26 Pacific Spirit Guest House
27 Johnson Heritage House B&B
28 Arbutus House B&B
34 London Guard Motel
35 Eldorado Motor Hotel
36 2400 Motel
40 Burnaby Cariboo RV Park
41 Chelsea Cottage B&B

48 Richmond RV Park
50 Delta Vancouver Airport Hotel & Marina
51 Holiday Inn Express
52 Delta Pacific Resort
53 Stay 'n Save Motor Inn

PLACES TO EAT
2 Salmon House on the Hill
7 Beach House at Dundarave Pier
13 Sailor Hagar's Brew Pub
14 Thai House Restaurant
17 Seven Seas Seafood Restaurant
18 The Pear Tree
19 Horizons Restaurant
30 Seasons in the Park
33 Sun Sui Wah
42 Punjabi Market; Zeenaz Restaurant; All India Sweets & Restaurant

Lynn Headwaters Regional Park

Mt Seymour Provincial Park

Lynn Canyon Park

Deep Cove

Bedwell Bay

Sasamat Lake

BELCARRA

Mt Seymour Pkwy

Belcarra Regional Park

Cates Park

Dollarton Hwy

Second Narrows Bridge

Berry Point

Burrard Inlet

Barnet Marine Park

Barnet Rd

Conferderation Park

Burnaby Mountain Park

PORT MOODY

Hastings Park

Hastings St

Curtis St

Simon Fraser University

Burnaby Mountain Pkwy

Clarke Rd

Como Lake Park

BURNABY

Trans-Canada Hwy

Lougheed Hwy

COQUITLAM

Burnaby Lake

Burnaby Lake Regional Park

Forest Glen Park

Deer Lake

Deer Lake Park

North Arm Fraser River

Central Park

Kingsway

Rumble St

Marine Way

NEW WESTMINSTER

Queen's Park

McBride Blvd

Pattullo Bridge

Sky Train

Queensborough Bridge

Fraser River

Annacis Island

Richmond Fwy

88 Ave

0   1.5   3 km
0   1   2 miles

MAP 3 DOWNTOWN VANCOUVER & WEST END

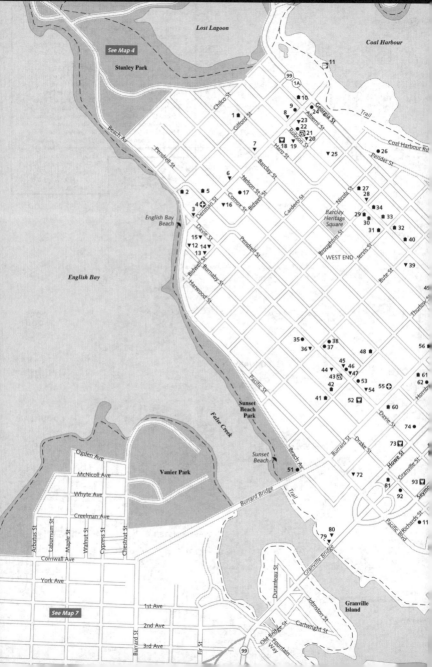

Lost Lagoon

Coal Harbour

See Map 4

Stanley Park

99
1A

Chilco St

Gilford St

Beach Ave

Pendrell St

English Bay Beach

English Bay

Pender St

Coal Harbour Rd

Georgia St
Alberni St
Robson St
Haro St

Barclay St

Nelson St

Comox St

Bidwell St

Denman St

Cardero St

Nicola St

Barclay Heritage Square

Broughton St

Jervis St

WEST END

Bute St

Thurlow St

Davie St

Burnaby St

Bidwell St

Pendrell St

Harwood St

Pacific St

Sunset Beach Park

False Creek

Vanier Park

Ogden Ave

McNicoll Ave

Whyte Ave

Creelman Ave

Cornwall Ave

York Ave

See Map 7

Arbutus St
Laburnum St
Maple St
Walnut St
Cypress St
Chestnut St

Sunset Beach

Burrard Bridge

Trail

1st Ave

2nd Ave

3rd Ave

Burrard St

Fir St

99

Durnanleau St

Granville Bridge

Old Bridge St
Mountain Way

Johnston St

Cartwright St

Granville Island

Burrard St

Drake St

Howe St

Granville St

Seymour St

Pacific Blvd

Richards St

Hornby St

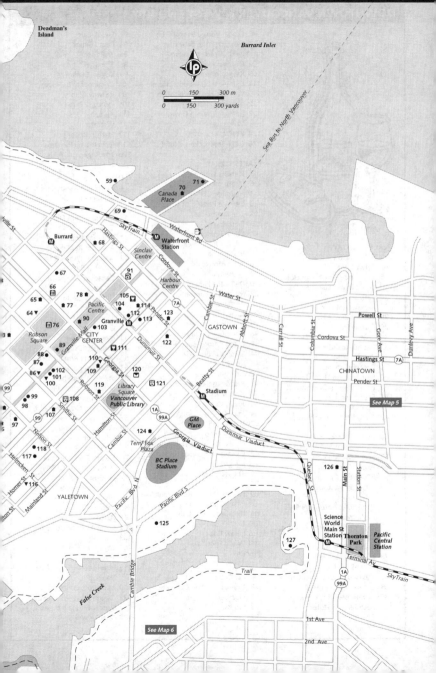

Deadman's
Island

Burrard Inlet

Sea Bus to North Vancouver

0   150   300 m
0   150   300 yards

59 ■

71 ■

70 ■
Canada
Place

69 ■

SkyTrain

Hastings St

Waterfront Rd

ville St

Burrard

M Burrard

68 ■

Waterfront
Station

Sinclair
Centre

Cordova St

91 ■
Harbour
Centre

Water St

Cambie St

GASTOWN

Powell St

67 ●

Abbott St

Carrall St

Columbia St

Cordova St

Gore Ave

Dunlevy Ave

66 ■

65 ■

78 ■

77 ■

105 ■
104 ■

Pacific
Centre

114 ■
112 ■
113 ■

123 ■

7A

See Map 5

CHINATOWN

Hastings St

7A

64 ▼

90 ■

103 ■

Granville

M Granville

Pender St

122 ■

Pender St

76 ■

Robson
Square

111 ■

CITY
CENTER

Dunsmuir St

Granville Mall

89 ■

88 ●
87 ●

86 ▼

102 ●
101 ●
100 ●

110 ■
109 ■

Georgia St

120 ■

Beatty St

M Stadium

Robson St

119 ■

Library
Square
Vancouver
Public Library

121 ■

GM
Place

Dunsmuir Viaduct

126 ■

Main St

Station St

99

99 ●
98 ●

97 ●

99

108 ■
107 ●

Smithe St

Hamilton St

1A

99A

Georgia Viaduct

118 ●
117 ●

116 ■

Nelson St

Helmcken St

Homer St

124 ■
Terry Fox
Plaza

BC Place
Stadium

Quebec St

YALETOWN

Mainland St

ton St

125 ●

Pacific Blvd N

Pacific Blvd S

Science
World
Main St
Station

M

Thornton
Park

Pacific
Central
Station

Cambie Bridge

Trail

127 ●

Terminal Av

SkyTrain

1A

99A

False Creek

1st Ave

See Map 6

2nd Ave

DOWNTOWN VANCOUVER & WEST END KEY

PLACES TO STAY
1 Buchan Hotel
2 Sylvia Hotel
5 Oceanside Apartment Hotel
10 Lord Stanley Suites on the Park
27 Riviera Motor Inn
29 Robsonstrasse Hotel
30 Barclay Hotel
31 Listel Vancouver; O'Doul's
32 Pacific Palisades Hotel
33 Tropicana Motor Inn
34 Greenbrier Hotel
40 Blue Horizon Hotel; Inlets
41 HI-Vancouver Downtown
42 Sunset Inn Travel Apartments
48 Colibri Bed & Breakfast
56 YMCA
60 Burrard Motor Inn
61 Sheraton Wall Centre Hotel
63 Wedgewood Hotel
65 Hotel Vancouver; 900 West; Griffins
68 Days Inn Vancouver Downtown
70 Pan Pacific Hotel; Five Sails Restaurant
77 Crowne Plaza Hotel Georgia; Chameleon Urban Lounge; Georgia St Bar & Grill
78 Metropolitan Hotel; Diva at the Met
81 Travelodge Vancouver Centre
83 Bosman's Motor Hotel
85 Royal Hotel; Royal Pub
90 Four Seasons Hotel; Chartwell
96 Global Village Backpackers
97 Hotel Dakota; Babalu; Fred's Uptown Tavern
107 Dufferin Hotel
109 Kingston Hotel
114 Cambie International Hostel
119 Westin Grand Hotel; Voda
122 Victorian Hotel
123 Ramada Limited Downtown Vancouver
124 YWCA
126 C&N Backpackers Hostel

PLACES TO EAT
3 Raincity Grill
6 Death by Chocolate
7 Marquee Grill
8 Café de Paris
12 The Boathouse
13 Balthazar
14 Liliget Feast House
15 Krishna Pure Vegetarian Restaurant
16 Brass Monkey
19 Safeway
20 De Dutch Pannekoek House
23 Musashi Japanese Restaurant
25 Capers
28 Noodle King Café
36 Hamburger Mary's
39 Bread Garden Bakery & Café
44 Stepho's Souvlakia
45 Kisha Poppo
47 Tiffany
49 Pezzo; Thai House Restaurant
50 Joe Fortes
54 Joe's Grill
57 Ichibankan
58 Cafe Il Nido
64 Canadian Maple Delights
72 Il Giardino di Umberto
75 Allegro
79 The Riley
80 C
84 Goulash House Restaurant & Pastry Shop
86 Kitto Japanese House
100 Notte's Bon Ton
106 Elbow Room
110 White Spot
116 Brix

BARS & CLUBS
18 Denman Station Cabaret
52 Numbers
73 Odyssey
92 The Yale
93 Luv-A-Fair
94 Lava Lounge
95 The Gate
98 The Roxy
99 Vogue Theatre
101 Commodore Ballroom
104 Railway Club
105 Piccadilly Pub
111 Au Bar
115 Wett Bar
117 Starfish Room
118 Richard's on Richards
125 The Rage; Yuk Yuk's

OTHER
4 Care Point Medical Centre
9 Bayshore Bicycles
11 Harbour Cruises
17 Denman Place Discount Cinema
21 The Mail Room
22 Alley Cat Rentals
24 Spokes Bicycle Rental & Espresso Bar
26 Canadian College of English Language
35 Little Sister's Book & Art Emporium
37 Money Mart
38 Gay & Lesbian Centre
43 Internet Coffee
46 Shoppers Drug Mart
51 Vancouver Aquatic Centre
53 Davie Laundromat
55 St Paul's Hospital
59 Seaplane Terminal
62 Rent-A-Wreck
66 Canadian Craft Museum
67 American Express
69 Waterfront Centre; Visitor Info Centre
71 CN IMAX Theatre
74 Pacific Cinémathèque
76 Vancouver Art Gallery
82 Lo-Cost Car Rental
87 Granville Cineplex Odeon
88 Chapters
89 Eatons
91 Kinko's
102 Granville Book Company
103 The Bay
108 Orpheum Theatre
112 Travel CUTS
113 International Travel Maps & Books
120 Main Post Office
121 Queen Elizabeth Theatre; Vancouver Playhouse
127 Science World

MAP 4 STANLEY PARK

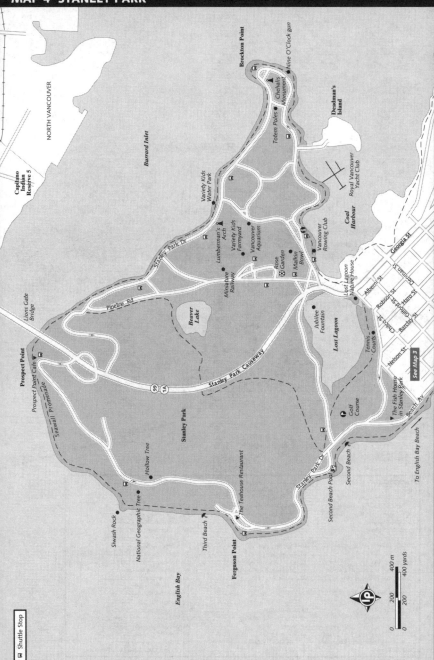

Shuttle Stop

NORTH VANCOUVER

Capilano Indian Reserve 5

Burrard Inlet

Brockton Point

Nine O'Clock gun

Chehalis Monument

Totem Poles

Deadman's Island

Royal Vancouver Yacht Club

Coal Harbour

Variety Kids Water Park

Lumberman's Arch

Variety Kids Farmyard

Vancouver Aquarium

Vancouver Rowing Club

Rose Garden

Malkin Bowl

Stanley Park Dr

Miniature Railway

Lost Lagoon Nature House

Georgia St

Lions Gate Bridge

Pipeline Rd

Beaver Lake

Jubilee Fountain

Lost Lagoon

Alberni St

Robson St

Gilford St

Chilco St

Nelson St

Barclay St

Denman St

Haro St

See Map 3

Prospect Point

Prospect Point Cafe

Stanley Park Causeway

99

1A

Tennis Courts

Seawall Promenade

Stanley Park

Golf Course

The Fish House in Stanley Park

Beach Av

Hollow Tree

The Teahouse Restaurant

Second Beach

Second Beach Pool

Stanley Park Dr

National Geographic Tree

To English Bay Beach

Siwash Rock

Third Beach

Ferguson Point

English Bay

0   200   400 m
0   200   400 yards

MAP 5 GASTOWN, CHINATOWN & EAST VANCOUVER

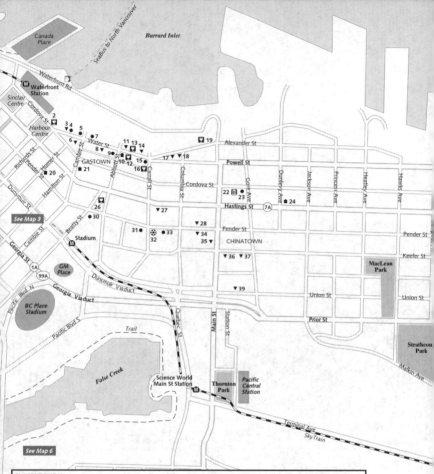

PLACES TO STAY
10 Dominion Hotel;
   Lamplighter's Pub
20 New Backpackers Hostel
21 Cambie International Hostel
24 Hotel Patricia
25 Waldorf Hotel
40 A Place at Penny's
43 Aberdeen Mansion

PLACES TO EAT
1 Cannery Seafood Restaurant
3 Raintree at the Landing
6 Water Street Café
8 Rossini's Pasta Palazzo
11 Old Spaghetti Factory
14 Brother's Restaurant
17 Jewel of India
18 Incendio
27 The Only Seafood Restaurant
28 Buddhist Vegetarian Restaurant
29 Pink Pearl

34 New Town Bakery & Restaurant
35 Kam's Garden Restaurant
36 The Gain Wah
37 Hon's Wun-tun House
38 Nick's Spaghetti House
39 Phnom Penh
41 El Cocal
42 Tony's Neighbourhood Deli & Café
45 Café du Soleil
46 Bukowski's
47 Juicy Lucy's Good Eats
48 Old Europe Restaurant
50 WaaZuBee Café
52 Clove Café & Record Bar
54 Café Deux Soleil

BARS & CLUBS
2 Steamworks Brewing Co
12 Sonar
13 Purple Onion
16 The Irish Heather
19 Alibi Room

26 Lotus Club; Charlie's Lounge;
   Chuck's Pub

OTHER
4 Inuit Gallery of Vancouver
5 Gastown Steam Clock
7 Hill's Indian Crafts
9 Western Canada Wilderness
   Commitee Store
15 Maple Tree Square; Gassy Jack Statue
22 Vancouver Police Centennial Museum
23 Firehall Arts Centre
30 International Village,
   Cinemark Tinseltown
31 Sam Kee Building
32 Dr Sun Yat-Sen Classical
   Chinese Garden
33 Chinese Cultural Centre of Vancouver
44 Magpie Magazine Gallery
49 Care Point Medical Centre
51 Commercial Drug Mart
53 Vicious Cycle Laundro & Leisurama

McGill St
McGill St
Nanaimo St
Eton St
Cambridge St
Oxford St
Dundas St
Triumph St
Pandora St
Pandora Park
Franklin St
1 ▼
Commissioner St
Wall St

Franklin St
25 ♠
Hastings St
▼ 29
7A
Pender St
To Second Narrows Bridge,
Playland &
Simon Fraser University
Ferndale St
Frances St
Turner St
Georgia St
Woodland Park
38 ▼
Templeton Park
Georgia St
Adanac St
Adanac St
Venables St
♠ 40

Parker St
Parker St
41 ▼
▼ 42
♠ 43
Napier St
William St
William St
Grandview Park
Charles St
44 ●
45 ▼
Kitchener St
46 ▼
▼ 47
Grant St
Graveley St
Il Mercato   49
Mall ✪
▼ 48
▼ 50
1st Ave
Grandview Viaduct
2nd Ave
Nanaimo St
● 51
3rd Ave
4th Ave
▼ 52
● 53
4th Ave
McSpadden Park
5th Ave
5th Ave
▼ 54
6th Ave
...ina Creek Park
7th Ave
8th Ave
To Burnaby,
Metrotown &
New Westminster
Broadway

Raymur Av
Glen Dr
Vernon Dr
McLean Dr
Woodland Dr
Commercial Dr
Salsbury Dr
Pender St
Victoria Dr
Semlin Dr
Lakewood Dr
Templeton Dr
Clark Dr
Odlum Dr
McLean Dr
Woodland Dr
Commercial Dr
Cotton Dr

LP
0   200   400 m
0   200   400 yards

MAP 6 GRANVILLE ISLAND & WEST SIDE

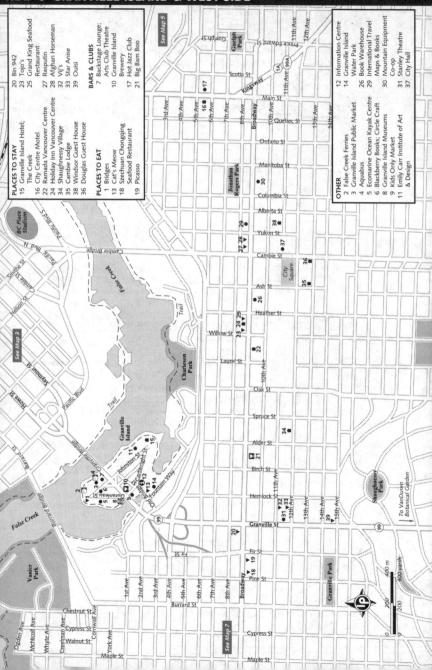

PLACES TO STAY
15 Granville Island Hotel;
   The Creek
16 City Centre Motel
22 Ramada Vancouver Centre
24 Holiday Inn Vancouver Centre
34 Shaughnessy Village
35 Cambie Lodge
38 Windsor Guest House
36 Douglas Guest House

PLACES TO EAT
1 Bridges
13 Cat's Meow
18 Szechuan Chongqing
   Seafood Restaurant
19 Picasso

20 Bin 942
23 Tojo's
25 Grand King Seafood
   Restaurant
27 Rasputin
28 Afghan Horseman
32 Vij's
33 Star Anise
39 Ouisi

BARS & CLUBS
7 Backstage Lounge;
   Arts Club Theatre
10 Granville Island
   Brewery
17 Hot Jazz Club
21 Big Bam Boo

OTHER
2 False Creek Ferries
3 Granville Island Public Market
4 Aquabus
5 Ecomarine Ocean Kayak Centre
6 Blackberry Books; Circle Craft
8 Granville Island Museums
9 Kids Only Market
11 Emily Carr Institute of Art
   & Design

12 Information Centre
14 Granville Island
   Water Park
26 Book Warehouse
29 International Travel
   Maps & Books
30 Mountain Equipment
   Co-op
31 Stanley Theatre
37 City Hall

MAP 7 KITSILANO

PLACES TO STAY
4 Hi-Vancouver Jericho Beach
7 Maple House
  Bed & Breakfast
8 Walnut House B&B
9 Mickey's Kits Beach Chalet

PLACES TO EAT
12 Nyala Restaurant
14 Topanga Cafe
16 Naam
17 Safeway
18 Vine Yard Restaurant
19 Capers
20 Romio's Greek Taverna
25 Sophie's Cosmic Cafe
26 Won More Szechuan
   Cuisine
28 Surat Sweet Restaurant
30 Montri's Thai Restaurant
35 Boleto/Ecco Il Pane
36 Lumiere

BARS & CLUBS
15 Darby's Pub
31 Cellar Jazz Café

OTHER
1 Vancouver Maritime Museum
2 H.R. MacMillan Space Centre;
  Vancouver Museum;
  Gordon MacMillan
  Southam Observatory
3 Ferry Terminal
5 Jericho Sailing Centre;
  Ecomarine Ocean
  Kayak Centre
6 Kitsilano Outdoor Pool
10 Women in Print
11 Kitsilano's Cyber Café
13 Great West Coin Laundromat
21 Duthie Books
22 Hope Unlimited
23 Ten Thousand Villages
24 Craftworks
27 Wanderlust
29 Fifth Avenue Cinemas
32 Kidsbooks
33 Banyen Books & Sound
34 Travel Bug

[Continued from page 101]
DOWNTOWN (Map 3)

The compact size of downtown Vancouver means that it's easy to get around on foot here; the only really steep streets are those that spill down to False Creek and English Bay on downtown's southwest end. A *lot* of people live right in downtown Vancouver, creating a vibrant community with a colorful array of neighborhood groceries, coffeehouses and drug stores. Unlike the downtown areas in a lot of North American cities (where the energy dies once the workers go home for the night), downtown Vancouver stays lively into the evening hours.

If you're looking for the center of downtown, go to **Robson St**, a crowded pedestrian scene full of intriguing shops and plenty of places to eat. Locals, international tourists and recent immigrants all throng here, giving the street the feel of a mini United Nations. Shops and restaurants stay open late, often until midnight in summer.

The Lookout!

Set 169m above the city atop Harbour Centre, The Lookout! (☎ 604-689-0421), 555 W Hastings St, boasts an excellent 360-degree view of Vancouver and beyond. Go on a clear day, when you'll be able to survey the city's surrounding mountains and waterscapes. (On a really good day, you might see Mt Baker in Washington State.) Tickets to the top cost $9/8/6 for adults/seniors/students; a family pass is $25. Tickets are good all day, so you can come back at night. Discounts are widely available; a hostel or auto-club card might knock down the price. The Lookout! is open 8:30 am to 10:30 pm daily, May through October; 9 am to 9 pm daily, November through April.

Vancouver Art Gallery

Despite near-constant controversy (including six executive directors in just over a decade), the city's principal art museum (☎ 604-662-4719), 750 Hornby St, still merits a visit. Once you enter the handsome late 19th-century stone building (formerly a courthouse), go straight to the 4th floor, which features works by Emily Carr, BC's best-known painter through the early to mid-20th century (see the boxed text 'The Life and Work of Emily Carr' in the Facts about British Columbia chapter). The permanent collection also features a good selection of art by Canada's famed Group of Seven. The museum gift shop sells plenty of cool posters, cards and gifts. The Gallery Café, which overlooks the Sculpture Garden, makes a great spot for coffee and a snack. Across the street on Robson Square, a series of waterfalls on the wall of the provincial courthouse offers a tranquil place for contemplation, day or night, as the rush of water drowns out the city's din.

The gallery is open 10 am to 5:30 pm daily (until 9 pm Thursday). The museum closes many Mondays from mid-October through Easter, unless a major exhibition is showing. Admission is $10/6 for adults/students with ID (except 5 to 9 pm Thursday, when there's a $5 suggested donation). Children 12 and under are free. A family pass costs $30. Major exhibitions may carry an admission surcharge.

Regularly scheduled exhibition tours take place daily, mid-June through September, and on Thursday evening and Saturday and Sunday afternoons the rest of the year. Exhibition tours in Japanese are available on selected Thursdays.

Canadian Craft Museum

Tucked off a quiet plaza near the Vancouver Art Gallery, this museum (☎ 604-687-8266), 639 Hornby St, is dedicated to the role of crafts in human culture. The permanent collection focuses on contemporary and historical works from Canada; touring shows and special collections frequently have a more international emphasis. The gift shop here carries some truly unique handmade gifts. The museum is open 10 am to 5 pm Monday to Saturday (until 9 pm Thursday) and noon to 5 pm Sunday; closed Tuesday from September through May. Admission is $5/3 adults/seniors and students (or by donation on Thursday evening). Children under 13 get in free.

Canada Place & Waterfront Station

Canada Place, the convention center with the distinctive white 'sails,' juts into the harbor at the foot of Howe St. Built to coincide with Expo '86, the complex contains the World Trade Centre, the Vancouver Trade and Convention Centre. the Pan Pacific Hotel, a cruise-ship terminal and the CN IMAX Theatre (☎ 604-682-4629), which shows movies daily in July and August and on weekday evenings and weekends the rest of the year; tickets cost $9.50/8.50/7.50 for adults/seniors/children four to 12. The northern end of Canada Place features promenade shops and a food court, plus good views across Burrard Inlet.

Just a block away from Canada Place on Waterfront Rd, you'll find Waterfront Station, the grand old Canadian Pacific Railway station. Once deteriorating, the now-restored building serves as the terminus for an entirely different kind of transportation – the SeaBus, which travels to North Vancouver. Waterfront Station is also a SkyTrain stop.

Science World

A fine place to spend a rainy day, Science World (☎ 604-443-7443), 1455 Quebec St, occupies the geodesic dome originally built for Expo '86. The high-tech playground includes interactive exhibits about the forces of nature, a Kidspace gallery aimed at children three to six, Internet access terminals, a 3D laser theater and a Visual Illusions space that showcases optical effects. The Alcan OMNIMAX Theatre features a 28-speaker digital sound system and one of the world's largest domed screens.

Science World is open 10 am to 6 pm daily, July and August; 10 am to 5 pm weekdays and 10 am to 6 pm weekends and holidays the rest of the year; closed December 25. Admission is $11.75/7.75 for adults/ seniors, students and children. Admission to the OMNIMAX Theatre is $10. Combination tickets are $14.75/10.50. To get there, take SkyTrain to the Science World-Main St station or Bus No 3, 8 or 19.

BC Place Stadium & GM Place

These two large sports arenas shore up the eastern edge of downtown. Both are unmistakable. A translucent dome-shaped roof covers BC Place Stadium (☎ 604-669-2300 for general information, 604-444-3663 for events), 777 Pacific Blvd S. The thin Teflon roof is 'air-supported,' which means that it's inflated by huge fans (no, not sports fans) and kept in place by crisscrossed steel wires – hence its quilted appearance.

Concerts, trade shows, sports events and other large-scale gatherings take place in this 60,000-capacity stadium, also the home of the BC Lions of the Canadian Football League (CFL). Hour-long stadium tours start at 11 am and 1 pm Tuesday and Friday, June through August. Meet at Gate H; the cost is $6/5 for adults/seniors, students and children six to 12.

The BC Sports Hall of Fame & Museum (☎ 604-687-5520), at Gate A, showcases top BC athletes, amateur and professional, with special galleries devoted to Terry Fox, who ran his 'Marathon of Hope' across Canada to collect money for cancer research (see boxed text), and Rick Hanson, who made a 'Man-in-Motion' wheelchair journey around the world to show what people with disabilities can do. The museum is open 10 am to 5 pm daily. Admission is $6/4 for adults/ children. A family ticket (up to four people) is $15.

Adjacent GM Place (☎ 604-899-7889), 800 Griffiths Way, is the city's major venue for professional sports; both the Vancouver Canucks of the National Hockey League (NHL) and the Vancouver Grizzlies of the National Basketball Association (NBA) play here. Bus Nos 2, 5, 15 and 17 access BC Place, while Nos 2, 5 and 17 stop at GM Place. SkyTrain's Stadium station serves both arenas.

Downtown Historic Railway

Take a step into the past on this old rail system, which travels between 1st Ave and Ontario St and Granville Island from 1 to 5 pm on Saturday, Sunday and holidays, mid-May to mid-October. The roundtrip

Terry Fox & the Marathon of Hope

People like Terry Fox don't come along all that often, and when they do their efforts often go unrecognized. However, Canadians were quick to applaud this Port Coquitlam resident who became a national hero in 1980.

In 1977, while studying kinesiology at Simon Fraser University, Fox lost his right leg to cancer. He was just 18. Inspired by a magazine article about a one-legged runner named Dick Traum who competed in the New York Marathon, Fox decided that he would start training as soon as he was able. After his recovery, he began to run every day, building up strength and developing his own technique. In January 1979, he ran his first half kilometer, and by August he was running 19km a day.

After two years, he was ready to run what he called the 'Marathon of Hope' across Canada, aiming to raise $1 from every Canadian for cancer research. With limited sponsorship and little media coverage, Fox began his run on April 12, 1980, at St John's, Newfoundland. By the time he reached Ontario, he'd become a household name, and donations poured in from around the country.

Fox averaged a remarkable 37km a day (he'd hoped to run 42km a day), most of it in pain, until a recurrence of cancer forced him to end his run near Thunder Bay, Ontario after 144 days and 5376km. The cancer had spread to Fox's lungs, and he died on June 28, 1981, just one month before his 23rd birthday. But his Marathon of Hope raised more than $24 million, surpassing his goal.

Fox's legacy lives on in the Terry Fox Run, an annual event held in September in towns and cities across the country. (The event continues to raise money for cancer research.) Also, a park and mountain in BC carry his name (near Hwys 16 and 5 in the central eastern part of the province near the Alberta border), as does an icebreaker (the MV *Terry Fox*), an 83km stretch of highway in Ontario between Nipigon and Thunder Bay (the Terry Fox Courage Hwy) and a $5 million scholarship fund established by the Canadian government (the Terry Fox Humanitarian Award). Monuments have been erected in his honor in Vancouver, Port Coquitlam, Ottawa and Thunder Bay.

— Chris Wyness

fare is $2/1 for adults/seniors and children. You can park free at the 1st Ave rail car barn.

STANLEY PARK (Map 4)

Vancouver's largest and much-beloved green space, Stanley Park (☎ 604-257-8400) is a 404-hectare cedar forest flanked by beaches that extend north and west of downtown. The park began as a military reserve in 1863, after Canadians became nervous about US occupation of the San Juan Islands in 1859. When these fears subsided, the lands were rededicated to use as a park. And what a park it is. Hiking, cycling and jogging trails meander through the woods. To experience one of the world's great urban walks, try the seawall walkway,

winding more than 9.5km along the park's shoreline. The three park beaches – Second Beach, Third Beach and English Bay Beach – attract lots of sunbathers and swimmers in summer; families also frolic in the outdoor swimming pool at Second Beach and in the Variety Kids Water Park at Lumbermen's Arch. Vista points afford stunning views of downtown Vancouver, the North Shore and the sea.

A well-known collection of **totem poles** sits on the east side of the park near Brockton Point. Also near here, the **Nine O'Clock Gun** has fired faithfully each evening for more than 100 years. Off the southern side near the Royal Vancouver Yacht Club looms **Deadman's Island**; it's said that a northern First Nations tribe once used the island as a camp for women captured in raids. Later a burial ground for aboriginal and Chinese people and Native Indians, it now serves as a naval reserve. Kids should enjoy the **Variety Kids Farmyard** and the **miniature railway** with a rain forest theme.

Lions Gate Bridge extends from the northern tip of the park. Just to its west sits **Prospect Point**, a popular spot for views of the First Narrows and passing ships. On the park's west side, the **National Geographic Tree**, a red cedar almost 30 meters around, is among the largest of its kind in the world – though it's not as well known as the nearby **Hollow Tree**.

Stanley Park is an easy walk from downtown; you can also take Bus Nos 23, 35, 56, 123 and 135. The free Stanley Park Shuttle runs 9:30 am to 6 pm daily, June through mid-September, with stops near many major sights. Stanley Park Horse-Drawn Tours (☎ 604-681-5115) offers narrated one-hour tours that depart every 20 to 30 minutes daily, mid-March through October, from the information booth on Stanley Park Dr, east of the Vancouver Rowing Club. The tours run 9:40 am to 5:20 pm in July and August, with slightly shorter hours the rest of the season, and cost $14.95/13.95/9.95 for adults/seniors and students/children.

Vancouver Aquarium

The Vancouver Aquarium (☎ 604-659-3474), Canada's largest, holds more than 8000 marine creatures and ranks as the country's biggest marine-mammal rescue and rehabilitation center. Currently, it's undergoing a true sea change: in 2000, aquarium officials announced their plan to end the live display of killer whales and to send Bjossa, a 23-year-old female orca who had lived in the aquarium since 1980, to Sea World in San Diego, California. But plenty of big creatures still live here, including beluga whales, Pacific white-sided dolphins, seals, otters and octopuses. Other exhibits include crocodiles, eels, piranhas and a wide variety of local sea life and freshwater fish.

The aquarium is open 9:30 am to 7 pm daily, July to early September, and 10 am to 5:30 pm daily the rest of the year. Admission is $13.85/11.70/9.15 for adults/seniors, students and teens/children four to 12. A family ticket costs $46. Visit the Web site www.vanaqua.org for information on special (but pricey) programs, such as the Night Lights sleepovers and Animal Adventures.

From downtown, follow Georgia St into Stanley Park and follow the signs, or take bus No 135 (daytime Monday to Saturday), 23 or 35 (evenings, Sundays and holidays). Bring money for parking if you drive.

Sea otters live at the Vancouver Aquarium.

Lost Lagoon Nature House

A brief stroll from bustling Robson St, the Stanley Park Ecology Society's nature house features interesting exhibits on park inhabitants. It's open daily except Tuesday, June through August, with weekend hours the rest of the year. Discovery Walks ($4) take place at 1 pm Sunday. Pre-registration is advised; call ☎ 604-257-8544.

Spanning the Decades

No Vancouver landmark is both as revered and reviled as the Lions Gate Bridge. This 842m span, rising 60m above the First Narrows and named for the twin mountain peaks north of Vancouver, opened in 1938 as the longest suspension bridge in the British Empire. About 5600 vehicles drove across that first day.

Flash forward 60 years. By 1998, the bridge carried 60,000 vehicles per day. Although its cables and towers remained strong and its lights (added in 1986) dazzling, its decking had deteriorated into a corroded mess. The province finally began replacing the entire bridge surface in the fall of 2000.

Although the bridge looks better than ever, it still only contains three lanes, with the center lane's direction changed as traffic conditions warrant (though any Vancouver driver will tell you that, at any given time, the center lane inevitably seems to be closed to vehicles traveling in your direction). Etiquette dictates you take turns merging on to the Lions Gate Bridge – and once you're up there, enjoy the view, but don't slow down. If you'd like to read a lovely essay, look for Douglas Coupland's 'Lions Gate Bridge, Vancouver, BC, Canada,' included in his book *Postcards from the Dead*.

GASTOWN (Map 5)

Vancouver's Victorian-era district takes its name from 'Gassy' Jack Deighton, a onetime English sailor who set up a saloon on the Burrard Inlet waterfront in 1867. When a village sprang up around his estab-lishment, people started calling the area Gassy's Town. (Today, a statue of Gassy Jack stands at Maple Tree Square, where Cordova and Water Sts meet.)

After the center of Vancouver moved elsewhere, Gastown gradually became a skid row, but in the 1970s the district's restoration pushed Vancouver's seedier characters a little farther south to Hastings St. The old Victorian buildings now house restaurants, boutiques, galleries and night-clubs. Old-fashioned lampposts, street vendors and buskers, or entertainers, add to the holiday feel of the area.

Possibly the most photographed object in Vancouver, the **Gastown Steam Clock** on Water St toots every 15 minutes, powered by the same system used to steam-heat many nearby office buildings. Although the clock looks old, it dates from the not-so-way-back days of 1977.

Housed in the city's former morgue and coroner's court on the fringes of Gastown, the **Vancouver Police Centennial Museum** (☎ 604-665-3346), 240 E Cordova St, tells the story of Vancouver's most infamous crimes and criminals in a suitably macabre setting. Displays include weapons, counter-feit money, forensic autopsy tools and a century's worth of drug paraphernalia. It's open 9 am to 3 pm weekdays and 10 am to

Gastown Steam Clock

LEE FOSTER

VANCOUVER & AROUND

3 pm Saturday, April through August. Admission is $5/3 for adults/seniors and children seven to 13.

Free Gastown walking tours take place at 2 pm daily, mid-June through August; meet at Maple Tree Square. Gastown itself is an easy walk from downtown or the SkyTrain Waterfront Station.

CHINATOWN (Map 5)

About 36,000 people of Chinese descent live in the area around W Pender St, roughly bordered by Abbott St and Gore Ave; thousands of others come here to shop, making this the third-largest Chinatown in North America, after San Francisco and New York.

For the most part, this is a real Chinese market and business district, full of stores with hanging ducks, bales of strange dried fish, exotic fruits and Asian remedies. The colors and smells, plus the street signs and the occasional old Chinese-style balcony, can make you believe for a second that you're in Hong Kong.

Chinatown is on the edge of Strathcona, Vancouver's most blighted area along Hastings and Main Sts. Since the recently arrived Hong Kong Chinese have colonized Richmond, a suburb of Vancouver, the center of Chinese Canadian business and culture has shifted there, at least in part. But Chinatown still throbs with life and remains a safe place to visit if you keep your wits about you.

Note that parking is almost nonexistent, but Chinatown is an easy walk from downtown; it's also on the No 3, 8, 19 and 22 bus lines and near the Stadium SkyTrain station. The Chinese Cultural Centre of Vancouver (☎ 604-687-0729), 50 E Pender St, leads inexpensive tours of the area.

Dr Sun Yat-Sen Classical Chinese Garden

A tranquil oasis amid Chinatown's bustle, this carefully planned garden (☎ 604-689-7133), 578 Carrall St, is the only full-scale Ming Dynasty-style garden outside China. Take the guided tour to best understand and appreciate its subtle design, which incorporates the Taoist principles of yin and yang.

Concerts take place on Friday evening in summer, and each fall and winter, the garden hosts the Mid-Autumn Moon Festival and Chinese New Year celebrations. Adjacent to the formal garden, the city's free Dr Sun Yat-Sen Park features a similar design.

The garden is open 9:30 am to 7 pm daily, June 15 through August 30 (when tours start on every hour); 10 am to 6 pm daily, May 1 through June 14 and all of September (tours six times daily); and 10 am to 4:30 pm daily, Oct. 1 through April 30 (tours four times daily). Admission is $7.50/6/5 for adults/seniors/students. A family ticket costs $18.

The Sam Kee Building

Recognized by *Ripley's Believe It or Not!* and the *Guinness Book of World Records* as the World's Narrowest Office Building, the building at the corner of Pender and Carrall Sts is easy to miss, not only due to its narrowness but also because it looks like the front of the larger, attached building behind. Built in 1913, it's only 1.5m wide and two stories tall. It results from a grudge: The city, intent on widening Pender St, neglected to pay Kee for this narrow strip of property, so he put up this slim building out of spite.

EAST VANCOUVER (Map 5)

Traditionally the working-class and non-British section of Vancouver, the area east of Main Street still attracts many immigrants, who make their homes here. Long the center of Vancouver's Italian community, **Commercial Dr**, or 'The Drive' as it's commonly called, remains one of the city's liveliest melting pots. The counterculture still thrives here as well, with earnest political conversations echoing among the many vegetarian cafés, bookstores, hemp shops and coffeehouses. Don't leave Vancouver without spending some time here.

Playland

Vancouver's amusement park (☎ 604-253-2311), on the Pacific National Exhibition Park grounds at Cassiar and Hastings Sts, offers such thrills and chills as a classic wooden roller coaster and the Hellevator, which shoots up a tower at 75km before sending riders in a free-fall toward the ground. Half of the 25 rides, though, cater to little tykes. Playland is open 11 am to 7 pm weekends from late April to mid-June and 11 am to 9pm daily from mid-June through mid-August (it's also open during the Pacific National Expo itself, which runs for two weeks in late August and early September). All-day passes cost $21 ($10 for small children or nonriding adults). To get there, catch bus No 4, 10 or 16 from downtown.

GRANVILLE ISLAND (Map 6)

On the southern side of False Creek, under the Granville Bridge, this small, formerly industrial island has turned into a busy blend of businesses, restaurants, galleries and theaters. The center of activity is the **Granville Island Public Market**, a food lover's dream made manifest, with dozens of greengrocers, fishmongers, butchers, bakers, cheese shops and other food merchants displaying their wares. It's open 9 am to 6 pm daily, from mid-May through mid-October, and Tuesday through Sunday the rest of the year.

The market faces a waterfront plaza that's nearly always filled with shoppers, frolicking children, buskers and swarms of pigeons and gulls. The free **Granville Island Water Park**, on the island's south side, offers more outdoor fun from May through September. The indoor **Kids Only Market**, meanwhile, lures young visitors with clowns, magicians, face-painters and stores featuring everything from fun wet-weather gear to toys and puppets.

Granville Island is also an arts center, home to the **Emily Carr Institute of Art & Design** (☎ 604-844-3800), 1299 Johnston St, which holds frequent exhibits in its galleries. The shops on the island include several commercial art galleries and craft studios, interspersed with recreational-equipment shops and ship chandlers. At night, the focus shifts from shopping to the performing arts, as several theater companies and live music clubs open their doors.

The **Granville Island Museums** complex (☎ 604-683-1939), 1502 Duranleau St, houses three collections under one roof: sport fishing, model ships and model trains. All are open 10 am to 5:30 pm daily. Admission, which includes entry to all three museums, is $6.50/5/3.50 for adults/seniors and students/children four to 12; a family ticket is $16.50.

The Granville Island Information Centre (☎ 604-666-5784), 1398 Cartwright St, is open 9 am to 6 pm daily. Parking can be very tight on Granville Island. Unless you must drive, consider taking the Aquabus or False Creek Ferries (see Getting Around, later in this chapter) or catching bus No 50 from Gastown or No 51 from Broadway and Granville St.

KITSILANO (Map 7)

The neighborhood of Kitsilano spreads across the southern shore of English Bay, roughly from Burrard St to UBC. During the 1960s and 70s, Kitsilano became a hippie enclave. But everyone and everything grows up; the hippies are now lawyers, and the neighborhood has gone genteel.

Kitsilano – usually referred to simply as 'Kits' – is still a fun area to explore, particularly along W 4th Ave and W Broadway, the primary commercial streets. One thing that hasn't changed in Kitsilano are the beaches. **Kitsilano Beach**, near Vanier Park, and **Jericho Beach**, farther west on W 4th Ave at Jericho Beach Park, remain two of the city's most popular places to gather and to worship the sun.

Vanier Park

Vanier Park, on English Bay south of False Creek and below the Burrard Bridge, boasts several museums and a great beach, along with a swimming pool, tennis courts and other sporting grounds. When the weather's fine, you'll see lots of people strolling, jogging, cycling, walking their dogs or simply sitting and watching the ships moving between English Bay and False Creek. To reach Vanier Park from downtown, catch the No 22 bus or take Aquabus or the False Creek Ferries from downtown or Granville Island.

Vancouver Museum This fine museum (☎ 604-736-4431), 1100 Chestnut St, vividly recounts both distant and recent Vancouver history. 'Go forward, look back' is the theme of the excellent orientation gallery, where exhibits include a look at the everyday life of First Nations people, plus artifacts of Vancouver at work and play – everything from an 1869 'bone-shaker' bicycle to a 1967 black-light poster from the Retinal Circus nightclub. The 'Vancouver Story' galleries examine the city's early settlement in greater depth. The changing exhibits are usually excellent, too, and many have a scope far beyond Vancouver. The museum is open 10 am to 5 pm daily (until 9 pm Thursday). Admission is $8/5.50 for adults/seniors and students; a family ticket is $25.

HR MacMillan Space Centre This facility (☎ 604-738-7827), part of the Vancouver Museum complex, features regularly changing shows projected onto a 20m-wide dome. These range from educational to entertaining (laser shows featuring musical hits). Other attractions include a virtual-reality simulator ride and a 'Cosmic Courtyard' of hands-on exhibits that let visitors launch a rocket, morph into a space alien and more.

The center is open 10 am to 5 pm daily, July and August; 10 am to 5 pm Tuesday to Sunday, September through June. Admission is $12.50/9.50/8.50 for adults/seniors and students/children five to 10; a family ticket is $40. Evening laser shows ($7.50) start at 9:30 pm Wednesday to Saturday, with additional shows at 10:45 pm Friday and Saturday. The Gordon Southam Observatory, on the grounds here, is open noon to 5 pm and 7 to 11 pm on weekends when skies are clear and volunteers are available (call ☎ 604-738-2855 to check). Admission is free.

Vancouver Maritime Museum For a glimpse of the city's rich seafaring heritage, stop at this museum (☎ 604-257-8300), 1905 Ogden Ave at the foot of Cypress St, a five-minute walk from the Vancouver Museum. Its signature exhibit is the *St Roch*, a 1928 Royal Canadian Mounted Police (RCMP) Arctic patrol sailing ship that was the first vessel to navigate the legendary Northwest Passage in both directions. Other displays tell of lighthouses, pirates, shipwrecks and more. The Children's Maritime Discovery Centre features hands-on activities. Classic wooden boats often anchor outside in Heritage Harbour. The museum is open 10 am to 5 pm daily, mid-May through early September; closed Monday the rest of the year. Admission is $7/4 for adults/children; a family ticket is $16.

ELSEWHERE IN VANCOUVER
University of British Columbia
Often just called UBC, this 400-hectare college campus (Map 2; ☎ 604-822-2211) with 32,000 students sits at the most westerly point of Vancouver. Forest still covers much of the grounds, particularly at Pacific Spirit Regional Park. Bus Nos 4 and 10 run to the university every 10 minutes or so from downtown; the journey takes about 30 minutes.

UBC Museum of Anthropology This well-done museum (☎ 604-822-3825), 6393 NW Marine Dr, contains outstanding art and artifacts that tell the story of BC's First Nations peoples. Highlights include works by Haida artist Bill Reid, especially his monumental yellow cedar carving of *Raven and the First Men*. Another exhibit focuses on Mungo Martin, who was born in the early 1880s, just before the Canadian government outlawed native practices in 1884. Martin struggled to preserve the traditions of his Kwakwaka'wakw people, eventually coming to UBC in 1949 to restore totem poles now on view at the museum.

The museum building itself is a work of art, designed by Arthur Erickson to mirror the post-and-beam structures of coastal First Nations people. The Great Hall's 15m walls of glass look out on still more totem poles and outdoor sculptures. The museum is open 10 am to 5 pm daily (until 9 pm

Tuesday). Several guided walks take place each day; call for details. Admission is $7/5/4 for adults/seniors/students (free on Tuesday between 5 and 9 pm); a family ticket is $20.

Nitobe Memorial Gardens Near the museum, these beautiful gardens (☎ 604-822-6038) reflect the designing talents of a prominent Japanese landscape architect. They're open 10 am to 6 pm daily, mid-March through mid-October; 10 am to 2:30 pm weekdays the rest of the year. Admission is $2.50/1.75/1.50 adults/seniors and students/children; enter free in winter.

UBC Botanical Gardens These lovely gardens (☎ 604-822-3928), 6804 SW Marine Dr near the corner of W 16th Ave, cover 28 hectares. The highlights include Canada's largest collection of rhododendrons and a 16th-century apothecary garden. A winter garden features plants that bloom in the cooler months, and a shop sells gardening gear and unusual plants. The gardens are open 10 am to 6 pm daily, mid-March to mid-October; 10 am to 2:30 pm daily the rest of the year. Admission is $4.50/2.25/1.75 for adults/seniors and students/children; it's free in winter.

Queen Elizabeth Park

The highest point in Vancouver, Queen Elizabeth Park (Map 2), at Cambie St and W 33rd Ave, sits atop 150m Little Mountain.

Bloedel Conservatory and the Seasons in the Park restaurant (see Places to Eat, later) are the primary attractions, but you'll also find stunning sunken gardens and many recreation facilities.

The domed **Bloedel Conservatory** (☎ 604-257-8570) takes in three climate zones and houses 500 species of gorgeous plants, though the 50 species of free-flying tropical birds often steal the show – especially Casey, an Amazon parrot who is quite a talker. It's open 9 am to 8 pm weekdays, 10 am to 9 pm weekends. Admission is $3.50/2/1.65 for adults/seniors/children.

To get to the park, take bus No 15 from Burrard or Robson Sts downtown.

VanDusen Botanical Garden

Get lost in a maze, gaze at rare ornamental plants and enjoy scenic views of Vancouver at this garden (Map 2; ☎ 604-878-9274), 5251 Oak St at W 37th Ave, not far from Queen Elizabeth Park. It's open 10 am to 9 pm, June through mid-August, with slightly shorter hours in May, late August and September. Admission is $5.50/2.75 for adults/seniors, students and children. To get there, take bus No 17 south on Burrard St from downtown.

ACTIVITIES

'You can ski in the morning and sail in the afternoon' must be the most common Vancouver cliché. But like most clichés, it's true.

It's Only Natural

No off-the-beaten-path destination, Wreck Beach – Vancouver's only nude sunbathing spot – attracts 100,000 people each year. The three main sections of the 6km beach appeal to different crowds. Gay men tend to congregate on the north end; the central section is full of people peddling food and other consumables; and the southern stretch is a throwback to the 1960s, with everyone just hanging loose and having a good time. For the most part, people don't come to Wreck Beach to have sex; if they do, it's done discreetly. Bear in mind, too, that going bare on this or any other Canadian public beach is technically illegal – but at Wreck Beach, Vancouver authorities are looking the other way.

Wreck Beach lies on the west side of the UBC campus; get there by taking NW Marine Dr south past the Rose Garden and the Museum of Anthropology to any of the trails marked No 4, 5 or 6.

You can also bike, scuba dive, golf, swim, skate, surf – and the list goes on. See the North Vancouver and West Vancouver sections, later in this chapter, for information on skiing and other activities at Grouse Mountain Resort, Cypress Provincial Park and Mount Seymour Provincial Park on the North Shore.

Cycling

Stanley Park's 9.5km seawall is probably Vancouver's favorite place to cycle. Rental bikes aren't available in the park, but many shops are just a block or two away, with rates running about $6 per hour, $14 for four hours or $20 to $25 per day. Choices include Bayshore Bicycles (Map 3; ☎ 604-688-2453), 745 Denman St; Spokes Bicycle Rental & Espresso Bar (Map 3; ☎ 604-688-5141), 1798 W Georgia St; and – probably cheapest of all – Alley Cat Rentals (Map 3; ☎ 604-684-5777), 1779 Robson St, where you can rent a beach-cruiser bike for less than $10 per day. Most bike shops also rent in-line skates, at prices slightly lower than those for bikes.

Swimming

Cool off at Second and Third Beaches in Stanley Park, at English Bay and Sunset Beaches downtown, or at Kitsilano and Jericho Beaches on the southern side of English Bay. Kits Beach is the largest and most popular; as many as 10,000 people may hit the sand here on a hot summer day. You can also swim in the outdoor heated saltwater pool (☎ 604-731-0011) here.

For serious swimmers, the Vancouver Aquatic Centre (Map 3; ☎ 604-665-3424), 1050 Beach Ave at the foot of Thurlow St downtown, offers an indoor heated swimming pool, whirlpool, diving tank, gym and sauna. You'll find another aquatic center located at UBC.

Kayaking

Ecomarine Ocean Kayak Centre (Map 6; ☎ 604-689-7575), 1668 Duranleau St on Granville Island, rents solo sea kayaks ($24 for two hours, $44 per day) and double kayaks ($34 for two hours, $64 per day). Its Jericho Beach location (Map 7; ☎ 604-222-3565), 1300 Discovery St, offers three-hour beginning kayaking classes ($49).

Windsurfing

Windsure Windsurfing School (Map 7; ☎ 604-224-0615), 1300 Discovery St at the Jericho Sailing Centre, rents boards and wetsuits and gives lessons ($29 and up for a two-hour group lesson).

Scuba Diving

You'll find the best scuba diving off the North Shore: at Cates Park on Deep Cove, up Indian Arm, at Lighthouse Park near West Vancouver and at Porteau Cove, 26km north of Horseshoe Bay. For equipment, training and trips, stop in at any of the Diving Locker's four Lower Mainland locations, including the shop at 2745 W 4th Ave in Kitsilano (☎ 604-736-2681).

Golf

Vancouver contains plenty of greens, including the small-scale pitch-and-putt courses at Stanley Park (Map 4; ☎ 604-257-8400) and Queen Elizabeth Park (Map 2; ☎ 604-874-8336). Other public courses in the city include Fraserview Golf Course (Map 2; ☎ 604-327-5616), off SE Marine Dr; McCleery Golf Course (Map 2; ☎ 604-257-8191), on SW Marine Dr; and the University Golf Club (Map 2; ☎ 604-224-1818), on the UBC campus.

Tennis

With more than 180 free public courts (including some at Stanley Park, Queen Elizabeth Park and Kits Beach Park), Vancouver offers plenty of places to play tennis. City courts are available on a first-come, first-served basis; you can only occupy a court for 30 minutes if someone's waiting.

ORGANIZED TOURS

Gray Line (☎ 604-879-3363) specializes in traditional bus sightseeing tours. The three-and-a-half-hour Deluxe Grand City Tour ($41/39/29 for adults/seniors/children) covers Stanley Park, Gastown, Chinatown and Queen Elizabeth Park. If you'd prefer a less structured itinerary, Gray Line's Decker/ Trolley tour ($25/24/14) allows riders to hop on and off buses at 22 designated stops; the ticket is good for two consecutive days. The Vancouver Trolley Company (☎ 604-801-5515) offers a similar service with 16 stops; one-day tickets cost $22/10 for adults/ children.

The X-Tour (☎ 604-609-2770) focuses on Vancouver's film-and-TV industry. For three hours, you ride around in a limo and look at past and current filming locations for such TV series as *The X-Files* and films like *Legends of the Fall*. At $145 per person, though, it's pretty pricey – especially since you're too late: *The X-Files* is now filmed in California.

West Coast Sightseeing (☎ 604-451-1600) runs the usual city bus tours, but it also offers a four-hour Native Culture Tour that visits various Vancouver museums and sights relating to the First Nations people. The cost is $45/43/27 for adults/seniors and students/children. The company also leads city tours in German and Mandarin.

Harbour Cruises (☎ 604-688-7246) offers 75-minute cruises ($18/15/6 for adults/ seniors and teens/children), as well as three-hour sunset dinner cruises ($60/50 for adults/children) around False Creek, English Bay and Burrard Inlet. Boats leave

from the operator's office, at the north foot of Denman St near Stanley Park.

Harbour Air Seaplanes (☎ 604-688-1277) features air tours aboard float planes, departing from its water terminal at the base of Burrard St (one block north of Canada Place). The least expensive flight ($76) tours the Vancouver area for 20 minutes.

Walking Tours

The best guided-tour bargain in town is probably Erik's City & Canyon Tour, available to guests of HI-Vancouver Downtown (see Places to Stay, later). The freewheeling daylong tour covers Vancouver's highlights, as well as Lynn Canyon Park on the North Shore, all for a mere $10 plus bus fare.

Walkabout Historic Vancouver (☎ 604-720-0006 or 439-0448) offers two different two-hour walking tours ($18). One covers downtown and Gastown; the other focuses on Granville Island.

SPECIAL EVENTS

Vancouver loves to party, with big events scheduled in nearly every month of the year, beginning with January's **Polar Bear Swim** (☎ 604-605-2304), a popular and chilly affair that takes place January 1 at English Bay Beach. In mid-February, Chinatown hosts a 15-day **Chinese New Year** celebration (☎ 604-687-6021), with dancers, music, fireworks and food.

Come spring, runners and walkers take to the streets for late April's **Vancouver Sun Run** (☎ 604-689-9441), one of the world's largest 10km races, which winds through downtown before finishing with a big party at BC Place Stadium.

May features two events: the **New Music West Festival** (☎ 604-684-9338), an international event with club crawls, band showcases, seminars and industry forums in early May; and the **Vancouver International Children's Festival** (☎ 604-708-5655), a family-oriented performing-arts festival that takes place in Vanier Park late in the month.

In mid-June, the **Alcan Dragon Boat Festival** (☎ 604-688-2382), on False Creek, attracts nearly 2000 competitors from around the world. At the end of the month, big-name stars and local favorites appear at the **duMaurier International Jazz Festival** (☎ 604-872-5200), one of the best in Canada.

On July 1, **Canada Day** celebrations take place at Canada Place (☎ 604-666-8477) and Granville Island (☎ 604-666-5784). At early August's **Symphony of Fire** (☎ 604-738-4304), an international fireworks extravaganza, countries compete to see who can ignite the biggest bangs off a barge in English Bay. Each show lasts about an hour, all set to music. Held the first weekend in August, **Pride** (☎ 604-687-0955) celebrates Vancouver's gay and lesbian communities. It culminates in a Sunday parade along Denman and Beach Sts, followed by a fair and entertainment at Sunset Beach.

The **Pacific National Exposition** (PNE; ☎ 604-253-2311), the second-largest fair in Canada, takes place from late August to early September at the Pacific National Exhibition Grounds at Hastings Park in East Vancouver.

The largest spectator sporting event in Canada, the **Molson Indy Vancouver** (☎ 604-280-4639 for tickets), held in early September, draws 350,000 spectators to watch pro race drivers negotiate the streets of downtown Vancouver. In mid-September, the **Vancouver Fringe Festival** (☎ 604-257-0350) presents drama, musical theatre, comedy and dance from around the world. From late September through early October, the **Vancouver International Film Festival** (☎ 604-685-0260) showcases 300 films from 50 nations.

During the December holiday season, the monthlong **Christmas at Canada Place** (☎ 604-666-8477) features ornate trees, wreaths and holiday window displays.

PLACES TO STAY

Vancouver is not a cheap place to stay during its summer season (May to September). You won't find any place to camp in the city itself (see North Vancouver, Burnaby and Richmond, later in the chapter, for camping possibilities in the suburbs), and you'll have to look far and wide for budget accommodations beyond the hostels. Most hotel rooms in Vancouver top $100. Because summer is so busy, you should make reservations weeks, even months, in advance if you have your heart set on a specific place to stay. The Super, Natural British Columbia reservations service (☎ 604-435-5622, 800-435-5662) can be a great help in finding reasonably priced accommodation. With many rooms at their disposal, its operators can often get you quite a good deal, at prices lower than what the hotels themselves may quote you.

Vancouver B&Bs often offer moderate prices, averaging $75 to $125 for a double with shared bathroom. Many are in the quiet residential neighborhoods of Kitsilano, Kerrisdale and Shaughnessy, all south of downtown. Because B&Bs come and go rather quickly, you may want to use a reservation service to locate a room. Old English B&B Registry (☎ 604-986-5069, fax 986-8810, vicki@bandbinn.com, 1226 Silverwood Crescent, North Vancouver, BC V7P 1J3) books about 25 inns; its Web site is www.bandbinn.com. In business since 1982, Town & Country B&B (☎/fax 604-731-5942, PO Box 74542, 2803 W 4th Ave, Vancouver, BC V6K 1K2) reserves rooms in about 30 different inns in Vancouver and Victoria. See www.townandcountrybedandbreakfast.com, its Web site.

Hostels

Most of the good hostels fill up throughout summer and remain quite busy the rest of the year, so it's wise to book ahead. Most have very limited parking, so it's best to arrive without a car.

Downtown (Map 3) A safe bet for budget travelers of all ages, *HI-Vancouver Downtown* (☎ 604-684-4565, 888-203-4302, fax 604-684-4540, van-downtown@hihostels .bc.ca, 1114 Burnaby St), on the corner of Thurlow St, contains 212 beds, with no more than four in a room. Scheduled activities abound, including a variety of local tours; the hostel also offers a free shuttle service to the bus and train station as well as to the Jericho Beach HI hostel. Facilities include a patio, Internet kiosks, library and games room. The low-key, hospitable hostel enjoys an excellent location, quiet but close to the action; it's a block from the shops and restaurants of Davie St and a short walk from anywhere else that's downtown. Quad rooms cost $20/24 per person for members/nonmembers. Private rooms for up to two people are $50/59; for three people, they run $63/72.

Global Village Backpackers (☎ 604-682-8226, 888-844-7875, gvbp@interlog.com, 1018 Granville St) is the newest and hippest hostel in town. Brightly painted and lively, it strikes a nice balance between the near-stodginess of the HI facilities and the grunginess of some other Vancouver hostels – though its Granville St location may be a bit *too* central for more mellow travelers. Features include 220 beds, a rooftop patio, nightly pub runs with no-lineup access to some of downtown's hottest clubs, good apartment and job boards, lockers, a bike storage room and a lounge with pool table. Bunks in quad rooms cost $22/25 with a hostel card/without. Private double rooms with a shared bath are $56/59; triple rooms with their own shower and toilet are $63/66. You can buy breakfast here for $2.95.

Right downtown, the *YMCA* (☎ 604-681-0221, 955 Burrard St) rents singles for $46/48 without TV/with TV and doubles for $55/57, all with bathrooms down the hall. A handful of family rooms cost about $75 (women and couples are allowed). Parking costs $7 per night, and small pets may stay for an extra $11 per night. Guests can use the Y's gym and pool facilities. A small, inexpensive restaurant off the lobby serves breakfasts and sandwiches.

The *YWCA* (☎ 604-895-5830, 800-663-1424 in Canada, hotel@ywcavan.org, 733 Beatty St) enjoys a good location near Sky-Train, BC Place and downtown. Everyone is welcome here — women, men, couples and families – and profits help fund the YWCA's local programs. The 155 rooms come in various configurations ranging from singles with lockable bathrooms down the hall ($56) to a room with five single beds ($147 for five). Doubles start at $66 with hall bath and run to $133 for two double beds and a private bathroom. Seniors, students and YWCA members can cut about 10% off all room rates. Amenities include in-room refrigerators, common kitchens, TV lounges and a laundry. Parking is $5 per day.

A little farther afield, the *C&N Backpackers Hostel* (☎ 604-682-2441, 888-434-6060, backpackers@sprint.ca, 927 Main St) does have some advantages, despite its less-than-ideal location: proximity to the bus and train stations, a laundry, an Internet room with a view, bike rentals and secure building access after 11 pm. An acceptable place to stay that seems to be improving, the hostel charges $12 per person to share a room with three to four beds. Private rooms cost $30 for one person, $35 for two.

Elsewhere in Vancouver 'Party here tonight!' screams a billboard on the side of the *Cambie International Hostel* (Map 5; ☎ 604-684-6466, 877-395-5335, fax 604-687-5618, info@cambiehostels.com, 300 Cambie St). It refers to the Cambie pub, but it also sums up the vibe at this Gastown-area bunkhouse. The ground floor is seriously rowdy, but the sleeping rooms are pretty nice, with four to six oversized beds and some en suite bathrooms and showers. Beds cost $20; there's technically a $25 rate for nonstudents or people without a hostel card, but it's rarely charged. No cooking facilities are available, but cheap eats are easy to come by in the bakery, café and saloon downstairs. (Guests' first breakfast is on the house.) Ask about free pick-up from the bus or train station or even Vancouver International Airport. The Cambie also runs a second, somewhat more sedate location downtown at 515 Seymour St (Map 3; ☎ 604-684-7757).

Also in the Gastown area, the seedy *New Backpackers Hostel* (Map 5; ☎ 604-688-0112, 347 W Pender St), also known as Vincent's, is the cheapest place in town, with shared space in six-bed dorm rooms for $10 and private rooms for $25/30 single/double. The staff is friendly, but the place truly is a dive. Trust your instincts here; if you check it out and sense you're better off paying a few more dollars elsewhere, do it.

Outdoorsy travelers will like the setting of the *HI-Vancouver Jericho Beach (Map 7;* ☎ *604-224-3208, 888-203-4303, fax 604-224-4852, van-jericho@hihostels.bc.ca, 1515 Discovery St)*, close to Jericho Beach Park on English Bay and about 20 minutes from downtown by southbound bus No 4 on Granville St. With 286 beds, it's the largest in Canada, though there still are never more than four beds to a room. Bunks cost $16 October through May, $17.50 June through September; nonmembers pay $20 year-round. The 10 private rooms – some very plain, others quite nice – all cost the same price: $45 for one or two people plus $22.50 for a third person. While you won't find any restaurants nearby, an on-premises café serves breakfast ($4.50 to $5.50) and dinner ($5.75 to $7), and kitchen facilities are available, too. Both Vancouver HI hostels offer additional information on the Web site www.hihostels.bc.ca.

University Housing

When students leave campus for the summer, the University of British Columbia rents out their rooms (although without the dirty socks and old pizza boxes, luckily). Available from about the first week in May to the end of August, rooms with shared bath cost $24/48 single/double; the self-contained apartments range from $69 (single) to $159 (four or five people). Year-round, you can rent one of the 47 condominium-style apartments for $99 to $159. The pleasant campus includes a cafeteria, restaurants, coin laundry, pub and sports facilities. For reservations, contact the Conference Centre (☎ 604-822-1010, fax 604-822-1001, reservation@housing.ubc.ca; Gage Towers, 5961 Student Union Blvd, UBC Campus, Vancouver, BC V6T 2C9) or visit the Web site www.conferences.ubc.ca. See Simon Fraser University under Burnaby, later in this chapter, for another campus option.

B&Bs

Just a short walk from Davie or Robson Sts downtown, *Colibri Bed & Breakfast (Map 3;* ☎ *604-689-5100, 877-312-6600, fax 604-682-3925, colibri@home.com, 1101 Thurlow St)* is a favorite among gay and lesbian travelers, though its location makes it ideal for anyone who seeks a central B&B. Rates start at $95/120, including a continental breakfast.

You'll find two moderately priced B&Bs in the Commercial Dr neighborhood of East Vancouver. *A Place at Penny's (Map 5;* ☎ *604-254-2229, 810 Commercial Dr)* offers studio ($95) and one-bedroom ($125) accommodations, each with private bath, equipped kitchen and a self-catered breakfast of fresh fruit and baked goods. The same innkeeper recently added rooms at similar prices in nearby *Aberdeen Mansion, (Map 5; 1110 Victoria Dr)*, a building that dates from 1910. Both are near the No 20 bus line.

The *Cambie Lodge (Map 6;* ☎ *604-872-4753, 888-872-3060, info@cambielodge.com, 446 W 13th Ave)*, at the former West Side location of Paul's Guest House, is now run by the same innkeeper who operates the nearby Windsor and Douglas guest houses. Despite extensive renovations, some rooms still come fairly cheap, with rates starting at $55 in summer, including breakfast. The staff say they speak English, Dutch, German, French, Swahili and Tagalo.

A big Victorian home with a front-porch sitting area, *Windsor Guest House (Map 6;* ☎ *604-872-3060, 888-872-3060, fax 604-873-1147, info@dougwin.com, 325 W 11th Ave)* contains 10 rooms ($75 to $105), some with private baths and all with cable TV. Rates include a full breakfast and free off-street parking. A sister property, *Douglas Guest House (Map 6; same phone as above, 456 W 13th Ave)* rents six rooms, including two suites that can sleep up to five people, for $75 to $125 double occupancy. The Garden Suite ($105) comes with its own kitchenette, bathroom and private entrance.

Also on the West Side, *Shaughnessy Village (Map 6;* ☎ *604-736-5511, fax 737-1321, info@shaughnessyvillage.com, 1125 W 12th Ave)* bills itself as Canada's largest B&B. A high-rise complex, it's actually an apartment building that happens to take travelers, but it's much nicer, safer and a lot more fun than the dumpy downtown crash pads that try to pass themselves off as budget hotels. Expect frumpy decor but amenities galore: a pool, exercise room, mini-golf, laundry, even a waterway for miniature yacht races. The rooms recall ship's cabins; they're packed with a fold-down bed, private bathroom, refrigerator and microwave, TV and clock radio, even a small balcony. Guests get a free breakfast in the onsite restaurant. Studio rooms cost $60/70 single/double in July and August; a few two-room suites are available for $99/109. Limited off-street parking is available, though the Broadway and Granville St shopping and dining districts are nearby.

In Kitsilano, the restored *Maple House Bed & Breakfast* (*Map 7;* ☎ *604-739-5833, fax 739-5877, info@maplehouse.com, 1533 Maple St*) offers rooms for $85 to $130. Close to the beach and Vanier Park, *Walnut House B&B* (*Map 7;* ☎ *604-739-6941, fax 739-6942, info@walnuthousebb.com, 1350 Walnut St*) rents three rooms ($105 to $150), all with en suite bathrooms, TVs, VCRs and well-stocked bookcases. Rates are similar at *Mickey's Kits Beach Chalet* (*Map 7;* ☎ *604-739-3342, 888-739-3342, fax 604-739-3342, mickeys@direct.ca, 2146 W 1st Ave*), where some rooms come with private balconies and others with fireplaces.

On the edge of the forest at Pacific Spirit Regional Park, the *Pacific Spirit Guest House* (*Map 2;* ☎ *604-261-6837, pspirit@vancouver.quik.com, 4080 W 35th Ave*) is a great spot for families, with children and small dogs welcome. Two rooms share a bath: one has a double bed and room for a cot ($15); the other has either one king or two twin beds. Rent one room for $75, or both for $135. Other amenities include a five-course breakfast, a hot tub, play area and access to a guest laundry, microwave and small fridge (often stocked with beverages). It's about a half-hour ride to downtown via the No 7 bus, four blocks away.

The *Chelsea Cottage B&B* (*Map 2;* ☎ *604-266-2681, fax 266-7540, chelsea@bc.sympatico.ca, 2143 W 46th Ave*), a homey spot in the Kerrisdale residential area, features two shared-bath rooms ($85/95) and

two private-bath rooms ($110/130), all with TVs and telephones. Also in Kerrisdale, the quaint, antique-filled *Johnson Heritage House B&B* (*Map 2;* ☎ *604-266-4175, fun@johnsons-inn-vancouver.com, 2278 W 34th Ave*) contains a variety of rooms ($85 to $180), each with its own excellent guest guide offering detailed lists of local restaurants and step-by-step directions for day trips to Victoria and Whistler. Both Chelsea Cottage and Johnson Heritage House are a short walk from the No 16 bus that travels downtown.

In Shaughnessy Heights, *Arbutus House B&B* (*Map 2;* ☎ *604-738-6432, fax 738-6433, stay@arbutushouse.com, 4470 Maple Crescent*) features an upscale feel but moderately priced rooms ($100 to $165). Bathrobes, slippers, afternoon tea and bedtime sherry are a few of the niceties you'll find at this elegant inn. It's a two-block walk to the Nos 8 and 16 bus lines and not much farther from an array of parks, gardens and historical homes.

Motels & Hotels

Downtown (Map 3) Vancouver's first B&B hotel, the *Kingston Hotel* (☎ *604-684-9024, 888-713-3304, fax 604-684-9917, 757 Richards St*) still offers a light morning meal of coffee, juice and toast. The very basic rooms cost $45 to $80 single or $55 to $95 double; the lower-priced rooms share bathrooms. Amenities include a coin-op laundry, TV lounge and sauna. Parking is available for $10 per night.

The *Victorian Hotel* (☎ *604-681-6369, 877-681-6369, 514 Homer St*) is a real find in Vancouver, offering reasonable prices in a 27-room European-style pension in a beautifully renovated historic building. Floral-print down duvets cover all the beds, and some of the rooms feature bay windows and kitchenettes. (All have phones and small TVs.) Shared-bath rooms start at $59/69 single/double; private-bath rooms begin at $89/99, including continental breakfast. Fenced parking is $8 per night. The Victorian also offers some plainer hostel-style accommodations in a separate, nearby building for $35/45.

The **Dufferin Hotel** (☎ 604-683-4251, 877-683-5522, fax 604-683-0611, reservations@ dufferinhotel.com, 900 Seymour St) rents rooms for $80/85. A few rooms with their own toilets but showers down the hall start at $55. There's free parking and a coffee shop and pub on the premises. The **Royal Hotel** (☎ 604-685-5335, 877-685-5337, fax 604-685-5351, frontdesk@attheroyal.com, 1025 Granville St) features a rich blue-and-gold decor with rates starting at $99 for rooms sharing semi-private, lockable baths and $129 for a room with private bath. Rates include a continental breakfast, plus welcoming cocktails in the hotel pub. A guest laundry is available, too. Both the Dufferin and the Royal pubs serve a primarily gay clientele, though they're straight-friendly.

The **Hotel Dakota** (☎ 604-605-4333, 888-605-5333, fax 604-605-4334, info@hoteldakota .com, 645 Nelson St) offers comfy rooms from $99 to $159. If you're into the club scene, note that taking a room here means free VIP admission to three popular clubs that are owned by the same company that manages the hotel: The Roxy, Babalu and Fred's Uptown Tavern.

Bosman's Motor Hotel (☎ 604-682-3171, 888-267-6267, fax 604-684-4010, bosmans@ bc.sympatico.ca, 1060 Howe St) isn't as hip, but it offers an extremely central location, plus free parking and an outdoor pool. Rooms, very nicely furnished for the price, start at $99/109. In a similar vein, the **Burrard Motor Inn** (☎ 604-681-2331, 800-663-0366, fax 604-681-9753, 1100 Burrard St) features a good downtown location, free secure parking and a pleasant courtyard. Singles/doubles are $94/104, though a few smaller rooms for one person cost $84. Add $5 for a kitchenette.

Among the chains, **Travelodge Vancouver Centre** (☎ 604-682-2767, 800-578-7878, fax 604-682-6225, 1304 Howe St) offers basic but fine rooms ($95/109), plus an outdoor pool. The **Ramada Limited Downtown Vancouver** (☎ 604-488- 1088, 888-389-5888, fax 604-488-1090, ramadalimiteddowntown@ bc.sympatico.com, 435 W Pender St) got a facelift recently, though the best sight here is the cascading neon waterfall sign outside.

Rates start at $139, including continental breakfast. Parking is $15 per night.

If you have money to burn, downtown Vancouver offers a number of top-end accommodations. Despite renovations, the **Crowne Plaza Hotel Georgia** (☎ 604-682-5566, 800-663-1111, fax 604-642-5579, hgsales @hotelgeorgia.bc.ca, 801 W Georgia St) still features plenty of Roaring 1920s ambience. Rooms start at $159. Amenities include a fitness center.

For a high-class room, look into the stylish **Sheraton Wall Centre Hotel** (☎ 604-331-1000, 800-663-9255, fax 604-331-1001, info@sheratonwallcentre.com, 1088 Burrard St), a newer 35-floor tower in the center of the city with a distinctly arty, modern atmosphere. Though published rates run from $180 to $400, rooms sometimes go for as low as $150, even in summer. The northwest-facing rooms feature incredible views.

At the **Days Inn Vancouver Downtown** (☎ 604-681-4335, 877-681-4335, fax 604-681-7808, welcome2@daysinn-va.com, 921 W Pender St), small but well-furnished rooms with mini-fridges start at $180. A complimentary downtown shuttle runs 7 am to 7 pm. Parking is $10 per night.

The **Wedgewood Hotel** (☎ 604-689-7777, 800-663-0666, fax 604-608-5348, info@ wedgewoodhotel.com, 845 Hornby St) is a business-oriented boutique hotel with 89 rooms, each slightly different. Rates start at $200/220. Niceties include balconies, home-made cookies, cordless phones and a health club. Ask for a Robson Square view.

The **Westin Grand Hotel** (☎ 604-602-1999, 888-680-9393, fax 604-647-2502, play@ westingrandvancouver.com, 433 Robson St) is a new all-suites hotel near BC Place, theaters and nightclubs. Rates run from about $200 to $350; ask about package deals that might give you a discount.

Despite the rising skyline, the **Hotel Vancouver** (☎ 604-684-3131, ☎ 800-441-1414, fax 604-691-1828, 900 W Georgia St) remains a city landmark recognizable outdoors by its green copper roof and noteworthy indoors for its smooth service and refined atmosphere. Guests can enjoy the excellent fitness facility and indoor pool, along with superb restaurants (900 West and Griffin's) and three varieties of afternoon tea: traditional, Asian and West Coast. Rooms start at $229/259.

Another well-appointed place, the *Metropolitan Hotel* (☎ 604-687-1122, 800-667-2300, fax 604-689-7044, reservations@ metropolitan.com, 645 Howe St) features oversized marble bathrooms, a health club with squash courts and an indoor pool. Rates start at $365, but ask about specials.

Although the regular rates at the *Pan Pacific Hotel* (☎ 604-662-8111, 800-663-1515 in Canada, 800-937-1515 in the USA, reservations@panpacific-hotel.com, 300-999 Canada Place) rank among Canada's most expensive, starting at about $400, sometimes the hotel offers city-side room discounts for BC residents ($175) and for AAA/CAA members ($275).

The *Four Seasons Hotel* (☎ 604-689-9333, 800-268-6282, fax 604-689-3466, 791 W Georgia St) sits above the Pacific Centre shopping complex. To get to the reception area, take the escalator to the left of the Buddha statue. Rates start at $420, but specials sometimes take them down to $300 or so. Expect every luxury here.

West End (Map 3) You can't get much closer to Stanley Park than the *Buchan Hotel* (☎ 604-685-5354, 800-668-6654, fax 604-685-5367, BuchanHotel@bc.sympatico .com, 1906 Haro St), a nicely appointed older hotel with rooms for $85/95 single/double; forego a private toilet, and rooms drop to $69/75. There's no parking on the premises.

The well-loved and slightly faded *Sylvia Hotel* (☎ 604-681-9321, fax 682-3551, 1154 Gilford St) enjoys a marvelous location on English Bay close to Stanley Park. Rooms here start at $65/95; suites with a separate bedroom, kitchen, and living area with a hide-a-bed cost $145. For bayside views in summer, try to reserve up to a year ahead. Parking is $7 per day. A restaurant here serves breakfast, lunch, and dinner.

Robson St is a favorite destination for many Vancouver visitors, and the *Barclay Hotel* (☎ 604-688-8850, fax 688-2534, info@ barclay.com, 1348 Robson St) is right in the

thick of it. Small but comfortable rooms with TV, phones and baths cost the (relatively) bargain price of $75/95. A continental breakfast costs $5. The downstairs lounge serves drinks.

Many former West End apartment buildings have become suite-style properties, with kitchens and a bit of room to spread out. You'll find quite a few along Robson St between Jervis and Nicola Sts. The *Tropicana Motor Inn* (☎ 604-687-5724, 1361 Robson St) may be the best deal, with high-rise one-bedroom suites ($99 to $139), free parking and a colorful indoor pool. The rooms are a bit more up-to-date at the *Riviera Motor Inn* (☎ 604-685-1301, 888-699-5222, fax 604-685-1335, 1431 Robson St), with suites for $128 and up, and the *Greenbrier Hotel* (☎ 604-683-4558, 888-355-5888, fax 604-669-3109, 1393 Robson St), where rates start at $148.

Nicer still, the *Blue Horizon Hotel* (☎ 604-688-4461, 800-663-1333, fax 604-688-4461, bluehorizon@ibm.net, 1225 Robson St) offers an array of large rooms ($159 and up), great views, balconies and an indoor pool. Apartment-style accommodations just a bit farther off the beaten path include *Sunset Inn Travel Apartments* (☎ 604-688-2474, 800-786-1997, fax 604-669-3340, sunsetinn@ accglobal.net, 1111 Burnaby St), with rates starting at $108/118, and the *Oceanside Apartment Hotel* (☎ 604-682-5641, 877-506-2326, fax 604-687-2340, oceansidehotel@ hotmail.com, 1847 Pendrell St), with one-bedroom suites ($130) and free parking.

Close to the Robson St action and Stanley Park, *Robsonstrasse Hotel* (☎ 604-687-1674, fax 685-7808, info@robsonstrassehotel .com, 1394 Robson St) offers studio kitchenettes for $169 and suites starting at $199, including secure free parking.

The high-rise *Lord Stanley Suites on the Park* (☎ 604-688-9299, 888-767-7829, fax 604-688-9297, info@lordstanley.com, 1889 Alberni St) features comfortable quarters ($190 and up) with full kitchens and access to a small fitness facility. The north-side rooms enjoy great views, but the south-facing suites cost a bit less and boast open balconies.

The **Listel Vancouver** (☎ 604-684-8461, 800-663-5491, fax 604-684-7092, moreinfo@ listel-vancouver.com, 1300 Robson St) is known as the 'art hotel'; rooms on the 4th and 5th 'gallery floors' feature original works. All rooms are modern, large and comfortably appointed, complete with window seats. Standard rooms cost $240, while gallery-floor rooms are $300.

The recently redone **Pacific Palisades Hotel** (☎ 604-688-0461, 800-663-1815, fax 604-688-4374, 1277 Robson St) wins guests over with its offbeat attitude, from the bright retro decor to the unusual mini-bar selections (Clif Bars, Cracker Jacks and travel games). Other amenities include a late-afternoon 'soul flow' reception (an updated, healthier take on the happy hour concept) and an onsite health club and pool complete with kids' play area. Rates start at $275, with suites for $325 and up, but ask about discounts.

Gastown, Chinatown & East Vancouver (Map 5) The **Dominion Hotel** (☎ 604-681-6666, 210 Abbot St) enjoys a good location in Gastown, though you'll want to ask for a room away from the noisy ground-floor Lamplighters Pub, especially on weekends. The rooms are well worn, but the Dominion is a fair value for the price: $50/60 single/double with a shared bath, $100/110 for an en suite room, including breakfast. There's also a room with four bunk beds that rent for $20 apiece.

Hastings St on either side of Main St is a less-than-wholesome part of town (especially at night), but the **Hotel Patricia** (☎ 604-255-4301, fax 254-7154, info@budgetpathotel .bc.ca, 403 E Hastings St) breaks rank. Large, clean and well-kept, the hotel offers a good value for the money; rooms start at $49/64/89/109 single/double/triple/quad. All have their own bathrooms, and some (like Room 507) offer knock-out views of downtown. There's free parking with video surveillance for your safety.

Just a few blocks west of Commercial Dr and close enough to the city center by bus, the **Waldorf Hotel** (☎ 604-253-7141, fax 604-255-8454, reservations@waldorfhotel.com, 1489 E Hastings St) offers rooms for $60/75, a good value for the money.

Granville Island & West Side (Map 6) Located near Granville Island's famed market, the **Granville Island Hotel** (☎ 604-683-7373, 800-663-1840, fax 604-683-3061, reservations@granvilleislandhotel.com, 1253 Johnston St) also puts you within a short stroll of galleries and night spots, as well as the water taxis to downtown. No two rooms are alike. Rates start at $209/219 single/double; ask about theater packages.

The **City Centre Motel** (☎ 604-876-7166, 800-707-2489, fax 604-876-6727, ctcmotel@ intergate.bc.ca, 2111 Main St), a 10-minute walk south of Pacific Central Station, rents rooms for $75, including free parking.

Overlooking downtown from the West Side, the **Ramada Vancouver Centre** (☎ 604-872-8661, 800-663-5403, fax 604-872-2270, ramada@direct.ca, 898 W Broadway) rents rooms with balconies for about $150. At the **Holiday Inn Vancouver Centre** (☎ 604-879-0511, 800-663-9151, fax 604-872-7520, holidayi@istar.ca, 711 W Broadway), rates start at $179. Check out the views from the 5th-floor sun deck.

Greater Vancouver (Map 2) You'll find a motel strip along Kingsway, a major road that branches off Main St southeast of E 7th Ave and continues through Burnaby all the way to New Westminster. This is a good part of the city to stay in if you don't mind being out of the center; all of the hotels and motels along here have plenty of free parking, the SkyTrain runs parallel to Kingsway (although it's about three blocks away at most points), and there's also regular bus service that will take you straight into the city center. Options along here include **London Guard Motel** (☎ 604-430-4646, 888-997-7773, fax 604-430-8951, 2227 Kingsway), where rooms start at $65; **2400 Motel** (☎ 604-434-2464, 888-833-2400, fax 604-430-1045, 2400motel@bc.sympatico.ca, 2400 Kingsway), with rooms for $72 and up; and **Eldorado Motor Hotel** (☎ 604-434-1341, fax 604 -434-5176, 2330 Kingsway), where rooms start at $79/89 single/double.

PLACES TO EAT

No matter what your tastes, Vancouver offers a cornucopia of fresh food served in some amazing settings. The city is especially well known for its seafood (including sushi, which some think is better here than in Japan) and dim sum, traditional Chinese food served in small portions. For that matter, tapas – small plates of all sorts of food, meant for sharing – remain the rage here, too. Best of all, you'll find a wide range of prices; you can eat very well for a little money, though you can also spend a lot.

Downtown (Map 3)

Budget If you're on a tight budget, you can always try fixing your own meals or buying prepared foods at the supermarket. Because so many people live in central Vancouver, you won't have trouble finding a grocery store; try the large chain *Safeway* (☎ 604-683-7687, 1766 Robson St) or the local chain Capers (☎ 604-687-5299, 1675 Robson St), which features fresh and organic foods.

Shopping center food courts often offer low prices and some variety. At the large food court at Waterfront Centre (across from Canada Place), more than a dozen vendors serve meals you can eat at indoor or outdoor tables.

International and regional chain restaurants all have an outpost or two downtown. BC's best-known chain, *White Spot* (☎ 604-662-3066, 580 W Georgia St), at Seymour St, serves good hamburgers and salmon burgers (about $7 to $9) and a wide variety of breakfast favorites ($5 to $9). Cheap greasy-spoon cafés and restaurants abound along Granville St; a few stand out. *Kitto Japanese House* (☎ 604-687-6622, 833 Granville St) is sometimes described as the McDonald's of Japanese food, but the food is good, fast and inexpensive ($6 to $8).

A European-style cake shop and tearoom, *Notte's Bon Ton* (☎ 604-681-3058, 874 Granville St) can't be beat for delicious pastries and cakes. Although it sits on an unfortunate stretch of Granville, *Goulash House Restaurant & Pastry Shop* (☎ 604-688-0206, 1065 Granville St) will reward you for the walk past adult video stores and seedy hotels with delicious food at reasonable prices. Try the stuffed cabbage rolls ($9.25), beef goulash ($11) or Wiener schnitzel ($11.95).

Canadian Maple Delights (☎ 604-682-6175, 769 Hornby St) specializes in all sorts of food using maple syrup, including 75 maple-syrup gifts to go. Breakfast items cost $3.25 to $8.95; later in the day, the menu features a wide array of soups, salads, sandwiches and appetizers ($3.95 to $6.95), as well as fondue and desserts ($1.50 to $6.95).

In the Yaletown area, the *Elbow Room* (☎ 604-685-3628, 560 Davie St) is a Vancouver institution for breakfast and lunch. The waiters are supposed to be abusive, but ours was merely surly. Breakfast runs until closing (4 pm weekdays, 5 pm weekends) and costs $2.75 to $8.25. Burgers start at $6.75, with the 'You've Got to be F—-king Kidding' burger priced at $10.95. Go and have fun.

More what you expect in Yaletown, *Brix* (☎ 604-915-9463, 1138 Homer St) offers eclectic, moderately priced food in a hip setting. Lunch ($9 to $12) includes a chicken spring roll with sour cherry compote ($8.95). Dinner features a tapas menu ($5 to $17) and entrees ($15 to $24) like seared venison atop a sweet-potato hash ($18.95).

Mid-Range & Top End For a romantic Italian dinner, try *Allegro* (☎ 604-683-8485, 888 Nelson St), which features paella ($14) and other entrees in the $12 to $19 range. *The Riley* (☎ 604-684-3666, 1661 Granville St) boasts a waterfront location on False Creek and friendly servers. Lunch offerings include pizzas and pastas ($11 to $14) and sandwiches ($8 to $13). Dinner ($8 to $23) features Malaysian tropical curry ($14) and caramelized halibut ($18).

The Umberto's chain of Italian restaurants has done a lot to put Vancouver on the cuisine map. The original restaurant, *Il Giardino di Umberto* (☎ 604-669-2422, 1382 Hornby St) still offers some of the city's best Tuscan cooking, updated with Canadian delicacies such as berries and wild game, all served in a lovely old house in the heart of downtown. Dinner items average $30, ranging from pasta (around $15) to the certified Angus beef Florentine ($70 for two). Lunch dishes run $11 to $16.

One of the best hotel restaurants in town, *Diva at the Met* (☎ 604-602-7788, 645 Howe St), in the Metropolitan Hotel, features an airy feel and multi-tiered seating. Lunch includes gourmet pizzas ($11 to $13) and a barbecued chicken club sandwich with red pepper and roasted garlic mayonnaise ($11.50). Dinner ranges from $16 to $34, with such offerings as a Moroccan spiced pork loin chop and oven-dried tomato couscous ($18.50) or barbecued salmon with caper berry butter sauce ($20.50).

The Pan Pacific's *Five Sails Restaurant* (☎ 604-662-8111, 300-999 Canada Place) is another memorable place to lighten your wallet. Dinner entrees ($28 to $36) include salmon in a potato crust with Atlantic lobster garnish ($28.50) and Fraser Valley duckling in Marsala sauce ($31.50). For lunch, consider the hotel's *Café Pacifico*, with mountain views and meals that cost $11 to $18.

Set on False Creek, *C* (☎ 604-681-1164, 1600 Howe St) has become the hottest new seafood restaurant in town. Its West Coast Dim Sum Business Lunch costs $18.50 per person (minimum two people); other midday selections include Dungeness crab and lemon myrtle cakes ($18). At dinner, look for more dim sum and main dishes ($24 to $39) like grilled octopus and bacon-wrapped scallops ($29), as well as an eight-course tasting menu ($90).

900 West (☎ 604-669-9378, 900 W Georgia St), in the Hotel Vancouver, features fresh local seafood and a top-notch wine list with about 75 varieties available by the glass. Lunch dishes (served weekdays) run $15 to $18; dinner main dishes cost $26 to $36, including Peace River caribou loin with huckleberry jus ($32). The hotel's less-formal restaurant, *Griffins*, serves a good, upscale breakfast. Try the Captain Vancouver eggs Benedict on toasted crumpets with

smoked salmon, chives and hollandaise sauce ($13.25).

Chartwell (☎ 604-689-9333, 791 West Georgia St), in the Four Seasons Hotel, is an expensive treat. Plates range from $20 for butternut squash risotto to $35 for Novia Scotia lobster. After ordering an entree, plus appetizers ($8 to $12) and an obligatory glass of wine, you'll be richer in calories than dollars. Lunch is a little less pricey ($17 to $21).

West End (Map 3)

Budget *Pezzo* (☎ 604-669-9300, 1100 Robson St) is a lively place for gourmet pizza by the slice ($3.50) or lasagna ($7.95). For Southeast Asian fare, head up the stairs to *Thai House Restaurant* (☎ 604-683-3383, 1116 Robson St), where most dishes average $14 and the lunch special is $7. Part of a popular local chain, *Bread Garden Bakery & Café* (☎ 604-688-3213, 812 Bute St), just around the corner off Robson St, offers lunchtime specials for about $5; you can also grab a quick breakfast here.

Noodle King Café (☎ 604-683-2913, 1429 Robson St) serves noodle and curry dishes ($6 to $9) at counter seats where you can watch the world go by. *Ichibankan* (☎ 604-682-6262, 770 Thurlow St) contains one of the best sushi bars in Vancouver, with items for $1.95 to $4.45; noodle dishes cost $5 to $7.

At breakfast, *De Dutch Pannekoek House* (☎ 604-687-7065, 1725 Robson St) will fill you up with Dutch pancakes. The dozen varieties range from a pancake topped with Dutch syrup ($6.60) to the 'Farmer's' version topped with ham, bacon, bratwurst, eggs, hash browns and (burp) hollandaise sauce ($12).

The nightly lines outside attest to the popularity of *Stepho's Souvlakia* (☎ 604-683-2555, 1124 Davie St), which offers great Greek casseroles and meat platters ($7 to $10). In the same neighborhood, *Joe's Grill* (☎ 604-682-3683, 1031 Davie St) is a local favorite for good, cheap food, including a $4 breakfast and burgers ($5 to $10). You can't have breakfast at *Tiffany* (☎ 604-685-9607, 1103 Davie St), but you can have weekend brunch for $4 to $10. At night, try the pastas and pizzas ($6 to $13).

Hamburger Mary's (☎ 604-687-1293, 1202 Davie St) stays open nearly 'round the clock, but it's at its best on a warm night, when you can sit outside and watch life go by at the Davie-Bute intersection. Look for a good variety of burgers, pasta dishes and salads in the $7 to $10 range. Breakfasts cost $6 to $8.

Krishna Pure Vegetarian Restaurant (☎ 604-688-9400, 1726 Davie St) offers one of the city's best buys: a 35-item all-you-can-eat buffet for $6.95 at lunch and $8.95 at dinner.

Mid-Range *Inlets* (☎ 604-688-4461, 1225 Robson St), at the Blue Horizon Hotel, features lots of outdoor seating and reasonable prices at breakfast ($5 to $9), lunch ($5 to $9) and dinner ($11 to $16). Cozy, casual and cheap, *Musashi Japanese Restaurant* (☎ 604-687-0634, 780 Denman St), between Robson and Alberni Sts, serves noodle dishes ($6 to $8), sushi plates ($6 to $12) and combination dinners ($14 to $16).

Forget the diet and let your willpower go for a walk at *Death by Chocolate* (☎ 604-899-2462, 1001 Denman St). Desserts start at $7; the signature dish, featuring a white chocolate tower, costs a steep $10.95. Feeling especially decadent? Try 'A Multitude of Sins' ($15).

A neighborhood favorite, the *Brass Monkey* (☎ 604-685-7626, 1072 Denman St) serves rock-crab ravioli ($9.75) and steamed Prince Edward Island mussels ($9). At the *Marquee Grill* (☎ 604-689-1181, 911 Denman St), a casually upscale spot in a converted movie theater, dinner features live music, plus a wide array of tapas ($5 to $11) and main dishes ($18 to $25). Lunch runs $7 to $11.

With its English Bay setting, *The Boathouse* (☎ 604-669-7375, 1795 Beach Ave) attracts both visitors and local business people. The bistro downstairs offers such dishes as halibut fish and chips ($12.99). At the slightly more formal dining room upstairs, fresh fish is available nightly ($16 to $19).

One of the West End's most intriguing new restaurants, *Balthazar* (☎ 604-689-8822, 1215 Bidwell St) contains plenty of hidden corners and alcoves, nice for conversation and romance. The Mediterranean and Moroccan menu includes tapas plates ($5 to $12) and entrees ($12 to $24).

The Japanese restaurant **Kisha Poppo** (☎ 604-681-0488, 1143 Davie St) specializes in all-you-can-eat dining. The lunch buffet ($11 weekdays, $12 weekends) has 30 items; for dinner ($18), there are 40 choices.

Top End For steaks, oysters, grilled fish and other staples of traditional Northwest cooking, go to *Joe Fortes* (☎ 604-669-1940, 777 Thurlow St), where most entrees, such as the swordfish or the crusted tuna, cost $20 to $25. The locals recommend *Cafe il Nido* (☎ 604-685-6436, 780 Thurlow St), tucked into a courtyard behind Manhattan Books & Magazines on Robson St, for tempting pasta dishes at lunch ($12 to $16) and dinner ($15 to $32).

O'Doul's (☎ 604-661-1400, 1300 Robson St), in the Listel Vancouver, fuses the cuisine of the Pacific Northwest and the American Deep South in such dishes as jambalaya with saffron risotto ($24). Breakfasts ($8 to $9) and lunches ($6 to $14) are more moderately priced. Live jazz accompanies the meals on Friday and Saturday night.

At *Café de Paris* (☎ 604-687-1418, 751 Denman St), an intimate French restaurant known for its peppercorn steak and pomme frites, lunch runs $10 to $18, while dinner entrees cost $18 to $25.

Raincity Grill (☎ 604-685-7337, 1193 Denman St), one of the West End's best-known and most popular restaurants, offers such choices as spaghetti and lamb meatballs and a low-calorie, low-fat 'spa fish' selection at lunch ($10 to $18). Dinner entrees ($14 to $34) include treats like Dungeness crab cakes with black-bean-chorizo-roasted-fennel hash and a lemongrass emulsion ($27).

Pacific Northwest dining doesn't get much more authentic than *Liliget Feast House* (☎ 604-681-7044, 1724 Davie St). The Native Indian cuisine and unique setting make this a real cultural experience, with dishes like venison steak ($22), arctic caribou tenderloin ($30) or one of the 'feast' dishes for two ($49).

Stanley Park (Map 4)

Stanley Park offers three restaurant choices, all of which tend to be pricey but worth the money, considering the setting and scenery. The *Prospect Point Cafe* (☎ 604-669-2737, *2099 Beach Ave)* features good views of the Lions Gate Bridge and Burrard Inlet, plus salmon (the specialty) in abundance; salmon steak is $17, and a salmon platter goes for $25. The café also serves Sunday brunch (11 am to 4 pm). The *Teahouse Restaurant* (☎ 604-669-3281, *7501 Stanley Park Dr)*, at Ferguson Point, enjoys wonderful views of English Bay and the North Shore. The menu includes seafood, lamb and duck; lunches run $12 to $18, and dinner entrees cost $17 to $28. Best of the lot, *The Fish House in Stanley Park* (☎ 604-681-7275, *8901 Stanley Park Dr)* charges $10 to $16 for entrees at lunch, $16 to $25 at dinner. People rave about the shiitake mushroom–dusted Chilean sea bass (for $22.95). During the early-bird special (5 to 6 pm Sunday to Thursday), you pay full price for one entree and get $15 off a second main dish.

Gastown (Map 5)

Italian food is really big in Gastown. *Rossini's Pasta Palazzo* (☎ 604-408-1300, *162 Water St)* serves 20 varieties of pasta ($11 to $12), along with steaks ($17 to $22) and weekday lunch specials ($7 to $8). The always-popular, usually crowded *Old Spaghetti Factory* (☎ 604-684-1288, *53 Water St)* offers soup-and-sandwich combos ($7.25), spaghetti ($8 to $10) and other main dishes ($11 to $14). The atmosphere is a bit more serene (though you needn't eat in silence) at *Brother's Restaurant* (☎ 604-683-9124, *1 Water St)*. Specialties include pasta ($9 to $14) and three cuts of prime rib ($16 to $25).

Raintree at the Landing (☎ 604-688-5570, *375 Water St)* seems like two restaurants in one: a cool bistro overlooking

Water St and a more upscale dining room with views of Burrard Inlet and the North Shore. Lunches cost $5 to $13; dinners ($16 to $25) include West Coast cioppino with house-grilled potato bread ($18.25). Also notable for fine dining, the *Water Street Café* (☎ 604-689-2832, *300 Water St)*, housed in one of the few buildings to escape the Great Fire of 1886, offers some outdoor seating right in the center of Gastown. Lunch costs $12 to $15, and dinners run $18 to $25.

A bit farther off the beaten path, *Jewel of India* (☎ 604-687-5665, *52 Alexander St)* charges $10 to $14 for main courses, including tandoori dishes, the house specialty (around $11). Lunch specials cost $7. Come for the live sitar music on Friday and Saturday evening. Adorned with some great original art, *Incendio* (☎ 604-688-8694, *103 Columbia St)* produces creative pizzas ($8 to $22) and excellent pasta ($9 to $12).

On the outskirts of Gastown, *The Only Seafood Restaurant* (☎ 604-681-6546, *20 E Hastings St)* opened its doors in 1912, making it one of the city's oldest restaurants. The rundown neighborhood makes it a pretty depressing place these days, but many locals still stop by for the clam chowder with bread ($3.25); salmon, cod and halibut cost $8 to $11.

Chinatown (Map 5)

Along Keefer St, the heart of Chinatown, you'll find lots of restaurants, including *The Gain Wah* (☎ 604-684-1740, *218 Keefer St)*, with 16 different varieties of *congee* (a rice or noodle soup loaded with goodies) starting at $3. Local favorite *Hon's Wun-tun House* operates several locations around town, with a Chinatown base at 108-268 Keefer St (☎ 604-688-0871). Expect a huge selection of noodle dishes for around $5.

Kam's Garden Restaurant (☎ 604-669-5488, *509 Main St)* specializes in wonton and barbecue dishes. Try a bowl of wonton soup ($4) or the dinner-for-one combination ($8). The *Buddhist Vegetarian Restaurant* (☎ 604-683-8816, *137 E Pender St)* serves chow mein ($8) and deluxe vegetarian dishes ($12). *New Town Bakery &*

Restaurant (☎ 604-681-1828, 158 E Pender St) features specials ($3 to $5) and a buffet lunch ($7) or dinner ($8); children eat for 65¢ per year of the child's age.

For Cambodian cuisine, go to *Phnom Penh* (☎ 604-682-5777, 244 East Georgia St), just off Main St, where most dishes average about $12.

Two excellent Asian restaurants outside Chinatown are worth noting. The *Pink Pearl* (☎ 604-253-4316, 1132 E Hastings St), a bit farther east, offers some of the best dim sum in town; come before 3 pm for the small plates. Later in the day, the menu shifts to Cantonese specialties. *Sun Sui Wah* (☎ 604-872-8822, 3888 Main St) is another Cantonese standout, with main dishes for $10 to $35.

East Vancouver (Map 5)

A hip and child-friendly eatery *Café Deux Soleil* (☎ 604-254-1195, 2096 Commercial Dr) offers 'kid food' selections ($2.50) and a play area on the small stage where acoustic musicians entertain on the weekend. Breakfasts run $4 to $7; after 5 pm, the night menu features such fare as a black bean roll-up ($7.25) and pesto burger ($6.75). Note that there's another restaurant a few blocks away called *Café du Soleil* (☎ 604-254-1145, 1392 Commercial St). The two share common origins and similar menus but are no longer related.

Clove Café & Record Bar (☎ 604-255-5550, 2054 Commercial Dr) is definitely one of Vancouver's most interesting Indian restaurants. Check out the vintage vinyl for sale while waiting for your meal, which includes mostly vegetarian dishes ($3 to $12 at lunch and dinner, $5 to $8 for Sunday brunch). It's closed Monday.

Old Europe Restaurant (☎ 604-255-9424, 1608 Commercial Dr) seems like a café you might find down a side street in Budapest. Choices include goulash and borscht ($4.95), veal stew with dumplings ($8.50) and Wiener schnitzel ($9.95).

A 21st-century hangout for beatniks, *Bukowski's* (☎ 604-253-4770, 1447 Commercial Dr) features a varied menu ($8 to $15), plus live jazz or blues Monday and Thursday night and spoken-word performances on Tuesday. *WaaZuBee Café* (☎ 604-253-5299, 1622 Commercial Dr) is another hip spot, serving great coffee and food ($8 to $12).

El Cocal (☎ 604-255-4580, 1037 Commercial Dr) specializes in Salvadoran and Brazilian food, with more familiar Mexican dishes thrown in for good measure. Selections include *feijoada* (pork stew) and *mukeka de peixe* (fish stew) for around $11. El Cocal also hosts an open-mic night for prose writers the second Monday of every month.

Juicy Lucy's Good Eats (☎ 604-254-6101, 1420 Commercial Dr), mainly a juice bar, offers healthy veggie and fruit concoctions (most about $4), plus a limited menu of soups, sandwiches, and 'rollies' (tortilla wraps). *Tony's Neighbourhood Deli & Café* (☎ 604-253-7422, 1046 Commercial Dr), open for lunch daily, charges about $6 for awesome panini sandwiches.

A few blocks away from the bustle, *Nick's Spaghetti House* (☎ 604-254-5633, 631 Commercial Dr) is Vancouver's classic Italian joint, serving large portions of old favorites like spaghetti and meat balls ($12), lasagna ($13) and rack of ribs served with spaghetti ($20).

Head north to the waterfront for a visit to the *Cannery Seafood Restaurant* (☎ 604-254-9606, 2205 Commissioner St), known for its terrific views and fresh fish (about 14 choices averaging $20). The extensive wine list may take you most of the evening to read.

Granville Island (Map 6)

For the best selection of only-in-Vancouver picnic provisions, head to the *Granville Island Public Market*, where you can buy all the appropriate fixings for a lunch in the great outdoors.

Among the sit-down restaurants, *Bridges* (☎ 604-687-4400, 1696 Duranleau St) remains the longtime favorite here, with a large outdoor deck and great views. Enjoy pub fare ($8 to $18) on the patio overlooking False Creek, or more serious Northwest cuisine in the upstairs dining room, where you can choose between à la carte entrees ($23 to $35) and the three-course fixed-price menu ($45).

By day, *Cat's Meow* (☎ *604-647-2287, 1540 Old Bridge St)* is a good spot for moderately priced lunches (fajitas and pizzas run $10 to $15) and weekend brunches ($4 to $10; design-your-own omelets cost $8.50). By night, it's a happening pub with frequent live music.

The Creek (☎ *604-685-7070, 1253 Johnston St)*, at the Granville Island Hotel, specializes in pizza (about $12) at lunch. Dinner selections ($16 to $26) include chipotle-rubbed rotisserie chicken ($18.95) and Szechwan poppy-seed rare ahi tuna ($22.95).

West Side (Map 6)

One of Vancouver's most interesting fine-dining areas, the Broadway & South Granville neighborhood (between Burrard and Main Sts on Broadway and 4th and 15th Aves on S Granville St) includes many creative upstarts and plenty of proven favorites. A New Orleans–style bistro, *Ouisi* (☎ *604-732-7550, 3014 S Granville St)* serves entrees like spicy pecan catfish crusted with orange chipotle cream ($14). Live jazz acts play several times a week. Ouisi offers lunch (mostly under $10) and dinner ($11 to $16) daily, as well as brunch on Saturday and Sunday.

Considered the high-water mark of Indian cuisine in Vancouver, *Vij's* (☎ *604-736-6664, 1480 W 11th Ave)* offers innovative food at reasonable prices. *Star Anise* (☎ *604-737-1485, 1485 W 12th Ave)* serves Pacific Rim cuisine for $20 to $32 at dinner, with some pre-theater specials.

Szechuan Chongqing Seafood Restaurant (☎ *604-734-2668, 1668 W Broadway)*, a longtime favorite, offers a staggering array of choices (nearly 200 dishes), many featuring fresh seafood, priced mainly $15 to $20. Delivery is available.

All the kitchen and dining staff at *Picasso* (☎ *604-732-3290, 1626 W Broadway)* work for the Option Youth Society, a nonprofit group that helps homeless teens move from street life to self-sufficiency. Eat here to benefit a good cause, but also to sample some tasty and inexpensive food. Breakfast (served 9:30 to 11 am weekdays) costs $5.95 to $7.25, while weekend brunch items run $4.95 to $7.95. Lunch (11 am to 3 pm weekdays) includes burgers ($6.95) and crab cakes ($7.95).

The tiny restaurant *Bin 942* (☎ *604-734-9421, 1521 W Broadway)* specializes in small plates and 'tapatisers' (mostly $9 to $10). Selections may include buffalo rib-eye steaks, sashimi-style ahi tuna and portobello mushroom cutlets. Pair the food with a selection or two from the wine list or 'hip hops' beer menu.

Grand King Seafood Restaurant (☎ *604-876-7855, 705 W Broadway)* features outstanding dim sum (about $4 per selection), sushi (starting at $1.50) and an array of Chinese entrees ($6 to $13 at lunch, $12 to $22 at dinner). *Tojo's* (☎ *604-872-8050, 777 West Broadway)*, on the 2nd floor, serves top-notch sushi and inventive, unusual Japanese entrees (around $18). A few tables enjoy great city views.

Rasputin (☎ *604-879-6675, 457 W Broadway)* brings fine Russian dining to Vancouver with dishes like cabbage rolls ($14), chicken Kiev ($19), and the evocatively named Rasputin's Feast ($25). *Afghan Horsemen* (☎ *604-873-5923, 445 W Broadway)* has been in business since 1974, which makes it one of the old-timers in this part of town. You can perch at either a standard table or join the communal seating on the floor. Main dishes cost $11 to $17.

Kitsilano (Map 7)

To purchase picnic fixings or other grocery items, stop in at *Safeway* (☎ *604-737-4875, 2315 W 4th Ave)* or at *Capers* (☎ *604-739-6676, 2285 W 4th Ave)*.

The neighborhood's hippie past lives on at the 24-hour *Naam* (☎ *604-738-7151, 2724 W 4th Ave)*, a funky restaurant serving stir-fries ($9), veggie burger platters ($8.50) and pizza ($10) and featuring live music every evening. Always packed, *Sophie's Cosmic Cafe* (☎ *604-732-6810, 2095 W 4th Ave)* is another Kitsilano classic, with breakfasts ($4 to $8) and offbeat dishes like 7-Up chicken kebabs ($7.75) and a BC oyster burger ($7.95). Try one of the delightful homemade desserts. An all-night option, the *Vine Yard Restaurant* (☎ 604-733-2420, 2296 W 4th Ave) offers breakfast around the clock, but you'll find eight different specials ($4 to $5) between 5 and 11 am.

The *Surat Sweet Restaurant* (☎ 604-733-7363, 1938 W 4th Ave) features vegetarian-only Gujarati Indian cooking; most dishes cost about $6. For spicy Chinese, try *Won More Szechuan Cuisine* (☎ 604-737-2889, 1944 W 4th Ave), which offers a $6 lunch special and other dishes for about $8.

Romio's Greek Taverna (☎ 604-736-2118, 2272 W 4th Ave) serves Mediterranean fare ($9 to $17) in an airy atmosphere. A good value, *Topanga Cafe* (☎ 604-733-3713, 2904 W 4th Ave) offers Californian-Mexican meals for $9 to $15.

Nyala Restaurant (☎ 604-731-7899, 2930 W 4th Ave) serves richly spiced Ethiopian food that is eaten without utensils – you use *injera* (flatbread) instead. Prices range from $9 for vegetarian dishes to $13 for most meat dishes; an all-you-can-eat vegetarian bonanza, offered Sunday and Wednesday, costs $10.95. The service is extraordinarily friendly.

Montri's Thai Restaurant (☎ 604-738-9888, 3629 Broadway) is widely considered the best Thai place in Vancouver, with superb pad Thai. Main dishes cost about $10 to $12.

One of the most highly regarded restaurants in Canada, *Lumiere* (☎ 604-739-8185, 2551 W Broadway) prepares a kind of French-fusion cooking that brings in the best of world cuisine and then drapes it in wonderful sauces. Menus vary seasonally, but there are usually several eight-course tasting menus for $55 to $75 (add $40 for wine).

Just a few doors down, *Boleto/Ecco il Pane* (☎ 604-739-1314, 2563 W Broadway) features a new six-course tasting menu each week for about $45. Main dishes ($16 to $19) include 'free-form lasagna' with asparagus and crab meat ($17.95); at lunch, get a panini sandwich ($9).

Greater Vancouver (Map 2)

Don't overlook *Seasons in the Park* (☎ 604-874-8008) and its lovely setting amid the gardens of Queen Elizabeth Park. A fine special-occasion choice, it offers lunch and weekend brunch ($9.50 to $22), as well as dinner ($14 to $24), which includes seafood, lamb and duck.

Spread out along Main St from E 48th to E 51st Aves, the Punjabi Market area is a great place to go for Indian food. *Zeenaz Restaurant* (☎ 604-324-9344, 6460 Main St) offers an all-you-can-eat buffet ($8 vegetarian, $10 with meat). It's closed Tuesday. Not to be outdone, the *All India Sweets & Restaurant* (☎ 604-327-0891, 6505 Main St) sets out a 45-item all-you-can-eat vegetarian buffet for $6.

ENTERTAINMENT

The best source of information on the arts and nightlife is *The Georgia Straight*, published every Thursday. *The West Ender* offers good general coverage, too, while *Xtra West* focuses on the gay scene. All are free and you can pick them up around town. For information about raves and other underground happenings, inquire at the music stores on Hastings and Seymour Sts.

Tickets for most events are available from TicketMaster (☎ 604-280-3311 for the performing arts, 280-4444 for concerts, 280-4400 for sports); many can also be ordered online at www.ticketmaster.ca. For details on upcoming performances and exhibitions, call the Arts Hotline (☎ 604-684-2787) or see the Alliance for Arts and Culture's Web site at www.allianceforarts.com.

Bars & Clubs

Downtown (Map 3) Some of the big downtown clubs also double as live-music venues for a wide array of touring acts. *Richard's on Richards* (☎ 604-687-6794, 1036 Richards St), often dubbed 'Dick's on Dicks,' has been a top dance and live-music club for many years. Other standbys include the *Roxy* (☎ 604-684-7699, 932 Granville St), with mainstream rock, and the *Starfish Room* (☎ 604-682-4171, 1055 Homer St).

The **Vogue Theatre** (☎ 604-331-7900, 918 Granville St), a converted cinema, also presents live music, as does **The Commodore** (☎ 604-739-4550, 868 Granville St), with its big bouncy dance floor. A hot spot for dancing in Yaletown, **Wett Bar** (☎ 604-662-7707, 1320 Richards St) features occasional live music showcases.

Au Bar (☎ 604-648-2227, 674 Seymour St) and **Voda** (☎ 604-684-3003, 433 Robson St), in the Westin Grand Hotel, are two of the newer and most chic nightclubs, both with frequent long lines and occasional celebrity sightings. Voda's street-side patio swarms with beautiful people on warm evenings. The inside of **Babalu** (☎ 604-605-4343, 654 Nelson St), the city's top Latin venue, looks like a salsa movie come to life. Neighboring **Fred's Uptown Tavern** (☎ 604-605-4350, 1006 Granville St) is a yuppie haunt. The clothes are casual, and so is the atmosphere.

The Yale (☎ 604-681-9253, 1300 Granville St) is one of the best blues bars in the city, if not the country. The Hotel Georgia houses both the **Chameleon Urban Lounge** (☎ 604-669-0806, 801 West Georgia St), which features a mix of jazz, trip hop and jungle music; and the **Georgia St Bar & Grill** (☎ 604-602-0994), where local jazz talent takes the stage.

At **Luv-A-Fair** (☎ 604-685-3288, 1275 Seymour St), you can groove to alternative and industrial dance music spun by DJs. **The Gate** (☎ 604-608-4283, 1176 Granville St) presents a mixture of swing, salsa and comedy. The **Piccadilly Pub** (☎ 604-682-3221, 620 W Pender St) features local rock and blues bands with a bit of house or acid jazz midweek. The **Railway Club** (☎ 604-681-1625, 579 Dunsmuir St) offers a variety of music seven nights a week and good original jazz on Saturday afternoon. **The Rage** (☎ 604-685-5585, 750 Pacific Blvd S), near BC Place, presents cutting-edge and Top 40 music and an occasional live band.

Gastown (Map 5) The **Purple Onion** (☎ 604-602-9442, 15 Water St) offers live jazz and blues in one room and DJ dance music in the other. **Lamplighter's Pub** (☎ 604-681-

6666, 210 Abbott St), in the Dominion Hotel, presents Top 40 bands and a Celtic night on Tuesday. **Sonar** (☎ 604-683-6695, 66 Water St) features a mixture of progressive house, soul, hip-hop, R&B, reggae and electronica. At **The Irish Heather** (☎ 604-688-9779, 217 Carrall St), you can sample the best Guinness in town, plus good food and occasional live music. Although the **Alibi Room** (☎ 604-623-3383, 157 Alexander St) is tucked well away from the main Gastown scene, it's well known among Vancouver's most hip club-goers, including many from the city's film industry. Expect good food in the upstairs dining room and techno music in the downstairs lounge. Screenplay readings take place the last Sunday of each month.

Elsewhere in Vancouver **Big Bam Boo** (Map 6; ☎ 604-733-2220, 1236 W Broadway), in the Broadway/South Granville area, presents live bands and Top 40 tunes. It's probably the most popular dance venue outside downtown, so go early to avoid the lines. The **Backstage Lounge** (Map 6; ☎ 604-687-1354, 1585 Johnston St), on Granville Island, features live music and a great selection of single-malt Scotches. Have a pint and a game of darts at **Darby's Pub** (Map 7; ☎ 604-731-0617, 2001 Macdonald St), at W 4th Ave in Kitsilano, where you can also hear live music Friday to Sunday. For good local jazz, try the **Cellar Jazz Café** (Map 7; ☎ 604-738-1959, 3611 W Broadway), in Kitsilano, or the **Hot Jazz Club** (Map 6; ☎ 604-873-4131, 2120 Main St), on the West Side.

Brewpubs

Play pool or admire the North Shore views at the **Steamworks Brewing Co** (Map 5; ☎ 604-689-2739, 375 Water St), in Gastown. Note that the beer is much better than the cuisine (a common brew-pub problem). **Granville Island Brewery** (Map 6; ☎ 604-687-2739, 1441 Cartwright St) offers tours and tastings 10 am to 4 pm daily.

Cinemas

Movie tickets typically cost about $9, but most theaters advertise discounted shows all day on Tuesday and until late afternoon on other days. Major first-run multiplex theaters include the downtown *Granville Cineplex Odeon* (Map 3; ☎ 604-684-4000, 855 Granville St); Alliance Atlantis' *Fifth Avenue Cinemas* (Map 7; ☎ 604-734-7469, 2110 Burrard St), in Kitsilano; and the *Cinemark Tinseltown* (Map 5; ☎ 604-806-0799, 88 W Pender St), in the Gastown area. The *Denman Place Discount Cinema* (Map 3; ☎ 604-663-2201, 1737 Comox St), on the West End, shows three films for $3 on Tuesday. The schedule at *Pacific Cinémathèque* (Map 3; ☎ 604-688-3456, 1131 Howe St) is so varied that it's best to think of it as an ongoing film festival.

Classical Music & Dance

The *Vancouver Symphony Orchestra* (☎ 604-876-3434 for information and tickets), the third-largest in Canada, performs more than 100 concerts annually at the Orpheum Theatre (Map 3), on Granville St at Smithe St. *Ballet British Columbia* (☎ 604-732-5003; 604-280-3311 for tickets), Vancouver's top dance troupe, takes the stage at the Queen Elizabeth Theatre (see Theater, later in this section). The season runs from October to May. *Vancouver Opera* (☎ 604-683-0222 or 280-3311 for tickets) also stages four annual productions at the Queen Elizabeth Theatre.

Comedy

Stand-up comics from around the city and North America appear at *Yuk Yuk's* (Map 3; ☎ 604-687-5233, 750 Pacific Blvd S). For laughs and competitive improvisational acting, you can't beat *TheatreSports League* (☎ 604-738-7013 or 687-1644 for tickets). These talented comics perform at the New Revue Stage (Map 6), 1585 Johnston St on Granville Island, across from the Arts Club Theatre's main stage. There are usually two shows Friday and Saturday: the classic improv set at 8 pm and a more ribald show at 11:45 pm.

Gay & Lesbian Venues

Vancouver's large gay population means there's a varied and ever-evolving club scene; for the latest, see the listings in *Xtra! West*. Downtown, *The Royal Pub* (Map 3; ☎ 604-685-5335, 1025 Granville St), in the Royal Hotel, is one of the top places to dance and dish, with occasional live music and a Tuesday-night bingo series that has raised more than $50,000 for local gay charities. Get there by 7:30 pm for a seat. Another popular spot, the *Dufferin Hotel* (Map 3; ☎ 604-683-4251, 900 Seymour St) hosts strip shows and drag karaoke.

Lava Lounge (Map 3; ☎ 604-605-6136, 1180 Granville St), open Wednesday through Sunday, features the ElectroLush Lounge on Thursday, with DJs, go-go dancers and a piano bar on other evenings. *Numbers* (Map 3; ☎ 604-685-4077, 1042 Davie St) is a multi-level men's cruise bar. *Odyssey* (Map 3; ☎ 604-689-5256, 1251 Howe St) has earned a reputation as the wildest gay dance club, with go-go boys and shower-room viewing.

On the far West End, *Denman Station Cabaret* (Map 3; ☎ 604-669-3448, 860 Denman St) is a lot of fun, with dancing, darts, drag acts and theme parties. It's mostly a men's scene, but women meet here on Friday.

Gastown's *Heritage House Hotel* (Map 5; ☎ 604-685-7777, 455 Abbott St) offers a variety of gay entertainment under one roof. Men congregate after work for drinks at Charlie's Lounge, although women take over Saturday for 'Forty and Fabulous.' Chuck's Pub features 'Guys in Disguise' on Friday and leather night on Saturday. Traditionally a women's venue, the Lotus Club has lately gone mixed.

Theater

All kinds of theater, from mainstream to fringe, are flourishing in Vancouver. At the Vancouver Playhouse, part of the Queen Elizabeth Theatre complex, the *Vancouver Playhouse Theatre Company* (☎ 604-873-3311) presents a six-play season from September to May. The Queen Elizabeth Theatre (Map 3), 600 Hamilton St, is itself a major venue for touring Broadway shows and other major productions.

The *Arts Club Theatre* (Map 5; ☎ 604-687-1644), another major organization,

Beach Blanket Bard

No one wants to be indoors on fine Vancouver summer evenings, so two theater groups present plays in the city's parks. The annual *Bard on the Beach* festival takes place from mid-June through September under an open tent at Vanier Park. Special events during the season typically include a salmon barbecue followed by Symphony of Fire pyrotechnics (see Special Events, earlier in the chapter) and a performance by the Vancouver Symphony Orchestra. For ticket information, call ☎ 604-739-0559 or visit the Web site www.bardonthebeach.org.

Theatre Under the Stars also stages several Broadway musicals at Stanley Park's Malkin Bowl from mid-July to mid-August each year. For tickets, call ☎ 604-687-0174 or see www.tuts.bc.ca.

performs on Granville Island and at the Stanley Theatre (Map 3), 2750 Granville Street. Michael J Fox and many other Canadian actors got their starts on an Arts Club stage. The *Firehall Arts Centre (Map 5; ☎ 604-689-0926, 280 E Cordova St)* puts on plays by Canadian and foreign playwrights, as well as dance presentations.

SPECTATOR SPORTS

From September through April, the Vancouver Canucks (☎ 604-899-4625) of the National Hockey League play at GM Place (Map 3), also the home of the Vancouver Grizzlies (☎ 604-899-4667) of the National Basketball Association. The BC Lions (☎ 604-589-7627), Vancouver's Canadian Football League team, play in BC Place Stadium (Map 3) from July to September. The Vancouver Canadians (☎ 604-872-5232), a single-A farm team for Major League Baseball's Oakland As, play a short-season (June through August) at Nat Bailey Stadium (Map 2), 4601 Ontario St, next to Queen Elizabeth Park. The Vancouver 86ers, a professional soccer team, play May through August at Swanguard Stadium (Map 2), at

the intersection of Boundary Rd and Kingsway in Burnaby. Tickets for the Grizzlies, Lions, Canucks and 86ers are available through TicketMaster (☎ 604-280-4400).

SHOPPING

Vancouver's central district contains some of the city's most dynamic shopping areas. On Robson St, the busiest shopping street in Vancouver, you can buy everything from couture to condoms, from Italian newspapers to fresh crab; you'll find lots of souvenir and gift shops here as well. Or you can buy nothing at all and simply enjoy the lively street scene.

The other major downtown shopping destination is Pacific Centre, a three-block-long underground shopping arcade that runs from Robson to Pender Sts between Granville and Howe Sts. Most of the stores are national and international chains, including The Bay and Eatons, the anchor store for the Pacific Centre.

Music fans will want to check out the shops on Seymour St north of Dunsmuir. Yaletown is the place to head for home furnishings and interior decorating. The old warehouse-district-gone-lofts is loaded with stylish design shops.

Gastown is a good place to look for First Nations art. Hill's Indian Crafts (Map 5; ☎ 604-685-4249), 165 Water St, features a good selection of carvings, prints, masks and cozy Cowichan sweaters. The Inuit Gallery of Vancouver (Map 5; ☎ 604-688-7323), 345 Water St, sells Inuit sculptures, drawings and tapestries and Northwest Coast Native Indian masks, carvings and jewelry. Should you be looking for vintage clothing, hemp products or cigars, you'll also find them in Gastown.

While in the Gastown-Chinatown area, check out the new International Village complex (Map 5), 88 W Pender St; it features everything from hip clothing stores to a TNT Supermarket, best described as a traditional Chinese market on steroids.

After Robson St, you won't find a more fun place to shop in Vancouver than Granville Island. The stalls at the warehouse-like public market (Map 6; ☎ 604-666-5784) overflow with fresh fish, vegetables, meats, cheeses, fresh-baked goods and everything else you might need to put together a meal. Merchants also sell fancy jams, syrups and other preserved foods that make good gifts; the fishmongers can pack fish for air shipment. Granville Island also is a good spot to shop for outdoor gear, books, and arts and crafts; Circle Craft (Map 6; ☎ 604-669-8021), 1666 Johnston St, sells lovely wearable art, pottery, jewelry and more.

Along W Broadway (one of the best spots in the country to go for outdoor equipment and clothing), you'll find Mountain Equipment Co-op (Map 6; ☎ 604-872-7858), 130 W Broadway, the biggest and best-known store in the area. You have to become a MEC member to buy in the store; lifetime memberships cost $5 and are available onsite. Shopping at MEC theoretically entitles you to a share in any future company surpluses, but such dividends are few and far between. Still, MEC is a hip, ecologically sensitive company that's worth checking out if you're in the market for outdoor gear.

True to its counterculture past, Kitsilano is Vancouver's best neighborhood for socially conscious shopping. The shop Craftworks (Map 7; ☎ 604-736-2113), 2112 W 4th Ave, sells handmade items created by people with disabilities. Ten Thousand Villages (Map 7; ☎ 604-730-6831), 2150 W 4th Ave, offers 'fairly traded' handicrafts from around the world; you'll find hammocks, drums, clothing and more. Hope Unlimited (Map 7; ☎ 604-732-4438), 2206 W 4th Ave, donates 10% of its profits to such charities as the YWCA, Children International and AIDS Vancouver. Its stock, 85% of which is Canadian-made, features home accessories and jewelry.

See the Burnaby section under Around Vancouver, later in this chapter, for information on the Metrotown complex, Greater Vancouver's biggest shopping destination.

GETTING THERE & AWAY

Since most people coming to BC arrive via Vancouver, we've covered details of air travel to and from here in the Getting There & Away chapter of this book. For more details on travel within the province, see the Getting Around chapter and the regional chapters that cover your BC destinations of choice.

Air
Vancouver International Airport (YVR) is about 10km south of the city on Sea Island, between Vancouver and the municipality of Richmond. The two recently merged major Canadian airlines – Air Canada and Canadian Airlines (☎ 888-247-2262) – dominate service; commuter subsidiaries fly to the smaller towns in the region. You'll have to pay an airport improvement fee ($5 to $15, depending on your destination) at the airport before your flight departs, unless your travel agent has already added it to your ticket. For complete information, see the Getting There & Away chapter.

The Vancouver area has three seaplane terminals: on the Fraser River, south of the main terminals at Vancouver International Airport; on the harbor near Canada Place; and in New Westminster. There's a helicopter terminal on the harbor near Waterfront Station.

Bus
The bus station is part of the train station: Pacific Central Station, 1150 Station St (see Train, below). Greyhound buses (☎ 800-661-8747, 604-482-8747) link Vancouver with Seattle and other cities in Canada and the USA. Greyhound does not offer service to Victoria. The following are sample one-way fares and average travel times to major western Canada destinations:

destination	time	fare
Banff	14 hours	$100
Calgary	16 hours	$117
Jasper	13 hours	$100
Kamloops	five hours	$47
Kelowna	six hours	$52
Prince George	12½ hours	$92
Prince Rupert	25 hours	$175

To/From Victoria Pacific Coach Lines (☎ 604-662-8074, 800-661-1725) runs buses to Victoria every hour 5:45 am to 8:45 pm during July and August and every two hours the rest of the year; the fare, including the ferry, is $26.50/51 one-way/roundtrip for adults, $17.50/33 for seniors and $13.25/25.50 for children five to 11. It's the same price from Vancouver International Airport; buses connect with the airport shuttle bus at Delta Pacific Resort in Richmond.

To/From Seattle Quick Coach Lines (☎ 604-940-4428) operates a shuttle bus to downtown Seattle for $32/58 one-way/roundtrip; the bus also makes stops at Seattle's Sea-Tac Airport and Bellingham Airport. Buses leave from most major hotels in downtown Vancouver. Bigfoot Adventure Shuttle (☎ 604-278-8224, 888-244-6673) also makes the Vancouver-Seattle run for $32/59, with service between major hostels in each city.

Train

Vancouver is the western terminus for Canada's VIA Rail (☎ 888-842-7245); it's also served by Amtrak (☎ 800-872-7245) trains from Seattle. You'll find the magnificent Pacific Central Station just off Main St, at 1150 Station St, between National and Terminal Aves southeast of downtown. The ticket office is open daily. The 'left luggage' counter is open 8 am to 10 pm. Lockers are available for $2 (small) and $4 (large). See the Getting There & Away and Getting Around chapters for more details on train service.

Car

If you're coming from the USA (Washington State), you'll be on I-5 until the border town of Blaine. At the border is the Peace Arch Provincial and State Park. The first town in BC is White Rock. Hwy 99 veers west, then north to Vancouver. Close to the city, it passes over two arms of the Fraser River and eventually turns into Granville St, one of the main thoroughfares of downtown Vancouver.

If you're coming from the eastern part of the province, you'll probably be on the Trans-Canada Hwy (Hwy 1), which takes the Port Mann Bridge over the Fraser River and snakes through the eastern end of the city, eventually meeting with Hastings St before going over the Second Narrows Bridge to North Vancouver. (Take a left on Hastings St for downtown Vancouver.)

If you're coming from Horseshoe Bay in the north, the Trans-Canada Hwy heads through West Vancouver and North Vancouver before going over the Second Narrows Bridge. In West Vancouver, you can follow the exit for Hwy 99; this will take you over Lions Gate Bridge into Stanley Park.

Ferry

BC Ferries (☎ 888-223-3779) provides service between the mainland and Vancouver Island. The main route runs from Tsawwassen (see Tsawwassen section, later in the chapter) to Swartz Bay, which is just north of Sidney. Between eight and 15 ferries travel in each direction daily, depending on the day and season. Ferries also go to Nanaimo from Tsawwassen and Horseshoe Bay. The one-way fare on all routes during peak times is $9/4.50 for adults/children, $2.50 for a bicycle and $32 for a car (driver not included).

Sunday afternoon, Friday evening and holidays are the busiest times for Vancouver Island crossings from both terminals, and people who plan to take their cars on the ferry must often wait one or two sailings for their turn. To avoid this, plan to cross at other times or reserve a space for your vehicle by calling ☎ 604-444-2890 or 888-724-5223 (in BC) or by visiting the Web site www.bcferries.com/res. BC Ferries also offers service from Tsawwassen to the major Gulf Islands. See the Southern Gulf Islands chapter for information on these routes.

GETTING AROUND

BC Transit (☎ 604-953-3333) produces two publications about getting around the city: the *Transit Guide*, a map of Greater Vancouver that shows bus, train and ferry routes, and *Discover Vancouver on Transit*, which lists many of the city's attractions and provides directions on how to get there (including Victoria). You can buy the former for $1.50 at newsstands and bookstores; pick up the latter for free at the Visitor Info Centre.

To/From the Airport

There are two ways of getting between the airport and downtown by bus – a city bus or the Vancouver Airporter. The mint-green Vancouver Airporter (☎ 604-946-8866, 800-668-3141) stops at Pacific Central Station and all major central hotels. Tickets cost $10 one-way, $17 roundtrip (with no time limit). You can purchase them from the driver. Buses leave the airport every 30 minutes 6:15 am to 12:15 am daily. The length of the journey varies with traffic and your ultimate destination. If Granville St is jammed – not unlikely – and your hotel is last on the route, it can take 90 minutes or more.

To get to the airport by city bus, take No 8 south on Granville St to 70th Ave. From there, transfer to bus No 100, bound for the airport. From the airport, do the reverse. The total travel time is one hour, and the fare is $3.50 on weekdays, $1.75 at night and on weekends. You need to have exact change.

A taxi between downtown Vancouver and the airport costs around $25.

To/From the Ferry Terminals

To get to Tsawwassen ferry terminal from downtown, take bus No 601 on Howe St to the Ladner Exchange, then bus No 640 to the ferry terminal. Allow about 75 minutes for the trip. To get to the Horseshoe Bay ferry terminal, take bus No 250 or 257 on Georgia St. The trip lasts about an hour, sometimes longer during rush hours.

Bus, SkyTrain & SeaBus

BC Transit (☎ 604-953-3333) offers three modes of public transportation: regular buses, the SkyTrain automated light-rail system and SeaBus ferries to North Vancouver.

The transit system is divided into three zones: the inner zone covers central Vancouver; the next zone includes the suburbs

of Richmond, Burnaby, New Westminster, North Vancouver, West Vancouver and Sea Island; the outer zone emcompasses Ladner, Tsawwassen, Delta, Surrey, White Rock, Langley, Port Moody and Coquitlam.

On weekdays before 6:30 pm, you pay a flat fare of $1.75/2.50/3.50 for one/two/three zones of travel, no matter whether you ride the regular buses, SkyTrain or SeaBus. (Discount fares, available to children ages five to 13 and seniors 65 and older, are $1.25/1.75/2.50.) At night and on weekends, all travel is $1.75 ($1.25 discount fare). When you pay your fare, you can ask the driver for a free transfer, good for 90 minutes.

Day passes, good for unlimited travel, cost $7; they're available at the Tsawwassen ferry terminal and at FareDealer outlets, which include the following retail stores: London Drugs, Money Marts, Mac's and other convenience stores. If you're staying a while, you might want to consider purchasing the 10-trip FareSaver Tickets or the monthly FareCards.

The wheelchair-accessible SkyTrain connects downtown Vancouver with Burnaby, New Westminster and Surrey. The SeaBus passenger-only catamarans zip back and forth across Burrard Inlet between Waterfront Station downtown and Lonsdale Quay in North Vancouver. For both, try to avoid rush hours, when many commuters crowd aboard.

Car

Vancouver has no expressways. On one hand, this means that the incredible vistas aren't marred by tangled layers of concrete interchanges – a refreshing change from other North American cities. But it also means that everyone must travel through the city on surface streets. Congestion is a big problem; few downtown streets have left-hand turn lanes, and traffic can back up for blocks during rush hours (about 7 to 9 am and 4 to 6 pm), especially with people trying to get onto Georgia St from the south. It's even worse on a wet or snowy day, so try to avoid driving in rush hour.

Then there's parking. It's hard to find places to park in most of the commercial and central residential areas; when you succeed, it often costs a fortune. Cars, especially those with non-BC license plates, are vulnerable to break-ins and thefts. Bottom line: You'd be wise not to bring a car to Vancouver. If you do, find a place where you can leave it parked, then use public transportation. Or park away from the center and catch a bus or SkyTrain downtown; it'll probably be quicker and better for your blood pressure, too.

Car Rental You'll have your pick of car-rental companies in Vancouver. Some offer discount coupons, which are available at various outlets, including the Visitor Info Centre (see Information, earlier). Check the Yellow Pages for a complete listing of car-rental companies. Some downtown agencies include the following (all of which operate counters at the airport as well):

Avis
   (☎ 604-606-2872), 757 Hornby St
Budget
   (☎ 604-668-7000), 1705 Burrard St
Hertz
   (☎ 604-606-4711), 28 Seymour St
Lo-Cost
   (☎ 604-689-9664), 1105 Granville St
National/Tilden
   (☎ 604-685-6111), 1130 W Georgia St
Rent-A-Wreck
   (☎ 604-688-0001), 1349 Hornby St
Thrifty
   (☎ 604-606-1666), 1400 Robson St

Taxi
Unless you're staying at a big hotel, you'll probably have to phone ahead for a cab. Companies include Black Top & Checker Cabs (☎ 604-671-1111, 731-1111 or 681-2181) and Yellow Cab (☎ 604-681-1111, 876-5555 or 255-6262).

Bicycle
Vancouver is a great cycling city. Several secondary-street bikeways run across town, giving people the option of traveling by cycle away from the main arteries. The Adanac Bikeway, for example, runs 5.5km from downtown to the eastern city limits; others include the Seaside Bike Route and the Cassiar Bikeway. For more information, call the Bike Hotline (☎ 604-871-6070). Bikes are allowed on the SeaBus, as well as on the ferries across False Creek. The Bicycling Association of BC publishes a cycling map of the city, available at the Visitor Info Centre and most bike shops.

Mini-Ferries
Two companies operate mini-ferry shuttles across False Creek. The False Creek Ferries (☎ 604-684-7781) stop at the Vancouver Aquatic Centre near Sunset Beach, as well as at Granville Island, at the Vancouver Maritime Museum at Kitsilano Point and at Stamp's Landing near the Cambie Bridge. Aquabus (☎ 604-689-5858) travels between Granville Island and downtown docks at Howe and Davie Sts, as well as to Stamp's Landing and Science World. The fare is $2 to $5, depending on your route. Day passes and multi-trip tickets are available.

Water Taxi
Burrard Water Taxi (☎ 604-293-1160) offers a 24-hour water-taxi service to the greater Vancouver maritime region.

Around Vancouver

Though Vancouver offers plenty of attractions to occupy visitors, most travelers find no shortage of reasons to explore beyond the city limits. Home to some of the metro area's best-known destinations, the suburbs feature entertainment and recreation opportunities for people of all interests.

NORTH VANCOUVER (Map 2)
• **population 125,220**
'North Van' is home to two of the metro area's biggest attractions: the Capilano Suspension Bridge and Grouse Mountain. Most visitors to Vancouver will want to set aside a half-day or so to cross Burrard Inlet and visit these marquee spots – or blow them off (together with their crowds) in favor of some less-ballyhooed but equally

worthy experiences. With the SeaBus terminal at hand, North Van also makes a good base for exploring downtown Vancouver.

Lonsdale Quay Market

At the center of the North Shore SeaBus terminal complex, this lively marketplace (☎ 604-985-6261) features a lower floor devoted to fresh and cooked food, with outdoor seating and frequent entertainment, and an upstairs area with specialty shops and several sit-down restaurants. A booth in the ferry terminal offers information on North Shore attractions. North Vancouver buses leave from here, too. The market is open 9:30 am to 6:30 pm daily (until 9 pm Friday). To get there, take the SeaBus from Waterfront Station in Vancouver.

Pacific Starlight Dinner Train

BC Rail runs dinner-train excursions from North Vancouver to Porteau Cove on Howe Sound from May through October. The ride and the three-course meal costs $84 ($100 for dome-car seating). Sunday lunch trips run in October and cost $70 ($80 for dome car). Trains leave from 1311 W 1st St. For more information or reservations, call ☎ 604-984-5500 or 800-363-3733 or email pass_info@bcrail.com.

Capilano Suspension Bridge

About 800,000 people cross this pedestrian bridge each year, arriving by the busload. The span – about 140m long and 70m above the Capilano River, with a 1333-person capacity – isn't the only thing to experience here; other attractions include a totem-pole carving house, nature trails, historical exhibits and live entertainment. Guided tours start every half-hour. But the crowds can be oppressive; many visitors leave wondering how much more beautiful the place would be if only there weren't so many people.

The bridge is open 8 am to dusk daily, mid-May through September; 9 am to 5 pm the rest of the year; closed December 25. Admission is $10.75/8.75/6.75/3.25 adults/seniors/students/children six to 12.

The best way to get here is via westbound bus No 246, which travels along Georgia St

in downtown Vancouver, to Ridgewood Dr and Capilano Rd, a block south of the park. Or take SeaBus from Vancouver's Waterfront Station to Lonsdale Quay. From there, take bus No 236 (May to September) or bus No 230 to Lonsdale Ave and 15th St, then bus No 232 to Edgemont Blvd and Capilano Rd, which is a block north of the park. If you're driving from Vancouver, head north over Lions Gate Bridge to Marine Dr in North Vancouver, then turn left (north) onto Capilano Rd.

Capilano Salmon Hatchery

This fish facility (☎ 604-666-1790), 4500 Capilano Rd, north of the suspension bridge, is most interesting from July to November, when you can see adult salmon swim through fish ladders past the Capilano River rapids to reach spawning grounds upstream. Exhibits tell the tale the rest of the year. Bus No 236 runs here from Lonsdale Quay.

Cleveland Dam

The dam (☎ 604-224-5739) creates Capilano Lake, which supplies much of Vancouver's drinking water. Here you'll see good views of the Lions, two peaks of the Coast Mountains. Admission is free, and there are picnic grounds. The dam is north of the salmon hatchery up Capilano Rd.

Grouse Mountain Resort

Billed as 'the Peak of Vancouver,' this resort (☎ 604-984-0661), 6400 Nancy Greene Way (the northern extension of Capilano Rd), is the city's most convenient ski area, as well as a popular summer destination. Bus no 236 from Lonsdale Quay runs right to the base.

The Skyride aerial tramway takes people up the mountain for 360-degree views from 1100m – as long as it's a clear day. The fare is $17.50/15.50/11.50/6.50 for adults/seniors/teens 13 to 18/children seven to 12; a family (two adults and two children) ticket is $45. Activities at the top include hiking, mountain biking, paragliding and helicopter tours. Don't miss the *Born to Fly* movie in the Theatre in the Sky; you can also view logger demonstrations and a gallery of chainsaw sculptures. The several dining options include The Observatory (fine dining), the Bar 98 Bistro (more casual fare) and the Hiwus Feasthouse (with First Nations storytelling, music and dancing).

Those who'd rather hike their way to the top can try the **Grouse Grind**, probably the most popular alpine hike in the Vancouver metro area. More of an outdoor gym than a wilderness trail, the 2.9km route has a very steep elevation gain of 853m, making this a good cardio workout. Very fit people make it up in about an hour, but 90 minutes is more typical. Wear boots and bug repellent and bring water. It's free to hike up; if you like, you can catch the Skyride down from the top for $5.

In winter, Grouse Mountain's activities include cross-country skiing, skating and sleigh rides. Don't forget downhill skiing: 22 ski runs are open 9 am to 10 pm daily from about December through April; call ☎ 604-986-6262 for snow conditions. All-day lift tickets cost $29/22/16 adults/seniors and teens 13 to 18/children seven to 12; for night skiing, the prices are $22/16/12. Lessons and rentals are available.

Lynn Canyon Park

It's only a third as long as the Capilano Bridge and not quite so high, either. But the good news is that not nearly as many people make the trek to Lynn Canyon suspension bridge, which means you might have it almost to yourself. Did we mention it's free? The park includes many hiking trails, pubs, picnic and swimming spots. It's open 7 am to dusk daily.

The **Lynn Canyon Park Ecology Centre** (☎ 604-981-3103), 3663 Park Rd, can educate you about the biology of the area through displays, films and slide shows. It's open 10 am to 5 pm daily, April through October, and noon to 4 pm the rest of the year, weekends only. To get to the park, take bus No 228 or 229 from Lonsdale Quay. Get off at Peters Rd; it's a 15-minute walk from there. If you're driving, cross Second Narrows Bridge, turn right on Lynn Valley Rd, then turn right (east) on Peters Rd, where you'll see signs that point the way.

Mt Seymour Provincial Park

Another quick escape from Vancouver, this park (☎ 604-924-2200) features several lakes, hiking trails and many scenic viewpoints. Some areas are very rugged, so visitors on overnight trips should register with park rangers. Mt Seymour Resorts (☎ 604-986-2261) operates a downhill ski area here in winter. To get to the park from Vancouver, cross the Second Narrows Bridge, turn right (east) on the Mt Seymour Parkway, then north on Mt Seymour Rd.

Deep Cove/Indian Arm

This protected area, which reaches far north of Burrard Inlet, offers some of the best kayaking and canoeing in Greater Vancouver. Lotus Land Tours (☎ 604-684-4922 or 800-528-3531) leads four-hour paddling trips in Indian Arm for $135 per person (half-price for children six to 11), including gear, transportation from Vancouver and a salmon barbecue lunch. Call 24 hours ahead. Deep Cove Canoe & Kayak Centre (☎ 604-929-2268), 2156 Banbury Rd, offers rentals, lessons and tours.

Places to Stay

Right by the Lions Gate Bridge, *Capilano RV Park* (☎ 604-987-4722, 295 Tomahawk Ave) offers spaces for tents ($27) and RVs ($34 to $38), complete with amenities – a pool, showers and laundry. It can be crowded. Wilderness camping is permitted at Mt Seymour Provincial Park, but there are no facilities.

A short walk from the Lonsdale Quay SeaBus terminal, the *Globetrotter's Inn* hostel (☎ 604-988-2082, globetrottersinn@ yahoo.com, 170 W Esplanade) attracts lots of skiers. Rent a dorm bed for $19 or a private room for $40 to $45. The array of amenities includes laundry, Internet access (just $2 per hour), kitchen access, bike rentals, an outdoor bouldering wall and a front porch where you can sit for a spell.

The *Capilano B&B* (☎ 604-990-8889, 877-990-8889, fax 604-990-5177, info@ capilanobb.com, 1374 Plateau Dr) offers guest rooms ($85 to $135) in a newer home. More of an upscale spot, *Thistledown House*

B&B (☎ *604-986-7173, 888-633-7173, fax 604-980-2939, info@thistle-down.com, 3910 Capilano Rd)* features five lovely rooms for $125 to $220, including breakfast and afternoon tea.

At the *Canyon Court Motel* (☎ *604-988-3181, 888-988-3181, fax 604-990-1554, info@ canyoncourt.com, 1748 Capilano Rd)*, close to Lions Gate Bridge, rates start at about $89. The *Grouse Inn* (☎ *604-988-7101, 800-779-7888, admin@grouse-inn.com, 1633 Capilano Rd)* charges $109 and up for regular rooms, $139 for rooms with kitchenettes. Amenities at both include a laundry and pool.

The *Lonsdale Quay Hotel* (☎ *604-986-6111, 800-836-6111, fax 604-986-8782, sales@ lonsdalequayhotel.bc.ca, 123 Carrie Cates Court)*, right on the waterfront, offers views of Vancouver. Rates start at about $140.

Places to Eat

Grab a quick bite from any of the many food vendors at Lonsdale Quay Market. Or head upstairs to either the British-style *Cheshire Cheese Inn* (☎ *604-987-3322)*, serving traditional food ($9 to $12), or the more upscale *Q Café* (☎ *604-986-6111)*, featuring great views of the city.

Most dishes at the *Thai House Restaurant* (☎ *604-987-9911, 180 W Esplanade)*, just above the quay, cost about $10, but watch for cheaper lunch specials. *Sailor Hagar's Brew Pub* (☎ *604-984-7669, 235 W 1st St)*, a couple of blocks up and over from the quay, not only produces some excellent beer, but also makes pretty good food, including sandwiches, burgers, pizza and fish-and-chips; the pub grub will set you back $8 to $12.

The next best thing to a dinner cruise is the *Seven Seas Seafood Restaurant* (☎ *604-987-3344)*, a floating eatery at the foot of Lonsdale quay, to the east of the quay. Built in 1941, what's now the Seven Seas used to be a ferry that traveled between North Vancouver and Vancouver before the Second Narrows Bridge was completed in 1957. Today, the restaurant serves a remarkable seafood smorgasbord for $40 Wednesday through Sunday.

WEST VANCOUVER (Map 2)
• population 40,900

This tony suburb has earned two spots in the records book: first, for having the highest per-capita income in Canada, and second (under the category 'dubious distinctions'), for producing Canada's first mall, the Park Royal Shopping Centre. You might be forgiven for thinking that the only thing West Vancouverites do is make and spend money, but look again: several lovely public parks, beaches and trails still exist amid the chic homes, shops and restaurants.

Parks

Some of the largest trees in Vancouver tower over **Lighthouse Park** (☎ 604-925-7200), which includes a rare stand of original coastal forest; you'll also see arbutus, a wide-leaf evergreen with orange colored peeling bark. About 13km of hiking trails wind through the park; the most popular one leads to the **Point Atkinson Lighthouse**, which commands a view of the inlet from its rocky perch. To get there, turn west (left) on Marine Dr after crossing Lions Gate Bridge and drive 9.5km. Or catch bus No 250 going west on West Georgia St.

Cypress Provincial Park (☎ 604-924-2200), located 8km north of West Vancouver off Hwy 99, features trails for hiking and mountain biking, along with several mountain lakes. You can do some downhill skiing at the Cypress Bowl Ski Area (☎ 604-926-5612), but it's better known for its cross-country trails.

Places to Stay & Eat

Wilderness camping is permitted in Cypress Provincial Park, but there are no facilities. For indoor accommodations, try the *Park Royal Hotel* (☎ 250-926-5511, fax 604-926-6082, 540 Clyde Ave)*, a small 30-room hotel that has the feel of an English country inn, complete with a pub. Rooms start at $150.

West Vancouver's Dundarave Pier offers a selection of light meals. For something more, try two of the metro area's most noted restaurants. With Vancouver at your feet, the *Salmon House on the Hill* (☎ 604-926-3212, 2229 Folkestone Way)* is tough to beat when it comes to views. Fresh fish dominates the menu ($19 to $29). *Beach House at Dundarave Pier (☎ 604-922-1414, 150 25th St)* also offers spectacular views, plus well-prepared seafood, lamb and steaks (entrees $16 to $31). Both places are open for lunch, dinner and Sunday brunch.

HORSESHOE BAY (Map 2)
The small coastal community of Horseshoe Bay marks the end of the North Shore. It's a pretty spot, with great views across the bay and up the fjord to distant glaciated peaks, but it's probably best known for its ferry terminal, with service to Bowen Island, Nanaimo on Vancouver Island and Langdale on the Sunshine Coast.

Whytecliff Park, at the far end of Marine Dr, attracts scuba divers and hikers. Trails lead to vistas and a gazebo, where you can watch the boat traffic wend its way in and out of Burrard Inlet.

If you're looking for a place to stay, try the *Horseshoe Bay Motel (☎ 604-921-7454, 6588 Royal Ave)*, about a five-minute walk from the ferry terminal. Basic rooms start at $75 for up to four people.

BOWEN ISLAND (MAP 1)
• population 3100

So you want to visit the Gulf Islands, but you don't think you have time. Consider a trip to Bowen Island, less than an hour from downtown Vancouver.

While you're on Bowen, you can stroll its waterfront boardwalks, which wind around buildings that date from the early 20th century. If you have something more adventurous in mind, Bowen Island Sea Kayaking (☎ 604-947-9266, 800-605-2925) offers several short **kayaking** tours, including a sunset paddle for about $49. Beginners are welcome, and the kayak shack is right by the ferry dock, so you needn't drive. Rentals and lessons are available, too.

Hiking trails and picnic grounds abound on Bowen, ranging from the five-minute stroll to the tables at Snug Cove to the 45-minute trek from the ferry dock to Killarney Lake, itself encircled by a 4km trail. The island also features several art galleries and

creature comforts like aromatherapy massage and reflexology at the Cottage (call ☎ 604-947-9161 for an appointment).

Places to Stay & Eat
A favorite destination for work-weary Lower Mainlanders, Bowen Island offers good visitor amenities. *Earthwoods Country Retreat (☎ 604-947-9712, earthwoods@ idmail.com, 1416 Westside Rd)* rents cozy rooms and cabins for $45/75 single/double. *Xenia (☎ 604-947-9816, fax 604-947-9076, xeniatlc@direct.ca)* is a soulful retreat center with a thousand-year-old Douglas fir tree, labyrinths and cabins ($85/110), including self-catered breakfast.

Union Steamship Company Marina (☎ 604-947-0707, ussc@direct.ca) offers moorage for boaters, plus indoor accommodations ($95 to $160). *Vineyard at Bowen Island (☎ 604-947-0028, staff@vineyard .bc.ca, 687 Cates Lane)* is a fancier B&B, with eight rooms for $95 to $225.

La Mangerie (☎ 604-947-2127) at Artisan Square, Artisan Lane off Grafton Rd, serves quiches, salads and other fare ($4 to $9.50). *Blue Eyed Mary's/The Breakfast Café (☎ 604-947-2583, 451 Bowen Trunk Rd)*, just up from the ferry dock, offers breakfast Friday through Sunday ($4 to $11) and a creative West Coast bistro-style dinner Thursday through Sunday ($12 to $20). *Doc Morgan's Inn (☎ 604-947-0808)*, at the Union Steamship Company complex on the boardwalk, serves both pub fare ($7 to $12) and more formal dinners ($15 to $23), as well as Saturday and Sunday brunch ($5 to $11).

Getting There & Around
BC Ferries serves Bowen Island from Horseshoe Bay, with about 16 sailings daily in each direction. The roundtrip fare for the 20-minute trip is $5.75/3 for adults/children; cars are $18.25.

BURNABY (Map 2)
• population 180,000

Burnaby, the city immediately east of Vancouver, is probably best known as the home of Metrotown, BC's biggest shopping complex and the second-largest mall in

Canada after the West Edmonton Mall. But that's not the only reason to visit.

Things to See & Do

Simon Fraser University, established in 1965, sits atop Burnaby Mountain, about 20km east of downtown Vancouver. Noted Canadian architect Arthur Erickson designed the university; his work remains controversial, thanks to his unusual use of space and perspective. Some of the worthwhile attractions here include the **Museum of Archaeology & Ethnology** (☎ 604-291-3325) and the **SFU Art Gallery** (☎ 604-291-4266). For information on university tours, call ☎ 604-291-3111. To get to campus, catch bus No 135 or 35 along Hastings St.

Near SFU, the lofty **Burnaby Mountain Park** offers some grand views of Greater Vancouver and its mountains and seascapes. If you're here, don't miss Kamui Mintara, 'Playground of the Gods,' a sculpture installation by the father-son team of Nuburi and Shusei Toko. The Tokos' work, reminiscent of the First Nations totems that stand nearby, reflects the story of Japan's aboriginal Ainu people and the gods who came down to Earth to give birth to them. The park also includes several trails, a rose garden and a well-regarded restaurant, Horizons (see Places to Stay & Eat, below).

The **Burnaby Village Museum** (☎ 604-293-6501) re-creates the atmosphere of a southwestern BC town between 1890 and 1925. The replica village contains an old schoolhouse, printing shop, drugstore and other establishments, along with a large, working steam-train model and a restored 1912 carousel that was built in Leavenworth, Kansas, probably with labor from the famous prison there. The 36 wooden horses look almost brand-new, but all were carved between 1912 and 1926. There's space for a wheelchair to ride along, too.

Burnaby Village is open daily from late April through mid-September. It's also open during the Christmas season (except Christmas Eve and Christmas Day). Admission is $6.60/4.45/4.55/3.95 for adults/seniors/teens/children six to 12. Carousel rides cost $1. To get there, take bus No 123

east on Hastings St or follow the signs from the Trans-Canada Highway. Burnaby Village is in Deer Lake Park, which also has a lake with summertime boat rentals ($10 per hour for single kayaks; $14 per hour for double kayaks, pedal boats, rowboats and canoes).

More than 500 stores comprise **Metrotown**, a combination of the Eaton Centre and Metrotown Centre (☎ 604-438-2444), two malls connected by a skywalk. A monument to rampant consumerism, Metrotown largely attracts avid shoppers, but even those bored out of their minds by malls might find something enticing here. Playdium (☎ 604-433-7529), for example, features dozens of interactive games and virtual-reality rides and a café where diners order from Hanna, the virtual hostess. SkyTrain runs right to the door from downtown Vancouver.

Places to Stay & Eat

Burnaby Cariboo RV Park (☎ 604-420-1722, toll-free reservation fax 800-667-9901, camping@bcrvpark.com, 7865 Cariboo Place) offers test sites ($22) and RV hookups ($30). Take Exit 37 off Hwy 1.

Simon Fraser University (☎ 604-291-4503) rents rooms from May to August. They're all fully furnished with shared bathrooms; singles cost $19 without bedding (bring your own sleeping bag), $31 with bedding; doubles with bedding are $51. The university also offers four-bedroom townhouse units for $115. You'll find cafeterias and a pub on campus. Contact Housing & Conference Services, Room 212, McTaggart-Cowan Hall, Burnaby, BC V5A 1S6.

If merely going to the mall isn't enough, you might want to stay there. *Holiday Inn Metrotown* (☎ 604-438-1881, 877-323-1177, fax 604-438-1883, holiday@direct.ca, 4405 Central Blvd), attached to the huge retail complex, rents rooms for $135 and up.

Many international food shops lie along E Hastings Ave (Hwy 7) in an area of Burnaby known as 'The Heights.' Here, too, is the *The Pear Tree* (☎ 604-299-2772, 4120 E Hastings Ave), a small place with a similarly small menu. Local diners rave about such fare as salmon with crushed sour-cream potatoes and star-anise butter sauce ($19.95).

Another popular upscale choice, the aptly named *Horizons Restaurant* (☎ 604-299-1155) sits atop Burnaby Mountain. Sunday brunch (11 am to 2 pm) features a made-to-order omelet bar ($13.95) with your choice of many ingredients, plus fresh fruit, muffins and more. Horizons also serves lunch ($8 to $15), available Monday to Saturday, and dinner nightly ($17.50 to $23.50), which includes seafood, steak and chicken and some smaller, less expensive vegetarian dishes.

NEW WESTMINSTER (Map 2)
• population 49,500
The oldest town in Western Canada, New Westminster was established in 1859 and briefly served as BC's capital city. Once the area's primary seaport, New Westminster still boasts districts with period charm along the Fraser River. The waterfront area at Westminster Quay Public Market & Esplanade is home to the new **Fraser River Discovery Centre** (☎ 604-521-8401), which interprets river history. It also just happens to share a building with the new **Royal City Star Riverboat Casino**, with 300 slot machines and 30 gaming tables. The New Westminster Visitor Info Centre (☎ 604-526-1905), 790 Quayside Dr, is next door.

Other attractions in town include the **Irving House Historic Centre**, (☎ 604-527-4640), 302 Royal Ave, a 14-room home built in 1865 for a riverboat captain on the Fraser River. One of the oldest structures in BC, the Irving House now functions as a museum of frontier life and furnishings. The adjacent **New Westminster Museum** tells the story of this historic township. Both sites are open 11 am to 5 pm Tuesday to Sunday, May through August; 1 to 5 pm weekends only the rest of the year. Admission is by donation.

Starline Tours (☎ 604-522-3506) offers **river cruises** to Harrison Hot Springs, Pitt Lake and Steveston for $42 and up. Paddlewheeler Adventures (☎ 604-525-4465) leads seven-hour cruises that include a stopover

at Fort Langley (about $55) and three-hour excursions (about $40). Most of the trips include lunch, and both companies operate off the docks at Westminster Quay.

If you want to stay overnight, the *Inn at Westminster Quay* (☎ 604-520-1776, 800-663-2001, fax 604-520-5645, 900 Quayside Dr), built over the water beside the Public Market, offers a Fraser River view from every room; rates start at $160/170 single/double. Restaurants and nightclubs line Columbia St near the waterfront.

You can reach New Westminster by taking SkyTrain.

RICHMOND (Map 2)
• population 149,000
Richmond has become closely identified with BC's recent influx of Hong Kong Chinese. But don't expect to find the bustling, slightly seedy charm of a Chinatown – everything here is upscale, sanitized and suburban.

For the real Richmond experience, drive along No 3 Rd and look for the many large shopping malls collectively known as **Asia West**: Yaohan Centre and Parker Place both feature gleaming Chinese stores filled with Chinese products and mostly Chinese shoppers, along with excellent Chinese food at very reasonable prices. To reach No 3 Rd in Richmond, take bus No 401, 403, 406 or 407 from Howe St in downtown Vancouver.

Canada's largest **Buddhist temple** (☎ 604-274-2822), 9160 Steveston Hwy between No 3 and No 4 Rds, welcomes visitors to view its gardens, murals and shrines. It's open 9:30 am to 5 pm daily; admission is free, but donations are welcome. Take bus No 403 from Howe St in Vancouver.

Places to Stay
The Richmond area is a good place to stay if you want to be near Vancouver International Airport. Many motels and hotels offer free shuttle service.

April to October, *Richmond RV Park* (☎ 604-270-7878, richmondrv@aol.com, 6200 River Rd) offers tent sites (starting at $17) and RV hookups ($23 to $26). *Holiday Inn Express* (☎ 604-223-9971, 800-465-4329, fax 604-214-8488, service@hi-express.bc.ca, 9351 Bridgeport Rd) rents out basic clean rooms for about $100. **Stay 'N Save Motor Inn** (☎ 604-273-3311, 800-663-0298, fax 604-273-9522, staynsave@staynsave.com, 10551 St Edwards Dr) charges $115/125 single/double in high season. For a touch more luxury, try the **Delta Vancouver Airport Hotel & Marina** (☎ 604-278-1241, fax 604-276-1975, 3500 Cessna Dr), where business-class rooms start at $155.

Steveston
In the southwest corner of Richmond, the old fishing village of Steveston makes a good day trip from Vancouver. You can almost smell the salt in the air as you stroll past Steveston's docks, where many anglers hawk fresh catch directly from their boats. A pleasant bike and pedestrian-only trail winds north and east of the village, offering you a chance to exercise.

The **Gulf of Georgia Cannery National Historic Site** (☎ 604-664-9009), 12138 4th Ave, which dates from 1894, features exhibits and entertaining tours led by former fisheries workers. You'll learn all you want to know about this once-powerful industry. The site is open 10 am to 5 pm daily, June through August, and Thursday through Monday during April, May, September and October. Admission is $5/3.75/2.50 adults/seniors/children six to 16.

Bus Nos 401, 406 and 407 go to Steveston from Howe St in downtown Vancouver. If you're driving, take the Steveston Hwy exit west off Hwy 99.

Places to Stay & Eat
Villager B&B (☎ 604-275-0550, villager@net-com.ca, 11111 6th Ave) rents two rooms for $65/85 single/double. **Steveston Hotel** (☎ 604-277-9511, 12111 3rd Ave) offers rooms with shared baths for about $40 and rooms with private baths for $75/85; suites go for $105 to $175.

Dave's Fish & Chips (☎ 604-271-7555, 3460 Moncton St) serves up delicious cod and halibut in its dining room or at its take-out window. Baskets start at $6; a second Dave's location on Steveston Landing charges more. **Pajo's**, on the dock, is another favorite for fish and chips. **Shady Island Restaurant** (☎ 604-275-6587, 3800 Bayview St), on the waterfront, offers casual fine dining with panoramic views. Burgers cost about $10, and other main dishes run $17 to $23.

DELTA (Map 1)
• **population 95,400**
Wild berries, sandhill cranes and trumpeter swans thrive in Delta's biggest attraction: **Burns Bog**, said to be the largest estuarine raised-peat bog on the west coast of the Americas. Although access is limited, the Burns Bog Conservation Society offers walking tours on an irregular schedule; call ☎ 604-572-0373 or 888-850-6264 for dates or more information.

ParkCanada RV Inns (☎ 604-943-5811, fax 604-943-0093, 4799 Hwy 17), on Nulelum Way northeast of the Tsawwassen ferry terminal, offers sites for $17 and up and free showers.

TSAWWASSEN (Map 1)
Yes, it's best known for the BC Ferries terminal that serves as Vancouver's main gateway to Victoria. But Tsawwassen also fronts on Boundary Bay, where **Centennial Beach Park** ranks among the Greater Vancouver area's best-kept secrets, with long stretches of lovely beach, excellent bird-watching and warm water for swimming at high tide. To get there, take Hwy 17 toward the Tsawwassen ferry terminal, then go south on 56th St to 12th Ave, then east to Boundary Bay Rd. Also nearby, albeit more expensive and crowded, is **Splashdown Water Park** (☎ 604-943-2251), on Hwy 17 just before the ferry terminal. Kids should enjoy the dozen-plus water slides.

Whistler & the Sunshine Coast

If you're looking for easily accessible adventure, it's hard to beat the regions north of Vancouver. No matter what your outdoor passion, chances are you can pursue it within a few kilometers of the Sea to Sky Hwy or on the lesser-known Sunshine Coast. But these regions also please less-active travelers who desire nothing more than stupendous scenery, memorable lodgings and a few good meals.

Sea to Sky Highway

Hwy 99, nicknamed the Sea to Sky Hwy, offers one of the prettiest drives in BC, with the blue panorama of Howe Sound on the southern portions and mountain scenery that rivals the Rockies stretching north from Squamish. Alas, the area's blessing – its proximity to the Vancouver metro area – is also its curse: it can get damned crowded up here, with plenty of infighting among outdoorsy types over who lays claim to the best recreational turf (eg, horseback riders vs mountain bikers, cross country skiers vs snowmobilers, etc).

The free magazine *99 North*, widely available along the route, offers comprehensive coverage of the area's sights and activities. 'The Mountain' radio station (107.1 FM in Squamish, 102.1 FM in Whistler) provides helpful reports on traffic and road conditions every 20 minutes. To hear reports from CBC Radio, tune into 1260 AM in Squamish, 100.1 FM in Whistler and 1240 AM in Pemberton.

Very occasionally – perhaps three times each winter – hazardous conditions force the Sea to Sky Hwy to close north of Squamish. But the closures are usually short – a few hours late at night, typically – and rarely snarl traffic.

For information on the BC Parks sites in this region, call ☎ 604-898-3678. For information on the BC Forest Service lands, call

Highlights

- Driving the beautiful Sea to Sky Hwy
- Skiing and snowboarding at Whistler and Blackcomb Mountains
- Sea kayaking in Howe Sound
- Experiencing high tide at Skookumchuck Narrows Provincial Park
- Paddling the Powell Forest Canoe Route

the Squamish Forest District (☎ 604-898-2100), or see the Web site www.for.gov.bc.ca/vancouvr/district/squamish.

LIONS BAY

You'll find some of Howe Sound's best **scuba diving** near Lions Bay; prime spots include Porteau Cove Marine Park, Christie Islet, Pam Rocks, Kelvin Grove and Bowyer Island. Sea to Sky Ocean Sports (☎ 604-892-3366), 37819 2nd Ave in Squamish, rents equipment and offers lessons and charter trips in these waters.

Just off Hwy 99, *Lions Bay General Store & Café* (☎ *604-921-6344*) features great views of Howe Sound and inexpensive soup, sandwiches and pizza. The general store stocks a good selection of fresh produce and gifts.

WHISTLER

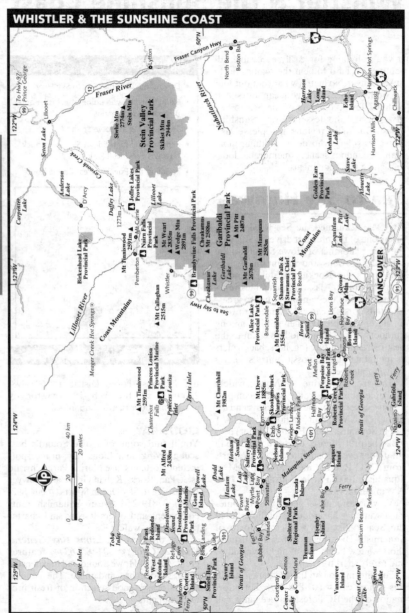

WHISTLER & THE SUNSHINE COAST

BRITANNIA BEACH

Another small way station along the Sea to Sky Hwy, Britannia Beach contains only one real attraction: the **BC Museum of Mining** (☎ 604-896-2233, 688-8735), which tells the story of the Britannia Mine. After opening in 1888, the mine went on to become the largest copper producer in the British Empire in the 1920s; it had produced more than 56 million tons of copper ore by the time it ceased operation in 1974.

A small train takes visitors into one of the mine's 360m tunnels, where you'll see demonstrations of the equipment and methods used to extract the ore. During the tour, you can also pan for gold and take a look at the huge Concentrator, itself a National Historic Site, along with a 235-ton 'super' mine truck. A 20-minute video presents the working and living conditions of the miners and their families.

The museum is open for tours 10 am to 4:30 pm Wednesday through Sunday in May, June, September and October; 10 am to 4:30 pm daily in July and August. The 90-minute tours leave at 10:30 and 11:30 am, 12:30, 1:30 2:30, 3:30 and 4:30 pm. Pre-booked tours are available the rest of the year, and the interpretation center and the

gift shop are open year-round. Admission is $10/8 for adults/seniors and students; kids under five are free. Gold-panning costs an extra $3.50 per person, but you're guaranteed to get a few flecks to take home.

If you're hungry for a bite to eat after your tour, you'll find a small collection of locally owned fast-food stands just north of the mining museum. *Mountain Woman Take Out* serves tasty burgers ($3 and up) and fish and chips for a few dollars more.

SQUAMISH
• **population 15,000**

Located about halfway between Vancouver and Whistler, Squamish enjoys an incredible natural setting. The Stawamus Chief looms over town to the southeast, its bulk nearly as great as Gibraltar. Mountains rise in most every other direction, too. A tiny harbor sits snugly between town and the monolith, and another arm of Howe Sound's headwaters – the Squamish River Estuary – cuts inland to the west.

For years, Squamish has primarily served as a forestry hub, but recreation has long been a big draw and general tourism is starting to catch up. A diverse group of visitors passes through this area every year:

WHISTLER

The Eagles Have Landed

One of the world's largest concentrations of bald eagles congregates in the Brackendale area, 7km north of Squamish, from late October to mid-February each year. As many as 3700 eagles gather along a 15km stretch of the Squamish River to feed on the dead salmon that float downstream after spawning.

The main viewing site is at Eagle Run, beside Government Rd north of Garibaldi Way and south of Depot Rd. Volunteer interpreters often staff the site on Saturday and Sunday afternoons during eagle season.

The Brackendale Art Gallery (☎ 604-898-3333), at the corner of Government and Depot Rds, offers helpful information about the eagle migration. While you're there, check out owner Thor Froslev's creations, sit a while in the splendid 'multireligious' chapel or have a bite to eat (noon to 5 pm daily in January; on Saturday, Sunday and holidays the rest of the year).

rock climbers, windsurfers, railroad history buffs and – in wintertime — birdwatchers eager to see hundreds of bald eagles.

Orientation & Information

If you're coming from Vancouver, turn left off Hwy 99 at the A&W Restaurant and McDonald's to reach Cleveland Ave and Squamish's small downtown. The well-stocked Visitor Info Centre (☎ 604-892-9244), 37950 Cleveland Ave, is near the far end of the street. You'll find the post office (☎ 604-892-3112) at 38064 Cleveland Ave.

The Squamish Public Library (☎ 604-892-3110), 37907 2nd Ave, includes a small art gallery. In addition to washers and dryers, Comfy's Coin Laundry (☎ 604-892-9870), 38201 Westway Ave, also contains computers (with email access), a coffee bar and kids' play area. For medical emergencies, go to Squamish General Hospital (☎ 604-892-5211), 38140 Behrner Dr.

Parks

At 335m, Shannon Falls ranks among Canada's highest and most beautiful waterfalls. A short hiking trail leads to the falls in the small **Shannon Falls Provincial Park**, along Hwy 99 just south of Squamish. A few picnic tables make this a good stopping point for lunch. In winter, when the falls freeze, ice climbers pick and pull their way to the top.

Just north of town, the **West Coast Railway Heritage Park** (☎ 604-898-9336) features one of Canada's best displays of historic rolling stock – about 65 cars, many of which have been converted to a walk-through museum of railroad history. The best exhibits include an excellent gallery of black-and-white photos by Charles Case and a three-car display showing the various stages of railroad car restoration. (The final example, the *British Columbia*, was bought for its scrap value of $400. Volunteers invested more than 80,000 hours and $360,000 into refurbishing it with the solid brass fittings and polished woods seen today.)

The park is open 10 am to 5 pm daily except Christmas Day and New Year's Day. Admission is $6/5 for adults/children. A family pass is $15. Add $2 per person or $5 per family for unlimited rides on the park's miniature railroad, which runs every half hour 11 am to 4 pm.

The small **Alice Lake Provincial Park** (☎ 604-898-3678) makes a nice base for exploring the area. The 6.5km Four Lakes Trail takes about two hours to trek, but if you only have a half hour to spare, you can hike to and around Stump Lake, the first one on the loop. Mountain bikes are not permitted on the Four Lakes Trail from May 1 to September 15. Sea to Sky Kayaking School (☎ 604-898-5498) offers rentals and lessons on Alice Lake.

Activities

Overlooking Squamish from a height of 652m, the Stawamus Chief is widely considered to be BC's best granite destination for **rock climbing**, with about 200 climbing routes. For information, guides or instruction, call Slipstream Rock & Ice (☎ 604-898-4891), 5010 Cheakamus Valley Rd; Vertical Reality Sports Store (☎ 604-892-8248), 38154 2nd Ave; or Squamish Rock Guides (☎ 604-898-1750).

You'll find some of western Canada's best **windsurfing** at Squamish Harbour, where winds from the mouth of the Squamish River can push sailboards to speeds as high as 60km/hr. (In fact, Squamish is a Coast Salish word meaning 'Mother of the Winds.') For information on weather and water conditions, call the Squamish Windsurfing Society (☎ 604-892-2235).

Mountain biking also draws lots of enthusiasts, who ride on more than 60 trails in the Squamish vicinity. Stop at Corsa Cycles (☎ 604-892-3331), 38128 Cleveland Ave, or Tantalus Bike Shop (see Getting Around, below) for information on the best routes.

Places to Stay

Both *Stawamus Chief Provincial Park* and *Alice Lake Provincial Park* contain campgrounds. Sites at the latter can be reserved by calling ☎ 800-689-9025 (604-689-9025 in Greater Vancouver). The private *Klahanie Campground* (☎ 604-892-3435) offers showers and laundry. Tent sites are $18, and RVs can park for $18 to $22.

The casual and friendly **Squamish Hostel** (☎ 604-892-9240, 800-449-8614, hostel@ mountain-inter.net, 38490 Buckley Ave) organizes rock-climbing and rafting trips and rents shared rooms for $15 ($40 for three nights) and two private rooms for $25. Amenities include bikes to borrow, a small rock climbing wall, fully equipped kitchen, laundry and rooftop deck. It's an easy walk from downtown.

Centrally located **Garibaldi Budget Inn** (☎ 604-892-5204, 888-313-9299, fax 604-892-3288, motorinn@mountain-inter.net, 38012 3rd Ave) caters to international travelers. Its small rooms include TV, phone and refrigerator for $44/49 single/double. A newer facility, **Super 8 Motel – Squamish** (☎ 604-815-0883, fax 815-0884, super8squamish@ uniserve.com, 38922 Progress Way) features an indoor pool and waterslide, fitness room, laundry and in-room refrigerators. Rooms cost about $90/110.

Sunwolf Outdoor Centre (☎ 604-898-1537, fax 898-1634, sunwolf@mountain-inter.net, 70002 Squamish Valley Rd) rents riverside cabins for $80. It offers rafting trips, eagle-viewing floats and guided fishing, hiking and mountain-biking trips.

The most upscale choice, the **Howe Sound Inn & Brewing Company** (☎ 604-892-2603, 800-919-2537, hsibrew@howesound .com, 37801 Cleveland Ave) features 20 welcoming rooms decorated with thick duvets and wood accents for $105. Some of the amenities include a sauna and outdoor granite climbing wall.

Places to Eat

Xanthine's Coffee & Tea (☎ 604-892-3443, 38134 Cleveland Ave), a local gathering spot, offers bagel sandwiches, salads and soups. At the **Roadhouse Diner** (☎ 604-892-5312), south of town on Hwy 99, you'll enjoy views of Shannon Falls while eating pasta and seafood dishes. Most lunch and dinner selections cost $5 to $12, but a few fancier dishes run up to $18. The diner serves breakfast Friday through Sunday.

North of town, the **Sunrise Japanese Restaurant** (☎ 604-898-2533, 40022 Government Rd) offers sashimi and noodle dishes for $7 and dinner combinations for $13.

The **Howe Sound Inn & Brewing Company** (see Places to Stay, above) contains two restaurants: a brew pub and its slightly more upscale cousin, the Red Heather Grill. At the brew pub, you can wash down burgers (about $9) and pizzas ($10-12), with one of the microbrewery's own beers (up to nine on tap) or a selection from its Scotch collection. A telescope on the patio is often trained on climbers making their ways up the Chief. The Red Heather Grill blends a fine-dining menu with a casual atmosphere featuring local art. Selections change weekly, but the menu usually includes several pastas ($11-13) and fresh cedar-plank-grilled halibut or salmon (about $16), all served with fresh bread made on the premises. The yeasty ale-and-cheddar bread is a standout.

Getting There & Around

Greyhound (☎ 604-898-3914) operates about six buses in each direction (northbound and southbound) daily. The fare from Vancouver is $8.25/16.50 one-way/roundtrip. Buses arrive and depart from the depot at 40446 Government Rd in Garibaldi Highlands; most of the buses also stop at the Chieftain Centre shopping plaza, along Pemberton Ave downtown.

BC Rail (☎ 800-339-8752 within BC, 800-663-8238 outside BC) offers train service to Squamish via the Cariboo Prospector, with one train daily in each direction. The fare from North Vancouver is $16/32 one-way/ roundtrip. BC Rail also operates the Royal Hudson Steam Train, a scenic ride from North Vancouver to Squamish, which runs Wednesday through Sunday, May through September; the basic roundtrip fare is $48/41/12.75 for adults/seniors and teens/ children five to 11. Passengers can also choose to take the MV Brittania ship back to Vancouver for $70/65/22 roundtrip.

Garibaldi Eco Adventure Centre (☎ 604-892-2088) offers a van shuttle service

WHISTLER

between Squamish and Whistler for $15 roundtrip. The company also books Squamish-area adventure tours; for details, visit its Web site at www.toursquamish.com.

Squamish Transit (☎ 604-892-5559) provides local bus service. For car rentals, go to Greg Gardner Motors (☎ 604-892-2277), 38684 Buckley Ave. Call Aaron Cabs (☎ 604-892-5995) for a taxi. Tantalus Bike Shop (☎ 604-898-2588), 40446 Government Rd, rents bikes for $15/35 per half-day/full day.

GARIBALDI PROVINCIAL PARK

East of both Squamish and Whistler, 195,000-hectare Garibaldi Provincial Park (☎ 604-898-3678) ranks among the Lower Mainland's largest parks. Best known for its hiking, Garibaldi includes more than 67km of developed trails that become cross-country ski routes in winter. Throughout the park, you'll find hike-in backcountry campsites ($3 to $5 per person).

Garibaldi has five main developed areas. To get to **Diamond Head**, turn east on Mamquam Rd, 4km north of Squamish; from there, it's a 16km drive over logging roads to a parking lot for the hiking and mountain-biking trail to Elfin Lakes (11km, three to five hours one-way); at Elfin Lakes, you'll find a first-come, first-served overnight shelter. Backcountry camping is also available at Red Heather (5km from the parking lot).

Black Tusk/Garibaldi Lake features beautiful alpine meadows and scenic mountain vistas. To get there, turn east off Hwy 99 37km north of Squamish or 19km south of Whistler. A paved 2.5km road leads to the Rubble Creek parking lot. From there, you can make the 9km, three- to four-hour one-way trek to Garibaldi Lake. You'll find backcountry campsites at Taylor Meadows and on the west shore of Garibaldi Lake.

The hike to **Cheakamus Lake** is among the park's most popular. You can reach the area via a road that runs 8.5km east from Hwy 99. (Look for the signs opposite Function Junction, a retail/industrial park on the south end of Whistler Valley.) The easy 3km hike takes 45 minutes to an hour with

minimal elevation gain; many people portage a canoe or kayak. Also in this area and just outside the provincial park, the BC Forest Service's 3000-hectare Whistler Interpretive Forest offers a wide variety of summer activities, ranging from hiking and mountain biking to kayaking and fishing.

The trail to **Singing Pass** leaves from the Whistler ski area. The 7.5km, two- to three-hour one-way hike heads up Fitzsimmons and Melody Creeks to the pass. From there, it's another 2km, one-hour trek to Russett Lake, where backcountry campsites are available.

To get to **Wedgemount Lake**, look for the parking lot 13km north of Whistler on the east side of Hwy 99. From here, it's a steep 7km, four- to six-hour hike to the glacial lake, but the climb will reward you with views of a 300m waterfall on Wedgemount Creek. Wedge Mountain (2891m), the highest in the park, rises to the south. Mountain-goat sightings are common in the area.

You can't take your dogs to Garibaldi Park, and the park also restricts the use of mountain bikes to certain trails. For more information, stop by BC Parks' district office at Alice Lake Provincial Park (see heading earlier in the chapter).

BRANDYWINE FALLS PROVINCIAL PARK

A popular day-use area 9km south of Whistler, this park features a 66m waterfall that spills 600 cubic meters of water per minute. A short trail leads to the falls' brink; another 7km trail leads to a suspension bridge that's also reachable via a much shorter trail from the BC Forest Service's Cal-Cheak Confluence Recreation Site (see Places to Stay under Whistler). Brandywine Falls Provincial Park also contains picnic areas, cross-country skiing and mountain-biking trails and a small campground with 15 sites ($12).

WHISTLER
• population 9000

The shorthand name 'Whistler' encompasses both the resort town 123km north of

Vancouver and the Whistler-Blackcomb ski resorts that have brought the town fame. Area residents eagerly await 2003, when the International Olympic Committee will announce its site decision for the 2010 Winter Games; Whistler is considered a top contender. But whether or not it gets the Games gig, Whistler will remain what many people believe is the best ski destination in North America. It's a beguiling spot in summer, too, with ample recreation options for every interest and far lower lodging prices than in winter.

Built almost entirely from scratch during the 1970s and '80s, Whistler tries to look much older. The massive hotels recall castles, and even shopping centers feature facades made out of venerable-looking quarried stone. But despite the contrived feel of Whistler Village, the skiers, shoppers and hikers who gather here lend the place a light, relaxing atmosphere.

Orientation

Whistler is divided into four main areas: Whistler Creekside, Whistler Village, Village North and Upper Village. If you're approaching south from the south, you'll enter at Whistler Creekside, the original Whistler base and home to a BC Rail train station. Although Whistler Creekside has been quiet in recent years, this subdued atmosphere promises to change, thanks to a $50-million project begun by Intrawest, the Whistler-Blackcomb resort owner.

The other three areas, which lie about 4km up the highway past Alta Lake, tend to blur into one large village. If you're driving, turn east (right) onto Village Gate Blvd, which divides Whistler Village (the base of Whistler Mountain) from Village North, and follow it to the end. You'll find large parking areas on the other side of Blackcomb Way, which divides the other two areas from Upper Village (the base of Blackcomb Mountain). The center of Whistler sprawls a bit, with hotels, restaurants, pubs and shops everywhere; start your explorations at Whistler Village, south of Village Gate Blvd and west of Blackcomb Way.

Information

The Whistler Chamber of Commerce (☎ 604-932-5528, fax 932-3755) has two Visitor Info Centres. One is at the intersection of Hwy 99 and Cheakamus Lake Rd at the entrance to the Whistler area. The other opened in Whistler Village in 2001, though the exact location hadn't been determined at press time. Both centers are open 9 am to 5 pm daily except Christmas Day.

For information on lodging and activities, contact Whistler's central reservation desk (☎ 800-944-7853) in the Whistler Conference Centre, just west of the Village Square on Golfers Approach. The conference center also houses Tourism Whistler's Activity & Information Centre. For more details, visit the Web site www.tourismwhistler.com.

The weekly *Pique Newsmagazine*, available free in Whistler and Squamish, offers the area's best news and entertainment listings, plus lots of feisty stories and ads for local restaurants and nightspots. The *Whistler Question* is a more traditional weekly newspaper. Glossy *Whistler* magazine, published twice annually, is a slick showcase for expensive clothing and real estate ads, with little helpful editorial coverage.

Money ATMs are widely available in Whistler. Exchange money at Custom House Currency Exchange (☎ 604-938-6658), 4227 Village Stroll, near the clock tower in Whistler Village.

Post & Communications The post office (☎ 604-932-5012) is at 106-4360 Lorimer Rd, near the corner of Blackcomb Way. Access email at Peaks Coffeehouse (☎ 604-905-2980), 4314 Main St near the Delta Whistler Village Suites, or at Whistler Cookie Co or Citta's Bistro (see Places to Eat, below).

Bookstores & Libraries Armchair Books (☎ 604-932-5557), on the square in Whistler Village, carries a good selection of fiction, nonfiction and regional titles. You'll find the Whistler Public Library (☎ 604-932-5564) in Village North, next to the Whistler Museum and Archives.

WHISTLER

WHISTLER

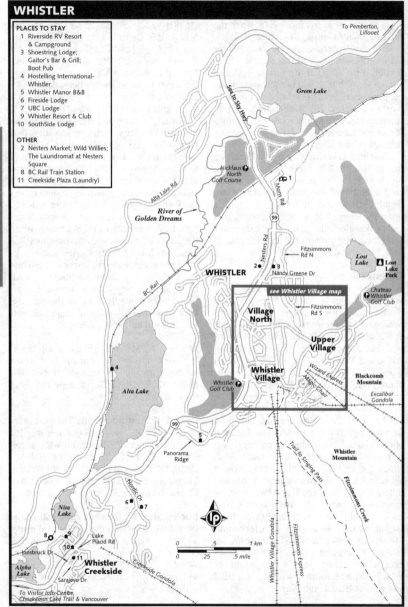

WHISTLER

PLACES TO STAY
1 Riverside RV Resort & Campground
3 Shoestring Lodge; Gaitor's Bar & Grill; Boot Pub
4 Hostelling International-Whistler
5 Whistler Manor B&B
6 Fireside Lodge
7 UBC Lodge
9 Whistler Resort & Club
10 SouthSide Lodge

OTHER
2 Nesters Market; Wild Willies; The Laundromat at Nesters Square
8 BC Rail Train Station
11 Creekside Plaza (Laundry)

To Pemberton, Lillooet

Green Lake

Sea to Sky Hwy

Moss Rd

Nicklaus North Golf Course

Alta Lake Rd

River of Golden Dreams

99

Nesters Rd

Fitzsimmons Rd N

Lost Lake

Lost Lake Park

2 3
Nancy Greene Dr

WHISTLER

see Whistler Village map

Fitzsimmons Rd S

Chateau Whistler Golf Club

BC Rail

Village North

Upper Village

Whistler Village

Whistler Golf Club

Wizard Express

Magic Chair

Blackcomb Mountain

Excalibur Gondola

4

Alta Lake

99

5

Panorama Ridge

Trail to Singing Pass

Whistler Mountain

Nordic Dr

Nita Lake

6 7

Fitzsimmons Creek

Fitzsimmons Express

8 9
Lake Placid Rd

10
11 **Whistler Creekside**

Innsbruck Dr

Alpha Lake

Sarajevo Dr

Creekside Gondola

Whistler Village Gondola

To Visitor Info Centre, Cheakamus Lake Trail & Vancouver

0   .5   1 km
0   .25   .5 mile

ROSS BARNETT

Point Atkinson Lighthouse at Lighthouse Park, West Vancouver

TERESA GAUDIO

Horseshoe Bay, where the mountains meet the sea

A winter sports paradise: Whistler Mountain

Summer skiing on Blackcomb Mountain

Away from it all in Garibaldi Provincial Park

Laundry Wash clothes at The Laundromat at Nesters Square (☎ 604-932-2960), 7009 Nesters Rd, or at Creekside Plaza (☎ 604-932-3980), 2010 Innsbruck Dr.

Medical Services The Town Plaza Medical Clinic (☎ 604-905-7089), 40-4314 Main St near the Delta Whistler Village Suites, offers walk-in services and extended hours. For emergencies, head to the Whistler Health Care Center (☎ 604-932-4911), 4380 Lorimer Rd.

Whistler Museum and Archives

This museum (☎ 604-932-2019), 4329 Main St in the Village North area, features exhibits on regional history, including the town's development as a resort. It's open 10 am to 4 pm Thursday through Sunday. Admission is $1; children and teens get in free.

Activities

Although many people think of Whistler as a huge winter playground (and it is!), the area also offers countless summer recreation opportunities. Intrawest Corporation (☎ 604-932-3434, 800-766-0449) owns and operates both Whistler and Blackcomb Mountains, both of which offer a range of year-round programs beyond skiing (see the Web site www .whistler-blackcomb.com).

Winter Whistler-Blackcomb sells more than 2.1 million lift tickets for **downhill skiing** and **snowboarding** each year, more than any other resort in North America. But the crowds can spread out here, since the resort encompasses one of the continent's largest ski areas, featuring more than 200 marked trails and 12 alpine bowls over 2800 hectares. The usually reliable snowfall, the vertical drop (1609m on Blackcomb, 1530m on Whistler) and the mild Pacific air combine to provide some of the most pleasant skiing to be found anywhere. The runs suit people of all abilities, too, with the terrain rated as 20% novice, 55% intermediate and 25% expert.

The regular ski season typically runs from mid-November until late April on Blackcomb Mountain and from late November until early June on Whistler Mountain. Blackcomb's Horstman Glacier is accessible from June through early August.

There are five mountain bases: Whistler Creekside, Whistler Village, Excalibur Village, Excalibur Base II and Upper Village Blackcomb. You'll find high-speed lifts at all of these locations; lines usually move quickly, though half-hour waits aren't uncommon on the busiest days. A one-day lift ticket costs $63/54/32 for adults/seniors and children 13 to 18/children seven to 12. The available lessons include a three-day

WHISTLER

Working at Whistler-Blackcomb

Whistler-Blackcomb hires several thousand people each year for seasonal jobs that range from ski-lift operators to food service personnel. October/November and February/March are the peak recruiting times; most jobs go to Canadian residents or people with Canadian work authorization, such as Australians and New Zealanders on working holiday visas. (See Work in the Facts for the Visitor chapter for details.) Hourly wages range from about $7.50 to $12, plus good benefits: a season ski pass to both mountains, 50% food discounts and free ski and snowboard lessons.

For information about job openings and applications, call ☎ 604-938-7366, fax 604-938-7838 or write Whistler-Blackcomb, 4896 Glacier Dr, Whistler BC, V0N 1B4, Canada. You can also visit the resort's Web site at www.whistler-blackcomb.com. Prospective employees can apply online, but everyone must interview in person, too.

Once you get a job, you need to find a cheap place to live, which isn't easy in Whistler. The resort makes some rooms available through its Glacier Residence program; rental rates range from $8.25 to $15 per person, per night. Call ☎ 604-938-7500 for information.

WHISTLER

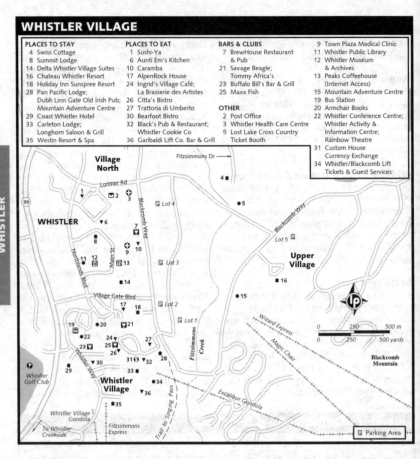

WHISTLER VILLAGE

PLACES TO STAY
4   Swiss Cottage
8   Summit Lodge
14 Delta Whistler Village Suites
16 Chateau Whistler Resort
18 Holiday Inn Sunspree Resort
28 Pan Pacific Lodge;
    Dubh Linn Gate Old Irish Pub;
    Mountain Adventure Centre
29 Coast Whistler Hotel
33 Carleton Lodge;
    Longhorn Saloon & Grill
35 Westin Resort & Spa

PLACES TO EAT
1   Sushi-Ya
6   Aunti Em's Kitchen
10 Caramba
17 AlpenRock House
24 Ingrid's Village Café;
    La Brasserie des Artistes
26 Citta's Bistro
27 Trattoria di Umberto
30 Bearfoot Bistro
32 Black's Pub & Restaurant;
    Whistler Cookie Co
36 Garibaldi Lift Co. Bar & Grill

BARS & CLUBS
7   BrewHouse Restaurant
    & Pub
21 Savage Beagle;
    Tommy Africa's
23 Buffalo Bill's Bar & Grill
25 Maxx Fish

OTHER
2   Post Office
3   Whistler Health Care Centre
5   Lost Lake Cross Country
    Ticket Booth

9   Town Plaza Medical Clinic
11 Whistler Public Library
12 Whistler Museum
    & Archives
13 Peaks Coffeehouse
    (Internet Access)
15 Mountain Adventure Centre
19 Bus Station
20 Armchair Books
22 Whistler Conference Centre;
    Whistler Activity &
    Information Centre;
    Rainbow Theatre
31 Custom House
    Currency Exchange
34 Whistler/Blackcomb Lift
    Tickets & Guest Services

beginners' program, children's lessons and women-only workshops. Ask about special multi-day rates and season passes. Note: Signs posted in the Whistler-Blackcomb resort parking lots warn people not to buy lift tickets 'from other than authorized ticket sales outlets.' If you fall for a scam and purchase forged tickets, you won't be able to use them at the lifts.

For gear rental, look into the Mountain Adventure Centres, which promise 'fine dining for your feet' – which means that you can choose from a wide array of high-performance snow-sports equipment and

switch as much as you want all day. You'll find the centers at four locations: Pan Pacific Lodge (☎ 604-905-2295); Blackcomb Daylodge (☎ 938-7737); the top of Whistler Mountain (☎ 905-2325); and the top of Blackcomb Mountain (938-7425),with yet another new location planned for Whistler Creekside.

If you prefer **cross-country skiing**, more than 28km of trails wind through Lost Lake Park and the valley. You can pick up trail maps and rent equipment throughout the resort area. The Lost Lake Cross Country Ticket Booth is north of Lorimer Rd, near its intersection with Blackcomb Way. Outdoor Adventures At Whistler (☎ 604-932-0647) offers **snowshoeing** tours, with all equipment included, starting at $39. TLH Heliskiing (☎ 250-558-5379, 800-667-4854) and Whistler Heli-Skiing (☎ 604-932-4105, 888-435-4754) lead helicopter treks to backcountry powder skiing.

Cougar Mountain (☎ 604-932-4086, 888-297-2222) specializes in wilderness adventures, including **snowmobiling**, **dog-sledding** and **backcountry fishing**. For a more laid-back adventure, try Blackcomb Horsedrawn Sleigh Rides (☎ 604-932-7631), which promises scenic tours of the area complete with hot chocolate and cowboy entertainment.

Summer From July through September, lifts remain open on both mountains, providing access to 48km of **hiking** trails. Summer sightseeing lift-ticket prices cost $22/19 adults/seniors and teenagers; children 12 and under ride free. The lifts run until 8 pm in July and August; after 5 pm, rides are $17/15 for adults/seniors and teens. Summer skiing and snowboarding lift tickets for Horstman Glacier cost $39/32 for adults/seniors and children. The ski village bustles with activity in summer, too; check out the climbing wall, trapeze swing and social scene at the base of Blackcomb Mountain.

Golfing fans come to play at Whistler's noted designer golf courses, which are generally open May through October. At Nicklaus North (☎ 604-938-9898), probably the most prestigious, greens fees start at $100.

Mountain biking is another popular summer pursuit, with more than 100km of single track in the area. The opportunities range from easy trails for recreational riders to hard-core mountain descents for experienced cyclists. Call Intrawest (☎ 604-932-

3434 or 800-766-0449) for information on tours, lessons and rentals. Wild Willies (☎ 604-938-8836), 7011 Nesters Rd, rents bikes and gives free bike tours of the valley daily in summer.

Many outfitters offer **horseback riding**, including Adventures on Horseback (☎ 604-894-6269) and the Whistler Outdoor Experience Co (☎ 604-932-3389). Whistler Air Services Ltd (☎ 604-932-6615, 888-806-2299) provides **flightseeing** float-plane trips to glaciers and alpine lakes. For **white-water rafting** on nearby rivers, contact Wedge Rafting (☎ 604-932-7171) or Whistler River Adventures (☎ 604-932-3532).

Special Events

Whistler is the setting for several major winter sports events, including the **Winter-Start Festival** in early December; the racing series from January through March; the annual **Whistler Gay Ski Week** in early February; and the **TELUS World Ski & Snowboard Festival** in mid-April.

In early June, the **Whistler Arts Experience** festival features workshops, gallery walks and entertainment. A fringe festival, **ArtRageous**, takes place at the same time. Music festivals happen all summer into early fall; these include the **Whistler Roots Weekend** in mid-July; the **Summit Concert Series**, with on-mountain performances during weekends in August; and the **Whistler Jazz & Blues Weekend** in mid-September. The festivities continue in fall, with such events as the **Alpine Wine Festival** in early September; **Oktoberfest** in mid-October; and **Cornucopia**, a food and wine festival in early November.

Places to Stay

There are many places to stay in Whistler, but few of them are cheap, and in the winter you'll be lucky to get a room at all on the weekend if you haven't booked well in advance.

The easiest way to secure a room is to use the central reservation service (☎ 604-664-5625, 800-944-7853 in North America, fax

WHISTLER

604-938-5758), which can book you a room at almost any of the area's hotels, lodges and condominiums (but none of the budget lodgings or B&Bs). Ask about package deals that can help cut the cost of accommodations and activities.

If you're on a budget, you probably won't want to come to Whistler in the second half of December or anytime during February and March, when most of the fancier rooms top $250. Top-end rates can dip by $100 or more during the early (mid-November to mid-December) and late (April) 'value' seasons. Rates quoted below are for the peak winter season, so expect much better deals at the pricier places the rest of the year.

Camping For cheap and rustic camping close to town, look for the BC Forest Services's *Cal-Cheak Confluence Recreation Site* about 10km south of Whistler on the east side of Hwy 99. Three separate areas contain 36 campsites ($10, or $5 for BC Forestry annual pass holders); the Cal-Cheak suspension bridge is a short walk from the south site.

Riverside RV Resort & Campground (☎ 604-932-5469, 877-905-5533, fax 604-905-5539, info@whistlercamping.com, 8018 Mons Rd) offers several amenities, including a hot tub, laundry, showers and shuttle service to Whistler Village. Rates are $20 for RV and tent sites with no hookups, $35 for RV sites with electric, water and sewer hookups, $125 to $150 for cabins that can sleep up to six people.

Hostels & Lodges It's rather remote, but *Hostelling International-Whistler* (☎ 604-932-5492, fax 932-4687, whistler@hihostels .bc.ca, 5678 Alta Lake Rd) enjoys a beautiful setting on Alta Lake, about 4km by foot from Whistler Village. Since the hostel can only accommodate 35 people, it's a good idea to book ahead, especially during ski season. Dorm bunks cost $18.50/22.50 for members/nonmembers. Amenities include canoes, bike rentals, Internet access and a dead-on view of Blackcomb Mountain. To get to the hostel, you can hoof it from the village (a 45-minute walk), or ride one of

the several daily buses. The BC Rail train (which follows the west side of Alta Lake) will stop at the hostel upon request.

SouthSide Lodge (☎ 604-932-3644, fax 932-0551, info@snowboardwhistler.com, 2121 Lake Placid Rd), very convenient to the Creekside area, offers 30 beds ($25 each) that are grouped five to a room. Each room comes with its own bathroom and shower, cable TV and VCR. Several budget lodges operate in the Nordic Estates area off Hwy 99 between Whistler Creekside and Whistler Village. *Fireside Lodge* (☎ 604-932-4545, 2117 Nordic Dr) and the *UBC Lodge* (☎ 604-932-6604, 822-5851 in Vancouver, 2124 Nordic Dr) both offers dormitory-style accommodations starting at about $25.

A 15-minute walk from the village, the *Shoestring Lodge* (☎ 604-932-3338, fax 932-8347, shoe@direct.ca, 7124 Nancy Greene Dr) rents both dorm beds ($26 and up) and motel-style rooms ($120). The place can get rowdy, with exotic dancers and bands in the on-premises Boot Pub, so ask for a room well down the hall if you want some peace and quiet.

B&Bs You'll find about 15 B&Bs in Whistler. The Visitor Info Centre can provide information about many of these.

Pleasant rooms, youthful innkeepers and a central location make *Whistler Manor* (☎ 604-932-2393, fax 932-7577, 3333 Panorama Ridge) a good choice. Rates range from $120 to $180 in winter, $80 to $130 in summer. *Swiss Cottage* (☎ 604-932-6062, 800-718-7822, fax 604-932-9648, swiss@ direct.ca, 7321 Fitzsimmons Dr) is also near the village, on a dead-end road with bikepath access. Rooms cost $100 to $150 in winter, $90 to $140 in summer (two-night minimum stay required year-round).

Hotels and Condominiums The *Whistler Resort & Club* (☎ 604-932-2343, fax 932-2969, reserve@rainbowretreats.com, 2129 Lake Placid Rd), in the Whistler Creekside area, suffers from a rather dated 1970s feel but offers some of the lowest prices in Whistler: $115 for a hotel room and $180 for a one-bedroom suite, double occupancy.

The nice amenities include a whirlpool and sauna and free use of canoes, tennis courts and bicycles in summer. The same company runs the **Carleton Lodge** (☎ 604-932-2343, fax 932-2969, reserve@rainbowretreats.com, 4290 Mountain Lane), in Whistler Village, where peak winter rates start at $270 for a one-bedroom suite.

Holiday Inn Sunspree Resort (☎ 604-938-0878, 800-229-3188, fax 604-938-9943, mail@whistlerhi.com, 4295 Blackcomb Way) boasts several appealing features: a central location within Whistler Village, an on-site concierge who can help with activity planning, and free meals for kids at several adjacent restaurants. Rates start at $229 for a studio room, which includes a fireplace and kitchenette.

Similar prices and amenities prevail, albeit with a slightly more upscale feel, at **Delta Whistler Village Suites** (☎ 604-905-3987, 888-299-3987, fax 604-938-6335, resdwvs@delta-whistler.com, 4308 Main St), in the Village North area. Studio suites go for $229.

The **Pan Pacific Lodge** (☎ 604-905-2999, 888-905-9995, fax 604-905-2995, whistler@panpacific-hotel.com, 4320 Sundial Crescent) overlooks the Whistler base area. Rooms with fireplaces, kitchens and soaker tubs start at $259. The boutique-style **Summit Lodge** (☎ 604-932-2778, 888-913-8811, fax 604-932-2716, reservations@summitlodge com, 4359 Main St), in Village North, offers studio suites with kitchenettes, balconies and fireplaces for $270. At the **Coast Whistler Hotel** (☎ 604-932-2522, 800-663-5644, fax 604-932-6711, reserve@direct.ca, 4005 Whistler Way), rooms start at $279, including the use of a heated pool, whirlpool and fitness center.

Westin Resort & Spa (☎ 604-905-5000, 888-634-557, fax 604-905-5589, reservations @westinwhistler.net, 4090 Whistler Way) is one of the resort's newest and biggest hotels, with 419 suite-style rooms starting at $329. Amenities include ski-in, ski-out access and a huge health club and spa with exotic equipment and treatments.

At the top of the price range, the **Chateau Whistler Resort** (☎ 604-938-8000,

800-441-1414, fax 604-938-2055, 4599 Chateau Blvd) beats the Westin Resort in size and cost, with 558 rooms starting at $399. Here you can enjoy the resort's own golf course and spa, as well as ski-in, ski-out access to Blackcomb Mountain.

Places to Eat
With more than 80 restaurants in Whistler, you'll have no trouble finding something good to eat. Resort Room Service (☎ 604-905-4711) delivers food from about 30 eateries for a charge of around $6. For a list of the selected restaurants, look in the local phone book, or call to request a menu guide.

Budget To prepare your own meals, shop for groceries at the reasonably priced **Nesters Market** (☎ 604-932-3545, 7019 Nesters Rd). For quick bites, try the **Whistler Cookie Co** (☎ 604-932-2962, 4268 Mountain Square) and **Auntie Em's Kitchen** (☎ 604-932-1163, 4340 Lorimer Rd). Both sell fresh baked goods, and the latter serves sandwiches and salads ($5 to $7.25).

Ingrid's Village Café (☎ 604-932-7000, 4305 Skiers Approach), just off the Village Square, makes a great stop for breakfast ($2 to $7) or lunch. Sandwiches start at $3.95, and several varieties of vegetarian burgers cost about $6.

Mid-Range On Whistler's Village Square, **La Brasserie des Artistes**(☎ 604-932-3569) serves a good breakfast all day, plus lunch and dinner (burgers and pastas are $9 to $12); it's also a good spot to kick back and have a beer, with plenty of outdoor seating on sunny days.

The cavernous **AlpenRock House** (☎ 604-938-0082, 4295 Blackcomb Way), under the Holiday Inn, features a fun atmosphere, good food, live music and dancing. Specialties include fondues and casseroles like Alper Magronen, a mess of macaroni, potatoes, Swiss cheese and homemade applesauce, starting at $7.95. You can bowl or play pool here, too.

At the Whistler base area, **Black's Pub & Restaurant** (☎ 604-932-6408, 4270 Mountain Square) is known for its pizzas ($8 to $14 for individual-size pies), which a lot of families enjoy in the downstairs dining room. The pub upstairs offers an excellent selection of microbrews and whiskies. Nearby, the **Garibaldi Lift Co Bar & Grill** (☎ 604-905-2220, 2320 London Lane) features huge burgers made to order, tasty margaritas and slopeside views.

Gaitor's Bar & Grill (☎ 604-938-5777), in the Shoestring Lodge, sets out a weekend brunch buffet ($11) on Sunday. At other times, this spot specializes in Mexican food, with quesadillas starting at $6, burritos for $9 to $11 and chicken chimichanga for $12.

The Mediterranean fare at **Caramba** (☎ 604-938-1879, 12-4314 Main St), in Village North, comes highly recommended by visitors and locals alike. Specialties include a wide array of pastas ($11 to $14), pizza (mostly $12) and rotisserie main dishes ($14 to $17, or $29 for the mixed grill for two).

On Village Square, the lively **Citta's Bistro** (☎ 604-932-4177, 4217 Village Stroll), pronounced 'Cheetah's,' serves up good, creative food; try the Cajun Caesar wrap, the beer-battered fish and chips ($9) or the Jim Beam-and-garlic steak ($19).

Sushi-Ya (☎ 604-905-0155, 230-4370 Lorimer Rd) offers a wide Japanese menu that includes sushi items ($1.75 to $3), noodle soups ($5 to $7), tempura dishes ($5 to $9) and sashimi selections ($8 to $24).

You'll find a vibrant social scene at the **Dubh Linn Gate Old Irish Pub** (☎ 604-905-4047), in the Pan Pacific Lodge at Whistler's base. Specialties include such soups as seafood corn chowder or Guinness-and-crab (each $7.95); sandwiches run $11 to $13, and main dishes cost $14 to $20.

Top End Every major hotel at Whistler contains a high-end dining room or two. More moderately priced than most hotel choices, **Trattoria di Umberto** (☎ 604-932-5858, 4417 Sundial Place), in the Mountainside Lodge, features dinner pastas ($11 to $13) and fish and meat dishes ($22 to $30). Lunch selections range from $7 to $14. The **Bearfoot Bistro** (☎ 604-932-3433, 4121 Village Green), in the Best Western Listel Whistler Hotel, has attracted attention with wild-game specialties and an impressive wine list. Main dishes cost $15 to $30.

Entertainment

You'd expect Canada's top ski resort to be a partying place, and it is. Après ski entertainment runs 4 to 7 pm, and many bars and clubs feature live music during those hours. The **Longhorn Saloon & Grill** (☎ 604-932-5999, 4290 Mountain Square), right at Whistler base, attracts crowds coming off the slopes. **Tommy Africa's** (☎ 604-932-6090) and the **Savage Beagle** (☎ 604-938-3337), under the same roof at 4222 Village Square, both draw a younger crowd of mostly 19-to-25-year-olds, while **Buffalo Bill's Bar & Grill** (☎ 604-932-6613, 4122 Village Green) attracts the 30-and-older set with occasional live music and comedy nights.

At **Maxx Fish** (☎ 604-932-1904, 4232 Village Stroll), the alternative spot in town, DJs spin a good variety of hip-hop, house and funk music. The **BrewHouse Restaurant & Pub** (☎ 604-905-2739, 4355 Blackcomb Way) creates such specialty beers as Twin Peaks Pale Ale and Lifty Lager; its big restaurant features early-bird dinner specials, 15 TVs and billiards. Live bands play frequently at the **Boot Pub** (☎ 604-932-3338), in the Shoestring Lodge, but the most popular performers here are the naked dancers of 'Das Boot Ballet,' appearing several nights each week.

Many establishments listed under Places to Eat, above, also see some lively nightlife, especially AlpenRock House, the Garibaldi Lift Co Bar & Grill, Dubh Linn Gate Old Irish Pub and Citta's Bistro.

The Rainbow Theatre screens first-run movies in the Whistler Conference Centre; call ☎ 604-932-2422 for showtimes.

Getting There & Away

Air Most people get to Whistler via ground transportation from Vancouver, which is the only option in winter. But June through September, Whistler Air (☎ 604-932-6615 or 888-806-2299) offers scheduled float-plane service between Whistler's Green Lake and Vancouver. The half-hour flights leave Vancouver's Harbour Air Terminal twice daily and cost $125 per person one-way.

Bus Greyhound Canada (☎ 604-932-5031, 800-661-8747) offers about six daily trips from Vancouver's Pacific Central Station to Whistler; the fare is $21/42 one-way/roundtrip. Most trips take 2½ hours, but the once-daily, early-morning Ski Express – with no stops between Horseshoe Bay and Whistler Creekside – arrives at Whistler Village in two hours. Buses stop at the main bus station, outside the Whistler Conference Centre. Tickets can be purchased either on the bus (in cash) or at Mail Boxes Etc, 4338 Main St in Village North (cash or credit cards). See the Web site www .whistlerbus.com for more details.

Shuttle Bigfoot Adventure Tours (☎ 604-278-8224 in Vancouver, 888-244-6673) runs a shuttle between central Vancouver and Whistler twice daily Tuesday, Thursday, Saturday and Sunday for $25/45 one-way/roundtrip (with open-ended return). Add $10 for service to Vancouver International Airport. Bigfoot also offers discounted lift tickets, as well as organized snowshoeing, ice-skating, snowmobiling and dog-sledding trips. Other, pricier shuttle services include Perimeter Whistler Express (☎ 604-266-5386 in Vancouver, 604-905-0041 in Whistler) and Vancouver Whistler Star Express (☎ 604-685-5546 in Vancouver, 604-905-7668 in Whistler).

Train BC Rail's Cariboo Prospector (☎ 800-339-8752 within BC, 800-663-8238 outside BC) runs one train daily each morning from North Vancouver to Whistler, with a return run in the evening. The trip takes 2½ hours. The one-way fare (including breakfast or dinner) is $32/29/20/6 for adults/seniors/children two to 12/children under age two. Reservations are required.

Getting Around

The WAVE (☎ 604-932-4020) offers bus rides around the Whistler area for $1.50, as well as a free shuttle service between Whistler Village, Village North and Upper Village. Buses are equipped with outside ski racks and bicycle racks.

For rental cars, contact Alamo Rent-A-Car (☎ 604-231-1409), Budget Rent-A-Car (☎ 604-932-1236) or Thrifty Car Rentals (☎ 604-938-0302).

Sea to Sky Taxi (☎ 604-932-3333 or 938-3333) provides taxi service. For limo service, call Sunshine Limousine Ltd (☎ 604-932-6995) or Town and Country Chauffeurs (☎ 604-932-6468).

PEMBERTON
• population 855
Just a short drive (32km) north of Whistler on Hwy 99, Pemberton has become a bedroom community for people priced out of the ski-town market. The cowboy hats start popping up here – you'll see more and more Wild West attire if you travel on to the Cariboo Chicoltin country in the northeast. For local information, stop at the Visitor Info Centre (☎ 604-894-6175), across from the Petro Canada station.

The area attractions include **Nairn Falls Provincial Park**, about 6km south of Pemberton along Hwy 99. The trail to the namesake falls (3km roundtrip) winds along steep banks overlooking the swift-flowing Green River, which may also be seen via an easy walk from the campground to Coudre Point. Another 4km roundtrip trail leads to One Mile Lake.

As you'd expect from the cowboy hats in town, **horseback riding** is a popular pastime. Poole Creek Stables (☎ 604-932-8666) and Adventures on Horseback (☎ 604-894-6269) offer trail rides and pack trips.

If you're willing to take a detour from the main highway, you'll find adventure aplenty via backcountry roads from Pemberton and points east. After a day of exercise, rest your weary bones at **Meager Creek Hot Springs**, 47km north of Pemberton via the Upper Lillooet River Rd. This world-class soaking site features Japanese-style bathing pools and interpretive trails. Geological hazards occasionally close Meager Creek, so inquire in Pemberton or call the Forest Service (☎ 604-898-2100) before setting out. Admission is $5 per person.

WHISTLER

Birkenhead Lake Provincial Park offers excellent wildlife watching, canoeing and fishing, plus an 85-site campground. It's 55km from Pemberton. Take the turnoff to D'Arcy at Mt Currie, 6km north of Pemberton on Hwy 99. The final 17km to the park are on a gravel road.

Places to Stay & Eat

Nairn Falls Provincial Park (☎ 604-898-3678) contains 92 campsites ($12). *Lillooet Lake Lodge* (☎ 604-905-9246), 12km off Hwy 99 east of Pemberton, rents tent sites ($20) and waterfront cabins ($80).

For those on a budget, the *Pemberton Hotel* (☎ 604-894-6313, fax 894-6655, 7423 Frontier St) offers a few single rooms with bathrooms down the hall for $30, plus rooms with private bathrooms that start at $50/60 single/double. About 6km north in the small community of Mount Currie, the *Hitching Post Motel* (☎ 604-894-6276) has 10 basic rooms for $45/57. For information on the 10 or so B&Bs in the Pemberton area, call or stop by the Visitor Info Centre.

Pony Espresso (☎ 604-894-5700, 1426 Portage Rd) is a funky eatery popular with everyone from Whistler commuters to longtime Pemberton locals. The bagel sandwiches (about $6 to $7) are scrumptious. Another good bet, the Outpost Restaurant (☎ 604-894-3340, 1392 Portage Rd) offers four kinds of Eggs Benedict on the weekends ($7.50), plus dinner selections ($11 to $19).

Getting There & Away

Greyhound Canada (☎ 604-894-6818, 800-661-8747) operates four daily bus trips from Vancouver's Pacific Central Station to Pemberton. Trips take about three hours; the fare is $22/44 one-way/roundtrip.

BC Rail's Cariboo Prospector (☎ 800-339-8752 within BC, 800-663-8238 outside BC) runs one train daily in each direction. The fare from North Vancouver is $40/80 one-way/roundtrip, including meals.

LILLOOET

• population 2058

The 101km stretch of Hwy 99 between Pemberton and Lillooet is a beauty, even

---

A Little Lillooet Lore

A former gold rush town, Lillooet served as 'Mile 0' on the old Cariboo Rd to the gold fields, meaning that all landmarks beyond here were named after their distance from Lillooet – hence unusual monikers like 70 Mile House and 100 Mile House.

Speaking of odd names, the Hwy 99 span over the Fraser River is formally known as the Bridge of the 23 Camels. Most miners bound for the Cariboo used horses, mules and oxen to haul their gear, but one prospector thought camels might work even better. Much to his surprise, they didn't work at all, and they smelled terrible, to boot. Still, the modern-day bridge builders didn't pass up the chance to memorialize this curious chapter of Lillooet's past.

---

more serpentine than the southern stretch of the Sea to Sky Hwy. The route crests near Joffre Lakes Provincial Park, where you can take a short hike to the first lake or follow a much more ambitious trail to the upper backcountry. After that, it's all downhill – at grades up to 17% – past Duffey Lake and along Cayoosh Creek.

Lillooet's mountainous setting belies its semi-arid climate, which sees some of the hottest temperatures in Canada. For local information, stop at the Visitor Info Centre (☎ 250-256-4308), 790 Main St, inside a converted church that also serves as a museum.

Activities abound. For **mountain biking**, contact Gravity Fed Adventures (☎ 250-256-7947), which leads guided trips out of Lillooet, using helicopters to reach the backcountry. Fraser River Jet Boat Adventures (☎ 250-256-4180) offers **scenic river trips** with historical commentary May through October. If you want to roll up your sleeves for some **gold panning**, Spirit River Holidays (☎ 250-256-4417) specializes in trips on the Fraser. **Golfing** at the nine-hole Sheep Pasture Golf Course, 5km south of Lillooet on Texas Creek Rd, presents a rare challenge: wooly mobile hazards.

Places to Stay & Eat
Cayoosh Creek Campground (☎ 250-256-4180, 877-748-2628, fax 250-256-4174, rjansen@lillonet.org), about 1km south of the Hwy 12 and 99 junction, offers 48 sites ($12 to $18), showers and lots of activities.

At the *Mile-0-Motel (☎ 250-256-7511, 888-766-4530, fax 250-256-4124, 616 Main St)*, you can wash your grubby clothes at the coin-op laundry; rooms start at $40/50 single/double. The *Hotel Victoria (☎ 250-256-4112, fax 256-4997, 667 Main St)* features nicely refurbished rooms, many with kitchenettes, for about $65/75.

You'll find the cheapest eats at the *farmer's market*, held at 10 am every Friday, May through October, next to the Mile-0-Motel. The reliable *Vic Café*, in the Hotel Victoria, offers breakfast and lunch, along with email access; later on, the hotel's dining rooms serve both fine-dining cuisine and pizza. *Dina's Place (☎ 604-256-4264, 690 Main St)* features Greek food, but it's overpriced ($10 to $20 for lackluster main dishes).

Getting There & Away
BC Rail's Cariboo Prospector stops at Lillooet once daily in each direction. The fare from North Vancouver is $67/134 one-way/roundtrip.

Sunshine Coast

Stretching from Langdale to Lund, the Sunshine Coast is a geographical orphan, separated from the rest of the Lower Mainland by the formidable Coast Mountains. Sunshine Coasters make full use of their scenic maritime location, enjoying everything from cruises into majestic Princess Louisa Inlet to kayaking and scuba diving in world-class settings.

Hwy 101 winds nearly the length of the coast, but the trip is interrupted by water between Earls Cove and Saltery Bay, where BC Ferries bridges the gap. Powell River, the region's largest town, is the jumping-off spot for ferries to Comox on Vancouver Island. Allow at least 90 minutes for the winding 84km drive from Langdale to Earls Cove, then 50 minutes for the ferry crossing to Saltery Bay. From Saltery Bay, it's a 35km drive to Powell River and another 23km from Powell River to Lund. Although you can get from Langdale to Powell River (including the ferry crossing) in about three hours, you'll want to allow more time for sightseeing or other activities en route.

GIBSONS
• population 4000

If you want to sample the Sunshine Coast on a day trip from Vancouver, or even an overnight excursion, Gibsons makes a fine destination. It's a short (5km) hop from Langdale, which in turn is only a 40-minute ferry ride from Horseshoe Bay (see the Vancouver & Around chapter). People still know Gibsons as the setting for *The Beachcombers*, a popular CBC series filmed here in the 1970s.

Orientation & Information
The town of Gibsons is divided into two sections: the visitor-oriented Gibsons Landing and Upper Gibsons, the commercial strip farther up the hill along Hwy 101 (the Sunshine Coast Hwy). The Gibsons Chamber of Commerce operates a tourist information desk (☎ 604-886-2325) outside the Sunnycrest Mall, just off Hwy 101 along the commercial strip; it's open 9 am to 5 pm daily. The chamber also staffs a seasonal information center at Gibsons Landing; it's open on weekends in June and daily in July and August.

You'll find the post office at the corner of Gower Point and Winn Rds. Laundromats and showers are available at the Gibsons Harbour headquarters and the Gibsons Marina.

Things to See & Do
The **Elphinstone Pioneer Museum** (☎ 604-886-8232), 716 Winn Rd across from the post office, displays an eclectic collection of bottles, period costumes, Native Indian baskets and seashells. It's open 10:30 am to 4:30 pm Tuesday to Saturday. Admission is by donation.

The **Sunshine Coast Maritime Museum** (☎ 604-886-4114 or 886-0866), Molly's Lane behind Gower Point Rd, includes a collection of model ships and other nautical exhibits. It's open 10 am to 4 pm daily in the summer and by chance or by appointment the rest of the year. Admission is free.

For a swim or a picnic, try the nice **Armours Beach**, just northeast of the village below Marine Dr, or **Chaster Park**, around the point on Ocean Beach Esplanade. (Follow Gower Point Rd.)

The sheltered harbors and islands of Howe Sound, near Gibsons, make an idyllic setting for **sea kayaking**. Sunshine Kayaking (☎ 604-886-9760) can get you started with rentals, lessons and a variety of tours.

Places to Stay

At **Lookout B&B** (☎ 604-886-1655, fax 886-1655, lookout@sunshine.net, 318 Shoal Lookout), on Gibsons Bluff at the far end of the village, you can survey the ocean where Howe Sound and the Georgia Strait meet. Rooms start at $75/85 single/double. The **Marina House B&B** (☎ 604-886-7888, marinahouse@sunshine.net, 546 Marine Dr), just 1km north of the village toward Langdale and tucked below the road, enjoys beach access and wonderful views of Shoal Channel; rooms start at $80/90.

Near the waterfront, the **Ritz Inn Motor Hotel** (☎ 604-886-3343, 800-649-1138, fax 604-886-8189, ritz_inn@dccnet.com, 505 Gower Point Rd) rents rooms for $70/79. Each room has kitchen facilities, but you'll be charged an extra $8 if you want to use the kitchen to cook your own meals. Up on Hwy 101, the **Cedars Inn** (☎ 604-886-3008, 888-774-7044, fax 604-886-3046, cedarsinn@ashler.com, 895 Sunshine Coast Hwy) offers similar prices.

Places to Eat

You'll find a good variety of restaurants in Gibsons. **Molly's Reach** (☎ 604-886-9710), at the intersection of Marine Dr and Gower Point Rd (you can't miss it), features harbor views and lots of *Beachcombers* memorabilia. It's open daily for breakfast (about $3 to $8), lunch ($6 to $8) and dinner, which

includes seafood specialties and other main dishes ($7 to $20).

You can buy fresh seafood right off the dock, or visit **Gibsons Fish Market** (☎ 604-886-8363, 292 Gower Point Rd), where you can sit at tables to enjoy fish and chips ($4.50 and up).

The decor is Tex-Mex, but meals are all over the map at **Howl at the Moon** (☎ 604-886-8881, 450 Marine Dr). This family-friendly spot serves steaks, pasta and seafood; most entrees cost $8 to $15. **The Flying Cow** (☎ 604-886-0301, 451 Marine Dr) makes a good vegetarian choice, with yummy soups (about $4) and omelets ($7 to $8).

At **Opa Japanese Restaurant** (☎ 604-886-4023, 281 Gower Point Rd), sit at one of the window seats overlooking the harbor, or pick up a boxed lunch or dinner to go. Dinner specials cost about $13. **Haus Uropa** (☎ 604-886-8326, 426 Gower Point Rd) specializes in German fare at lunch ($4 to $11) and dinner ($10 to $17). Even the kids can get their own Wiener schnitzel and fries ($5.75). **Jack's Lane Bistro & Bakery** (☎ 604-886-4898, 546 Sunshine Coast Hwy), just up the hill from the landing, is noted for its Mediterranean fare and fresh-baked goods.

Getting There & Around

BC Transit's Sunshine Coast Transit System (☎ 604-885-6899) serves the Lower Sunshine Coast from Langdale to Secret Cove. The one-way fare is $1.50/1 for adults/seniors and children. For complete information, see the transit schedules at the Web site www.suncoastcentral.com.

Malaspina Coach Lines (☎ 604-886-7742, 877-227-8287) travels between Vancouver's Pacific Central Station and the bus depot at 1009 Gibsons Way twice a day. The fare is $15.50/23 one-way/roundtrip, which includes the Horseshoe Bay–Langdale ferry.

BC Ferries (☎ 888-223-3779) offers about eight daily sailings between Horseshoe Bay and Langdale. In peak season, the 40-minute trip costs $8/4 for adults/children; cars are $27.75. This fare covers either a roundtrip between Horseshoe Bay and Langdale, or a one-way through-trip from Horseshoe Bay to Langdale and then from Earls Cove to Saltery Bay (the northern Sunshine Coast ferry). Allow 90 minutes for the 84km drive from Langdale to Earls Cove.

ROBERTS CREEK
• population 2500

During the Vietnam War era of the late 1960s and early '70s, many US residents opposed to the conflict headed north to Canada. Quite a few settled in the Roberts Creek area, 7km northwest of Gibsons, and the area retains a strong counterculture feel.

Roberts Creek Rd, off Hwy 101, leads to the anti-commercial center of town, where you'll find a post office, general store, library and several shops and restaurants. But the true heart of Roberts Creek is probably its community hall, which frequently hosts concerts, dances and lectures. Check the placards around town to see what's playing.

Head for **Roberts Creek Provincial Park**, just west of town off Hwy 101, for a day at the beach or a quick picnic stop. Canadian Wilderness Ecotours Ltd (☎ 604-885-0238, 877-350-5862) specializes in off-the-beaten-track tours to such places as the Caren Range (home to some of Canada's oldest trees, 1800-year-old yellow cedars); the Tetrahedron Range; and the Stoltman Wilderness. But one of the company's most popular tours is its two-hour evening stroll to hear owls hooting (and to hoot back at them) on nearby Mt. Elphinstone. Dates and times for tours vary; call or visit the Web site www.wildernessecotours.com for a schedule.

Places to Stay & Eat

Roberts Creek Provincial Park (☎ 604-898-3678) includes 25 campsites ($12), available May through September. *Moon Cradle Backpackers Retreat* (☎ 604-885-0238, 877-350-5862, fax 604-885-6640, mooncradle@ uniserve.com, 3125 Sunshine Coast Hwy) is the only hostel on the lower Sunshine Coast, and it's a good one. Innkeepers Shaeah Fialkow and Richard Biel, both dedicated environmentalists, have created a welcoming home in the woods. (Rich also co-owns Canadian Wilderness Ecotours,

mentioned above.) A dorm bunk (in hand-crafted cedar beds, no less) costs $20 for students and hostel members, $25 for everyone else. The hostel also rents private rooms ($25/45 single/double for students and members, $30/55 for nonmembers). Amenities include a free all-organic continental breakfast, shoulder massage, kitchen access (vegetarian food only, please) and drum circles and bonfires in summer.

Roberts Creek eats and hangs out at the *Gumboot Garden Café* (☎ 604-885-4216, 1057 Roberts Creek Rd). Breakfast selections range from homemade granola ($2.40) to a salmon omelet ($7.75). At lunchtime, burritos cost $6.25 to $7.25. Evenings bring fine dining for reasonable prices, such as organic chicken with lemon-ginger dipping sauce ($14). One of the Sunshine Coast's most upscale choices, *Creekhouse* (☎ 604-885-9321, 1041 Roberts Creek Rd) serves dinner Friday through Sunday. Most main dishes cost about $20; the $47 fresh-seafood platter feeds two.

Getting There & Away

Malaspina Coach Lines (☎ 877-227-8287) runs two buses daily to Roberts Creek. The fare from Vancouver is $17/26 one-way/ roundtrip, including passage aboard the Horseshoe Bay–Langdale ferry.

SECHELT
• population 8000

The second-largest town on the Sunshine Coast, Sechelt enjoys a waterside setting on a narrow isthmus amid several bays. Parks and beaches abound. This area has long been an important stronghold of the Coast Salish people; in 1986, the Sechelt Band became the first in modern Canada to attain self-government.

Sechelt's downtown area is centered around the intersection of Hwy 101 and Wharf Ave. From here, if you're coming from Roberts Creek, turn right for Porpoise Bay or left for Halfmoon Bay and the Earls Cove ferry. The Sechelt & District Chamber of Commerce (☎ 604-885-0662) operates a Visitor Info Centre in the Trail Bay Mall, 5755 Cowrie St.

SUNSHINE COAST

The post office (☎ 604-885-2411) is at the corner of Dolphin and Inlet Sts. The Daily Roast coffee shop (☎ 604-885-4345), 5547 Wharf St, offers free email access for patrons. Sechelt Coin Laundry (☎ 604-885-3393), 5660 Dolphin St, is open until 6 pm Monday to Saturday; closed Sunday.

Things to See & Do

At the **Davis Bay** beach, on the south side of Sechelt, you can fish off the long pier or go for a swim. With a good kayak launch and a sandy beach, **Porpoise Bay Provincial Park**, northeast of downtown, makes an ideal base camp for paddlers and cyclists exploring the Sunshine Coast. The park also offers interpretive programs.

The Sechelt First Nations band has its headquarters at the **House of Hewhiwus** (☎ 604-885-8991), on the south end of town. This impressive complex includes a theater, a museum and gift shop.

The **Sunshine Coast Arts Centre** (☎ 604-885-5412), at the corner of Trail Ave and Medusa St, displays art in its gallery and holds cultural events in its performance space. Sechelt also hosts the Festival of the Written Arts (☎ 604-885-9631), a major Canadian literary gathering held each August at the Rockwood Centre on Cowrie St.

If you're here for the **cycling**, Mountain High Cycle/Trail Bay Sports (☎ 604-885-2512), 5504 Trail Ave, offers bike rentals and maps. On the Edge (☎ 604-885-4888, 877-322-4888), based in nearby Halfmoon Bay, leads guided mountain-biking trips, art-studio cycle tours, kayak-and-bike combo trips and more. To rent gear or take lessons in **scuba diving**, try the Diving Locker (☎ 604-885-9830), 5567 Dolphin St; or Suncoast Diving & Watersports (☎ 604-740-8006), 5395 Selma Park Rd. Pedals &

Paddles (☎ 604-885-6440), at Tillicum Bay on Sechelt Inlet, offers canoe and kayak rentals, lessons and trip planning.

Places to Stay

South of Sechelt, **Wilson Creek Campground** (☎ 604-885-5937, 800-565-9222, fax 604-885-5445, 4314 Hwy 101) offers 37 sites ($15 to $20) year-round. **Porpoise Bay Provincial Park** (☎ 604-898-3678), 4km north of Sechelt, features a separate area set aside for hikers and cyclists ($9), plus regular sites for everybody else ($17.50). From July through September, you can reserve a spot by calling ☎ 800-689-9025 (604-689-9025 in Greater Vancouver).

Ask the Visitor Info Centre to give you a list of Sechelt's numerous B&Bs, where rooms cost $90 to $120.

Downtown, the **Cozy Court Motel** (☎ 604-885-9314, fax 885-7723, 5522 Inlet Ave) offers moderately priced rooms ($50/55 for a single/double) just four blocks from the beach. Guest rooms are older at **Blue Sky Motel** (☎ 604-885-9987, 4726 Hwy 101), but they're right across Hwy 101 from the beach. You'll pay $55/58/68 single/double/kitchenette.

On the waterfront downtown, **Driftwood Inn** (☎ 604-885-5811, fax 885-5836, driftwood-inn@sunshine.net, 5454 Trail Ave) charges $79/84. At Davis Bay, **Bella Beach Inn** (☎ 604-885-7191, 800-665-1925, fax 604-885-3794, 4748 Hwy 101), each room comes with an ocean view and either a patio or balcony for $79/89.

Places to Eat

You'll find three of Sechelt's best restaurants in a downtown plaza at 5530 Wharf Ave. **Wild Flour Bakery** (☎ 604-740-9998) specializes in decadent baked goods made with fresh ingredients. **Sun Fish Café**

(☎ 604-885-0237) serves tasty salads and sandwiches (about $7) and main dishes ($9 to $17). The **Old Boot Eatery** (☎ 604-885-2727) features a wide menu of pastas ($9 to $11), pizza (about $12), seafood ($13 to $15) and steaks and ribs (about $17).

The Wharf (☎ 604-885-7285, 4748 Hwy 101), at the Bella Beach Inn, offers both Japanese and Canadian food, with dinner served from 5 pm daily except Thursday. **Pebbles** (☎ 604-885-5811, 5454 Trail Ave), at the Driftwood Inn, features a wide menu with seafood specialties. Meals are reasonably priced at lunch ($4 to $9), though a bit pricey at dinner ($15 to $23).

Getting There & Away
Malaspina Coach Lines (☎ 877-227-8287), 5653 Wharf St, stops twice daily at Sechelt. The fare from Vancouver is $18.75/29.50 one-way/roundtrip, including the Horseshoe Bay–Langdale ferry.

EGMONT & EARLS COVE
It's a lovely drive northwest of Sechelt to these communities at the top of the Lower Sunshine Coast. Several companies run full-day boat trips up Jervis Inlet to the rugged fjords of **Princess Louisa Inlet** and **Chatterbox Falls**, including Malibu Yacht Charters (☎ 604-883-2003), and the Egmont Water Taxi (☎ 604-883-2092). Try also Sunshine Coast Tours (☎ 604-883-2456). For a good hike, try **Skookumchuck Narrows Provincial Park**, near Egmont, at high tide, when the ocean roars in or out of the narrows.

BC Ferries (☎ 250-386-3431, 888-223-3779) offers about eight daily sailings between Earls Cove and Saltery Bay. In peak season, the 50-minute trip costs $8/4 for adults/children; cars cost $27.75; this fare covers either a roundtrip between Earls Cove and Saltery Bay or a one-way through-trip from Horsehoe Bay to Langdale and then from Earls Cove to Saltery Bay.

POWELL RIVER
• population 14,000

Powell River is a gritty industrial town anchoring the top of the Sunshine Coast. Most travelers pass through quickly on a circle tour of the Sunshine Coast and Vancouver Island, but those who linger will find low-cost amenities and a good array of recreational opportunities.

Powell River lies 31km north of the Saltery Bay ferry terminal. Hwy 101 becomes Marine Ave through downtown. The Townsite area north of downtown is home to the huge Pacific Paper mill. From there, Hwy 101 continues on to its terminus at Lund, 23km north.

The Powell River Visitor Info Centre (☎ 604-485-4701), 4690 Marine Ave, stays open year-round. You'll find the post office (☎ 604-485-5552) at 4812 Joyce Ave; there's also a postal services counter, plus ATMs and a grocery store, in the Town Centre Mall, 7100 Alberni St (enter on Joyce Ave). Access email at Armourtech (☎ 604-485-6423), 4717 Marine Ave, or at the Powell River Public Library (☎ 604-485-4796), 4411 Michigan Ave.

You can do laundry at Atwater Laundromat (☎ 604-485-2023), 4454 Willingdon Ave. For medical emergencies, go to Powell River General Hospital (☎ 604-485-3211), 5000 Joyce Ave.

Things to See & Do
Willingdon Beach, west of downtown, is a pleasant place to pass time. Across Willingdon Ave from the beach, the **Powell River Museum** (☎ 604-485-2222) contains a replica of a shack once occupied by Billy Goat Smith, a hermit who lived (with his goats) in the area in the early 20th century. Ask about the museum's treasure hunt if you're traveling with children. The museum is open 9 am to 5 pm daily, June through August, and weekdays the rest of the year. One of the province's oldest movie houses, the **Patricia Theatre** (☎ 604-483-9345), 5848 Ash St in Townsite, offers a glimpse of the past – there's even a carousel out back.

The 180km **Sunshine Coast Trail** from Saltery Bay to Sarah Point includes 27 shorter trails; all are shown on the excellent Powell River Visitor Map ($2), available at the Visitor Info Centre. The same map

SUNSHINE COAST

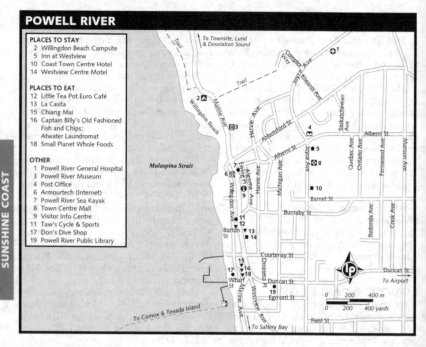

POWELL RIVER

PLACES TO STAY
2 Willingdon Beach Campsite
5 Inn at Westview
10 Coast Town Centre Hotel
14 Westview Centre Motel

PLACES TO EAT
12 Little Tea Pot Euro Café
13 La Casita
15 Chiang Mai
16 Captain Billy's Old Fashioned
   Fish and Chips;
   Atwater Laundromat
18 Small Planet Whole Foods

OTHER
1 Powell River General Hospital
3 Powell River Museum
4 Post Office
6 Armourtech (Internet)
7 Powell River Sea Kayak
8 Town Centre Mall
9 Visitor Info Centre
11 Taw's Cycle & Sports
17 Don's Dive Shop
19 Powell River Public Library

details the 57km Powell Forest Canoe Route, which connects 12 lakes via easily portaged trails.

For information on the ample **scuba diving** around Powell River, contact Don's Dive Shop (☎ 604-485-6969), 6789 Wharf St, which leads guided dives and rents gear. Taw's Cycle & Sports (☎ 604-485-2555), 4597 Marine Ave, rents bikes and offers sound advice on local **mountain biking**, campsites and hiking. Powell River Sea Kayak (☎ 604-485-2144), 6812E Alberni Place, rents boats and leads a range of **kayaking** tours, from two-hour paddles to multi-day trips into Desolation Sound.

Places to Stay

At *Willingdon Beach Campsite* (☎ 604-485-2242, 4845 Marine Ave), the facilities include showers, laundry, walk-in tent sites ($15) and full hookups ($20). The *Old Courthouse Inn & Hostel* (☎ 604-483-4000, 6243 Walnut St), in the Townsite section, offers dorm-style bunks for $17, shared-bath rooms for $27/35 single/double, and private-bath rooms for $35/44. The rate includes linens and towels and kitchen access – though there's a great little café on the ground floor. All rooms are nonsmoking. Ask about low-cost pick-ups from the bus or ferry.

Beacon Bed & Breakfast (☎ 604-485-5563, 877-485-5563, fax 604-485-9450, beacon@aisl.bc.ca, 3750 Marine Ave), south of town toward Saltery Bay, features a waterfront setting and on-site massage therapy. Double rooms cost $75 to $135.

The *Inn at Westview* (☎ 604-485-6281, fax 485-2622, theinnatwestview@prcn.org, 7050 Alberni St) offers basic rooms with balconies for $48/52. At the *Westview Centre Motel* (☎ 604-485-4023, 877-485-4023, fax 604-485-7736, 4534 Marine Ave), downtown, rates start at $50/ 58. *Coast Town Centre Hotel* (☎ 604-485-3000, 800-663-1144, fax 604-485-3031, 4660 Joyce Ave) boasts an

(Way) Down on the Farm

For a few days of backcountry hiking and canoeing, consider the HI *Fiddlehead Farm* (☎ 604-483-3018, fax 485-3832, retreat@ fiddleheadfarm.org), about 20km up Powell Lake from town and accessible only by boat. The hostel charges $36 for a bed in the house, $28 for camping; rates include all meals and canoe use. If you're willing to do two hours of chores, you'll only have to pay $22. Make arrangements at least one week in advance so the owners can schedule your boat transportation ($20 roundtrip). For reservations, call (make sure you let the phone ring 10 times) or write to Box 421, Powell River, V8A 5C2.

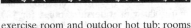

exercise room and outdoor hot tub; rooms start at $69/89.

Powell Lake is popular for houseboating. Plan to spend about $700 (four days) or $1000 (a week) for a cruiser that can sleep six people or more. Outfitters include Papa Bear's Vacations (☎ 604-483-8224, fax 853-3135) and Sunquest Houseboat Rentals (☎ 604-485-4043). Inquire at the Visitor Info Centre about floating cabins and B&Bs near the Sunshine Coast Trail and Powell Forest Canoe Route.

Places to Eat

Small Planet Whole Foods (☎ 604-485-9134, 4449 Marine Ave), a vegetarian deli/café, offers sandwiches ($4 to 5) and desserts ($1 to $3). *Captain Billy's Old Fashioned Fish and Chips* (☎ 604-485-2252) has been dishing the fish ($6.45 for two pieces) near the ferry terminal for more than 25 years. It's open daily from April through September.

La Casita (☎ 604-485-7720, 4578 Marine Ave) features Mexican combo plates ($7 to $12). It's closed Sunday. *Little Tea Pot Euro Café* (☎ 604-485-5955 Willingdon Ave) serves homemade soups (about $4) and lunch specialties (mostly $7 to $8) and hosts Sunday-afternoon poetry readings. Take a quick trip

to Thailand at *Chiang Mai* (☎ 604-485-0883, 4463 Marine Ave), which offers lunch ($6.50 to $7.50) and dinner ($7 to $13).

In Townsite, the *Old Courthouse Café*, in the Old Courthouse Inn & Hostel, displays lots of local artwork and serves breakfast, lunch and dinner at budget prices. On Powell Lake past Townsite, the *Shinglemill Pub* (☎ 604-483-2001, 6233 Powell Place) offers good, moderately priced bistro-type food accompanied by great views.

Getting There & Around

Pacific Coastal Airlines (☎ 800-663-2872) flies to Powell River from Vancouver for $99 one-way; book 10 days ahead for a cheaper ($69) fare. The Powell River Airport, 7576 Duncan St, is about 2km from downtown.

Malaspina Coach Lines (☎ 877-227-8287) operates bus service between Vancouver and Powell River, with two trips daily in each direction. The fare is $30.25/60.50 one-way/roundtrip, with the two ferry rides included. Buses stop at the Coast Town Centre Hotel.

BC Transit's Powell River Regional Transit System (☎ 604-485-4287) offers local bus service for $1.50/1 adults/seniors and children.

BC Ferries (☎ 250-386-3431 or 888-223-3779) offers four daily sailings between Powell River's Westview ferry terminal and Comox on Vancouver Island. The boats are often overloaded, especially on the mid-day sailing, so plan to arrive at least an hour before departure if you're driving. The 75-minute crossing costs $7.50/3.75 one-way for adults/children; cars cost $25. See the Getting Around chapter for information on discounted Sunshine Coast Circle Pac tickets, which offer savings if you plan to travel up the entire Sunshine Coast, over to Vancouver Island, and back to Vancouver, or vice versa.

For taxi service, call Powell River Taxi (☎ 604-483-3666).

TEXADA ISLAND

The largest of the Gulf Islands, Texada is mainly a limestone-mining and logging stronghold, but it does contain a few B&Bs and restaurants. BC Ferries takes the 35-minute trip from Powell River 10 times daily in each direction; the roundtrip fare is $5/2.50 for adults/children. Cars cost $12.75.

Shelter Point Regional Park (☎ 604-486-7228), 19km from the ferry dock, offers 47 campsites ($13 to $15) with showers and good access to fishing, boating, hiking and diving. *Texada Shores B&B* (☎ 604-486-7388, 2790 Sanderson Rd), in Gillies Bay, rents self-contained waterfront suites with kitchen access for about $60. Pick up a copy of the island brochure and map in Powell River or on the ferry for more information on Texada visitor services.

LUND & BEYOND

Lund, at the northern end of Hwy 101, serves as a staging point for trips to **Desolation Sound** and tropical-like **Savary Island**. Desolation Sound got its name from Captain George Vancouver, who thought the region's seascapes seemed remote and forbidding. With its many sheltered bays, 8256-hectare Desolation Sound Provincial Marine Park offers plenty of boating, fishing, kayaking and swimming opportunities. You can only get to the sound by boat; you'll find ramps at Lund and Okeover Arm Provincial Park.

Sometimes called 'the Hawaii of the North,' Savary Island features sandy beaches galore and a few visitor accommodations (although most cottages are private retreats). For more information, visit the Web site www.savary.bc.ca. For access to the island, call Lund Water Taxi (☎ 604-483-9749), which charges $6.50/13 one-way/roundtrip (half-price for children six and under). The same company can provide land taxi service on the island by request.

Eagle Adventures (☎ 604-483-4033) offers guided tours to Savary Island and the Copeland Islands, as well as bike, kayak and canoe rentals. Pristine Charters (☎ 604-483-4541) does fishing trips and dining cruises.

Places to Stay & Eat

At *Cedar Lodge B&B Resort* (☎ 604-483-4414, 9825 Malaspina Rd), a European-style pension, rooms start at $45/50 single/double. The nicely refurbished *Lund Hotel* (☎ 604-414-0474, 1436 Hwy 101) reopened in summer 2000 with waterside rooms for $89; rooms facing town are $79. *Desolation Resort* (☎ 604-483-3592, fax 483-7942, desolres@prcn.org, 2694 Dawson Rd) features cedar chalets on Okeover Inlet ($120 and up).

Nancy's Bakery (☎ 604-483-4180), on the Lund pier, serves breakfast and lunch. Try the gooey cinnamon rolls. *Flo's Starboard Café*, on the waterfront, offers home cooking (mostly $5 to $9). The upscale *Laughing Oyster* (☎ 604-483-9775, 10052 Malaspina Rd) features excellent food ($8 to $29) and good views. The wide menu includes everything from seafood to steaks to salads.

Vancouver Island

The largest island off the coast of the Americas, Vancouver Island stretches 450km and has become home to more than 500,000 people, most of whom live along the southeast coast. A mountain range runs down the center of the island, its snowcapped peaks framing forests, lakes and streams. The coastline is rocky and tempestuous in some places, sandy and calm in others. It rains only about 25 inches a year in Victoria but 300 inches a year in Port Alberni, just 75km due north. Overall, however, the island enjoys the mildest climate in Canada.

For years, Vancouver Island has been dependent on its natural resources. But in the 1990s, amid falling lumber prices and depleted fishing stocks, many small communities lost much of their livelihood. Towns have had to find ways to adapt, with mixed success. Tourism has proven the salvation for many communities, but other areas, surrounded by clear-cuts, have less success luring visitors.

Vancouver Island is a popular destination, and Victoria in particular draws crowds in midsummer, but the island is also a major haven for 'snowbirds,' who travel here in winter to escape colder climes. You can save money and avoid the heaviest crowds by traveling in spring and fall, which are also quite pleasant.

Victoria

• **population 318,000**

Victoria, British Columbia's provincial capital, lies at the southeast end of Vancouver Island, 90km southwest of Vancouver. Although bounded on three sides by water, it is sheltered from the Pacific Ocean by the Olympic Peninsula, across the Strait of Juan de Fuca, in Washington State.

Despite its reputation as a genteel city of Anglophiles, Victoria has attracted a broad range of international settlers who have brought their own cuisine and customs and

created a city that is nearly as cosmopolitan as Vancouver. Plenty of travelers come to Victoria for its heavily publicized major attractions: the Butchart Gardens, high tea at the Empress, shopping on Government St. But many others use Victoria as a springboard for outdoor adventures, including kayaking the Inner Harbour or hiking the West Coast Trail, a few hours farther afield.

HISTORY

James Douglas, chief factor for the Hudson's Bay Company, chose the location of present-day Victoria to replace Fort Vancouver along the Columbia River, an area that was being overrun with US pioneers bent on settling the Oregon territory. In 1842, Douglas strode off the SS *Beaver* at

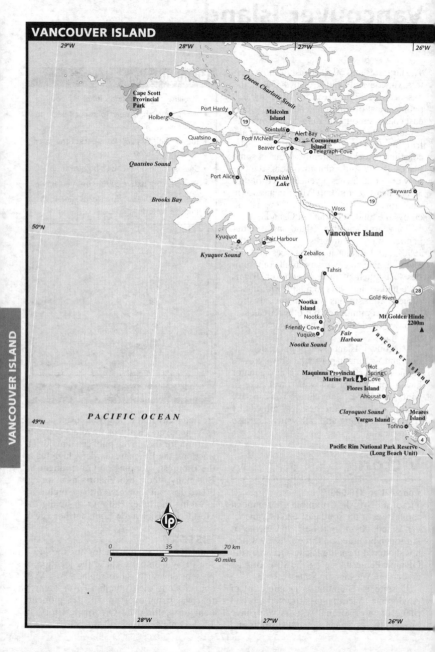

VANCOUVER ISLAND

29°W   28°W   27°W   26°W

Queen Charlotte Strait

Cape Scott
Provincial
Park

Port Hardy

Holberg

Malcolm
Island

Sointula   Alert Bay

Quatsino   Port McNeill   Cormorant
Island

Beaver Cove   Telegraph Cove

Quatsino Sound

Port Alice

*Nimpkish
Lake*

Brooks Bay

Sayward

Woss

50°N

Kyuquot   Fair Harbour   **Vancouver Island**

Kyuquot Sound   Zeballos

Tahsis

Gold River

Nootka
Island   Mt Golden Hinde
2200m

Nootka

Friendly Cove   *Fair
Harbour*

Yuquot

Nootka Sound

Maquinna Provincial
Marine Park   Hot
Springs
Cove

Flores Island

Ahousat

Clayoquot Sound   Meares
Island

Vargas Island   Tofino

Pacific Rim National Park Reserve
(Long Beach Unit)

PACIFIC OCEAN

49°N

0   35   70 km
0   20   40 miles

28°W   27°W   26°W

VANCOUVER ISLAND

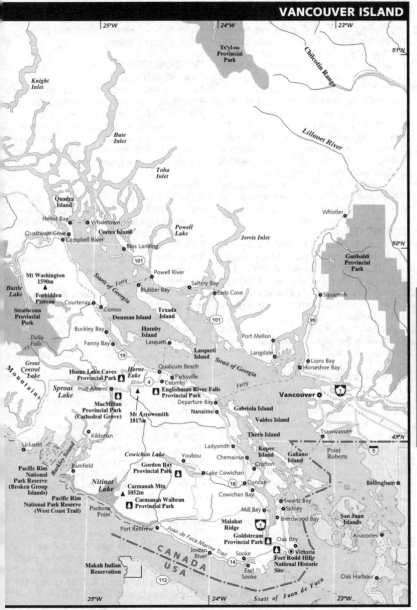

VANCOUVER ISLAND

Clover Point, crossed present-day Beacon Hill Park and chose a fort site at what is now Bastion Square. (Fort Victoria was erected the following year.) But things didn't really start hopping until the gold rush of 1857. As miners stormed the outpost, the town grew almost overnight.

Still, Victoria remained a scruffy, muddy place until the 1860s. Incorporated in 1862, the city became provincial capital of the newly created British Columbia in 1866. The completion of the Canadian Pacific Railroad and the city's sublime setting (Rudyard Kipling once described Victoria as 'Brighton Pavilion with the Himalayas for a backdrop') ensured Victoria's future popularity. Tourism and the provincial government continue to be Victoria's major employers.

ORIENTATION

The Inner Harbour is Victoria's focal point, surrounded by the Empress Hotel, Parliament Buildings and the Royal British Columbia Museum. From the Inner Harbour, Wharf St leads north to Bastion Square. Two blocks east, Government St attracts lots of tourists.

One full block east of Government St, Douglas St is downtown's main north-south thoroughfare. Fort St, a one-way street heading east, is another major artery. Following Fort St east up the hill and then along Oak Bay Ave will lead you through the 'tweed curtain' to the wealthier, very British area of Oak Bay, about 3km from downtown.

Both Douglas and Blanshard Sts lead north out of the city – the former to the Trans-Canada Hwy (Hwy 1) and Nanaimo, the latter to the Patricia Bay (Pat Bay) Hwy (Hwy 17), Sidney and the BC Ferries terminal at Swartz Bay. Hwy 17 also is the route to Butchart Gardens, about 21 km north of Victoria. Hwy 1A is an alternate route (via Gorge and Craigflower Rds) to either the Trans-Canada Hwy or Hwy 14, the road to Sooke and Port Renfrew.

Maps

The *Official Victoria Free Map* includes discounts to local attractions. AAA/CAA and MapArt both publish good street maps. BC Transit's free *Explore Victoria By Bus* leaflet tells you how to get to attractions by public transportation.

INFORMATION
Tourist Offices

Near the water at the Inner Harbour, the Visitor Info Centre (☎ 250-953-2033, fax 382-6539), 812 Wharf St, is open 8:30 am to 7:30 pm daily, June 15 through September 30; 9 am to 5 pm daily the rest of the year (except Dec 25). For more information, visit the Web site www.tourismvictoria.bc.ca.

Money

ATMs are everywhere, including at major bank branches along Douglas St. For money exchange, try Custom House Currency Exchange (☎ 250-389-6007); its six locations include 815 Wharf St, across from the Visitor Info Centre; the BC Ferries terminal at Swartz Bay; and Victoria International Airport.

You can also change money at American Express (☎ 250-385-8731), 1203 Douglas St. Many downtown businesses accept US and even other foreign currency, but the exchange rate is not usually as favorable as the exchange rate you can get via an ATM withdrawal.

Post & Communications

You'll find the main post office (☎ 250-953-1352) at 714 Yates St between Blanshard and Douglas Sts. Victoria CyberCafé (☎ 250-995-0175), 1414-B Douglas St, offers Internet access for 14¢ per minute or $8 per hour. Cyber Station of Victoria (☎ 250-386-4687), 1113 Blanshard St, provides access for 20¢ per minute; it's open until 10 pm Monday to Saturday.

Media

The *Times Colonist* is the daily newspaper. The weekly *Monday Magazine* features arts and entertainment news. Tune your radio dial to 90.5 FM for the CBC. Other popular area radio stations include 'The Q' at 100.3 FM and 'The Ocean' at 98.5 FM.

Travel Agencies

Travel CUTS has two Victoria locations: downtown at 634 Johnson St (☎ 250-995-8556) and in the University of Victoria student union (☎ 250-721-8634).

Bookstores

Munro's Books (☎ 250-382-2464), 1108 Government St, is a longstanding independent bookseller. The local outpost of the megachain Chapters (☎ 250-380-9009), 1212 Douglas St, is open 9 am to 11 pm daily. Wells Books (☎ 250-360-2929), 824 Fort St, specializes in nautical fare.

Libraries

You'll find the main branch of the Greater Victoria Public Library (☎ 250-382-7241) at 735 Broughton St.

Universities

In the city's northeast section, the University of Victoria campus can be reached via a 20-minute ride from downtown on bus No 14.

Laundry

A small coin-op laundry with showers sits right under the main Visitor Info Centre, on the waterfront level. The Laundry (☎ 250-598-7977), 1769 Fort St, contains Internet terminals so you can check your email while you do the wash. A bit closer to downtown, the Maytag Homestyle Laundry (☎ 250-386-1799), 1309 Cook St, is open 7 am to 10 pm daily.

Luggage Storage

You can leave your luggage in lockers beside the bus station, 700 Douglas St. Tokens for the lockers, obtained inside the station, cost $2 per 24 hours. Signs say it's unsafe to leave bags overnight.

Medical Services

For minor medical needs, head to Mayfair Walk-In Clinic (☎ 250-383-9898), 3147 Douglas St. It's open daily, with no appointment necessary. Royal Jubilee Hospital (☎ 250-595-9200, 595-9212 for emergencies) is at 1900 Fort St.

Emergency

Dial ☎ 911 for fire, police or ambulance.

Dangers & Annoyances

At night, prostitutes and drunks often frequent Broad St between Yates and Johnson Sts. Some drunks also hang out on the corner of Yates and Douglas Sts. Panhandlers work downtown Victoria day and night.

THINGS TO SEE & DO
Royal British Columbia Museum

This acclaimed museum (☎ 250-387-3701, 953-4629 for recorded information), 675 Belleville St, is well worth a few hours or even half a day of your time. The 2nd-floor 'Living Land, Living Sea' gallery includes an impressive wooly mammoth reconstruction and a walk-through exhibit of realistic seashore, forest and river environments. (If you can't get to a tide pool in person, here's a good place to mingle with sea creatures like sea stars and anemones.) Nearby, the 'Open Ocean' mimics an undersea voyage, with animation, special effects and film sequences based on actual deep-sea dives.

On the 3rd floor, the First Peoples exhibit hall is packed with carvings, canoes, beadwork, basketry and more. Hushed tones prevail as visitors wander through the displays of totem pole sections, a model of the 19th-century Haida village of Skedans and a recreation of Nawalagwatsi, 'the cave of supernatural power.' Elsewhere on the 3rd floor, you can learn about BC's European and Asian history. Here, you'll find a walk-through model of Captain Vancouver's *Discovery*, an old-time movie theater and a working water wheel in the gold rush exhibit.

The museum complex includes an IMAX theater, gift shop and café. It's open 9 am to 5 pm daily (except Dec 25 and Jan 1), with IMAX screenings from 9 am to 8 pm. Museum admission is $8/5 adults/seniors, students and children six to 18. The family rate is $21. A combination ticket, good for the museum and IMAX, costs $15.50/12.50/13.50/11.25 for adults/seniors/students/children.

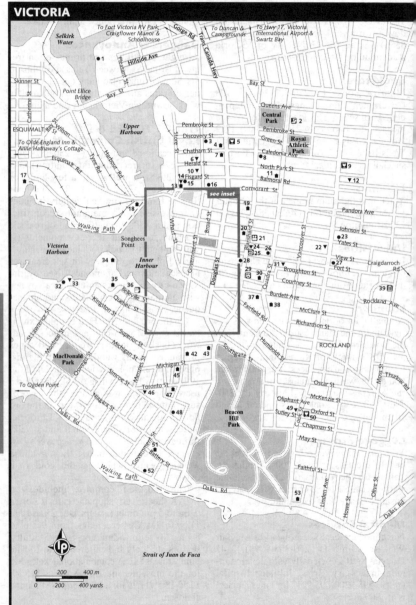

VICTORIA

Selkirk Water

To Fort Victoria RV Park;
Craigflower Manor &
Schoolhouse

Gorge Rd

To Duncan &
Campgrounds

To Hwy 17, Victoria
International Airport &
Swartz Bay

Hillside Ave

Trans Canada Hwy

●1

Pleasant St

Bay St

Skinner St

Catherine St

Point Ellice
Bridge

Bay St

Queens Ave

Central
Park

☒2

ESQUIMALT

St Wilson

Esquimalt Bay

Upper
Harbour

Pembroke St

Pembroke St

Royal
Athletic
Park

To Olde England Inn &
Anne Hathaway's Cottage

Esquimalt Rd

Harbour Rd

Tyee Rd

Discovery St

●3 4

☒5

Green St

Caledonia Ave

Chatham St

7

●8

17

Herald St

6 ▼

North Park St

☒9

10 ▼

14 Fisgard St

11 ●

Balmoral Rd

▼12

18

15

●16

13

Cormorant St

see inset

Walking Path

Songhees
Point

19

Pandora Ave

Victoria
Harbour

Inner
Harbour

Wharf St

Broad St

20

Johnson St

21

Blanshard St

●23

Yates St

34

Government St

Douglas St

24 ▼

26

22 ▼

View St

25

●27

Fort St

Craigdarroch
Rd

32

▼33

35

28

29

30

31 ▼

Broughton St

Courtney St

Quadra St

Vancouver St

Belleville St

36

Quebec St

Kingston St

Burdett Ave

39

37

38

Fairfield Rd

Rockland Ave

McClure St

ROCKLAND

Strawberry St

Montreal St

Oswego St

MacDonald
Park

Superior St

Michigan St

Richardson St

Humboldt St

Southgate St

Moss St

Thurlow Rd

To Ogden Point

Simcoe St

Menzies St

Michigan St

●42 43

45

Oscar St

McKenzie St

Niagara St

Toronto St

47

Oliphant Ave

49 ▼

Oxford St

Beacon
Hill
Park

☒50

Sutley St

Chapman St

●48

May St

Government St

51

Battery St

Faithful St

Linden Ave

Olive St

Dallas Rd

● 52

53

Dallas Rd

Walking Path

Dallas Rd

LP

N

0   200   400 m

0   200   400 yards

Strait of Juan de Fuca

VICTORIA

PLACES TO STAY
4 Paul's Motor Inn
7 Traveller's Inn
11 Victoria Backpackers Lodge
13 Swans Hotel; Swans Brewpub;
   Neptune Soundbar
17 Spinnakers Guesthouse;
   Spinnakers Brewpub
18 Ocean Pointe Resort
19 Ocean Island Backpackers Inn
20 Dominion Hotel
30 YM-YWCA
34 Laurel Point Inn
35 Admiral Motel
37 Cherry Bank Hotel;
   Bowman's Spare Rib House
38 Abigail's Hotel
40 Craigmyle Guest House
42 Birdcage Walk Guest House
43 Shamrock Motel
45 Holland House Inn
47 James Bay Inn
51 Battery Street Guest House
53 Dashwood Manor
58 Best Western Carlton Plaza; BJ's Lounge
60 Hotel Douglas
63 Isabella's Guest Suites
65 HI Victoria Hostel
94 Strathcona Hotel;
   Sticky Wickets Pub; Legends
101 Magnolia Hotel & Suites

105 Chateau Victoria
106 Quality Inn Downtown
110 Empress Hotel
119 Crystal Court Motel
121 Queen Victoria Inn

PLACES TO EAT
6 Herald St Café
10 Foo Hong Chop Suey
12 Mount Royal Bagel Factory
14 Tamami Sushi
22 Pluto's Mesquite Diner
24 Baan Thai
31 Blue Fox Café
33 Barb's Place
46 The Bent Mast
49 Cook Street Fish & Chips
56 Green Cuisine
61 John's Place
62 Chandler's Seafood Restaurant
64 Il Terrazo
68 Friends of Dorothy
69 Day & Night
72 Wharfside Eatery
73 Suze Restaurant & Lounge
74 Periklis
76 Growlie's
86 Camille's Fine Westcoast Dining
87 Koto Japanese Restaurant
91 Le Petit Saigon

92 Pagliacci's
100 Sam's Deli
102 Smitty's Family Restaurant
104 Milos
108 Milestone's

BARS & CLUBS
5 The Island Icehouse
9 Thursdays
50 Flying Beagle Pub
66 Steamers Public House
67 Axis
77 Boom Boom Room
83 Liquid
84 D'arcy McGee's
89 Fever
90 Hermann's Jazz Club

OTHER
1 Point Ellice House & Gardens
2 Crystal Pool & Fitness Centre
3 Sports Rent
8 Frank White's Scuba Shop
15 Bean Around the World
16 McPherson Playhouse
21 Capital 6 Cinema
23 Maytag Homestyle Laundry
25 Cyber Station of Victoria
27 BC Ferries Information Office
28 Mocambo Coffee
29 Royal Theatre
32 Fisherman's Wharf
36 Inner Harbour Ferry Terminal
39 Art Gallery of Greater Victoria
41 Craigdarroch Castle
44 Government House
48 Carr House
52 Ogden Point Dive Centre
54 E&N Railiner Station
55 Ocean River Sports
57 Travel CUTS
59 Victoria CyberCafé
70 Main Post Office
71 Odeon Theatre
75 Sasquatch Trading Company
78 Maritime Museum
80 Chapters
81 American Express
82 Cuda Marine Adventures
85 Victoria Bug Zoo
88 Munro's Books
93 Rogers' Chocolates
95 Greater Victoria Public Library
96 SpringTide Whale Watching Tours;
   British Colony Adventures
97 Custom House Currency Exchange
98 Harbour Rentals
99 Canadian Impressions
103 Vic Theatre
107 Visitor Info Centre; Prince of Whales
109 Miniature World
111 Victoria Harbour Ferry
112 Royal London Wax Museum
113 Pacific Undersea Gardens
114 Bus Station
115 Crystal Garden
116 Parliament Buildings
117 Royal BC Museum
118 Thunderbird Park
120 Helmcken House & St Anne's
   Pioneer Schoolhouse

VANCOUVER ISLAND

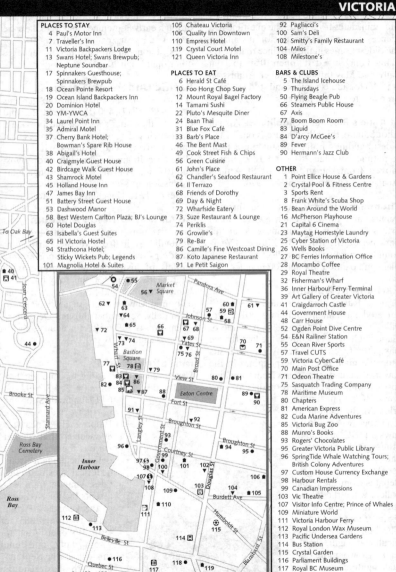

Helmcken House This house (☎ 250-361-0021), in Eliot Square beside the Royal BC Museum, dates from 1852. The one-time residence of an early town doctor, it's among the oldest homes in the province to have remained unchanged. It's open 10 am to 5 pm daily, mid-May through October. Admission is $5/4/3 for adults/seniors and students/children five to 12. A family ticket is $12.

St Anne's Pioneer Schoolhouse Also in Eliot Square, this schoolhouse is one of the oldest buildings in Victoria still in use. Built sometime between 1840 and 1860, it was moved from the grounds of St Anne's Academy to its present site in 1974.

Thunderbird Park Visit June through August, and you may catch Native Indian artists at work in the carving shed at this park beside the Royal BC Museum. Year-round, you can view a collection of both plain and painted wooden totem poles.

Parliament Buildings

Francis Rattenbury designed the multi-turreted Parliament Buildings, 501 Belleville St, which date from 1898. A statue of Captain George Vancouver, the first British navigator to circle Vancouver Island, sits atop the main dome. The paintings in the lower rotunda depict scenes from Canadian history, while the upper rotunda's art portrays BC's main industries. At the Legislative Chamber, where all the laws of BC are made (there is no Senate in the provincial parliament), you can view the debates from the public gallery when the legislature's in session, which varies from year to year. The buildings are spectacular at night, thanks to the glow of more than 3000 lightbulbs.

The Parliament Buildings, also called the Legislative Buildings, are

George Vancouver

open 8:30 am to 5 pm daily, with free 35-minute guided tours offered daily, June through early September, and weekdays the rest of the year (call ☎ 250-387-3046 for times). Phone ahead for tours in languages other than English.

Pacific Underseas Gardens

A sort of natural aquarium, the gardens (☎ 250-382-5717), 490 Belleville St, descend beneath the water's surface and provide a glass-enclosed view of sea creatures and human divers who interact with them. Hours are 10 am to 7 pm July and August and 10 am to 5 pm September through June. Admission is $7/6.25/5/3.50 adults/seniors/students (12 to 17)/ children (five to 11).

Royal London Wax Museum

This wax museum (☎ 250-388-4461), 470 Belleville St in front of the Parliament Buildings, contains more than 300 wax models of historical and contemporary figures. It's open 9:30 am to 5 pm daily, January through mid-May; 9 am to 7:30 pm daily, mid-May through August; 9:30 am to 6 pm daily, September through December. Admission is $8/7/6.50/3 for adults/seniors/students/children six to 12.

Miniature World

Usually more interesting to children than adults, this attraction (☎ 250-385-9731), 649 Humboldt St on the northern side of the Empress Hotel, features 80 scenes that depict various themes in exact detail, including a circus, historical sites and fairy tales. A model train represents the development of the Canadian Pacific Railway from 1885 to 1915. It's open 9 am to 9 pm daily, mid-June through early September, with shorter hours the rest of the year. Admission is $8/7/6 adults/students/children.

Crystal Garden

Fashioned after London's Crystal Palace by architect Francis Rattenbury, the 1925 Crystal Garden (☎ 250-381-1213), 713 Douglas St, puts on a show with colorful tropical-style gardens and many exotic animals, including the world's smallest monkeys and waves of free-flying butterflies. The popular attraction is open 8:30 am to 8 pm daily in July and August; 9 am to 6 pm daily in May, June, September and October; 1 am to 4:30 pm daily from November through April. Admission costs $7.50/6.50/4 for adults/seniors/children five to 16; a family ticket is $20.

Bastion Square

On the site of old Fort Victoria between Government and Wharf Sts, Bastion Square once held the courthouse, jail, gallows and a brothel, but the square's old buildings have since turned into restaurants, nightclubs, boutiques, galleries and offices. You can purchase handcrafted local wares at the ongoing Bastion Square Festival of the Arts, held Wednesday to Sunday, June through September, and Thursday through Sunday in April and May.

The **Maritime Museum** (☎ 250-385-4222), 28 Bastion Square, explores all aspects of Vancouver Island's seafaring past and present. Housed in an 1889 building that once served as BC's first provincial law courts, the museum features more than 400 ship models dating back to 1810; displays on piracy, shipwrecks and navigation; and the *Tilikum*, a converted dugout canoe that John Voss sailed almost completely around the world from 1901 to 1904. It's open 9:30 am to 4:30 pm daily. Admission is $5/4/3/2 for adults/seniors/students/children.

Victoria Bug Zoo

Anyone fascinated by creepy crawlers will love this place (☎ 250-384-2847), 1107 Wharf St, and even people who loathe bugs may come away with a new appreciation of them. All kinds of insects, from giant desert hairy scorpions to perpetually pregnant Australian stick insects to leaf-cutter ants, live in a sprawling series of Plexiglas tubes here. You'll see several dozen of the world's most unusual insects and spiders – and if looking isn't enough, you can touch and even hold many of them, too. Informative guides tell how the bugs eat, mate, give birth and more. The zoo is open 9:30 am to 5:30 pm Monday to Saturday and 11 am to 5:30 pm Sunday. Admission is $6/5/4 for adults/seniors and students/children three to 16.

Chinatown

Set on the northern edge of downtown, Victoria's small Chinatown is the oldest in Canada. A selection of mostly inexpensive restaurants and authentic Asian markets line Fisgard St, the main thoroughfare. Look for Fan Tan Alley, a narrow passageway between Fisgard St and Pandora Ave, which was a good spot to buy opium in the 1800s.

Fisherman's Wharf

Just west of the Inner Harbour, Fisherman's Wharf bustles with fishing boats and pleasure craft coming and going. Buy fresh seafood from the boats, or stop by Barb's Place for fish and chips (see Places to Eat later in this chapter).

Starting from Fisherman's Wharf, the **Scenic Marine Drive** skirts the coast along Dallas Rd and Beach Dr. You'll see several parks and beaches along the way, though access to the shore is restricted in many places because of private homes right on the coastline. The Gray Line double-decker bus includes Marine Drive in its tour (see Organized Tours, later in this chapter). You can also begin the drive at Beacon Hill Park.

Beacon Hill Park

South of downtown via Douglas St, this 61-hectare park offers an oasis of trees, gardens, ponds, pathways and playing fields. A tall totem pole here is among the world's highest; you'll also find a 100-year-old cricket pitch, a wildfowl sanctuary and children's petting zoo. The southern edge overlooks the ocean. Look for a staircase down to the beach off the walking path across Dallas Rd. The park is an easy walk from downtown; you can also take bus No 5.

Carr House

South of the Inner Harbour, a short walk or trip on bus No 5 or 11 leads to the birthplace of Emily Carr, BC's best-known painter (see the boxed text 'The Life and Work of Emily Carr' in the Facts about British Columbia chapter). Carr House (☎ 250-383-5843), 207 Government St, features displays on her life and work, including some of her paintings, many of which incorporated subject matter drawn from the culture of Vancouver Island's coastal First Nations people. The house is open 10 am to 5 pm daily, late May through mid-October. Admission is $5/4/3 for adults/seniors and students/children six to 18; a family ticket is $12.

Art Gallery of Greater Victoria

About 1km east of the downtown area, the art gallery (☎ 250-384-4101), 1040 Moss St just off Fort St, features good collections of Asian art, pre-Columbian Latin American objects and contemporary Canadian paintings. It's open 10 am to 5 pm Monday to Saturday (until 9 pm Thursday), 1 to 5 pm Sunday. Admission is by donation on Monday; otherwise, it's $5/3 for adults/seniors and students; children under 12 get in at no cost. Take bus No 10, 11 or 14 from downtown.

Government House

This house (☎ 250-387-2080), 1401 Rockland Ave, is the official residence of the province's lieutenant governor. It's closed to the public, but visitors are welcome to stroll the impressive grounds from dawn to dusk daily. Look for the extensive gardens and lily pond. To get there, take bus No 1 from downtown.

Craigdarroch Castle

Near Government House, but off Fort St, this opulent house (☎ 250-592-5323), 1050 Joan Crescent, was built in the mid-1880s by coal millionaire Robert Dunsmuir. It later served as a military hospital and college. Now completely restored, the castle boasts exquisite stained glass and a good view from the top floors. It's open 9 am to 7 pm daily in summer, 10 am to 4:30 pm daily the rest of the year. Admission is $8/5.50/2.50 for adults/students/children six to 12. Take bus No 11 or 14.

Olde England Inn & Anne Hathaway's Cottage

Set among 2 hectares of gardens in Esquimalt (on the other side of Victoria's Inner Harbour), this gimmicky but effective recreation of an English Tudor village (☎ 250-388-4353), 429 Lampson St, includes replicas of Shakespeare's birthplace and the thatched cottage of his wife, Anne Hathaway, complete with authentic 16th-century antiques. It's open daily for tours, April through October; call for current hours. Admission is $8.50/4.50 for adults/children. Take bus No 24 or 25.

Point Ellice House & Gardens

Built in 1861, this beautifully kept house (☎ 250-380-6506), 2616 Pleasant St off Bay St at the Point Ellice Bridge, retains a superb collection of Victorian furnishings and decorations. It's open noon to 5 pm daily, mid-May to mid-September. Admission is $5/4/3 for adults/seniors & students/children (six to 12 years). Take bus No 14.

Craigflower Manor & Schoolhouse

Built in 1856, the restored Georgian-style farmhouse (☎ 250-383-4627), at Craigflower and Admirals Rds northwest of the city, used to be the central home in the first farming community on Vancouver Island. Admission also includes a visit to the historic schoolhouse. The farmhouse is open noon to 4 pm daily, mid-May through September. Admission is $5/4/3 for adults/seniors and students/children. A family ticket is $10. Take bus No 10 or 14.

Fort Rodd Hill National Historic Site

This scenic 18-hectare park (☎ 250-478-5849), 603 Fort Rodd Hill Rd off Ocean Blvd, is the only national historic site on Vancouver Island. Built in the late 1890s to protect Esquimalt Harbour and the Royal Navy yards, Fort Rodd Hill contains **Fisgard**

Lighthouse, Western Canada's first. It has been in continuous use since 1860. The site is open 10 am to 5:30 pm daily, March through October; 9 am to 4:30 pm daily, November through February. Admission is $3/2.25/1.50 for adults/seniors/children. The park is about 11km northwest of the city. Bus No 50 comes within 2km of the park.

ACTIVITIES
Scuba Diving
Good shore dives near Victoria include **Saxe Point Park**, off Esquimalt Rd; the **Ogden Point Breakwater**, just south of Beacon Hill Park off Dallas Rd; **10 Mile Point**, near Cadboro Bay; and the entire **Saanich Inlet**, which contains Willis Point Park. **Race Rocks**, 18km southwest of Victoria Harbour, offers superb scenery both above and below the water. Diving charters and dive shops in Victoria provide equipment sales, service, rentals and instruction. Good resources include Frank White's Scuba Shops' downtown location (☎ 250-385-4713), 1855 Blanshard St, and Ogden Point Dive Centre (☎ 250-380-9119), 199 Dallas Rd. The latter maintains a Web site at www.divevictoria.com.

Swimming
Crystal Pool & Fitness Centre (☎ 250-361-0732), 2275 Quadra St, contains a pool, sauna and whirlpool. **Thetis Lake Municipal Park**, off the Trans-Canada Hwy northwest of town (about a 20-minute drive), is another good spot for a dip.

Kayaking
Ocean River Sports (☎ 250-381-4233), 1437 Store St, rents canoes and kayaks and offers guided trips, locally and island-wide. British Colony Adventures (☎ 250-216-5646), 950 Wharf St, leads local guided tours starting at $55. Sports Rent (☎ 250-385-7368), 611 Discovery St, rents canoes and kayaks for about $30 per day.

Windsurfing
Board sailing is big in **Cadboro Bay**, near the university, and at **Willows Beach** in Oak Bay. To hop on board contact Excel Water-sports (☎ 250-383-8667), 2001 Douglas St, for local information.

Whale-Watching
About a dozen outfitters offer trips out into Georgia Strait to watch orcas (killer whales) and other marine wildlife. A three-hour excursion costs about $75 to $85 for adults. For information and reservations, browse the brochures at the Visitor Info Centre. Outfitters include Seacoast Expeditions (☎ 250-383-2254), 45 Songhees Rd at the Ocean Pointe Resort; Prince of Whales (☎ 250-383-4884), 812 Wharf St, just below the Info Centre office; Cuda Marine Adventures (☎ 250-995-2832), on the Wharf St pier; and SpringTide Whale Watching Tours (☎ 250-386-6016), 950 Wharf St.

ORGANIZED TOURS
Gray Line (☎ 250-388-5248), 700 Douglas St, features many kinds of tours, including its basic 90-minute double-decker bus trip ($17.50/8.75 for adults/children). Tally-Ho Sightseeing (☎ 250-383-5067) offers tours in a large, horse-drawn wagon for $14/8.50/6 for adults/students/children under 17. If you want to rent an entire small carriage (which seats up to six), you'll pay $60 for 30 minutes, $105 for an hour or $150 for 90 minutes. Victoria Carriage Tours (☎ 250-383-2207) leads tours in horse-drawn carriages that seat four ($85 for 45 minutes, $105 for an hour). Both carriage companies board at the corner of Belleville and Menzies Sts.

Victoria Harbour Ferry (☎ 250-708-0201) offers a 45-minute tour ($12/6 for adults/children). Passengers can hop on and off as they like at regular stops such as Fisherman's Wharf and Spinnakers Brewpub.

Pacific Wilderness Railway Co (☎ 250-381-8600, 800-267-0610) runs trips aboard vintage railroad coaches from Victoria to the top of the mountainous Malahat area. Prices for the two-hour tours in open-air cars (three times daily, June through September, with less-frequent runs in May and October) start at $29/19/5 for adults/children six to 12/children five and under. (Air conditioned and first-class seating is available.) The company also offers lunch

On the Ale Trail

Oh-so-refined Victoria has earned a robust reputation as a serious beer-drinking town. The Victoria Ale Trail tour offers you a prime chance to visit brewpubs and microbreweries, learn about the brewing process, sample finished ales and lagers, and cap it all off with a gourmet dinner of inspired beer-and-food pairings.

The tour takes place the first Saturday night of each month and costs $119 per person. Stops include the Harbour Canoe Club, Hugo's Grill & Brew Club, the Lighthouse Brewing Company, Spinnakers Brewpub, the Strathcona Hotel, Buckerfield's Brewery and Vancouver Island Brewery. Special lodging rates are available. For more information, call First Island Destinations & Travel Ltd (☎ 250-658-5367) or see the Web site www.firstislandtours.com.

($99) and five-course dinner ($149) trips to the noted restaurant at the Aerie Resort atop the Malahat.

Walking Tours

Victoria Bobby Walking Tours (☎ 250-995-0233) features a 75-minute city walk led by a retired, uniformed London police officer. It departs from the Visitor Info Centre at 11 am daily, May through September. Tours cost $10; children 12 and under go for free when accompanied by a grown-up. Reservations are recommended.

Bird's Eye View Walking Tours (☎ 250-592-9255) offers guided strolls through the Empress Hotel. The tours ($7) leave at 10 am daily, May through mid-October.

The Old Cemeteries Society leads a regular series of walking tours (about $5 each). Call ☎ 250-598-8870 to hear recorded information.

SPECIAL EVENTS

Major events in Victoria include the TerrifVic Jazz Party in late April; the Victoria Day Parade and Swiftsure International

Yacht Race in late May; the Victoria Flower and Garden Festival in mid-June; Jazzfest International and Folkfest, both held in late June and early July; Canada Day celebrations on July 1; the Victoria Shakespeare Festival, which lasts from mid-July through mid-August; First People's Festival, held the first weekend in August; the Classic Boat Festival in early September; and the Great Canadian Beer Festival in early December.

PLACES TO STAY

You'll have trouble finding reasonably priced rooms from mid-May through September. Make reservations as soon as you know your travel plans. Tourism Victoria's room-reservation service (☎ 800-663-3883) may be able to help.

Camping

Fort Victoria RV Park (☎ 250-479-8112, fax 479-5806, info@fortvicrv.com, 340 Island Hwy), on Hwy 1A, is the closest to town, 6.5km from the city center. The park caters mainly to RVs ($27 to $29), but it does have a few tent sites ($23). Bus No 14 or 15 from downtown stops right at the gate.

The year-round **Thetis Lake Campground** (☎ 250-478-3845, fax 478-6151, petisa@home.com, 1938 W Park Lane), on Rural Route 6 off the Trans-Canada Hwy, is about a 20-minute drive northwest of the city center. You can shower and do your laundry here, or take a dip in the nearby lake. A site for two people is $16; electric hookups are an extra $2. The campground is about 1.5km from the No 50 bus route.

See the Southern Vancouver Island section, later in the chapter, for more camping options in the Victoria vicinity.

Hostels

Victoria is a hosteller's dream town, with accommodations to suit every age and taste. The only drawback is that places fill up fast in high season; reservations are essential in summer and advised year-round.

A newer spot, **Ocean Island Backpackers Inn** (☎ 250-385-1785, 888-888-4180, fax 250-385-1780, get-it@oceanisland.com, 791 Pandora Ave) enjoys a splendid location in central Victoria. Full of life and art, this big old building features about 155 beds and spacious kitchen facilities; amenities include Internet access ($1 for 15 minutes) and free morning coffee. Both the young and the young-at-heart will feel right at home. Dorm rooms cost $20 ($16.50 with a hostel card or student ID), and 12 or so private rooms are $40.

The *HI Victoria Hostel* (☎ 250-385-4511, 888-883-0099, fax 250-385-3232, victoria@ hihostels.bc.ca, 516 Yates St) also sits in a convenient location, near the Inner Harbour and all the major sights. (There's a chance it may move to new, larger quarters in 2001 or 2002, so ask when you book.) Bunks in the barracks-style dorm rooms cost $16.50/ 20.50 members/nonmembers; a few private rooms cost $37 to $44 double occupancy. Reservations are a must. In peak season it's advisable to register before 4 pm.

Much smaller, the *Victoria Backpackers Lodge* (also known as the Turtle Refuge) (☎ 250-386-4471, turtlerefuge@hotmail.com, 1608 Quadra St) offers dormitory beds for $13 and several comfortable private rooms for $30/40 single/double. The hostel features luggage storage, a laundry, no curfew and a good edge-of-downtown location.

The *YM-YWCA* (☎ 250-386-7511, 880 Courtney St) are both in the same building, but the residence is only for women. A dorm bunk with bedding costs $20. Private single rooms cost $38.50, though they're often fully booked with long-term boarders. Guests enjoy free use of the Y's heated swimming pool and other fitness facilities, plus access to a coin-op laundry. You don't get any kitchen privileges here, but you can buy cheap breakfasts and lunches in the cafeteria downstairs. Reservations are essential. Parking is limited. Enter the building on Broughton St.

Selkirk Guest House International (☎ 250-389-1213, selkirkvictoria@hotmail .com, 934 Selkirk Ave), over the Johnson St Bridge in Esquimalt, offers a family atmosphere in the country but close to town. Rates are $18 for dorm beds, $40 to $80 for private rooms, with linens provided; the $80 room includes its own bathroom and

kitchen. Outside, look for a dock on the Gorge Waterway (with boats that guests can use), plus a tree house and trampoline, a waterfront hot tub and endless kilometers of nearby walking, running and cycling paths (including the Galloping Goose Trail). It's a half-hour walk or short drive to downtown. Take Bus No 14 from Douglas St (it stops two blocks away) or hop aboard the harbor ferry. Check in after 4 pm unless you make prior arrangements.

A family atmosphere also prevails at *Hannah's House* (☎ 598-7323, 1729 Oak Bay Ave), available to visitors from May 1 through mid-September. (University of Victoria students stay here the rest of the year.) Several dorm rooms sleep four to six people, with beds for $18. Private rooms cost $40. Linens are provided. Amenities include access to a kitchen and a porch with a barbecue. It's a 20-minute walk from downtown; you can also take the No 1 or 2 bus. Plan to check in by 4 pm. There's no curfew.

The *University of Victoria* rents rooms from May through August. Singles/doubles are $38/50, including breakfast; parking costs $5 per weekday, nothing on weekends. While you stay, you can use university facilities, including several licensed cafeterias. Contact Housing & Conference Services (☎ 250-721-8395), University of Victoria, PO Box 1700, Victoria, BC V8W 2Y2.

Cat's Meow Mini Hostel (☎ 250-595-8878, 1316 Grant St) offers six dorm beds ($17.50) and two private rooms ($40 to $43). The accommodations are plainer than most, but rates include a continental breakfast. No kitchen is available, though guests with camp stoves can cook in the backyard and eat at the picnic table. Owner Daphne Cuthill generously helps guests plan their Victoria visit. Check in between 4 and 7 pm or by prior arrangement.

B&Bs

Victoria is packed with B&Bs, with rates ranging from about $50 to $200. For help finding one, contact Victoria Vacationer B&B (☎ 250-382-9469, 1143 Leonard St, Victoria, BC V8V 2S3) or inquire at the Visitor Info Centre.

VANCOUVER ISLAND

Most Victoria B&Bs fall in the higher price ranges, with a few exceptions. *Marion's B&B* (☎ 250-592-3070, 1730 Taylor St) offers four small rooms with comfy beds for $40/60. The good breakfasts are enormous, and the owners are friendly. It's a 10-minute bus ride from downtown; take No 27 or 28 to the Myrtle St stop.

The moderately priced *Battery Street Guest House* (☎ 250-385-4632, 670 Battery St), south of downtown and one block from Beacon Hill Park, offers rooms for $65 to $125. At the *Craigmyle Guest House* (☎ 250-595-5411, 1037 Craigdarroch Rd), about 1km east of downtown next to Craigdarroch Castle, rates start at $65/80. Each room has its own bathroom, but it's located across or down the hall.

Convenient to the Inner Harbour, *Birdcage Walk Guest House* (☎ 250-389-0804, 877-389-0804, fax 250-389-0348, 505 Government St) offers five guest rooms with private bathrooms in a historic home for $100 to $150. Each room also includes cooking facilities, and some are suitable for small families.

In the same neighborhood, the delightful and small *Holland House Inn* (☎ 250-384-6644, 800-335-3466, 595 Michigan St) rents 16 rooms for $145 and up. Each has its own bathroom, phone and TV.

Spinnakers Guesthouse (☎ 250-386-2739, 308 Catherine St), on the northwest side of the harbor, offers rooms in three nearby guesthouses ($149 and up). You're right next to Spinnakers Brewpub (see Brewpubs & Bars under Entertainment, later), so you can sample all that good beer.

Dashwood Manor (☎ 250-385-5517, 800-667-5517, 1 Cook St) enjoys an excellent location by the ocean and Beacon Hill Park. Each of the 14 handsome rooms has its own bathroom; breakfast comes from the stocked in-room refrigerator, with fresh croissants delivered each morning. Summer rates start at $165; full ocean views cost $195.

Motels & Hotels

Budget & Mid-Range You won't find any budget-level motels in downtown Victoria in the high season, but a few possibilities lie nearby. The Gorge Rd area northwest of downtown features several lower-cost motels, including the *Fountain Inn* (☎ 250-385-1361, 356 Gorge Rd E), with rooms for $40 to $60. At the *Casa Linda Motel* (☎ 250-474-2141, 364 Goldstream Ave), a modest place toward Sooke, rooms cost $55/60 single/double.

If you can afford to spend a little extra, the downtown area contains several moderately priced options. Up the hill behind the Inner Harbour, the *Cherry Bank Hotel* (☎ 250-385-5380, 800-998-6688, cherrybank @pacificcoast.net, 825 Burdett Ave) dates back to 1897 – and it shows. The faded rooms in this one-time brothel won't suit everyone, but the prices should please, especially considering the central location: $60/68 with shared bathroom, $80/88 with private bath. Prices include breakfast, but rooms lack TVs and telephones.

One of the best values in the center of town, the *Crystal Court Motel* (☎ 250-384-0551, fax 384-5125, mbscott@vanisle.net, 701 Belleville St) boasts a good location across from the bus station and Crystal Garden. Rooms are $75/78 (add $2 for a kitchen).

Walking distance from downtown, *Paul's Motor Inn* (☎ 250-382-9231, 1900 Douglas St) rents rooms for $75. Amenities include a 24-hour restaurant and parking. The *Traveller's Inn* chain operates six motels in Victoria; the locations closest to downtown include 1850 Douglas St at Caledonia Ave (☎ 250-381-1000) and 710 Queens Ave at Douglas St (☎ 250-370-1000, 888-753-3774). The high-season rates of $79/89 include a skimpy breakfast. Look for discount coupons, widely available on the ferries, at visitor centers and in the official BC Accommodations guide.

The centrally located *Hotel Douglas* (☎ 250-383-4157, 800-332-9981, fax 250-383-2279, stay@hoteldouglas.com, 1450 Douglas St) offers some budget rooms without private toilets for $50. Regular rooms start at $85/105. You'll find a 24-hour café in the lobby, with a restaurant and pub next door.

A bit more upscale, the *Strathcona Hotel* (☎ 250-383-7137, 800-663-7476, fax 250-383-6893, lou@strathconahotel.com, 919 Douglas

VANCOUVER ISLAND

St) charges $79/99 and up. It's a bustling place with several popular bars and a restaurant; ask for a room away from the action. Parking is $2 per night.

The **Shamrock Motel** (☎ 250-385-8768, 800-294-5544, fax 250-385-1837, 675 Superior St) enjoys a great location across from Beacon Hill Park. Rooms, all of which come with kitchenettes, rent for $99/119.

Top End Most hotel rooms in Victoria top $100 May through September, so you'll find the most choices in this category. The rates listed apply to the high season, with better deals abounding the rest of the year; many of these places fall in the mid-range or even budget bracket from October through April.

A few blocks from the Inner Harbour, **James Bay Inn** (☎ 250-384-7151, 800-836-2649, fax 250-385-2311, 270 Government St) should make for a favorite choice. Rooms at the well-kept older hotel start at $106 in summer but dip to $56 at other times. The totally renovated **Dominion Hotel** (☎ 250-384-4136, 800-663-6101, fax 250-382-6416, dominion@dominion-hotel.com, 759 Yates St) offers charming rooms that start at $119/129, plus $5 per day for parking. Come mid-October through April, however, a double room, three-course dinner and continental breakfast for two can cost as little as $49 midweek, $59 weekends. Even the Inner Harbour hotel rates drop steeply in the off-season: at the **Admiral Motel** (☎ 250-388-6267, 888-826-4725, 257 Belleville St), a room priced at $169/179 in July costs $79/89 in November. You get the idea.

The **Best Western Carlton Plaza** (☎ 250-388-5513, 800-663-7241, carlton@direct.ca, 642 Johnson St) is a refurbished older hotel with rooms starting at $109. **Quality Inn Downtown** (☎ 250-385-6787, 800-661-4115, 850 Blanshard St) offers rooms for $135 to $170 ($10 extra for kitchenettes).

Isabella's Guest Suites (☎ 250-381-8414, 537 Johnson St) features an excellent off-street location and modern romantic verve in one of Victoria's busiest shopping and dining areas. The two apartment-like suites ($135 each) include huge beds, complete kitchens, claw-foot tubs and enclosed showers, wood floors and classy furnishings. The per-night price goes down for longer stays, which are encouraged. Rates include breakfast. Il Terrazo next door will deliver room-service dinners on request.

Queen Victoria Inn (☎ 250-386-1312, 800-663-7007, info@queenvictoriainn.com, 655 Douglas St) offers one of the best values in this price category, with rooms for $135 and up, most including kitchens and many with good views. The nearby **Chateau Victoria** (☎ 250-382-4221, 800-663-5891, reservations@chateauvictoria.com, 740 Burdett Ave), just up the hill from the Empress, rents rooms for $150 and up. Both these high-rise hotels contain indoor pools and fitness facilities.

Swans Hotel (☎ 250-361-3310, 800-668-7926, fax 250-250-361-3491, reservations@swanshotel.com, 506 Pandora Ave) is in a gem of a downtown building by the waterfront. Studio suites start at $159; much nicer one-bedroom suites go for $179.

Across the Inner Harbour from downtown and the Parliament Buildings, and with tremendous views of both, the **Ocean Pointe Resort** (☎ 250-360-2999, 800-667-4677, 45 Songhees Rd) combines luxury-class rooms (starting at $159) with spa and sports facilities.

Rates at the seaside **Oak Bay Beach Hotel** (☎ 250-598-4556, 1175 Beach Dr) start at $189. In summer, the hotel provides a shuttle service into the city center and offers lunchtime cruises.

Laurel Point Inn (☎ 250-386-8721, 800-663-7667, reservations@laurelpoint.com, 680 Montreal St) guards the entrance to the Inner Harbour. Amenities include saunas, an indoor pool, balconies and good views; rates start at $190.

Abigail's Hotel (☎ 250-388-5363, 800-561-6565, innkeepeer@abigailshotel.com, 906 McClure St) makes a good romantic retreat. The Tudor-style mansion's 22 rooms are stocked with fresh flowers, goose-down duvets and other niceties. Rates start at $199, including a three-course breakfast (served in your room, if you like) and evening hors d'oeuvres.

The **Empress Hotel** (☎ 250-348-8111, 800-441-1414, 721 Government St) is practically synonymous with Victoria. Built in 1908 and surrounded by lovely gardens, the Empress attracts lots of honeymooners, bus-tour groups and well-heeled travelers. Rates are all over the map, depending on season and demand, but plan on paying about $239 for a room facing the city, more for a harbor view.

Magnolia Hotel & Suites (☎ 250-381-0999, 877-624-6654, magnoliahotel@bc.sympatico.ca, 623 Courtney St) is among the newest and most deluxe places in Victoria. Catering mainly to a business clientele, its 66 well-appointed rooms start at $239.

PLACES TO EAT
Victoria is a great dining town, with everything from tea rooms and pubs to cutting-edge Pacific Rim cuisine. Prices vary widely, so it's easy to eat cheap at one meal and splurge at the next, if you desire.

Budget
The pancake breakfast at **Smitty's Family Restaurant** (☎ 250-383-5612, 850 Douglas St), near the Empress, costs about $6. You can get the same thing for about half the price at **Day & Night** (☎ 250-382-5553, 622 Yates St), a few blocks away.

Growlie's (☎ 250-383-2654, 615 Yates St) features 10 varieties of eggs Benedict with such creative toppings as spinach, chicken breast or back bacon. Other local favorites for breakfast and lunch include the often-crowded **John's Place** (☎ 250-389-0799, 723 Pandora Ave) and the **Blue Fox Café** (☎ 250-380-1683, 101-919 Fort St).

Despite its proximity to the high-rent district (the Inner Harbour), **Sam's Deli** (☎ 250-382-8424, 805 Government St) offers reasonable prices, with $6 sandwiches big enough for two. Follow your nose to **Mount Royal Bagel Factory** (☎ 250-380-3588, 1115 North Park St), where the aroma of fresh Montreal-style bagels wafts out the door. Enter on Grant St.

Pluto's Mesquite Diner (☎ 250-385-4747, 1150 Cook St), a few blocks from downtown in a converted gas station, serves breakfast (mostly $5 to $7) until 2 pm and a variety of burgers, quesadillas and Mexican platters ($7 to $11) for lunch and dinner.

The several food carts on Market Square, at the corner of Johnson and Wharf Sts, offer quick bites on sunny days. **Green Cuisine** (☎ 250-385-1809, 560 Johnson St), indoors on the courtyard level, boasts a delicious vegetarian buffet.

Friends of Dorothy (☎ 250-381-2277, 615 Johnson St) offers burgers and pasta, plus old-fashioned main dishes like meat loaf ($8.25). In Chinatown, the small and basic **Foo Hong Chop Suey** (☎ 250-386-9553, 564 Fisgard St) serves good, simple Cantonese food ($5 to $8).

Barb's Place (☎ 250-384-6515, 310 St Lawrence St), housed in a shack on Fisherman's Wharf, offers fish and chips starting at about $7. **Cook Street Fish & Chips** (☎ 250-384-1856, 252 Cook St) is another reliable choice.

While exploring the James Bay neighborhood, look for **The Bent Mast** (☎ 250-383-6000, 512 Simcoe St), a neat little spot open late every night. The menu includes soups ($5), salads ($6 to $8) and a selection of main dishes (about $10). Wash it all down with some BC beers. The Bent Mast features live music most nights, starting at about 9:30 pm.

Mid-Range
Re-Bar (☎ 250-360-2401, 50 Bastion Square) is a happening spot with an eclectic, international menu (heavily vegetarian, with most dishes $7 to $12) and an onsite bakery. Lunch is served daily and dinner is available Tuesday to Saturday.

Le Petit Saigon (☎ 250-386-1412, 1010 Langley St) offers recommendable Vietnamese meals for $10 to $17. **Baan Thai** (☎ 250-383-0050, 1117 Blanshard St) is the best place in town for authentic Thai cuisine ($8 to $15).

Suze Lounge & Restaurant (☎ 250-383-2829, 515 Yates St) serves drinks and dinner nightly, starting at 5 pm. The menu includes pizza ($10 to $13), pasta ($12 to $13) and about four featured Pacific Northwest dishes ($17 to $19).

The ornate Parliament Buildings, Victoria

Native art at Thunderbird Park, Victoria

Alfresco dining on Bastion Square, Victoria

An easy day on Long Beach in Pacific Rim National Park, Vancouver Island

Colorful Butchart Gardens, Vancouver Island

Fisgard Lighthouse, Victoria

You can dine on the indoor-outdoor patio at the **Wharfside Eatery** (☎ 250-360-1808, 1208 Wharf St), which specializes in fresh seafood ($20 to $25) but also serves up pizza ($15 to $19) and hamburgers (starting at $10).

Bustling and popular, **Il Terrazzo** (☎ 250-361-0028, 555 Johnson St) is the best place in town for Italian pastas, grilled meats and tempting pizza. Most main dishes cost $8 to $16 for lunch (served daily except Sunday) and $15 to $30 for dinner. A bit less expensive, **Pagliacci's** (☎ 250-386-1662, 1011 Broad St) features a clever movie-theme menu, with pasta starting at $11 and other main dishes for $17 to $20. Live music acts play Sunday through Wednesday evenings.

Herald St Café (☎ 250-381-1441, 546 Herald St) serves delicious pastas for $9 to $12 at lunch and $15 to $19 at dinner. It also offers vegetarian dishes, great desserts and about 350 wine selections.

The well-established **Chandler's Seafood Restaurant** (☎ 250-385-3474, 1250 Wharf St) specializes in ocean fare, with dinner prices ranging from $15 for smoked-salmon pasta to $30 for the Victoria Seafood Platter. Lunch is available, too ($10 to $13).

Victoria has a number of good Greek restaurants, but **Milos** (☎ 250-382-5544, 716 Burdett Ave) is the best known. Try the roast lamb (about $15). Belly dancers perform at 8 pm nightly during the busy season. Many locals recommend **Periklis** (☎ 250-386-3313, 531 Yates St), with similar entertainment but lower prices.

Head to **Bowman's Spare Rib House** (☎ 250-385-5380, 825 Burdett Ave), in the Cherry Bank Hotel, for rib dinners ($17 for a full rack) and steaks ($14 to $18).

Milestone's (☎ 250-381-1244, 812 Wharf St), right on the harbor below the Visitor Info Centre, features a good view of both the Parliament Buildings and the Inner Harbour, plus lots of tapas plates ($4 to $7), sandwiches ($8 to $11) and main dishes ($12 to $18); the BC salmon ($15) is among the best.

Koto Japanese Restaurant (☎ 250-382-1514, 510 Fort St) serves mainly seafood and offers a sushi and salad bar; main courses cost $16 to $26. **Tamami Sushi** (☎ 250-382-3529, 509 Fisgard St) serves sushi-for-two for $35 and single pieces for about $2.

Among Victoria's most inventive restaurants, **Camille's Fine Westcoast Dining** (☎ 250-381-3433, 45 Bastion Square) combines seasonally changing Northwest ingredients with eclectic, international cuisine.

Top End

The Empress Hotel (☎ 250-384-8111), 721 Government St, is the top-tier dining spot in town, with three notable options. **Kipling's**, the most casual choice, sets out buffets at breakfast ($19), lunch ($18) and dinner ($24). The **Bengal Lounge** features curry specials ($16 to $18) and terrific atmosphere, with a tiger skin above a blazing fireplace and ample leather furniture. It's open daily for lunch, Sunday through Thursday

Tea Time, Victoria Style

Nothing says Victoria like taking afternoon tea at the Empress Hotel (see Places to Stay), where mouthwatering scones, fresh berries in Devonshire cream and decadent pastries are all on the menu. If you'd like to indulge, plan to reserve ahead by calling ☎ 250-384-8111 at least several days in advance during the busy season. You'll want to skip the rest of your meals that day, not just because you'll be stuffed, but because this experience doesn't come cheap: $32 per person ($15 for children four to 11).

Victoria's other tea rooms don't cost nearly so much. Best known is The **Blethering Place Tea Room & Restaurant** (☎ 250-598-1413, 2250 Oak Bay Ave), where the name means 'to sit around and talk about nothing in particular.' Full afternoon tea here costs $13 to $15 per person, with many tarts and scones available à la carte for about $3. A historic site, the **Point Ellice House & Gardens** (☎ 250-380-6506, 2616 Pleasant St) offers tea in a charming setting; the $16.95 tab includes a tour, and you can even play croquet afterward.

for dinner. The best deal offered at the formal *Empress Room* is the three-course menu priced at $40, or $30 between 5:30 and 6:30 pm. (It costs about $72 with wines that have been selected to highlight each course.) Otherwise, the main courses start at $30. Reservations are advised at every Empress restaurant.

ENTERTAINMENT
Brewpubs & Bars
For some of the best beer in BC, go to *Spinnakers Brewpub & Restaurant* (☎ 250-386-2739, 308 Catherine St), where they've also got a great deck with views of the Inner Harbour. *Swans Brewpub* (☎ 250-361-3310, 506 Pandora St) takes up half the main floor of Swans Hotel. Visit Thursday for Celtic music.

It doesn't make its own beer, but the *Sticky Wicket Pub* (☎ 250-383-7137, 919 Douglas St), in the Strathcona Hotel, offers an extensive selection of international beer on tap as well as creative food, seating for families and a rooftop patio with beach volleyball courts. A bit away from downtown, the *Flying Beagle Pub* (☎ 250-382-3301, 301 Cook St) serves up good grub, accompanied by many beers on tap.

Coffeehouses
Caffeine isn't the only stimulus at *Mocambo Coffee* (☎ 250-384-4468, 1028 Blanshard St), where philosophy discussions take place at 7 pm Tuesday and poets hold forth at 7:30 pm Friday. *Bean Around the World* (☎ 250-386-7115, 533 Fisgard St) is a rejuvenating refuge in one of Victoria's busiest districts.

Theater & Performing Arts
Big venues in town include *McPherson Playhouse* (☎ 250-386-6121, 3 Centennial Square), on the corner of Pandora Ave and Government St. The elegant *Royal Theatre* (☎ 250-386-6121, 805 Broughton St) hosts a range of musical performances, including ballet, dance and concerts, many performed by the resident Victoria Symphony (☎ 250-385-6515) and the Pacific Opera Victoria (☎ 250-386-6121).

Other theaters worth checking out are the *Belfry* (☎ 250-385-6815, 1291 Gladstone Ave), northeast of the downtown area, and the *Phoenix Theatre* (☎ 250-721-8000), on the University of Victoria campus.

Live Music
Touring acts appear a few times each month at *Legends* (☎ 250-383-7137, 919 Douglas St) and *The Island Icehouse* (☎ 250-382-5853, 1961 Douglas St), in the Horizon West Hotel. For good local bands of all types, head to *Steamers Public House* (☎ 381-4340, 570 Yates St), *Thursdays* (☎ 250-360-2711, 1821 Cook St) or *Swans Brewpub* (listed above). *D'arcy McGee's* (☎ 250-380-1322, 1127 Wharf St) features live Celtic music Friday and Saturday. For blues and jazz, head to the *James Bay Inn* (☎ 250-384-7151, 270 Government St). Check out the calendar in *Monday Magazine* to see what's happening when you visit.

Dance Clubs
Bastion Square has long been ground zero for clubbers, who throng to *Liquid* (☎ 250-385-5333, 15 Bastion Square), a hot spot for Top 40 and hip-hop music. Across the street and down the stairs beside the Wharfside Restaurant, the *Boom Boom Room* (☎ 250-381-2331, 1208 Wharf St) packs in a young crowd with regular theme nights.

Neptune Soundbar (☎ 250-388-5758, 1601 Store St), downstairs at the Swans Hotel, is the city's club of choice for electronica and other alternative grooves. Gays and lesbians often head to *BJ's Lounge* (☎ 250-388-0505, 642 Johnson St). Victoria also has an excellent rave scene; check *Monday Magazine* or inquire at any cool record store for information.

Cinemas
Admission at commercial cinemas such as the *Capitol 6 Cinema* (☎ 250-384-6811, 805 Yates St) and the *Odeon Theatre* (☎ 250-383-0513, 780 Yates St) is typically about $8 to $9, reduced to $5.25 on Tuesday. The *Vic Theatre* (☎ 250-383-1998, 808 Douglas St) screens classic movies on weekend afternoons for just $1. The University of Victo-

ria's *Cinecenta* (☎ 250-721-8365) features recently released and classic independent films in the Student Union Building. Admission is $6.50/5.50/4.50 for adults/students/ seniors and children; all seats are $3.50 for Sunday matinees.

SHOPPING

On Government St, the main downtown shopping thoroughfare, an interesting mix of local and chain retailers compete for the visitors' dollars. Notable spots include the famously rich Rogers' Chocolates (☎ 250-384-7021), 913 Government St; Canadian Impressions (☎ 250-383-2641), 811 Government St, which sells crafts by First Nations people; and Sasquatch Trading Company (☎ 250-386-9033), 1233 Government St, where you'll find a good selection of hand-knitted Cowichan sweaters, unique to BC.

Eaton Centre (☎ 250-382-7141), on Government and Douglas Sts between Fort and View Sts, can be fun to stroll around even if you aren't looking to spend money. The complex includes five floors and 100 shops, plus restaurants, fountains and a rooftop garden.

GETTING THERE & AWAY

Air

Victoria International Airport (YYJ) is in Sidney, about 26km north of the city off the Patricia Bay Hwy (Hwy 17). Airlines serving Victoria include the recently merged Air Canada (☎ 250-360-9074, 888-247-2262, www.aircanada.ca) and Canadian Airlines (☎ 888-247-2262), with daily service to Vancouver and Seattle; Horizon Air (☎ 800-547-9308, www.horizonairlines.com), with regular service between the cities of Victoria and Seattle, Port Angeles and Bellingham; North Vancouver Air (☎ 800-228-6608, www.northvanair.com), with flights to Vancouver, Whistler, Tofino, Campbell River and Powell River; and WestJet Airlines (☎ 800-538-5696, www.westjet.com), with flights to Vancouver and other Western Canadian cities.

West Coast Air (☎ 250-388-4521, 800-347-2222, www.westcoastair.com) and Harbour Air Seaplanes (☎ 250-384-2215, 800-665-0212, www.harbour-air.com) offer seaplane flights to Vancouver Harbor.

Bus

The bus station is at 700 Douglas St. Pacific Coach Lines (☎ 250-385-4411, 800-661-1725) operates buses to Vancouver every hour between 6 am and 6 pm (until 9 pm on Friday and Sunday) during July and August and every two hours from 6 am to 8 pm the rest of the year; the fare, which includes the ferry, is $26.50/51 one-way/roundtrip for adults, $17.50/33 for seniors and $13.25/25.50 for children five to 11. It's the same price to Vancouver International Airport; buses connect with the airport shuttle bus at Delta Pacific Resort in Richmond. For more details, visit their Web site at www.pacificcoach.com.

Laidlaw Coach Lines (☎ 250-385-4411) covers Vancouver Island. Six or seven buses a day travel to Nanaimo; from there, two buses go on to Tofino and one or two buses to Port Hardy. Call for details or see the Web site www.victoriatours.com.

Although Greyhound has no service on Vancouver Island or from Victoria to the mainland, it does maintain an office (☎ 250-385-5248) in the bus station where you can purchase tickets for buses departing from Vancouver.

Train

The Esquimalt & Nanaimo Railiner, or E&N Railiner, operated by VIA Rail (☎ 250-383-4324, 800-561-8630), connects Victoria with points north, including Duncan, Nanaimo, Parksville and Courtenay. There is one train in each direction per day – northbound from Victoria at 8:15 am, southbound from Courtenay at 1:30 pm. The scenic journey takes about 4½ hours. The *Malahat*, as the train is known, is very popular, so book ahead. Seven-day advance purchases are cheaper.

Full schedules are available at www.viarail.ca or in person at travel agencies or the Visitor Info Centre. The E&N Railiner station, 405 Pandora Ave, is near the corner of Johnson and Wharf Sts. To get there, take bus No 6, 24 or 25.

VANCOUVER ISLAND

Ferry

BC Ferries (☎ 250-386-3431, 888-223-3779) operates service to the mainland from Swartz Bay, 27 km north of Victoria via the Pat Bay Hwy (Hwy 17). Ferry schedules are widely available around town. BC Ferries' information office, 1112 Fort St, is open 8:30 am to 4:30 pm weekdays.

The trip between Swartz Bay and Tsawwassen near Vancouver takes 95 minutes, with sailings every hour between 7 am and 10 pm in July and August. (In the off-season, sailings begin on every odd hour between 7 am and 9 pm.) The peak-season one-way fare is $9/4.50 for adults/children; a car is $32. To reserve a spot for your vehicle, call ☎ 888-724-5223 in BC or 604-444-2890 outside BC, or visit their Web site at www .bcferries.com.

BC Ferries also operates between Swartz Bay and five of the southern Gulf Islands: Galiano, Mayne, Saturna, Salt Spring and North Pender. Schedules vary by season and destination, with more frequent sailings in July and August. The peak-season roundtrip fare is $6/3 for adults/children; a car is $20.25 ($19.25 for a car to Salt Spring Island).

Three passenger-only ferry services and one car-ferry service serve Washington State from the Inner Harbour ferry terminal at 430 Belleville St. The ferry MV *Coho*, operated by Black Ball Transport (☎ 250-386-2202), sails to Port Angeles, just across the Strait of Juan de Fuca. Fares are calculated in US dollars, but Canadian currency is accepted: the Canadian rate is about $10.35 for a walk-on passenger ($5.15 for children five to 11). A car and driver cost about $43. The trip takes about 1½ hours. Mid-June through mid-September, four boats a day leave Victoria, departing at 6:10 and 10:30 am and 3 and 7:30 pm. The rest of the year, boats leave at 10:30 am and 4 pm only.

The passenger-only *Victoria Express* (☎ 250-361-9144) also goes to Port Angeles from the Inner Harbour terminal, departing two to three times daily from late May through early October; the roundtrip fare for the one-hour journey is about $37/15 for adults/children five to 11.

Victoria Clipper and *Victoria Clipper II*, run by Clipper Navigation (☎ 250-382-8100), sail to Seattle in water-jet-propelled catamarans; the journey takes about three hours. In summer, the fare costs about $88/147 one-way/roundtrip. The passenger-only *Victoria Star*, operated by Victoria Cruises (☎ 800-443-4552), makes a trip to Bellingham and back daily, June through September.

See the Sidney section, later in this chapter, for information on ferry service to the San Juan Islands in the US.

GETTING AROUND
To/From the Airport

Airporter shuttle buses (☎ 250-386-2525) provide service between the airport and all area hotels and B&Bs. It runs every half-hour from 4:30 am to midnight daily and costs $13/11.70 for adults/seniors and students. A taxi to the airport from downtown costs about $40. City bus No 70 passes within 1km of the airport.

To/From the Ferry Terminals

Bus No 70 goes to the BC Ferries terminal at Swartz Bay. Bus No 75 travels to the Washington State Ferry dock in Sidney.

Bus

BC Transit buses (☎ 250-382-6161) run frequently and cover a wide area. The normal one-way fare is $1.75 ($2.50 if you travel into a second zone, such as the suburbs of Colwood or Sidney). Have exact change ready. All-day passes ($5.50/4 adults/seniors and students) are not sold on buses but are available from convenience stores and the Visitor Info Centre.

Car

Shop around for the best rental prices. All major rental companies have offices at the airport and in and around the downtown area, including Avis (☎ 250-386-8468), 1001 Douglas St; Budget (☎ 250-953-5300) 757 Douglas St; Enterprise (☎ 250-475-6900), 2507 Government St; National/Tilden (☎ 250-386-1213), 767 Douglas St; and Thrifty (☎ 250-383-3659), 625 Frances Ave.

Taxi

Call Empress Taxi (☎ 250-381-2222), Victoria Taxi (☎ 250-383-7111) or Blue Bird Cabs (☎ 250-382-3611). Or try two-seat human-powered Kabuki Kabs (☎ 250-385-4243), which cost $1 per minute.

Bicycles

For bike rentals, contact Harbour Rentals (☎ 250-995-1661), 811 Wharf St, which also rents scooters, and Sports Rent (☎ 250-385-7368), 611 Discovery St.

Mini-Ferry

Victoria Harbour Ferry provides service to the Empress Hotel, Visitor Info Centre, Ocean Pointe Resort, Fisherman's Wharf, Spinnakers Brewpub and other stops on the Inner Harbour and Gorge waterway. Fares start at $3/1.50 for adults/children under 12; prices vary depending on how far you travel.

Southern Vancouver Island

Beyond Victoria, Southern Vancouver Island's attractions range from world-famous gardens to tide pools, with plenty of coastal hiking trails and excellent bicycling routes for outdoor types.

SAANICH PENINSULA

Southern Vancouver Island's transportation hub, this peninsula (north of Victoria on Hwys 17 and 17A) contains Victoria International Airport and offers ferry connections to the Southern Gulf Islands and the USA's San Juan Islands. It also boasts several major attractions.

Butchart Gardens

With all the raw and rugged natural beauty in British Columbia, it's a bit ironic that these 20 hectares of elaborate, manicured gardens (☎ 250-652-5256, 652-4422), 800 Benvenuto Ave in Brentwood Bay, rank among the province's top tourism draws. Every year visitors come in droves to visit the Butchart grounds, created by the family of a local cement manufacturer beginning in 1904.

You can wander through the gardens in about 1½ hours, but avid gardeners may want to linger much longer. If time is short, don't miss the truly impressive Sunken Gardens and the peaceful Japanese Garden. Consider coming in the evenings from June 15 to September 15, when the grounds are lit and live musical entertainers perform. Fireworks are set off to music each Saturday night in July and August. Special holiday entertainment and displays take place every November and December.

The gates open at 9 am daily; closing times vary by season. (Gates officially close at 10:30 pm, mid-June through early September, though guests can stay an hour past that once they're in the park.) Admission also varies seasonally; mid-June through September, it's $16.50/8.25/2 for adults/teens 13 to 17/children five to 12. At other times of year, adult admission ranges from $7.75 to $12.75. Three restaurants on the grounds serve everything from quick bites to fine dining. The visitor center offers strollers, cameras and umbrellas on loan, as well as luggage storage and visitor guides in 19 languages.

Located about 21km north of Victoria, the gardens can be reached via bus No 75 from downtown Victoria, though it's a slow trek. Better to take the $4 one-way express shuttle from Gray Line (☎ 250-388-5248), which operates as many as 11 times daily. If you're driving, follow the Patricia Bay Hwy (Hwy 17) north.

Victoria Butterfly Gardens

Close to Butchart Gardens, this lesser-known attraction (☎ 250-652-3822), 1461 Benvenuto Ave, features more than 300 free-flying butterflies from 30 species. Wait for the similar but slightly less-expensive Butterfly World at Coombs if you're traveling up island. This spot is open 9 am to 5 pm daily, March through October (call for off-season hours); admission is $8/7/4.50 for adults/seniors and students/children six to 12 years old.

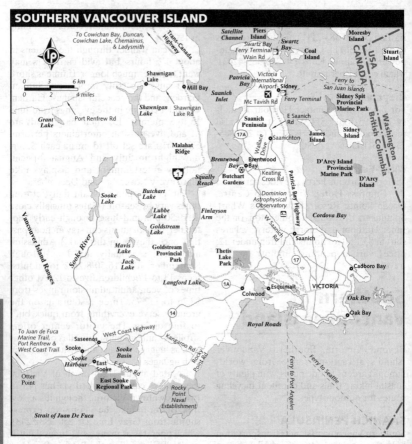

SOUTHERN VANCOUVER ISLAND

Dominion Astrophysical Observatory

Perched on Little Saanich Mountain, this facility (☎ 250-363-0012), 5071 W Saanich Rd, boasts a 183cm research telescope and features exhibits about major telescopes around the world. Visitors are welcome 9 am to 6 pm Sunday through Friday and 9 am to 11 pm Saturday; try to come between 7 and 11 pm each Saturday from April to October, when there are guided tours (and observations, clear skies permitting). Members of the Royal Astronomical Society also gather here on Saturday night, and they're more than happy to talk about the night skies.

Places to Stay & Eat

Western Motel 66 (☎ 250-652-4464, *2401 Mt Newton X Rd*), in Saanichton, makes a good budget base for the Saanich Peninsula, just a few kilometers from Butchart Gardens, Sidney and the airport and ferry terminals. Rooms cost $48/63 single/double in the summer. You can eat at one of the popular *White Spot* chain restaurants next door. Among the many area B&Bs, *Wintercott Country House* (☎ 250-652-2117, *wintercott @*

bc.sympatico.ca, 1950 Nicholas Road), in Saanichton, draws repeat visitors to its quiet country setting. The three bedrooms, each with private bath, cost $75/95.

Sidney
• **population 11,000**

Situated at the north end of the Saanich Peninsula near the airport and ferry terminal, Sidney is often seen as a way station to somewhere else. But the town itself features an offshore provincial park and seven bookstores, possibly the most per capita in BC. It's also the northern terminus of the Galloping Goose Trail (see the boxed text).

Sidney's two visitor information centers (10382 Patricia Bay Hwy; Fifth St S at Lochside Ave) stay open from March 1 through November 30. Tanners (☎ 250-656-2345), 2436 Beacon Ave, is the biggest of Sidney's bookstores, with an excellent map department and thousands of magazine titles.

Things to See & Do The **Sidney Spit Provincial Marine Park** is a great spot for swimming, sunbathing and beachcombing. A passenger ferry (☎ 250-727-7700) runs between the Beacon Ave wharf and Sidney Spit Provincial Park from May 15 to September 30. Ferries depart Sidney on the hour and the park on the half-hour from 9 am to 5 pm Monday to Thursday and until 6 pm Friday to Sunday (7 pm weekends during July and August). The roundtrip fare is $9/7/6 for adults/seniors/children six to 12.

If you want to do some **cycling** on the Galloping Goose Trail, rent a bike at True Value Hardware (☎ 250-656-8611), 2488 Beacon Ave. Go **whale-watching** with Sea Quest Adventures (☎ 250-656-7599).

Places to Stay & Eat Camping ($12) is available at *McDonald Provincial Park*, near the Swartz Bay ferry terminal, and *Sidney Spit Provincial Park*, accessed by the passenger ferry from Sidney.

The *Waterfront Hotel Sidney* (☎ 250-656-1131, 888-656-1131, 2537 Beacon Ave) offers streetside rooms ($60) and waterfront rooms ($70), including continental breakfast. Rooms at *Victoria Airport Travelodge*

(☎ 250-656-1176, 2280 Beacon Ave) start at $75/115 single/double.

Classical Treats (☎ 250-655-1166, 2505 Beacon Ave) is open daily for breakfast and lunch, with refined live music (perhaps a harpist or hammer dulcimer player) most Thursday evenings. Sidney has three Greek restaurants in its small downtown; locals say the budget-priced *Maria's Souvlaki* (☎ 250-656-9944, 9812 2nd St) is the best. *Café Mozart* (☎ 250-655-1554, 2470 Beacon Ave) is the fine-dining choice; entrees cost from $15 to $20.

Don't despair if the parking lot is full at *Mary's Bleue Moon Café* (☎ 205-655-4450, 9535 Canora Rd), just across from the airport in Sidney. This locally popular place is a lot bigger than it looks from the outside, and there's more parking across the street. Mary's serves breakfast, lunch and dinner daily, with nothing on the menu more than $14.

Getting There & Away The Washington State Ferries (☎ 250-381-1551), 2499 Ocean Ave, offers service from Sidney through the

---

The Galloping Goose

Stretching from Swartz Bay to the Sooke area, the 100km Galloping Goose/Peninsula trails system ranks among the best cycling/pedestrian routes in BC (and it's the province's first designated route along the 15,000km Trans Canada Trail, now complete).

The Galloping Goose, named for a noisy gas railcar that ran between Victoria and Sooke in the 1920s, is built mostly on abandoned Victoria & Sidney and Canadian National railway beds. Four bus lines along the route – Nos 50 (Goldstream), 61 (Sooke), 70 (Pat Bay Hwy) and 75 (Central Saanich) – are bike-rack equipped. For a brochure with maps or more information, ask at area Visitor Info Centres or call the Capital Region District Parks office at ☎ 250-478-3344. The Greater Victoria Cycling Coalition's Web site at www.gvcc.bc.ca is a good place to look for regional cycling information.

VANCOUVER ISLAND

US San Juan Islands to Anacortes on the Washington mainland. The one-way fare for the two-hour trip is about $13.50 per passenger; the fare for a car and driver costs $36 to $61, depending on the season.

THE MALAHAT

Just north of Victoria on the Island Hwy, this mountainous area makes a nice day trip from the city. **Goldstream Provincial Park** (☎ 250-391-2300), 19km north of Victoria, is best known for its chum salmon spawning season (late October through December). You'll also find good fishing and hiking, along with human- and natural-history exhibits at the park's Freeman King Visitor Centre.

Places to Stay & Eat

Often considered the nicest campground near Victoria, *Goldstream Provincial Park* (☎ 250-391-2300), just off Hwy 1, has nearly 160 sites ($18.50). Some may be reserved; call ☎ 800-689-9025 (☎ 604-689-9025 in Greater Vancouver). To get to Goldstream, take bus No 50; transfer to No 58 at the Canwest Shopping Centre.

KOA-Victoria West (☎ 250-478-3332), about 25km north of Victoria on Hwy 1, has a heated swimming pool June through August. Rates range from $25 for tent sites to $48 for a simple cabin.

One of BC's finest lodgings, *The Aerie Resort* (☎ 250-743-7115, 800-518-1933, aerie@relaischateaux.fr, 600 Ebedora Lane) is 35km north of Victoria off Hwy 1. With fewer than two dozen rooms and stupendous views, The Aerie is a retreat unto itself, yet not so far from Victoria that you can't drive in for a visit. Rooms run $250 to $325 June through September. The Aerie's acclaimed dining is a high-flying affair, too: $32 to $35 per person for the three-course lunch or $55 to $75 per person for six-course vegetarian, tasting or seven-course fixed-price dinner menus.

SOOKE

• **population 4100**

A scenic 34km drive (or bus ride on No 61) west of Victoria, the Sooke area is noted for its natural beauty and good recreational opportunities. If you're traveling west from here, note that there are no gas stations on Hwy 14 between Sooke and Port Renfrew.

The **Sooke Potholes** make a great spot for swimming and picnicking. Look for the turnoff east of town on Hwy 14, then follow the winding road north for several kilometers. The **Sooke Regional Museum** and Sooke Visitor Info Centre (☎ 250-642-6351), both at 2070 Phillips Rd, are open 9 am to 5 pm daily year-round.

East Sooke Regional Park offers outstanding hikes, from short strolls to the beach to the 10km Coast Trail. For longer treks, consider hiring a guide from either the Twin Ventures Association/EcoFuns (☎ 250-642-4342) or Nature Calls EcoTours (☎ 250-361-4453).

The Ocean Kayak Institute (TOKI; ☎ 250-642-2159), 5449 Sooke Rd, offers **kayaking** lessons, rentals, guide training and a range of short and multi-day tours. For **cycling**, rent bikes at Sooke Cycle & Surf (☎ 250-642-3123), 6707 West Coast Rd.

Places to Stay & Eat

Just up the road from the visitor center, *Sooke River Flats Campsite* (☎ 250-642-6076) is open April through September, with tent and RV sites for $15 and limited electrical hookups for $2 more. Coin-op showers make this a popular spot for people who've just finished hiking the West Coast or Juan de Fuca Trails. *French Beach Provincial Park* (☎ 250-391-2300), 20km west of Sooke, offers 69 sites for $12; some can be reserved by calling ☎ 800-689-9025 (604-689-9025 in Greater Vancouver). It, too, fills up with hikers.

Sooke has more than 60 bed and breakfasts, most costing about $65 to $75 a night, including a dozen or so on the Galloping Goose Trail. Stop at the Visitor Info Centre to see the displays many have posted.

Rooms at the *Sooke Harbour House* (☎ 250-642-3421, fax 250-642-6988, 1528 Whiffen Spit Rd) cost a bundle ($300 and up May through October, including full breakfast and picnic lunch), but few places compare for an anniversary or other special occasion. Some rooms have private outdoor hot tubs; all have fireplaces and inspired individual decor. The seaside dining room is open to the public for dinner (main courses $27 to $38; fixed-price menu about $60) by reservation. For less formal dining, check out *Good Life Bookstore Café* (☎ 250-642-6821, 2113 Otterpoint Rd) or *Fox's Grill* (☎ 250-642-2643, 5449 Sooke Rd).

JUAN DE FUCA MARINE TRAIL

The West Coast Trail is still considered BC's preeminent long-distance coastal hike, but the 47km Juan de Fuca Marine Trail has become a worthy alternative. Unlike the WCT, the Juan de Fuca doesn't require hiking reservations (at least not yet), and it features several access points so you don't have to tramp the whole length.

From east to west, access points from Hwy 14 are at China Beach, 63km from Victoria and just west of Jordan River; Sombrio Beach; Parkinson Creek; and Botanical Beach. There are six established campsites en route, with fees of $5 per person per night (cash only, exact change); most through-hikers take four days to make the complete trek. The most difficult part of the trail is the stretch from Bear Beach campsite to Chin Beach, but any part can be a major slog, with slippery tree roots and mud. For detailed information on planning a trip, contact BC Parks' South Vancouver Island District (☎ 250-391-2300) or visit the Web site www.bcparks.gov.bc.ca. West Coast Trail Express (☎ 250-477-8700) provides shuttle service between Victoria and the trailheads.

Nature Calls Eco Tours (☎ 250-361-4453) offers four-day guided treks along the Juan de Fuca for $595 per person, including meals and transportation from Victoria. Guide Larry Hall and his staff also lead one-day, 10km 'West Coast Wonders' hikes along a moderate section of the trail. These cost $85, including lunch. Canadian Wilderness Ecotours (☎ 250-642-1834) has similar programs.

China Beach is an especially nice spot for a day trip along the Juan de Fuca. An easy 15-minute walk from the parking lot leads

Juan de Fuca

One of southwest BC's most prominent geographical features, the Strait of Juan de Fuca off the south coast of Vancouver Island, actually was named for a Greek explorer, Apostolos Valerianos, who probably never saw the place. Valerianos somehow got the Spanish moniker Juan de Fuca as a nickname. In a 1596 stopover in Venice, he supposedly told Englishman Michael Lok of a trip he'd made up the Pacific coast from Mexico, during which he'd discovered a strait at about 48 degrees latitude. Much later, Captain Charles Barkeley found the strait and, recalling Lok's story, named it for Juan de Fuca.

to a sandy beach and water warm enough for wading. You'll find a waterfall at the western end of the beach.

PORT RENFREW
• population 400

May through September, this sleepy community at the end of Hwy 14 hums with activity as hikers prepare to tackle (or arrive to recuperate from) the West Coast Trail. The added popularity of the year-round Juan de Fuca Marine Trail has given Port Renfrew a bit more business in the off-season.

For information on the West Coast Trail, see the Pacific Rim National Park section, later in this chapter. Visitors looking for a short hike will enjoy the 2.7km loop to Botanical Beach, known for its tide pools. (Allow about 90 minutes, and go at low tide.) Seafoam Kayak Rentals (☎ 250-647-0019), next to Pacheedaht Campground, rents single or double kayaks by the hour or day.

Places to Stay & Eat

Many hikers stay at *Pacheedaht Campground* (☎ 250-647-0090), where sites run $5 to $20. *Bill's International Bunkhouse* (☎ 250-647-0022) offers beds ($25), a washer and dryer and shared bath. Both lie near the West Coast Trailhead on the

Pacheedaht Reserve; get there on Tsono-qua Rd, which heads north off Hwy 14 on the outskirts of Port Renfrew. The *Port Renfrew Hotel* (☎ *250-647-5541*), at Snuggery Cove, offers simple rooms (about $30) with a shared bath and shower, as well as a laundry across the street.

Arbutus Beach Lodge (☎ *250-647-5458*), a waterfront B&B, includes a hikers' room that sleeps five ($85 for two, plus $15 per extra person). Other rooms range in price from $65 to $95. The *West Coast Trail Hotel* (☎ *250-647-5565*) offers nice motel-style rooms for $70 to $100. The red-roofed *Lighthouse Neighbourhood Pub & Restaurant* (☎ *250-647-5543*) serves hamburgers ($7 to $9), pasta ($11 to $12) and seafood ($12 to $15).

Cowichan Valley

Just over the Malahat from Victoria, this valley is home to the Cowichan nation, BC's largest aboriginal group, with about 4500 people. Duncan and points west offer outstanding recreation. The valley is also the gateway to Carmanah Walbran Provincial Park, noted for its giant trees. Cowichan means 'land warmed by the sun,' and this area enjoys the highest average annual temperatures in Canada.

COWICHAN BAY
• population 2795

A short loop drive east of Hwy 1 leads to this small working seaside town. Check out the **Marine Ecology Centre** (☎ 250-748-4522), where you can view a whole range of live sea critters , some through microscopes, some in hands-on touch tanks. Though it's nothing fancy, it's still worth the price of admission ($3/2 for adults/kids five to 12; families are $7).

Dream Weaver B&B (☎ *250-748-7688, 888-748-7689, 1682 Botwood Lane*), a newly built Victorian-style home, offers rooms for $70 to $130. *Cookies 'n' Cream* (☎ *250-746-6822, 1721 Cowichan Bay Rd*) offers soups, sandwiches, coffee and tea in addition to scrumptious sweet treats.

DUNCAN
• population 5330

Duncan town leaders and the Cowichan people have worked together to make this the 'City of Totems,' with several dozen examples of this West Coast art form on view along its streets.

The Visitor Info Centre (☎ 250-746-4636), 381A Trans-Canada Hwy, is open 9 am to 5 pm daily, mid-April through mid-October.

One of Vancouver Island's best First Nations attractions, the **Cowichan Native Village** (☎ 250-746-8119), 200 Cowichan Way, immerses visitors in the tribe's culture. Try your hand at carving or beading, learn about salmon's importance in Cowichan culture and see a multimedia show on the tribe's 'Great Deeds.' Admission is $10/6/4 for adults/seniors and students/children 12 and under. First Nations people get in for $5; a family pass costs $20. It's a dollar or two more to add on a visit to the craft center. You can also eat light meals here. Call to check upcoming dates for midday salmon barbecues ($28.50 for adults) and Coast Salish feasts ($39.50), accompanied by live entertainment.

About 3km north of Duncan, the **BC Forestry Discovery Centre** (☎ 250-715-1113, 2892 Drinkwater Rd) features both indoor and outdoor exhibits on its 40 hectares. Here you can stroll through a stand of 55m-tall Douglas firs that were present before Captain Cook arrived in 1778, take rides on a working steam train, visit a bird sanctuary, hike nature trails or view a replica of an old logging camp; the facilities also include picnic areas and a playground. It's open 10 am to 6 pm daily, May through early September, with limited hours the rest of the year. Admission is $8/7/4.50 for adults/seniors and students/children five to 12.

Places to Stay & Eat

Set along the river just off Hwy 1, *Duncan RV Park & Campground* (☎ *250-748-8511, 2950 Boys Rd*) has sites for $12 to $19. Rooms at the *Duncan Motel* (☎ *250-748-2177, 2552 Alexander St*) are a good value at $44/49 single/double, while the *Falcon Nest Motel* (☎ *250-748-8188, 5867 Trans-Canada*

Hwy) offers a heated outdoor pool and rooms for $44/50. Head to downtown Duncan for some good local food, including Friday night's East Indian buffet at the 1950s-style *Good Rock Café* (☎ *250-748-4252)*, at Government and Jubilee Sts.

Getting There & Away

Island Coach Line buses (☎ 250-746-4841) travel between Duncan and Victoria for $10 one-way. The station is in the Village Green Mall at 180 Central Way. A 70-minute train trip between Duncan and Victoria on the E&N Railiner (☎ 250-383-4324, 800-561-8630) costs $12.

Ferries sail from the small town of **Crofton**, 16km northeast of Duncan on Hwy 1A, to Vesuvius Bay on the north end of Salt Spring Island (see Salt Spring Island's Getting There & Around section in the Southern Gulf Islands chapter).

COWICHAN LAKE & AROUND

Cowichan Lake is the largest freshwater lake on Vancouver Island, 22km west of Duncan via Hwy 18. Back roads along the way parallel the lovely Cowichan River.

Small Lake Cowichan (population 2900) maintains a Visitor Info Centre (☎ 250-749-3244) at 125-C South Shore Rd.

Recreational activities abound in **Cowichan River Provincial Park**, a preserve stretching from the Glenora area south of Duncan to the village of Lake Cowichan. Highlights include a 20km hiking trail (the western stretch east from Skutz Falls makes a good short hike) and advanced-level kayaking in Marie Canyon. Look for railroad exhibits at the **Kaatza Station Museum** in Saywell Park, next to the Lake Cowichan Visitor Info Centre.

Gordon Bay Provincial Park, on the south shore of Cowichan Lake, offers good swimming, fishing and boating. Nitinat Lake, west of Cowichan Lake, is one of the best windsurfing spots on Vancouver Island; for information, visit the Web site www.island.net/~nitinat. Pachena Bay Express (☎ 250-728-1290) runs shuttles to and from Nitinat by reservation only; call for schedules and fares.

A Fitting Legacy

Randy Stoltmann ranks high among the mythical figures of BC's backcountry. Stoltmann stumbled on the giant trees of the Carmanah Valley on a 1988 hiking trip. Learning they were slated to be logged, he argued for the preservation of these majestic trees, and his determined efforts led to the establishment of the Carmanah Walbran Provincial Park in 1990. Stoltmann died in a mountaineering accident in 1994, but his legacy lives on in Carmanah's Randy Stoltmann Commemorative Grove. He was also an author and wrote several notable hiking guides, including *Hiking the Ancient Forests of British Columbia & Washington.*

Places to Stay & Eat

Lakeview Park Municipal Campground (☎ *250-749-3350)*, about 3km west of town on South Shore Rd, is on the southern shore of Cowichan Lake. It features sites for $15, plus showers, toilets and free firewood. *Gordon Bay Provincial Park*, about 14km from Lake Cowichan on South Shore Rd, has 126 sites ($18).

Greendale Lodge (☎ *250-749-6570, 8012 Greendale Rd)*, in Lake Cowichan, offers six cabins ($65 to $95) in a parklike setting with wildlife and river access. *Sahtlam Lodge and Cabins* (☎ *250-748-7738, 5720 Riverbottom Rd W)*, in Duncan, is a little more upscale, with rates of $135 to $180 and fine dining by reservation Thursday through Sunday night. It enjoys a convenient location near the Cowichan River and Trans-Canada trails. The *Rail's End Pub* (☎ *250-749-4001, 109 South Shore Rd)* in Lake Cowichan, features tasty meals and a model-train display.

CARMANAH WALBRAN PROVINCIAL PARK

This 16,450-hectare park boasts some of the last remaining old-growth forest on Vancouver Island, including 95m-tall spruce trees and cedars more than 1000 years old.

VANCOUVER ISLAND

Unfortunately, the park can only be reached via a slow, dusty drive over active logging roads. (It's best to travel on weekends or evenings, when the loggers aren't working.)

From Gordon Bay Provincial Park (about 40km off Hwy 1), follow South Shore Rd to the Nitinat Main Rd. Follow Nitinat Main to its junction with Junction South. Turn left onto South Main and continue to the Caycus River Bridge. South of the bridge, stop at the safety checkpoint (it monitors logging-truck traffic). Turn right and follow Rosander Main for 29km to the park. Once you're there, it's a relatively short hike of an hour or so (in good weather) into the tallest trees. Campsites with tent pads, tables and water are provided, but there are no other services nearby. (The closest phone and gas station are on the Didtidaht Reserve, 33km away.)

Nature Calls Eco-Tours (☎ 250-361-4453) leads day trips ($110) into the Carmanah from Victoria on the third Sunday of each month from May through September. Advance reservations are essential. Canadian Wilderness Ecotours (☎ 250-642-1834) offers guided three- and four-day hikes in the region ($350 and up).

Follow the Yellow Point Road

The Yellow Point Rd, a back route between Ladysmith and Nanaimo, makes a good detour from the Trans-Canada Hwy. Follow the signs to **Crow & Gate** (☎ 250-722-3731), the oldest British-style pub in the province. Sample tasty steak-and-kidney pie and Cornish pasties in a highly authentic atmosphere.

The **Yellow Point Lodge** (☎ 250-245-7422, 3700 Yellow Point Rd), 24 km south of Nanaimo, draws many vacationing BC residents with its log lodge and cabins. Activities include kayaking, tennis, swimming, and mountain biking, with all meals included in the daily rate of $110 to $185 per person. No children under 14 are allowed.

CHEMAINUS
• **population 4000**

Chemainus' sawmill shut down in 1983, but rather than submit to a slow death, town officials commissioned a large outdoor mural of local history. People took notice, and 33 murals now adorn city buildings. Chemainus has since done quite well; there's even a new sawmill, along with many shops and galleries.

The Visitor Info Centre (☎ 250-246-3944), 9796 Willow St, is open May through August; if it's closed, look for informational exhibits across the street in Waterwheel Park.

While you're in town, sign on with Chemainus Heritage Tours for a 30-minute murals tour, which costs $5/4/2 for adults/seniors/teens/children 12 and under. Take in a play at the brightly painted **Chemainus Theatre** (☎ 250-246-9820, 800-565-7738).

BC Ferries provides frequent daily service to nearby **Thetis Island**, known for its warm-water beaches, and **Kuper Island**, a Native Indian reserve with no visitor amenities. The roundtrip fare is $5/12.75 per passenger/vehicle.

Places to Stay & Eat
Bald Eagle RV Park Campground (☎ 250-246-9457, 8705 Chemainus Rd), 5km south of town on the Chemainus River, includes tent sites ($16) and hookups ($20). *Hummingbird House B&B* (☎ 250-245-8412, 11120 Chemainus Rd) offers two rooms in a modern oceanfront home, both with private bathrooms, for $45/60 single/double. Rooms at the Victorian-style *Bird Song Cottage* (☎ 250-246-9910, 9909 Maple St) cost $80/105. The *Fuller Lake Chemainus Motel* (☎ 250-246-3282, 9300 Trans-Canada Hwy) charges $55/65.

LADYSMITH
• **population 6500**

Ladysmith was named one of the prettiest small towns in Canada by *Harrowsmith Country Living* magazine. Its revitalized main street features many restored buildings from the late 19th and early 20th centuries.

The Visitor Info Centre (☎ 250-245-2112), 26 Gatacre St, is supplemented in the summer months by an information booth on the Trans-Canada Hwy. The **Black Nugget Museum** (☎ 250-245-4846), 12 Gatacre St, houses old-time memorabilia in a former hotel. **Transfer Beach Park** attracts lots of swimmers and picnickers.

Recently renovated, century-old *Lady-smith Inn* (☎ 250-245-8033, fax 245-8390, 640 1st Ave) rents rooms for $51/63 single/double. *Steam Whistle's Tap & Grille* (☎ 250-245-0693, 626 1st Ave) features an eclectic menu, with dishes for $6 to $15.

Nanaimo & Around

• population 73,000

The second largest city on Vancouver Island, with two BC Ferries terminals, Nanaimo offers plenty of sights and recreation right around town, with many more attractions only a short drive or ferry ride away.

A number of First Nations bands once shared the area, which was called 'Sne-Ny-Mos,' a Salish word meaning 'meeting place.' Coal was discovered in 1852, and mining dominated the town for 100 years. Mining has declined in importance, and tourism and forestry now power the area's economy. Nanaimo's Marine Festival and World Championship Bathtub race takes place each July.

ORIENTATION

Nanaimo, about 110km north of Victoria, has done a superb job revitalizing its downtown waterfront, adding eateries and pubs around the inner harbor, which extends north along the Newcastle Island Channel from the Boat Basin area near Harbour Park Mall. The impressive Port Theatre performing arts complex anchors one end of the waterfront on the corner of Bastion and Front Sts. The city center lies behind the harbor, with most shops on Commercial St and Terminal Ave. Also noteworthy is the Old City Quarter, a small section of downtown bordered by Fitzwilliam, Selby and Wesley Sts.

To the south, Nicol St, the southern extension of Terminal Ave, leads to the Trans-Canada Hwy and BC Ferries Duke Point terminal via Hwy 19 East. To the north, Terminal Ave forks – the right fork becomes Stewart Ave (Hwy 1) and leads to the BC Ferries terminal in Departure Bay; the left fork becomes Hwy 19A, which heads up island to Courtenay, Campbell River and Port Hardy. N Island Hwy, as 19A is known in town, has quite a few shopping malls, including the Woodgrove Centre, the largest on Vancouver Island. If you want to blow through town, the Nanaimo Parkway (Hwy 19) skirts the city's west side.

INFORMATION

Far from the city center, Nanaimo's Visitor Info Centre (☎ 250-756-0106, 800-663-7337, fax 250-756-0075) is at 2290 Bower Rd, 1km off Hwy 19 at Northfield Rd. It's open 8 am to 7 pm daily, May to September; 9 am to 5 pm weekdays and 10 am to 4 pm weekends the rest of the year. In summer, an information office stays open daily in The Bastion on the waterfront (see Things to See & Do, below). For more local information, visit www.tourismnanaimo.com. You'll find the headquarters of Tourism Vancouver Island (☎ 250-754-3500, fax 754-3599) on the 2nd floor of 335 Wesley St in the Old City Quarter. Its Web site is www.islands.bc.ca.

You'll find major banks on Commercial St downtown. Change foreign currency at Money Mart (☎ 250-753-1440), 164 Nicol St.

The main post office is in Harbour Park Mall at Front St and Terminal Ave. Tanis' Web Café (☎ 250-714-0302), 129 Bastion St, offers Internet access ($5.50 per hour) from 8:30 am to 7 pm weekdays and 10 am to 6 pm Saturday.

Of several good used bookstores along Commercial St, the most interesting is the Literacy Naniamo Bookstore (☎ 250-754-8982), 22 Commercial St, where profits go to help people learn to read. Spiritwood Books (☎ 250-753-2789), 99 Commercial St, has a good selection of New Age and metaphysical titles. You'll find a branch of the Chapters chain in the Woodgrove Centre at N Island

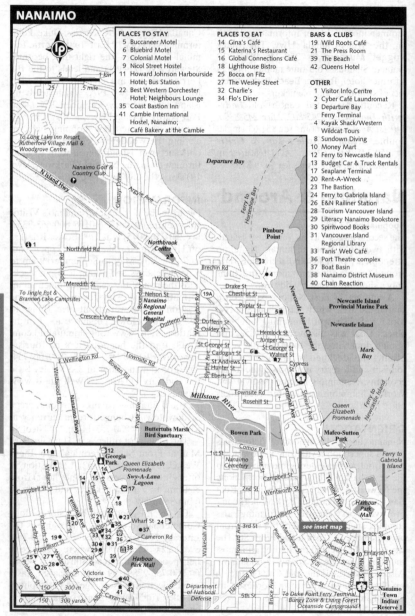

NANAIMO

PLACES TO STAY
5   Buccaneer Motel
6   Bluebird Motel
7   Colonial Motel
9   Nicol Street Hostel
11 Howard Johnson Harbourside
    Hotel; Bus Station
22 Best Western Dorchester
    Hotel; Neighbours Lounge
35 Coast Bastion Inn
41 Cambie International
    Hostel, Nanaimo;
    Café Bakery at the Cambie

PLACES TO EAT
14 Gina's Café
15 Katerina's Restaurant
16 Global Connections Café
18 Lighthouse Bistro
25 Bocca on Fitz
27 The Wesley Street
32 Charlie's
34 Flo's Diner

BARS & CLUBS
19 Wild Roots Café
21 The Press Room
39 The Beach
42 Queens Hotel

OTHER
1   Visitor Info Centre
2   Cyber Café Laundromat
3   Departure Bay
    Ferry Terminal
4   Kayak Shack/Western
    Wildcat Tours
8   Sundown Diving
10 Money Mart
12 Ferry to Newcastle Island
13 Budget Car & Truck Rentals
17 Seaplane Terminal
20 Rent-A-Wreck
23 The Bastion
24 Ferry to Gabriola Island
26 E&N Railiner Station
28 Tourism Vancouver Island
29 Literacy Nanaimo Bookstore
30 Spiritwood Books
31 Vancouver Island
    Regional Library
33 Tanis' Web Café
36 Port Theatre complex
37 Boat Basin
38 Nanaimo District Museum
40 Chain Reaction

VANCOUVER ISLAND

chain in the Woodgrove Centre at N Island Hwy and Dickinson Rd.

The main Nanaimo branch of the Vancouver Island Regional Library (☎ 250-753-1154) is at 90 Commercial St.

Boat Basin Laundromat (☎ 250-754-8654) is in the Harbour Park Mall. North of the city center, Cyber Café Laundromat (☎ 250-729-8124), 210-2000 N Island Hwy on the east side of the Northbrook Centre, features Internet access and a cappuccino bar.

Nanaimo Regional General Hospital (☎ 250-754-2121) is at 1200 Dufferin Crescent, northwest of the downtown area. Dial ☎ 911 for police, fire or ambulance.

THINGS TO SEE & DO

The **Nanaimo District Museum** (☎ 250-753-1821), 100 Cameron Rd overlooking downtown, traces the growth of the city, with exhibits on the First Nations people, the Hudson's Bay Company and coal mining. It's open 9 am to 5 pm daily, mid-May through early September; 9 am to 5 pm daily except Monday and major holidays the rest of the year. Admission is $2/1.75/75¢ for adults/seniors and students/children under 12.

Built by the Hudson's Bay Company in 1853 for protection from the local Native peoples, **The Bastion**, on Front St at the corner of Bastion St, was never used but for the odd firing of a cannon to quell a disturbance. It's now open 9 am to 5 pm Wednesday through Sunday in July and August. Admission is $1. Get there at noon to see and hear the cannon.

Just offshore of downtown, **Newcastle Island Provincial Marine Park** features picnicking, cycling, hiking and beaches. A grand pavilion contains a restaurant and hosts occasional dances; call ☎ 250-753-5141 or 755-1132 for information on upcoming events.

Ferries run to Newcastle on sunny weekends in March and April and daily from May 1 to mid-October; roundtrip fares are $4.75/3.75 for adults/seniors and children five to 12. The 10-minute trips leave the dock at Nanaimo's Maffeo-Sutton park every hour on the hour from 10 am to 7 pm (9 pm on weekends) and return from Newcastle Island on the half-hour.

About 3km south of Nanaimo on Hwy 1, the small **Petroglyph Provincial Park** features some ancient Native Indian carvings in sandstone. Most are now barely visible, but there are castings from which you can make rubbings.

Set on and around a bridge spanning the Nanaimo River south of town, the **Bungy Zone** (☎ 250-716-7874), 35 Nanaimo River Rd off Hwy 1, offers a full menu of thrills. One jump is $95, or you can become a lifetime member for $100 and get jumps for $25 apiece. Other activities include the Ultimate Swing ($50) and Zip Line ($25). You can camp on the premises for $10 per tent if someone jumps ($10 per head if no one leaps). Zone staff will pick you up free from either local BC Ferry terminal if at least one person in your group pays for a full-price jump.

ACTIVITIES

Nanaimo and its nearby islands offer some of the best **scuba diving** in BC. Dive enthusiasts recently sunk the *Cape Breton* World War II supply ship northwest of Gabriola Island, creating the area's newest and largest artificial reef. For information on dive sites, or for guides, lessons or equipment, visit Sundown Diving (☎ 250-753-1880, 888-773-3483), 22 Esplanade.

The Kayak Shack/Western Wildcat Tours (☎ 250-753-3234) offers sea **kayaking** lessons, rentals and tours from its headquarters near the Departure Bay terminal.

Nanaimo's Parkway Trail extends 20km along Hwy 19, the city's bypass route, and offers opportunities for **cycling, in-line skating, jogging** and **walking**. The trail accesses many parks, including Buttertubs Marsh Sanctuary and Morrell Sanctuary, both good for **bird-watching**. Ask for a map at the Visitor Info Centre.

PLACES TO STAY
Camping
Space is limited at *Newcastle Island Provincial Marine Park* (☎ *250-753-3481*), where there are only 18 walk-in tent sites ($12) and no reservations. There's more room, plus showers and laundry at the 193-site *Living Forest Oceanside Campground & RV Park* (☎ *250-755-1755, 6 Maki Rd*), south of town off Hwy 1. Sites here cost $16 for tents and $19 for full hookups. *Jingle Pot Campsites & RV Park* (☎ *250-758-1614, 4012 Jingle Pot Rd*), 8km north of Nanaimo off Hwy 19, offers showers, laundry and sites for $12 to $18. At *Brannen Lake Campsites* (☎ *250-756-0404, 4228 Briggs Rd*), also north of town off Hwy 19, you can camp on a working farm; sites are $16 to $19.

Hostels
The homey *Nicol St Hostel* (☎ *250-753-1188, fax 753-1185, nanaimohostel@home.com, 65 Nicol St*) is a five-minute walk from the Harbour Park Mall. Hosts John and Moni Murray offer tent sites ($10), dorm beds ($15) and private rooms (about $40). Amenities include linens and towels, a coin-op laundry and kitchen privileges. The backyard features great views, an airy outdoor shower, barbecue facilities and a fun mural created by past guests. Families would feel at home here. Reservations are advised. Plan to check in between 4 and 11 pm.

The *Cambie International Hostel, Nanaimo* (☎ *250-754-5323, 877-395-5335, nanaimo@cambiehostels.com, 63 Victoria Crescent*) enjoys an even more central location, but it can't match the Nicol St Hostel for ambience. Beds in four-person dorm rooms cost $25 ($5 less with a student ID or hostel card). Each dorm room has its own

toilet. There are no cooking facilities, but Cambie throws in free breakfast at its downstairs café. The pub downstairs is one of Nanaimo's rowdiest, so ask for a room well away from the noise.

B&Bs
Nanaimo's B&Bs are far from the city center. Good choices include the *Beach Estates* (☎ *250-753-3597, 800 Beach Dr*), with rooms for $38 to $65, and *Long Lake B&B* (☎ *250-758-5010, 240 Ferntree Place*), which charges $80 to $110.

Hotels
A helpful front desk and good-sized rooms await travelers at the *Bluebird Motel* (☎ *250-753-4151, 995 N Terminal Ave*), where rooms cost about $46/53 single/ double. Across the street, the tiny *Colonial Motel* (☎ *250-754-4415, 950 N Terminal Ave*) rents rooms (some with kitchenettes) for $49/55 and up and offers kayak rentals. The *Buccaneer Inn* (☎ *250-753-1246, info@ thebuccaneerinn.com, 1577 Stewart Ave*), the closest motel to the Departure Bay ferry terminal, welcomes divers to its comfortable rooms ($49/59), some with ocean views.

Howard Johnson Harbourside Hotel (☎ *250-753-2241, 800-663-7322, 1 N Terminal Ave*) isn't on the waterfront, but it does have an outdoor pool and rooms starting at $88. Downtown, the refurbished and historic *Best Western Dorchester Hotel* (☎ *250-754-6835, 800-661-2449, 70 Church St*) features rooms and suites with harbor views starting at $90. Across the street, the *Coast Bastion Inn* (☎ *250-753-6601, 800-663-1144, 11 Bastion St*) has well-appointed rooms starting at $85 weekends and $115 weekdays. *Long Lake Inn Resort* (☎ *250-758-1144, 800-565-1144, 4700 N Island Hwy*) is just 3 km north of Nanaimo, but it has a resort feel, with a swimming beach, marina and canoe rentals. Rooms cost $110 to $150.

PLACES TO EAT
Budget
For self-catering, try Thrifty Foods, located in the Harbour Park Mall, or the downtown

VANCOUVER ISLAND

Nanaimo farmers' market, held 10 am to 2 pm every Friday, late May through mid-October, at Pioneer Waterfront Plaza, near the Bastion.

Naniamo's best bet for breakfast is the *Café Bakery at the Cambie* (☎ 250-754-5323, 63 Victoria Crescent), where $3 buys a breakfast of bacon, eggs, toast and hash browns. Locals throng here for the freshly baked bread and pastries, including an outstanding version of the town's signature sweet, the Nanaimo bar.

Prices are similar at *Charlie's* (☎ 250-753-7044, 123 Commercial St), where you'll find $3 breakfast specials, $5 soup-and-sandwich deals and gourmet ice cream. Down the street and just a bit more pricey, *Flo's Diner* (☎ 250-753-2148, 187 Commercial St) serves omelets, burgers, and a 'Big-Ass Breakfast' for about $7. In a previous incarnation, Flo's was owned by the father of jazz star (and local girl-made-good) Diana Krall.

Global Connections Café, aka the Funky Diner (☎ 250-753-3366, 10 Front St), features great views and a creative international menu with items from $5 to $9. *Bocca on Fitz* (☎ 250-753-1799, 427 Fitzwilliam St) is an upscale coffeehouse serving soups, salads and sandwiches.

Mid-Range & Top End

One of the most romantic spots in town, *Katerina's Restaurant* (☎ 250-754-1351, 15 Front St) offers Greek fare and seafood for $10 to $17. Just around the corner, the brightly colored *Gina's Café* (☎ 250-753-5411, 47 Skinner St) is a local favorite for its lively atmosphere and Mexican combination plates ($9 to $10).

The *Green Garden Restaurant* (☎ 250-753-2828), in the Harbour Park Mall, stays open until 3 am Friday, Saturday and Sunday. It features smorgasbord spreads for lunch ($7.50), dinner ($10.50) and Sunday brunch ($9.50).

An eight-minute ferry ride from the south end of Nanaimo's harbor, the *Dinghy Dock Floating Pub* (☎ 250-753-2373) serves seafood or barbecued fare for lunch ($6 to $8) and dinner ($8 to $12). The ferry

costs $4/3 roundtrip for adults/seniors and children.

Among the most upscale eateries in Nanaimo, *The Wesley Street* (☎ 250-753-4004, 1-321 Wesley St) offers creative selections like yam-crusted salmon grilled in a curried orange cream ($19.50). The *Lighthouse Bistro* (☎ 250-754-3212, 50 Anchor Way), on the waterfront, features a white-linen atmosphere with dinner selections for $9 to $30, including pastas, lamb and veal schnitzel. The pub upstairs has lower prices and a more casual feel. From either floor, watch seaplanes taking off and landing.

ENTERTAINMENT

The *Port Theatre* (☎ 250-754-8550, 125 Front St) presents local and touring fine-arts performances. For nightlife, young adults hit *The Beach* (☎ 250-754-7900, 37 Gordon St), while *The Press Room* (☎ 250-716-0030, 150 Skinner St) is popular with an older crowd.

Live music by local and regional acts can often be heard at the *Queens Hotel* (☎ 250-754-6751, 34 Victoria Crescent) and *Wild Roots Café* (☎ 250-753-0200, 299 Wallace St). *Neighbours Lounge* (☎ 205-716-0505, 70 Church St), in the basement of the Best Western Dorchester Hotel, caters to the area's gay and lesbian community.

Major movie houses include the 10-screen *Avalon Cinema Centre* (☎ 250-390-5021, 6631 N Island Hwy), in the Woodgrove Centre, and the *Caprice Grand 8 Theatres* (☎ 250-741-9000, 4750 Rutherford Rd), in the Rutherford Village Mall, which is off the N Island Hwy.

GETTING THERE & AWAY
Air

Most flights to Nanaimo are via seaplane, with the terminal right downtown on the harbor. Companies include Baxter Aviation (☎ 250-754-1066) and Harbour Air (☎ 250-714-0900, 800-665-0212). The fare for the Nanaimo-Vancouver run is about $50 one-way, though roundtrip specials as low as $78 are often available.

Nanaimo Collishaw Air Terminal (☎ 250-245-2157) is a 15-minute drive south of town on Hwy 1. Pacific Coastal Airlines (☎ 800-665-1177) offers scheduled flights to and from Vancouver.

Bus
Laidlaw Coach Lines (☎ 250-753-4371) connects Nanaimo with points north and south; the one-way fare to or from Victoria is $17.50. The station is behind the Howard Johnson Harbourside Hotel at 1 N Terminal Ave north of the centre at Comox Rd.

Train
The E&N Railiner (☎ 800-561-8630) passes through once a day in each direction and stops at the station at 321 Selby St. The one-way fare to Victoria is $21. Tickets can be purchased from the conductor.

Ferry
BC Ferries has two Nanaimo terminals with service to the Vancouver area. Sailings from Departure Bay go to Horseshoe Bay. The 39km trip takes 80 to 95 minutes, depending on the ship. Fares and sailings vary seasonally, but in peak season (late June through mid-September), there are about 11 trips each way. Bet on about eight daily peak-season sailings between Duke Point and Tsawwassen. The trip takes two hours. The fares for both routes are the same: $9/4.50/32 for adults/children five to 11/cars. To reserve a spot on either route, call ☎ 888-724-5223 in BC or 604-444-2890 outside BC, or visit the Web site www.bcferries.com.

GETTING AROUND
BC Transit Bus No 2 goes to the Departure Bay ferry terminal. No city buses run to Duke Point. Local bus fares are $1.75; day passes cost $4.50. For more information, call ☎ 250-390-4531 or pick up a transit guide at the tourist office. All buses pass through the Harbour Park Mall, located at Front St and Terminal Ave.

The shuttle company Nanaimo Seaporter (☎ 250-753-2118) provides door-to-door service to the Departure Bay ferry terminal for $6 and to the Duke Point terminal for $14; fares are good for either one or two people traveling together.

Rental agencies include Budget Car & Truck Rentals (☎ 250-754-7368), 33 S Terminal Ave, and Rent-a-Wreck (☎ 250-753-6461), 227 Terminal Ave. For taxi service, call AC Taxi at ☎ 250-753-1231. Taxi fares to/from Departure Bay are about $8; for Duke Point, plan on about $25.

Chain Reaction (☎ 250-754-3309), 12 Lois Lane, down the steps between Victoria Crescent and the Harbour Park Mall, rents bicycles and offers good information on local cycling.

GABRIOLA ISLAND
Considered the most northerly of the Southern Gulf Islands, Gabriola Island makes a fine trip from Nanaimo for an afternoon or longer. Hundreds of artists live on the island, but it's just as well known for its scenery and recreation.

For local information, look for 'Gabriola Gertie' (see Things to See & Do, below) on the ferry dock in Nanaimo; chances are, she'll be handing out island maps and brochures. The Visitor Info Centre (☎ 250-247-9332), 575 North Rd in the Folklife Village Shopping Centre, is open May through September. See its Web site at www.gabriolaisland.org.

Things to See & Do
A small park area, **Malaspina Galleries** is known for its unusual sandstone caves formed by wind and tides. It's 1km off Taylor Bay Rd; make the first left turn as you leave the ferry dock. Not far away, **Gabriola Sands Provincial Park** includes shaded Taylor Bay Beach and sandy Pilot Bay Beach, separated by a grassy field and picnic area. On the island's opposite, southeast end, **Drumberg Provincial Park** offers good swimming, while **Brickyard Beach** features tide pools and clam-digging.

The **Gabriola Museum** (☎ 250-247-9987), 505 South Rd, has indoor historical exhibits ($2) and an outdoor Petroglyph Park with reproductions of rock art found elsewhere on the island. About a dozen Gabriola artists open their studios to the public. Among them, FOGO Folk Art (☎ 250-247-8082), 3065 Commodore Way, features Bob and Dee Lauder's practical, sometimes profane and always whimsical wooden carvings. ('Gabriola Gertie' is their creation, as is 'Monique' at Page's Marina.)

For information on **scuba diving**, visit Gabriola Reefs Dive Shop (☎ 250-247-8443), at Silva Bay Marina, which offers gear and guides.

Places to Stay & Eat

Convenient to the ferry, *Gabriola Campground* (☎ 250-247-2079) has 28 beachside campsites ($14). *Casa Blanca By the Sea* (☎ 250-247-9824, 1707 El Verano Dr) offers a bed-and-breakfast room for $50/60 and a large self-contained suite with kitchen ($80), along with kayak rentals and guided tours starting at $25.

Surf Lodge (☎ 250-247-9231, fax 250-247-8336, surflod@island.net, 885 Berry Point Rd) features rooms ($85 to $105) and cabins ($95 to $165). The lodge's Sunset Lounge serves great fish and chips ($8.75). Bald eagles often perch high in the treetops just outside. *Allegro Café* (☎ 250-247-2077), in the Folklife Village Shopping Centre, serves breakfast ($3.25 to $7.50) until 3:30 pm, plus lunch (mostly $5 to $7) and prime rib on Sunday evening ($12 to $14).

Getting There & Away

Pacific Spirit Air offers daily seaplane flights from Vancouver to Silva Bay. The 12-minute flight costs $130 roundtrip. BC Ferries travels between Nanaimo and Gabriola Island about 15 times daily. The peak-season roundtrip fare for the 20-minute trip is $5/12.75 per passenger/car. The Nanaimo dock is near the Harbour Park Mall.

Central Vancouver Island

Vancouver Island's midsection includes some of its greatest recreational assets: long stretches of sand at Parksville and Qualicum Beach, windswept Pacific Rim National Park, Clayoquot Sound near Tofino and more.

PARKSVILLE, QUALICUM BEACH & AROUND

Parksville (population 10,000) and Qualicum Beach (population 7000) and the coast toward Comox have become major vacation destinations as well as departure points for Tofino and the rest of the island's west coast via Hwy 4, just south of Parksville, or Hwy 4A from Qualicum Beach.

Look for Visitor Info Centres at 1275 E Island Hwy in Parksville (☎ 250-248-3613) and at 2711 W Island Hwy in Qualicum Beach (☎ 250-752-9532). For more local information, visit www.oceansidetourism.com. For information on parks, contact the Strathcona District Office (☎ 250-954-4600) of BC Parks in Rathtrevor Beach Provincial Park (see Places to Stay, below). The Parksville After-Hours Clinic (☎ 250-248-7200), 154 Memorial Ave, handles minor medical needs until 9 pm daily.

Things to See & Do

Aside from the beaches, most of the area's attractions lie inland; many are open only from March through October. At Coombs, 8km west of Parksville, check out the goats grazing on the roof of the **Old Country Market** (☎ 250-248-6272, 2326 Alberni Hwy) or visit **Butterfly World** (☎ 250-248-7026, 1080 Winchester Rd), where you can walk through a tropical garden filled with butterflies and birds; admission is $6/5/4.50/3.50 for adults/seniors/students/children.

Englishman River Falls Provincial Park, about 13km southwest of Parksville at the end of Errington Rd, features a short hiking trail past two beautiful waterfalls. Nearby, the **North Island Wildlife Recovery Centre** (☎ 250-248-1274), 1240 Leffler Rd, includes a wildlife museum and exhibits on its efforts to rehabilitate bald eagles and black bears. Admission is $3/2 for adults/children.

At **MacMillan Provincial Park**, 28km west of Parksville on Hwy 4, you can picnic on Cameron Lake or walk short trails through the magnificent Cathedral Grove, a forest with huge Douglas firs and red cedars, some 800 years old. Some of the grove's one-time tallest trees now rest on the forest floor, victims of a severe windstorm in 1997.

VANCOUVER ISLAND

Crazy for Caves

Home to some of Vancouver Island's best limestone caves, **Horne Lake Caves Provincial Park**, 12km off Hwy 19 north of Qualicum Beach, offers tours of varying lengths and difficulty daily in July and August and on weekends in June and September. Trips range from easy, 90-minute interpretive hikes of Riverbend Cave ($15/12 for adults/children under 12) to the five-hour 'High Adventure' expedition in basic caving ($79; ages 15 and up only) or the seven-hour 'Underground Extreme' trip for those with prior rope experience ($110). Experienced spelunkers can tackle the caves on their own, with equipment available for rent. Bring warm clothing and sturdy shoes. Don't drink much at breakfast, because there is no toilet until you're back in daylight. Call ☎ 250-248-7829 for reservations (necessary for all programs except the first-come, first-served Riverbend Cave hikes) or ☎ 250-757-8687 for tour information.

Places to Stay

Camping With 2000m of sandy beach, **Rathtrevor Beach Provincial Park**, 3km south of Parksville off Hwy 19, is the area's most popular campground. Sites cost $12 to $18.50. You can camp, too, at **Englishman River Falls Provincial Park**, on Errington Rd, and **Little Qualicum Falls Provincial Park**, 19km west of Parksville on Hwy 4. Both charge $15.

Riverbend Resort & Campground (☎ 250-248-3134, 800-701-3033, 1-924 E Island Hwy), in Parksville, offers tent sites ($15), full hookups ($21) and cottages ($55 to $88). The common area is stocked with games and videos for rainy days. **Tranquility Woods** (☎ 250-954-1661, 2080 Errington Rd), in Errington, includes campsites ($14 to $23) and cabins with hot tubs ($69 to $119).

B&Bs Stays of more than one night are encouraged at **Naturally By the Falls Health Retreat B&B** (☎ 250-248-4788, 877-302-2255, 1180 Englishman River Rd), in Errington, an organic farm where owner Maria Matias is happy to help her guests develop better health habits. The very comfy guest rooms cost $79 to $99.

Motels The rooms at **Englishman River Motel** (☎ 250-248-6532, 762 E Island Hwy),

in Parksville, may be well-worn, but the prices ($50/60 single/double), the kitchen and the riverside setting still make them a good value. The nicer **Paradise Sea Shell Motel** (☎ 250-248-6171, 877-337-3529, 411 W Island Hwy), in Parksville, charges $60/80, which includes beach access and continental breakfast. The **Old Dutch Inn** (☎ 250-752-6914, 800-661-0199, 2690 Island Hwy W), in Qualicum Beach, features an indoor pool and rooms for about $80. The **Sand Pebbles Inn** (☎ 250-752-6974, 2767 Island Hwy W), in Qualicum Beach, rents rooms for $85 to $119, some with kitchens and a patio or balcony overlooking the water.

Beachside Resorts **Pacific Shores Nature Resort** (☎ 250-468-7121, fax 469-2001, 1-1600 Stroulger Rd), in Nanoose Bay, offers a variety of options, from standard motel rooms ($80) to condo-style suites and townhouses ($110 to $260), all brightly decorated and well furnished. Canoe and kayaks are available, and mountain bikes may be rented; other amenities include hot tubs, a large indoor pool, fitness room and convenience store/deli.

Set amid forests but close to the beach, **Tigh Na Mara Resort Hotel** (☎ 250-248-2072, 800-663-7373, 1095 Island Hwy E) offers lodge rooms, cottages and condos starting at $110, plus a fitness room, indoor pool and watercraft rentals.

Places to Eat
After you've gawked at the goats, enter Coombs' *Old Country Market (2326 Alberni Hwy)* for sit-down meals ($4 to $7) or gourmet picnic goods to go. *Shoot the Breeze* (☎ 250-752-0301, 694 Memorial St), in Qualicum Beach Village, is a casual café with breakfast ($4 to $7), sandwiches ($5) and pastas and quesadillas ($8 to $11). *Sand Pebbles Restaurant* (see Places to Stay, above) serves lunch ($6 to $10) and dinner ($7 to $19). *Tigh Na Mara Resort Restaurant* offers fine dining in the evenings ($14 to $21).

Getting There & Away
The bus company Laidlaw Coach Lines stops in Parksville (☎ 250-248-5332) and Qualicum Beach (☎ 250-752-9532). The one-way fare from Nanaimo to Parksville is $7.50; from Victoria, it's $25. E&N Railiner (☎ 250-383-4324, 800-561-8630) stops at Parksville ($26/52 one-way/roundtrip from Victoria) and Qualicum Beach ($28/56).

PORT ALBERNI & AROUND
• population 19,500
The gateway to Vancouver Island's west coast, Port Alberni was built on natural resources. More than 300 commercial fishing boats work out of the area, most catching salmon.

The Alberni Valley Visitor Info Centre (☎ 250-724-6535, fax 724-6560) is at 2533 Redford St. For medical help, go to West Coast General Hospital (☎ 250-723-2135), 3841 8th Ave. Do laundry at West Coast Cleaners (☎ 250-723-6733), 4487 Gertrude St.

Things to See & Do
Port Alberni's big draw is **Lady Rose Marine Services** (☎ 250-723-8313, 800-663-7192 April through September), which runs day trips up Barkley Sound to Bamfield, Ucluelet and the Broken Group Islands on the 100-passenger *Lady Rose* and 200-passenger *Frances Barkley*. The Bamfield run takes place 8 am to 5:30 pm Tuesday,

Thursday and Saturday year-round, as well as Friday and Sunday during July and August; it costs $20/40 one-way/roundtrip. There's a coffee shop on board. Bring a sweater or jacket, even if it's warm in Port Alberni.

The working packet freighters make numerous stops en route to deliver mail and supplies, with a 60- to 90-minute layover in Bamfield. Taking a ride on one of them is an enjoyable, scenic way to spend a lazy day, as well as a practical means of returning from the West Coast Trail's north end at Bamfield. From October to May, kayakers and canoeists can request a stop at the Broken Group Islands. The company also makes a separate run to Ucluelet ($23/45) and the Broken Group Islands ($20/40) on Monday, Wednesday and Friday from June through September. That trip leaves at 8 am and returns about 7 pm, with a 90-minute stop in Ucluelet. See www.ladyrosemarine.com for more information.

In town, **Harbour Quay**, at the foot of Argyle St, contains shops, restaurants and an observation tower. The **Alberni Valley Museum** (☎ 250-723-2181), 4255 Wallace St, features impressive exhibits, including beautifully woven goods and a spectacular Chinese paper lion headdress. It's open 10 am to 5 pm Tuesday to Saturday (until 8 pm Thursday); suggested donation is $3.

McLean Mill Historic Site is Canada's only heritage sawmill, family-operated from 1926 to 1965. Get there on the **Alberni Pacific Railway Steam Train**, which runs hourly from 11 am to 4 pm weekends in July and August. Trains depart the restored 1921 station at the entrance to Harbour Quay; fares are $3/2 for adults/children.

Places to Stay
Arrowvale Campground (☎ 250-723-7948, 5955 Hector Rd), on the Somass River 6km west of Port Alberni, offers 45 sites ($15 to $20), plus showers, swimming, a playground, farm tours and laundry. A riverview cottage sleeps up to four ($130 double occupancy; two or more nights $95 each). Sites ($12) are primitive at *Stamp River Provincial Park*, 14.5km west of Port Alberni on

Doing Della Falls

At 440m tall, Della Falls is the highest in Canada, and getting there can be an epic experience in itself. Although it's set deep within Strathcona Provincial Park, you'll have the easiest time reaching Della from Port Alberni.

Take Hwy 4 about 13km west of town to Great Central Lake Rd. You'll then need to boat to the trailhead across 35km Great Central Lake, either in your own vessel (canoeists should plan on seven to 12 hours) or via a shuttle (see below). From there, it's a 16km hike to Della Falls; plan on five to eight hours one way, with 510m change in elevation. All told, set aside a minimum of two days to make the trip via boat shuttle, four if you're paddling a canoe.

Ark Resort (☎ 250-723-2657), 11000 Great Central Lake Rd in Port Alberni, offers a water-taxi service to the trailhead for $90 per person roundtrip. The resort also includes campsites and rents boats, canoes and camping gear for Della-bound trekkers. For more information, visit the Web site www.arkresort.com.

Nanaimo-based Western Wildcat Tours (☎ 250-753-3234) leads guided four-day, three-night hikes to Della Falls and on to high-alpine Love Lake ($588 per person), with about 10 departures from late June through early September. Learn more at www.bcwildcat.com.

Beaver Creek Rd, a small wooded campground near a waterfall. Salmon migrate through here in late August.

It's smoky and spartan, but the **Personal Touch Hostel** (☎ 250-723-2484, 4908 Burde St) fills Port Alberni's need for cheap beds. You pay $15 for a bed, $35 for a bed and three square meals a day. The **Riverside Lodge** (☎ 250-724-9916, 5065 Roger St), convenient to the bus station, charges $59/65 single/double. A few kitchenettes are available for $8 more. There are no in-room phones, but there is a coin laundry, and the

owners are friendly and helpful. The **Esta Villa Motel** (☎ 250-724-1261, 800-724-0844, 4014 Johnston Rd) features rooms starting at $52/65, a pleasant barbecue and picnic grounds.

Places to Eat

Open at 5 am, the **Blue Door Café** (☎ 250-723-8811, 5415 Argyle St) draws an early-morning crowd of fisherfolk; it's a handy spot to grab breakfast before boarding the Lady Rose. **Paradise Café** (☎ 250-724-5050, 4505 Gertrude St) serves daily specials at breakfast ($3.99 to $4.99), lunch ($6.49) and dinner ($8.99). Under the tower at Harbour Quay, the **Clockworks Restaurant** (☎ 250-723-8862, 41-5440 Argyle St) prepares seafood platters for two at lunch ($16.95) and dinner ($49.95, including lobster tails). Other main dishes cost about $5 to $9 at lunch and $10 to $17 at dinner.

Getting There & Around

Laidlaw Coach Lines (☎ 250-724-1266), 4541 Margaret St, runs buses from Port Alberni to Ucluelet ($15) and Tofino ($17.50).

Rental cars are available through Budget (☎ 250-724-4511), 3500 3rd Ave, and Rent-a-Wreck (☎ 250-724-6565), 4521 10th Ave. For cab rides, call United Cabs (☎ 250-723-2121) or Fairway Taxi (☎ 250-723-3511). Contact Port Alberni Transit (☎ 250-723-3341) for local bus information.

See Things to See & Do, above, for information on boat service to Bamfield, Ucluelet and the Broken Group Islands.

BAMFIELD
• population 520

A gateway to the West Coast Trail and a layover point on the *Lady Rose* or *Frances Barkley*, tiny Bamfield is the most remote town many travelers visit on their Vancouver Island journey. The community lies on both sides of Bamfield Inlet. It's divided into Bamfield East (where you'll arrive if you take the 100km drive west from Port Alberni) and Bamfield West (where you'll spend your *Lady Rose* layover on the boardwalk). The Bamfield Chamber of Commerce (☎ 250-728-3006) maintains a

Visitor Info Centre on Grappler Rd in Bamfield East and a Web site at www .alberni.net/bamcham.

For a short stroll at Bamfield West, try **Brady's Beach Trail**. Broken Island Adventures (☎ 250-728-3500, 888-728-6200) specializes in **scuba diving** throughout Barkley Sound.

Places to Stay & Eat
The First Nations–run *Pachena Bay Campground* (☎ 250-728-1287), about 3 km from Bamfield East on Port Alberni Rd, features a splendid setting, with showers and sites for about $15. *Marie's Bed & Breakfast* (☎ 250-728-3091 or 728-3411) offers rooms for $50/80 single/double. *Bamfield Trails Motel* (☎ 250-728-3231), near the dock at Bamfield East, is popular with West Coast Trail hikers; rooms run about $100.

Bamfield Lodge and Cottages (☎ 250-728-3419), on the boardwalk at Bamfield West, charges $100 for cottages that sleep up to four. There's an espresso bar on the deck outside. Lady Rose Marine Services passengers on layover at Bamfield West will also find sandwiches for sale at the Bamfield General Store or gourmet food to go from *The Lunch Box* (☎ 250-728-3036), a bit farther down the boardwalk.

TOFINO & AROUND
• population 1200

The most appealing end-of-the-road town on Vancouver Island, Tofino sits at the terminus of Hwy 4. Its population doubles in summer as people come to visit nearby Pacific Rim National Park, Hot Springs Cove and other natural attractions.

Tofino sits on Clayoquot (Clay-Kwot) Sound, one of the most scenic areas on Vancouver Island. Dotted with islands and rimmed by mountains, Tofino's setting is both serene and spectacular. And did we mention the wildlife? If you want to see whales, sea lions and other maritime creatures, this is a top place to go.

You'll find Tofino 122km west of Port Alberni via a winding, narrow road. If you drive, do so in the daytime, both for safety's sake and for the pleasure of enjoying the

scenery. And consider coming in April or September, when there are fewer crowds and lower lodging rates.

Information
The Visitor Info Centre (☎ 250-725-3414, fax 250-725-3296), 380 Campbell St, is open 9 am to 7 pm daily, May to September. Its Web site is www.island.net/~tofino. The *Long Beach Maps* brochure offers helpful listings for Tofino, Ucluelet and Pacific Rim National Park.

The Sound is a local magazine distributed around Tofino and on the Web at www.island.net/~thesound. The post office is on First St. The Tofino Laundromat, 448 Campbell St, is open 9 am to 9 pm.

Hot Springs Cove
One of BC's best day-trip destinations, Hot Springs Cove is the best-known part of Maquinna Provincial Marine Park, 37km north of Tofino. Most sojourners travel by Zodiac boat, watching for whales and other sea critters en route, though seaplane service

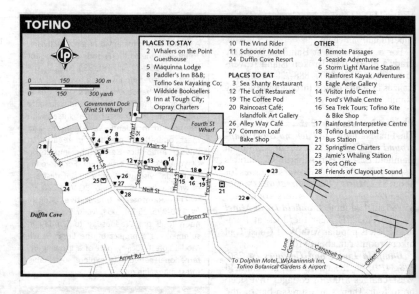

TOFINO

PLACES TO STAY	10 The Wind Rider	OTHER
2 Whalers on the Point Guesthouse	11 Schooner Motel	1 Remote Passages
5 Maquinna Lodge	24 Duffin Cove Resort	4 Seaside Adventures
8 Paddler's Inn B&B;		6 Storm Light Marine Station
Tofino Sea Kayaking Co;	PLACES TO EAT	7 Rainforest Kayak Adventures
Wildside Booksellers	3 Sea Shanty Restaurant	13 Eagle Aerie Gallery
9 Inn at Tough City;	12 The Loft Restaurant	14 Visitor Info Centre
Ospray Charters	19 The Coffee Pod	15 Ford's Whale Centre
	20 Raincoast Café;	16 Sea Trek Tours; Tofino Kite
	Islandfolk Art Gallery	& Bike Shop
	26 Alley Way Café	17 Rainforest Interpretive Centre
	27 Common Loaf	18 Tofino Laundromat
	Bake Shop	21 Bus Station
		22 Springtime Charters
		23 Jamie's Whaling Station
		25 Post Office
		28 Friends of Clayoquot Sound

is available. From the boat landing, you can hike 2km over boardwalks to a series of natural hot pools perfect for soaking.

Many outfitters make the run to Hot Springs Cove. Remote Passages (☎ 725-3330, 800-666-9833), 71 Wharf St, is one of the more ecologically minded companies, with guides well versed in the natural history of Clayoquot Sound. Its six- to seven-hour Hot Springs Explorer trip costs $89/59 for adults/children. Tofino Air Lines (☎ 250-725-4454) flies to Hot Springs Cove (about $155 roundtrip for a three-seat Cessna, $220 for a six-seat Beaver). Magna Helicopters (☎ 250-726-8946, 877-999-4356) charges $125 to $150 per person for a roundtrip flight to the cove, with a four-hour layover, though it's a more rugged hike from the helipad than it is from the boat dock.

For overnight stays, there are a few primitive campsites near the hot-springs boat landing. The Hesquiaht First Nation operates *Hot Springs Lodge* (☎ 250-670-1106), in the community of Hot Springs Cove. Its six rooms cost $100 ($75 in the off-season) and come with kitchenettes, hide-a-beds and

satellite TV. The innkeepers will ferry you to the Hot Springs Cove boardwalk at your convenience, and you can also enjoy a private beach here. You can only get to the lodge by water-taxi ($60/40 for adults/children roundtrip).

Meares Island
Visible from Tofino, Meares Island is home to the Big Tree Trail, a 400m boardwalk stroll through old-growth forest, including a red cedar tree that's been standing for 1500 years. The island was the site of a key 1984 anti-logging protest that kicked off the modern environmental movement in Clayoquot Sound. Rainforest Boat Shuttle (☎ 250-725-3793) runs a 2½-hour trip to Meares Island for $20/5 for adults/children under 12. Sea Trek Tours (☎ 250-725-4412, 800-811-9155), 411-B Campbell St, operates 90-minute trips that feature a glass-bottom boat ride for $25/20/15/5 for adults/seniors and students/children six to 12/children two to five.

Ahousat
Located on remote Flores Island, Ahousat is home to the Wild Side Heritage Trail, a

moderately difficult path that traverses 10km of forests, beaches and headlands between Ahousat and Cow Bay. Walk the Wild Side (☎ 250-670-9586, 888-670-9586), a First Nations business, leads guided hikes on the route. It's a 40-minute water-taxi ride from Tofino to Ahousat; Cougar Island Taxis (☎ 250-670-9692 or 726-8427) makes the run for $45 roundtrip.

Tofino Botanical Gardens
This new attraction (☎ 250-725-1237), 1084 Pacific Rim Hwy, features the native plants of Clayoquot Sound and several theme gardens, along with bird-watching blinds and a tree house for kids. It's open 9 am to dusk daily; admission is $6/5/2 for adults/students/ children. Three-day passes and 'sweat-equity' admissions are available, and anyone arriving without a car gets a dollar off.

Activities
Kayaking Tofino Sea Kayaking Co (☎ 250-725-4222, 800-863-4664), 320 Main St, offers tours ($40 and up), rentals, lessons and a great bookstore called Wildside Book-sellers. Remote Passages (☎ 250-725-3330, 800-666-9833) operates similar day trips. Rainforest Kayak Adventures (☎ 250-725-3117, 877-422-9453), 316 Main St, specializes in four- to six-day guided tours and instructional courses for beginner and intermediate paddlers; prices start at $650.

Surfing Tofino is a swell place to surf (pun intended) or to learn how. Inner Rhythm Surf Camp (☎ 250-726-2211) features a variety of adult and youth surf classes and camps starting at $59, plus food and lodging. See the Web site www.innerrhythm.net for more details. Blue Planet (☎ 250-726-7854) offers four-hour surfing classes ($69) or a two-day retreat ($395). Surf Sister (☎ 250-725-4456, 877-724-7873) is BC's only all-female surf school, with two-day courses for $195, including gear rentals.

Fishing Clayoquot Sound features year-round fishing for chinook salmon, plus seasonal catches of halibut, steelhead and coho salmon. Guides include Ospray Charters

(☎ 250-725-2133, 888-286-3466), 350 Main St, and Springtime Charters (☎ 250-725-2351), 586 Campbell St.

Whale-Watching You're likely to see whales on any trip to Hot Springs Cove or Flores Island or sometimes even from shore in Tofino, but you can also book a trip devoted to their pursuit. Go from March to May, when they migrate through the area, though many whales linger through summer. Many local outfitters run two- to three-hour trips (for about $50 to $70), including Adventures Pacific Charters (☎ 250-725-2811, 888-486-3466), Jamie's Whaling Station (☎ 250-725-3919, 800-667-9913), Remote Passages (☎ 250-725-3330, 800-666-9833) and Seaside Adventures (☎ 250-725-2292, 888-332-4252). Forde's Whale Centre (☎ 250-725-2132), 411 Campbell St, has a small museum at its trip headquarters.

Storm-Watching From mid-October through March, Tofino offers a front seat to watch some of the most spectacular storms on the North American West Coast. Many visitors are content to watch the pounding surf from their hotel rooms, but Long Beach Nature Tours Company (☎ 250-726-7099) offers guided hikes to safe viewing spots for $160 (half-day) or $320 (full day); rates cover up to five people.

Places to Stay
Tofino's budget lodging scene has brightened in recent years, but you still won't find many rooms under $100 from May through September, so you will want to book way ahead.

Camping You'll find several good, albeit pricey, choices south of Tofino. *Bella Pacifica Resort & Campground (☎ 250-725-3400)*, 3km south of Tofino on Pacific Rim Hwy, has forest sites ($27) and beachfront sites ($36). *Mackenzie Beach Resort (☎ 250-725-3439, 1101 Pacific Rim Hwy)* charges $30 for tent sites and $35 for full hookups; a variety of sleeping rooms and cottages cost $139 to $239. Also south of town, the *Crystal Cove Beach Resort*

(☎ *250-725-4213, 1165 Cedarwood Place*) offers sites starting at $30 and log cottages beginning at $160. Also see Places to Stay & Eat under Pacific Rim National Park, earlier in the chapter.

Hostels One of the nicest and newest hostels in Canada, the *Whalers on the Point Guesthouse* (☎ *250-725-3443, fax 725-3463, info@tofinohostel.com, 81 West St*) sits right by the ocean in Tofino's west end. Built specifically as a hostel in 1999, this handsome HI affiliate features a game room, bike rentals, surfboard lockers and spacious kitchen, dining and lounging areas. Bunks in the four-bed shared rooms cost $22/24 for HI members/nonmembers. Private rooms and suites for two to five people are $66 to $99 for members, $70 to $109 for nonmembers.

The Wind Rider (☎ *250-725-3240, fax 725-3280, whole@island.net, 231 Main St*) is a nonprofit, women-only retreat house best suited to groups of women traveling together, although individual backpackers are welcome. Rates start at $25 for a shared room and $60 for private rooms; rent the whole house (which sleeps nine) for $250. Kitchen facilities and linens are provided, and there's a deck and Jacuzzi.

B&Bs The best budget choice, the *Paddlers Inn B&B* (☎ *250-725-4222, 800-863-4664, paddlers@island.net, 320 Main St*) is run by the Tofino Sea Kayaking Co and sits right above its store; rates ($50/60 single/double) include the makings of a self-catered continental breakfast. For a more deluxe experience, head for the *Inn at Tough City* (☎ *250-725-2021, fax 725-2088, cityinn@cedar.alberni.net, 350 Main St*), a lovely place where rooms with decks cost $130 to $165. Toward Pacific Rim National Park, *BriMar B&B* (☎ *250-725-3410, 1375 Thornberg Crescent*), on Chesterman Beach south of Tofino, features three ocean-view rooms for $110 to $160.

Motels and Resorts At the *Dolphin Motel* (☎ *250-725-3377, fax 725-3374, 1190 Pacific Rim Hwy*), about 3km south of town near Chesterman Beach, rooms (all with refrigerators) begin at $79/99 for one bed/two beds. *Schooner Motel* (☎ *250-725-3478, fax 725-3499, 311-312 Campbell St*), downtown overlooking the bay, rents rooms (some with kitchens) for $95/125 and up. Some rooms come with views of the sound at the *Maquinna Lodge* (☎ *250-725-3261, 800-665-3199, fax 250-725-3433, 120 First St*), where rates start at $115.

Best Western Tin Wis Resort (☎ *250-725-4445, 800-661-9995, fax 250-725-4447, tinwis@mail.island.net, 1119 Pacific Rim Hwy*) offers beach access and rooms that start at $160. At the *Duffin Cove Resort* (☎ *250-725-2448, 888-629-2903, duffin@island.net, 215 Campbell St*), near the water and downtown, accommodations range from studio rooms ($165) to oceanside cabins ($300).

Middle Beach Lodge (☎ *250-725-2900, fax 725-2901, lodge@middlebeach.com*), on the Pacific Rim Hwy, offers everything from forest-facing rooms ($105) to deluxe cabins ($400). All include a continental breakfast. Many rooms in the main lodge are on a par with those at the *Wickaninnish Inn* (☎ *250-725-3100, 800-333-4604, fax 250-725-3110, wick@wickinn.com*), on Osprey Lane south of town. Exquisitely furnished, the Wickaninnish's guest rooms ($340 to $420) feature push-button gas fireplaces, two-person hot tubs and private balconies. On Quait Bay northeast of Tofino, *Clayoquot Wilderness Resort* (☎ *250-726-8235, PO Box 130, Tofino V0R 2Z0*) is an adventure lodge specializing in horseback riding and fishing; rates run $350 to $430 with meals.

Places to Eat

The *Common Loaf Bake Shop* (☎ *250-725-3915, 180 First St*) is a low-key local gathering spot with second-floor atrium seating and tasty homemade muffins, cookies, breads and cakes. The *Alley Way Cafe* (☎ *250-725-3105*), tucked in the yard behind the corner of First and Campbell Sts, serves a range of all-day breakfasts, Mexican-style dishes and various vegetarian meals under $8. If you're planning a day trip, you can get sandwiches to go for about $6 at *The Coffee Pod* (☎ *250-725-4246, 151 Fourth St*). Cafe

Pamplona (☎ 250-725-1237), at the Tofino Botanical Gardens, serves light meals, including excellent soups, for about $4.

The Loft Restaurant (☎ 250-725-4241, 346 Campbell St) is a reliable spot for breakfast ($4 to $7), lunch ($5 to $12) and dinner ($14 to $18). The *Sea Shanty Restaurant (☎ 250-725-2902, 300 Main St)* offers good food and terrific views, especially at sunset. *The Raincoast Café (☎ 250-725-2215, 120 Fourth St)* features bistro-style dining with small dishes ($5 to $11) and larger plates ($12 to $24, mostly seafood).

The *Pointe Restaurant (☎ 250-725-3100)*, at the Wickanninish Inn, ranks among BC's very best, with both fixed-price dinners ($70; $50 vegetarian) and à la carte main dishes ($24 to $39). Reservations are essential at dinner. Lunch is less expensive ($10 to $21), with such fare as a grilled wild sockeye salmon BLT on black-currant cornmeal toast ($14).

Entertainment

The *Sandbar Pub (☎ 250-725-3261, 120 First St)*, downstairs in the Maquinna Lodge, is Tofino's nightlife hot spot. The Tofino Botanical Gardens (see that section, earlier) hosts occasional live music events; call for details.

Shopping

The longhouse-style Eagle Aerie Gallery (☎ 250-725-3235), 350 Campbell St, displays work by noted artist Roy Henry Vickers, who lived in Tofino for many years. Island-folk Art Gallery (☎ 250-725-3130), Fourth and Campbell Sts, features a nice array of paintings and jewelry. Storm Light Marine Station (☎ 250-725-3342), 316 Main St, sells or rents outdoor and camping gear; you can relax at the coffee bar and deck out back.

Getting There & Around

North Vancouver Air (☎ 800-228-6608) flies to Tofino year-round from Vancouver ($300 roundtrip) and Victoria ($265). The Tofino Airport is south of town off the Pacific Rim Hwy. Sound Flight (☎ 800-825-0722) and Northwest Seaplanes (☎ 800-690-0086) run scheduled high-season float-plane service

between the Seattle, Washington, area and Tofino; the fare is about US$195 one-way with a seven-day advance purchase.

Laidlaw Coach Lines (☎ 250-725-3431) operates daily bus trips to Tofino's station (450 Campbell St), with two runs daily in summer. The one-way fare is $30 from Nanaimo, $47.50 from Victoria.

IslandLink (☎ 250-726-7779, 877-954-3556) runs a once-daily shuttle between Tofino and Nanaimo's Departure Bay BC Ferries terminal ($79 roundtrip). The company also shuttles passengers between Tofino and Ucluelet ($9/12 one-way/roundtrip), with stops at the Tofino Airport and within Pacific Rim National Park (at Long Beach, Greenpoint and the Wickaninnish Centre). See schedules posted locally.

For taxis, call Tofino Taxi (☎ 250-725-3333). Tofino Car Rentals (☎ 250-725-1221, 800-593-9389) rents cars and vans, and Tofino Kite & Bike Shop (☎ 250-725-1221), 441A Campbell St, rents and repairs bicycles.

PACIFIC RIM NATIONAL PARK RESERVE

With rain forests of huge cedar and fir trees, and tremendous waves rolling in from across the ocean, Pacific Rim National Park Reserve has become one of BC's top attractions. The 50,000-hectare park includes three units: the Long Beach area between Tofino and Ucluelet, the Broken Group Islands in Barkley Sound and the famous West Coast Trail.

For casual visits to the Long Beach Unit, you won't need anything beyond the map in this book and perhaps a stop at the park information center on Hwy 4 just inside the southern boundary. If you drive in, park use fees must be paid at the Wickaninnish Centre or at a trailhead parking lot; the cost is $3 per vehicle for two hours or $8 per vehicle per day, good until 11 pm. If you plan to stay more than a few days, an annual pass is available for $42 per vehicle ($31.50 for seniors). Parks Canada's Great Western Pass also is honored. There's no charge to drive through the park to Tofino.

For trips to the Broken Group Islands or the West Coast Trail, get updated, detailed information from Parks Canada (☎ 250-726-7721, fax 726-4720, pacrim_info@pch.gc.ca); you can also write to Pacific Rim National Park Reserve, PO Box 280, Ucluelet, BC V0R 3A0; or visit the Web site at www.harbour.com/parkscan/pacrim.

Long Beach Unit

Easily accessed by Hwy 4, the Long Beach Unit attracts the largest number of visitors in the park. Start with a stop at the **Wickaninnish Centre**, with interpretive exhibits on the park's cultural and natural history. (The center was named for a chief of the Nuu-chah-nulth tribe, who have lived in the Long Beach area for centuries.) Then try one or more of the trails that range in length from 100m to 5km. They include:

Radar Hill 100m climb to a former World War II installation

Schooner Cove 2km trail through old- and second-growth forests, with beach access

Long Beach Easy walking at low tide and great scenery along the sandy shore

Spruce Fringe 1.5km loop trail featuring hardy Sitka spruce trees

Rain Forest Trail Two 1km interpretive loops through old-growth forest

South Beach 1km roundtrip through forest to a pebble beach, accessed behind the Wickaninnish Centre

Bog Trail 800m interpretive loop around a moss-layered bog

Wickaninnish Trail 5km shoreline and forest trail, accessed behind the Wickaninnish Centre

Tread carefully over slippery rocks and roots and never turn your back on the surf. Avoid swimming near rocks or in areas where water currents seem to push you off-shore. The safest place to swim is the north end of Long Beach, where surf guards patrol the beach during July and August.

Places to Stay & Eat The only park-run site, ***Green Point Campground*** (☎ *800-689-*

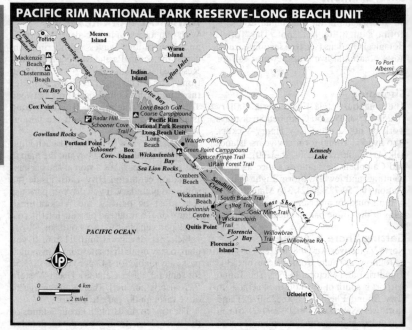

PACIFIC RIM NATIONAL PARK RESERVE-LONG BEACH UNIT

VANCOUVER ISLAND

Templar Channel
Tofino
Meares Island
Browning Passage
Warne Island
Mackenzie Beach
Chesterman Beach
Indian Island
Tofino Inlet
To Port Alberni
Cox Bay
Grice Bay
Cox Point
Long Beach Golf Course Campground
Pacific Rim National Park Reserve Long Beach Unit
Radar Hill
Schooner Cove Trail
Gowlland Rocks
Portland Point
Warden Office
Green Point Campground
Spruce Fringe Trail
Rain Forest Trail
Kennedy Lake
Schooner Cove
Box Island
Wickaninnish Bay
Sea Lion Rocks
Long Beach
Combers Beach
Sandhill Creek
Wickaninnish Beach
South Beach Trail
Bog Trail
Lost Shoe Creek
Wickaninnish Centre
Gold Mine Trail
PACIFIC OCEAN
Quitis Point
Wickaninnish Trail
Florencia Bay
Willowbrae
Willowbrae Rd
Florencia Island
Ucluelet

0   2   4 km
0   1   2 miles

9025 for reservations) is 18km from Tofino and 20km from Ucluelet along Hwy 4. The 94 drive-in sites ($20) can be reserved up to three months ahead; it's first-come, first-served for the 20 walk-in sites ($14). You'll have to get along without showers or hookups here. Fires are allowed at the drive-in sites. Another camping option within the park boundaries (but run privately) is the **Long Beach Golf Course Campground** (☎ *250-725-3332)*, near Grice Bay, where the 53 sites cost $20.

For food, try the **Wickaninnish Centre Restaurant**, which offers lunch ($8 to $13) and dinner ($13 to $26) with views of Long Beach. It's open 11 am to 10 pm March through October.

Broken Group Islands

This unit includes about 100 islands at the entrance to Barkley Sound. Broken Island Adventures (☎ 250-728-3500, 888-728-6200) runs **sightseeing trips** from Sechart (three hours for $38, including lunch) or Bamfield (6½ hours for $85, including lunch). Children eight to 15 pay half-fare, and younger children ride free.

The Broken Group Islands are an increasingly popular **kayaking** destination, but visitors must know what they're doing – or sign on with a guided trip. Eco West Adventures (☎ 250-748-0511, 888-326-9378) leads five-day tours for $700 per person. Wildheart Adventures (☎ 250-722-3683) offers four-day trips for $549.

Kayakers should travel in groups of three or more; thoroughly read Parks Canada's informational sheets on potential hazards; and call the boating safety information line (☎ 800-267-6687) before setting out. Do-it-yourselfers must obtain marine charts 3670 and 3671, which cost $20 each and are available at marine shops or from the Canadian Hydrographic Service (☎ 250-363-6358, fax 363-6841, chartsales@pac.dfo-mpo.gc.ca); write to Chart Sales, Institute of Ocean Sciences, 9860 Saanich Rd, PO Box 6000, Sidney, BC V8L 4B2.

Designated camping areas ($5 per person per night) are located on eight islands: Hand, Turret, Gibraltar, Willis, Dodd, Clarks, Benson and Gilbert. The maximum stay at any single site is four nights; the maximum stay in the Broken Group Islands as a whole is 14 nights. The campsites have solar composting toilets, but garbage must be packed out.

Getting There & Away Toquart Bay is the principal launching spot, accessed via a 16km gravel logging road off Hwy 4, 12km northeast of the Pacific Rim Hwy junction. You'll also find a BC Forest Service campsite at the launch.

Lady Rose Marine Services (☎ 250-723-8313, 800-663-7192 from April to September) transports kayakers and their gear to Sechart Whaling Station Lodge (☎ 250-720-7358), the company's base in the Broken Group Islands. There, rooms with shared baths are available from June through September for $40/60 single/double ($65/110 including meals). The company also runs a water taxi from Sechart and Toquart Bay to several of the Broken Group Islands for $20 to $45 per person, depending on the pick-up and drop-off points. You can rent canoes and kayaks at Sechart, too.

West Coast Trail

The third and most southerly section of the park is the 75km West Coast Trail, one of Canada's best-known and toughest hiking routes. Originally constructed as an escape route for shipwreck survivors, the trail runs between Pachena Bay (☎ 250-728-3234), near Bamfield on the north end, and Gordon River (☎ 250-647-5434), near Port Renfrew on the south. Hikers must be able to manage rough terrain, rock-face ladders, stream crossings and adverse weather conditions. Plan on six to eight days to hike the entire route.

Some people do a day hike or even hike half the trail from Pachena Bay (considered the easier end of the route), but each overnight hiker must have a permit, and only 52 people can begin the trail on any given day, 26 in each direction. To apply, call the Super Natural British Columbia Reservation Service (☎ 800-663-6000 in the US and Canada, 604-663-6000 in Greater Vancouver,

250-387-1642 worldwide). As of 2000, hikers can call March 1 and request any starting date in May; April 1 for any start date in June; May 1 for July; June 1 for August; and July 1 for September. When you call, be ready with an intended start date and two alternate dates, the name of the trailhead from which you intend to start, the number of hikers in your party (maximum 10) and a Visa or MasterCard number. The nonrefundable reservation fee ($25 per hiker) includes a trail guide and map.

Permits also are available through a waiting-list system; six of each day's 26 available spaces are set aside to be used on a first-come, first-served basis at each trailhead. Waiting-list spaces are allocated at 1 pm each day from both of the registration centers, and people who land the spaces can start hiking that day. But from July to mid-September, hikers sometimes wait up to three days to get a permit via the waiting list. Day hikers are allowed on the trail from each end, but they must obtain a free day-use permit, available from the registration centers.

In addition to the $25 reservation fee, you'll pay a $70-per-person trail use fee plus two ferry fees totaling $25, payable when you sign in at the registration center. Hikers can sign in as early as 3:30 pm the day before they start; if they plan to arrive after 1 pm of their start date, they must notify the registration center before 1 pm to save their space. Each overnight hiker must attend a one-hour orientation session before setting out on the trail; these are held four times daily.

Once on the trail, hikers must do the following: use good, reliable gear (especially well-broken-in boots); practice low-impact camping; carry tide tables and a watch; treat or boil all water collected from streams; cook on a lightweight backpackers' stove; and pack out all garbage. All supplies must be packed in, too; Parks Canada recommends lightweight, nutritious, low-odor foods. Hikers can camp at any of the designated sites along the route, most of which have solar-composting outhouses. Theoretically, there's nowhere to buy supplies on the

trail, though soda, beer and food are sometimes available at the Nitinat Narrows Ferry and at a store just south of the Carmanah Lighthouse.

Hikers who want to hike only the easier half of the trail from Pachena Bay to Nitinat Narrows can leave from Nitinat Lake. Make advance arrangements for a ride from West Coast Trail Express (see Getting There & Away, below).

A few companies lead guided through-hikes on the West Coast Trail; Parks Canada keeps a list, beginning in January each year. Tsusiat Tour Company (☎ 888-875-1833) offers one-day guided trips through the Nitinat Narrows to such sites as Hole in the Wall, Tsusiat Falls, Clo-oose Bay, Cheewaht Reserve and the Carmanah Lighthouse, all on the West Coast Trail. These cost $195 per person, including lunch and transportation to and from Lake Cowichan.

Getting There & Away It takes 90 minutes to drive from Port Alberni to Bamfield (Pachena Bay) on a gravel logging road. It's a two-hour drive on paved Hwy 14 from Victoria to Port Renfrew (Gordon River). West Coast Trail Express (☎ 250-477-8700) offers roundtrip shuttle-bus service to Bamfield and Port Renfrew from Victoria and Nanaimo. See details at www.trailbus.com. Pachena Bay Express (☎ 250-728-1290) operates shuttle service from Port Alberni to Bamfield and Pachena. Lady Rose Marine Services (☎ 250-723-8313; 800-663-7192 from April to September) runs a passenger ferry to and from Bamfield.

UCLUELET
• population 1700

Something of a poor relation to the northerly Tofino, Ucluelet doesn't match Tofino's charm, mainly due to the extensive forest clear-cutting that's readily visible from town on clear days. Still, Ucluelet which lies 100km west of Port Alberni remains a bustling place with plenty of visitor services at generally cheaper prices than in Tofino. The Visitor Info Centre (☎ 250-726-4641, fax 726-4611), at the Hwy 4 junction, is open June through August.

Attractions in town include **Big Beach**, with tide pools, shells, kelp beds and a gazebo shelter; access the beach via a 600m trail from Bay St. The **Wild Pacific Trail** winds past the scenic lighthouse at Amphitrite Point and connects with a boardwalk trail at He-Tin-Kis Park.

Killer whales migrate past Ucluelet.

Subtidal Adventures (☎ 250-726-7336), 1950 Peninsula Rd, and Canadian Princess Resort (see Places to Stay, below) offer **whale-watching** trips. For **sea kayaking**, contact Majestic Ocean Kayaking (☎ 250-726-2868), 1786 Peninsula Rd, which leads half-day to multi-day trips. Pristine Adventures (☎ 250-726-4477) offers guided **canoeing** and **black bear–watching** trips for $75 and up.

Places to Stay
The **Ucluelet Campground** (☎ 250-726-4355, 260 Seaplane Base Rd) has sites ($16 and up) with hot showers and flush toilets. **Agape Bed & Breakfast** (☎ 250-726-7073, 246 Lee St), 4km north of Ucluelet and a five-minute walk from Pacific Rim National Park, offers rooms starting at $40/55 single/double. The innkeepers speak five languages. Rooms with shared baths go for $30 and up at the **Ucluelet Hotel** (☎ 250-726-4324, 250 Main St). Across from the bus depot, **Pacific Rim Motel** (☎ 250-726-7728, 1755 Peninsula Rd) rents rooms for $75 and up. The **West Coast Motel** (☎ 250-726-7732, 247 Hemlock St) offers rooms and suites (some with kitchenettes) overlooking the harbor, plus an indoor pool and gym; rates start at $79.

Canadian Princess Resort (☎ 250-726-7771, 800-663-7090, fax 250-598-1361, obmg@pinc.com, 1948 Peninsula Rd) charges $80 to $185 for double rooms. The lower rate rents a tiny but charming stateroom with shared bath in a survey ship moored in Ucluelet Harbour; the pricier digs are in the main lodge on shore. **A Snug Harbour Inn** (☎ 250-726-2686, 888-936-5222, fax 250-726-2685, asnughbr@island.net, 460 Marine Dr) is an upscale romantic retreat; rooms start at $200.

The recently opened **Roots Lodge** (☎ 250-726-2700, 888-594-7333, info@reefpoint.com, 310 Seabridge Way) bills itself as an adventure travel lodge with lots of fun activities and rooms for $205 and up. It's part of the ongoing Reef Point recreational development on Spring Cove and – surprise – it's endorsed by the increasingly omnipresent Canadian conglomerate that shares its name.

Places To Eat
Gray Whale Ice Cream & Delicatessen (☎ 726-2113, 1950 Peninsula Rd) serves sandwiches, salads and pastries; you can also arrange a fishermen's picnic, available for pick-up as early as 5:30 am. **Blueberries Café** (☎ 250-726-7707, 1627D Peninsula Rd) is open for breakfast ($5 to $9), lunch ($7 to $9) and dinner ($12 to $21); $12.95 buys crab cakes with curried raisin mayo and dill linguine. **Matterson Restaurant** (☎ 250-726-6600, 1682 Peninsula Rd) features a refined farmhouse atmosphere with lace curtains and home-baked goods. Breakfasts ($4 to $9) include build-your-own omelets; lunch runs $6 to $9, dinner $9 to $19.

Getting There & Away
Laidlaw Coach Lines provides bus service to Ucluelet from Nanaimo ($27.50 one-way) and Victoria ($45). See Tofino, earlier, for more transportation options.

DENMAN & HORNBY ISLANDS
Southernmost of the so-called Northern Gulf Islands, both Denman and Hornby offer excellent access to outdoor activities. Both islands publish annual map brochures,

VANCOUVER ISLAND

available at area Visitor Info Centres, or on the ferry (see Getting There & Around, below). For Denman Island information, call ☎ 250-335-1636 or see the Web site www.denmanis.bc.ca. For Hornby information, visit www.hornbyisland.com.

Denman's attractions include three provincial parks: **Fillongley**, with easy hiking and beachcombing; **Boyle Point**, where sea lions and eagles are often seen or heard; and **Sandy Island**, only accessible by water from Denman's northern tip. Among Hornby's provincial parks, **Tribune Bay** features a long sandy beach with safe swimming, while **Helliwell** offers notable hiking and offshore scuba diving.

For **kayaking** rentals, contact Denman Island Sea Kayaks (☎ 250-335-2505), 1536 Northwest Rd, or Hornby Ocean Kayaks (☎ 250-335-2726). Inter-Island Charters (☎ 250-335-2321 or 335-3120) offers **fishing** and **sightseeing** charters as well as water-taxi service.

Places to Stay
On Denman, campsites cost $15 at *Fillongley Provincial Park*. On Hornby, camp at *Ford's Cove* (☎ 250-335-2169), where sites cost $14/22 for tents/RVs, and at *Bradsdadland Waterfront Camping* (☎ 250-335-0757, 2105 Shingle Spit Rd), where sites cost $20 to $23, plus $1 for each utility hookup.

Denman Island Guest House (☎ 250-335-2688, 3806 Denman Rd) is 400m from the ferry landing, up the hill and on the left. The 1912 farmhouse, a combination hostel/B&B, charges $20 per person; the rate drops to $15 for the third night of a stay. Some private digs are available for $40 for one person or $50 for two. You can rent bikes, including one with a kid-trailer.

Aimed at adults who enjoy camping but hate the hassles, *Breatheasy Vacations* (☎ 250-335-2944, 6580 Central Rd), on Hornby Island, offers five weatherproof cedar 'bunkies' with two twin beds for $49 a night (single or double) from May through mid-September. The bunkies share an outdoor kitchen, privy, shower facilities and a glassed-in guest pavilion with an ocean view. Guests need to bring their own

bedding and food. Breatheasy also rents a cottage with bathroom and kitchen for $700 per week, or $125 per night from May to mid-June. Optional guided hiking tours are available.

GreenHill B&B (☎ 250-335-1957, 10225 Greenhill Rd), on Denman, has rooms for $35/40 single/double, with beaches and kayak rentals close by. *Sea Breeze Lodge* (☎ 250-335-2321), at Tralee Point on Hornby Island, features cottages overlooking the ocean; on-site activities include tennis, kayaking and fishing. Weekly room-and-board rates from mid-June through mid-September are $768 per adult (based on double occupancy); children stay and eat for $276 to $474 per week, depending on age. Ford's Cove (mentioned above) also offers cottages with equipped kitchens for $495 per week for a family of four.

Places to Eat
The Denman Island General Store (☎ 250-335-2293) and the Hornby Island Co-op General Store (☎ 250-335-1121) are good places to stock up on groceries. *Café On the Rock* (☎ 250-335-2999), next door to the Denman Island General Store, serves good vegetarian meals and homemade pie. *Cockburns*, at the Denman Island Guest House (see Places to Stay), offers reasonably priced breakfasts, with light meals later in the day. The Hornby Island Resort's *Wheelhouse Restaurant* (☎ 250-335-0136) is open daily for lunch and dinner, with soups and salads ($3.50 to $6.50) and main courses ($6 to $10).

Getting There & Around
BC Ferries offers service to Denman and Hornby Islands from the Buckley Bay terminal, 75km north of Nanaimo between Qualicum Beach and Courtenay. Island Coach Lines buses will stop at Buckley Bay on request. In high season, expect about 19 sailings per day from Buckley Bay to Denman Island and about 14 trips from Denman to Hornby. Each trip takes about 10 minutes; the roundtrip fare on either route is $4.50/2.25/11.25 for adults/children/cars. The last ferry from Hornby back to

Denman leaves at 6 pm. Service from Denman to Buckley runs much later.

Island Rides Transportation (☎ 250-334-6518) offers taxi service on Hornby Island. Bike and scooter rentals are available at the Denman Island General Store (☎ 250-335-2293), as well as at Hornby Island Bike Shop (☎ 250-335-0444), on Central Rd near the Co-op.

COMOX VALLEY

The Comox Valley includes Courtenay (population 20,000) and Comox (population 12,000), important supply hubs for trips to Mt Washington, 32km west of Courtenay, and to Strathcona Provincial Park. Comox also is the departure point for BC Ferries service to the Sunshine Coast on the mainland (see the Whistler & the Sunshine Coast chapter).

The Comox Valley Visitor Info Centre (☎ 250-334-3234, 888-357-4471), 2040 Cliffe Ave in Courtenay, distributes information on both cities and the surrounding area. Its Web site is www.tourism-comox-valley .bc.ca. You'll find the main Courtenay post office (☎ 250-334-4341) at 219 4th St. You can access email at Joe Read's Bookstore & Internet Café (☎ 250-334-9723), 2760 Cliffe Ave in Courtenay. Do laundry at Courtenay Centre Home Style Laundry (☎ 250-334-0875), 4-2401 Cliffe Ave.

Things to See & Do

Known as *the* place to ski on Vancouver Island, **Mt Washington Alpine Resort** (☎ 250-338-1386) stays open year-round. From early December to late April, the resort features 50 Alpine ski runs, plus a snowboard park, cross country and snowshoe trails and a snow-tubing park. Full-day lift rates for Alpine and Nordic skiing and boarding are $44/36/23 for adults/seniors and teens/children seven to 12. Passes to the tubing area cost $10 for three hours, $15 for a full day. Introductory programs in snowboarding or downhill, cross-country or telemark skiing go for $30 to $60, including a lift ticket, rental equipment and a two-hour lesson. For information on the many other packages available, see the Web site at www.mtwashington.bc.ca. Call ☎ 250-338-1386 for details on shuttle service from the Comox Valley.

The Mt Washington summer season runs from late June through early September. Activities include **horseback riding, fly-fishing** and **chair-lift rides**, which cost $10/8 for adults/seniors and children seven to 18; a family pass is $29, and a rider with a mountain bike pays $15. For an easy, rewarding hike into adjacent Strathcona Provincial Park, take the 2.2km **Paradise Meadows Loop Trail** from the Nordic ski area parking lot. (See the Strathcona Provincial Park section, later in this chapter, for more information.) Lodging (central reservations at ☎ 888-231-1499) and food are available year-round on the mountain.

In Courtenay, the attractions include the **Courtenay and District Museum** (☎ 250-334-3611), 360 Cliffe Ave, best known for its life-size replica of an elasmosaur, a prehistoric marine reptile first discovered in this area. It's open daily May through September, Tuesday through Saturday the rest of the year; admission is by donation. The **Puntledge Hatchery** (☎ 250-338-7444), about 5km west of Courtenay via Lake Trail and Powerhouse Rds, features exhibits on the development of salmon and steelhead trout. It's open year-round, with free admission.

Miracle Beach Provincial Park (☎ 250-755-2483), 22km north of Courtenay, contains hiking trails and a sandy beach. For **scuba diving**, contact Pacific Pro Dive & Watersports (☎ 250-338-6829), 2270 Cliffe Ave in Courtenay, a full-service shop with trips, tours, lessons and gear.

Places to Stay

Courtenay Riverside Hostel (☎ 250-334-1938, wandstar@yahoo.com, 1380 Cliffe Ave) offers dorm beds ($16) and private rooms ($35), with kitchen and laundry facilities, Internet access, and linens and towels provided. It's in a good location close to parks and downtown; ask about free pickup service from the Powell River ferry and discount ski packages for Mt Washington.

Comox Lake Hostel (☎ 250-338-1914, comoxlakehostel@telus.net, 4787 Lake Trail

Rd), a homey place 6km west of Courtenay, makes a fine rural retreat. You can literally hike into Strathcona Provincial Park, or take one of the shorter walks to the Puntledge River, waterfalls and swimming holes. Camping costs $10 per person per night; a bed is $17. Kitchen and laundry facilities are available, as are bikes, barbecue pits and area adventure tours. Arrange ahead for pick-up at either the train station ($3) or the ferry ($6).

Greystone Manor B&B (☎ 250-338-1422, 4014 Haas Rd) sits 2km from Courtenay amid English gardens. Rooms with private baths start at $60/80 single/double.

Courtenay's *River Heights Motel (☎ 250-338-8932, 1820 Cliffe Ave)*, one of the area's most reasonably priced spots, offers well-worn but acceptable rooms ($40/45). In Comox, budget rooms are available at the *Evergreen Resort Motel (☎ 250-339-3102, 1950 Comox Ave)*, where rates start at $40/50, and at *Port Augusta Inn & Suites (☎ 250-339-2277, 2082 Comox Rd)*, with rooms for $50/60 and up.

Rooms at the more expensive *Best Western Collingwood Inn (☎ 250-338-1464, 1675 Cliffe Ave)* start at $82/92. The *Coast Westerly (☎ 250-338-7741, 1590 Cliffe Ave)*, in Courtenay, features an indoor pool and exercise room, with rooms priced at $109/119 and up.

Places to Eat

The Atlas Café (☎ 250-338-9838, 250 6th St), in Courtenay, is the area's best choice, with a wide international menu and reasonable prices ($6 to $12). The *Bar None Café (☎ 250-334-3112, 244 4th St)*, in Courtenay, serves gourmet vegetarian fare. In Comox, try the *Leeward Neighborhood Pub (☎ 250-339-5400, 649 Anderton Rd)* for homemade soups and chowders ($3 to $6), burgers (about $7) and pastas ($9 to $12).

Getting There & Around

Air Canada (☎ 888-247-2262) and Pacific Coastal (☎ 800-663-2872) serve the Comox Valley Regional Airport in Comox. An advance-purchase roundtrip fare from Vancouver costs about $160.

The bus company Island Coach Lines (☎ 250-334-2475) serves Courtenay; the one-way fare is $35 from Victoria, $17.50 from Nanaimo. Courtenay is also the end of the line for VIA Rail's E&N Railiner (☎ 800-561-8630), 899 Cumberland Ave. The fare from Victoria costs $40/80 one way/roundtrip.

BC Ferries offers service from the Little River terminal near Comox to Powell River on the mainland. There are only four sailings a day and no reservations, so arrive an hour ahead of time to ensure boarding. The one-way fare for the 75-minute sailing is $7.50/3.75/25 for adults/children/cars. Circle Pac tickets offer discounted rates for travelers who are making a full loop of Vancouver Island and the mainland; see the Getting Around chapter for details.

Cars are available from Rent-a-Wreck (☎ 250-334-2060), 334 Ryan St in Courtenay, and Budget (☎ 250-338-7717), 1555 Comox Rd in Courtenay. Call ☎ 250-339-5453 for local bus information.

CAMPBELL RIVER
• population 30,700

Vancouver Island's northernmost population and trading center, Campbell River is a hot spot for salmon fishing and scuba diving, as well as a supply depot for adventures in the wilderness areas to the north and west and the main departure point for Strathcona Provincial Park.

For local information, stop at the Visitor Info Centre (☎ 250-287-4636, fax 286-6490), 1235 Shoppers Row, or visit the Web site www.campbellrivertourism.bc.ca. Access email at the OnLine Gourmet (☎ 250-286-6521), 970 Shoppers Row. A coin-op laundry and showers are available from 7 am to 11 pm daily behind the Rip Tide Pub, 1340 Island Hwy.

Things to See & Do

The well-done **Museum at Campbell River** (☎ 250-287-3103), 470 Island Hwy, features a good collection of First Nations masks, an 1890 pioneer cabin and video footage of the Ripple Rock explosion, the world's largest-ever human-created, non-nuclear blast.

(Ripple Rock, a submerged mountain in the Seymour Narrows north of Campbell River, caused more than 100 shipwrecks before it was blown apart in 1958. An overlook on Hwy 19 shows what's left of it.) The museum is open 10 am to 5 pm Monday to Saturday and noon to 5 pm Sunday, mid-May through September; noon to 5 pm Tuesday to Sunday the rest of the year. Admission is $2.50/2/7.50 for adults/seniors and students/families.

Campbell River calls itself the 'Salmon Capital of the World.' You can wet a line right off the downtown Discovery Pier or go deep-sea **sport fishing** with an outfitter. Get a list from the Visitor Info Centre, or just stroll down the dock to see what's available.

The HMCS *Columbia*, sunk near Campbell River, is a major draw for **scuba diving**. Contact Beaver Aquatics Limited (☎ 250-287-7652), 760 Island Hwy, for information, gear and lessons. From July through October, Paradise Found Adventure Tours (☎ 250-923-0848) leads **snorkeling** trips to see migrating salmon in the shallow pools and slow-running waters of the Campbell River.

You'll find excellent spots for **mountain biking** near town, including the Snowden Demonstration Forest, 10km west, and the Pump House trail systems. Get details at Urban Lemming Adventure Sports (☎ 250-286-6340), 151 Dogwood St.

Places to Stay & Eat

Camping ($12) is available at *Elk Falls Provincial Park*, 10km west of Campbell River on Hwy 28; at *Loveland Bay Provincial Park*, 19km northeast at Campbell Lake; and *Morton Lake Provincial Park*, 19km north off Hwy 19.

Above Tide Motel (☎ 250-286-6231, 361 Island Hwy) is a quiet place to stay south of downtown, with ocean views and rates starting at $49/59 single/double. North of downtown, *Rustic Motel* (☎ 250-286-6295, 800-567-2007, 2140 N Island Hwy) rents rooms for $60/70 (add $10 for a kitchen). *Painter's Lodge Holiday & Fishing Resort* (☎ 250-286-1102, 1625 MacDonald Rd) ranks among the fanciest places to sleep

and eat, with lots of activities and rooms starting at $160.

For food, try the *Bee Hive Café* (☎ 250-286-6812, 921 Island Hwy), in business since 1929; its new waterfront location blends modern food and contemporary decor with historical photos of Campbell River. Stop in for breakfast ($7 to $9), lunch ($5 to $13) or dinner, when selections include salmon for $15 or a seafood platter for $17. The local outlet of *Fogg n' Suds* (☎ 250-286-4944, 205-489 S Dogwood St) offers a good selection of salads ($5 to $9), wraps and burgers ($7 to $10) and main dishes ($8 to $16). *Chan's Kitchen* (☎ 250-286-6776, 1891 Island Hwy) features a wide menu of Chinese dishes ($6.75 to $14).

Getting There & Around

Canadian Regional (☎ 888-247-2262) and Pacific Coastal (☎ 800-663-2872) provide scheduled air service to Campbell River from Vancouver for about $160 roundtrip. Kenmore Air float planes (☎ 800-543-9595) operates flights from Seattle for about US$360 roundtrip. Air Rainbow (☎ 250-287-8371, 888-287-8366) offers float-plane service from Vancouver for about $420 roundtrip.

Island Coach Lines (☎ 250-287-7151), on the corner of 13th Ave and Cedar St, runs one bus north daily to Port Hardy ($52.50 one-way) and four buses south to Victoria ($40).

For trips in town, call Al's Taxi at ☎ 250-287-7666 or rent a bike on the sea walk (look for the little red building). Local bus information is available at ☎ 250-287-7433.

QUADRA & CORTES ISLANDS

Quadra Island is a quick hop from Campbell River via BC Ferries; Cortes Island is a bit more remote. Together, they're often called the 'Discovery Islands' for their location in the Discovery Passage.

Each island's annual map/brochure is available at area Visitor Info Centres and on the ferries. An information booth behind the Quadra Credit Union, 657 Harper Rd, stays open from mid-June to early September. The *Discovery Islander* is a free newspaper distributed on both islands. Information is also available at www.discoveryislands.bc.ca, www.quadraisland.bc.ca and at www.cortesisland.com. There are ATMs on both islands.

Things to See & Do

Located at Quadra Island's Cape Mudge, the acclaimed **Kwagiulth Museum and Cultural Centre** features a fascinating collection of items used in potlatches, along with early photos of traditional Kwakwaka'wakw villages. It's open 10 am to 4:30 pm Monday through Saturday and noon to 4:30 pm Sunday, June through September; 10 am to 4:30 pm Tuesday to Saturday the rest of the year. Admission is $3/2/1 for adults/seniors/children six to 12.

Hollyhock (☎ 800-933-6339), a retreat center at Manson's Landing on Cortes Iszland, offers innovative workshops on yoga, meditation, massage, songwriting and many other topics. Most of these programs last four to six days and cost about $325 to $600, with accommodations and meals extra (starting at $66 per person per day for camping to $143 for a room with private bath, double occupancy).

Quadra's **Rebecca Spit Provincial Park** offers good swimming and boating access. On Cortes, **Manson's Landing Provincial Park** boasts abundant shorebirds and shellfish, and **Smelt Bay Provincial Park** makes a great place to watch the sun set. Nearby **Mittlenatch Island Nature Park**, sometimes called the Galapagos of Georgia Strait for its natural diversity, can be seen on guided walks led by longtime area guide George Sirk (☎ 250-935-6926, fax 935-6929).

Activities

Seven **hiking** trails of varying length wind their way around the island, as noted on the local map/brochure. Quadra Sun Rentals (☎ 250-285-3601) offers canoe rentals and guided tours of the island's chain of freshwater lakes, while Island Cycle (☎ 250-285-3627) has bike rentals. For **sea kayaking**, consider a tour with Coast Mountain Expeditions (☎ 250-287-0635) or Coastal Spirits Wilderness Expeditions (☎ 250-285-2895).

Abyssal Diving Charters & Lodge (☎ 250-285-2420, 800-499-2297 in North America, fax 250-285-2427, ian@abyssal.com), just up the hill from the Quathiaski Cove ferry dock, is Quadra's top source for **scuba diving**, offering everything from rental gear and dives to accommodations in a gorgeous creekside lodge.

On Cortes, the T'ai Li Lodge (☎ 250-935-6749) offers five-day learn-to-kayak retreats from May to September each year; prices start at $490 ($415 with your own camping gear).

Places to Stay

On Cortes, camp at **Smelt Bay Provincial Park** (☎ 800-689-9025 for reservations) for $12 and at **Gorge Harbour Marina Resort** (☎ 250-935-6433), on Hunt Rd, for $10 to $18; the latter also has coin-op laundry and showers, plus sleeping rooms that go for $45 and up.

Set in a big farmhouse on 33 acres, **Quadra Island Backpackers' Hostel** (☎ 250-285-3557, 1225 Heriot Bay Rd) includes tent sites ($10), dorm beds ($16) and a simple cottage ($40). **A Traveler's Rural Retreat** (☎ 250-287-9232) also offers limited hostel-style accommodations on Quadra Island. Call ahead for details.

Coastal Spirits B&B (☎ 250-285-2895, 1069 Topcliff Rd), on Quadra, has three rooms, all with private baths, for $60 and up. The **Yum Yum Tree B&B** (☎ 250-285-2491, 660 Heriot Bay Rd), on Quadra right by the ferry to Cortes, offers very nice rooms ($75 to $110), each with a kitchenette, balcony and TV. Quadra's **Tsa-Kwa-Luten Lodge** (☎ 250-285-2042, 800-665-7745), on Lighthouse Rd close to the beach, is a First Nations–owned resort featuring Native art, architecture and food; rates start at $90/115.

Set amid tall trees, **Cortes Island Motel** (☎ 250-935-6363), at Manson's Landing, is a good value, with rooms starting at $59/69 single/double; most come with kitchens.

Places to Eat

On Quadra, head to the small shopping plaza close to Quathiaski Cover ferry dock, where you'll find pizza at **Lovin' Oven II**

(☎ 250-285-2262) and good Mexican food at **Wacko Taco** (☎ 250-285-2777).

The Tak (☎ 250-935-8555, 7 Sutil Point Rd), near Manson's Landing on Cortes, is open nightly for dinner; look for burgers ($7.50) and such specials as snapper fillet with roasted red pepper sauce ($11.95). Other good bets on Cortes include **Caffé Suzanne** (☎ 250-935-6866), with waterfront dining right on Squirrel Cove, and the **Floathouse Restaurant** (☎ 250-935-6631), at Gorge Harbour Marina.

Getting There & Around
BC Ferries offers about 16 daily sailings from Campbell River to Quathiaski Cove on Quadra Island. The roundtrip fare for the 10-minute trip is $4.50/2.25/11.50 for adults/children/cars. Expect about six daily sailings from Heriot Bay on Quadra to Whaletown on Cortes Island; the 45-minute journey costs $5.50/2.75/13.75 for adults/children/cars roundtrip. The last ferry from Cortes back to Quadra leaves before 6 pm.

The Cortes Connection (☎ 250-935-6911) provides shuttle bus service from Campbell River to Cortes Island via the ferry. It runs six times a week in summer (daily except Sunday) and three times a week the rest of the year. Reservations are advised. The ride costs $12 one-way, plus the ferry fare listed above.

Since both Quadra and Cortes are fairly large islands, it's something of a challenge to get around without a car. Check to see if your hotel or other accommodation offers pick-up service from the ferry terminal. For a taxi, call Quadra Taxi (☎ 250-285-3598).

STRATHCONA PROVINCIAL PARK
By far the largest provincial park on Vancouver Island, 250,000-hectare Strathcona Provincial Park (☎ 250-337-2400) is BC's oldest protected area. Campbell River is the main access point, with Hwy 28 between Campbell River and Gold River cutting across the Buttle Lake district. The park's Forbidden Plateau area is reached via Courtenay, as is the popular Mt Washington alpine resort area, just outside the park.

Della Falls, Canada's highest waterfall, also lies within Strathcona, but it's easiest to get to it by way of Port Alberni. Mt Golden Hinde (2200m), the highest point on Vancouver Island, occupies the center of the park west of Buttle Lake.

Strathcona is a hiker's park. In the Forbidden Plateau area, notable trails include the **Paradise Meadows Loop** (2.2km, 45 minutes), an easy walk through wildflower meadows; the summit of **Mt Albert Edward** (6.5km, five hours); and **Mt Becher** (5km, two hours), with great views of the Comox Valley, the Strait of Georgia and the Coast Mountain Range. Don't attempt the 9km, unmaintained **Comox Glacier Trail** unless you're an advanced hiker or a mountaineer.

In the Buttle Lake area, easy walks include the stroll to **Lady Falls** (900m, 20 minutes) and the trail along **Karst Creek** (2km, 45 minutes), which winds past sinkholes, disappearing streams and beautiful waterfalls. For a more challenging hike, try the **Elk River Trail** (11km, five hours), which follows the Elk River Valley to Landslide Lake, or **Flower Ridge Trail** (6km, five hours), with great alpine scenery.

Strathcona has two campgrounds, both in the Buttle Lake area. **Buttle Lake Campground** offers both first-come, first-served and reservable sites. The swimming area and the nearby playground make this a good choice for families. Sites are $15; there are also some marine camping sites for $8. **Ralph River Campground**, 26km south of the Hwy 28 junction, features first-come, first-served sites for $12. Backcountry sites throughout the park cost $3 per person.

Strathcona Park Lodge
Begun in 1959 as an outdoor education center, this family-run business (☎ 250-286-3122, fax 286-6010, info@strathcona.bc.ca), on Hwy 28, still takes teaching as its mission. For most of the year, the lodge welcomes schoolchildren for weeklong introductions to the natural world. But in summertime, the lodge becomes a base camp for travelers – especially families – eager to experience the outdoors with few distractions.

Strathcona runs a variety of programs. Its Alpine to Ocean Adventures ($260 to $1325) feature hiking, canoeing and sea-kayaking trips to remote locales. Family Adventure Week, aimed at people with children ages six to 13, includes a full menu of activities capped off by an overnight canoe trip ($730 per adult, $520 per child, including meals and lodging).

Most visitors stay a week, but you'll find some overnight accommodations ranging from a double room with shared bath ($40) to a cabin that sleeps 12 ($275). The dining-hall meals include both buffet options (breakfast and lunch $9 each, dinner $16; half-price for children under 12) and table service. You can rent kayaks and canoes or spend your time sampling the nearby hiking trails. Strathcona Park Lodge also operates a chalet at Mt Washington.

GOLD RIVER
• population 1750

Gold River made big news in 1999, when the Bowater paper mill shut down and wiped out about 80% of the town's tax base. The company bought the homes of employees who chose to leave town, then turned around and sold them at bargain prices. Retirees and a few telecommuting types snapped up the homes, forever changing the face of this carefully planned town.

Gold River is at the end of Hwy 28, 89km west of Campbell River. The Visitor Info Centre (☎ 250-283-2418), at the corner of Hwy 28 and Scout Lake Rd, is open from mid-May through early September.

Things to See & Do

Gold River is a major **caving** destination. Upana Caves, north of town on the gravel road toward Tahsis, have 15 known entrances and 450m of passages. Ask at the Visitor Info Centre about organized and self-guided tours.

Nootka Sound Service (☎ 250-283-2325) uses the *Uchuck III*, a very loud converted WWII mine-sweeper, for trips to remote villages and settlements in Nootka Sound and Kyuquot Sound. Year-round, passengers can go on a one-day trip to **Tahsis** (departs

Tuesday at 9 am; $45/42/23 for adults/seniors/children seven to 12) or a two-day trip to **Kyuquot**, with overnight accommodations and a self-catered breakfast (departs Thursday at 7 am; $195/310 single/double plus $70 per child). Once at Kyuquot, you can take a one-hour wild-otter–watching guided tour for $15 (minimum five people). From July through mid-September, the company also offers day trips to **Friendly Cove**, where Captain Cook first met Chief Maquinna and the Mowachaht people in 1778. These leave Wednesday and Saturday at 10 am ($40/20 for adults/children); the Saturday trips have a longer layover, up to three hours, at Friendly Cove.

Places to Stay & Eat

For camping or budget accommodations in Gold River, try the *Peppercorn Motel* (☎ 250-283-2443), on the far side of town, which offers tent sites ($10), RV hookups ($18) and simple rooms (starting at $49) with refrigerators, coffeemakers and televisions but no phones. The *Ridgeview Motor Inn* (☎ 250-283-2277, 800-989-3393, 395 Donner Court) features upscale rooms ($89 to $125), plus a restaurant and pub and a hospitality room where guests can do some light cooking. You'll find good food at *Charlie's Family Restaurant* (☎ 250-283-9025), where the menu includes sandwiches ($6 to $10), pizza ($6 and up) and dinners ($10 to $18).

North Vancouver Island

Of the half million people who live on Vancouver Island, fewer than 20,000 reside north of Campbell River – even though this region takes up about half the island's land mass.

SAYWARD & WOSS

These two crossroads are the only towns with services in the nearly 200km stretch of Hwy 19 between Campbell River and Port McNeill. The *Fisherboy Park & Motel*

(☎ 250-282-3204), at Sayward Junction, has campsites ($12) and simple rooms ($49/55 single/double). ***Schoen Lake Provincial Park*** *(☎ 250-954-4600)*, 12km on a rough road from Hwy 19 south of Woss, offers 10 primitive sites in a mountain setting ($9). At the ***Rugged Mountain Motel*** *(☎ 250-281-2280)*, in Woss, rates start at $50/60; there's an adjacent gas station and café.

TELEGRAPH COVE
About 190km north of Campbell River, as Hwy 19 nears Port McNeill, you'll find the small community of Telegraph Cove, a major base for wildlife-watching tours.

Killer whales like to migrate through Johnstone Strait, between Sayward and Alert Bay. Stubbs Island Charters (☎ 250-928-3185, 800-665-3066) runs daily **whale-watching** trips near the strait's famous Robson Bight Ecological Reserve, where the orcas congregate from July to September. Four-hour trips cost $65/59 for adults/seniors and children; add $8 for lunch. From late August through late October, Tide Rip Tours (☎ 250-339-6294, 888-643-9319) leads groups on trips from Telegraph Cove up Knight Inlet on the BC mainland to see grizzly bears. Discovery Expeditions (☎ 250-758-2488, 800-567-3611) offers four- to six-day sea-kayaking tours from Telegraph Cove and elsewhere in BC, as well as short-term kayak rentals.

Places to Stay & Eat
Telegraph Cove Resorts *(☎ 250-928-3105, 800-200-4665)* offers campsites for $18 to $23 a night and a variety of indoor lodging with kitchens. Accommodations range from a simple room for two ($49) to a cabin for nine people ($250); vintage hotel-style rooms in the 1912 Wastell Manor house run $95 to $175. TVs and telephones are nowhere in sight. The Wardlaw House ($225) sleeps eight and features an amazing view of Johnstone Strait. The resort's ***Killer Whale Café*** is the only restaurant at Telegraph Cove, serving breakfast ($6 to $7), lunch ($8 to $12) and dinner ($15 to $20). There's also a convenience store and a pub with old-time photos of Telegraph Cove.

At ***Alder Bay Campsite*** *(☎ 250-956-4117)*, close to Telegraph Cove, waterfront sites cost $16 to $26. ***Hidden Cove Lodge*** *(☎ 250-956-3916)*, 7km from Telegraph Cove, rents rooms for $12, including breakfast. Look for the signs for both of these on the road between Telegraph Cove and Hwy 19.

PORT MCNEILL
• population 2700
A gateway to the nearby island communities of Alert Bay and Sointula, Port McNeill also makes a good base for helicopter tours and scuba-diving and fishing trips. You'll find the Visitor Info Centre (☎ 250-956-3131, fax 956-4633) at 351 Shelley Crest.

For a low-key stay, try ***Tranquil Space B&B*** *(☎ 250-956-2002, 2702 Brockington Place)*, where rates start at $45, including a self-catered breakfast. More deluxe, ***Seeview B&B*** *(☎ 250-956-4818, 2291 Quatsino Crescent)* still offers reasonable prices ($65 to $95), with a full breakfast, hot tub, rec room and garden. The ***Haida-Way Motor Inn*** *(☎ 250-956-3373, 1817 Campbell Way)* charges $70/86 single/double, with free email access in the lobby. Its ***Northern Lights Restaurant*** serves pricey dinners ($13 to $30) and cheaper breakfasts and lunches. The ***McNeill Inn*** *(☎ 250-956-2466, 1597 Beach Dr)* offers reasonably priced meals ($3 to $7 at breakfast and lunch, $5 to $12 at dinner), plus rooms starting at $70/80.

Getting There & Away
Air Rainbow (☎ 250-956-2020) offers float-plane service to and from Vancouver and Seattle. Laidlaw Coach Lines (☎ 250-949-7532) travels to Port McNeill from Victoria ($82.50 one-way) and Nanaimo ($65 one-way). Rainbow Express Water Taxi Service (☎ 250-956-8294), on Beach Dr, offers kayak support and fishing charters. See Getting There & Away under Alert Bay, below, for information on BC Ferries service to Alert Bay and Sointula.

ALERT BAY
• population 600
Situated on 5km-long Cormorant Island, the village of Alert Bay is a fascinating

VANCOUVER ISLAND

blend of old fishing settlement and Native community, offering a glimpse of the more remote First Nations settlements in BC's north (though it remains within easy access of Vancouver Island). For local information, contact the Visitor Info Centre (☎ 250-974-5024), 116 Fir St, open all year, or visit the Web site www.alertbay.com.

The **U'Mista Cultural Centre** (☎ 250-974-5403), a 2km walk from the BC Ferries dock, features an impressive collection of masks and other items used by the Kwakwaka'wakw nation during their potlatches. Singing, dancing and barbecues take place in the warmer months; call ahead for dates and details. Other Native points of interest include a burial ground, ceremonial big house and what is probably the world's tallest (53m) totem pole. It's sometimes possible to catch modern-day totem pole carvers at work around town, too.

Walk through giant cedar trees and mosses at **Alert Bay Ecological Park** (also known as Gator Gardens), on the island's north side. (You can ask for a map of the park at the Visitor Info Centre.) Seasmoke and Sea Orca Expeditions (☎ 250-974-5225) offers **whale-watching** expeditions aboard its classic yacht. The cost ($70/40 for adults/children three to 12) also includes on-board refreshments.

Places to Stay & Eat
About a 40-minute walk west from the BC Ferries dock, the *Gwakawe Campground* (☎ 250-974-5556) is the nicest on the island, with sites for $12. *Pacific Hostelry* (☎ 250-974-2026, 549 Fir St) , in a former church across the street from the beach facing Johnstone Strait, can fit only 12 people, so call ahead for reservations. A bed costs $15.

The *Orca Inn* (☎ 250-974-5322, 289 Fir St) contains a half-dozen small rooms ($50/60) with showers and TVs but no phones. The *Old Customs House* (☎ 250-974-2282, 119 Fir St) offers three rooms that share a bath and kitchen access for $50 to $65. Both these places have restaurants downstairs. *On the Beach Cottage* (☎ 250-974-5225, 66 Fir St) is a charming retreat suitable for up to six people. The cottage

comes with a full kitchen and bath plus a private deck facing the ocean. The rate for two is $95.

Getting There & Away
BC Ferries offers service from Port McNeill to Alert Bay (45 minutes) on Cormorant Island and Sointula on Malcolm Island (25 minutes). Check the schedule carefully; it's one of the ferry system's most confusing, but there are about 11 departures daily, with alternating sailings for each island. The roundtrip fare is $5.50/2.75/13.75 for adults/children/cars.

From Mid-June through September, Sea Orca Expeditions (☎ 250-974-5225) runs a passenger-only ferry that serves Alert Bay, Sointula, Alder Bay and Telegraph Cove. The roundtrip fare between Alert Bay and Telegraph Cove runs $20/10 for adults/children.

MALCOLM ISLAND
Alert Bay–bound travelers may also want to plan a visit to neighboring Malcolm Island and the town of Sointula (population 635), a onetime socialist commune founded in 1901 by Finns, for whom the town's name meant 'harmony.' Not as tourist-oriented as Alert Bay, Sointula nonetheless has some visitor amenities. Wayward Wind Charters (☎ 250-973-6307) offers **whale-watching** tours on a sailboat ($70, including lunch), as well as accommodations in log cabins (starting at $50/60 single/double).

The *Malcom Island Inn* (☎ 250-973-6366, 210 1st St) includes a restaurant and rooms (starting at $52/57). *Ocean Bliss Bed & Breakfast Cottages* (☎ 250-973-6121), at 1st and Rupert St, charges $60 to $80, with meals beyond breakfast available for an extra charge.

PORT HARDY
• population 5300
This small town at the northern end of Vancouver Island is best known as a departure point for BC Ferries trips up the Inside Passage to Prince Rupert. The Visitor Info Centre (☎ 250-949-7622, fax 949-6653) is at 7250 Market St.

You won't find much in town except a small **museum**, 7110 Market St, which is open 10 am to 5 pm Monday to Saturday, but the area around Port Hardy offers good **salmon fishing, scuba diving** and **wildlife-watching**. North Island Diving & Water Sports (☎ 250-949-2664), on the corner of Market and Hastings Sts, rents and sells equipment and runs courses. Sea Legend Charters (☎ 250-949-9525) and Catala Charters (☎ 250-949-7560, 800-515-5511) both operate a variety of adventure tours for divers, hikers and sightseers. For **kayaking** rentals and tours, contact Odyssey Kayaking (☎ 250-902-0565) or North Island Kayak (☎ 250-949-7707).

Places to Stay & Eat

Port Hardy fills up most nights from June through September, so book ahead. Campgrounds include **Wildwood Campsite** (☎ 250-949-6753), on the ferry terminal road, with sites for $15; **Sunny Sanctuary Campground** (☎ 250-949-8111, 8080 Goodspeed Rd); and **Quatse River Campground** (☎ 250-949-2395, 5050 Hardy Bay Rd), where a portion of the proceeds goes toward salmon preservation.

At **This Old House Bed & Breakfast** (☎ 250-949-8372, 8735 Hastings St), near the bus depot and restaurants, rates start at $40/70 single/double. **Kay's B&B** (☎ 250-949-6776, 7605 Carnarvon Rd) is another good deal, with four bedrooms for $42/61. **C-View Bed & Breakfast** (☎ 250-949-7560, 6170 Hardy Bay Rd) can accommodate two people ($75) to five ($120) in its rooms. **Oceanview Bed & Breakfast** (☎ 250-949-8302, 7735 Cedar Place) features lovely views; rates start at $75/85.

The **North Shore Inn** (☎ 250-949-8500, 7370 Market St) is depressing and overpriced at $79/93. Much nicer are the **Glen Lyon Inn** (☎ 250-949-7115, 6435 Hardy Bay Rd) and the **Quarterdeck Inn** (☎ 250-902-0455, 6555 Hardy Bay Rd), both new inns with waterfront rooms for about $100.

Getting There & Around

Pacific Coastal Airlines (☎ 250-949-6353, 800-663-2872) offers air service to Port Hardy.

Laidlaw Coach Lines (☎ 250-949-7532), on the corner of Market and Hastings Sts, runs one bus a day to Victoria ($92.50) and Nanaimo ($75). North Island Transportation, operating out of the same office, runs a shuttle bus to/from the ferry terminal for $5 one-way. The bus will pick you up and drop you off wherever you're staying.

From mid-May to mid-October, BC Ferries sails the *Queen of the North* up the Inside Passage to Prince Rupert on spectacular, 15-hour daylight trips. Discovery Coast Passage ferries also sail from Port Hardy, en route to Bella Coola. Reservations are essential for both; see the Getting Around chapter for details. The ferry terminal is 3km south of town across Hardy Bay.

CAPE SCOTT PROVINCIAL PARK

About 70km west of Port Hardy over an active logging gravel road, this remote park with pristine beaches offers challenging hiking and wilderness camping for those wishing to get away from it all. One of the most accessible spots is the undisturbed expanse of sandy beach at San Josef Bay, less than an hour's walk along a well-maintained trail. Beyond this, things get serious. The eight-hour, 24km slog to wild Cape Scott, an old Danish settlement at the park's far end, weeds out the Sunday strollers. Just submit totally to the 'goddess of mud' and rewards will come to you; Nels Bight Beach, a camping spot six hours down the trail, is one of them. Wildlife is abundant.

Note that the west coast of this northern tip of the island is known for strong winds, high tides and heavy rain (up to 500cm per year). You'll need to take all supplies and equipment if you're camping (strictly backcountry; $3 per person). Gear should be windproof and waterproof, and you'll need to purify all water before drinking it.

VANCOUVER ISLAND

Southern Gulf Islands

When Canadians refer to British Columbia as 'lotus land,' the Gulf Islands are often what they have in mind. The mild climate, abundant flora and fauna, relative isolation and natural beauty combine to make the islands an escapist's dream destination. Indeed, the islands have attracted many retirees, artists or counterculture types who shun the nine-to-five grind of mainland life.

If you actually lived here, you might have to worry about having your well run dry in summer or finding a viable means of making a living. But as a visitor, you'll only encounter the abundant charms that make the Gulf Islands one of BC's most popular destinations. Scuba diving, sailing and kayaking are all popular pastimes, but the islands also offer such land-based pleasures as hiking, horseback riding and gallery hopping.

The Gulf Islands include about 200 islands in all, lying northeast of Victoria and southwest of Tsawwassen in an archipelago that spills over into the San Juan Islands of Washington State. Most of the islands are small, and nearly all of them are uninhabited. Just five of the larger islands receive BC Ferries service; their populations range from fewer than 400 (Saturna Island) to about 12,000 (Salt Spring Island).

This chapter covers the six most popular islands. If you have access to a boat, you'll enjoy checking out the many smaller islands scattered throughout the archipelago. The waters off **Wallace Island Provincial Marine Park**, west of Galiano Island, offer superb paddling conditions. **Cabbage Island Marine Park**, off Saturna's south end, presents opportunities for swimming, fishing and wilderness camping. Portland Island, about 5km north of Swartz Bay, doubles as **Princess Margaret Provincial Marine Park**, with primitive campsites, picnic areas, hiking trails and good kayak landings at Arbutus Point and Shell Beach.

Lodging is tight on all the ferry-served islands, so you must make reservations, especially in high season. You'll find many options in Tourism BC's accommodations directory (see the Accommodations section of the Facts for the Visitor chapter), but quite a few smaller B&Bs are not listed. For information on B&Bs on Salt Spring Island, stop by the Visitor Info Centre in Ganges; on the other islands, pick up the brochures published by each island, which are generally available on the ferries. The free twice-monthly newspaper *Island Tides* also carries some advertisements for lodgings. Canadian Gulf Islands Reservations (☎ 888-539-2930) handles bookings for more than 100 B&Bs, inns, cottages and other accommodations. If you plan to camp, bring a propane stove

Highlights

- Seeing the islands by boat – be it kayak, ferry or under sail
- Hiking – or driving – to a mountain lookout for panoramic views
- Visiting artists in their studios
- Exploring Montague Harbour Provincial Marine Park on Galiano Island
- Shopping the Saturday market at Ganges on Salt Spring Island
- Scuba diving at first-class sites throughout the Gulf Islands

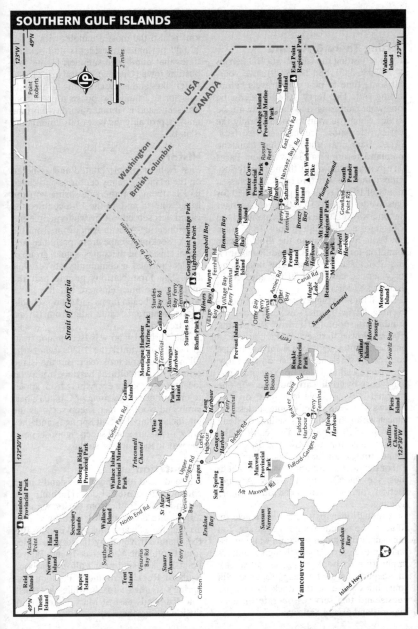

SOUTHERN GULF ISLANDS

0 2 4 km
0 1 2 miles

123°W
49°N

Point Roberts

USA
CANADA

Washington
British Columbia

Waldron Island

East Point Regional Park

Tumbo Island

Cabbage Island Provincial Marine Park

Russell Reef
East Point Rd

Winter Cove Provincial Marine Park
Lyall Harbour
Narvaez Bay Rd
Mt Warburton Pike
Saturna Island
Ferry Terminal
Saturna Beach
Breezy Bay
Plumper Sound
South Pender Island

Gowlland Point Rd

Georgia Point Heritage Park & Lighthouse Point

Campbell Bay
Fernhill Rd
Mayne
Bennett Bay
Horton Bay
Samuel Island

Mayne Island
Village Bay Ferry Terminal
Village Bay
Miners Bay

Mt Norman Regional Park
North Pender Island
Browning Harbour
Beaumont Provincial Marine Park
Bidwell Harbour

Sturdies Bay Rd
Galiano Bay Rd
Sturdies Bay
Sturdies Bay Ferry Terminal
Bluffs Park

Montague Harbour Provincial Marine Park

Ferry to Tsawwassen

Strait of Georgia

123°30'W

Amies Rd
Otter Bay
Canal Rd
Magic Lake
Otter Bay Ferry Terminal
Prevost Island

Swanson Channel

Moresby Island

Ferry
Portland Island
Moresby Passage
To Swartz Bay

Dionisio Point Provincial Park

Alcala Point

Reid Island
Thetis Island

Hall Island
Norway Island
Kuper Island

Secretary Islands

Bodega Ridge Provincial Park

Porlier Pass Rd

Wallace Island Provincial Marine Park

Wallace Island

Southey Point

Trincomali Channel

Wise Island

Galiano Island

Ferry
Montague Harbour
Parker Island

Ferry Terminal
Long Harbour

Beddis Beach

Ruckle Provincial Park

Beaver Point Rd

Long Harbour
Long Harbour Rd

Ganges Harbour

Upper Ganges Rd
Ganges

Beddis Rd

Salt Spring Island

Mt Maxwell Provincial Park
Mt Maxwell Rd

Fulford-Ganges Rd
Fulford Harbour
Ferry Terminal

Fulford Harbour

Piers Island

Satellite Channel
123°30'W

St Mary Lake
North End Rd
Vesuvius Bay

Vesuvius Bay Rd
Ferry Terminal
Erskine Bay

Stuart Channel

Crofton

Sansum Narrows

Vancouver Island

Cowichan Bay

Island Hwy

49°N

since fires generally aren't allowed on the Gulf Islands.

Getting There & Around

If you're visiting the islands via BC Ferries (☎ 250-386-3431, 888-223-3779), give yourself some time to plot your travels before setting out. The ferry schedules can be somewhat confusing, and there may not be service when you want to go. Generally, the ferries offer more frequent service from Swartz Bay (near Victoria) than from the mainland terminal at Tsawwassen. Fares vary by season; from July through early September, the one-way fare from Tsawwassen to a Gulf Island is $9 per person ($4.50 for ages five to 11), plus $35.50 for a passenger car; one-way fares back to the mainland are $5/2.50 for adults/children and $18.25 for a car. From Swartz Bay to the Gulf Islands, roundtrip fares are $6/3 for adults/children and about $20 for a car. The interisland ferry service costs $3/1.50 for adults/children plus $7 for a car.

You'll find the biggest crowds on Friday-evening ferries from Tsawwassen and on Sunday-afternoon ferries from the islands. You're allowed to reserve vehicular spaces on these routes, so if you want to be sure your car or truck has a place on the ferry, it's wise to call and sign up. You must pay in advance by credit card, but you won't be charged any reservation fees on the Tsawwassen–Gulf Islands routes unless you cancel within five days of sailing or don't show up ($10 penalty). You can't make reservations for the Swartz Bay–Gulf Islands routes, nor for interisland ferries.

For detailed information on ferry schedules, see the Getting There & Around section under each individual island heading.

Although it helps to have a vehicle on some of the islands, it's not necessary. You can usually find lodgings within walking distance of each ferry dock (though again, it's imperative to book rooms in advance). Innkeepers of more far-flung properties will sometimes drive to the dock to pick up guests, and taxi services operate on each major island except Saturna.

SALT SPRING ISLAND

The largest Southern Gulf Island (180 sq km) is also the most populous, with about 12,000 permanent residents and several times that number in summer. Home to a bustling town (Ganges), several large freshwater lakes and many charming farmsteads, Salt Spring Island also boasts a prominent arts scene and a vibrant Saturday-morning market, probably the best of its kind on the islands.

History

First Nations people hunted and gathered on the island for many centuries and called it 'Klaathem' for the salt springs on the island's north end. In the 19th century, the island was settled not by white people but by pioneering African Americans from the USA. Seeking escape from prejudice and social tensions in the States, a small group of settlers formed a community at Vesuvius Bay. The First Nations people and the blacks sometimes clashed, but the latter stuck it out, began farms and set up schools. More immigrants came later from Britain and Ireland.

Salt Spring Island was BC's major fruit-growing area until the 1930s, when the Okanagan region took over. But the island retains its agricultural heritage today, as local farms produce everything from apples to organic cheese to some of Canada's best lamb and wool. In fact, sheep serve as the unofficial symbol of Salt Spring Island; they graze in pastures, and sheep signposts point the way to local artists' studios.

Orientation

All roads lead to Ganges, the island's main commercial center: Long Harbour Rd, which handles traffic from the Tsawwassen ferry; Fulford-Ganges Rd, used by visitors arriving from Swartz Bay; and Vesuvius Bay Rd, mainly traveled by those who sailed from Crofton on Vancouver Island. Beaver Point Rd, accessed near Fulford Harbour, leads to Ruckle Provincial Park on Salt Spring's southeast reach, while the North End Rd winds past St Mary Lake toward the island's northern tip.

Information

The helpful staff at the Ganges Visitor Info Centre (☎ 250-537-5252), 121 Lower Ganges Rd, offers heaps of information, including a free self-guided map to art studios, as well as binders with listings for the island's 100 or so B&B accommodations. The office is open 10 am to 4 pm daily.

You can find ATMs at the Fulford Inn, 2661 Fulford-Ganges Rd, and in Ganges at Thrifty Foods and at all major-bank branches.

The Ganges post office (☎ 250-537-2321), 109 Purvis Lane, sits across the parking lot from Mouat's Clothing Co in central Ganges; there are also post offices at Fulford Harbour and Vesuvius Bay.

Salt Spring Books (☎ 250-537-2812), 104 McPhillips in Ganges, offers email access for 10¢ per minute. The island has two weekly newspapers: *The Driftwood* and *The Barnacle*.

Coin-operated laundries in Ganges include Mrs. Clean (☎ 250-537-4133), next to Centennial Park, and New Wave (☎ 250-537-2500) at Moby's Marine Pub, 124 Upper Ganges Rd. Moby's also has coin-op showers.

Dial ☎ 911 for any fire, police or medical emergencies. Lady Minto Hospital (☎ 250-538-5545), 135 Crofton Rd, serves Salt Spring's medical needs.

Ganges

Ganges, the principal village, sees more action during the day than at night, when many visitors return to accommodations elsewhere. Still, you can find a bit of nightlife, especially at the ever-popular Moby's Marine Pub (see Places to Eat, later).

Ganges' well-known **Market in the Park** (☎ 250-537-4448) features wares from local artists, craftspeople and farmers. It takes place 8 am to 4 pm every Saturday, April through October. For the finer arts, try the Gallery Walks, held 5 to 9 pm every Friday, mid-March through late September. Participants simply take their time strolling among the Ganges galleries. ArtSpring (☎ 250-537-2102), 100 Jackson Ave, offers a full calendar of performing arts events.

The Salt Spring **Festival of the Arts** (☎ 250-537-4167) takes place each July, when local and touring artists present music, theater and dance performances. For information on other local activities, see the Parks & Beaches and Activities sections, below.

Parks & Beaches

In Ganges, the parks include **Rotary Maritime Park**, on Ganges Harbour, where you can launch kayaks and other small boats, and **Mouat Park**, behind the ArtSpring center, which features walking trails and a golf course where you fling Frisbees instead of hitting golf balls. Camping is no longer permitted in Mouat Park.

Not far south of Ganges via Cranberry and Mt Maxwell Rds, **Mt Maxwell Provincial Park** contains one of the Gulf Islands' most accessible viewpoints. It's about 9km off the main road, on a route safe for all but large RVs and trailers. Baynes Peak (588m) caps the park and offers sweeping views of Salt Spring Island and beyond. (Keep an eye on children and pets near the steep drop-offs.)

Ruckle Provincial Park (☎ 250-653-4115) ranks among the best parks in the Gulf Islands, with good camping and a beautiful shoreline along Beaver Point. Set on the site of one of the oldest family farms in British Columbia (established in 1872), the park still contains an active farmstead. If you can't camp overnight or longer, spend some time walking around the farm; it's the best way to enjoy a brief visit. Ruckle also features some easy hiking trails through forests and along the shore and offers opportunities for fishing, bicycling and boating.

Salt Spring Island has about two dozen public beach access points, with a full list available from the Visitor Info Centre (see Information, earlier). Popular spots include Beachside Dr alongside Long Harbour, Southey Point at the island's north end and Beddis Beach on the island's east side, noted for good swimming and sunbathing. Head to Erskine Bay or Vesuvius Bay for lovely sunsets.

Activities

The narrow, winding and steep roads here don't discourage many people from **cycling**. Pick up the *Cycling Map of Salt Spring Island* (50¢) at the Visitor Info Centre to find the best local routes. Another good publication, *Salt Spring Out Of Doors* costs less than $5 and includes details on hiking trails, beach-access points, historic sites, berry picking and more. Salt Spring Kayaking (☎ 250-653-4222), 2923 Fulford-Ganges Rd at Fulford Wharf, rents bicycles for $5/25 per hour/day. You'll pay an extra $10 for delivery to your ferry or accommodations.

Several companies can outfit you for **kayaking**. Salt Spring Kayaking (see above paragraph) rents kayaks for $12/20 single/double per hour. The company offers three-hour guided introductory paddles for $50 ($30 for children ages eight to 16); two-hour sunset or full-moon harbor tours at Fulford or Ganges ($30); and multi-day trips starting at $250. Sea Otter Kayaking (☎ 250-537-5678), 1186 North End Rd, offers similar trips that depart from the foot of Rainbow Rd at Ganges Harbour. If you'd rather have someone else be skipper, Herberg Charters (☎ 250-537-9321, 888-293-1603) features **boat trips** by the hour, day or longer.

Wild Rovers Expeditions (☎ 250-537-4532) leads small-group backwoods expeditions on Salt Spring Island and Vancouver Island. See its Web site at www.gulfislands/wildrovers.

For **golfing**, head to Salt Spring Island's two nine-hole courses: Blackburn Meadows (☎ 250-537-1707), 269 Blackburn Rd, and Salt Spring Island Golf Club (☎ 250-537-2121), 805 Lower Ganges Rd.

Salt Spring Guided Rides (☎ 250-537-5761) offers **horseback riding** on Mt Maxwell. Prices start at $20 for a half-hour ride.

Places to Stay

Ruckle Provincial Park (☎ 250-391-2300) offers 70 primitive, mostly walk-in campsites near the ocean ($12) on a first-come, first-served basis. A few campsites are also available at Cottage Resort and Lakeside Gardens (see below).

Tucked away in the woods, the ***Salt Spring Island Hostel*** (☎ 250-537-4149, hostel@saltspring.com, 640 Cusheon Lake Rd), a Hostelling International affiliate, offers beds in dorm rooms and tipis for $15.50/19.50 members/nonmembers; a family room in the main lodge costs $50/60. But most families will probably want to sleep in the charming tree house ($50/60). The family room and tree-house prices cover two adults; kids cost an extra $12.50 each. Another adults-only tree house makes a great romantic retreat at $60 for two. Amenities include Internet access, kitchen facilities, communal campfires and a short trail to one of the prettiest waterfalls in the Gulf Islands, plus bike or scooter rentals for $15 per day.

B&B choices abound on Salt Spring. Breakfast is tasty at the pastoral ***Old Farmhouse B&B*** (☎ 250-537-4113, farmhouse@saltspring.com, 1077 North End Rd), near St Mary Lake, a restored century-old farmhouse with four guest rooms ($150 to $170), all with private bathrooms and balconies.

Island Escapades (☎ 250-537-2537, 888-529-2567, fax 250-537-2532, escapades@saltspring.com, 118 Natalie Lane) offers B&B accommodations starting at $125/150 single/double, plus packages featuring kayaking, sailing or rock climbing.

Motel accommodations are in somewhat limited supply on Salt Spring, but there are a few good choices. The ***Seabreeze Inn*** (☎ 250-537-4145, fax 537-4323, seabreeze@saltspring.com, 101 Bittancourt Rd) offers quiet rooms overlooking Ganges Harbour and a few kitchenettes; prices start at $70 single or double. The ***Fulford Inn*** (☎ 250-653-4432, 2661 Fulford-Ganges Rd) charges $50/77 for its eight basic rooms. A two-bedroom suite with kitchen rents for $100, with discounts for stays of more than one night.

One of several resorts along St Mary Lake, ***Lakeside Gardens*** (☎ 250-537-5773, lakesidegardens@saltspring.com, 1450 North End Rd) offers RV and tent sites for $18 (plus hookups if needed), cabanas with lofts ($50) and fully equipped cottages ($90). Boat and canoe rentals are available.

The *Cottage Resort* (☎ 250-537-2214, 175 Suffolk Rd), also on St Mary Lake, features a sandy swimming beach, free canoes and rowboats and housekeeping cottages for $100 to $170, depending on the size.

The health-oriented *Salty Springs Spa & Seaside Resort* (☎ 250-537-4111, fax 537-2939, 1460 North Beach Rd), near Vesuvius Bay, features upscale seaside chalets with fireplaces starting at $189; some have kitchens. The indulgent activities here include massages, body wraps, yoga and more. *Seido-En Forest House* (☎ 250-653-2311, fax 653-2310, seido-en@uniserve.com, 124 Meyer Rd) is a Japanese-style retreat usually rented by the week for $900. Amenities include a full kitchen, indoor sunken tub, outdoor shower, two patios and lots of privacy. The most upscale choice on the island, *Hastings House* (☎ 250-537-2362, fax 537-5333, hasthouse@saltspring.com, 160 Upper Ganges Rd) features 17 rooms starting at $310 and a restaurant that's among the best on the islands.

Places to Eat
Embe Bakery (☎ 250-537-5611, 174 Fulford-Ganges Rd) serves scrumptious muffins, breads and other baked goods, beginning at 5 am daily. The hip *Treehouse Café* (☎ 250-537-5379, 106 Purvis Lane), close to the Ganges waterfront, features outdoor tables and reasonable prices ($2 to $7) for breakfast and lunch. In July and August, it stays open for dinner as well, with live music some evenings.

Also in Ganges, *Moby's Marine Pub* (☎ 250-537-5559, 124 Upper Ganges Rd) offers a winning combination: a lively atmosphere, excellent views of Ganges Harbour and good food, with such dishes as a crab quesadilla ($9.50), 'Lamburghini' (lamb burger with mango chutney for $8.25) and halibut and chips in three sizes ($7.25 to $11.25). On Sunday, come for brunch in the morning or live jazz in the evening.

At *Alfresco Waterfront Restaurant* (☎ 250-537-5979), in Ganges' Grace Point Square, you can dine on burgers ($8 to $10),

pastas (from $13) and seafood ($13 to $17) indoors or on the patio.

On Salt Spring's south end, the *Fulford Inn* (see Places to Stay, above) serves such meals as stir-fried pork and fettuccini ($10) and roast lamb ($13) for lunch and dinner daily. For lighter bites, try *Rose's Café* (☎ 250-653-9222), at the Fulford ferry landing.

Shopping
If you're looking for unusual souvenirs, try the batik jackets and hand-painted rain boots at Mouat's Clothing Co (☎ 250-537-5551), 106 Fulford-Ganges Rd. Mouat's Home Hardware (same phone number) is a classic old-fashioned hardware emporium that sells a little bit of everything.

Jill Louise Campbell Fine Art (☎ 250-537-1589, 800-474-6705), 3-110 Purvis Lane in Ganges, features the artist's lovely watercolors, while Pegasus Gallery of Canadian Art (☎ 250-537-2421, 800-668-6131), also in the Mouat's complex, offers an extensive selection of paintings, jewelry, basketry and carvings.

Getting There & Around
Several seaplane companies serve Salt Spring: Seair (☎ 800-447-3247), Pacific Spirit Air (☎ 800-665-2359) and Harbour Air (☎ 800-665-0212), all of which offer daily scheduled flights between the Vancouver area and the Gulf Islands. The fare to Ganges is about $60/120 one-way/roundtrip.

Most visitors arrive by boat, a convenient way to travel since Salt Spring has no fewer than three BC Ferries terminals: at Long Harbour, Fulford Harbour and Vesuvius Bay. The boats sail twice daily between Tsawwassen and Long Harbour (sometimes more in summer); for Friday and Saturday sailings, make advance reservations by calling ☎ 250-386-3431 or 888-223-3779. Ferries travel more frequently between Tsawwassen and Swartz Bay, where you can transfer to a boat bound for Salt Spring's Fulford Harbour. Swartz Bay–Fulford ferries run about eight times a day. There also are more than a dozen daily sailings between Vesuvius Bay and Crofton, roughly midway between Victoria and Nanaimo.

It's best to have a car on Salt Spring Island, but Silver Shadow Taxi (☎ 250-537-3030) offers cab service by advance reservation. Gulf Islands Water Taxi (☎ 250-537-2510) provides seaborne service and a variety of Gulf Islands day tours.

Heritage Car & Truck Rentals (☎ 250-537-4225), at the Ganges Marina, rents scooters and cars, with free pick-up and drop-off at the ferry terminals or seaplane ports.

NORTH & SOUTH PENDER ISLANDS

Recreation trumps the arts on the Pender Islands – actually two islands joined by a short bridge. You may see some artists' studios here, but the more than 1000 islanders prefer to spend their time playing in the glorious natural surroundings. The Penders fall in the geographical center of the Gulf and San Juan Islands – and this, locals would have you believe, makes them the center of the universe. It's an undeniably spectacular place, where the sea, sky and neighboring islands all seem close enough to touch.

Information

If the Visitor Info Centre (☎ 250-629-6541), 2332 Otter Bay Rd on North Pender, isn't open when you arrive, you'll still find a helpful informational board listing the location and phone numbers of lodgings and other businesses.

You won't find ATMs anywhere on the Penders, so come prepared. The post office is in the small Driftwood Centre shopping plaza, at the corner of Bedwell Harbour and Razor Point Rds on North Pender. The community library (☎ 250-629-3722) sits on North Pender's Bedwell Harbour Rd. For medical emergencies, try the local health center (☎ 250-629-3233), on North Pender's Canal Rd shortly before the bridge to South Pender.

Things to See & Do

Prior Centennial Provincial Park, on North Pender, features a short walking trail and forested campsites that draw many cyclists. It's just a few hundred meters away from **Medicine Beach**, a good sunbathing spot at Bedwell Harbour.

Just over the bridge to South Pender, take the moderately steep, hour-long hike up and down **Mt Norman** (255m) for some grand views of the San Juan Islands, Vancouver Island and (on a clear day) Washington State's Cascade Mountains.

If you want to lounge on the sand, the nicest beaches include **Hamilton Beach** in Browning Harbour on North Pender and **Mortimer Spit** on South Pender. Watch for the more or less tame deer around the islands.

Several resort swimming pools allow nonguests to go **swimming** for a small fee. Check at Bedwell Harbour Island Resort or Otter Bay Marina (see Places to Stay, below). For **golfing**, try Pender Island Golf & Country Club (☎ 250-629-6659), 2305 Otter Bay Rd in North Pender; it's open to the public.

Cycling is popular on the Penders, but use caution on the winding, narrow roads. Rent bikes at Otter Bay Marina, Cooper's Landing, Bedwell Harbour Island Resort or the Driftwood Auto Centre (part of the Driftwood Centre).

Kayak Pender Island (☎ 250-629-6939), 2319 MacKinnon Rd at Otter Bay Marina on North Pender, offers guided **kayaking** tours ($35 for adults, $30 for children) and lessons ($50). Other available adventures include women's full-moon outdoor paddles,

Mt Norman hiking tours and overnight kayak and camping trips. Call ahead for reservations.

Places to Stay

Prior Centennial Provincial Park (☎ 250-391-2300) has 17 campsites ($12); reserve by calling ☎ 800-689-9025 (604-689-9025 in Greater Victoria). Sites also are available at Beaumont Provincial Marine Park on South Pender, but the park is only reachable by private boat.

On North Pender, close to the ferry terminal, **Otter Bay Marina** (☎ 250-629-3579, 2319 MacKinnon Rd) rents a dozen large, waterproof tents that sleep up to four people for $35. They're carpeted, and they come with two cots. A single furnished cabin with cooking facilities can accommodate up to three people for $75. **Port Browning Marina Resort** (☎ 250-629-3493, 4605 Oak Rd) offers campsites ($10 per tent), double rooms ($50) and cottages that can sleep up to four ($80). The amenities at both Otter Bay and Port Browning include showers, laundry facilities, a swimming pool and a store.

If you subscribe to the local belief that the Penders are the center of the universe, then Shark Cove – where the two islands meet – must be nirvana. At this very spot, **Cooper's Landing** (☎ 250-629-6133, 888-921-3111, info@cooperslanding.com, 5734 Canal Rd), on North Pender, offers a magical combination of reasonably priced accommodations and abundant recreation. Now an HI hostel, this former scuba-diving lodge still offers trips for experienced divers, along with bike rentals, kayak rentals and lessons, nature tours and trips in voyageur canoes, which can seat about a dozen people or more. The Mt Norman trailhead is a 10-minute walk away. A sauna or massage might not sound bad after all that activity, so Cooper's Landing offers those, too.

Dorm beds cost $20/30 members/nonmembers. Outside, tipis that each sleep about six people comfortably are $15. Upstairs in the main lodge, a room with skylights, great views and its own bathroom across the hall costs $64/85 double occupancy (it can sleep up to five people; add $20/15 per extra adult/child). Below the main floor, a self-contained unit perfect for a small family includes its own bathroom, kitchen and dining area and rents for $64/85 double occupancy. Bring your own linens, or pay the hostel's small rental fee. All guests enjoy access to the communal kitchen.

Betty's Bed & Breakfast (☎ 250-629-6599, Bettysb-b@direct.ca, 4711 Buccaneer Rd) sits on the shores of North Pender's Magic Lake, a popular retirement home area. Rates start at $60 and include the use of mountain bikes and a rowboat.

The adults-only **Oceanside Inn** (☎ 250-629-6691, oceanside@penderisland.com, 4230 Armadale Rd), on North Pender, is an upscale B&B with great views (especially from the private cliffside hot tubs over the bay). All rooms have private bathrooms and rent for $130 and up.

Inn on Pender Island (☎ 250-629-3353, 800-550-1572, 4709 Canal Rd), a small motel in the woods on North Pender, is popular with cyclists. The comfortable but simple rooms (no phone or TV) cost $70/80 single/double in summer ($90 for a suite with a refrigerator). A few cabins – with private hot tubs or porches with good views – sleep up to three people for $130. These are stocked with kitchen appliances and dishes, a wood-burning stove, and a small TV with VCR. The inn also features a hot tub and door-to-door delivery of the continental breakfast.

On South Pender, the **Bedwell Harbour Island Resort & Marina** (☎ 250-629-3212, 800-663-2899, fax 250-629-6777, bedwell@islandnet.com, 9801 Spalding Rd) makes an excellent choice for family vacations, with an oceanfront pool, kids' day-care programs, playground, canoe and bike rentals, coin-op laundry, a tennis court and a wide variety of rooms. In summer, you'll pay $119 for a standard room, $159 for a studio cabin, $179 for a two-bedroom cabin with a small porch and $269 for a deluxe two-bedroom villa.

Strictly for adults, **Pender Lodge** (☎ 250-629-3221, 1329 MacKinnon Rd), on North Pender, rents housekeeping cottages ($110

SOUTHERN GULF ISLANDS

A Gulf Islands National Park?

For all their beauty and renown, BC's Southern Gulf Islands seem strikingly vulnerable to commercial development, since local and national officials have taken so few steps toward protecting parcels of land here – until recently, that is. The Canadian and BC provincial governments now hope to establish a national park that incorporates parts of Mayne, Saturna and the Pender Islands, as well as several smaller surrounding islands that are currently provincial marine parks.

At public hearings held on the Gulf Islands in 2000, most residents expressed strong support for the plan. Although it's still in its formative stages, the proposed park has been growing steadily, now that the government's gotten busy buying tracts of privately owned land through the Pacific Marine Heritage Legacy project. For information on the park's progress, call ☎ 888-812-7778 (☎ 250-363-8569 in Victoria) or visit the Web site www.harbour.com/parkscan/pmhl.

to $150) very close to the ferry landing and the Islanders restaurant. Amenities include an outdoor pool, tennis court, shuffleboard and ocean views. Children aren't permitted unless the entire lodge is rented for a family reunion.

Places to Eat

If you're waiting for your BC Ferries ship to come in, grab a bite at **The Stand** (☎ 250-629-3292, 1371 Otter Bay Rd), with sandwiches and hamburgers for $4 to $8.50. **Memories at the Inn** (☎ 250-629-3353), adjacent to the Inn on Pender Island (see Places to Stay, above), serves both excellent pizza ($7 to $20) and fine-dining fare like peel-and-eat prawns steamed in Kokanee beer ($9), chicken linguine ($14) and barbecued ribs ($18).

On South Pender, the **Bedwell Harbour Island Resort & Marina** (see Places to Stay, above) includes a fine-dining restaurant

(entrees $14 to $29) and a bistro with less-expensive fare. The small and refined **Islanders Restaurant** (☎ 250-629-6811, 1325 MacKinnon Rd), on North Pender, features a range of unusual dishes, from an open-faced shrimp sandwich ($9.95) to wild Arctic musk ox ($25.95).

Shopping

Galloping Moon (☎ 250-629-6020), 1325 MacKinnon Rd, features local arts and crafts, including clothes, candles, gargoyles, gift foods, linens and a lot more. Shop around, or just grab a cup of coffee and sit in the garden. Silk 'n' Petals (☎ 250-629-3432), in the Driftwood Centre on North Pender, is another good gift shop; it's open daily. A handful of local artists open their studios to the public, while several more welcome visitors by appointment. See the annual island map brochure (available at the Visitor Info Centre) for listings.

Getting There & Around

BC Ferries (☎ 250-386-3431, 888-223-3779) offers transportation from the Penders to Tsawwassen (once or twice daily; reservations are suggested on weekends), Swartz Bay (about seven or eight times Monday to Saturday; four times Sunday), Galiano and Mayne Islands (two to four times daily), Salt Spring Island/Long Harbour (once or twice daily) and Saturna Island (once or twice daily except Sunday).

Since you can find several lodging options close to the ferry dock, a car isn't an absolute necessity. If you have no wheels and your accommodations host can't pick you up, you can always catch a ride with Pender Island Taxi (☎ 250-629-6050).

SATURNA ISLAND

The most lightly populated island, Saturna is a bit harder to reach than the other main Gulf Islands. To many people, however, this inaccessibility makes it all the more attractive as a remote and tranquil escape for a few days or more.

For the latest local information, pick up a copy of the annual Saturna Island map brochure on one of the BC Ferries or see wwww.saturnatourism.bc.ca. The post office is at the Saturna General Store, 101 Navarez Bay Rd. Don't look for banks or medical services on Saturna Island – you won't find any. Dial ☎ 911 for emergencies.

Things to See & Do

Winter Cove Provincial Marine Park, on the island's north side, features a sandy beach and offers access to fishing, boating and hiking. At the top of **Mt Warburton Pike**, you'll find a wildlife reserve with feral goats and fine views, though you'll also have to look at a mess of telecommunications equipment.

Saturna, like the other Gulf Islands, has its share of resident artists. See the annual map brochure for a listing of those who invite visitors to their studios, usually by appointment. Gallery Rosa (☎ 250-539-2866), 111 East Point Rd, offers a good selection of local works. It's open weekend and holiday afternoons.

Affiliated with the Saturna Lodge, the Saturna Island Vineyards winery (☎ 250-539-5139) offers tours and tastings 11 am to 4:30 pm daily, May through September. It's only a short stroll from the lodge (see Places to Stay, below).

For **swimming**, try Veruna Bay near Winter Cove, Russell Reef off the east side of the island or East Point Regional Park, where you can also experience some of the best **whale-watching** in the Southern Gulf Islands. Saturna Sea Kayaking (☎ 250-539-5553), in Boot Cove (only a five-minute walk from the ferry), offers **kayaking** lessons and rentals, along with good paddling advice for Saturna and surrounding islands.

Places to Stay

There are no campgrounds on Saturna Island and no more than a dozen places to stay indoors, so it's important to book well ahead for a stay here. **Breezy Bay B&B** (☎ 250-539-2937, breezybay@gulfislands .com, 131 Payne Rd), on a small farm less than 1.5km from the ferry terminal, rents rooms for $60/75 single/double. Innkeeper Renie Muir takes a special interest in the people and culture of India, and many photos of her travels decorate the walls. In the morning, guests can look forward to a filling farm-style breakfast of delicious local ingredients.

East Point Resort (☎ 250-539-2975) offers six cottages on the waterfront, with private sandy-beach access and forested trails. Rates start at $80, with a seven-day minimum in high season.

Upscale yet unpretentious, **Saturna Lodge** (☎ 250-539-2254, 888-539-8800, fax 250-539-3091, saturnalodge@hotmail.com, 130 Payne Rd) offers fine dining on the premises. Rooms cost $135 to $195, including a gourmet breakfast. All guests enjoy access to a garden hot tub, bicycles, bocce, badminton and croquet.

Places to Eat

A small café in the **Saturna General Store** (☎ 250-539-2936, 101 Navarez Bay Rd) serves soups, wraps and other light meals for $4 to $7. Here you can also pick up a picnic featuring locally made Haggis Farm baked goods, fresh produce and deli items. The **Lighthouse Pub** at the Saturna Point Store (☎ 250-539-5725, 102 East Point Rd) is another popular spot for a quick bite.

For fine dining, head to the restaurant at the **Saturna Lodge** (☎ 250-539-2254), which features dinner nightly in summer and Thursday through Sunday in spring and fall. A three-course meal costs $30. The jazz brunch that's served one Sunday a month starts at $14.

Getting There & Around

BC Ferries (☎ 250-385-3431, 888-223-3779) sails to Lyall Harbour on Saturna, but to get there from Tsawwassen, you must either sail through Swartz Bay or transfer at Mayne Island. Either way, plan to spend two to four hours on most of the roundabout voyages, some of which don't dock at Saturna until nearly 10 pm. BC Ferries leave Tsawwassen for Saturna via Swartz Bay or Mayne Island twice daily on weekdays and once daily on weekends. You can reserve vehicle space on these ferries; ask for a 'through-fare' ticket if you travel from Tsawwassen to Saturna via Swartz Bay. The ferries sail to Saturna from Swartz Bay four times per day on Saturday and Monday through Thursday, five times on Friday and twice on Sunday, but no vehicle reservations are accepted for the ferry from Swartz Bay.

You don't absolutely need a car on Saturna, since you can find lodgings near the ferry terminal. To arrange taxi service, contact Saturna Island Shuttle & Touring (☎ 250-539-5359). It's best to call ahead for reservations.

MAYNE ISLAND

If you're a geographer or an anthropologist, you won't find a much more interesting spot on the Gulf Islands than Mayne Island. First off, for the natural-history buffs, the bay fronts on Active Pass, a narrow channel that's the tightest squeeze on the Tsawwassen–Swartz Bay BC Ferries route. The human history of the island is also unique. In the 19th century, gold rushers congregated here, halfway between Vancouver Island and the Fraser River, to fortify themselves for the rest of their trip. Today, Mayne Island has attracted a number of resident artists, musicians and writers, plus plenty of professional people who have set up second (and third) homes on this less-visited island.

Information

On the ferry en route to the island, pick up a free Mayne Island brochure, which contains current listings of places to stay, eat and play, plus a good map. You'll also find an information panel set up just past the Village Bay ferry terminal on the right-hand side. For more local information, visit the Web site www.geocities.com/~mayneisland.

There are no ATMs on Mayne Island. The post office is at Tru Value Foods on Village Bay Rd in the Miners Bay area. The Mayne Library (☎ 250-539-2673) is here, too; it offers Internet access, and it's open 11 am to 3 pm Wednesday, Friday and Saturday. Miners Bay Books (☎ 250-539-3112), 400 Fernhill Rd behind the Springwater Lodge, carries a good selection of new and used books for adults and children.

Make sure you wash your clothes before you come, since you won't find any laundries on the island. For all emergencies, dial 911. The Health Centre (☎ 250-539-2312) is at the intersection of Fernhill and Felix Jack Rds.

Things to See & Do

The **Plumper Pass Lock-up** (☎ 250-539-5286) at Miners Bay once served as a jailhouse for late-19th-century rowdies. Now it's a museum, open 11 am to 3 pm Friday through Monday, late June through early September or by appointment. About two dozen **artists' studios** operate on Mayne, with wildly varying hours. A brochure available across the island lists their addresses and phone numbers. Fernhill Centre, 574 Fernill Rd (about halfway between Miners Bay and Bennett Bay), includes several galleries and gift shops featuring local works.

The hour-long roundtrip hike to the top of **Mt Parke** will reward you with great 360-degree views of Active Pass, the Gulf Islands and beyond. The trailhead is at the end of Montrose Drive, near Fernhill Centre.

If you're looking for good **beaches**, head to Dinner Bay Park, on Mayne's south shore; Campbell Bay, on the northeast side; or Georgina Point Heritage Park and Lighthouse Point at the island's northern tip.

Mayne's back roads offer some of the best **cycling** in the Gulf Islands. You can rent bikes from Tinkerers B&B (☎ 250-539-2280) in Miners Bay and from the Bayview Bed & Breakfast (☎ 250-539-2924, 800-576-2115), 764 Steward Dr, on the island's east side.

Mayne Island Canoe & Kayak Rentals (☎ 250-539-2667 or 539-0077) offers **kayaking** instruction and fast-boat pick-ups at remote locations for people who don't want to paddle back to Mayne. The company operates year-round and provides free ferry pick-ups and drop-offs for clients.

For sea-based sightseeing, try Island Charters (☎ 250-539-5040), which offers full-day or half-day **sailboat cruises** aboard a 33-foot (10m) vessel ($135 and up for two people, including lunch).

Places to Stay

Mayne Island Kayak & Canoe Rentals (☎ 250-539-2667), at Seal Beach near Miners Bay, offers tent camping, with a hot tub and showers. *Fernhollow Campground* (☎ 250-539-5253, 640 Horton Bay Rd) permits tent pitching in a quiet location on the island's east side. There are no RV facilities on Mayne Island.

Along Sunset Place in Miners Bay, the *Tinkerers B&B* and *Till Eulenspiegel Guesthouse B&B* share ownership (☎ 250-539-2280, tinkerers@gulfnet.pinc.com) and an international clientele. The staff speaks Spanish and German as well as English, and the owners offer language-practicum programs. But if that's not your thing, you can simply laze about the hammock, enjoy the sea views or go for a bike ride. Rates range from $65 to $95.

The *Root Seller Inn* (☎ 250-539-2621), a self-catering budget B&B at Miners Bay, attracts cyclists and other active guests. Rooms start at $50/75 single/double.

The *Springwater Lodge* (☎ 250-539-5521, springwaterlodge@netscape.net) was built on Miners Bay in the 1890s; it's now possibly the oldest continuously operating hotel in BC, a good place to sleep and an even better place to eat. The facilities include five sleeping rooms with shared bath ($40), plus several two-bedroom cabins with sleeper sofa, stove, coffeemaker, refrigerator and sun deck ($85 in summer).

The pleasant *Mayne Inn Hotel* (☎ 250-539-3122, 494 Arbutus Dr), a small waterfront hotel on Bennett Bay, features inexpensive rooms with a view and a TV but no phone. Rates start at $50/60. Also in the Bennett Bay area, *Blue Vista Cottages* (☎ 250-539-2463, 877-535-2424, 563 Arbutus Dr) offers one- and two-bedroom housekeeping cabins, all with decks and some with fireplaces, for $50 and up.

Oceanwood Country Inn (☎ 250-539-5074, fax 539-3002, oceanwood@gulfislands .com, 630 Dinner Bay Rd) is the luxe property on Mayne Island. All rooms come with private bathrooms and views of the Navy Channel; the best of the bunch feature whirlpool tubs and private balconies. Rooms start at $160, and breakfast, as well as afternoon tea, is included.

Places to Eat

Dolphins (☎ 250-539-3324) offers short-order food service by the ferry dock at Village Bay. Quick, inexpensive meals are also the order of the day at *Manna Bakery Café* (☎ 250-539-2323), next to Tru Value Foods, where you can get coffee and baked goods, soup for $3.50 or a sandwich for not much more. *Miners Bay Café* (☎ 250-539-9888) features lots of vegetarian options (mostly $3.50 to $7) plus excellent take-out pizza on Friday and Saturday evening.

Springwater Lodge (☎ 250-539-5521) draws loyal locals and visitors alike for its reasonably priced fare, including breakfast ($3.75 to $7.25), lunch ($6.25 to $10) and dinner (nightly specials run about $17). At the *Mayne Inn Hotel* (☎ 250-539-3122) you can eat on a deck overlooking Bennett Bay. Breakfast choices range from granola ($2.95) to eggs Benedict ($7.95). Sandwiches ($6 to $8) and burgers ($8 to $10) are available at lunch, while dinner selections include fish and chips ($7.95), halibut burgers ($8.95) and creative quesadillas (about $9).

The restaurant at the swank *Oceanwood Country Inn* (☎ 250-539-5074) is one of the best in the Gulf Islands. Four-course dinners of Pacific Northwest cuisine cost about $42.

Getting There & Around

BC Ferries (☎ 250-386-3431 or 888-223-3779) docks at Village Bay, on Mayne Island's west side. Ferries arrive from Tsawwassen about twice daily. Reservations are encouraged all week long, and they're necessary for the Friday-evening and Saturday-morning sailings. Service from Swartz Bay is more frequent, about five or six times daily. You can also travel by ferry between Mayne and Galiano, Salt Spring, Saturna and the Pender Islands.

On Mayne, it's easy to make do without a car, especially if you stay in the Miners Bay area. Midas Taxi Service (☎ 250-539-3132 or 539-0181) operates cabs daily except Wednesday, plus island tours for $25 per hour.

GALIANO ISLAND

Despite its proximity to Tsawwassen (it's the closest of the major Southern Gulf Islands), the long and narrow Galiano Island has an uncrowded feel. Only about 1000 people live here, most of them on the southeast side of the island near Sturdies Bay. Wilderness prevails elsewhere, from the sheer rock cliffs below Bodega Ridge to the many small islands just off Galiano's coast. The island's excellent beaches include the superlative Montague Harbour Provincial Marine Park.

Information

As always, look for the helpful island map brochure on the ferry, or stop by the information shack on your right-hand side as you leave the ferry terminal at Sturdies Bay. For more information, call the Galiano Chamber of Commerce (☎ 250-539-2233), see the island's Web site at www.galianoisland.com, send email to info@galianoisland.com or write to PO Box 73, Galiano Island, BC V0N 1P0.

Galiano Island has no banks or ATMs. The post office is at the Daystar Market (☎ 250-539-2505), near the junction of Sturdies Bay and Porlier Pass Rd. You'll find no laundries on the island. The Health Care Centre (☎ 250-539-3230) is on Burrill Rd south of Sturdies Bay Rd. Dial ☎ 911 in an emergency.

Parks & Beaches

With its sheltered setting, **Montague Harbour Provincial Marine Park** is one of the two best provincial parks in the Southern Gulf Islands. (The other is Ruckle Provincial Park on Salt Spring.) A trail leads from the campground along a long stretch of crushed-shell beach where First Nations people once shucked their seafood harvest. Today, it's a superb spot to watch a sunset. Take care not to walk on the sand spits, where rare black oyster-catcher birds lay their eggs April through August.

Bluffs Park boasts great views of Active Pass, along with 5km of hiking paths. You can access the park by rough but passable Bluff Rd, which leads between Burrill and Georgeson Bay Rds. Known for its abundant and colorful bird life, **Bodega Ridge Provincial Park** also contains the highest point on the island, the 382m Bodega Hill. Kayakers like to camp at **Dionisio Point Provincial Park**, at the island's far northwest end; the park can only be reached by boat or via the hiking trail from Devina Dr.

Activities

For good **scuba diving** near Galiano, head to Alcala Point, home to friendly wolf eels; the anemone walls at Race Point and Baines Bay; a swim-through cave at Matthews Point; and the sunken Point Grey tugboat. For gear and tours, contact Galiano Island Diving (☎ 250-539-3109), 1005 Devina Dr, or Lead Foot Diving & Water Sports (☎ 250-539-5341 or 888-609-6924), at Montague Marina. Lead Foot also offers one-hour **harbor tours** for $15/12 adults/seniors and children six to 14.

Kayaking is terrific off Galiano Island. Gulf Island Kayaking (☎ 250-539-2442), at Montague Marina, specializes in half-day trips (about $40) and two- to seven-day camping tours (starting at $155 without meals, $245 fully catered). The Sutil Lodge (☎ 888-539-2930) provides kayak rentals, lessons, and guided tours starting as low as $20.

If you're here for **horseback riding**, Bodega Resort (☎ 250-539-2677) offers 75-minute trail rides year-round, weather permitting, for $20 per person. You must make reservations. The island's narrow, hilly roads make **cycling** a challenge, but if you're up for it, rent bikes at Galiano Bicycle Rental & Repair (☎ 250-539-9906), 36 Burrill Rd near Sturdies Bay. For something different, try the **scooter** rentals ($22 per hour) at Montague Marina.

Places to Stay

Montague Harbour Provincial Marine Park (☎ 250-391-2300), about 9.5km from the Sturdies Bay ferry terminal, includes 25 primitive drive-in and 15 walk-in campsites for $15 each. To make reservations, call ☎ 800-689-9025 (or 604-689-9025 in Greater Vancouver).

Idyllic Arts Retreats

Galiano Island offers two unusual retreats for travelers hooked on books or cinema. Bibliophiles should enjoy the Weekends for Readers, hosted by the legendary Celia Duthie, now retired from the Vancouver bookstore that bears her name. Held at the Bodega Resort, these weekends allow ample time for avid book lovers to read and talk about beloved (or not-so-beloved) tomes. Each features a noted author, with past guests including mystery writer William Deverell, poet Susan Musgrave and writer/designer Barbara Hodgson. A readers' weekend costs $300/500 single/double occupancy, with most meals provided. For more information, call ☎ 250-539-2764 or visit the Web site www.duthiebooks.com/galiano.

The Gulf Islands Film & Television School bills itself as a 'film, video and animation boot camp.' Mainly, it offers courses for kids ages 10 to 19, but adults, too, can sign up for weeklong programs in drama and documentary filmmaking. Every student leaves with a complete, original video. The cost is $595 plus $245 for room and board. For details, call ☎ 250-539-3290 or see GIFTS' Web site at www.youthfilms.com.

There are no hostels on Galiano, but at *Glenn Gulch Farm* (☎ 250-539-5218, ggfarm @island.net, 1721 Porlier Pass Rd), you can exchange six hours of chores at a working organic farm for basic bed and board. Call ahead or just stop by. Even if you don't stay here, you can drop by the farm to stock up on fresh produce, free-range poultry and pork, cut flowers and more.

Galiano has quite a few B&Bs. One of the oldest, *Sutil Lodge* (☎ 250-539-2930, 888-539-2930, reservations@gulfislands.com, 637 Southwind Dr) dates from the 1920s. Since it's near the beach at Montague Harbour, the lodge offers free use of canoes, plus on-site kayak rentals. Rates start at $60/75 single/double. Ask about the spring package ($89 per person), which includes two nights' lodging, breakfast and a four-hour guided kayak tour.

The plush rooms at *Galiano Lodge* (☎ 250-539-3388, 877-530-3939, galianolodge @gulfislands.com, 134 Madrona Dr) are among the best deals on Galiano. They all include fireplaces, patios and a continental breakfast buffet (but no TVs, phones or housekeeping services) for $75 to $150. A few simpler rooms outside the main lodge cost $50. Just a five-minute walk from the ferry terminal, the lodge offers beach access.

The two-story log cottages at *Bodega Resort* (☎ 250-539-2677, 120 Cook Rd) can sleep up to six people. The fully furnished cottages start at $80 double occupancy, plus $20 per extra adult or $10 per child. Two rooms in the main lodge go for $40/60, including breakfast. Innkeepers Barb Geary and Steve Ocsko are friendly folks; Steve also is a talented stone carver whose works adorn the grounds. You'll find plenty of hiking and horseback riding here, and children will enjoy watching the sheep.

The *Woodstone Country Inn* (☎ 250-539-2022, 888-339-2022, 743 Georgeson Bay Rd) offers Galiano's most upscale accommodations, with 12 big rooms that start at $110/120. Most come with fireplaces.

Places to Eat

Arrive early at the ferry so you can sample the delicious Indonesian and German food – yes, that's right – offered by *Max & Moritz Spicy Island Food House* (☎ 250-539-5888). Dishes include pita breakfast sandwiches ($2.50 to $4.50), Berliner currywurst ($3.50) and the awesome ayam bumbu kacang ($7.50), a grilled chicken breast with peanut sauce, rice and veggies. Bring your own plate (or cup, for drinks) and get 25¢ off.

The *Hummingbird Pub* (☎ 250-539-5472, 47 Sturdies Bay Rd) features live entertainment on summer weekends and an outdoor picnic and barbecue area. Get a fish-and-chips picnic to go for $10.

At the other end of the spectrum, the **Woodstone Country Inn** (see Places to Stay, above) offers fine dining, with three-course dinners for $22 to $29. You must make reservations. Another upscale choice, *La Berengerie* (☎ 250-539-5392), on Montague Rd just east of Clanton Dr, serves four-course West Coast–influenced French dinners for $25. Meals are offered weekends only; call ahead for reservations.

Getting There & Around

BC Ferries (☎ 250-386-3431 or 888-223-3779) serves Sturdies Bay on the island's east side. Boats bound for Galiano leave twice daily from Tsawwassen; reservations are essential for the Friday-evening and Saturday-morning boats. Ferries from Swartz Bay arrive at Galiano four times a day. There's also service between Galiano and Salt Spring, Mayne and the Pender Islands.

Go Galiano Island Shuttle (☎ 250-539-0202) meets the ferries daily in July and August and on weekends in May, June and September. Rides cost $3 per person between Sturdies Bay and Montague Harbour. (Dogs ride free!) The shuttle also makes a run to and from the Hummingbird Pub each evening ($4 roundtrip), in addition to offering standard taxi service around the island.

Fraser Valley

The Fraser Valley takes its name from Simon Fraser, who explored the river that now bears his name in 1808. (See the boxed text 'They Charted BC' in the Facts about British Columbia chapter.) Most travelers rip through the Fraser Valley, eager to get to Vancouver and points west or the Rockies to the east. But the valley's small towns, deep canyons, wild rivers and accessible wilderness areas deserve a closer look; many make excellent day or weekend trips from Vancouver.

Two roads parallel the Fraser River on its final flow to the ocean. The Trans-Canada Hwy (Hwy 1) south of the river handles most of the traffic; although occasionally scenic, it's mostly a no-nonsense, limited-access freeway. Hwy 7, by contrast, meanders

Highlights

- Exploring history at the Kilby Store & Farm or Fort Langley

- White-water rafting on the rapids of the Fraser, Chilliwack, Thompson or Nahatlatch Rivers

- Camping and hiking at Golden Ears or Manning Provincial Parks

- Taking a leisurely country drive on the meandering Hwy 7

through farmland and small towns north of the Fraser for one of the Lower Mainland's prettiest drives. At Hope, Hwy 1 becomes the slow road, heading north through the Fraser River Canyon. Towns and parks in this chapter are listed roughly west to east, then north from Hope.

GOLDEN EARS PROVINCIAL PARK

Although dwarfed in size by Garibaldi Provincial Park to its north, 55,900-hectare Golden Ears Provincial Park (☎ 604-924-2400) is still among BC's largest. The park was named for Mt Blanshard's twin peaks, which sometimes seem to glow in the sun. Golden Ears is just north of Maple Ridge, about an hour's drive from Vancouver via the Lougheed Hwy (Hwy 7). No road runs between the adjacent Golden Ears and Garibaldi Parks, which are separated by mountains.

Lovely Alouette Lake, once a Native fishing area, is Golden Ears' centerpiece. Here you'll enjoy good opportunities for fishing, as well as canoeing, windsurfing and water-skiing.

Hikers of all abilities should find a trail to suit them. If time is short, stroll along the Spirea Nature Trail, on the right side of the main park road before the Alouette Lake turnoffs. Longer trails include the strenuous Alouette Mountain Trail (10km, five hours one-way, 1000m elevation change); the easier Alouette Valley Trail (7km, three hours one-way, little elevation gain); and the popular Lower Falls Trail along Gold Creek (2.7km, one hour one-way, minimal elevation change), with a 10m waterfall and good sunbathing spots along the way.

Golden Ears contains about 400 campsites ($18.50) at its Alouette and Gold Creek Campgrounds, both on Alouette Lake. Reservations are a good idea on summer weekends; call ☎ 800-689-9025 (☎ 604-689-9025 in Greater Vancouver). Backcountry camping is also permitted ($5 per person).

FRASER VALLEY

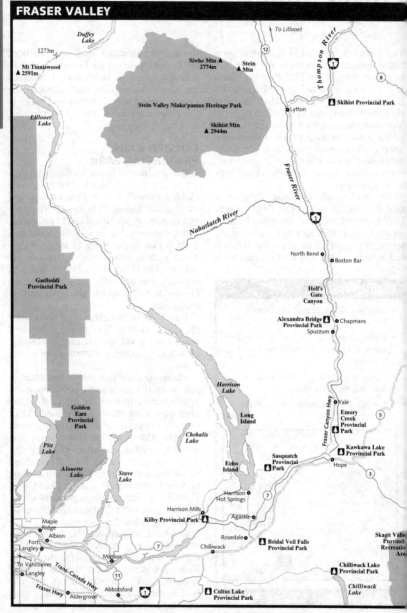

To Lillooet

Thompson River

Duffey Lake

1273m

Mt Tinniswood
▲ 2591m

Siwhe Mtn ▲
2774m   ▲ Stein Mtn

Skihist Provincial Park

Lillooet Lake

Stein Valley Nlaka'pamux Heritage Park

Skihist Mtn
▲ 2944m

Lytton

Fraser River

Nahatlatch River

Garibaldi Provincial Park

North Bend   ● Boston Bar

Hell's Gate Canyon

Alexandra Bridge   ● Chapmans
Provincial Park
Spuzzum

Harrison Lake

Long Island

Golden Ears Provincial Park

Yale

Emory Creek Provincial Park

Chehalis Lake

Pitt Lake

Echo Island

Sasquatch Provincial Park

Kawkawa Lake Provincial Park

Alouette Lake

Stave Lake

Hope

Harrison Hot Springs

Maple Ridge

Albion

Fort Langley

Harrison Mills

Kilby Provincial Park

Agassiz ●

Rosedale ●

Bridal Veil Falls Provincial Park

Skagit Valley Provincial Recreation Area

To Vancouver   Trans-Canada Hwy

Langley

Mission

Chilliwack

Chilliwack Lake Provincial Park

Fraser Hwy   Aldergrove

Abbotsford

Cultus Lake Provincial Park

Chilliwack Lake

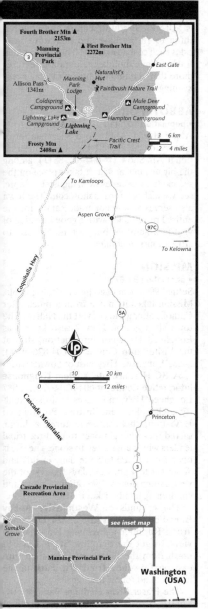

LANGLEY & FORT LANGLEY

Your basic sprawling suburb, Langley (population 83,173) nonetheless boasts one cool attraction: the 19-screen Famous Players Colossus Langley movie theater (☎ 604-513-8747), 200 St at Hwy 1, which looks like a spaceship ready to launch. The lobby resembles the bridge of a spacecraft. Patrons buy tickets from 'aliens' and enjoy drinks at a cocktail lounge called 'The Pod.' High-tech and interactive games round out the entertainment offerings.

Fort Langley (pop 2,578) is something else again, as picturesque a village as you'll find on the Lower Mainland. You can while away a fine afternoon by exploring Fort Langley's museums and shops. For information, stop by the old Canadian National Railway station at the north end of town or call ☎ 604-888-1477.

Fort Langley National Historic Site

On November 19, 1858, James Douglas stood in the Big House here and read the proclamation creating the colony of British Columbia. So Fort Langley (☎ 604-513-4777) can stake a solid claim to being the birthplace of BC, and this is one of only a handful of national historic sites in the province.

Fort Langley's importance dates back even farther than 1858. In 1827, 25 Hudson's Bay Company employees established a trading post downstream of the present fort site. From the start, they were a multicultural lot: British, Hawaiian, French Canadian, Métis and Iroquois. They worked together (and with the local Stolo Salishan people) to supply the already-established First Nations trading network with furs, blankets, tools and farm produce, the latter raised right at the fort.

The fort was moved to its existing site in 1839. It burned down the next year but was swiftly rebuilt. Today, the site contains seven buildings, including one – the 1840s storehouse – that is an original. A 10-minute video explains the post's history. While you're here, you should also take time to view the excellent collection of prints by artist Paul Kane, who traveled to the Pacific

Northwest in the 1840s to record the ways of the region's First Nations tribes just before the influx of European settlers changed the Natives forever. Kane's work is every bit the equal of the much better known US painter George Catlin.

Fort Langley National Historic Site, 23433 Mavis Ave just east of Glover Rd (the main street in Fort Langley), is open 10 am to 5 pm daily March through November. Admission is $4/3/2 for adults/seniors/children six to 16. (Children five and under get in free.) The fort hosts several special events each year, including an old-fashioned Canada Day bash on July 1. On the first weekend in August, the observance of BC Day includes Brigade Days, which feature a campout by historical re-enactors and an arts festival.

Places to Stay & Eat

You'll find chain hotels near Hwy 1 in Langley, but for a more memorable stay, go to Fort Langley. *Fort Camping Resorts* (☎ *604-888-3678, 9451 Glover Rd*), on an island in the Fraser River, includes a pool, playground, showers and laundry. Rates start at $18.

Eagle's Reach Bed & Breakfast (☎ *604-888-4470, 800-393-9888, fax 604-888-4773, eagles@istar.ca, 24658 87 Ave*) enjoys river and mountain views and offers a three-course breakfast. Rooms start at $70/90 single/double.

Also in Fort Langley, *Wendel's Books & Fresh Food Café* (☎ *604-513-2238, 103-9233 Glover Rd*) offers a daily breakfast ($4 to $7), plus sandwiches, wraps and quesadillas ($6 to $7). If you're just in the mood for a light snack, you can order coffee drinks, fruit smoothies and baked goods. A block or so away, the *Lampliter Gallery Café* (☎ *604-888-6464, 9213 Glover Rd*) offers a slightly more formal experience for lunch and dinner.

ALDERGROVE

• **population 9500**

The **Greater Vancouver Zoological Centre** (☎ 604-857-9005), 5048 264 St, houses more than 900 animals from about 200 species,

including rhinos, lions, tigers, elephants and apes. It's open 9 am to dusk daily; admission is $10.50/7.50 adults/seniors and children three to 15. Parking and miniature train rides each cost an extra $2. The zoo's annual 'Lights Alive' holiday celebration features more than a million lights on display every evening in December.

ABBOTSFORD

• **population 107,410**

Along Hwy 1, Abbotsford attracts a lot of visitors for the annual Abbotsford International Air Show (☎ 604-852-8511), among the biggest in Canada. It takes place on the second full weekend each August. For more, see www.abbotsfordairshow.com. The town also serves as a major trade center for the entire Fraser Valley, with a good selection of visitor amenities but not much else to attract tourism dollars.

MISSION

• **population 31,677**

Settled 9000 years ago by the Stolo people, Mission takes its name from a much later Catholic attempt to convert the Natives. The town sits right on Hwy 7, also known as Lougheed Hwy. For information, stop at the Visitor Info Centre (☎ 604-826-6914), 34033 Lougheed Hwy, east of downtown.

A BC Heritage site, **Xaytem Longhouse Interpretive Centre** (☎ 604-820-9725), 35087 Lougheed Hwy, showcases Stolo spirituality, archaeology and history. Pronounced HAY-tum, the center features a large, sacred rock, thought once to be three tribal leaders who were turned to stone. The site is open from 10 am to 5 pm daily in July and August, 2 to 4 pm weekdays the rest of the year. Admission is $6/5 adults/seniors and children. A family ticket is $13.

The grounds of **Westminster Abbey** Benedictine monastery, 33224 Dewdney Trunk Rd, offer a sweeping Fraser Valley view. To get there, follow Stave Lake St north from the Lougheed Hwy, then turn east on Dewdney Trunk Rd. Park in the main lot and follow the signs.

The **Fraser River Heritage Park** (☎ 604-826-0277), off Stave Lake Rd just north of

Crossing the Fraser

The farther you venture up the Fraser Valley, the more you'll want to think about the spots where you can cross the river, since there aren't many. Hwy 1 fords the Fraser south of Coquitlam. The next crossing opportunity to the east is the free Albion ferry between Fort Langley, on the south bank, and Maple Ridge, on the north. The boat runs every 15 minutes between about 6 am and 10:30 pm, then every half hour until about 1 am. During midday, you'll probably have to watch one or two sailings before your turn comes; at rush hours (around 8 am and 5 pm), the wait may be longer. A snack bar helps travelers whittle away the spare time.

You'll find another bridge on Hwy 11 between Abbotsford and Mission, and one more between Rosedale and Agassiz. This span provides access to Harrison Hot Springs, and it's the last crossing until the Trans-Canada Hwy (Hwy 1) swings north just west of Hope.

the Lougheed Hwy, features outdoor concerts Wednesday and Friday evenings June through August. The grounds also include a hilltop restaurant. Mission Raceway Park (☎ 604-826-6315), off London Ave just west of the bridge to Abbotsford, features **drag racing** April through October.

HARRISON MILLS
• population 100

A worthwhile stop, this crossroads town off Hwy 7, about 40km east of Mission, contains the **Kilby Store & Farm**, best known for its restored (and truly impressive) 1920s general store. Other delights here include a parlor where you can work a jigsaw puzzle, a barnyard full of farm animals, a playground and a tearoom with lunch and snack fare (mostly $2 to $6). While you're here, try on some period clothing. Kilby is open 11 am to 5 pm daily. Admission is $6/5/3 for adults/seniors/children six to 14; a family pass costs $16. Guided tours are available for parties of five or more for an extra $1 per person; call ahead to arrange.

You'll find about 21 campsites ($12) at nearby **Kilby Provincial Park** (☎ 604-824-2300). This beautiful spot right on Harrison Bay contains a boat launch.

HARRISON HOT SPRINGS
• population 1060

Set on expansive Harrison Lake, once a shortcut to the Cariboo gold fields, Harrison Hot Springs has been a resort area since the 1880s. It also occupies a prominent place in local mythology: rumor has it that Sasquatch, or 'Bigfoot,' lives here. Indeed, many visitors to the region have claimed to see the hairy creature stomping around the backcountry.

Many area hotels pipe in mineral water from the local springs, but campers or others not sleeping in town can soak their weary bones at the indoor **Harrison Public Pool**, open 9 am to 9 pm daily. Admission is $7/5 adults/children. The Visitor Info Centre (☎ 604-796-3425), 499 Hot Springs Rd, is open May through October.

Places to Stay & Eat

Sasquatch Provincial Park (☎ 604-824-2300), 6km north of Harrison Hot Springs via Hwy 7, contains 177 sites ($12). Close to the town beach, **Bigfoot Campgrounds** (☎ 604-796-9767, 800-294-9907, 670 Hot Springs Rd) features showers, laundry facilities and sites that start at $15.

The modest **Glencoe Motel & RV Park** (☎ 604-796-2574, fax 604-796-9572, glencoe2 @uniserve.com, 259 Hot Springs Rd) offers campsites ($16 to $20) and motel rooms ($45/50). **Quality Hotel-Harrison** (☎ 604-796-5555, 888-265-1155, fax 604-796-3731, sales@harrisonhotsprings.com, 190 Lillooet Ave) offers basic rooms ($90 and up) and whirlpool rooms (starting at $130). The high-rise **Harrison Hot Springs Resort** (☎ 604-796-2244, 800-663-2266, fax 604-796-3682, info@harrisonresort.com, 100 Esplanade) features its own outdoor mineral pools and rooms for $150 and up.

If you're craving a quick bite, try the snack bars and cafés at the Harrison Village Mall plaza. *Ashoka Canadian & Indian Cuisine* (☎ *604-796-5555)*, in the Quality Inn, offers a 21-item buffet for about $12. Not far from town at the junction of Hwys 7 and 9, the sunny yellow *Giggleberry Station* (☎ *604-796-5505)* serves breakfast and lunch (mostly $4 to $6).

CHILLIWACK & AROUND
• population 62,582

Farmland, rivers and lakes surround Chilliwack, on Hwy 1 about 100km east of Vancouver, making the area a big outdoor playground. For information on recreation opportunities, inquire at the Visitor Info Centre (☎ 604-858-8121), 44150 Luckakuck Way (Hwy 1 exit 116), which is open year-round.

Hyak Wilderness Adventures (☎ 604-734-5718, 800-663-7238) and Chilliwack River Rafting (☎ 604-824-0334, 800-410-7238) offer **white-water rafting** trips on the Chilliwack River, parts of which can be floated year-round.

Cultus Lake, 8km south of Chilliwack via Vedder Rd, is a good spot for sunbathing and more serene water sports. Cultus Lake Canoe Rentals (☎ 604-858-8841) rents canoes, kayaks and paddleboats on the main beach. For good camping ($18.50) and hiking, go to **Cultus Lake Provincial Park**; popular treks include Teapot Hill Trail (5km, two hours roundtrip) and the Giant Douglas Fir Trail (45 minutes roundtrip).

A pretty cascade of water tumbles over the rocks at the 122m **Bridal Veil Falls**, east of Chilliwack on Hwy 1 exit 135. Water slides and theme parks surround the falls. The more subdued **Minter Gardens** (☎ 604-794-7191), at the junction of the Trans-Canada Hwy and Hwy 9, features specialty plantings and a maze.

HOPE
• population 7000

Established as a Hudson's Bay Company fort, Hope remains a major hub for the Fraser Valley. Hwys 1, 3 and 5 converge here, and a number of reasonably priced restaurants and motels have sprung up near the crossroads.

Hope's biggest asset is its scenic river setting, with mountain views all around. Ironically, though, city planners established riverside **Centennial Park** near the city center, then planted so many trees and hedges that visitors can see neither the river nor many of the mountain peaks. Tourism officials say the hedges are a windbreak, but we think they ought to grab a machete and reveal the river vistas, if only in a few places.

From Hope, the toll road Coquihalla Hwy (Hwy 5) heads north to Kamloops. You'll find few service stations along the way, so leave with a full tank. The Crowsnest Hwy (Hwy 3) sweeps south through Manning Provincial Park on its way to the Okanagan Valley.

Information
The Visitor Info Centre (☎ 604-869-2021), 919 Water Ave, is open 9 am to 5 pm daily; there are helpful information kiosks outside if you arrive after hours.

For regular mail, go to the post office, 777 Fraser Ave. To check email, go to Erica Press (☎ 604-869-5678), 366-C Wallace St. You'll find the Fraser Valley Regional Library (☎ 604-869-2313) at 1011 6th Ave. Do laundry at Speedie Laundromat (☎ 604-869-9715), 409 Wallace St. For medical help, head to Fraser Canyon Hospital (☎ 604-869-5656), 1275 7th Ave.

Things to See & Do
Local artist Pete Ryan has created two dozen or so **chainsaw carvings** around town, many of them in Memorial Park, between 3rd and 4th Aves and Park and Wallace Sts. Built in 1861, **Historic Christ Church**, at the corner of Park St and Fraser Ave, ranks among the oldest churches in BC; it's still used for regular services. The **Othello Quintette Tunnels**, a 15-minute drive east on Kawkawa Lake Rd, were cut for the Kettle Valley Railway between 1911 and 1919 and have since been featured in several movies, including *First Blood*, the

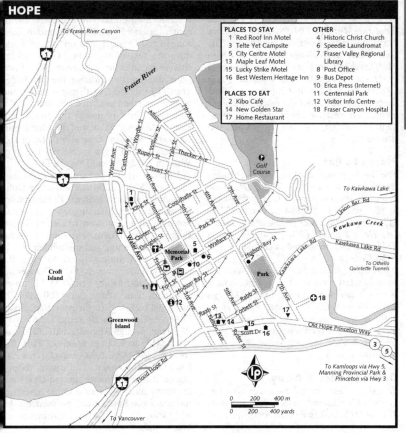

HOPE

PLACES TO STAY
1 Red Roof Inn Motel
3 Telte Yet Campsite
5 City Centre Motel
13 Maple Leaf Motel
15 Lucky Strike Motel
16 Best Western Heritage Inn

PLACES TO EAT
2 Kibo Café
14 New Golden Star
17 Home Restaurant

OTHER
4 Historic Christ Church
6 Speedie Laundromat
7 Fraser Valley Regional Library
8 Post Office
9 Bus Depot
10 Erica Press (Internet)
11 Centennial Park
12 Visitor Info Centre
18 Fraser Canyon Hospital

first 'Rambo' movie. A short drive southeast on the Crowsnest Hwy leads to the site of the 1965 Hope Slide, which killed four people after a small earthquake caused part of Johnson Peak to crumble.

Places to Stay
The Stolo First Nations band runs the *Telte Yet Campsite* (☎ 604-869-9481, 600 Water Ave), adjacent to the city's Centennial Park – and there are no hedges to block the river views here. Amenities include showers, a self-serve laundry and a small children's play area. Sites cost $12 to $19, and day

users can pitch a picnic for $3. Remember the mosquito repellent.

Hope's overabundance of motel rooms means that prices are good. The *City Centre Motel* (☎ 604-869-5411, 455 Wallace St) features big rooms with TVs and mini-fridges but no phones for $40/45 single/double. For the same price, *Lucky Strike Motel* (☎ 604-869-5715, 504 Old Hope Princeton Way) offers the same amenities plus telephones and clock radios.

You can soak in the indoor pool and hot tub at *Maple Leaf Motor Inn* (☎ 604-869-7107, fax 869-7131, 377 Old Hope Princeton

Way), where rooms cost $50/55 (a few bucks more for the kitchenettes). The *Red Roof Inn Motel* (☎ 604-869-2446, 477 Hwy 1) offers similar amenities and prices. The *Best Western Heritage Inn* (☎ 604-869-7166, fax 869-7106, 570 Old Hope Princeton Way) serves people who want to spend $99/109 for a room not much nicer than those available at half the price. Amenities include an exercise room and spa, continental breakfast, in-room fridges and on-site laundry.

Places to Eat
The basic home cooking at the *Home Restaurant* (☎ 604-869-5558, 665 Old Hope Princeton Way) is popular for breakfast ($5 to $8), lunch ($5 to $8) and dinner ($7 to $12). *New Golden Star* (☎ 604-869-9588, 377 Old Hope Princeton Way) features a wide Chinese menu; most dishes cost $6 to $11. *Kibo Café* (☎ 604-869-7317, 267 King St), a smart little place, offers Japanese food for $6 to $13. Eat outside if the weather is nice. A few kilometers outside town, *Skinny's Grille* (☎ 604-869-5713, 63810 Flood Hope Rd) features a creative menu (main dishes include a Greek phyllo pastry or Sole Neptune, each $12) and occasional live entertainment as well.

Getting There & Away
Five daily buses from Vancouver arrive at Hope's Greyhound depot, 833 3rd Ave. The fare is $19/37 one-way/roundtrip.

MANNING PROVINCIAL PARK
This 70,000-hectare park (☎ 250-840-8836), about 30km southeast of Hope via Hwy 3, ranks among BC's most popular and highly developed provincial parks. It provides a habitat for more than 200 species of birds plus abundant mammals; you're almost certain to see black bears (but no grizzlies) here. Manning also marks the usual end of the 4240km **Pacific Crest Trail** from Mexico to Canada via the Sierra and Cascade Mountains in the US. PCT through-hikers can often be found swapping tales inside the Bear's Den pub in the Manning Park Resort in September and October.

Interpretive hikes and programs abound for information, stop at the park visitor center (open 8:30 am to 4:30 pm daily, mid-June to mid-October; 8:30 am to 4 pm weekdays the rest of the year). Good hiking choices include the Lightning Lake Loop (9km, 2½ hours roundtrip); the Dry Ridge Trail (40 minutes), with great views and wildflowers; the Paintbrush Nature Trail (20 minutes), which begins at the Naturalist's Hut on Blackwall Peak; and the wheelchair-accessible Sumallo Grove Trail (about 25 minutes), lined by impressive stands of Western red cedar and Douglas fir.

You can fly-fish for trout in Lightning Flash and Strike Lakes or angle for Dolly Varden in the Sumallo River. Prime country for winter sports, Manning features a small downhill ski and snowboard area at Gibson Pass and about 100km of groomed trails for cross-country skiing and snowshoeing.

Plenty of people stay outdoors at the park's four campgrounds ($12 at Coldspring, Hampton and Mule, $18.50 at Lightning Lake); for reservations, call ☎ 800-689-9025 or ☎ 604-689-9025 in Greater Vancouver. Others opt for a comfy room (about $100 mid-June through August), chalet ($105) or cabin ($135 to $200) at *Manning Park Resort* (☎ 250-840-8822, 800-330-3321, fax 250-840-8848). The chalets and cabins, though placed in an unfortunate parking-lot setting, are nicely furnished inside. Other amenities include a good restaurant, horseback rides and canoe, kayak, rowboat and mountain-bike rentals.

Greyhound buses stop four times daily at Manning Park. The fare from Vancouver is $30/60 one-way/roundtrip.

FRASER RIVER CANYON
North of Hope, Hwy 1 heads into the impressive steep-sided scenery of the Fraser River Canyon, with plenty of places to stop and enjoy the view.

Founded by the Hudson's Bay Company, **Yale** (pop 300) marked the farthest point that paddle wheelers could go during the gold rush days; it also was a major work camp during construction of the Canadian Pacific Railway. The Yale Museum (☎ 604-

863-2324) is open 10 am to 5 pm daily, May to September. Admission is $4.50/3.50/2.50 for adults/seniors/children six to 14; a family pass costs $12. Gold-panning and walking tours cost a few dollars more.

At **Alexandra Bridge Provincial Park**, 1km north of the town of Spuzzum, an open-grate suspension bridge, built in 1926, spans the Fraser River. It's free to cross, and the area makes a nice picnic spot.

Hell's Gate Airtram (☎ 604-867-9277), 31km north of Yale in Hell's Gate Canyon, is a tourist trap to be sure, but fun nonetheless. If you look beyond the many gift shops, you'll find genuinely educational displays on Simon Fraser's 1808 passage through the canyon and on modern-day salmons' struggle to swim upriver to their ancestral spawning grounds. Come in May or June, when the fast-running Fraser rumbles beneath the Airtram and bridge. If you eat inside the Salmon House Restaurant (entrees $4.25 to $12.50), ask for a window table, where you might see humming-birds flit about in the greenery outside. The Airtram is open 9 am to 6 pm daily, mid-June through early September, with slightly shorter hours the rest of its season (April through October). Admission is $10/8.50/6.50 for adults/seniors/children six to 18; a family pass costs $26.50.

LYTTON
• population 366

Lytton marks the spot where the clear-running Thompson River meets the cloudy Fraser. It's a major outfitting point for rafting trips, as well as the gateway to the Stein Valley. The helpful staff at the Visitor Info Centre (☎ 250-455-2523), 400 Fraser St, offers heaps of information on area recreation. While you're there, stop in at the town's small museum next door. Also worth a look are the fine Native crafts at the Siska Art Gallery and Museum (☎ 250-455-2219), off Hwy 1 south of town.

Stein Valley Nlaka'pamux Heritage Park

Considered the last major unlogged wilderness in southwestern BC, this area gained provincial protection in 1995; it's jointly managed by BC Parks and the Lytton First Nations. To immerse yourself in the woods, you can hike eight to 10 days down the demanding 80km-long valley from Lytton to Lizzie Lake near Pemberton, or simply enjoy some good day hikes from the Lytton end. Stop at the Lytton Visitor Info Centre for a map and directions to the trailhead, which is accessed by a free ferry over the Fraser; the boat runs continually from 6:30 am to 10:15 pm daily. If you plan a through-hike, pick up a copy of the *Stein Valley Wilderness Guidebook* by Gordon R White at the Lytton visitor center.

White-Water Rafting

One-day trips on the popular Fraser and Thompson Rivers cost about $85 to $100 per adult. Lytton-based Kumsheen Raft Adventures (☎ 800-663-6667) offers both power trips (where you hang onto a motorized, wildly bucking raft) and paddle trips (where you dig in and help propel the raft through the rapids). Either way, you'll get soaked. Other area outfitters, most of which shun motorized trips, include Fraser River Raft Expeditions (☎ 800-363-7238) and REO Rafting Adventure Resort (☎ 800-736-7238), both of which run the lesser-known but very fast Nahatlatch River near Boston Bar; Hellsgate Rafting Adventures

(☎ 888-434-2837); and Hyak River Rafting (☎ 800-663-7238).

Places to Stay & Eat

Skihist Provincial Park (☎ 604-851-3000), on Hwy 1 east of Lytton, features 56 sites ($15) and a hiking trail with good views of the Thompson River Canyon. *Kumsheen Rafting Resort* (☎ 250-455-2296), 6km east of Lytton, rents campsites ($6 to $9 per person) or furnished cabin tents that can sleep up to four people ($79). You can eat at the restaurant here, too.

Indoor accommodations in Lytton include budget-priced rooms at the *Totem Motel & Lodge* (☎ 250-455-2321, fax 455-6696, 320 Fraser St) and the *Braeden Lodge Motel* (☎ 250-455-2334, 800-732-5392, 223 Main St).

Stop's (☎ 250-455-2101, 520 Main St) offers email access and packs picnics to go for about $5.

Getting There & Away

Greyhound buses stop in Lytton twice daily from each direction. The fare from Vancouver is $35/70 one-way/roundtrip.

Thompson-Okanagan

Summer travelers coming to this region from the Lower Mainland marvel at the seemingly impossible shift in climate, especially in the dry, hot Okanagan Valley. Put away your raincoat and bust out the shorts – just when you thought it wasn't going to happen, wham-o – you find summer. This fertile valley, dominated by orchards, wineries and warm lakes, gets more than 2000 hours of sunshine a year. When it rains, it doesn't last long and the splash is actually refreshing after you've spent days lolling around on the hot beach. Three 'sister cities' – Penticton, Kelowna and Vernon – attract the majority of visitors. Like migrating birds, tourists and British Columbians alike flock here in summer – to sip wine, play golf, hike or mountain bike in the dry hills, or simply flake out on one of the many sandy beaches. In winter, when dry, fluffy snow falls, the climate stays mild, the sun still shines and snow sports take over.

The Thompson Valley follows the three stems of the great Thompson River, past trout-filled lakes, cattle ranches and lovely lolling valleys. Kamloops, at the north end of the Coquihalla Hwy (Hwy 5), is the major service junction, with highways sprouting in all directions.

The Thompson-Okanagan territory falls under the Kamloops Forest Region, comprised of seven separate districts: Clearwater, Kamloops, Lillooet, Merritt, Penticton, Salmon Arm and Vernon. For topographic maps and backcountry trail and camping information, contact the Kamloops Forest Region (☎ 250-828-4131, fax 828-4154), 515 Columbia St in Kamloops. You can also visit the Ministry of Forests' Web site, www.for.gov.bc.ca.

Highlights

- Eating a freshly picked Penticton peach
- Discovering Okanagan Valley wineries
- Mountain biking on the abandoned Kettle Valley Railway
- Ripping and shredding on the slopes at Apex, Big White and Sun Peaks
- Singing and dancing at the annual Kamloops Powwow
- Swimming in Shuswap Lake, then napping on the white-sand beach

Okanagan Valley

The Okanagan, which runs about 180km north-south between the Monashee Mountains in the east and the Cascade Mountains in the west, is one of many beautiful valleys carved out by glaciers. Long ago, the valley bottom was filled with water, but over time, land shifted and water evaporated, creating a series of lakes, the longest of which is Okanagan Lake. The valley gets little rain and lots of sunshine, making it a vacation hotspot for anyone tired of mountain and coastal rain.

The Okanagan is a significant retirement center, attracting seniors from across Canada. This, in some measure, is responsible for the large growth of Kelowna, Penticton and Vernon, the area's major towns, all of which show unfortunate signs of growing pains. The downtown cores and beaches are

259

THOMPSON-OKANAGAN

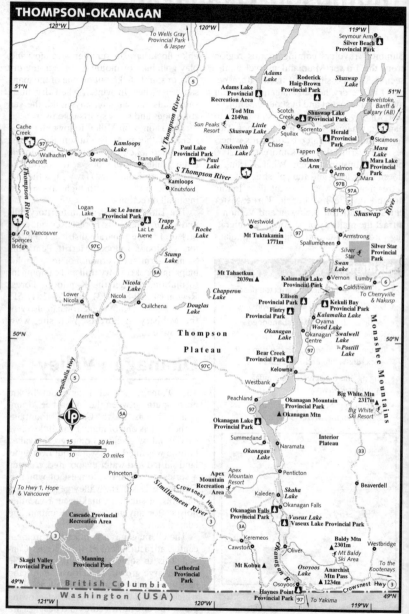

THOMPSON-OKANAGAN

120°W · 120°W · 119°W

To Wells Gray
Provincial Park
& Jasper

Seymour Arm
Silver Beach
Provincial Park

51°N

Adams
Lake

Roderick
Haig-Brown
Provincial Park

Shuswap
Lake

Adams Lake
Provincial
Recreation Area

51°N

To Revelstoke,
Banff &
Calgary (AB)

Tod Mtn
2149m

Scotch
Creek

Shuswap Lake
Provincial Park

Sun Peaks
Resort

Little
Shuswap Lake

Squilax

Sorrento

Herald
Provincial
Park

Sicamous

Cache
Creek

Kamloops
Lake

Paul Lake
Provincial Park

Niskonlith
Lake

Chase

Tappen

Mara
Lake

Mara Lake
Provincial Park

Walhachin

Tranquille

Paul
Lake

Salmon
Arm

Salmon
Arm

Mara

Ashcroft

Savona

S Thompson River

97B

97A

Kamloops

Knutsford

Enderby

Shuswap

Thompson River

Logan
Lake

Lac Le Juene
Provincial Park

Trapp
Lake

Roche
Lake

Westwold

Mt Tuktakamin
1771m

Spallumcheen

Armstrong

97

Silver Star
Provincial
Park

To Vancouver

Spences
Bridge

97C

Lac Le
Juene

Silver
Star

Swan
Lake

5

Stump
Lake

Mt Tahaetkun
2039m

Kalamalka Lake
Provincial Park

Vernon

Lumby

6

5A

Nicola
Lake

Chapperon
Lake

Ellison
Provincial Park

Fintry
Provincial Park

Kekuli Bay
Provincial Park

Coldstream

To Cherryville
& Nakusp

Lower
Nicola

Nicola

Quilchena

Douglas
Lake

Kalamalka Lake

Oyama

Wood Lake

Merritt

Thompson

Okanagan
Lake

Okanagan
Centre

Swalwell
Lake

Monashee

50°N

Plateau

Bear Creek
Provincial Park

Postill
Lake

50°N

Coquihalla Hwy

97C

Kelowna

5

Westbank

Big White Mtn
2317m

Mountains

Peachland

97

Okanagan Mountain
Provincial Park

Big White
Ski Resort

Okanagan Mtn

5A

Okanagan Lake
Provincial Park

Summerland

Naramata

Interior
Plateau

33

0   15   30 km

0   10   20 miles

Okanagan
Lake

Princeton

Apex
Mountain
Recreation
Area

Apex
Mountain
Resort

Penticton

Beaverdell

To Hwy 1, Hope
& Vancouver

Crowsnest Hwy

Kaleden

Skaha
Lake

Simikameen River

3

Okanagan Falls
Provincial Park

Okanagan Falls

Cascade Provincial
Recreation Area

3A

Vaseux Lake

Vaseux Lake Provincial Park

Skagit Valley
Provincial Park

Manning
Provincial Park

Keremeos

Baldy Mtn
2301m

Westbridge

Cawston

Oliver

Mt Baldy
Ski Area

To the
Kootenays

Cathedral
Provincial
Park

Mt Kobau

Osoyoos
Lake

Anarchist
Mtn Pass
1234m

Crowsnest Hwy

3

49°N

British Columbia

Osoyoos

Haynes Point
Provincial Park

97

To Yakima

49°N

Washington (USA)

121°W · 120°W · 119°W

still intact, but outlying areas are often dominated by strip malls, superstores and other signs of urban sprawl.

But the region remains incredibly scenic, with rolling, scrubby hills, narrow blue lakes and clear skies. Near Osoyoos, close to the US border, cactuses grow on desert slopes that receive only 250mm of rain a year. Warm lakes, fresh fruit and sandy beaches draw people to Penticton and Kelowna. Vernon, with a smaller population and fewer tourists, is surrounded by excellent provincial parks. The entire region fills with visitors in summer; throughout July and August, expect all types of accommodation to be tight.

Fruit Orchards & Vineyards

The region's fertile soil and heavy irrigation, combined with the relatively warm climate (summers tend to be hot and dry), have made the Okanagan the country's top fruit-growing area. About 100 sq km of orchards bear fruit in the region, which contains 85% of Canada's orchards.

During April and May, the entire valley comes alive with blossoms. In late summer and autumn, the orchards drip with delicious fresh fruit. Stands dotting the roads sell the best and cheapest produce in Canada.

So-called 'agri-tourism' has become very popular – you can visit farms, orchards and wineries throughout the valley. *Tours of Abundance*, a widely distributed free guide, lists the many orchards and wine tastings. The drive north along Hwy 97 from Osoyoos passes an almost endless succession of orchards, farms and fruit stands. The slow-moving tourists and retirees on this route will give you plenty of time to smell the apples, peaches, and, yes, even the roses.

If you wish to tie your trip to a specific fruit, the approximate harvest times are as follows:

fruit	harvest times
strawberries	mid-June to early July
raspberries	early July to mid-July
cherries	mid-June to mid-August
apricots	mid-July to mid-August
peaches	mid-July to mid-September
pears	mid-August to late September
apples	early September to late October
grapes	early September to late October

Work There's work fruit picking; it's hard and the pay isn't great, but you don't always need a work permit and you'll meet lots of young people. You can expect to make anywhere from $48 to $185 per day, depending on the crop, the employer and whether or not you have experience (which isn't necessary). The season starts first around Osoyoos, where the weather is warmer, and moves north with the crops.

Arrive early and shop around. To get started, register at the Ki-Low-Na Friendship Society (☎ 250-763-4905), 442 Leon Ave in Kelowna. Talk to Marv Baker, who coordinates casual labor workers throughout the Okanagan.

OSOYOOS
• population 4140

Osoyoos sits at the edge of dark-blue Osoyoos Lake, amid stark, dry, rolling hills at the southern end of the Okanagan Valley. The skies are sunny, the waters warm and the air dry, which is quite a shocker if you're coming from the coast. With its hot, dry weather, the Osoyoos region produces the earliest and most varied fruit and vegetable crops in Canada. Look for roadside stands selling cherries, apricots, peaches, apples and other fruit. There are also many vineyards in the area.

The word 'Osoyoos' is a butchering of the Native word 'soyoos,' meaning 'sand bar across,' for the thin strip of land that almost cuts Osoyoos Lake in half. Why the 'O' got added is a little uncertain; some suggest that it comes from the involuntary 'oh' you gasp as you come over the hill into the scenic valley.

A small town at heart, Osoyoos has become a big resort. In 1975, in cooperation with the provincial government, the locals adopted a theme to beautify the town. Because of the climate, topography and agriculture, they chose a Spanish motif.

THOMPSON-OKANAGAN

Though the adoption wasn't an overwhelming success, some businesses and houses maintain this look.

Osoyoos' 'pocket desert,' which runs about 50km northward to Skaha Lake and stretches about 20km across at its widest point, marks the northern extension of the Mexican Sonoran Desert. The flora and fauna found here are remarkably similar to their counterparts (at 600m elevation) two borders south. Averaging less than 200mm of rain a year, the area creates prime habitat for the calliope hummingbird (the smallest bird in Canada), as well as rattlesnakes, painted turtles, coyotes, numerous species of mice and various cactuses, desert brushes and grasses. This is Canada's only desert.

In a province where all the superlatives that describe scenery work overtime, the stretch of road between Osoyoos and Penticton has to rank as one of the more deserving recipients of praise. And the scenery isn't too shabby as you head west out of town, toward the Okanagan Highlands, either.

Orientation & Information

Osoyoos is at the crossroads of Hwy 97, heading north to Penticton, and the Crowsnest Hwy (Hwy 3), running east to the Kootenay region and west to Hope. The US border, cutting through Osoyoos Lake, is just 5km to the south.

The Visitor Info Centre (☎ 250-495-7142, 888-676-9667, fax 250-495-6161) is slightly northwest of town, on the corner where the Crowsnest Hwy branches off westward from Hwy 97, next to the Husky gas station. It's open 9 am to 5 pm daily in summer, weekdays only at other times.

Things to See & Do

The Desert Centre (☎ 250-495-2470), 3km north of Osoyoos off Hwy 97, sits on 27 hectares of the Antelope Brush ecosystem, a fragile extension of the Sonora and Mojave Deserts. Estimates suggest that only 9% of this endangered ecosystem is left in the world – the rest of it has been either overgrazed, used for agriculture or turned into golf courses and housing developments for urban sun-lovers. A new facility, the Desert Centre features interpretive kiosks along raised boardwalks that meander through the dry land. Though plenty of unique animals live here – such as Great Basin pocketmice, spadefoot toads and tiger salamanders – most of them are active only at night. But during the day, you can still learn a lot, as well as hear plenty of birdsong and the occasional tickle of a rattlesnake's tale. The center offers 90-minute guided tours throughout the day; it's open 9 am to 7 pm daily in summer. Admission is $5/2 for adults/children. You'll get a shade umbrella, but bring a hat and drinking water – this is, after all, the desert. For more information about the ecosystem or the center, check out the Web site www.desert.org.

The climate makes Osoyoos Lake among the warmest lakes in the country, and every summer thousands of people lounge on the sandy beaches and splash around in the water. If you're sunburned or plain sick of the hot sun, the small Osoyoos Museum (☎ 250-495-2582), in Gyro Community Park, will fill a couple of hours with its displays on natural history, the Inkaneep people, orchards and irrigation. It's open 10 am to 3:30 pm daily from June to September; admission is $2.

If you have a car, follow Hwy 97 north to Oliver and stop off at the many wineries and fruit stands along the way (see the boxed text 'Okanagan Valley Wineries'). In winter, take the rough Camp McKinney Rd from Oliver east to the Mt Baldy Ski Area (☎ 250-498-4086), which has cross-country trails and 11 downhill runs with a vertical drop of 420m. With lift tickets only $28, it's one of the cheapest places to ski in BC.

On the south side of the Crowsnest Hwy 8km west of town, look for the spotted lake, a weird natural phenomenon. In the hot summer sun, the lake's water begins to evaporate, causing its high mineral content to crystallize, leaving white-rimmed circles of green on the water.

Three kilometers farther west along Hwy 3, look for a gravel Forest Service road that will take you to the summit of **Mt Kobau**, where you'll enjoy superb views of the town and desert to the east, the **Similkameen Valley** to the west and the US border to the south. The bumpy road to the summit is 20km long, but the views are well worth it. Amateur and professional astronomers flock here every August for the Mt Kobau Star Party, during which they set up telescopes, use red lights only and marvel at the night sky. For information, write to the Mt Kobau Astronomical Society at PO Box 20119 TCM, Kelowna, BC V1Y 9H2.

East of Osoyoos along the Crowsnest Hwy, the **Anarchist Mountain Lookout** also offers excellent views from 700m up.

Places to Stay

Camping *Haynes Point Provincial Park* (☎ *250-494-0321*), jutting into the lake 2km south of downtown, contains the most sought-after sites. In fact, short of using a shotgun you're not likely to get in until next year. However, some of the 41 sites ($18.50) are reservable through BC Parks (☎ 800-689-9025), so you might be able to nab a spot if you plan early.

A good alternative where there are usually vacancies, the *Inkaneep Campground & RV Park* (☎ *250-495-7279*) is on the Osoyoos Indian Reserve, 4km east of town. (Turn north off Hwy 3 at 45th St.) Tent sites cost $18 ($19 for a waterfront spot). You'll find laundry facilities, watersports rentals and good beach access here. It's open May to September.

On the east side of town along Lakehore Dr, you'll pass by a slew of RV parks with 'family camping only,' meaning you must be able to put up with screaming children and be in bed by 10 pm. Among them is *Cabana Beach Campground* (☎ *250-495-7705, 2231 E Lakeshore Dr*), 2.5km off Hwy 3. It rents small cabins by the week ($305 to $380) and offers tent spaces for $19.

Motels Most of the central beachside motels line motel row on Main St (Hwy 3) at the eastern end of town. Most of them drastically drop their rates from September to June. In summer, the *Adriatic Motel* (☎ *250-495-3250, 5505 Main St*) features an indoor pool and whirlpool and basic but clean rooms for $65.

At the *Richter Pass Motor Inn* (☎ *250-495-7229, 7506 Main St*), you'll pay $64 and up for newly renovated rooms, or $110 for a one-bedroom suite. Across the way, the *Desert Motor Inn* (☎ *250-495-6525, 7702 Main St*) features an outdoor pool and tidy rooms, with rates starting at $75 for a standard room and $94 for a suite.

Nearby, the *Poplars Motel* (☎ *250-495-6035, 6404 Cottonwood Dr*) rents nice rooms with kitchenettes for $85 to $140. The *Sun Beach Motel* (☎ *250-495-7766, 7303 Main St*) offers large, six-person rooms with patios starting at $100.

West of town, at the junction of Hwys 3 and 97, *Plaza Royale Motor Inn* (☎ *250-495-2633, 8010 Valiant Lane*) features standard rooms with balconies for $75/85 single/double, plus an outdoor pool.

Places to Eat

The *Osoyoos Burger House* (☎ *250-495-7686, 6910 Main St*) – actually on 62nd Ave – serves soups, sandwiches and burgers for less than $6. See if you can resist the gooey cheese aroma coming from *Mami's Pizza* (☎ *250-495-6838, 8515 Main St*). Small pizzas start at $10.

Grab a beer and a burger on the west side of town at the *Burrowing Owl Pub* (☎ *250-495-3274, 7603 Spartan Ave*), where a patio overlooks the lake. Burgers and fish and chips are $7, steaks $16. For the best food in town, head to *Campo Marina* (☎ *250-495-7650*), at the Richter Pass Motor Inn on Main St (see Places to Stay). Authentic Italian pasta dishes average $10. You can also get fish, chicken and steak. The restaurant is open for dinner only and closes on Monday.

Getting There & Away

The Greyhound station is in Chucker's Convenience Store (☎ 250-495-7252), 6615 Lakeshore Dr (Hwy 3) east of town at the east end of the motel strip. Buses run daily

Okanagan Valley Wineries

Wine lovers agree that there's nothing more wonderful than wandering around a lush orchard on a hot summer day, sipping wine and admiring the view. Well, welcome to casual connoisseur heaven. With lots of sunshine and fertile soil, the Okanagan is BC's largest and oldest wine-producing region. The area is known for its white wines, produced mostly in Kelowna and North Okanagan, and for its classic reds, made in the South Okanagan, mainly around Penticton and along the 'Golden Mile' in Oliver.

The valley celebrates its bounty twice a year. The four-day Spring Wine Festival in early May focuses on the previous year's wines, while the 10-day Fall Wine Festival in early October celebrates the harvest and crush. Pick up a copy of *Okanagan Wine Festivals* or find out more by calling ☎ 250-861-6654 or visiting www.owfs.com.

A great way to tour wineries is by bicycle, on the Tour de Vine (☎ 250-492-3600, 800-663-1900), which coincides with the Spring Wine Festival. The guided trips cost $35 (including a bag lunch) or $75 (including lunch at a winery). You can bring your own bike or rent one for $20. For more information, see www.tour devine.bc.ca.

The Okanagan Valley Wine Train (☎ 888-674-8725) departs Kelowna and takes passengers on a six-hour tour through Vernon to Armstrong. There, you'll disembark for a buffet dinner and live entertainment. The train passes many wineries but doesn't stop for tastings or tours. It runs from May to October and costs $60/70 for standard/first-class service, including dinner.

You can also tour the wine country on your own. Many wineries offer free tastings and tours, while some charge a nominal fee. Most are open to the public from May to November, during which time the valley is alive with blossoming trees and crowds of tipsy wine tasters. On the facing page is a complete list of Okanagan wineries.

Okanagan Valley Wineries

North Okanagan
Bella Vista Vineyards
(☎ 250-558-0770), 3111 Agnew Rd
in Vernon

Gray Monk Estate Winery
(☎ 250-766-3168), 1055 Camp Rd
in Okanagan Centre

Kelowna
Calona Vineyards
(☎ 250-762-3332), 1125 Richter St

CedarCreek Estate Winery
(☎ 250-764-8866), 5445 Lakeshore Rd

House of Rose
(☎ 250-765-0802), 2270 Garner Rd

Pinot Reach Cellars
(☎ 250-764-0078), 1670 Dehart Rd

Quails' Gate Estate Winery
(☎ 250-769-4451), 3303 Boucherie Rd

Slamka Cellars
(☎ 250-769-0404), 2815 Ourtoland Rd

St Hubertus Estate Winery
(☎ 250-764-7888), 5225 Lakeshore Rd

Summerhill Estate Winery
(☎ 250-764-8000), 14870 Chute Lake Rd

Mission Hill Winery
(☎ 250-768-7611), 1730 Mission Hill Rd
in Westbank

Peachland
First Estate Cellars
(☎ 250-767-9526), 5031 Cousins Rd

Hainle Vineyards Estate Winery
(☎ 250-767-2525),
5355 Trepanier Bench Rd

Summerland
Scherzinger Vineyards
(☎ 250-494-8815), 7311 Fiske St

Sumac Ridge Estate Winery
(☎ 250-494-0451), 17403 Hwy 97

Penticton
Hillside Estate
(☎ 250-493-4424), 1350 Naramata Rd

Poplar Grove Winery
(☎ 250-492-4575), 1060 Naramata Rd

Naramata
Kettle Valley Winery
(☎ 250-496-5898), 2988 Hayman Rd

Lake Breeze Vineyards
(☎ 250-496-5659), 930 Sammet Rd

Lang Vineyards
(☎ 250-496-5987), 2493 Gammon Rd

Nichol Vineyard
(☎ 250-496-5962), 1285 Smethurst Rd

Red Rooster Winery
(☎ 250-496-4041), 910 Debeck Rd

Okanagan Falls
Blue Mountain Vineyards
(☎ 250-497-8244)

Hawthorne Mountain Vineyards
(☎ 250-497-8267), Green Lake Rd

Stag's Hollow Winery & Vineyards
(☎ 250-497-6162), 2215 Sun Valley Way

Wild Goose Vineyards
(☎ 250-497-8919), Sun Valley Way

Oliver
Burrowing Owl Vineyards
(☎ 250-498-0621), 100 Burrowing Owl Place

Carriage House Wines
(☎ 250-498-8818),
32764 Black Sage Rd

Domaine Combret Estate Winery
(☎ 250-498-6966), Road No 13

Gehringer Brothers Estate Winery
(☎ 250-498-3537), Road No 8

Gersighel Wineberg
(☎ 250-495-3319), 29690 Hwy 97

Golden Mile Cellars
(☎ 250-498-8330), 14130 316A Ave

Hester Creek Estate Winery
(☎ 250-498-4435), 13163 326th St

Inniskillin Okanagan Vineyards
(☎ 250-498-6663, 800-498-6211),
Road No 11

Jackson-Triggs Vintners
(☎ 250-498-4981), 38619 Hwy 97

Tinhorn Creek Vineyards
(☎ 250-498-3743), 32830 Tinhorn
Creek Rd

THOMPSON-OKANAGAN

THOMPSON-OKANAGAN

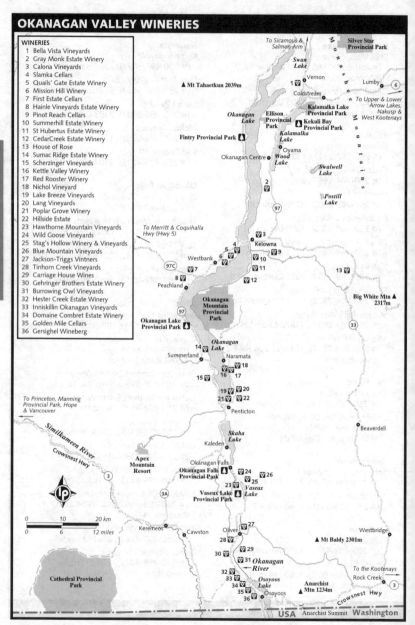

OKANAGAN VALLEY WINERIES

WINERIES
1 Bella Vista Vineyards
2 Gray Monk Estate Winery
3 Calona Vineyards
4 Slamka Cellars
5 Quails' Gate Estate Winery
6 Mission Hill Winery
7 First Estate Cellars
8 Hainle Vineyards Estate Winery
9 Pinot Reach Cellars
10 Summerhill Estate Winery
11 St Hubertus Estate Winery
12 CedarCreek Estate Winery
13 House of Rose
14 Sumac Ridge Estate Winery
15 Scherzinger Vineyards
16 Kettle Valley Winery
17 Red Rooster Winery
18 Nichol Vineyard
19 Lake Breeze Vineyards
20 Lang Vineyards
21 Poplar Grove Winery
22 Hillside Estate
23 Hawthorne Mountain Vineyards
24 Wild Goose Vineyards
25 Stag's Hollow Winery & Vineyards
26 Blue Mountain Vineyards
27 Jackson-Triggs Vintners
28 Tinhorn Creek Vineyards
29 Carriage House Wines
30 Gehringer Brothers Estate Winery
31 Burrowing Owl Vineyards
32 Hester Creek Estate Winery
33 Inniskillin Okanagan Vineyards
34 Domaine Combret Estate Winery
35 Golden Mile Cellars
36 Gersighel Wineberg

to Vancouver and Calgary and north up the valley to Kelowna and Penticton.

AROUND OSOYOOS

The small town of **Keremeos**, surrounded by orchards and known for its wineries and fruit stands, lies about 25km west of Osoyoos along the Crowsnest Hwy. Just 4.5km farther west is the turnoff to Ashnola River Rd, which leads 21km to **Cathedral Provincial Park** (☎ 250-494-6500), a 33,272-hectare mountain wilderness area characterized by unusual basalt and quartz monzonite rock formations. The park offers excellent backcountry camping and hiking around wildflower meadows and turquoise lakes.

Three steep trails lead to the park's core area around Quiniscoe Lake and the gorgeous *Cathedral Lakes Lodge* (☎ 250-492-1606, 888-255-4453). From here, myriad trails venture off in all directions. Look for mule deer, mountain goats and California bighorn sheep.

You can stay at the lodge or in cabins. Lodge rooms range from $246 to $366 for two nights, including meals, use of canoes and the hot tub. Cabins range from $192 to $306, also for two nights and including all of the above. You can also stay at the backcountry campsite for $5.

For lodge guests and campers, the lodge operates a jeep shuttle from its parking lot to the 2000m-high Quiniscoe Lake and the lodge itself, saving you the steep 16km trek up. The return trip is free if you stay at the lodge and costs campers $55 ($65 in July and August). You must reserve a pick-up ahead of time.

PENTICTON

• population 33,000

Penticton, the southernmost of the three Okanagan sister cities, sits directly between Okanagan Lake and Skaha Lake, which are connected by the Okanagan River Channel. Also between the two lakes is Main St, a long, built-up strip of eateries and motels.

To the Salish, Pen-Tak-Tin means 'place to stay forever,' an idea that many people took to heart. Between 1975 and 1985, the population rose from 13,000 to 25,000.

Almost 60% of the population is over the age of 65, but despite the high number of retirees, the town exudes a young, sporty feel, generated perhaps by the plethora of annual festivals that draw tourists en masse. Maybe it's the excellent mountain biking and the world-class climbing on Skaha Bluffs or maybe it's just the long, sunny, lakeside days. In Penticton the sun shines for an average of 600 hours in July and August – about 10 hours a day – and that's more than it shines in Honolulu! It's not surprising, then, that the number-one industry is tourism.

The good weather shaped the town's history as well. Penticton became an official townsite in 1892, while several nearby mine claims were being developed. Fruit companies started buying up land in the early 1900s, the industries grew and by the 1930s Penticton's location and climate were gaining a reputation. It soon became a vacation destination. The downtown is undergoing something of a revival, particularly along the small Front St. Close by, Okanagan Beach boasts about 1300m of long sandy beach, with average water temperatures of about 22°C, making this a good spot to cool your heels for a day or two.

Orientation

The downtown area lies just to the south of Okanagan Lake. Parkland surrounds much of the lake. Lakeshore Dr W runs west beside the lake from downtown to Riverside Dr and Hwy 97. The main street is fittingly called Main St, a north-south route flanked on its east side by Ellis and Van Horne Sts and on its west by Martin and Winnipeg Sts. The downtown area extends for about 10 blocks southward from the lake. Important streets running west to east include Westminster Ave W and Nanaimo and Wade Aves. Most banks, restaurants and bars are contained in this area.

South of downtown, Martin St merges to join Main St. The road continues straight, becoming S Main St, and forks off to the right to become Skaha Lake Rd, which then turns into Hwy 97. At the southern end of town, you'll find the 1.5km-long Skaha Beach, with sand, trees and picnic areas.

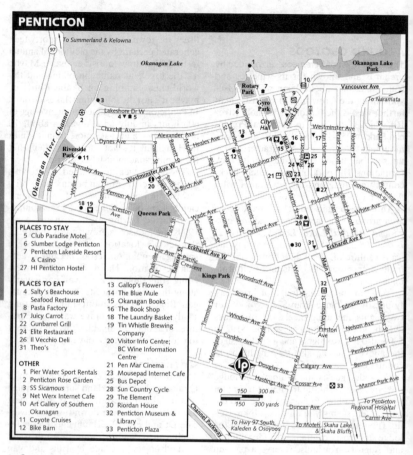

PENTICTON

PLACES TO STAY
5   Club Paradise Motel
6   Slumber Lodge Penticton
7   Penticton Lakeside Resort
    & Casino
27 HI Penticton Hostel

PLACES TO EAT
4   Salty's Beachouse
    Seafood Restaurant
8   Pasta Factory
17 Juicy Carrot
24 Gunbarrel Grill
26 Il Vecchio Deli
31 Theo's

OTHER
1   Pier Water Sport Rentals
2   Penticton Rose Garden
3   SS Sicamous
9   Net Werx Internet Cafe
10 Art Gallery of Southern
    Okanagan
11 Coyote Cruises
12 Bike Barn

13 Gallop's Flowers
14 The Blue Mule
15 Okanagan Books
16 The Book Shop
18 The Laundry Basket
19 Tin Whistle Brewing
    Company
20 Visitor Info Centre;
    BC Wine Information
    Centre
21 Pen Mar Cinema
23 Mousepad Internet Cafe
25 Bus Depot
28 Sun Country Cycle
29 The Element
30 Riordan House
32 Penticton Museum &
    Library
33 Penticton Plaza

Information

The Visitor Info Centre (☎ 250-493-4055, 800-663-5052, fax 250-492-6119), 888 Westminster Ave W next to the convention center, is open 8 am to 8 pm daily in summer. The rest of the year, it's open 9 am to 5 pm weekdays and 11 am to 5 pm weekends.

The main post office is used by businesses and for distribution. To send mail and buy stamps, you should go to one of the small postal outlets like Gallop's Flowers, 187 Westminster Ave W downtown. You'll find other outlets at Embassy Cleaners in the Cherry Lane Shopping Centre, 2111 Main St at Warren Ave, and at Plaza Card & Gift in the Penticton Plaza, 1301 Main St. The IGA supermarket, 1160 Government St, also offers postal services.

If you need to check your email or surf the Web, try the Mousepad Internet Café (☎ 250-493-2050), 320 Martin St, which has a helpful staff. Net Werx Internet Café (☎ 250-490-0571), 151 Front St, is a smaller, quiet place to surf the Web and sip a latte.

Penticton's library (☎ 250-492-0024), 785 Main St next to the museum, is open 10 am to 5 pm Monday to Saturday (until 9 pm on Tuesday and Thursday) and 1 to 5 pm Sunday.

The Book Shop (☎ 250-492-6661), 242 Main St, features a huge collection of second-hand books. Across the street, Okanagan Books (☎ 250-493-1941), 233 Main St, offers a good selection of regional books and magazines.

The *Penticton Herald* is the daily newspaper. The free *Western News Advertiser*, published biweekly, covers community events.

Coin-operated laundry services include The Laundry Basket, 976 Eckhardt Ave W, a couple blocks from the Info Centre. It's open 8 am to 5 pm daily. The Plaza Laundromat, 1301 Main St in Penticton Plaza, is open 7 am to 10 pm daily.

In summer, public restrooms are open at both Skaha and Okanagan Lake beaches. The Penticton Regional Hospital (☎ 250-492-4000) is south of downtown at 550 Carmi Ave.

Things to See & Do

History buffs can visit the SS *Sicamous* (☎ 250-492-0403), 1099 Lakeshore Dr W, an old stern-wheeler, which sits dry-docked at the western end of the beach. The *Sicamous* carried passengers and freight on Okanagan Lake from 1914 to 1936. Now nicely restored, it features a model of the Kettle Valley Railway and historic photos of the Okanagan, taken while the area was being settled. The site is open 9 am to 9 pm daily in the heart of summer, 10 am to 5 pm weekdays the rest of the year (though hours are limited in winter). Admission is $4/1 for adults/children.

If you want to take some time out to smell the roses, you can stroll around the **Penticton Rose Garden**, beside the *Sicamous*, for free. The paved **Okanagan River Channel Biking & Jogging Path** follows the channel from lake to lake. It's great for running, walking, cycling or in-line skating.

The **Art Gallery of Southern Okanagan** (☎ 250-493-2928), at the east end of Front St, displays an excellent collection of regional, provincial and national artists. Ex-

hibits change every six weeks. The gallery is open 10 am to 5 pm Tuesday to Friday, 1 to 5 pm weekends. Admission is $2.

The **Penticton Museum** (☎ 250-490-2451), 785 Main St at the library complex, is an excellent small-town museum with well-done, pleasingly eclectic displays, including a large natural-history exhibit on animals and birds indigenous to BC. It's open 10 am to 5 pm Monday to Saturday. Admission is by donation.

Of the many area **wineries**, Hillside Cellars (☎ 250-493-4424), 1350 Naramata Rd northeast of downtown, is the closest. It's open 9 am to 9 pm daily. Nearby is Lake Breeze Vineyards (☎ 250-496-5659), 930 Sammet Rd in Naramata. It's open 10 am to 6 pm daily. The **BC Wine Information Centre** (☎ 250-490-2006), in the same building as the Visitor Info Centre at 888 Westminster Ave W, sells quality wines from local vineyards and dispenses lots of information on area vineyards. Free tastings take place from 2 to 4 pm Saturday year-round.

Activities

Watersports Both Okanagan and Skaha Lakes enjoy some of the best windsurfing conditions in the Okanagan Valley. Pier Water Sport Rentals (☎ 250-493-8864), at the end of Martin St beside the Penticton Lakeside Resort & Casino, rents windsurfing boards and catamarans for $12 and $25 per hour. The other equipment available for hourly rental includes kayaks and canoes ($15), pedal boats ($10) and ski boats ($60).

Parasail Penticton (☎ 250-492-2242) offers rides on both lakes. You start on the beach and a speedboat pulls you up 50m into the air. It costs $40 for a 10-minute ride, but people say the sensation and views are worth the money.

Coyote Cruises (☎ 250-492-2115), 215 Riverside Dr, rents inner tubes that you can float on all the way down the Okanagan River Channel to Skaha Lake. The trip takes nearly two hours; Coyote Cruises buses you back, all for $10. You can also bring your own inner tube or swim down the channel – though it takes an average swimmer about four hours – but you'll have to figure out how to get back.

Mountain Biking The dry climate and rolling hills around the city combine to offer some excellent mountain biking terrain. Get to popular rides by heading east out of town, toward Naramata. Follow signs to the city dump and Campbell's Mountain, where you'll find lots of single-track and a dual-slalom course, both of which aren't too technical. Once you get there, the riding is mostly on the right side, but once you pass the cattle guard, it opens up and you can ride anywhere. Also check out Three Blind Mice, which you reach by following Riddle Rd up to the old Kettle Valley Railway tracks.

Rent bikes and pick up a wealth of information at either of Penticton's well-stocked bike shops. The Bike Barn (☎ 250-492-4140), at the corner of Westminster Ave W and Brunswick St, rents bikes for $25 to $35 per day. Sun Country Cycle (☎ 250-493-0686), 533 Main St, charges $15 for a half day, $25 for a full day. Both shops are open 9 am to 5:30 pm daily except Sunday, when the staff go out and ride.

In summer, the fast quad chairlift at Apex Mountain Resort zips riders and their bikes to the top of the mountain (see Apex Mountain Resort in the Around Penticton section, later). You can explore the backcountry or simply get a rush from following a trail down again. All-day chairlift passes cost $15. Bike rentals are $20 for a half day, $25 for a full day.

Rock Climbing Propelled by the dry weather and compact gneiss rock, climbers from all over the world come to the Skaha Bluffs to enjoy a seven-month climbing season on more than 400 bolted routes. The rock is compact but still has plenty of holes to make the climbing excellent for experienced and novice climbers. You'll need a car or a ride to get to the Bluffs. Follow S Main St toward Skaha Lake. Just before the playground and beach parking lot, turn right on Crescent Hill Rd and then right again onto

Valleyview Rd. Proceed for a few kilometers until you see a dirt road on the right and a sign directing you to the parking area. From there, you'll see the bluffs, though most of the climbing happens on the back side of the rock, so you'll have to follow the well-marked trail around.

Skaha Rock Adventures (☎ 250-493-1765) offers advanced, technical instruction and introductory courses for anyone venturing into a harness for the first time. The one-day course Intro to Rock costs $95, though the price goes down if you cajole others into joining you.

Special Events

Penticton is the city of festivals, which happen almost nonstop throughout the summer. In July, be sure to catch the **Beach Blanket Film Festival**. Bring a lawn chair or blanket and kick back to watch the movie screen, which is set up on – yes on – Skaha Lake. For more information, see the Web site www.beachblanketfilmfest.org.

The city's premier event is the **Peach Festival** (☎ 800-663-5052), basically a weeklong party that has taken place in early August since 1948. The festivities include sports activities, novelty events, street music and dance, nightly entertainment and a major parade that's held on Saturday.

Another long-standing annual event that usually runs the second week in August is the **BC Square Dance Jamboree** (☎ 250-492-5856), which attracts about 3500 dancers who kick it up on an enormous dance floor in Kings Park from 8 to 11 pm six nights in a row. The jamboree also features street dances, dances held at both lakes – in the water! – pancake breakfasts and other activities.

At the end of August, hard-core athletes are put through their paces in Canada's only **Ironman Triathlon** (☎ 250-490-8787), where more than 1700 athletes swim 3.9km, cycle 180km and then, just for the heck of it, run a full marathon (42km). The race takes an average of 10 to 12 hours to complete. For those of us with a little less energy, many excellent spots are set up alongside the course so we can watch the action.

Places to Stay

Camping You'll find many tent and trailer parks in the area, especially south of town, around Skaha Lake. Many are just off Hwy 97. Most charge about $17 to $25 for two people in a tent. This is in no way wilderness camping, but it's a cheap place to stay. The beach closes at midnight and stays that way until 6 am.

Hostels The excellent *HI Penticton Hostel* (☎ 250-492-3992, fax 492-8755, penticton@ hihostels.bc.ca, 464 Ellis St) enjoys a convenient location right downtown, just south of the Greyhound bus depot. Facilities include private rooms, kitchen, laundry, patio and an Internet kiosk. Hostel guests qualify for discounts on bike rentals, rock-climbing courses, restaurant meals and groceries. The hostel also arranges a wine tour that includes lunch and tastings at four different wineries, all for about $25. Also ask about fruit-picking work, as many orchards contact the hostel looking for short-term pickers. The office is open 7 am to noon and 5 pm to midnight daily. Dorm beds cost $16/20 for members/nonmembers.

B&Bs The Visitor Info Centre keeps a long list of local B&Bs. A long-time Penticton family runs the historic *Riordan House* (☎ 250-493-5997, 689 Winnipeg St), which features four rooms filled with antiques. Guests get housecoats and slippers to wear around the house. All rooms ($50 to $85) come with queen-size beds.

Many of Penticton's B&Bs are in nearby Kaleden, which can be reached by following Hwy 97 south. Nature lovers will like the reclusive *Three Gates Farm B&B* (☎ 250-497-8833). The log house sits on 77 acres amid pine trees and flowering meadows. The two rooms range from $70 to $85.

Apex Alpine Guest Ranch (☎ 250-492-2454), on Green Mountain Rd, is 22km west of Penticton and 12km from the Apex ski area. It offers horseback riding and hiking on nearby trails. The cost of $60 per person per day includes meals. You can also go the B&B route, which costs $60 per couple.

Motels & Hotels Because Penticton hosts so many crowd-attracting festivals, the city is absolutely chock full of motels. Lakeshore Dr W and S Main St/Skaha Lake Rd contain most of the local motels. The *Club Paradise Motel* (☎ 250-493-8400, 1000 Lakeshore Dr) sits across the street from the Okanagan Lake beach, though no rooms look out on the lake. Still, the accommodations are clean and include free coffee. Double rooms range from $55 to $65; two-bedroom suites cost $120. Also fronting the lake but closer to the downtown area is the restful *Slumber Lodge Penticton* (☎ 250-492-4008, 800-663-2831, 274 Lakeshore Dr W), where rooms start at $88 and climb up to $300 for four-bedroom suites. There is also a room equipped for people with disabilities.

Penticton Lakeside Resort & Casino (☎ 250-493-8221, 800-663-9400, 21 Lakeshore Dr W), a large high-rise on the lake, features extensive facilities, including a restaurant, bar and outdoor barbecue area. The Vegas-style casino opened in spring 2000. In peak season (July and August), rooms facing the park cost $151; lakeside rooms run up to $166.

Down at the Skaha end of town, the *Beachside Motel* (☎ 250-492-8318) is all about location. Just a block from Skaha Beach, it features an outdoor picnic area, indoor pool and fairly average rooms starting at $74 ($82 with a kitchenette). Two-bedroom suites with kitchenette go for $102. *Log Cabin Motel* (☎ 250-492-3155, 3287 Skaha Lake Rd), also close to the beach, offers very nice grounds, an outdoor pool and clean rooms starting at $85. Accommodations in one of the older, four-person cabins with kitchenettes start at $68.

Places to Eat

Penticton definitely has its share of good eats. Nearly all the downtown restaurants are on or near Main St, and the revival of the downtown core has brought an increase in choice, though one local said, 'This town changes restaurants as often as people change underwear.' Here are a few places with staying power.

For anyone needing a carrot juice or wheat-grass fix, **The Juicy Carrot** (☎ 250-493-4399, 254 Ellis St) serves a variety of smoothies ($2.50), juices and vegetarian fare like the Buddha salad and veggie burgers, both for $4.50. For the best sandwich in town, go to **Il Vecchio Deli** (☎ 250-492-7610, 317 Robinson St), where veggie or meat sandwiches are a steal at $3.

The **Elite Restaurant** (340 Main St) (though the address is not on the building) features a 1950s pink neon sign and standard diner fare. Eggs with hash browns and toast cost $4.50; a full-course dinner is $8.

The **Pasta Factory** (☎ 250-493-5666, 75 Front St) features excellent Italian food and a patio. Lunch entrees average $8, and dinner meals are $11 to $13. For excellent, authentic Greek food, try **Theo's** (☎ 250-492-4019, 697 Main St), where a tasty chicken souvlaki will run you $13.

Cool in summer and cozy in winter, the Gunbarrel Grill (☎ 250-490-0573), upstairs in the city center building at Main St and Wade Ave, serves pasta, salads and grilled items. Dinner entrees average $14. For a taste of seafood with a Caribbean flair, head to **Salty's Beachouse Seafood Restaurant** (☎ 250-493-5001), at the west end of Lakeshore Dr W. The fish-grotto atmosphere and large patio make it a relaxing place to swallow some steamed clams ($9) or swordfish ($14).

If you're in the southern part of town and in the mood for good Thai food, try **Boa Thong** (☎ 250-770-9791, 2985 Skaha Lake Rd), where the killer pad Thai costs $8.50. **La Casa Ouzeria** (☎ 250-492-9144, 2406 Skaha Lake Rd) is an old local favorite with Greek and Italian standards for $9 and up.

Entertainment

The Tin Whistle Brewing Company (☎ 250-770-1122, 954 W Eckhardt Ave) brews its own ales and offers free tours and tastings from 11 am to 5 pm daily.

The **Barking Parrot** (☎ 250-493-9753), in the Penticton Lakeside Resort, attracts a local crowd that lounges around at the outdoor tables and snacks on food and drinks. Every Wednesday, comedy night starts at 8 pm ($5 cover). **The Element** (535 Main St) is a hot dance club that usually charges a cover of around $5. **The Blue Mule** (218 Martin St), near the corner of Westminster Ave W, features country music and dancing.

The **Pen Mar Cinema** (☎ 250-492-5974, 361 Martin St) contains four theaters that show mainstream movies. Admission is $7.50 for adults, $4 for seniors and kids.

Getting There & Around

The small Penticton Regional Airport is served by Canadian Regional and Central Mountain Air (☎ 888-247-2262 for both), with daily flights from Vancouver and Calgary. Regional planes fly to small towns throughout BC.

The Greyhound bus depot (☎ 250-493-4101), at 307 Ellis St on the corner of Nanaimo Ave one block east of Main St, contains a cafeteria and luggage lockers. The building is open 6 am to 5 pm daily. Popular bus destinations include:

destination	time	fare
Vancouver	6½ hours	$50
Kelowna	1¼ hours	$12
Vernon	2¼ hours	$17
Nelson	six hours	$41
Banff	11 hours	$67
Calgary	12 hours	$84

If you're driving, take Hwy 97 north from Osoyoos or south from Kelowna. Hwy 3, running east-west through the southern part of the province, also passes through Penticton.

For local bus information, contact Penticton Transit (☎ 250-492-5602) or go to the Visitor Info Centre and pick up a copy of the leaflet Rider's Guide, which lists routes and fares. The one-way fare is $1.35; a day pass costs $3.25. The lake-to-lake shuttle bus runs along both waterfronts from 9 am to 6:50 pm daily. Also, bus No 3 travels from the corner of Wade Ave and Martin St down South Main St to Skaha Lake.

AROUND PENTICTON
Apex Mountain Resort
Apex Mountain Resort (☎ 250-292-8222, 877-777-2739, info@apexresort.com), 33km west of Penticton off Green Mountain Rd, features 60 downhill runs catering to all levels of ability, though the mountain is known for its plethora of double-black-diamond and technical runs. The crowds are smaller than at nearby Big White Mountain in Kelowna, and the high-speed quad chair hauls skiers and boarders up quickly, keeping the lines short. Close to the village you'll find 30km of accessible cross-country trails. Lift tickets cost $42. Inquire about package deals at Penticton motels.

Apex is also a popular summer spot, when the downhill trails open up to horse-back riders, hikers and mountain bikers.

Vaseux Wildlife Centre
Just south of Okanagan Falls, watch for the small sign at the north end of Vaseux Lake, which lies about 22km south of Penticton on Hwy 97. You'll see lots of birds here, and you might catch a glimpse of bighorn sheep or the northern Pacific rattlesnake. From the center, you can hike to the Bighorn National Wildlife Area and the Vaseux Lake National Migratory Bird Sanctuary, where more than 160 bird species nest.

You can camp at one of the 12 year-round sites on the east side of the lake, which is popular for bass fishing, swimming and canoeing in summer. In winter, people head to the lake for skating and ice fishing. *Camping* costs $12.

Dominion Radio Astrophysical Observatory
Studying the distribution of gas in the Milky Way, the Dominion Radio Astrophysical Observatory (☎ 250-490-4355) uses various radio telescopes to detect radio-wave energy in the universe. A giant, seven-antenna telescope takes photos of the 'radio sky,' allowing scientists to study things like celestial gas clouds.

The observatory is open for self-guided tours year-round. In winter, it's open 9 am to 5 pm weekdays. In summer, the observatory adds weekend hours (10 am to 5 pm). Scientists conduct guided tours from 2 to 5 pm on Sunday. Visiting the observatory is free. To get there, head about 10km south on Hwy 97 from Penticton. Drive 9km up White Lake Rd to reach the observatory parking lot.

SUMMERLAND
• population 11,150
A small lakeside resort town 18km north of Penticton on Hwy 97, Summerland features some fine 19th-century heritage buildings. You can tour the **Summerland Trout Hatchery** (☎ 250-494-3346), 13405 Lakeshore Dr, from 8:30 to 11:30 am and 1:30 to 4:30 pm daily for free. One of the few BC hatcheries used to stock lakes, this one focuses on rainbow, eastern brook and kokanee trout. While you're in town, head to **Giant's Head Mountain**, an extinct volcano south of the downtown area, for great views of Okanagan Lake.

The **Agricultural Research Station**, 7km south of Summerland on Hwy 97, was designed for the study of fruit trees, their growth, diseases and production. You can enjoy your lunch on picnic grounds surrounded by an ornamental garden displaying a wide variety of plants and trees. The grounds are open 8 am to 8 pm daily, April to October; 8 am to 5:30 pm daily the rest of the year.

KELOWNA
• population 98,000
The Okanagan's major city, Kelowna sits midway between Vernon and Penticton along the east side of 136km-long Okanagan Lake. The rounded, scrubby hills typical of the valley encircle Kelowna, gradually growing greener the closer you get to town, which (unusually) is the greenest area around, thanks to its many gardens and parks (65!). Beneath skies that are almost always clear, terraced orchards and bright green golf courses line the slopes of Kelowna's rolling hills, and sandy beaches rim the dark-blue water of the lake.

THOMPSON-OKANAGAN

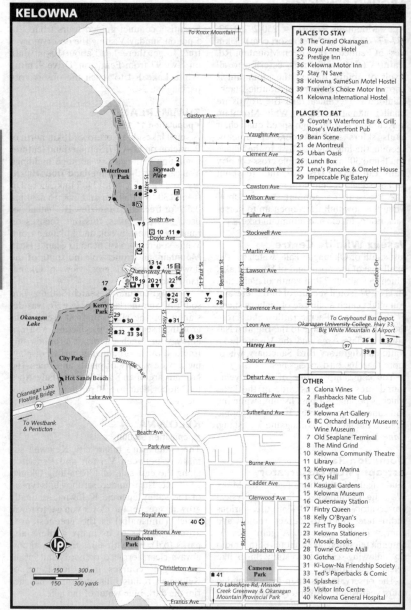

KELOWNA

PLACES TO STAY
3 The Grand Okanagan
20 Royal Anne Hotel
32 Prestige Inn
36 Kelowna Motor Inn
37 Stay 'N Save
38 Kelowna SameSun Motel Hostel
39 Traveler's Choice Motor Inn
41 Kelowna International Hostel

PLACES TO EAT
9 Coyote's Waterfront Bar & Grill;
  Rose's Waterfront Pub
19 Bean Scene
21 de Montreuil
25 Urban Oasis
26 Lunch Box
27 Lena's Pancake & Omelet House
29 Impeccable Pig Eatery

OTHER
1 Calona Wines
2 Flashbacks Nite Club
4 Budget
5 Kelowna Art Gallery
6 BC Orchard Industry Museum;
  Wine Museum
7 Old Seaplane Terminal
8 The Mind Grind
10 Kelowna Community Theatre
11 Library
12 Kelowna Marina
13 City Hall
14 Kasugai Gardens
15 Kelowna Museum
16 Queensway Station
17 Fintry Queen
18 Kelly O'Bryan's
22 First Try Books
23 Kelowna Stationers
24 Mosaic Books
28 Towne Centre Mall
30 Gotcha
31 Ki-Low-Na Friendship Society
33 Ted's Paperbacks & Comic
34 Splashes
35 Visitor Info Centre
40 Kelowna General Hospital

Throughout the summer, scores of tourists come through to sip wine, play in the lake, hike the hills or simply laze around in the ample sunshine (the sun shines here for nearly 2000 hours each year). Summer days are usually dry and hot, the nights pleasantly cool. Winters are snowy but dry, making nearby Big White a big attraction for skiers and snowboarders. Kelowna's popularity as a tourist destination lends the town a distinct resort feel.

The town's population has more than doubled in the last 30 years, partly due to its thriving economy. The combination of excellent weather and agricultural prowess make Kelowna the biggest producer of BC wines. Along with tourism and agriculture, high-tech manufacturing now helps drive the economy. Even without the tourists, there are plenty of people around to spend money, play golf and sip wine. In fact, more millionaires per capita reportedly live in Kelowna than anywhere else in Canada.

History

Kelowna, an Interior Salish word meaning 'grizzly bear,' owes its settlement to a number of oblate missionaries who arrived in 1858, hoping to convert the Natives. One of the priests, Father Charles Pandosy, established a mission in 1859 and planted the area's first apple trees along the banks of L'Anse au Sable, what is now known as Mission Creek. He is Canada's lesser-known equivalent of the USA's Johnny Appleseed.

An increasing trickle of settlers followed his lead, and his agricultural success led to the first full-scale planting of apples in 1890. This was, after all, ideal pioneer country, with lots of available timber to build houses, a freshwater creek and prime, grassy lands that were just begging for the cattle to come munching. Successful cattle-raising and fruit-growing brought even more settlers and the town began to take shape.

In 1892, the townsite of Kelowna was established; it quickly became an economic hub. In 1905, the town was incorporated, just in time for the orchard boom, when trees spread like weeds through the entire Okanagan Valley. The Kettle Valley Railway finally chugged through in 1916, connecting Kelowna to Canadian Pacific Railway (CPR) lines at Hope and Midway and opening up an exporting trade from the Okanagan Valley.

With the completion of the Okanagan Lake Floating Bridge in 1958, Kelowna experienced yet another growth spurt. Growing pains are evident in the barrage of motels and strip malls that plague the eastern end of town. Ignore all that and you'll find that the lakeside, downtown area and surrounding orchards make Kelowna a stunning, surprisingly cosmopolitan city.

Orientation

The large City Park on the lake's edge forms the western boundary of town. Starting from the big white modern sculpture

Did You Shoot the Ogopogo?

Okanagan Lake is said to contain a monster similar to that of Loch Ness but known as Ogopogo. The Native Indians, who first reported it, would offer the creature sacrificial animals before venturing on the lake. The Visitor Info Centre claims it will pay a million dollars to anyone able to catch the famed Ogo on film. Occasional claimed sightings have proved especially unverifiable.

'Sails,' which was put in by helicopter in 1997, and the model of Ogopogo, the mythical lake monster who sits at the edge of City Park, Bernard Ave runs east and is the city's main drag. Other important thoroughfares are Water, Pandosy and Ellis Sts, all running north-south. South of town, Pandosy St becomes Lakeshore Rd.

Hwy 97, called Harvey Ave in town, marks the southern edge of the downtown area; it heads west over the bridge toward Penticton. East of downtown, Harvey Ave becomes a rather unattractive 15km strip lined with service stations, shopping malls, motels and fast-food restaurants. This unfortunate blast of urban sprawl resulted from the city's fast growth, lack of city planning and the growing population's need for more amenities. Past the sprawl, Harvey Ave is again called Hwy 97 and heads northeast toward Vernon.

At the northern end of Pandosy St, where it meets Queensway Ave, you'll find the town clock tower, which stands in a fountain that marks the civic center. At the north edge of the city, The Grand Okanagan, a giant lakeside structure, sits across from Skyreach Place, Kelowna's coliseum.

Information

The Visitor Info Centre (☎ 250-861-1515, 800-663-4345, fax 250-861-3624), 544 Harvey Ave (Hwy 97) near the corner of Ellis St, offers extensive local and regional information. It's open 8 am to 5 pm weekdays and 10 am to 4 pm weekends, with longer hours in summer.

Most of the town's banks are on Bernard Ave, between Water and Ellis Sts.

You'll find postal outlets in Kelowna Stationers (☎ 250-762-2009), 297 Bernard Ave; Towne Centre Stationary & Card Shop (☎ 250-868-8480), in the Town Centre Mall, 565 Bernard Ave; Capri Tobacco (☎ 250-860-2627), 1835 Gordon Ave; The Card Corner (☎ 250-763-9542), 3155 Lakeshore Rd; and Orchard Park Shoppers Drug Mart (☎ 250-860-3764), in the Orchard Park Mall on Harvey Ave at Cooper Rd.

Surf the Web or check your email at The Mind Grind (☎ 250-763-2221), 1340 Water St, which serves good cappuccino, sandwiches and ice cream.

Kelowna's library (☎ 250-762-2800), 1380 Ellis St, was cleverly designed to look like an open book. Once you see it, you'll notice that the back of the building is the spine, which opens up toward the front of the building, like the fanned pages of a book. Okay, so it takes a little imagination . . .

Mosaic Books (☎ 250-763-4418), 411 Bernard Ave, sells maps (including topographic ones), atlases and travel and activity guides, plus books on Native Indian history and culture. In the spirit of competition with the massive Chapters bookstore, it now features a good selection of magazines and a coffee bar.

Ted's Paperbacks & Comics (☎ 250-763-1258), 269 Leon Ave one block up from City Park, sells used books and an eclectic mix of collector comics. First Try Books (☎ 250-763-5364), 426B Bernard Ave, is a used bookstore whose bookmark reads, 'In literature as in love, we are astonished at what is chosen by others.'

The *Kelowna Daily Courier* prints an events calendar called 'Showtime' every Thursday. The biweekly community paper is the *Capitol News*.

For medical care, go to Kelowna General Hospital (☎ 250-862-4000), 2268 Pandosy St at Royal Ave.

Things to See & Do

A part of the civic center complex, the **Kelowna Museum** (☎ 250-763-2417), 470 Queensway Ave at Ellis St, showcases Kelowna's ethnographic and natural history. The exhibits and the museum itself are gearing up for a much-needed face-lift, which promises some refreshing new works. The museum is open 10 am to 5 pm Tuesday to Saturday (also open on Monday in July and August). Admission is free.

After you've checked out the museum, take a lovely and peaceful stroll around the beautifully manicured Kasugai Gardens. The Circle of Friendship sculpture marks the entrance to the Japanese garden, which is sandwiched between the museum and City Hall.

The **Kelowna Art Gallery** (☎ 250-979-0888), 1315 Water St, features the work of many local artists, including exhibits by Okanagan University College students. The light, airy gallery makes a nice place to wander around. It's open from 10 am to 5 pm Tuesday to Saturday, 10 am to 9 pm Thursday and 1 to 5 pm Sunday.

Located in an old packinghouse, the **BC Orchard Industry Museum** (☎ 250-763-0433), 1304 Ellis St, recounts the conversion of the Okanagan Valley from ranchland to orchards. The exhibits show just about everything you can do with fruit, from seeds to jam. It's open 10 am to 5 pm Monday to Saturday and noon to 5 pm Sunday (closed Sunday and Monday in winter). Admission is by donation.

Tucked away in the same building is the **Wine Museum** (☎ 250-868-0441), which is primarily an attempt to market high-quality BC wines.

If you're interested in wine, be sure you take a tour of one of the local **wineries** (see the boxed text 'Okanagan Valley Wineries,' earlier in the chapter). Several vintners in and near Kelowna offer tours and free samples. Calona Wines (☎ 250-762-9144), 1125 Richter St right in Kelowna, is one of BC's largest producers and was the first in the Okanagan; it started in 1932. It's open 10 am to 5 pm daily. In Westbank, about 13km southwest of Kelowna, you can visit Mission Hill Winery (☎ 250-768-7611), 1730 Mission Hill Rd off Boucherie Rd, which offers tours, tastings and sales 10 am to 5 pm daily (until 7 pm in summer). CedarCreek Estate Winery (☎ 250-764-8866), 5445 Lakeshore Rd, is open 9:30 am to 5:30 pm daily.

For an **orchard tour**, stop at Kelowna Land & Orchard Co (☎ 250-763-1091), 3002 Dunster Rd, one of many local orchards open for tours. Admission includes a 40-minute wagon ride ($7 for adults, free for children under 12). You can also buy fruit and baked goods here.

The major historic site in the area is the **Father Pandosy Settlement**, where some original buildings survive on the spot where the oblate priest set up his mission in 1859.

The church, school, barn, one house and a few sheds from what was the first white settlement in the Okanagan have been restored. The site is small, well away from the center of town and there's not a lot to see, but it's free. To get there, go south along Lakeshore Rd, then east on Casorso Rd to Benvoulin Rd. It's open 8 am to sundown daily, April to October.

At the foot of Bernard Ave, behind the model of Ogopogo, the old ferry boat **Fintry Queen** (☎ 250-763-2780) is moored in the lake. Now converted into a restaurant, it also provides lake cruises from June to September. The 90-minute cruise costs $9.

Parks & Beaches

City Park & Promenade, the central downtown park, is excellent. Slide into the water from the sandy **Hot Sands Beach**, read under one of the many shade trees or just marvel at the flower gardens blooming with tulips and enjoy the soothing view across Okanagan Lake. Given the bucolic setting and the warm lake water (just slightly cooler than the summer air), it's no wonder would-be fruit pickers are sitting around picking only guitars.

At 650m long, the **Okanagan Lake Bridge**, just west of City Park, is Canada's longest floating bridge; it's supported by 12 pontoons and has a lift span in the middle so that boats up to 18m high can pass through.

From Bernard Ave, the lakeside promenade extends north past the marina, lock and artificial lagoon to The Grand Okanagan and a condominium complex that boasts a blend of Canadian and Spanish architectural styles. The promenade is good for a stroll, skate or jog in the evenings. The promenade joins City Park with the equally bucolic Waterfront Park, just to the north.

You'll find several beaches south of Okanagan Lake Bridge along Lakeshore Rd. **Gyro Beach**, at the south end of Richter St, attracts lots of locals. The Okanagan Shuswap Nudist Society (☎ 250-492-0295) provides information on local buff beaches.

For information on other local parks, see Activities, below.

Activities

Watersports Fishing is possible on Okanagan Lake and many of the 200 lakes near Kelowna. You'll need a $16 license, available from local sporting goods stores and gas stations. You can rent speedboats (starting at $52 per hour), arrange fishing trips and cruises or rent windsurfing gear at Kelowna Marina (☎ 250-861-8001), at the lake end of Queensway Ave. Windsurfers take to the water from the old seaplane terminal, near the corner of Water St and Cawston Ave.

Hiking & Mountain Biking You'll find excellent hiking and fat-tire riding all around town. To get started, pick up the excellent *Heritage Walking Tour* brochure from the Visitor Info Centre. While you're there, ask for directions to **Mission Creek Greenway**, a meandering, 18km wooded path following the creek. It makes for a nice, mellow bike ride. Hike or ride up **Knox Mountain**, which sits on the north end of the city. Along with bobcats and snakes, the mountain has good trails and rewards you with excellent views from the top.

Definitely worth exploring by foot or by bike is the **Kettle Valley Railway**, which affords fantastic views of the Myra Canyon. The trail follows the old railway tracks through tunnels and over old trestles. To reach the railway, follow Harvey Ave (Hwy 97) east to Gordon Dr. From there, turn right on KLO Rd and follow it all the way to the end of McCulloch Rd. About 2km after the pavement ends, you'll come to a clearing where power lines cross the road. Turn right on the Myra Forest Service Rd and follow it for 8km to the parking lot. You'll see the trailhead, and the first trestle is about a 15-minute walk from there.

Monashee Adventure Tours (☎ 250-762-9253, 888-762-9253) offers biking or hiking tours of the railway trestles. The easy 20km ride or 4½-hour, 10km hike crosses the trestles and tunnels over Myra Canyon. Tours are accompanied by local guides, who give excellent historical accounts of the area. The $100 price includes a bike, lunch and shuttle to the trails.

The 10.5-sq-km **Okanagan Mountain Provincial Park**, south of Kelowna off Lakeshore Rd, is a popular spot for hikers, bikers and horse riders. Many of the trails date from the days of the fur trade. About 8.5km northwest of Kelowna, **Bear Creek Provincial Park** offers opportunities for hiking, as well as windsurfing, fishing, swimming, and wilderness camping. From Kelowna, cross the floating bridge and go right (north) on Westside Rd.

Skiing & Snowboarding Unlike other year-round mountain resorts in the area, **Big White Ski Resort** (☎ 250-765-3101, 800-663-2772, snow report ☎ 250-765-7669) at Big White Mountain, 55km east of Kelowna off Hwy 33, functions solely as a winter resort. The highest ski resort in the province features 840 hectares of runs, which are covered in deep dry powder for excellent downhill and backcountry skiing, and deep gullies that make for excellent snowboarding. There is also night skiing. Adult lift tickets cost $44. Because of Big White's distance from Kelowna, most people stay up here. The resort includes numerous restaurants, bars and hotels and a couple of hostels (see Places to Stay, later).

Special Events

With the influx of summer tourists comes an influx of festivals. In July, keep an ear open for the **Mozart Festival** (☎ 250-762-3424), which features everything from professional orchestral concerts to free music outdoors. On July 1st, the city strums its collective guitar and celebrates Canada Day with the **Kelowna Folk Fest** (☎ 250-763-9747). For more drama, keep your eyes peeled for summer performances by **Shakespeare Kelowna** (☎ 250-878-0444) and the annual August **Fringe Festival** (☎ 250-860-7330). In September, look out for the colorful **Dragon Boat Festival** (☎ 250-868-1136).

Places to Stay

As in the rest of the Okanagan Valley, accommodation here can be difficult to find in summer; it's best to book ahead or arrive early in the day.

Camping Camping is the cheapest way to stay in the area, though you'll be a fair way from town. The best place is *Bear Creek Provincial Park*, 9km north of Kelowna off Westlake Rd, on the west side of the lake. The campground offers 122 shady sites close to the park's 400m-long beachfront area. Sites cost $18.50 and fill up fast. *Okanagan Mountain Provincial Park*, south of Kelowna off Lakeshore Rd, also offers camping, but you have to hike in to access sites. To contact either park, call ☎ 250-494-0321.

Numerous privately owned places surround Kelowna, especially in Westbank and south along Lakeshore Rd. The grounds are usually crowded and the sites close together. To get to Westbank, head west along Hwy 97 over Okanagan Lake Bridge and then turn off at Boucherie Rd. Follow this for quite a while and you'll hit the so-called 'resort area.' This area is quite far from town – you'll need a car. Sites cost $15 to $25.

Closer to town, *Willow Creek Family Campground* (☎ 250-762-6302, 3316 Lakeshore Rd) boasts its own beach, a fire pit and proximity to shops and restaurants. Sites cost $16.

Hostels The *Kelowna International Hostel* (☎ 250-763-6024, fax 763-6068, kelownahostel@silk.net, 2343 Pandosy St), on the corner of Christleton Ave, is a short walk from the beach, though about 12 blocks from the downtown core. An old, spiffed-up house, the place feels relaxed and neighborly. Amenities include dorm-style and private rooms, laundry, Internet access, a clean kitchen and a large outside deck. Dorm beds cost $15, private rooms $35.

The *Kelowna SameSun Motel Hostel* (☎ 250-763-9814, 877-562-2783, fax 250-868-9373, samesun@silk.net, 245 Harvey Ave) enjoys a very central location, near the corner of Hwy 97 and Abbott St. Housed in an old motel, this hostel definitely caters to the young backpacker crowd, with volleyball courts, a barbecue and bike rentals. Beds are $17. Both of the above hostels offer free pick-up at the bus depot.

SameSun also provides a daily shuttle service to the Big White Ski Resort, where it runs the *SameSun Ski Resort Hostel* (☎ 250-765-7050), in the Alpine Center on the top of the mountain, so you can ski or board right to the door. Dorm beds cost $19, and ski packages can be arranged. If you're looking for rest and lots of sleep, don't count on it here, as the hostel is known for its party atmosphere.

Also at Big White are *Bumps* and its next-door neighbor, the larger *Bumps Too* (☎ 250-765-2100, 888-595-6411, fax 250-765-3035, bigwhitehostels@canada.com), run by Big White Hostels in the village. Close to restaurants and nightlife, the two-part hostel offers ski/snowboard lockers, laundry, Internet access, more than 40 private rooms ($19.50) and plenty of dorm-style beds ($15). Only open during ski season (October to early May), the hostel runs a shuttle service from Kelowna to the mountain. For more information, visit the Web site www.bigwhitehostels.com.

University Housing The north Kelowna campus of *Okanagan University College* (☎ 250-470-6055, 3180 College Way) opens up its residences to the public from May to August. Though it's a ways from town, it's close to the airport, and buses run regularly to and from downtown. Singles cost $32; suites with kitchens and private bathrooms are $50/60 single/double, and suites for four are $115. The price includes linens and a continental breakfast.

B&Bs Kelowna contains more than 60 B&Bs, which range from luxurious lakeside retreats to farmhouses in the middle of vineyards. The Visitor Info Centre keeps a substantial list of all the B&Bs affiliated with the Chamber of Commerce.

For an excellent lesson in Kelowna history, visit the *Historic Manor House* (☎ 250-861-3932, 2796 KLO Rd). Only a ten-minute drive from town, this beautiful heritage home sits on a still-working apple orchard – one of Kelowna's first. A double room costs $105.

On the other side of the spectrum, *Caps Lakeside B&B* (☎ 250-764-4222, 4460 Lakeland Rd), also 10 minutes from downtown, is an elegant beachfront home right on the lake, with rooms for $115 to $140.

Motels & Hotels Most of the motels lie along Hwy 97 north of the downtown area, especially at Harvey Ave and Gordon Dr. You'll find some good choices not far past the Hwy 33 junction. *Western Budget Motel* (☎ 250-763-2484, 2679 Hwy 97 N) is the cheapest, with rooms starting at $43/48 single/double; it accepts pets for an extra $5. The *Traveler's Choice Motor Inn* (☎ 250-762-3221, 800-665-2610, 1780 Gordon Dr) features a pool, Jacuzzi and continental breakfast. Rooms cost $85/95. The *Stay 'N Save* (☎ 250-862-8888, 800-663-0298, 1140 Harvey Ave) is a well-run place with comfortable rooms starting at $89. Nearby, the *Kelowna Motor Inn* (☎ 250-762-2533, 800-667-6133, 1070 Harvey Ave) boasts an indoor pool. Regular rooms start at $79/99; two-bedroom suites cost $120 to $145.

Royal Anne Hotel (☎ 250-763-2277, 888-811-3400, fax 250-764-2636, 348 Bernard Ave), in an excellent location just one block east of City Park, contains the popular Sergeant O'Flaherty's Pub. Good rooms start at $129/179. Also enjoying a good location is the more upscale *Prestige Inn* (☎ 250-860-7900, fax 860-7997, 1675 Abbott St), on the corner of Harvey Ave. Theme rooms and Jacuzzi suites range from $100 to $280.

If you stay at *The Grand Okanagan* (☎ 250-763-4500, 465-4651, fax 763-4565, reserve@grandokanagan.com, 1310 Water St), you might never have to leave the resort. The lakeside hotel takes up a couple of city blocks and contains everything from shops to a gym, pools, restaurants and a casino. But it ain't cheap. Room rates range from $259 to a whopping $370. You could always have a cocktail at the bar and pretend you're staying there . . . .

Places to Eat
Join the hip and happenin' locals and start your morning off with a coffee and muffin from the *Bean Scene* (☎ 250-763-1814), at the bottom of Bernard Ave, just a block from City Park. *Lena's Pancake & Omelet*

House (533 Bernard Ave) serves cheap breakfast specials and all types of pancakes and omelets ($5 and up) daily. The *Impeccable Pig Eatery* (☎ 250-762-0442, 1627 Abbott St) offers great breakfasts and vegetarian lunches but no dinners (it closes at 4 pm). At *Lunch Box* (☎ 250-862-8621, 509 Bernard Ave), near the corner of Ellis St, you can sit outside and enjoy its excellent salads, sandwiches ($5) and the Montreal smoked-meat sandwiches ($6) that rival the real thing.

An excellent choice for health-conscious travelers is *Urban Oasis* (☎ 250-762-2124, 1567 Pandosy St), which specializes in 'high-energy food.' The friendly staff will hook you up with fresh juices, power shakes or delicious veggie wraps ($5.50).

The lively atmosphere and great lakeside patio may be the best thing about *Rose's Waterfront Pub* (☎ 250-860-1141, 1352 Water St), a popular beer-swilling spot for the locals with pretty standard pub fare (burgers for $8). Upstairs in the same building, *Coyote's Waterfront Bar & Grill* (☎ 250-860-1226) also features a great deck and serves good Southwest cuisine like grilled ribs ($13).

The excellent restaurant *de Montreuil* (☎ 250-860-5508, 368 Bernard Ave) has dedicated itself to buying whatever it can from local growers. A two-course dinner is $30, but well worth the splurge. It's open for lunch weekdays and for dinner nightly.

Entertainment
The Royal Anne Hotel contains a popular pub, *Sergeant O'Flaherty's*, that's frequented by all types – visitors, workers and locals. Locals describe the place as 'delightful, raucous, fun-filled and vibrant,' and there's often impromptu dancing. Enter from the rear of the hotel on Queensway Ave. *Kelly O'Bryan's* (☎ 250-861-1338), on the corner of Bernard Ave and Mill St, features a popular upstairs 'paddy-o' and good Guinness on tap.

Partying types can choose from a few hoppin' nightspots in Kelowna. For anyone who fondly remembers the tight jeans and big hair of the '80s, *Flashbacks Nite Club*

(☎ *250-861-3039, 1268 Ellis St*), in a former cigar factory, brings those halcyon days back. You can play pool or enjoy the live music. The cover charge varies depending on who's playing. The dance clubs *Splashes* (☎ *250-762-2956*) and *Gotcha* (☎ *250-860-0800*), across the street from each other on Leon Ave, draw crowds. The cover charge is usually $5, but be warned: it leaps to $20 on long weekends.

The Sunshine Theatre Company (☎ 250-763-4025) stages a range of productions at the *Kelowna Community Theatre*, on the corner of Water St and Doyle Ave. Free *concerts*, featuring everything from rock to classical music, take place in downtown's Kerry Park on Friday and Saturday nights during summer and in City Park on Sunday afternoons in summer.

Skyreach Place This 6000-seat coliseum, which opened in August 1999, is Kelowna's venue for big events. Surrounded by the Kelowna Art Gallery, the planned Kelowna Community Arts Centre on Cawston Ave and the BC Orchard Industry Museum, Skyreach Place acts as the cornerstone for the city's intentional 'culture corner.'

Skyreach is the home arena for the WHL (World Hockey League) Kelowna Rockets (who play in fall and winter) and for the lacrosse-playing Okanagan Thunder (who play in spring and summer). When no one's playing a game here, the stadium hosts big-name music stars – everyone from BC-boy Bryan Adams to finger-snappin' Tom Jones and soulful Ray Charles. To find out what's happening at Skyreach, call the information line (☎ 250-979-0888) or look up the Web site www.skyreachplace.com.

Getting There & Away

The airport is about 20km north of town on Hwy 97. Air Canada and Canadian Airlines (☎ 888-247-2262 for both) operate daily flights to Vancouver, Calgary and Edmonton. The discount carrier WestJet (☎ 250-491-5600) flies to those cities plus Victoria. Horizon Airlines (☎ 800-547-9308) flies nonstop to Seattle. Regional airlines link the city to smaller cities around BC.

The Greyhound bus depot (☎ 250-860-3835) 2366 Leckie Rd is north of the downtown area, off Hwy 97. Daily buses travel to other points in the Okanagan Valley, as well as Kamloops (three hours, $22), Vancouver (six hours, $48), Calgary (11 hours, $72) and Prince George (11 hours, $79). The station contains a restaurant and coin lockers. It's open 7 am to 6 pm weekdays, 7 am to 5 pm Saturday and 11 am to 4 pm Sunday. To get there, take city bus No 10 from Queensway Station, Queensway Ave between Pandosy and Ellis Sts. It runs every half hour, roughly, from 6:30 am to 9:45 pm. From the depot, use the free phone to call the hostels or hotel to request a pick-up.

Getting Around

To/From the Airport The Kelowna Airporter bus (☎ 250-765-0182) charges $12. The one-way fare in a taxi is about $22. From downtown, take city bus No 9, 10 or 11 to the Orchard Park Mall. Transfer to a No 23, which will take you to the airport.

Bus For information about local buses, call Kelowna Regional Transit Systems (☎ 250-860-8121) or pick up a copy of *Kelowna Regional Rider's Guide* from the Visitor Info Centre. There are three zones for bus travel, and the one-way fare in the central zone is $1.25. A day pass for all three zones costs $4.25. All the downtown buses pass through Queensway Station, on Queensway Ave between Pandosy and Ellis Sts.

Car & Taxi All the major car rental companies operate agencies in Kelowna. These include Budget (☎ 250-712-3380), 1328 Water St; Rent-A-Wreck (☎ 250-763-6632), 2702 Hwy 97 N; and Thrifty Car Rentals (☎ 250-765-2800), 1980 Springfield Rd.

For taxi service, try Kelowna Cabs (☎ 250-762-4444 or 762-2222) or Checkmate Cabs (☎ 250-861-1111 or 861-4445).

VERNON
• **population 32,000**

Vernon, the most northerly of the Okanagan's 'Big Three,' lies in a scenic valley encircled by three lakes: the Okanagan,

Kalamalka and Swan. But unlike Penticton and Kelowna, Vernon developed because of its roads, not its lakes. Once the hub of the Okanagan Valley, Vernon used to be a major crossroads town that connected the valley with the rest of the interior. Fur traders first used its strategic location, and an onslaught of gold prospectors followed them, streaming up the valley to the Cariboo district. Later cattle were brought in, and in 1891 the railway arrived. But it was in 1908, with the introduction of large-scale irrigation, that the town took on an importance that was more than transitory. Soon the area was covered in orchards and farms.

With a friendly and artsy community and stunning Kalamalka Lake, Vernon is possibly the most underrated city in the Okanagan. Its growth has been slower than that of its sister cities, so it hasn't been hit as hard by the blight of uncontrollable urban sprawl. Though forestry remains the city's primary industry, Vernon's population is surprisingly cosmopolitan, with a multicultural bent provided by populations of Germans, Chinese and First Nations people, the last of whom occupy a reserve to the west of town.

Downtown Vernon doesn't have many attractions, though an ongoing community project to paint murals depicting the area's history is starting to add some color. If downtown doesn't knock your socks off, take one of the surrounding tree-lined country roads to Ellison, Kalamalka Lake, Fintry and Silver Star Provincial Parks, and you'll find endless outdoor activities.

Orientation

Surrounded by rolling hills, downtown Vernon is a clean, neat, quiet place on Hwy 97. Main St, also called 30th Ave, rarely bustles. To the north of 30th Ave, 32nd Ave is an important thoroughfare, as is 25th Ave to the south. At 25th Ave, Hwy 6, which leads southeast to Nelson and Nakusp, meets Hwy 97, which runs north-south, becoming 32nd St in Vernon and bisecting the city. On 32nd St, north of 30th Ave, you'll find a commercial strip with service stations, motels and fast-food outlets.

The other major north-south street is 27th St, which eventually joins Hwy 97 north of town. On 27th St is the provincial courthouse, the city's most impressive structure. All the downtown sights are within easy walking distance of each other.

Information

Vernon has two Visitor Info Centres, and both are a bit of a hike to get to if you don't have a car. The main Visitor Info Centre (☎ 250-542-1415, 800-665-0795, fax 250-542-3256), 701 Hwy 97 S, is about 5km north of town. The other one is on 6326 Hwy 97 N near the southeastern shore of Swan Lake. Both are open 8:30 am to 6 pm daily. Also check out www.vernontourism.com online for more information.

The main post office (☎ 250-545-8239), 3101 32nd Ave, is on the corner of 31st St opposite the civic center. For Web surfing try Grizzly Internet (☎ 250-558-4568), 3207 31st Ave.

Vernon's public library (☎ 250-542-7610), 3001 32nd Ave, is next door to the Vernon Museum.

Bookland (☎ 250-545-1885), 3400 30th Ave, sells topographical maps of the region plus travel guides and books on activities in the Okanagan Valley and BC. If you're looking for magazines or foreign newspapers, The Front Page (☎ 250-260-3713), 3222 30th Ave, offers an excellent selection.

Vernon publishes two newspapers, including the *Vernon Morning Star*, a thrice weekly paper you can pick up anywhere. It features listings of goings-on around Vernon and neighboring North Okanagan communities. The weekly *Sun Review* offers local commentary and feature stories.

For a little Hawaiian vibe while you watch your clothes go round and round, try the Hawaiian-decorated Aloha Coin Wash (☎ 250-545-8022), downtown at 2800 34th St; it's open 8 am to 10 pm daily. You can also put your stuff through the wringer at Kal Lake Coin Laundry (☎ 250-549-2400), 1800 Kalamalka Lake Rd.

For medical care, go to the Vernon Jubilee Hospital (☎ 250-545-2211), 2101 32nd St.

Things to See & Do

Built entirely of local granite, the **Provincial Courthouse** (☎ 250-549-5422) sits majestically at the eastern end of the downtown area, on the corner of 30th Ave and 27th St. **Polson Park**, off 25th Ave and next to 32nd St, bursts with spring and summer flowers. If it's hot outside, this is a good, cool rest spot, thanks to the shade and trickling Vernon Creek. The Japanese and Chinese influence is evident in the gardens and the open, cabana-like structures dotting the park, at one end of which is a floral clock.

Behind Polson is a **skateboard park** and the **Interior Space & Science Center** (☎ 250-545-3644), where science buffs and little kids can check out interactive science exhibits. Admission is $5/4 for adults/children.

The **Vernon Museum** (☎ 250-542-3142), 3009 32nd Ave at 31st St (behind the glockenspiel-like clock tower), displays historical artifacts from the area, including old carriages and clothes, a good antique telephone collection and lots of archival photos of the area and the locals. It's open 10 am to 5 pm Monday to Saturday; admission is free. Vernon's library is right next door.

The **Vernon Art Gallery** (☎ 250-545-3173), 3228 31st Ave, boasts impressive exhibits and knowledgeable staff. It's open 10 am to 5 pm weekdays and 11 am to 4 pm Saturday. Admission is by donation.

Named for wildlife painter Allan Brooks, who lived in Vernon before he died, the **Allan Brooks Nature Centre** (☎ 250-260-4227) features interactive displays on the North Okanagan's diverse ecosystems. It's open 9 am to 9 pm daily from May through September (closed in winter). Admission is $3/2 for adults/children. To get there, follow 34th St until it becomes Mission Rd. Follow that for about 2km, then turn left onto Allan Brooks Road. Follow signs to the center.

Provincial Parks

Kalamalka Lake This 8.9-sq-km park lies on the eastern side of warm, shallow Kalamalka Lake (simply called 'Kal' by the locals), south of town. The park offers great swimming at Jade and Kalamalka beaches, good fishing and public picnic areas. A network of mountain biking and hiking trails take you to places like Cougar Canyon (apparently a bit of a misnomer as no one has ever reported seeing a cougar), where the rock climbing is excellent. There are no campgrounds in the park. To get there from downtown, follow Hwy 6 east to the Polson Place Mall, then turn right on Kalamalka Lake Rd and proceed to Kal Beach. You can also ride bus No 1 from downtown.

Ellison A 15-minute drive takes you to this beautiful park on Okanagan Lake, 16km southwest from Vernon. Ellison includes campsites, more hiking and biking trails and the only freshwater marine park in western Canada. Scuba divers can plunge into the warm water to explore a sunken wreck or come face to face with a giant perch. You can rent scuba gear in Vernon at the dive shop Innerspace (☎ 250-549-2040), 3103 32nd St. Ellison is also known for its world-class rock climbing. To get to Ellison from downtown, go west on 25th Ave, which soon becomes Okanagan Landing Rd. Follow that and look for signs to the park.

Silver Star A provincial park 22km northeast of Vernon, Silver Star doubles as a year-round resort. Boasting a built-up Victorian-style village, hotels, lots of great restaurants and more than 600 hectares of snowy terrain, Silver Star Mountain Resort (☎ 250-542-0224, 542-1745 for a snow report, 800-663-4431) attracts every level of skier and boarder from late October to early April. Lift tickets are $48.

Starting at the end of June – the official start of the summer season – the chairlifts start running again, and ski runs become excellent hiking and mountain-biking trails. Stunning views let you see all the way west to the Coast Mountains.

With plans for a new hostel right in the village, Silver Star is making the mountain resort more accessible to budget travelers.

To get to Silver Star, take 48th Ave off Hwy 97, just northeast of downtown. For up-to-date information, check out the Web site www.silverstar.com.

Places to Stay

Camping By far the best campground is at *Ellison Provincial Park*, 16km southwest of Vernon. The park features a developed beach, underwater marine park and good hiking and biking trails. Its 71 campsites fill up early, so it's a good idea to call ahead. *Kekuli Bay Provincial Park*, which opened in summer 2000, is 11km south of Vernon off Hwy 97. Though trees have been planted throughout the campground, it'll take a few years before they'll offer any shade. As a result, the 69 sites are fully exposed to the scorching summer sun. The park is, however, right on the western shore of Kalamalka Lake, so cooling down is an easy saunter off the boat-launch dock.

Fintry Provincial Park, a 54km drive southwest of Vernon on the west side of Okanagan Lake, lies a little farther out of town but has 150 campsites, a beach and great hiking trails. To get there, follow Hwy 97 northwest of Vernon (toward Kamloops), then turn left on Westside Rd. For general information on all three parks above, call ☎ 250-494-6500. For reservations, call ☎ 800-689-9025.

There are lots of privately owned campgrounds that may lack a knee-deep-in-wilderness experience but offer easy access to Kalamalka and Okanagan Lakes. These, too, get crowded in the height of summer. One of the closest campgrounds to town is *Swan Lake RV Park* (☎ 250-545-2300, 7255 Old Kamloops Rd), 5km north of Vernon, where tent sites start at $16. Head west along 43rd Ave then turn right (north) onto Old Kamloops Rd. Two kilometers south of town, *Dutch's Tent & Trailer* (☎ 250-545-1023, 15408 Kalamalka Lake Rd) charges $17 and up for sites; it's open year-round.

Hostels The beautiful *HI Lodged Inn* (☎ 250-549-3742, 888-737-9427, fax 250-549-3748, lodgedinn@telus.net, 3201 Pleasant Valley Rd) is just a few minutes' walk from downtown. A large yard with plant species endemic to the area surrounds the old heritage building, making the city's only hostel a convenient and relaxing place to hang out. The facilities include a large kitchen, coin laundry and clean, spacious dorm-style and private rooms. Dorm beds cost $15/19 for members/nonmembers.

The hostel also acts as the community's travel resource center, with a good library and excellent map room. If you're looking for adventure while in Vernon, this is the place to come, as the hostel works with local organizations to arrange paragliding, skydiving, climbing and hiking trips, plus winery tours and interpretive tours of the area's flora and fauna. You can rent bikes for $30 per day.

B&Bs Vernon has lots of B&Bs, many located on the surrounding hills and on local farms. For a complete listing, contact the Visitor Info Centre. Close to downtown is *Tuck Inn* (☎ 250-545-3252, 3101 Pleasant Valley Rd), a large, white Victorian house with doubles for $75, including full breakfast. Up in the hills, *Melford Creek Country Inn & Spa* (☎ 250-558-7910, 7810 Melford Rd), 1km off Silver Star Rd, features a huge indoor spa area and pool. Rooms start at $79.

Motels & Hotels You'll find many, many motels in and around Vernon, especially north of downtown along 32nd St (Hwy 97). Downtown, the *Schell Motel* (☎ 250-545-1351, 2810 35th St), on the corner of 30th Ave, contains a heated pool and sauna. Rooms cost $56/65 single/double ($8 extra with a kitchen). The reliable *Travelodge* (☎ 250-545-2161, 800-578-7878, 3000 28th Ave) charges $64/74 for its standard rooms.

Farther north, the *Comfort Inn* (☎ 250-542-4434, 800-228-5150, 4204 32nd St) features an indoor pool and whirlpool. Rooms start at $79/89. The *Best Western Vernon Lodge* (☎ 250-545-3385, 800-663-4422, 3914 32nd St), on the corner of 39th Ave, boasts an indoor tropical garden, a restaurant and Checkers Pub. Rooms cost $99/109 and up.

Places to Eat

For a small town, Vernon abounds with eateries, particularly little coffee shops and sandwich places. Whether you're craving caffeine or a solid dose of local gossip, *Bean*

Scene (☎ *250-558-1817, 2923 30th Ave*) is definitely the place to be. The hub of what's happening in town, the café offers good coffee and teas served by a friendly staff.

A popular lunch place downtown, *Johnny Appleseed* (☎ *250-542-7712, 3018 30th Ave*) serves good soups, sandwiches ($6) and veggie specials, though the cranky staff should probably spend more time relaxing at the Bean Scene. *Little Tex Cafe & Bistro* (☎ *250-558-1919, 3302B 29th St*) is small, but the portions are big. Try the fantastic salsa or the excellent quesadillas ($8 and up).

J-Don (☎ *250-558-6939, 2900 30th Ave*) is known for its good prices and Japanese dons (rice bowls), which start at $5.50. One block west, *The Italian Kitchen Company* (☎ *250-558-7899, 2916 30th Ave*) offers good Italian entrees (around $12) served on red-and-white checkered tablecloths. *Pandora's Bistro* (☎ *250-558-6198, 2908 29th Ave*), the only openly gay-friendly restaurant in town, prepares tasty vegetarian food, including the Veggie Pies (a bargain at $5.25).

For a lively pub atmosphere, try *Sir Winston's Pub* (☎ *250-549-3485, 2705 32nd St*), with good beer and standard pub fare, such as burgers ($8).

If you're in the mood for a little spice, try *Amarin Thai* (☎ *542-9300, 2903 31st St*), where the delicious green curry will set you back $9.25. A favorite with locals, *Eclectic Med* (☎ *250-558-4646, 3117 32nd St*) lives up to its name, with yummy foods from around the world. Dinner-sized Thai chicken salad is $11; the Moroccan lamb is $19.

Entertainment
The best outdoor patio in town sits right on Kalamalka Lake at *Alexander's Beach Pub* (☎ *250-545-3131*), right beside the Kal Lake beach.

One of the few nightclubs in town, *Club XS* (☎ *250-558-5370, 2933A 30th St*) attracts some decent bands and a lively, eclectic crowd. The younger set boogies the night away at *Club Rio* (☎ *250-549-7448*), on the corner of 29th Ave and 29th St.

The Vernon Jazz Society puts on a show every second Saturday at the *Vernon Club*, above Nolan's Pharmacy on 30th St. For show information, call ☎ 250-549-1228 or visit www.vernonjazz.homestead.com.

The local *movie theater* is in the Polson Place Mall, at the junction of Hwy 6 and 27th St.

Getting There & Around
BC bus service radiates in all directions from the Greyhound bus depot (☎ 250-545-0527), 3102 30th St at 31st Ave. The station contains a restaurant and offers baggage storage, though there are no lockers. The building is open 6:15 am to 10 pm daily, but closes between 1:15 and 2:15 pm and between 4 and 5 pm.

For information about local buses, contact Vernon Regional Transit System (☎ 250-545-7221), 4210 24th Ave, or pick up a copy of *Vernon Regional Rider's Guide*, which offers details of fares and routes, from the Visitor Info Centre. All buses leave downtown from the bus stop at 31st St and 30th Ave. For Kalamalka Lake, catch bus No 1; for Okanagan Lake, take bus No 7. The one-way fare is $1.50, and a day pass costs $3. In the unlikely event you'll need a cab, call Vernon Taxi (☎ 250-545-3337).

AROUND VERNON
The **O'Keefe Historic Ranch** (☎ 250-542-7868), 12km north of Vernon on Hwy 97 in Spallumcheen, was home to the O'Keefe family from 1867 to 1977. Among other things, you'll see the original log cabin, a general store, old farm machines and St Ann's, probably the oldest Roman Catholic church in the province. The ranch offers a good introduction to life in the valley before the region was taken over by the fruit-growing industry. The ranch is open 9 am to 5 pm daily, May to October. Admission is $6/4 for adults/children.

On Hwy 97A, 23km north of Vernon, you'll come across **Armstrong** (population 3900), known mostly for its cheese and excellent farmer's market. Thirteen kilometers farther north is **Enderby** (population 3010), on the banks of the Shuswap River. Rock climbers scale the vertical rocks at Enderby Cliffs, north of town. For more information, contact the Enderby Visitor Info Centre (☎ 250-838-6727).

East of Vernon on Hwy 6, farms and forests line the road to **Lumby** (population 1900) and **Cherryville** (population 1000), about 20km and 48km from Vernon, respectively. Outdoor opportunities abound, and the many lakes draw lots of anglers. From Cherryville, you can drive northeast on the Sugar Lake Rd to the backcountry wonderland of remote **Monashee Provincial Park**. Hwy 6 also heads east over a scenic road to **Needles**, where you catch the ferry to the Kootenays (see the Kootenays chapter). For area information, contact the Lumby Visitor Info Centre (☎ 250-547-2300).

Thompson Valley

The spectacular North Thompson and South Thompson Rivers converge at Kamloops and become the Thompson River, a major tributary of the Fraser River, which spills into the ocean near Richmond. Long used as vital transportation links, these rivers carved out the geographic and human history of this region. Kamloops, a major highway junction and service center, is the largest town in the Thompson Valley. East of Kamloops, just north of the Okanagan Valley, is the Shuswap, an area known for houseboating and summer fun on scenic Shuswap Lake. West of Kamloops, the Thompson River passes through rolling green hills and beautiful ranchlands to Ashcroft, Cache Creek and Logan Lake. South is Merritt, the last stop on the Coquihalla Hwy (Hwy 5) before the road heads south to Hope and back to Vancouver. This entire area is rich in Shuswap First Nations history and culture. It is a place where lakes and rivers converge, highways connect and cattle thrive.

THE SHUSWAP

Shuswap ('shoe-swap') Lake is in the shape of a lazy H, lying on its side, or maybe just drunk and falling over. Can you picture it? The top right arm of the lake is Seymour Arm, and below it is Anstey Arm. At the bottom left is Salmon Arm (also the name

Saluting the Sockeye

Sockeye salmon are some of the most hard-core travelers around. These wily fish travel from the Adams River to the Pacific Ocean and back again in what is one of nature's most miraculous and complete cycles of life. It all starts on the shallow riverbed in Roderick Haig-Brown Provincial Park, a massive breeding ground for sockeye salmon. Since glaciers carved out river valleys, pairs of male and female sockeye have fought starvation, currents and grueling rapids to return from the ocean to the place of their birth. In early fall, the lower Adams River hosts a frenzy of spawning salmon.

Each spawning female lays about 4000 eggs, many of which do not survive; either they're unsuccessfully fertilized or killed off by rainbow trout and other predators. The ones that do survive spend the winter tucked into the gravel on the riverbed, waiting out frost and weather while slowly growing in the soft, jelly-like casing of the eggshell. In spring, the eggs hatch and tiny salmon fry – measuring about 2.5cm in length – emerge and float downriver to spend their first year in Shuswap Lake. Though the calm lake water keeps the fry safe from the rushing currents of the river, only one out of four fry eludes the hungry jaws of predators. Survivors of that ordeal grow in the lake, becoming smolt. These hardy fish, up to 10cm long, begin the long journey to the mouth of the Fraser River, which they follow all the way to the Pacific Ocean. Once in the salty water, the salmon grow up to 3kg, needing size and agility to escape more ravenous predators like killer whales, seals and commercial fishermen. Once they've reached maturity, about four years after

of the town). The top left of the H is the thick thumb of the lake, whose tip breaks off, like a hangnail, into Little Shuswap Lake. Salmon Arm, on the Trans-Canada Hwy, is the main service center at the lake, though nearby Sicamous proclaims itself the 'houseboat capital of Canada.' On the north shore of the lake, you'll find two excellent provincial parks, more camping and accommodations.

The area around the lakes is picturesque, with green, wooded hills and farms. The grazing cattle and lush, cultivated land make a pleasant change of scenery no matter which direction you're coming from. Many provincial parks dot the area, offering an abundance of water-related activities. Accommodations are tight in the height of summer, so if you're coming in July and August, try to phone ahead.

Salmon Arm contains the area's main Visitor Info Centre (☎ 250-832-2230, 877-725-6667), 751 Marine Park Dr NE at Harbourfront Drive. The smaller Sicamous Visitor Info Centre (☎ 250-836-3313), 110 Finlayson St, also provides area information.

The Greyhound bus depot (☎ 250-832-3962), 50 10th St SW in Salmon Arm, is one block north of the Trans-Canada Hwy. You can use the luggage lockers if you need to store some stuff. Buses leave daily going east and west.

Roderick Haig-Brown Provincial Park

This provincial park on the north shore of Shuswap Lake takes its name from Roderick Haig-Brown (1908-1976), a British Columbian naturalist and angler who devoted much of his life to conserving sockeye salmon. Look for his many books in BC bookstores. The 1059-hectare park protects either side of the Adams River from the northwest side of Shuswap Lake to Adams Lake. If you're here in October, you'll see the bright red sockeye running upriver to spawn (see the boxed text 'Saluting the Sockeye'). The fish population peaks every four years, when as many as two million fish crowd the Adams' shallow riverbeds. The years 2002 and 2006 will see the next big spawns. Interpretive displays tell all about

THOMPSON-OKANAGAN

Saluting the Sockeye

their birth, a biological signal as sharp as intuition takes hold and the salmon know it's time to make the great journey back home.

Of every 4000 eggs produced at Roderick Haig-Brown Provincial Park, only two fish survive long enough to make the long, grueling journey home to spawn. When the internal alarm rings, the sleek, silvery ocean sockeye stop eating as they reach the Fraser's freshwater mouth. From here on, for the next 21 days, the fish rely on body fat and protein to energize their 29km-a-day swim over rocks and raging rapids.

Scraped, beaten and torn, the fish slowly turn a bright crimson red, a color they'll carry like cloaks until they reach the spawning grounds. There, the red heads turn a deep green, the male's snout elongates and his teeth get sharper, ready to fend off intruders as he and the female, now heavy with eggs, search for a place to nest. But good real estate on the shallow riverbed is hard to come by, and the pairs of fish fight like crazed parents to find a sheltered spot to nest. The female digs her nest by furiously flopping her tail while simultaneously laying eggs. The male quickly swims by, dropping a shower of milt to fertilize the eggs. The female then covers the nest with gravel. Upon completion of this exhausting ordeal of recreation, the hardy couple quietly dies, leaving their eggs to follow in this incredible journey.

Though the salmon spawn annually, every four years a mass migration occurs that far overshadows the intermittent-year spawns. In these years, up to two million sockeye return home.

this great event. You can hike in the park but camping is not permitted.

Activities

Two **white-water rafting** companies run the Adams River, which is mostly a Class III river (which means it'll get your adrenaline pumping but won't send you into cardiac arrest). Adams River Rafting (☎ 250-955-2447, 888-440-7238), in Scotch Creek at 3993 Squilax-Anglemont Rd, operates a mellow two-hour trip for $44. Shuswap Whitewater Rafting (☎ 250-955-2800), just down the street, offers a similar experience.

Houseboating can be a fun way to explore the Shuswap, especially during the height of summer, when the lake looks like a little village with a bunch of floating houses. Most houseboats are totally self-contained, with kitchens and running water. Some even come with hot tubs and water-slides. Most rent by the week, can sleep about 10 people and cost around $1200 for the week. Fuel is extra, and you have to bring your own food. If you want to rent houseboats, your best bet is to pick up a list of rentals at the Visitor Info Centres in Salmon Arm or Sicamous.

Places to Stay

Camping For information on all Shuswap provincial parks, call ☎ 250-851-3000. *Herald Provincial Park*, 25 minutes northwest of Salmon Arm, sits on the homestead of one the Shuswap's first farmers. It features sandy beaches, waterfalls and 51 sites ($18.50). To get there, turn off the Trans-Canada Hwy onto Sunnybrae Rd. *Shuswap Lake Provincial Park*, on the north shore at Scotch Creek, offers excellent wooded sites on the lake and no shortage of them: the park contains a whopping 272 campsites ($18.50). For reservations at both parks, call ☎ 800-689-9025. You can also camp by the water at *Silver Beach Provincial Park*, which sits at the head of Seymour Arm near the old gold-rush town of Seymour City. With only 35 sites, it's a little quieter.

Hostels The *HI Squilax General Store & Caboose Hostel* (☎ 250-675-2977, squilax@

jetstream.net), about 10km east of Chase and 45km west of Salmon Arm, touts itself as a 'rustic experience,' complete with a resident population of Yuma bats (they sleep outside). Though it seems downright dirty compared to other BC hostels, it can make a good rural hub for exploring the area. Plus, if you've ever wanted to explore the rear of a train, here's your chance: the dorm-style beds are in old cabooses, strewn about the lawn next to Shuswap Lake. The main building contains private rooms and a communal kitchen. Readers enjoy the campfires at night, and budget travelers appreciate the cheap accommodations (hard to find in this area). Beds cost $14/18 for members/nonmembers; add $4 for a private room.

B&Bs The Visitor Info Centre keeps a complete list of area B&Bs. *The Trickle Inn* (☎ 250-835-8835, trickle@jetstream.net, 5290 Trans-Canada Hwy), 11km west of Salmon Arm in Tappen, is a nice place to splurge. Victorian rooms in a 1907 farmhouse start at $100/125 single/double; rates include a delicious breakfast.

Motels & Hotels Many motels line the Trans-Canada Hwy on either side of Salmon Arm. Among the cheaper ones, the *Salmon River Motel* (☎ 250-832-3065, 910 40th St), 1km west of town, offers barebones rooms for $54/59 single/double. On the eastern outskirts of town, the *McGuire Lake Inn* (☎ 250-832-2129, 620 Trans-Canada Hwy) features a good pub, a pool and large clean rooms starting at $70/75. At the *Best Western Villager West Motor Inn* (☎ 250-832-9793, 800-528-1235, 61 10th St), next to the Greyhound station, rooms start at $73/80.

The incredibly beautiful *Quaaout Lodge Resort* (☎ 250-679-3090, 800-663-4303, quaaout@quaaout.com), on Little Shuswap Lake, was designed and built by the Little Shuswap Band, a part of the Shuswap First Nations, in 1992. The building that contains the entrance area and dining room resembles a *kekuli*, or winter house, which is usually buried in the ground. First Nations art decorates the hotel, and the kitchen serves up gourmet meals based on traditional foods and cooking methods. On the lodge grounds are four giant teepees, each one facing a different direction in a symbolic gesture of respect to the earth. Ask the staff about the sweat lodge and the mid-July powwow. Rooms for one or two people start at $150. To get there, follow the Trans-Canada Hwy west to the north shore and look for signs.

Places to Eat

Get good coffee at *Hazbeanz* (☎ 250-804-0855, 371 Alexander St NE) or down the street at *The Chocolate Bean* (☎ 250-832-6681). *Jiggers Bar & Grill* (☎ 250-832-9797, 620 Trans-Canada Hwy), at the McGuire Lake Inn, serves good burgers ($8) and large portions of pasta ($10). For yummy Thai food, try *Poe Thong Thai* (☎ 250-832-0699, 131 Hudson Ave). Over on the north shore in Scotch Creek, *Finz Bar & Grill* (☎ 250-995-0900) has a great patio overlooking the marina. Its large menu includes meal-sized Caesar salads for $7 and Greek Pizza for $9.

KAMLOOPS

• population 85,000

Sitting at the confluence of the North Thompson, South Thompson and Thompson Rivers, Kamloops (or 'Loops,' as it's called by the locals) has always served as an important crossroads. The Shuswap Natives used the rivers and many lakes for transportation and salmon fishing. Fur-traders arrived in 1811, trading European goods with Shuswaps all along the riverbanks and carrying disease as they went. (By the time the Oblate missionaries arrived in 1842, the Native populations had dwindled by a third.) Overlanders, on their way to the Cariboo gold fields, passed through on rafts. The rivers fed the first farms. The Canadian Pacific Railway arrived in 1885, and by 1890 Kamloops had become a bustling transportation center.

The highways took over where the rivers left off. The Trans-Canada Hwy (Hwy 1) cuts east-west through town, the Yellowhead Hwy (Hwy 5) heads north to Jasper, Hwy 5A travels south and the Coquihalla Hwy (Hwy 5) heads southwest to Vancouver.

With its strategic location, the city has grown rapidly since the late 1960s and has turned into the major service and industrial center in the district, thanks to the primacy of the forestry, agriculture and manufacturing industries. An estimated 30,000 head of cattle live around Kamloops and two of Canada's largest manufacturers of ginseng are based here.

Kamloops is spread over a large area of lakes and dry, rolling hills. The downtown core is quiet, clean and pleasant.

Orientation & Information

Train tracks separate the Thompson River's edge from the downtown area. Next to the tracks, running east-west, is Lansdowne St. The other principal streets are Victoria St (the primary shopping area) and Seymour St, both parallel to and south of Lansdowne. Several blocks farther south, the Trans-Canada Hwy runs through the neighborhood of Sahali. You can reach the north shore via the Overlander Bridge (called Blue Bridge by the locals) or the Red Bridge on the north end of downtown. On the northwestern corner of the city, over the pedestrian walkway on Lansdowne St and 3rd Ave, is the Riverside Coliseum and Riverside Park, a pleasant spot for a picnic or stroll. Across from the park's shoreline, the North Thompson River meets the South Thompson River. Together they form the Thompson, flowing west into Kamloops Lake.

The Visitor Info Centre (☎ 250-374-3377, 800-662-1994, fax 250-828-9500) is at 1290 W Trans-Canada Hwy (exit 368) on the southwest side of town. It's open 8 am to 6 pm daily in summer, 9 am to 6 pm weekdays at other times. The city's Web site is www.city.kamloops.bc.ca.

The main post office (☎ 250-374-2444) is at 301 Seymour St, on the corner of 3rd Ave. You'll find the Kamloops public library (☎ 250-372-5145) at 465 Victoria St. Merlin Books (☎ 250-374-9553), 448 Victoria St across from the art gallery, is a great local bookstore with regional books, maps, magazines and newspapers.

THOMPSON-OKANAGAN

KAMLOOPS

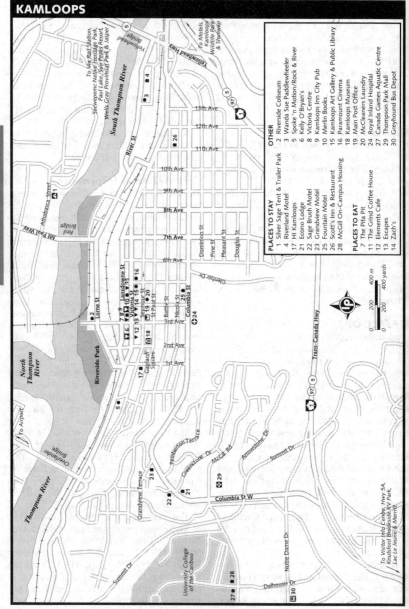

PLACES TO STAY

1 Silver Sage Tent & Trailer Park
4 Riverland Motel
17 HI Kamloops
21 Econo Lodge
22 Sage Brush Motel
23 Grandview Motel
25 Fountain Motel
26 Scott's Inn & Restaurant
28 McGill On-Campus Housing

PLACES TO EAT

7 The Pita Pit
11 The Grind Coffee House
12 Elements Cafe
13 Escapes
14 Zach's

OTHER

2 Riverside Coliseum
3 Wanda Sue Paddlewheeler
5 Spoke 'n Motion/Rock & River
8 Kelly O'Bryan's
9 Victoria Centre
10 Kamloops Inn City Pub
15 Merlin Books
15 Kamloops Art Gallery & Public Library
16 Paramount Cinema
18 Kamloops Museum
19 Main Post Office
20 McCleaners Laundry
24 Royal Inland Hospital
27 Canada Games Aquatic Centre
29 Thompson Park Mall
30 Greyhound Bus Depot

Newspapers include *Kamloops Daily News* and *Kamloops This Week*, a twice-weekly paper that lists community events.

To wash your clothes, try McCleaners Laundry (☎ 250-372-9655), 437 Seymour St. For medical care, go to the Royal Inland Hospital (☎ 250-374-5111), 311 Columbia St.

Things to See & Do

Many brick and stone buildings in the downtown core date back to the late 1800s, including the restored 1887 **St Andrews Presbyterian Church**, now the oldest public building in town. Pick up a copy of the *Kamloops Heritage Walking Tour* from the Visitor Info Centre. The **Kamloops Museum** (☎ 250-828-3576), 207 Seymour St at 2nd Ave, explores the area history, from the early Shuswaps to the missionaries, from the Overlanders (who passed through on their way to find gold in the Cariboo) to the arrival of the railroad. The video library includes movies on bears and salmon, as well as the history of mapmaker and river namesake David Thompson. The museum is open 9 am to 4:30 pm Tuesday to Saturday; admission is by donation. **Kamloops Art Gallery** (☎ 250-828-3543), 465 Victoria St, in the same industrial-style building as the public library, features an impressive collection of local, regional and national artists. Admission is $3/2 for adults/children.

The **Kamloops Wildlife Park** (☎ 250-573-3242), 17km east on the Trans-Canada Hwy, contains an interesting population of wild things, including Brazilian cockroaches, birds of prey, grizzly bears, camels and more, oh my. A little train toodles around the park in summer. It's open 8 am to 6 pm daily in July and August, 8 am to 4:30 pm daily the rest of the year. Admission is $6.75/3.75 for adults/children.

North of downtown on the Kamloops Indian Reserve, the **Secwepemc Native Heritage Park** (☎ 250-828-9801), 355 Yellowhead Hwy, is the most interesting site in Kamloops. Here you can view a movie about the Secwepemc, or 'the people,' who were called Shuswap by white settlers because the white men couldn't get their tongues around Secwepemc (pronounced sha-**quat**-mic). Outside, the site has recreated traditional winter and summer houses and the Kamloops Powwow arbor. Inside, a museum outlines the history and the culture of the Secwepemc People, along with informative ethnobotany displays depicting how berries, leaves and roots were used for food and medicine. The park is open 8:30 am to 4:30 pm weekdays, October to May; 8:30 am to 8 pm weekdays and 10 am to 6 pm weekends during summer. Admission is $6/4 for adults/children and includes the excellent guided tours. Ask about the annual **Powwow**, a major event held here every August. Unfortunately, there is no city bus to the park.

A big tourist draw is the *Wanda Sue* **Paddlewheeler** (☎ 250-374-7447), a restored stern-wheeler that takes passengers on a two-hour cruise down the Thompson River. You can also do dinner cruises. The boat leaves from a terminal at the Old Yacht Club, 1140 River St at the foot of 10th Ave. Be there an hour before your sailing to get tickets, which cost $11.50/6.50 for adults/children. *Wanda Sue* runs at various times throughout the day from May to September. Call for times.

If you are in the mood for a swim, the **Canada Games Aquatic Centre** (☎ 250-828-3655), 910 McGill Rd near University College of the Cariboo, is an excellent facility

Coyotes call Paul Lake Provincial Park home.

with a pool, steam room, hot tub and sauna. You can drop in for $5.

Hikers and beach-lovers flock to **Paul Lake Provincial Park**, only 30 minutes north in Kamloops' brushy grasslands. Mountain bikers like to do the 20km trip around Paul Lake, while fisher types try for Gerard or rainbow trout. This is a protected habitat for falcons, bald eagles, coyotes and mule deer, so keep your eyes peeled. To reach the park, take Hwy 5 north for 5km, then turn onto Pinantan Rd and drive for 19km. The 213-hectare **Lac Le Jeune Provincial Park**, 37km south of Kamloops on the Coquihalla Hwy (Hwy 5), is popular for camping, swimming and rainbow-trout fishing on Lac Le Jeune (French for 'the young lake'). In winter, the park connects to the Stake Lake cross-country ski trails.

Sun Peaks Resort

This relatively new resort (☎ 250-578-7232 800-807-3257, info@sunpeaksresort.com), built on Tod Mountain 53km northeast of Kamloops, is fast becoming a year-round recreation spot, though it rarely looks more picturesque than in winter, when snow blankets the small village full of restaurants and shops. The mountain boasts 80 runs, six chairlifts, a snowboard park and 881m of vertical rise. BC Olympian Nancy Greene runs the ski school. More than 78% of the runs are novice or intermediate, making the resort more family-oriented. Lift tickets cost $46/26 for adults/children. The Sun Peaks International Hostel offers the only cheap accommodations (see Places to Stay, later).

Ski rentals are available on the mountain (☎ 250-578-5430) or at Spoke 'n Motion (☎ 250-372-3001), 194 Victoria St. The summer bike shop turns into a complete ski shop in winter, renting ski packages for $25 and snowboards (with boots) for $20. You can also rent telemark and cross-country skis.

In summer, the quad chair keeps running, taking hikers and mountain bikers up top to play around on the snowless runs. The ride up costs $12, or $25 with a bike.

Places to Stay

Camping The *Silver Sage Tent & Trailer Park* (☎ 250-828-2077, 771 Athabasca St E), northeast over the river, is nothing special but it's quiet. You can see across the river to downtown, which is walkable from the campground. The facilities include campsites ($15 and up), a coin laundry and showers. *Knutsford Brookside RV Park* (☎ 250-372-5380) lies 12km southwest of town, on Hwy 5A (the Kamloops to Princeton Hwy). All facilities are available, including showers and a coin laundry; a site for two people starts at $17.

You can also camp in the two nearby provincial parks (☎ 250-851-3000). *Paul Lake Provincial Park*, 24km northeast of Kamloops, offers nice sites on the north end of Paul Lake for $12. *Lac Le Jeune Provincial Park*, 37km south of town, has flush and pit toilets but no showers. The 144 sites, each with a picnic table and fire pit, cost $15. For directions to these two parks, see Things to See & Do, earlier.

Hostels The spacious *HI Kamloops* (☎ 250-828-7991, fax 828-2442, kamloops@ hihostels.bc.ca, 7 W Seymour St), on the corner of 1st Ave, is in the beautiful old courthouse close to downtown. Built in 1909 by Honeyman and Curtis (the same folks who designed the Empress in Victoria), the grand courthouse was constructed with local brick and imported granite and slate. It opened as a hostel in 1992 and retains the courthouse feel, especially when the sun shines through the stained-glass windows. Common areas include a lounge and dining room in the original courtrooms, where you can sit in the jury box and reenact the sentencing of outlaws like Billy Minor. The hostel also has a huge kitchen, computers for Internet access and coin-laundry facilities. The office is open 8 am to 1 pm and 5 to 10 pm. Dorm beds cost $16/20 for members/ nonmembers; private rooms start at $40/43. The hostel is often full in summer, so it's a good idea to reserve ahead. From the Greyhound bus depot, take local bus No 3 ($1.25) to the corner of Seymour St and 3rd

Ave, then walk two blocks west, or you can walk the entire way in about 30 minutes.

The **Sun Peaks International Hostel** (☎ 250-578-0057, sunpeakshostel@canada com, 1140 Sun Peaks Rd), up at the ski hill, occupies an old A-frame wood lodge in a prime location, just across the road from the quad chairlift. Amenities include a communal kitchen, lounge and laundry facilities. The hostel arranges group ski/snowboard lessons, hikes and social events, as well as transportation to and from Kamloops. At $20 per night, it is by far the cheapest place to stay on the mountain. Check out the Web site at www.sunpeakshostel.com.

University Housing From May to August, **McGill On-Campus Housing** (☎ 250-372-7778, fax 372-2757, mcgillhousing@telus net), at University College of the Cariboo, rents out student rooms. Each single room comes with its own fridge, microwave and hotplate but you'll have to share a bathroom. This is a good option if the hostels are booked up. Rooms cost $25 per night, with a two-night minimum stay.

B&Bs The Visitor Info Centre keeps a full list of B&Bs.

Motels & Hotels You'll find most motels on Columbia St, west of the downtown area, and on the Trans-Canada Hwy east of town. On the west side, the **Econo Lodge** (☎ 250-372-8235, 800-589-1988, 775 Columbia St W) offers clean no-frills rooms for $50/55 single/double. One of the better values in town is **Sage Brush Motel** (☎ 250-372-3151, 888-218-6116, sagebrushmtl@hotmail.com, 660 Columbia St W), where rooms start at $50/60. The **Grandview Motel** (☎ 250-372-6312, 800-210-6088, info@grandviewmotel com, 463 Grandview Terrace) features a pool and a large patio with outdoor barbecues, but don't take the name too literally: the 'grand view' is of the valley and the pulp mill on the other side of the river. Rooms start at $71/81.

Closer to downtown, **Scott's Inn & Restaurant** (☎ 250-372-8221, 800-665-3343, 551 11th Ave) contains an indoor pool, a welcoming cafe and average rooms that start at $50/60. Scott's has also taken over an old motel across the street and rents out rooms there for a month at a time.

Right downtown across from the hospital, the **Fountain Motel** (☎ 250-374-4451, 888-253-1569, 506 Columbia St) offers basic rooms for $56/62. About a kilometer east of the core, just before the highway junction, the **Riverland Motel** (☎ 250-374-1530, 800-663-1530, 1530 River St) features nice rooms overlooking the Thompson River, plus an indoor pool and hot tub. Most rooms have kitchenettes and start at $65/75, including a continental breakfast.

You can swim in the heated pool at the **Thrift Inn** (☎ 250-374-2488, 800-661-7769, 2459 Trans-Canada Hwy), east of town; rooms cost $43/50. The **Courtesy Inn Motel** (☎ 250-372-8533, 800-372-8533, 1773 Trans-Canada Hwy) features an indoor pool, sauna and very comfortable rooms starting at $65/77.

Places to Eat

Along and around Victoria St, numerous places offer meals or just coffee. The **Victoria Centre** (228 Victoria St) contains a food court with some cheap eats. Start your day with a cup of joe from **The Grind Coffee House** (☎ 250-828-6115, 476 Victoria St), at 5th Ave, or go west a block to **Zach's** (☎ 250-347-6487), a mellow coffeehouse that bakes its own bagels. For a healthy, light and cheap lunch, stop by the **Pita Pit** (☎ 250-377-7482, 330 Victoria St). Giant veggie pitas cost $4.25; meaty versions are $5.50.

An excellent place to have lunch and write a postcard, **Elements Cafe** (☎ 250-372-1341, 229 Victoria St) shows off local artists' work in a colorful space. This spot features an open-to-anyone jam night on Thursday and music or improvisational theater (called 'theater sports') on Friday and Saturday. The lunch portions are small but rightly priced at $5 for salads and $6 for wraps; dinner costs more.

One of the best spots for a delicious meal in a comfortable setting is just up the street

THOMPSON-OKANAGAN

at *Escapes* (☎ 250-377-7700, 357 Victoria St).
You can either sit by the fire upstairs in the
pub or at a table downstairs in the restaurant. The menu is the same either way.
Burgers are $9, a veggie sandwich is $8 and
a tuna steak dinner is $15.

Entertainment

Kelly O'Bryans (☎ 250-828-1559, 244 Victoria St) is a merry Irish pub with cheap
burgers and well-poured pints. The *Kamloops Inn City Pub* (345 Victoria St) occupies Kamloops' first fire hall, which dates
back to 1905. The atmospheric spot features
pool tables and a good lineup of crusty
locals sitting at the bar. It's dark, dingy and
smoky but, hey, it's historic.

Getting There & Away

Kamloops Airport is 7km northwest of
town on Kamloops' north shore. Air BC
and Canadian Regional (☎ 888-247-2262 for
both) fly to Kamloops daily from Vancouver.

The Greyhound bus depot (☎ 250-374-1212), 725 Notre Dame Dr, is southwest of
the downtown area off Columbia St W. The
building, which contains a cafeteria and
luggage lockers, only closes between 3 and
5 am. Many buses leave daily for Vancouver, Calgary, Jasper, Edmonton, Prince
George and Kelowna.

The VIA Rail station (☎ 800-561-8630),
11km north of town off the Yellowhead
Hwy, is only open 30 minutes prior to departures. Every week, three trains go south
to Vancouver, and three trains go east to
Jasper, Edmonton and beyond. For Prince
George, you must transfer in Jasper. The
privately operated *Rocky Mountaineer* tour
train stops here overnight on its various
trips.

Getting Around

For information about local bus routes, call
Kamloops Transit Service (☎ 250-376-1216)
or pick up a *Rider's Guide* from the Visitor
Info Centre. The main stop, where you can
catch any bus, is at the Thompson Park
Mall, at Lansdowne St and 6th Ave. The
one-way fare is $1.25.

For a taxi, call Yellow Cabs (☎ 250-374-3333) or Kami Cabs (☎ 250-554-1377).

AROUND KAMLOOPS

Heading west, the Trans-Canada Hwy
passes by Kamloops Lake, following the
Thompson River as it winds its way through
rolling hills and green river valleys. En
route, the road goes by **Walhachin**, essentially just a valley now. Between 1907 and
1914, a group of English settlers created
their own agricultural haven here, successfully tilling the dry land and building their
own irrigation flume to carry water to the
thriving orchards. After WWI called away
most of the men, a massive storm ripped out
the flume and destroyed this little utopia
almost overnight. If you look across the
valley, you can still see the indentation from
the flume. A sign along the highway tells the
story.

Heading west, you'll hit **Ashcroft** (population 1900), a cattle-ranching community
surrounded by sagebrush and tumbleweeds.
When the railroad rolled through in the
1880s, Ashcroft was already a small farming
community settled by gold-rushers, who realized early that they weren't going to find
any gold. In the 1960s, it became a big
copper mining town, but when the price of
copper dropped in the '80s, two mines
closed and the population shrank. Only the
farmers were left sitting pretty.

Just north of Ashcroft is **Cache Creek**
(population 1140), a tiny town prospectors
rushed through on their way to find gold in
the Cariboo. The story goes that the minors
would hide their gold or cache in a nearby
creek. Locals insist that there are still unclaimed stashes of gold buried deep in the
creek bed.

Following the scenic Hwy 97C south will
take you to the young town of **Logan Lake**
(population 2600), built in the early 1970s as
a company town for the large open-pit
copper mine. Before you come into town,
look for the striking turquoise lake alongside the highway. It's actually a 'slag pond,'
essentially a giant bathtub used for cleaning
copper. There's also a viewpoint overlook-

ing the massive mine. The Visitor Info Centre (☎ 250-523-6225) is the town's biggest attraction – it's housed in a mining shovel parked next to a giant ore-hauling truck. From Logan Lake, Hwy 97C heads south to Merritt.

MERRITT
• population 3000

Nestled in the pretty Nicola Valley 115km north of Hope, Merritt offers the only services along the Coquihalla Hwy (Hwy 5) between Hope and Kamloops. Before the first-stage completion of the 'Coq' (as the highway's called locally) in 1986, Merritt was a small town that didn't see much action.

Motels sprung up with the building of the highway, and that's pretty much all the action Merritt sees today – car traffic. Until July, that is – when the toe-stompin' **Merritt Mountain Music Festival** two-steps into town. This four-day country music festival attracts up to 100,000 hootin' and hollerin' cowboy-hat clad dudes who camp on the festival grounds. Beware that motels fill up during this week.

From Merritt, Hwy 97C heads east to the Okanagan or northwest to the Cariboo. Before continuing on, stop by the excellent Visitor Info Centre (☎ 250-315-1342) at the junction of the Coquihalla and Hwy 97C.

Here you can pick up information from all over the province. It's also a good idea to check road conditions before going south or north, as road conditions on the Coquihalla can get nasty any time of year. Be forewarned that there's a toll booth on the Coquihalla midway between Merritt and Hope; cars pay $10.

Places to Stay & Eat

At the north end of town (exit 290 off the Coquihalla Hwy), the **Merritt Motor Inn** (☎ 250-378-9422, 3561 Voght St) features an indoor pool, sauna and clean rooms for $55/65 single/double. Nearby, the **Coquihalla Motor Inn** (☎ 250-378-3567, 800-353-3571, 3571 Voght St) contains a pool with a hot tub and nice rooms for $60/71. For a neat ranching experience, try the **Quilchena Hotel** (☎ 250-378-2611, hotel@quilchena.com), 20km northeast of Merritt off Hwy 5A. This working ranch boasts gorgeous guest rooms, a Victorian dining room, a saloon and its own airstrip. Rooms start at $75. Check it out on the Web at www.quilchena.com.

Consume coffee, sandwiches and desserts and play pool at **Javalanche** (☎ 250-378-1888, 2144 Quilchena Ave). For Chinese food, you can't go wrong at the **Canada Cafe** (☎ 250-378-5551, 2055 Quilchena Ave), where wonton soup is $5 and chicken chow mein is $8.

THOMPSON-OKANAGAN

The Kootenays

The Kootenay region of BC is dominated by four mountain ranges: the Rockies and Purcells in the east and the Selkirks and Monashees in the west. Almost anywhere you look, you'll see snow-covered peaks. Wedged between the parallel mountain chains is an incredibly scenic series of lakes, rivers and thinly populated valleys. Dense populations of grizzly and black bears, elk, moose and deer thrive here, so you stand a good chance of seeing wildlife if you visit. National and provincial parks throughout the area preserve much of the varied terrain and make it accessible for visitors.

Highlights

- Gazing at wildflowers on the Meadows in the Sky Parkway

- Soothing your sore muscles in the warm waters of Nakusp Hot Springs

- Skiing nothing but powder at Kimberley and Fernie Alpine Resorts

- Plucking guitars or dancing to the bongo beats in groovy Nelson

- Getting goose bumps on a rafting roar down the Kicking Horse River

- Canoeing on one of the long, slender Kootenay lakes

Traversing the high mountain passes has always been a challenge and a necessity. Evidence shows that First Nations people crossed the snowy peaks and canoed turbulent river waters to trade with neighboring tribes more than 10,000 years ago. Later, starting in the early 1800s, European explorers fought treacherous conditions to conquer, then map, the craggy passes.

During the 1890s, prospectors found rich mineral deposits, and boomtowns sprang up like daisies in the silver-rich Slocan Valley and around Rossland, where the mountains were studded in gold, as well as near Kimberley, where prosperous claims of lead and zinc populated the area. Soon stern-wheelers plied the Kootenays' long lakes, carrying minerals to smelters or to waiting trains.

Today, people still come here to explore the region's rich natural bounties. Visitors travel to the Kootenays to soak in the many area hot springs, to ski and snowboard at spectacular mountain resorts, to relive the mining history or to play in the rivers and lakes.

The Kootenays fall under the Nelson Forest Region, comprised of six separate districts: Arrow, Boundary, Columbia, Cranbook, Invermere, Kootenay Lake. For topographic maps and backcountry trail and camping information, contact the Nelson Forest Region (☎ 250-354-6200, fax 354-6250), 518 Lake St in Nelson. You can also obtain information from the Ministry of Forests' Web site at www.for.gov.bc.ca.

West Kootenays

East of the busy Okanagan Valley, the western boundary of the West Kootenays region follows the 230km-long Arrow Lake. The southern boundary is near the US border at Grand Forks and Creston. The eastern boundary follows the 145km-long Kootenay Lake, which is nestled in the scenic valley between the Selkirk and Purcell Mountains.

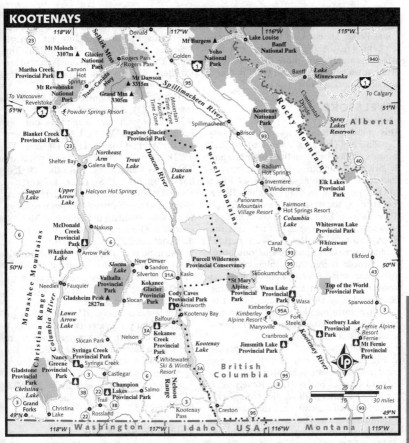

The Trans-Canada Hwy (Hwy 1) marks the northern boundary. Several ferries across lakes and rivers connect highways throughout the region (see the boxed text 'Kootenay Ferries,' later in this chapter).

Stern-wheeler transportation on the long lakes in the late 1800s and early 1900s connected the area to the US via rivers and lakes. Later, trains added to the transportation network by carrying goods to and from the stern-wheeler ports. Busy ports included pretty Nakusp on Upper Arrow Lake and Kaslo on Kootenay Lake, where today you can visit the world's oldest surviving stern-

wheeler. The Slocan Valley boomed with silver mines during the late 1800s, and during WWII more than 20,000 Japanese Canadians were forced into Japanese internment camps throughout the valley. Today, the Slocan is one of the most picturesque parts of the province.

The area around Castlegar and Grand Forks is rich in Russian Doukhobor history (see the Castlegar section, later in this chapter), and Rossland's Red Mountain, once famous for gold discoveries, is now one of the province's best ski areas. Revelstoke, at the north end of the West Kootenays, is the world capital for heli-skiing and the gateway to Mt Revelstoke and Glacier National Parks. The striking town of Nelson, the center of the region, boasts an active artist community, and more than one third of the town's buildings have been restored to their Victorian glory.

REVELSTOKE
• population 8500
This small mountain city on the Trans-Canada Hwy (Hwy 1), 70km east of Sicamous, is nestled between the Monashee and Selkirk mountain ranges and sits at the confluence of the rushing Illecillewaet River and the wide, slow-moving Columbia River. It perches on the western edge of Mt Revelstoke National Park, which is about halfway between the Okanagan Valley and the Rocky Mountains. Revelstoke's natural landmarks make it a picturesque, outdoorsy place, whose recreational splendor is not lost on the active, friendly community. Neat wooden houses and tiny gardens line the quiet residential streets. A recent effort to revitalize downtown heritage buildings has paid off, giving the alpine community a sense of historical dignity.

Originally known to First Nations people as 'Big Eddy,' for the respite it offered canoe travelers, the town was later named for Edward Charles Baring (Lord Revelstoke), the British financier who came through with a much-needed cash advance that saved the Canadian Pacific Railway (CPR) from bankruptcy. The coming of the CPR in the 1880s, and later the opening of the Trans-Canada Hwy in 1962, made Revelstoke a viable transportation hub. Today, more and more people use the town as a base from which to venture to the mountains to ski and snowboard, hike, bike or simply gaze at snowy peaks and alpine meadows.

Orientation & Information
Revelstoke is south of the Trans-Canada Hwy. Victoria Rd runs parallel to the railway tracks that run along the northeast end of town. The main streets include 1st St and Mackenzie Ave. Grizzly Plaza, between Mackenzie and Orton Aves, is a pedestrian precinct and the heart of downtown, where free live music performances take place in the evenings throughout July and August. Life-size bronze grizzly bears flank the plaza. The paved Revelstoke River Trail (an excellent place to walk or jog) runs along the river at the south end of town.

The Visitor Info Centre (☎ 250-837-5345, fax 837-4223), 206 Campbell Ave, is open 8:30 am to 4:30 pm weekdays only. In summer, a second Visitor Info Centre opens on the Trans-Canada Hwy (☎ 250-837-3522); it's staffed from 9 am to 5 pm daily. The Parks Canada regional office (☎ 250-837-7500), 301 3rd St, offers information about Mt Revelstoke and Glacier National Parks; it's open 8 am to 4:30 pm weekdays. In the same building, the Friends of Mt Revelstoke & Glacier (☎ 250-837-2010) distributes books and maps of the parks.

The main post office is next door. Grizzly Book & Serendipity Shop (☎ 250-837-6185), 208 Mackenzie Ave, sells magazines, a wide selection of metaphysical literature and some regional books.

The few coin-operated laundries in town include Family Laundry (☎ 250-837-3938), 409 1st St, which stays open until 8 pm Monday to Saturday (5 pm on Sunday). The newer Selkirk Laundry, 100 Boyle Ave, is open until 9 pm daily.

Queen Victoria Hospital (☎ 250-837-2131) is on the southeast side of town on Newlands Rd.

Things to See & Do
The **Revelstoke Railway Museum** (☎ 250-837-6060, 877-837-6060), in a beautiful building right off Victoria Rd downtown, contains restored steam locomotives, including one of the largest steam engines ever used on CPR lines. Photographs and artifacts document the construction of the CPR, pay tribute to its hardy workers and relate the railway's ongoing financial woes. Volunteer railway engineers are often on hand to recount stories about the heyday of rail travel. Check out the museum's Web site at www.railwaymuseum.com.

The museum bookstore carries a vast selection of books about the building of the

REVELSTOKE

To Trans-Canada Hwy
(Hwy 1) & Hwy 23S

Bend St

Bend St

Mt Revelstoke
National Park

To Mt Revelstoke &
Meadows in the Sky Parkway

Summit Pkwy

To Canyon Hot Springs,
Glacier National Park,
Golden & Calgary

Trans-Canada Hwy

Columbia River

Centennial
Park Dr

To Revelstoke
River Trail

To Hospital, Airport &
Powder Springs Resort

PLACES TO STAY
3 Mountain View Motel
7 HI Revelstoke Traveller's Hostel
   & Guest House
14 Powder Springs Inn
20 Regent Inn
24 Daniel's Guest House

PLACES TO EAT
13 Frisby Ridge Teriyaki Restaurant
15 Bertz Outdoor Equipment & Café
16 Tony's Roma
17 Manning's Restaurant
18 Blue Beary Patch
21 Three Bears' Bistro

OTHER
1 Visitor Info Centre (Seasonal)
2 Courthouse
4 Revelstoke Railway Museum
5 Family Laundry
6 Selkirk Laundry
8 Revelstoke Museum
9 Canadian Avalanche Centre
10 Parks Canada Office; Friends of
   Mt Revelstoke & Glacier
11 Post Office
12 Visitor Info Centre
19 Grizzly Book & Serendipity Shop
22 High Country Cycle & Sports
23 Library

THE KOOTENAYS

CPR, which was instrumental – if not essential – in linking Canada (see the boxed text 'Canadian Pacific Railway's Iron Link'). The museum is open 9 am to 8 pm daily in July and August; 9 am to 5 pm daily from April to June and September to October; 9 am to 5 pm weekdays from November to March. Admission is $5/2 for adults/children.

Revelstoke Museum (☎ 250-837-3067), in the brick building on the corner of 1st St and Boyle Ave, holds a permanent collection of furniture and historical odds and ends, including mining, logging and railway artifacts that date back to the town's estab-

lishment in the 1880s. It's open 10 am to 5 pm daily in July and August and 1 to 4 pm weekdays at other times. It's worth a few minutes and the suggested $2 donation.

BC Hydro (☎ 250-837-6211) runs free tours of the 175m-high **Revelstoke Dam** on the Columbia River, 4km north of town off Hwy 23 and adjacent to Columbia View Provincial Park. A 'talking wand' leads you through a gallery of photos and information on hydroelectricity and the building of the dam. The highlight of the tour is the ride up the elevator to the Dam Crest Lookout, where an illuminated topographic map shows the vast Columbia River system. Though fairly boring for non-engineer types, the tour is free and makes a good rainy-day activity. You can also tour Hydro's **Mica Dam**, 149km north of Revelstoke in a bend of the Columbia River, at the end of Hwy 23.

Canyon Hot Springs (☎ 250-837-2420), 35km east of Revelstoke along the Trans-Canada Hwy, make a great spot for a quick visit. The site consists of a hot pool (42°C) and a larger, cooler swimming pool (32°C). The springs are open 9 am to 9 pm daily, May to September; 9 am to 10 pm daily in July and August. Admission is $5.50/4.50 for adults/children, including a locker and shower; a day pass is $7.50/6. You can rent a bathing suit and towel.

Nearby Tourist Traps
Between Revelstoke and Sicamous lie many kitschy roadside attractions of the kind popular several decades ago. Some prime examples, all on the Trans-Canada Hwy, include **Three Valley Gap Ghost Town** (☎ 250-837-2109), 19km west of Revelstoke; the **Enchanted Forest** (☎ 250-837-9477), 32km west; and **Beardale Castle Miniatureland** (☎ 250-836-2268), 42km west. The first combines historical buildings, a stage show, a motel and more in a large complex; the second involves numerous fairies and other figures scattered around a forest; the third displays handcrafted tiny towns and teensy trains. If you're in the mood to buy tacky trinkets or hunks of fudge, you'll get your fill at any of these places.

Activities
White-Water Rafting Apex Rafting Company (☎ 250-837-6376, 888-232-6666), which maintains an office at Canyon Hot Springs, runs mellow, two-hour guided trips on the Illecillewaet River in spring and summer. They're perfect for first-time rafters or for anyone wanting to just kick back and enjoy the scenery. Trips cost $42/32 for adults/children.

Mountain Biking Once the snow melts, ski runs become excellent mountain-biking

trails. Pick up a copy of the *Biking Trail Map* from the Visitor Info Centre or High Country Cycle & Sports (☎ 250-814-0090), 188 Mackenzie Ave, where you can also rent bikes for $30 per day.

If you're looking for sheer fun, maximum views and minimal effort, Summit Cycle Tours (☎ 250-837-3734) will drive you and your bike 27km up Mt Revelstoke, drop you off and let you coast down alongside wildflower-filled alpine meadows. The 2½-hour trip costs $49, including bike rental and transportation.

Skiing & Snowboarding Sandwiched in between the vast but relatively lesser-known Selkirk and Monashee mountain ranges, Revelstoke draws serious snow buffs looking for untracked powder and no crowds. Whether you ski, board or just like to romp around in the snow, Revelstoke's long, snowy winter season and experienced tour operators give you plenty of options.

For **downhill skiing** at a modest price, head to Powder Springs Resort (☎ 877-991-4455, 250-837-3199 in winter only). This small ski hill on Mt Mackenzie, just 4km southeast of Revelstoke, lacks the multiple chairlifts of bigger resorts, but its heavy snowfall (up to 1200cm), access to back-country slopes and relatively cheap lift tickets make it a spectacular spot. Tickets cost $24 on weekdays and $28 on weekends, and kids always ski free. You can get incredible deals if you stay at the hostel or at Powder Springs Inn (see Places to Stay, later in this section). Rentals are also available at the mountain. Skis (and boots) cost $20 per day, and snowboard packages are $25.

A popular but expensive way to find fresh powder is by **heli-skiing**, where a helicopter takes you high into the alpine to ski or snowboard steep slopes, deep powder and even glaciers. Selkirk Tangiers Helicopter Skiing (☎ 250-837-5378, 800-663-7080, selkirk@rockies.net) runs three-, five- and seven-day trips ranging from $2400 to $5500. You can get much cheaper rates if you go standby, either calling the night before or the same day. For more information, see www.selkirk-tangiers.com online.

Is It Me, or Is That Mountain Moving?

As you marvel at all the snowy peaks, take a second to realize that you are in the pumping heart of avalanche country, where heavy slides of falling snow have enough power and weight to crush an entire city. An avalanche, whose name is derived from the French verb 'avaler' (to swallow), occurs when a slab of snow separates from more stable snow or ground cover. This most often happens when there's a dramatic shift in temperature or when there's a heavy snowfall or, for that matter, heavy snowmelt.

Watching a distant avalanche is perhaps one of the most spectacular sights in nature. Up close, an avalanche can be the most thunderous and frightening exertion of power you'll ever encounter – and you want to be well out of the way. Avalanches kill more people in BC each year than any other natural phenomenon. Whether you're backcountry ski touring or simply hiking in the alpine, you should definitely find out the scoop before you venture into unknown terrain.

The Canadian Avalanche Association (CAA) operates the Canadian Avalanche Centre (☎ 250-837-2435), at the corner of 1st St and Campbell Ave in Revelstoke. It analyzes avalanche trends, weather patterns and avalanche accidents. If you're planning on doing any trips in the backcountry, you'll want to contact the CAA first. The 24-hour avalanche information line is ☎ 800-667-1105. For more information, write the CAA at PO Box 2759, Revelstoke, BC V0E 2S0, or check out the Web site www.avalanche.ca.

Canadian Mountain Holidays or CMH (☎ 800-661-0252) offers more upscale trips; prices vary depending on season and trip length. CMH maintains a Web site at www.cmhski.com.

Though sometimes called 'the poor man's heli-skiing,' **snow-cat skiing** isn't exactly cheap. Snow cats are giant, heated tractors that easily navigate ice and snow, allowing you to reach some pretty pristine alpine conditions. CAT Powder Skiing (☎ 250-837-5151, 800-991-4455, catski@junction .net) offers packages, including accommodations and meals at Powder Springs Inn (see Places to Stay). Prices range from $800 to $2200 (two to five days). Rates are a little cheaper in March, November and December. You can also try your luck at going standby, which costs about $300 per day. For more information, visit the Web site www.catpowder.com.

For **cross-country skiing**, head to the Mt MacPherson Ski Area, 7km south of town on Hwy 23. You'll pay $5 to use the 22km of groomed trails. You can rent classic or skate skis from The Nordic Connection (☎ 250-837-6168).

Places to Stay

Blanket Creek Provincial Park (☎ 250-825-3500, 800-689-9025 for reservations), 25km south of Revelstoke along Hwy 23, includes 64 campsites with flush toilets and running water but no showers. Find the same facilities and 25 sites at *Martha Creek Provincial Park* (☎ 250-825-4421), 16km north of town on Hwy 23. The camping fee at both parks is $12.

Many private campgrounds lie east and west of Revelstoke along the Trans-Canada Hwy. *Canyon Hot Springs Resort* (☎ 250-837-2420, canyon@revelstoke.net), 35km east, offers full facilities, including showers, laundry, a café and a grocery store. Tent sites cost $19; log cabins for two people start at $89.

In town, *Daniel's Guest House* (☎ 250-837-5530, 313 1st St E), a 100-year-old three-story house and backpacker hangout, charges $15 for dorm beds and $30 for private rooms. It's only open June through October.

The immaculate and comfortable *HI Revelstoke Traveller's Hostel & Guest House* (☎ 250-837-4050, 888-663-8825, fax 250-837-6410, 400 2nd St W) features free

Internet access, $5-a-day bike rentals, several kitchens and bulletin boards loaded with local information. Dorm beds cost $17/19 for members/nonmembers. Private rooms are $23/30 single/double. Through the hostel you can also arrange heli-skiing or snow-cat skiing at reduced rates. In winter, $19 gets you a dorm bed and a lift ticket to Powder Springs – the deal of the century. For more information, check the Web site www.hostels.bc.ca.

Motels in town include the **Mountain View Motel** (☎ 837-4900, 1017 1st W), where the large, clean rooms come with a fridge, TV and free coffee. Rates are $50 to $65.

The owners of the **Powder Springs Inn** (☎ 250-837-5151, 800-991-4455, 200 3rd St W) also run the snow-cat skiing operation (see Activities, earlier), so this motel with a restaurant has become a hub for skiers and snowboarders. The inn also offers fishing packages. Rooms start at $55 in summer, $39 in winter. Also in town is the restored **Regent Inn** (☎ 250-837-2107, 112 1st St W), where a lot of the heli-skiers stay in winter. The hotel contains a Jacuzzi, sauna, restaurant and bar. Its comfortable rooms cost $99 to $139, including a continental breakfast.

You'll find a collection of big chain motels and hotels along the Trans-Canada Hwy, but stay in town if you want to get the vibe of this cool mountain community.

Places to Eat

Outdoor gear and java junkies will get their fill of both at **Bertz Outdoor Equipment & Café** (☎ 250-837-6575, 217 Mackenzie Ave), where you can shop for a backpack while sipping your coffee. Breakfast is a must across the street at the **Blue Beary Patch**. It opens early, and a good, hearty breakfast with toast, sausage, hash browns and eggs goes for $5.50. **Three Bears Bistro** (☎ 250-837-9575, 114 Mackenzie Ave) features a good outdoor patio on the plaza where you can consume sandwiches ($5) and big salads ($7). The bistro serves lunch and dinner in the summer but closes at 6 pm in winter.

For a small town, Revelstoke has more than its share of Chinese restaurants. The best is **Manning's Restaurant** (☎ 250-837-

3200, 302 Mackenzie Ave), where one-person combo plates cost $7.75. Sushi lovers should check out **Frisby Ridge Teriyaki Restaurant** (☎ 250-837-5449, 201A 1st Ave W), where sushi combos start at $5.25. Popular with the local folks, **Tony's Roma** (☎ 250-837-4106, 306 Mackenzie Ave) serves up classic Italian fare such as veggie lasagna ($9) and fettuccine with shrimp ($9.50). Meals come in two sizes: medium or regular. The medium is plenty.

Getting There & Away

The Revelstoke Airport, on the southeast side of town, services charters. The Greyhound bus depot (☎ 250-837-5874), 1899 Fraser Dr, is west of town, just off the Trans-Canada Hwy. It has storage lockers, but beware, the depot closes from 1 to 3 pm on weekends. Four buses head east daily, and five go west.

MT REVELSTOKE NATIONAL PARK

This relatively small (260 sq km) national park, just northeast of Revelstoke in the Clachnacudainn Range of the Selkirk Mountains, comes alive with blankets of wildflowers in summer. The Selkirks are known for their jagged, rugged peaks and steep valleys. From the 2223m summit of Mt Revelstoke, the views of the mountains and the Columbia River valley are excellent. To get to the summit, take the 26km **Meadows in the Sky Parkway**, 1.5km east of Revelstoke off the Trans-Canada Hwy. Open when enough snow melts (usually not until July), the paved road winds through lush cedar forests and alpine meadows and ends at Balsam Lake, within 2km of the peak. From here, walk to the top or take the shuttle, which runs from 10 am to 4:20 pm daily.

There are several good hiking trails from the summit. You can camp only in designated backcountry campsites, and you must have a $6 Wilderness Pass camping permit (in addition to your park pass), which is available from Parks Canada in Revelstoke (☎ 250-837-7500) or from the Rogers Pass Centre (☎ 250-814-5233) inside Glacier

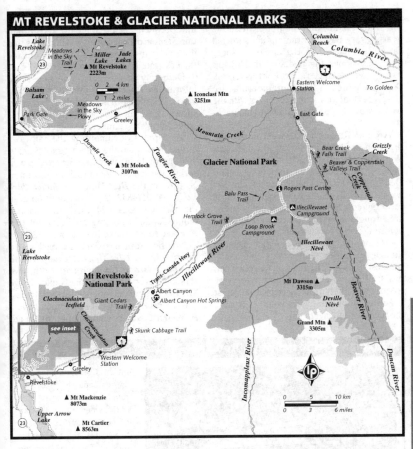

MT REVELSTOKE & GLACIER NATIONAL PARKS

National Park. There are no 'front-country' campgrounds in the park. Much of the summer is rainy, so check that tent for leaks.

There's good cross-country skiing and snowshoeing in the very long winters, but avalanches and bad weather require you to have the right gear and be prepared for anything. Be sure to stop off at the Parks Canada office before venturing out into the backcountry.

Admission to both Mt Revelstoke and Glacier National Parks (the two are administered jointly) is $4/2 for adults/children per day. If you plan to spend more than a few day in the national parks, you may want to consider buying an annual pass for $35/18, which is valid in all of Canada's national parks. See the National Parks section in the Facts about British Columbia chapter for more information about national park fees.

GLACIER NATIONAL PARK

About halfway between Revelstoke and Golden lies this 1350-sq-km park that contains more than 430 glaciers. If you think the other mountain parks have been wet, then you'll like this place. It only rains here twice a week – once for three days and then again for four. It's the same in winter; it snows nearly every day, and the annual snowfall can be as much as 23m. Because of the sheer mountain slopes, this is one of the world's most active avalanche areas. For this reason, skiing, caving and mountaineering are closely regulated; you must register with the park warden before venturing into the back-country.

Around Rogers Pass, you'll notice the many snow sheds protecting the highway. With the narrow road twisting up to 1330m, this is a dangerous area, sometimes called Death Strip; an unexpected avalanche can wipe a car right off the road. Still, the area is carefully controlled, and sometimes snows are brought tumbling down with artillery before they fall by themselves.

In summer, the road is clear of snow, though you can encounter rains even on the sunniest of days. Whether you travel by car, bus, trail or bicycle (more power to you), Rogers will likely rank as one of the most beautiful mountain passes you'll ever have the pleasure of traversing.

At the east side of the park is the dividing line between Pacific Standard and Mountain Standard Time zones, which means that if it's noon in the park, it's 1 pm just outside the east gate (heading into Alberta).

Definitely plan to spend some time at the informative **Rogers Pass Centre** (☎ 250-814-5233), 72km east of Revelstoke. The center shows films on the park and organizes guided walks in summer. Also check out the CPR displays documenting the railway's efforts to conquer the pass. It's open 8 am to 8:30 pm daily in summer, 9 am to 5 pm in spring and fall and 7 am to 5 pm in winter. Next door, the **Best Western Glacier Park Lodge** (☎ 250-837-2126), the only hotel in the park, contains a 24-hour coffee shop, a dining room, swimming pool and hot tub. Average rooms range from $100 to $250.

Not far from here are the park's two campgrounds: *Illecillewaet Campground* and *Loop Brook Campground*. Both have running water and flush toilets and charge $13. Backcountry campers must stick to designated backcountry sites and must have a $6 Wilderness Pass camping permit (in ad-

Canadian Pacific Railway's Iron Link

British Columbia had an almost separate existence from the rest of Canada until 1885, when the Canadian Pacific Railway (CPR) made its way over the treacherous Rockies. These rails for the first time linked the disparate territories of the west and east and played an instrumental role in cementing the unity of the nation.

Running the rails through the Rockies was an enormous challenge that was accomplished by the labor of thousands of immigrant laborers who endured harsh conditions to complete the dangerous job. Hundreds of workers were killed by disease and accident. Among the challenges they faced were the horrific avalanches of Rogers Pass, which swept away people and trains like toys. Eventually huge tunnels and snow sheds were laboriously constructed to protect the trains. East of the town of Field in Yoho National Park (see the Rockies chapter), the gradients were so steep that

dition to your park pass), which is available from the Parks Canada regional office in Revelstoke or from the Rogers Pass Centre. The $2 booklet *Footloose in the Columbias* is an excellent guide to hiking in both of the parks and is available in the bookstore at Rogers Pass.

NAKUSP

• population 2000

Quiet and pretty Nakusp, sitting about midway up the long Upper Arrow Lake, is the main town in the valley south of Revelstoke. The dry, picturesque valley follows a chain of lakes between the Monashee and Selkirk mountain ranges. Nakusp, a First Nations word meaning 'sheltered bay,' was a major steamship port during the Slocan mining boom in the 1890s. Steamships carried ore up to the CPR tracks in Revelstoke. When the boom subsided and new highways took business away from the stern-wheelers, the economy shifted to forestry and pole-making. At one time, most of Canada's wood poles came out of Nakusp. The last great stern-wheeler to ply

the lake's waters was the SS *Minto*, which was retired in 1954.

This very attractive portion of the province enjoys a relatively low profile, so it's surprisingly and refreshingly not overrun with tourists. Good camping and hiking areas, pleasant travel roads and nearby hot springs make Nakusp a fine place to spend a couple of days. If you're in the area on a Wednesday night in summer, stop by Recreation Park on the east side of town and listen to some free live music in the park bandstand.

Southwest of Nakusp, Hwy 6 splits, heading southwest to Fauquier past Arrow Park, the official dividing line between Upper and Lower Arrow Lakes, and to the free ferry from Fauquier to Needles. Once on the other side, you'll climb over the 1189m-high Monashee Pass en route to Vernon in the Okanagan Valley (see the Vernon section in the Thompson-Okanagan chapter). You'll pass campgrounds and a few small provincial parks along this route.

The Nakusp Visitor Info Centre (☎ 250-265-4234, 800-909-8819), 92 W 6th Ave,

Canadian Pacific Railway's Iron Link

any braking problem caused trains to run away down the hill, where they would eventually fly off the tracks and kill passengers. To solve this problem, two huge spiraling tunnels were built inside the granite mountains so that the grades were cut in half to a much more manageable 2.2%. These remain in use and are an internationally recognized engineering marvel.

Along with the trains, the CPR built grand hotels in Calgary, Banff, Lake Louise, Vancouver and elsewhere to encourage tourists and business travelers to ride the line and explore the region. People jumped at the chance to experience such rugged wilderness and still sip tea in luxury. The line was completed on November 7, 1885, and it carried passengers for over a hundred years until government stinginess cut back on rail service. Today, the route is still traversed by CPR freight trains and the occasional (and expensive) *Rocky Mountaineer* cruise train. West of Calgary, the Trans-Canada Hwy parallels much of the route.

There are four excellent places to learn about the history of this rail line in BC: A lookout from the Trans-Canada Hwy 8km east of Field offers a good view of the lower of the two spiral tunnels, with explanatory displays on how they work; the museum area inside the Rogers Pass Centre in Glacier National Park shows the hazards of avalanches and features a model of the entire route over the Rockies; the free publication *Snow War*, available at Rogers Pass, details the railway's efforts to beat the winter; and the railway museum in Revelstoke (see the Revelstoke section) documents the construction history of the entire CPR.

housed behind an original paddle wheel, is open year-round. Next door, a museum houses neat displays on early settlement, the flooding of the Arrow Lakes and the stern-wheeling days. It's open 12:30 to 4:30 pm daily in May and June and 10 am to 5 pm daily in July and August. For local news, pick up the weekly *Arrow Lakes News*. The Arrow Lakes Hospital (☎ 250-265-3622) is at 97 1st Ave, on the east end of town.

Hot Springs

The tranquil **Nakusp Hot Springs** (☎ 250-265-4528) lie about 12km northeast of Nakusp off Hwy 23. A mere 2km from the spring's source, the clean pools are drained daily so they don't smell or collect sediment. Though the squeaky clean pools tend to ruin some of the natural vibe, the gorgeous scenery reminds you that you are steeping deep in nature. One-time soaks cost $5.75, or come and go as much as you want all day for $8.50. Facilities include showers, changing rooms and lockers. The springs are open daily year-round; they close at 10 pm in spring and summer and at 9:30 pm in winter.

If you don't have a car, the Nakusp Regional Transit System (☎ 250-265-3674) offers scheduled bus service from the community services building at 205 6th Ave NW. On Monday, the bus leaves town at 10 am and departs from the springs at 11:30 am. On Wednesday, the stay at the springs is longer, with the bus leaving downtown at 11 am and departing the springs at 2:25 pm. If you have a group of people, call and ask if the bus driver will take you at other times. The fare is $1.25 each way. You can also walk to the springs via the easy-going but long 8km Kuskanax Interpretive Trail. Ask at the Visitor Info Centre for details.

The resort **Halcyon Hot Springs** (☎ 250-265-3554, halcyon@cancom.net), 32km north of Nakusp on Hwy 23, caters to every budget, with accommodations that range from campsites ($15) and camping cabins ($70 for two) to luxurious chalets ($145 to $205). You don't need to stay here to enjoy the hot springs, which sit high on a balcony above

---

Kootenay Ferries

The long Kootenay and Upper and Lower Arrow Lakes necessitate some ferry travel. All ferries are free.

Upper Arrow Lake Ferry (☎ 250-837-8418) runs year-round between Galena Bay (49km south of Revelstoke) and Shelter Bay (49km north of Nakusp) on Hwy 23. The ferry trips, which take 30 minutes, run daily every hour on the hour from Shelter Bay and every hour on the half hour from Galena Bay. The last crossing of the day leaves Shelter Bay at midnight and Galena Bay at 12:30 am.

Needles Ferry (☎ 250-837-8418) crosses Lower Arrow Lake between Fauquier (57km south of Nakusp) and Needles (135km east of Vernon) on Hwy 6; the trip take five minutes. The ferry runs every day, leaving from Fauquier every 30 minutes on the hour and the half hour. From Needles, it runs on the quarter and three-quarter hour. The ferry travels 24 hours a day, though after 10 pm it leaves on demand only.

Kootenay Lake Ferry (☎ 250-229-4215) sails between Balfour on the west arm of Kootenay Lake (34km northeast of Nelson) and Kootenay Bay. Its 45-minute crossing makes it the world's longest free car ferry. In summer, the ferry leaves every 50 minutes between 9:20 am and 5:40 pm; after that, and in winter, it leaves every hour and 40 minutes. Final sailings are at 12:20 am from Balfour and at 1 am from Kootenay Bay.

Upper Arrow Lake. Single dips cost $6/4 for adults/children; day passes are $9/6. You can rent towels for $2.50. For more information, go to www.halcyon-hotsprings.com.

Anyone wishing to soak for free should ask around about two nearby natural hot springs: **St. Leon's**, a favorite with locals for its seclusion and kidney-shaped pools, and **Halfway**, 24km north on Hwy 23. Getting to both undeveloped springs requires driving on logging roads and a little hiking. Ask at the Visitor Info Centre for specific directions as these spots are, after all, secluded.

Places to Stay & Eat

You can pitch a tent in the cramped campground at the *Nakusp Hot Springs* (☎ 250-265-4528), where the tent sites cost $12, including showers and firewood. If the sites there are sold out, check out *Coachman Campsite* (☎ 250-265-4212), right at the hot springs turnoff on Hwy 23. It's more of an RV park but has showers, a pool and tent sites for $12 to $15. Camp right in town at the *Village of Nakusp Campsite* (☎ 250-265-4019), at the north end of Recreation Park (on the corner of 8th Ave and 4th St); it's open from late April to October. The facilities include flush toilets, showers and wooded sites for $15. Nearby *McDonald Creek Provincial Park* (☎ 250-825-3500), 10km south of town on Hwy 6, lies on the east shore of the lake. The park includes 38 campsites with dry toilets but no showers. You can pitch a tent for $10.50.

The historic *Leland Hotel* (☎ 250-265-4221, 96 4th Ave) overlooks the lake and contains a restaurant and pub. The small, basic rooms range from $35 to $55. Also downtown, the *Selkirk Inn* (☎ 250-265-3666, 800-661-8007, 210 6th Ave) is a clean place to spend the night, with rooms for $50 to $69.

Grab your coffee at *Kicking Horse Coffee*, on the corner of Broadway St and 5th Ave. Open early for the loggers, *Guesthouse Café & Bakery* (☎ 250-265-4707, 87 4th Ave) serves up a hearty breakfast for $6 or sandwiches for $5. *Broadway Deli & Bistro* (☎ 250-265-3767, 408 Broadway St), one of the friendliest places in town, serves good breakfasts for $5.25, plus salads, sandwiches and yummy burritos for $7 at lunch. Look for the big pink pig. For beer and burgers ($8), or if you're looking for somewhere open late, head to *Wylie's Pub* (☎ 250-265-4944, 401 Broadway St).

NEW DENVER & AROUND
• population 580

Southeast of Nakusp, Hwy 6 rolls 47km to New Denver, Silverton, Sandon and the lovely Slocan Valley. Note that there are no gas stations on this stretch of highway.

A major boomtown in the heyday of the Silvery Slocan Mines and originally named Eldorado, New Denver grew quickly with seemingly endless potential, enough (it was felt) to rival the also-booming Colorado town. This optimism shrank as the boom subsided, and New Denver is now just a twinkle in its namesake's eye. But greatness is a subjective thing; New Denver's quiet, progressive and artistic community lives surrounded by gorgeous mountain peaks on the shoulder of beautiful Slocan Lake. Ask anyone who lives here and they'll tell you, it doesn't get better than this. Nearby Silverton (population 240), also boomed but went bust. The pretty spot is scarcely more than a ghost town now.

There is no Visitor Info Centre in New Denver, but the Chamber of Commerce runs a de facto information booth in summer, though its location changes every year. The best place to get information is at the Valhalla Inn (see Places to Stay & Eat, later in this section).

Things to See & Do

The Silvery Slocan Museum, 202 6th Ave in the historic Bank of Montreal building, features well-done displays from the booming mining days, including a rare bank vault. It's open 10 am to 5 pm daily in July and August and weekends only in spring and fall.

Sandon, a **ghost town** on Hwy 31A between New Denver and Kaslo, features historic buildings restored to reflect the exciting and greedy days when the silver mines boomed. Check out where the action happened at Molly Brown's Brothel, have a snack at the Tin Cup Café (☎ 250-358-2606) or peruse the Sandon Museum in the historic general store building. Sandon is open 10 am to 6 pm daily, June through September.

Near Sandon, you can get one of the best views of the Slocan Valley from the Idaho Lookout, a 2244m-high viewpoint above the ghost town. A rough logging road leads up to a parking lot. From there, an easy 30-minute (one-way) hike takes you to this awesome vista. In July and August, spare

Relocation Camps

In 1942, more than 20,000 Japanese Canadians where forced from their coastal homes, herded into animal stalls at Vancouver's Hastings Park, then sent to remote 'relocation camps' throughout BC's interior.

The **Nikkei Internment Memorial Centre** (☎ 250-358-7288), 306 Josephine St in New Denver, sits on the site of one of 10 former internment camps in the Slocan Valley. Today, it is a peaceful place built and cared for by the Kyowakai Society, which a group of internees formed in 1943. The center includes a beautiful Japanese garden and remains the only internment camp organization still in operation. It's open 9:30 am to 5 pm daily, June through September. Admission is $4/2 for adults/children.

your poor car from navigating the bumpy road and take the shuttle from Sandon. Ask at the museum for information. For less of a hike, try the **K&S Railway Historic Trail**, which also starts in Sandon. The 5km trail dallies along, passing interpretive signs, old mine shafts and remnants of the railway. You'll also get good views of the surrounding mountains.

Valhalla Provincial Park

A stunningly scenic position in the verdant Slocan Valley, along with lakeside seclusion, makes this 49,600-hectare area one of the province's best parkland jewels. Located southeast of New Denver just east of Hwy 6, the park encompasses most of the Valhalla Range of the Selkirk Mountains. The range takes its name from the Norse mythological palace for slain warriors. Ochre rock paintings along the shoreline are believed to represent the dreams and visions of ancient Arrow Lakes Indians, who treasured the natural sanctuary.

You can drive 30km along Hwy 6 and marvel at the jaw-dropping vistas of the Valhallas' sharp, snow-covered peaks. Or you can enjoy even better views by packing your backpack for a day hike or overnight trip. Slocan Lake serves as the park's eastern boundary; its other sides butt up against more rugged peaks and dense forest. You can only access the main areas of the park by boat or commercial water taxi; these travel across Slocan Lake from three points along Hwy 6: New Denver, northeast of the park; Silverton, to the east; and Slocan, to the southeast. In New Denver, Kingfisher Water Taxi (☎ 250-358-2334) charges $15 per person for a roundtrip to the Nemo Creek Trailhead, a good point of departure for day hikes. The price goes up if there are fewer than four people on the trip, so try to hook up with other hikers.

Valhalla was protected as parkland in 1983, mostly due to the intense efforts of the Valhalla Wilderness Society (☎ 250-358-2333, vws@vws.org), an advocacy group that formed in the '70s to save the Valhalla Range from logging. Since then, the now-thriving group has also successfully campaigned to protect the Khutzeymateen Grizzly Sanctuary near Prince Rupert (see the North chapter) in 1993 and the nearby White Grizzly Wilderness in 1995. The Valhalla Wilderness Society office, 307 6th St in New Denver, is a great place to learn more about current issues and to get excellent park topographic maps and helpful trail information.

Places to Stay & Eat

Camping with flush toilets and showers is available at the *Village of New Denver Municipal Campground* (☎ 250-358-2316), near the marina at the bottom of 3rd Ave. Waterfront sites cost $14. The *Silverton Campsite* offers some nice $10 sites right on the lake, though there are pit toilets and no showers.

The lively *Valhalla Inn* (☎ 250-358-2228, valhallainn@netidea.com, 509 Slocan Ave) is somewhat of a hub, with a pub, restaurant and good-sized rooms. Rates range from $55 to $80.

For a unique experience, sleep in a cozy tipi at the *Valhalla Lodge & Tipi Retreat*

(☎ *250-365-3226, fax 365-3264, valhalla@ knet.kootenay.net*), on the west shore of Slocan Lake. A beachfront tipi for two people costs $118, which includes a round-trip boat shuttle from the town of Slocan, the use of a canoe and access to a communal kitchen and sauna. You have to stay a minimum of two nights and bring your own food. The only way to reach the retreat is by boat shuttle.

On 6th Ave in New Denver you'll find two good stops for breakfast or lunch. *The Apple Tree (☎ 250-358-2691)*, beside the museum, attracts friendly locals who lounge on the outdoor patio. A little farther east is the *Panini Bistro & Delicatessen (☎ 250-358-2830)*, where you can order a European breakfast for $5.50 or a baguette sandwich for $7.50.

KASLO
• population 1065

Unlike what happened in surrounding towns in the Slocan Valley, it was timber, not silver, that lured the first European settlers to Kaslo. But it was the fervor in the nearby mines that prompted the first timber-claim holders to sell off small parcels of what is now the Kaslo townsite.

In 1895, the Kaslo & Slocan Railroad, backed by the US-based Great Northern Railroad, brought Kaslo out of isolation by linking it with the silver mines in the Slocan. With the building of hotels, bars and brothels, the population boomed along with the mines.

Once the mining slowed, Kaslo became a thriving fruit-growing community noted especially for its cherries, some of which were said to be the size of plums. During WWII, the *New Canadian*, a newspaper serving all the Canadian Japanese internment camps, was published in Kaslo.

Today, Kaslo's tree-lined streets, restored Victorian buildings and access to outdoor activities make it a worthwhile stop for travelers. The helpful staff at the Visitor Info Centre (☎/fax 250-353-2525), 324 Front St, can give you great information on hiking and mountain-biking trails in the area.

Things to See & Do
In its early days, the town's isolated location on the north arm of Kootenay Lake made steamship travel to Nelson significant. Today, the 1898 SS *Moyie*, the world's oldest surviving sternwheeler, is now a museum (☎ 250-353-2525) and National Historic Site, moored permanently on the downtown lakeside. It's open 9:30 am to 5 pm daily from mid-May to Mid-October. Admission is $5/2 for adults/children.

The **Kootenay Star Museum** (☎ 250-353-2115), 402 Front St, contains artifacts and displays about mining history; it's open 9 am to 5 pm daily. Admission is by donation.

The beautifully restored **Langham Cultural Centre** (☎ 250-353-2662), 477 A Ave, features displays by local artists and live music performances. Call to see what's happening while you're in town.

If you're looking for the scoop on outdoor activities, another must-stop is Discovery Canada Outdoor Adventure Inc (☎ 250-353-7349, 888-300-4453, discover@ netidea.com). The company, which maintains an office on Front St, runs guided hiking tours (starting at $60), mountaintop concerts by moonlight ($35) and courses on mountaineering. The staff can tell you almost anything you'd want to know about hiking in the Selkirk or Purcell Mountains.

Places to Stay
View the *Kaslo Municipal Campground (☎ 250-353-2311)* at Vimy Park as an absolute last resort if you can't find camping anywhere else. Sites lie on little more than a grassy parking lot and cost $13. You'll have better luck, although it's not wilderness camping, at *Mirror Lake Campground (☎ 250-353-7102)*, 5km south of Kaslo on Hwy 31, and at *Davis Creek & Lost Ledge Provincial Parks (☎ 250-825-3500)*, 25km north of Kaslo on Hwy 23, both of which offer lakeside sites for $12.

The lovingly built and cozy *Kootenay Lake Backpackers Hostel (☎ /fax 250-353-7427, klhostel@pop.kin.bc.ca, 232 B Ave)* is a European-style hostel with a big common kitchen, patio and yard. Dorm beds cost

THE KOOTENAYS

$15. Private rooms are $26/32 single/double. You can also access the Internet, do laundry and rent kayaks, canoes and bikes.

The **Mariner Inn** (*☎ 250-353-7171, 430 Front St*) contains a pub and restaurant with a patio overlooking the lake. The small, clean rooms cost $50. For B&B listings, pick up a copy of *North Kootenay Lake B&B Directory* from the Visitor Info Centre.

NELSON
• population 10,000

Surrounded by the Selkirk Mountains and snug up against the west arm of Kootenay Lake, Nelson, at the junction of Hwys 6 and 3A, is the heart of the Kootenays.

The town was born in the late 1800s, when two down-on-their-luck brothers from Washington sat bemoaning their bad fortune on top of Toad Mountain, just southwest of what is now Nelson. While the brothers rested, some of their party found the copper-silver deposit that later became the Silver King Mine. A town began to build up around the ore-rich mine, and its mass production prompted two transcontinental railways to serve Nelson, in order to carry the goods away to smelters. When this proved too costly, the mining company built its own smelter, which only lasted as long as the ore. Finally, the smelter buildings were destroyed in a massive fire in 1911, and like most mined-out towns, Nelson turned to its forests.

In 1977, Nelson was elected guinea pig for the government's pilot project on heritage conservation. Today the picturesque town nestled in the hillside boasts more than 350 carefully preserved and restored late-19th- to early-20th-century buildings.

The town's charm and location lure many people who are seeking city culture but small-town lifestyle. The active, artsy community fancies itself a sophisticated eccentric, lucky enough to live in paradise. The renowned Kootenay School of the Arts, the Selkirk School of Music and a school of Chinese medicine draw an interesting and eclectic mix.

The town's friendly, laid-back character is inviting. At any given time you can hear people talking about spirituality or tofu. And that sweet smell in the air? Yup, you guessed it – Nelson is known (unofficially, of course) for growing excellent pot.

Regardless of what activity you're after, be it kayaking on Kootenay Lake, skiing at Whitewater or checking out local arts, Nelson makes a great base for exploring the region.

Orientation & Information

Nelson sits on the west arm of Kootenay Lake. As it travels down from the north, Hwy 3A becomes a series of local streets before heading west to Castlegar. Hwy 6, which skirts the west side of downtown, also goes to Castlegar or south to the small lumber town of Salmo before connecting with Hwy 3 and heading to Creston and the East Kootenays.

Baker and Vernon Sts are the two main downtown thoroughfares. Baker St has many shops and restaurants, while Vernon St holds government buildings, including city hall, the courthouse and the post office. The Visitor Info Centre (*☎ 250-352-3433, fax 352-6355*), 225 Hall St, is open 8:30 am to 8 pm daily in summer; 8:30 am to 5 pm weekdays and 10 am to 5 pm weekends the rest of the year.

The post office (*☎ 250-352-3538*) is at 514 Vernon St. Free Internet access is available at the library, on the corner of Stanley and Victoria Sts. You can also check email or surf the net at The Net Idea (*☎ 250-352-3512*), 625 Front St, just west of the Visitor Info Centre.

For an excellent selection of local books, topographic maps and magazines, go to Oliver's Books (*☎ 250-352-7525*), 398 Baker St. Packrat Annie's (*☎ 250-354-4722*), upstairs at 411 Kootenay St, carries a good array of used books.

For a good sense of the local scene, pick up a copy of the *Daily News*. You'll find events listings posted at the Kootenay Co-Op store, 295 Baker St, where you can also look for advertisements for rides elsewhere in BC.

Do your laundry at the Plaza Laundromat (*☎ 250-352-6077*), 616 Front St, and at

NELSON

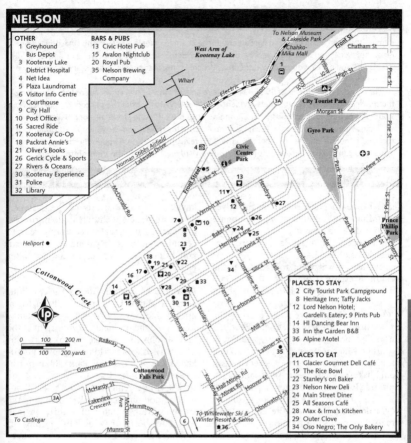

OTHER
1 Greyhound
  Bus Depot
3 Kootenay Lake
  District Hospital
4 Net Idea
5 Plaza Laundromat
6 Visitor Info Centre
7 Courthouse
9 City Hall
10 Post Office
16 Sacred Ride
17 Kootenay Co-Op
21 Packrat Annie's
26 Gerick Cycle & Sports
27 Rivers & Oceans
30 Kootenay Experience
31 Police
32 Library

BARS & PUBS
13 Civic Hotel Pub
15 Avalon Nightclub
20 Royal Pub
35 Nelson Brewing
  Company

PLACES TO STAY
2 City Tourist Park Campground
8 Heritage Inn; Taffy Jacks
12 Lord Nelson Hotel;
  Gardeli's Eatery; 9 Pints Pub
14 HI Dancing Bear Inn
33 Inn the Garden B&B
36 Alpine Motel

PLACES TO EAT
11 Glacier Gourmet Deli Café
19 The Rice Bowl
22 Stanley's on Baker
23 Nelson New Deli
24 Main Street Diner
25 All Seasons Café
28 Max & Irma's Kitchen
29 Outer Clove
34 Oso Negro; The Only Bakery

THE KOOTENAYS

the Esso Village Coin-Op (☎ 250-352-3524), 524 Nelson Ave.

The Kootenay Lake District Hospital (☎ 250-352-3111) is at 3 View St.

Things to See & Do

Lakeside Park is a popular spot where you can hang out or walk along the trail that runs through the park. In summer, brave souls swim in chilly, glacier-fed Kootenay Lake. **Streetcar No 23**, one of the town's originals, has been restored and now follows a 2km track from under the bridge (at the north end of Lakeside Park) to the wharf at the foot of Hall St. It runs noon to 6 pm daily in summer and on weekends only in spring and fall. Tickets are $2/1 for adults/children.

Almost a third of Nelson's buildings have been restored to their high- and late- Victorian architectural splendor, so you'll definitely want to pick up a copy of the *Heritage Walking Tour* leaflet from the Visitor Info Centre. Even if you're not a big history buff, you'll appreciate this step back in time as you stroll around town.

For more history, go to the **Nelson Museum** (☎ 250-352-9813), on the corner of Nelson Ave and Anderson St, which features

Remembering Roxanne

Remember Daryl Hannah, Steve Martin and those charming street scenes in the smash-hit movie *Roxanne*? Well, you're not alone. The blooming gardens, seemingly great weather and colorful streets left audiences worldwide wondering, 'Where is this charming little town and how can we move there?'

Throughout the summer of 1986, Daryl, Steve and an army of film crews buzzed about making the movie on Nelson's quiet streets. Evidence is still everywhere, from the photogenic fire hall on Ward St and the Victorian houses on Carbonate St to the cafés and stores all along Baker St.

The number of visitors to the town quadrupled after the movie, and the Chamber of Commerce received hundreds of calls from people wishing to relocate to Nelson. Though the frenzy is all but gone, you can still pick up a copy of the *Roxanne Walking Tour* from the Visitor Info Centre.

displays on early Natives, settlers, the Silver King Mine and boating history. It's open 1 to 6 pm daily in summer. The rest of the year, it's open 1 to 4 pm daily except Sunday. Admission is $2.

Beer lovers will want to check out the **Nelson Brewing Company** (☎ 250-352-3582), 512 Latimer St. Call to find out about the frequent tours and tastings.

One of the biggest events in Nelson is the **International Street Performers Festival**. Known by locals as 'Street Fest,' the three-day affair, which happens the third weekend in July, features a variety of street artists, from buskers and mimes to poets and craftmakers. Baker St becomes a pedestrian mall, and performers from all over the world do their thing on the crowd-lined streets. For more information, call ☎ 250-352-7188 or visit www.streetfest.bc.ca on the Web.

Activities

Kayaking Kootenay Kayak Tours (☎ 250-229-4959, 877-229-4959), located in nearby Balfour, offers kayaking trips ranging from hour-long paddles to multi-day camping trips around large Kootenay Lake. A three-hour guided trip costs $50, or you can rent kayaks ($44/64 single/double) and go out on your own for half a day. Check out the Web site www.kootenaykayak.com.

Rivers & Oceans (☎ 250-354-1241) arranges higher-end rafting and white-water

kayaking expeditions around the province. The store, in an old church at the north end of Baker St, is a great place to buy gear, to get information on kayaking on the Slocan and Kootenay Rivers or to contact other paddlers.

Hiking & Mountain Biking The two-hour climb to **Pulpit Rock**, practically in town, affords fine views of Nelson and Kootenay Lake. Find the trailhead on your right at the end of Johnstone Rd (in the northern part of town). Excellent hikes abound at **Kokanee Creek Provincial Park**, 20km northeast of town off Hwy 3A. Stop in at the park's visitor center (☎ 250-825-4212) for information on specific hikes, including the Canyon Trail, which winds through lush forest to views of waterfalls spilling off Kokanee Glacier. Eight trails begin right at the visitor center. Lake-filled **Kokanee Glacier Provincial Park** boasts 85km of some of the area's most superb hiking trails. The two-hour hike to Kokanee Lake is wonderful and can be continued to the glacier. Call ☎ 250-825-3500 to find out about current trail conditions.

Most of this area's mountain-biking trails wind up from Kootenay Lake along steep and rather challenging hills, followed by stomach-emptying downhills. Trail names like 'Boneyard' and 'Fat Chance' make the whole idea a little daunting for anyone but advanced riders, but there are some intermediate trails for those wishing to end the day free of open wounds. The best way to find out about trails is by chatting up the folks at one of the bike shops. Gerick Cycle & Sports (☎ 250-354-4622), 702 Baker St, rents road bikes ($20 per day) and mountain bikes ($29 to $39 per day). The Sacred Ride (☎ 250-362-5688), 213 Baker St, has knowledgeable staff. Both of the shops sell *Your Ticket to Ride*, an extensive trail map, for $10.

Skiing & Snowboarding Known for its heavy powdery snowfall, which averages 1000cm per year, **Whitewater Ski & Winter Resort** (☎ 250-354-4944, 352-7669 for a snow report), 12km south of Nelson off Hwy 6, features good skiing and boarding. Yet to be bulldozed by the massive resort-building dollars that turn small ski towns into flashy resorts throughout the province, Whitewater maintains its small-town charm. Whitewater has only two chairs and a rope tow, but they can take you to an elevation of 396m and some great powdery snow. Lift tickets cost $37; the HI Dancing Bear Inn offers a package that gets you a lift ticket and night's sleep for $49.

The First Chair Shuttle (☎ 250-354-1994) runs daily trips from Nelson to the mountain. It picks up passengers at all downtown hotels, including the hostel, at around 8:30 am. It leaves Whitewater at 3:40 pm. Shuttle tickets cost $6 each way. Hitchhiking is also a relatively safe and usually easy method of transportation up the mountain.

Morning Mountain (☎ 250-352-9969), off Hwy 3A north of town, is another ski area geared toward families. The **Apex-Bush Cross Country Ski Area** (☎ 250-354-4292), about 12km south of Nelson, offers 25km of classic and skating tracks for novice to expert skiers. Look for signs at the turnoff to Whitewater, just off Hwy 6.

Before doing any backcountry skiing, be sure to stop in at Kootenay Experience (☎ 250-354-4441), 306 Victoria St. Open only in winter, the store rents backcountry equipment and sells gear and topographic maps.

Places to Stay

Camping For convenient camping, try the downtown *City Tourist Park* (☎ 250-352-7618), at High and Willow Sts. The sites ($14) aren't spectacular, but there are showers, flush toilets and laundry facilities.

The Redfish and Sandspit Campgrounds at *Kokanee Creek Provincial Park* (☎ 250-825-4212, 800-689-9025 for reservations), 20km northeast of Nelson off Hwy 3A, contains 132 wooded tent sites with toilets and showers. The park has its own visitor center and offers daily interpretive programs, especially on the land-locked kokanee salmon that spawn in the creek. The pretty sites cost $17.50.

Excellent and accessible backcountry camping is available at *Kokanee Glacier Provincial Park*. Call ☎ 250-825-3500 to find out about trail and site conditions. For any backcountry camping in the area, pick up a copy of *Arrow and Kootenay Lake Forest Districts Recreation Map*, which you can get at the Kokanee Creek Provincial Park visitor center or by calling the Nelson Forest Region office at ☎ 250-354-6200.

Hostels Perhaps the best place to stay in the Kootenays, the central *HI Dancing Bear Inn* (☎ 250-352-7573, fax 352-9818, dbear@netidea.com, 171 Baker St) makes a great home away from home where travelers of all ages will feel comfortable. The beautifully renovated hostel bustles with activity, but the rooms are quiet and immaculate. The comfortable living room makes a great place to read a book or find out about local happenings. The hostel has Internet access, some good books about regional history, a communal kitchen and laundry facilities. Skiers and boarders can stay at the hostel and get a lift ticket to Whitewater, all for $49. Beds cost $17/20 for members/nonmembers; family rooms and doubles start at $34. Check out the hostel's Web site at www.dancingbearinn.com.

B&Bs Right downtown, *Inn the Garden B&B* (☎ 250-358-3226, fax 352-3284, 408 Victoria St) offers guest rooms in a lovingly restored Victorian home. Rooms for two people range from $75 (shared bath) to $150 (private bath). Ask at the Visitor Info Centre for a listing of Nelson B&Bs, many of which start at $55.

Hotels You can find a variety of motels at the highway intersections, including the *Alpine Motel (☎ 250-352-5501, 888-356-2233)*, 1120 Hall Mines Rd near Observatory St in the south part of town. Rooms, which are large, cost $55/60 single/double or $85 for a double with a kitchenette.

Nelson's best hotel options are right in town. The *Heritage Inn (☎ 250-352-5331, fax 352-5214, info@heritageinn.org, 422 Vernon St)* has a pub, restaurant and nightclub, making the hotel somewhat of a hub, whether you stay here or not. As in most heritage buildings, the rooms are small but clean and full of character. Standard room rates, including breakfast, are $58/64. Down the street, the *Lord Nelson Hotel (☎ 250-352-7211, fax 352-2445, 616 Vernon St)* offers similar accommodations for cheaper prices. Rates start at $46/56. The premises include a restaurant, pub and beer and wine store.

Places to Eat

Java junkies will kiss the earth in front of *Oso Negro (☎ 250-532-7761, 522 Victoria St)*, which brews the best coffee this side of Vancouver. This locally owned 'micro-roaster' serves up over 18 blends of socially conscious organic coffee – and it's strong and delicious. In the same building, pick up a boiled bagel or muffin from *The Only Bakery (☎ 250-354-1200)*.

For hearty breakfasts, head to *Stanley's on Baker (☎ 250-354-4458, 402 Baker St)*, where the yummy scrambled tofu will set you back $5.50. Also good for breakfast is *Gardeli's Eatery (☎ 250-352-5570)*, in the Lord Nelson Hotel.

Order an excellent sandwich ($4) at *Nelson New Deli (☎ 250-352-3354, 491 Baker St)*. The artsy *Glacier Gourmet Deli Café (☎ 250-354-4495, 621 Vernon St)* serves good salads and light meals, including salmon burgers ($6) and chili ($4.50). Stop

by for live jazz music on Friday and Saturday night.

People-watching is best on the smoke-free sidewalk patio at *Main Street Diner (☎ 250-354-4848, 616 Baker St)*. A big plate of fish and chips is $9, and burgers are $8. Garlic lovers should head straight to the *Outer Clove (☎ 250-354-1667, 536 Stanley St)*, where dinners, including a good vegetarian selection, range from $8 to $16. A Nelson must-stop is *The Rice Bowl (☎ 250-354-4129, 301 Baker St)*. This popular spot specializes in Japanese and Thai dishes, including sushi and noodles. A full-size rice bowl, filled with veggies and sauce, is $7.50.

A little more upscale, *Max & Irma's Kitchen (☎ 250-352-2332, 515A Kootenay St)* serves large calzones and pasta dishes for $11. If you're in the mood to splurge, the *All Seasons Café (☎ 250-352-0101, 620 Herridge Lane)* is well worth every penny. The fresh menu, excellent service and outdoor heated courtyard make for a delicious night out. Dinners range from $14 to $25.

Entertainment

Nelson has its share of places to pound a pint or party down. Most are within walking distance of each other. A good beer-sipping pub (though not downtown), *Bogustown Neighbourhood Pub (☎ 250-354-1313, 712 Nelson Ave)* features a fun, relaxed atmosphere, pub food, pool tables and a good patio. Also check out the brews at the *9 Pints Pub*, in the Lord Nelson Hotel.

If you're into more of a party scene, head to the *Civic Hotel Pub (☎ 250-352-5121, 705 Vernon St)* or to *The Royal Pub (☎ 250-352-2449, 330 Baker St)*, where there's live music and karaoke. If you're looking for dancing, check out *Taffy Jacks*, in the Heritage Inn, or *Avalon Nightclub (☎ 250-354-4823, 198 Baker St)*, in the old Savoy Hotel.

Getting There & Around

The Greyhound bus depot (☎ 250-352-3939), at 1112A Lakeside Dr, is in the Chahko-Mika Mall. Two buses depart daily for Calgary via Fernie and for Vancouver via Kelowna. There are no lockers, but you can leave your stuff at the counter for $1 per day. The depot is open 6 am to 8:30 pm daily, with afternoon closures on weekends.

It's easy to walk anywhere in Nelson, though you'll have to contend with some steep uphills. You can also take the Nelson Transit System buses (☎ 250-352-8201) just about anywhere in town. The main stop is on the corner of Ward and Baker Sts. Bus No 2 will take you to the Chahko-Mika Mall or Lakeside Park. No 10 goes to the North Shore and to the Kootenay Lake ferry. For times, pick up a copy of the *Rider's Guide* bus schedule at the Visitor Info Centre.

AROUND NELSON
Formerly a booming mining town, tiny Ainsworth, 46km north of Nelson on Hwy 31, today is home to only 100 people, most of whose livelihood comes from tourism generated by **Ainsworth Hot Springs** (☎ 250-229-4212, 800-668-1171). The springs boast the highest mineral content of any hot springs in Canada. Along with the usual pool, you can also soak in a former mine shaft that is now a hot-water-filled cave. One-time soaks cost $6.50; a day pass is $10. It's open 10 am to 9:30 pm daily year-round.

High in the Selkirk Mountains, **Cody Caves Provincial Park** can be accessed by a forest service road off Hwy 31, 4km north of Ainsworth. At the caves, an underground stream flows through ancient limestone and past impressive stalactites, soda straws, stalagmites and waterfalls. You can only explore the caves with a guide. Hiadventure Corp (☎ 250-353-7425) runs one-hour tours that cost $12/8 for adults/children. Helmets, coveralls and gloves are provided, but be sure to wear study shoes and warm clothes.

CASTLEGAR
• population 7300

Castlegar, a sprawling town known primarily as a highway junction – Hwys 3 and 3A merge here – sits on the Kootenay River at the southern end of Lower Arrow Lake. Recent development has robbed the town of any charm or character it may once have had, though you can still find a decent bowl of borscht.

Castlegar's history centers around the more than 5000 Doukhobors, members of a Russian Christian pacifist sect who followed their leader, Peter Verigin, west from Saskatchewan between 1908 and 1913. The Doukhobors, small groups of peaceful, communal-living people, had begun to reject the teachings of the Russian Orthodox Church during the 18th century. They refused ritual worship, believing instead that god's spirit lived within each individual and that it was up to individuals, not an outside god, to have peaceful and harmonious lives. The church shunned the Doukhobors, exiling them to cold, barren corners of Russia, where the church hoped the group would fizzle out. But the Doukhobors thrived, and in 1898 and '99, 7500 members immigrated to Canada, first to Saskatchewan and then to Castlegar and nearby Grand Forks.

Though many Doukhobors have integrated into Canadian society, some still live on communal farms, and the Russian influence is still evident throughout this area, in the dozens of borscht restaurants.

Orientation & Information
Head to the north end of Columbia Ave to see downtown Castlegar. In the southern part of town, you'll find the year-round Visitor Info Centre (☎ 250-365-6313, fax 365-5778, cdcoc@kootenay.net), 1995 6th Ave at 20th St. The town maintains a Web site at www.castlegar.com.

Things to See & Do
The reconstructed **Doukhobor Historical Village** (☎ 250-365-6622), on the east side of the Columbia River off Hwy 3A, is little more than a couple of buildings, a statue of Tolstoy and a small museum that you can afford to miss. A restaurant used to sit on the grounds, and though the signs remain, the building now sits empty and is an apt symbol for the slumping tourist attraction. The museum is open daily, May through September. Admission is $3/2 for adults/children.

A somewhat brighter light in the Doukhobor legacy is **Zuckerberg Island**

Heritage Park. The island, officially named 'Emerald Island' (though no one calls it that), was the home of Alexander Feodorovitch Zuckerberg, a Russian teacher brought in to educate the Doukhobor children. Today, the park contains a suspension bridge, trails and restored buildings, including the former chapel house, which is open daily in July and August. The park is open during daylight hours year-round. Admission here is by donation.

The **Castlegar Museum** (☎ 250-365-6440), 400 13th Ave, housed in an old train station, features an interesting display on the history of the West Kootenay Power & Light Company, including diving gear used by early company workers. In the middle of the display is a mint-condition 1929 Harley Davidson motorcycle that has nothing to do with the power company but is pretty darn cool. Upstairs is a well-done display of early Castlegar inhabitants. The museum hours are 10 am to 5 pm daily in July and August, 10 am to 5 pm Monday to Saturday at other times. Admission is by donation.

The giant **Keenleyside Dam**, 8km northwest of Castlegar on the Columbia River, opened in 1968. The second of three Columbia River Treaty dams built by BC Hydro to harness power generated by the river, this concrete- and earth-filled dam stands 52m tall. BC Hydro runs a free, 45-minute guided tour about the building of the dam, its massive reservoir (the Arrow Lakes) and the dam's generators, which supply power to Washington and Oregon in the US, as well as BC. Tours run on the hour from 9 am to 3 pm daily, May to August; note that there is no noon tour. During the rest of the year, call ☎ 250-365-5299 to arrange a tour. To get to the dam, follow Arrow Lakes Dr west of Castlegar.

Places to Stay & Eat

Syringa Creek Provincial Park (☎ 250-825-3500, 800-689-9025 for reservations) sits on Lower Arrow Lake, 17km northwest of Castlegar off Broadwater Rd on the north side of the Columbia River. It offers 60 campsites ($15), a long beach, swimming

and good hiking. It's open April to October. West of town, *Nancy Greene Provincial Park* (☎ 250-825-3500), at the junction of Hwys 3 and 3B, is a quiet and rustic campground with pit toilets and 10 sites for $9.

In summer, find cheap accommodations at Selkirk College's **Kekuli House Residence** (☎ 250-365-1227, 301 Frank Beinder Way). The private rooms come with single beds but shared bathrooms and kitchen. You'll pay $20 if you have your own bedding or $35 for supplied linen. The turnoff to the college is across from the airport, off Hwy 3A.

Being a major highway junction, Castlegar has its share of motels. Close to downtown and right on the river is the *Twin Rivers Motel* (☎ 250-365-6900, 1485 Columbia Ave). Basic rooms cost $48/58 single/double. At the junction of Hwys 3A, 3 and 22, the comfortable and clean *Days Inn* (☎ 250-365-2700) contains a dining room and beer store. Rooms start at $65.

Great restaurants do not abound in this town, though you'll find a decent full breakfast ($7) or lunch sandwich ($5.25) at *Cafe Friends* (☎ 250-365-0846, 1102 3rd St). *Annie's Cafe* (☎ 250-365-1151), on the corner of Columbia Ave and 3rd St, offers good muffins, coffee and sandwiches for $6.

Though everyone claims to have the best borscht in town, the winner appears to be *Weezie's Borscht Hut* (☎ 250-304-2633, 2816 Columbia Ave), at the south end of Castlegar. The small restaurant serves up a large bowl with bread and cheese for $5.25 or Russian specialties like meat-filled cabbage rolls for $10.95. Weezie also serves sandwiches and breakfasts.

Getting There & Away

Canadian Regional Airlines and Air BC (☎ 888-247-2262 for both) fly from Vancouver to the Castlegar Airport, on Hwy 3A southeast of town.

Greyhound (☎ 250-368-8400) rolls into Castlegar, with daily buses heading west along the Crowsnest Hwy or east to Nelson and points beyond. The bus depot (☎ 250-365-7744) is at 365 Columbia Ave.

ROSSLAND
● population 4000

This gorgeous mountain town, 27km south-west of Castlegar and only 11km north of the US border, is perched high in the Rossland Mountains, a southern buttress of the Monashee Range.

At 1023m, this high-elevation town sits in the eroded crater of an ancient mineral-rich volcano. The area was first encountered by Europeans in 1865, when builders of the historic Dewdney Trail passed by and simply marveled at the reddish mineral stains on nearby Red Mountain. Prospectors didn't come sniffing around for another 25 years. It wasn't until 1890 that a guy named Joe Moris decided to do more than marvel and finally tapped into the incredibly rich gold deposits that induced Rossland's birth. After old Joe's discovery, the town built up quickly. Sourdough Alley (today's Columbia Ave) became the province's wildest and toughest main thoroughfare, and by 1895, 7000 residents and hundreds of prostitutes could take their pick of 42 saloons. By 1929, most of the claims were mined-out, and the boom shrank to a whisper, but in less than 45 years, Rossland had produced $165 million worth of gold.

Today, Rossland has become a cool small town whose sporty inhabitants take full advantage of the area's bounty. Skiing has long been a top attraction, and the Red Mountain Resort boasts some of the best technical trails in the world. Canadian Olympic gold medalists Kerrin Lee-Gartner and Nancy Greene (namesake of the park) hail from Rossland.

Information
The Visitor Info Centre (☎ 250-362-7722) is located in the museum building, at the junction of Hwys 22 and 3B. It's open 9 am to 5 pm daily, mid-May to Mid-September closed the rest of the year). For some good information, visit www.rossland.com on the internet.

For books and regional information, stop by Gold Rush Books & Espresso (☎ 250-362-5333, 800-668-0140), 2063 Washington St.

Things to See & Do
With its excellent displays on mining history, the **Rossland Historical Museum** (☎ 250-362-7722), beside the Visitor Info Centre on the site of the former Black Bear Mine, merits a stop. At the museum, you can sign up for the 45-minute tour of the famed Le Roi Mine. This guided underground tour gives you a good idea of the toil the early hard-rock miners had to endure. Tours leave every 90 minutes in May, June and September or every half hour in July and August. A ticket for the museum and mine tour costs $8/5 for adults/children; a museum-only ticket is $4/3.

Dubbed 'Canada's Mountain Bike Capital,' Rossland features a well-developed and extensive trail system that radiates right from downtown. Much of the **mountain biking** is for hard-core types who refer to themselves as 'Rubberheads,' but there are mellower trails also accessible from town. As usual, bike shops are the best places to go for information. Powderhound (☎ 250-362-5311), 2040 Columbia Ave, offers bike rentals for $15 to $35 per day depending on how much suspension you want. The Sacred Ride (☎ 250-362-5688), 2123 Columbia Ave, has friendly staff and a local bike club.

Only 5km north of downtown of Hwy 3B, **Red Mountain Ski Resort** (☎ 250-362-7384, 362-5500 for a 24-hour snow report, 800-663-0105, reservations@ski-red.com) includes 1590m-high Red Mountain and 2040m-high Granite Mountain, for a total of 485 hectares of powdery terrain. Geared mostly toward intermediate and advanced skiers and snowboarders, the area is known for its steep, tree-filled runs. Get details on the Web site www.ski-red.com.

Daily lift tickets cost $42. Ski and snowboard rentals are available on the mountain at Le Roi's Sports Shop (☎ 250-362-7124). Skis and snowboard packages cost $31 per day. In town, you can rent ski packages ($27 and up) at Powderhound (☎ 250-362-5311), 2040 Columbia Ave. Snowboard packages start at $30 per day. Take your skis along on the local bus (250-364-0261), which goes to and from Red Mountain in the winter.

Across the highway from Red Mountain, **Black Jack Cross Country Area** (☎ 250-362-9465) boasts 25km of groomed skating and classic trails. Day passes cost $7. You can rent cross-country equipment for $20 at High Country Sports (☎ 250-362-9000), in the Red Mountain Motel.

Places to Stay & Eat

HI Mountain Shadow Hostel (☎ 250-362-7160, 888-393-7160, mshostel@kootenay.net, 2125 Columbia Ave) definitely attracts the ski-bum/snowboarder crowd in the winter. Things quiet down in summer, though at $17 a night, it's always pretty busy. Along with ski posters, topographic maps line the walls of the common living room and kitchen, offering a good perspective on the surrounding mountains. In winter, the hostel has ski packages.

The following rates cover the peak season, which means winter in Rossland. Most hotels substantially lower their rates the rest of the year, so it's worthwhile to call ahead. The *Uplander Hotel* (☎ 250-362-7375, 800-667-8741) contains two dining rooms, the popular Powder King Pub and basic but comfortable rooms starting at $90 for two. At the base of Red Mountain is the gorgeous *Ram's Head Inn* (☎ 250-363-9577, 877-267-4323, ramshead@powerlink.com). A large common room with vaulted ceilings and a hefty stone fireplace, an outdoor hot tub, a games room and cozy guest rooms make a stay here a real treat. Rooms range from $76 to $120, and you can get good package deals in the ski season.

Join the mountain bikers for coffee and a $5 breakfast at *Clansey's* (☎ 250-362-5273), next door to Powderhound on Columbia Ave. For great views and good pub food, head to *The Flying Steamshovel* (☎ 250-362-7323, 2003 2nd Ave). Across the street is *Idgie's Restaurante* (☎ 250-362-0078, 1999 2nd Ave), known for its excellent pizza and lasagna.

AROUND ROSSLAND

West of Rossland, the lovely **Christina Lake** is a good place to stay for a day or two, especially if you're camping at **Gladstone Pro-**vincial Park. The Texas Creek Campground in the park, on the north end of Christina Lake, offers campsites for $12 year-round. It lies 10km east of Christina Lake off Hwy 3 and can be tricky to find, so keep a good eye out for the signs for East Lake Dr and then follow it for a kilometer to the campground.

Farther west, you'll hit the pretty border town of **Grand Forks** (population 4000), known for its borscht and relatively abundant sunshine. The town was a by-product of the Phoenix Mine, once the biggest copper-producing smelter in BC. Some of the Doukhobors who settled in Castlegar came here, and their influence still lends character and good food to the town.

TRAIL
• **population 8000**

Just a short glide down the hill from Rossland lands you in the lap of Trail, possibly the most toxic place you'll find in BC. This industrial town, 27km southwest of Castlegar at the junction of Hwys 3 and 3A, is the home of Cominco, the world's largest smelter of silver, zinc and lead. Dark plumes of smelter smoke dominate the skyline, giving the town a brown, gauzy glow and a rather rotten-eggish smell. The area's normally lush vegetation is stunted here, killed off 60 years ago by the smelter's toxic emissions. Though operations run 'cleaner' today, it's no wonder Trail suffers from an astonishingly high rate of juvenile cancer.

An interesting mishmash of houses squeezes together along the cliffs by the Columbia River. Juxtaposed with the smelter buildings, these give the town a strikingly different character. The many Italian immigrants who came here at the end of the 1800s to work in the mines have also left their mark and their descendants in Trail.

The Visitor Info Centre (☎ 250-368-3144, fax 368-6427), 200-1199 Bay Ave, sells forestry maps and offers free Internet access. It's open 9 am to 5 pm daily in summer, 9 am to 5 pm weekdays the rest of the year. The Greyhound bus depot (☎ 250-368-8400), 1355 Bay St, is right downtown.

If the pollution doesn't discourage you, you can take a free tour of the **Cominco** smelter. The 2½-hour tours meet at 10 am at the Cominco Interpretive Center in the Visitor Info Centre before heading up to the smelter (you'll need your own transportation up there). Wear long pants, sleeves and close-toed shoes. Cameras are not allowed.

Champion Lakes Provincial Park (☎ 250-422-4200), about 26km northeast of Trail off Hwy 22, encompasses a chain of three lakes. The campground here includes 95 sites ($15) with good beach access and flush toilets. To reserve, call ☎ 800-689-9025.

CRESTON
• population 4900
Following the Crowsnest Hwy 3 east from Trail as it skirts the US border, you'll climb over the incredibly scenic, 1774m Kootenay Pass and roll down into Creston, the center of a green, fruit-growing district. The fertile soil and mild weather create perfect growing conditions for Spartan and Macintosh apples. Other thriving crops include asparagus, peaches, cherries and canola.

Only 11km north of the US border, Creston serves as a gateway to the Kootenays from Washington and Idaho in the US. The Visitor Info Center (☎ 250-428-4342, fax 428-9411, dresofc@kootenay.com), 711 Canyon St, is open 9 am to 5 pm weekdays year-round; it's also open on weekends in the summer. Its helpful Web site is www.crestonbc.com. Buses bound for points east and west leave daily from the Greyhound bus depot (☎ 250-428-2767), 125 16th Ave N.

Things to See & Do
The interesting **Stone House Museum** (☎ 250-428-9262), 219 Devon St, is a thick-walled structure with animal figures and even car windshields embedded into the walls. It offers guided tours from 10 am to 3:30 pm daily, May to September. Admission is $2.

Beer connoisseurs will want to take the free hour-long tour through the **Columbia Brewery** (☎ 250-428-9344), where BC's famed Kokanee beer is brewed and bottled. Tours depart at 9:30 and 11 am and 1 and 2:30 pm weekdays, from mid-May to mid-September. The tour includes a free tasting.

Just off Canyon St at 11th Ave, take a look at the building **murals** that depict the region's agricultural character.

An absolute must-see is the spectacular **Creston Valley Wildlife Management Area** (☎ 250-428-3259), 11km west of Creston along Hwy 3. These 7000 hectares of prime waterfowl habitat sit on protected provincial land 17 times larger than Vancouver's Stanley Park. More than 100,000 migrating birds use the area to flock, nest and breed. The fertile floodplain is filled with birdsong, and the marshy wetlands attract the province's largest populations of black terns, white-fronted geese and blue herons. The area earned Ramsar designation in 1994, an honor bestowed on wetlands of 'international importance,' as stated by an intergovernmental treaty signed in Ramsar, Iran in 1971 to protect world wetlands. You can walk along a 1km boardwalk to a watchtower for $3 or go on a one-hour guided canoe tour for $5. Regardless, bring your binoculars.

Places to Stay & Eat
Summit Creek Campground & Recreation Park (☎ 250-428-7441), close to the wildlife center west of town, attracts visiting birders and offers tenting sites ($12.50), showers, flush toilets and daily interpretive programs. It's open May through September. About 5km east of town, *Little Joe's Campground & Fruit Stand* (☎ 250-428-2954, 4020 Hwy 3) features nice sites ($15) surrounded by cedar trees, plus showers and flush toilets. *Scottie's RV Park & Campground* (☎ 250-428-4256, 800-982-4256), right in town across from Columbia Brewery, offers non-secluded but convenient sites for $15.

A good deal, the *Mountain View Inn* (☎ 250-428-4418, 1441 Northwest Blvd), west of downtown at the same turnoff as the Stone House Museum, offers individual cabins that overlook the valley; these cost $54/58 single/double. A popular spot right in town is the *Hacienda Inn* (☎ 250-428-2224, 800-567-2215, 800 Northwest Blvd), which includes a lounge and a restaurant. Large rooms come with a TV and small fridge for $54/59 single/double.

THE KOOTENAYS

Find time to have a meal and a moment on the patio at the excellent ***Kootenay Rose Coffeehouse & Vegetarian Restaurant*** (☎ 250-428-7252, 129 10 Ave N), where you can get salads and sandwiches with soup for $5.25. The ***Garden Bakery*** (☎ 250-428-2740, 1025 Canyon St) serves a sandwich and doughnut lunch for $5. For something more substantial, check out ***Peppers Pub***, in the Hacienda Inn.

East Kootenays

The East Kootenays lie between the Purcell Mountains in the west and the Rocky Mountains in the east. Golden, in the north, sits between Glacier and Yoho National Parks, while Cranbrook, in the south, serves as the major highway crossroads. Defined by its numerous rivers – including the Columbia, Kootenay and Kicking Horse – the area teems with creeks and lakes that are perfect for fly-fishing. River dams generate much of the province's (and Washington's and Oregon's) hydroelectricity. The 16km-long Columbia Lake, at Canal Flats, is the source of the great Columbia River, which winds around BC and Washington State before spilling into the Pacific Ocean in Oregon.

Recently, the East Kootenays region has become a world-class ski and snowboard area, with substantial resorts popping up at Fernie, Kimberley, Panorama and Golden.

CRANBROOK
• population 19,000

Despite its position at the base of the Steeples Range of the Rocky Mountains and in the rolling foothills of the Purcells, this city, which lies 106km northeast of Creston, is not a very attractive place. Its role as the commercial and administrative center of the East Kootenays has made the city prone to rapid development and sprawl. The comely downtown core is overshadowed by 'The Strip,' a 2km slice of Hwy 3 called Cranbrook St as it runs through town, which is dominated by fast-food chains, auto-parts stores, malls and roadside motels.

Tourism types say that Cranbrook's 2228 hours of yearly sunshine make it the sunniest place in the province, which is a redeeming factor, especially since you'll find abundant outdoor activities on nearby lakes and mountains. The regional airport, which lies 14km northeast of the city on Hwy 95A, and the convergence of Hwys 3 and 95A make Cranbrook a relatively busy transportation hub.

Fly-fishing: a popular sport here

Information
The Visitor Info Centre (☎ 250-426-5914, 800-222-6174, fax 250-426-3873), 2279 Cranbrook St N, is open 8:30 am to 7 pm weekdays and 9 am to 5 pm weekends during the summer. The rest of the year, it is open from 8:30 am to 4:30 pm weekdays only. A summer information center at the south end of town on Hwy 3 is open 9 am to 5 pm weekdays in June, July and August.

THE KOOTENAYS

Okanagan Lake, the centerpiece of the Okanagan Valley

Blue sky above, sagebrush below: sweeping vistas from the Trans-Canada Hwy

The Victorian streets of Nelson in the Kootenays

Revelstoke River Trail: a nice spot for a walk

Scaling the rocks near Vernon

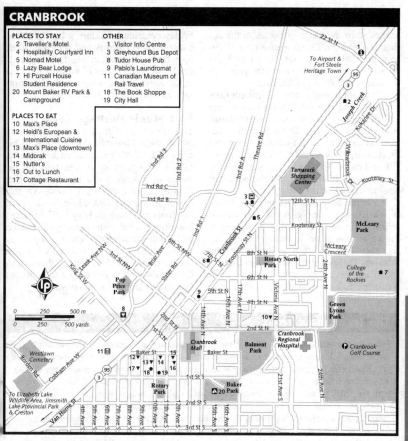

CRANBROOK

PLACES TO STAY
2 Traveller's Motel
4 Hospitality Courtyard Inn
5 Nomad Motel
6 Lazy Bear Lodge
7 HI Purcell House Student Residence
20 Mount Baker RV Park & Campground

PLACES TO EAT
10 Max's Place
12 Heidi's European & International Cuisine
13 Max's Place (downtown)
14 Midorak
15 Nutter's
16 Out to Lunch
17 Cottage Restaurant

OTHER
1 Visitor Info Centre
3 Greyhound Bus Depot
8 Tudor House Pub
9 Pablo's Laundromat
11 Canadian Museum of Rail Travel
18 The Book Shoppe
19 City Hall

THE KOOTENAYS

The *Cranbrook Daily Townsman* is the local paper, but you'll also see a lot of *Calgary Sun* papers around, reflecting the East Kootenays' close affiliation with Alberta. The Book Shoppe (☎ 250-426-3415, 800-665-9880), 33 10th Ave S downtown, sells topographic maps, magazines and regional books.

Do your laundry at Pablo's Laundromat, 323 Kootenay St N; it's open 8 am to 9 pm daily.

For medical care, go to the Cranbrook Regional Hospital (☎ 250-426-5281), 24th Ave N at 2nd St N.

Things to See & Do

Though most of Cranbrook's attractions are the mountains and lakes outside of the city, you'll find a few things to do in town. The **Canadian Museum of Rail Travel** (☎ 250-489-3918) is a neat vestige of prosperous and luxurious 'Trans-Canada Limited' rail-travel days. Some 80,000 sq ft of delicately restored train cars sit parked at 1 Van Horne St N, alongside Hwy 3. You can see before-and-after photo displays as you tour the station house (circa 1900), business and sleeping cars and elaborate parlors decorated with mahogany and walnut paneling, brass fixtures and plush carpets. The Dining Car Tearoom is a good last stop where you can nibble on scones, slurp ice cream or sip tea in the authentic dining car. The museum is open 10 am to 6 pm daily in summer, 10 am to 5 pm Tuesday to Saturday the rest of the year. Admission is $6/3 for adults/children.

At the south end of town, **Elizabeth Lake Wildlife Area** is a small waterfowl refuge for species such as Canada geese, mallards, wood ducks and teals. Other birds that migrate through the area include yellowhead blackbirds, black terns, killdeer and coots. Elk and moose frequently roam around the marshy land. It's free to visit the park, but be sure to stick to the trails.

A couple of annual festivals give Cranbrook cause to whoop it up. The second weekend in June, 200 shiny antique cars cruise around town while bystanders relive the 1950s and '60s at **Rockin' in the Rockies**. The popular **Sam Steele Days**, a four-day party, takes place on the third weekend in June. The whole town comes out in costume to celebrate the hardy founder of Fort Steele. Events include a Friday pancake breakfast, a baseball tournament, logger sports and the Sam Steele Sweetheart Pageant, in which a local 11th-grader wins the honor of saluting the town in the Saturday morning parade. For more information, call ☎ 250-426-4161.

Fort Steele Heritage Town

This town was named for the diplomatic North West Mounted Police (later to become the RCMP) superintendent Samuel Steele, who worked to ease tensions between gold seekers and the Ktunaxa First Nations during the East Kootenay gold rushes in the late 1800s. Fort Steele, 14km north of Cranbrook on Hwy 93/95, became a boomtown, filled with commercial ventures and passing miners; its commercial prowess seemed solid. However, only 10 years after the boom, the BC Southern Railway chose Cranbrook as a more apt spot to go to, and Fort Steele all but fell into obscurity.

The Truth about Trout

Fishing types who visit BC boast about the eager schools of fish that practically leap out of the water, onto fishing lines and into garlic- and butter-soaked cooking pans. They bolster this talk with day-dreamy visions of sitting in a boat on a glassy early-morning lake or of delicately dancing a fly rod on a babbling brook, all of which add to the romantic notion that BC lakes are stocked with fish. Well, in fact, they are, though not as naturally as you might think.

Few people realize that the provincial government's Ministry of Environment, Lands and Parks (MELP) plays a major role in keeping the fish count up. Anglers catch an estimated nine million freshwater fish every year. To keep up with angler demand, more than 1100 lakes and streams are augmented with 12 million fish born and raised in metal containers in fish hatcheries throughout the province. Five major hatcheries produce inland fishes, including steelhead trout, anadromous cutthroat, brook char, land-locked kokanee salmon, rainbow trout and westslope cutthroat.

Fish eggs are captured from wild spawning fish that get trapped in pens on their way to their native spawning grounds. They are transported to a hatchery, where hatchery staff pushes the eggs or sperm out of their abdomens. Except for the kokanee salmon, which die after spawning, the fish are held until they are mature enough to spawn again and then returned to their native spawning streams. Some fish don't get to go home; these unlucky vertebrates are kept at the hatchery, where they continue to be artificially spawned.

The fertilized eggs from these wild salmon are stacked in incubation trays with freshwater running through to emulate stream water and provide oxygen to the eggs. Four to six weeks later, embryonic trout – called alevin – poke their disproportionately giant black eyes out of the egg case.

Unlike most tourist traps, Fort Steele Heritage Town is well done. The ghost town literally comes alive from late June to September, when colorful characters wearing 1890s costumes walk the streets, convincingly re-creating the town's heyday. The 60-plus historical buildings once again become functional, so you can watch blacksmiths at work, shop at the H Kershaw & Son General Store or get in a gunfight at the saloon. Horse shows and live performances take place at the theater and in the streets. For show times, call the 24-hour information line (☎ 250-426-7352). The site is open 9:30 to 5 pm daily in May and June, 9 am to 8 pm daily from July through October. A two-day pass (you can't buy a one-day pass) costs $7.50/4.50 for adults/children. A reduced pass ($3.75/2.25) buys you admission from 5:30 to 8 pm for one evening only.

Places to Stay

Cranbrook's municipal campground is now called the *Mount Baker RV Park & Camp-ground* (☎ 250-489-0056, 877-501-2288, 1501 1st St S), but be aware that it still appears on many maps and in the minds of locals as the 'municipal park.' Open from April through October, the campground includes showers, flush toilets and about 70 (40 serviced, 30 unserviced) fairly treeless sites for $18. Other camping options include the *Jim-smith Lake Provincial Park* (☎ 250-422-4200), off Hwy 3 at the southern end of Cranbrook. The 29 good, shady sites and beach access make this a better option than the city campsite, though there are only pit toilets and no showers. Sites cost $12.

If you want to be closer to Fort Steele, you and everyone else's screaming children could camp just outside the heritage town gate at the *Fort Steele Resort & RV Park* (☎ 250-489-4268). There's a restaurant and store along with dull, loud sites for $18. A much better bet is to turn off Hwy 93/95 onto Fort-Steele-Wardner Rd and follow it for 16km to *Norbury Lake Provincial Park* (☎ 250-422-4200). With plenty of shade and

---

The Truth about Trout

About four weeks after that, the alevin, now called fry, shed the yolk sac and begin feeding. The fry are transferred to large steel troughs, where an automatic feeder dispenses food. The growing fry are finally moved to net enclosures in rearing ponds to prepare for their return to the wild. The entire hatchery is kept squeaky clean to prevent any parasites or contaminants – which could later invade lakes and streams and eventually other animals, including humans – from entering the fish.

Before stocking lakes or streams, biologists need to consider factors such as how many people are fishing in a certain lake, how the increase in fish will impact vegetation or other animals such as the fish's predators or its prey. Fish are transported in special trucks that feed the fish into the stream through a large pipe. Helicopters and small airplanes carry fish to higher-elevation lakes or to streams inaccessible by road.

Learn more about this fascinating augmentation of nature by visiting one of the freshwater fish hatcheries.

The **Kootenay Trout Hatchery** (☎ 250-429-3214), 45km east of Cranbrook along the Bull River, raises about three million rainbow, brook and cutthroat trout a year, mostly to bolster the fish populations in order to keep up with anglers' demands. Here you'll see how the fertilized eggs are captured and raised from fry to fish until they're able to return to local rivers and lakes. The hatchery is open 8 am to 4 pm daily. To get there from Cranbrook, take Hwy 3 toward Fernie and turn left onto the Fort Steele-Wardner Rd. Look for signs.

Regardless, next time you get lost in thoughts of squiggly worms, lazy days and bountiful fish, remember that nature's bounty doesn't always reproduce as fast as we want it to.

THE KOOTENAYS

the Steeples Range looming nearby, this is an excellent spot. The facilities include 46 sites ($12) and pit toilets but no showers.

Non-camping budgeters should check out the College of the Rockies' *HI Purcell House Student Residence* (☎ 250-489-8282, fax 489-8240, 2700 College Way), which opens to the public in summer. The private rooms come with a desk and single bed, plus access to a shared bathroom and kitchen. You'll pay $19/31 single/double. Add $5 if you need linen.

Cranbrook has no shortage of roadside motels, all with pretty clean, standard rooms. Among the cheapest are *Lazy Bear Lodge* (☎ 250-426-6086, 621 Cranbrook St N), with rooms starting at $43/48. The *Hospitality Courtyard Inn* (☎ 250-489-4124, 1209 Cranbrook St N) offers VCRs in each room and free movie rentals. Rooms cost $45/50 ($5 extra for a kitchenette). Down The Strip, the large *Traveller's Motel* (☎ 250-426-4208, 888-489-1456, 2000 Cranbrook St N) is farthest from the train tracks. Rooms rent for $48/58.

Nicer rooms and friendly staff are on hand at the *Nomad Motel* (☎ 250-426-6266, 800-863-6999, 910 Cranbrook St N). Rooms here cost $59/69, including a continental breakfast.

Places to Eat

You can find any kind of fast food and standard diners along The Strip, but the best places to eat are downtown. The most popular spot for breakfast is the *Cottage Restaurant* (☎ 250-426-6516, 13 9th Ave S) where a full breakfast with eggs, bacon, hash browns and toast costs $5. It's closed Sunday.

For good coffee, salads and deli sandwiches, head to *Max's Place*, which has two locations: downtown (☎ 250-489-3538, 21 10th Ave S) and close to the college (☎ 250-426-6885, 301 Victoria Ave). Another reliable spot for sandwiches downtown is *Out to Lunch* (☎ 250-489-5434, 5 12th Ave S), though it closes at 4 pm and isn't open on weekends. To pick up bulk snacks for hiking or camping, stop by *Nutter's* (☎ 250-426-5519, 1107 Baker St).

Heidi's European & International Cuisine (☎ 250-426-7922, 821C Baker St) serves large portions of vegetarian spaetzle ($12) and Wiener schnitzel ($15). Taste some flavorful Korean food at *Midorak* (☎ 250-489-4808, 1015 Baker St), where lunches average $8 and dinners go for about $12. It's closed on Monday.

For beer, pub food and a lively atmosphere, try *Tudor House Pub* (☎ 250-489-1169, 22 Briar Ave NW), on the west side of the highway.

Getting There & Around

Canadian Regional Airlines and Air BC fly to the Cranbrook Airport (☎ 250-426-7913) from Vancouver daily. Central Mountain Air offers flights from Calgary. For information about any of these airlines, call Air Canada (☎ 888-247-2262).

The Greyhound bus depot (☎ 250-489-2465) is at 1229 Cranbrook St N at Theatre Rd. Three buses depart daily for Vancouver (16 hours, $95) in the west and Calgary (eight hours, $54) in the east. The station has lockers and is open 7 am to 6 pm weekdays, 7 am to 3 pm Saturday and 10:30 am to 2:30 pm Sunday.

Though there's been talk of it for a long time, Cranbrook currently has no local transit service. For taxi service, call Star Taxi (☎ 250-426-3888) or Sun City Cabs (☎ 250-426-1111).

Cranbrook has all the major car rental companies. Among them are:

Budget
(☎ 250-489-4371), 1024 Cranbrook St N

Hertz
(☎ 250-489-1115), airport

National Car Rental
(☎ 250-489-0911), 217 Cranbrook St N;
(☎ 250-489-3689), airport

Rent-A-Wreck
(☎ 250-426-3004), 703D Cranbrook St N

FERNIE

The Elk Valley, comprised of Fernie, Sparwood and Elkford, sits in the rain shadow of the Rocky Mountains' Lizard Range.

Constant winter storms travel over the Rockies and dump vast amounts of snow on the area, making it a powdery paradise for skiers and snowboarders. The growing town of Fernie (population 5082), 93km east of Cranbrook, is nestled between the high peaks of the Three Sisters Mountains (not to be confused with the more renowned mountains in Alberta) and Mt Fernie. The town experienced a devastating fire in 1908, which resulted in a brick-and-stone building code. Thus, today you'll see many fine late-19th- and early-20th-century buildings, many of which were built out of local yellow brick, giving the town an appearance unique in the East Kootenays.

The area has a rich economic history of mining and logging, activities which are now giving way to winter tourism. Elaborate plans are already well under way for the Fernie Alpine Resort, which could be both a blessing and a curse for the small town. While younger locals think the new industry is good for Fernie, many older residents fear the mountain resort community will grow too quickly and draw tourist dollars away from the main town.

Downtown Fernie lies southeast of Hwy 3. Many shops and services can be found on 7th Ave, which runs parallel to the highway. The Visitor Info Center (☎ 250-423-6868, fernie@elkvalley.net) is east of town off Hwy 3, just past the Elk River crossing. It is open 9 am to 7 pm daily in summer and 9 am to 5 pm weekdays the rest of the year. For medical emergencies, go to the Fernie District Hospital (☎ 250-423-4453), at the east end of 5th Ave past the police station.

Fernie Alpine Resort

A five-minute drive from downtown Fernie, BC's fastest-growing ski hill,' which develops hope will eventually rival Whistler, gets a whopping 875cm of snow per year on average. Managed by Resorts of the Canadian Rockies – the same folks who run Alberta's Lake Louise and who are fast developing Kimberley Alpine Resort – the Fernie Alpine Resort (☎ 250-423-4655, 800-258-7669) is undergoing massive resort-style growth to turn it into a year-round

Check Your Watch

Like Alberta and Idaho, the East Kootenays lie in the Mountain Time Zone, unlike the West Kootenays and the rest of BC, which fall in the Pacific Time Zone. If you're heading west on the Trans-Canada Hwy (Hwy 1) from Golden, the time changes at the east gate to Glacier National Park. Or, as you travel west on the Crowsnest Hwy (Hwy 3), the time changes between Cranbrook and Creston. Mountain Time is always an hour ahead of Pacific Time. For example, when it's noon in Golden and Cranbrook, it's 11 am in Glacier National Park and Creston.

attraction. For now, its 97 runs, five bowls and almost endless dumps of powder draw droves of skiers and snowboarders looking for unspoiled terrain. Lift tickets cost $54/43 for adults/children. For 24-hour snow reports, call ☎ 250-423-3555. More information is available on the Web site www .skifernie.com.

To get to the resort from town, follow Hwy 3 west and turn right onto Ski Hill Rd. Most hotels run shuttles daily, and hitchhiking is easy and relatively safe.

Rent ski or snowboard equipment in town for $28 per day at Fernie Sports (☎ 250-423-3611). The resort charges $33 for skis and $29 for snowboards.

Heavy snowfalls dramatically increase avalanche danger. If you are planning on doing any backcountry touring, be sure to stop by the Guides Hut (☎ 250-423-3650), 671 2nd Ave, where you can get the scoop on weather, rent avalanche kits, get topographic maps and find out about organized backcountry tours.

Activities

White-Water Rafting Whether you're looking to soak up some rays or get soaked by the river, two rafting companies offer trips on the Bull and Elk Rivers. Canyon Raft Company (☎ 250-423-7226, 888-423-7226) and Mountain High River Adventures

(☎ 250-423-5008, 877-423-4555) both offer day trips on either river for $75 or half-day floats for $49. The trips include all the gear and lunch.

Hiking Great hiking trails radiate in all directions from Fernie. The excellent and challenging Three Sisters Hike winds through forests and wildflower-covered meadows, along limestone cliffs and scree slopes. The 2744m summit offers incredible 360-degree views of the Elk Valley, Fisher Peak and surrounding lakes. From the Visitor Info Centre, take Dickens Rd to Hartley Lake Rd and follow it to the lake. Turn left onto the dirt track and follow it 3km to the trailhead. Allow at least four hours each way. Another hike affording spectacular views, the Hosmer Mountain Trail, is also off Hartley Lake Rd (there is a parking area and a well-marked trailhead). This moderate hike takes about 2½ hours one-way.

Mountain Biking The best thing about mountain biking in Fernie is the choice of terrain, from easy toodles along trails in Mt Fernie Provincial Park to steep granny-gear uphills and log-jumping downs. *The Secret of Single Track* is a good local map with trail descriptions. Pick it up at bike shops or at the Visitor Info Centre. Get the lowdown from local riders at Fernie Sports (☎ 250-423-3611), 1191 7th Ave, where you can rent front-suspension bikes for $25 per day. For good information and bike tuning, go to the ski-shop-turned-summer-bike-shop SV Ski Base (☎ 250-423-6464), 442 2nd Ave.

Places to Stay

Three kilometers west of town, *Mt Fernie Provincial Park* (☎ 250-422-4200, 800-689-9025 for reservations) offers 38 sites ($12), flush toilets, waterfalls, a self-guided interpretive trail and access to mountain-bike trails. Sites are $12.

Winter is Fernie's busy season, when it gets tougher and more expensive to find places to stay. Prices listed below are peak winter rates. If you're booking ahead of time, Fernie Tourism operates a central reservations line (☎ 250-423-9207, 888-754-7325) and a Web site (www.fernietourism.com) to help people find accommodations or packages. Sometimes you'll get good deals, though you may have better luck looking on your own. Ask at the Visitor Info Centre for a listing of B&Bs.

The cheapest place in town is the *HI Raging Elk Hostel* (☎ 250-423-6811, fax 250-423-6812, raginelk@elkvalley.net, 892 6th Ave). Though the rooms are crowded and run-down, the hostel enjoys a central location and offers ski packages starting at $55 for a bed and a lift ticket. Carbo-load on the free pancake breakfast in the morning. Beds cost $18/22 for members/nonmembers. Private rooms for two cost $30 in summer, $60 in winter.

Just off the highway, the *Snow Valley Motel* (☎ 250-423-4421, 877-696-7669, fax 250-423-7437, 1041 7th Ave) rents large, clean rooms with TV and free coffee. Amenities include shuttle service to the mountain, an eight-person hot tub and friendly staff who know a lot about the town. Rooms cost $59/64 single/double. The *Three Sisters Motel* (☎ 250-423-4438, 877-326-8888, fax 250-423-6220, threesis@kootenaycable.com, 441 Hwy 3) features large rooms, a pool and hot tub. Rooms cost $70/80, but if you're traveling with more than two people, ask about the triple and quad rooms, which can be a good deal if you have enough people. Rooms at the *HI 3 Lodge* (☎ 250-423-4492, 800-667-1167, fax 250-423-6004, hithree@cancom.net, 891 Hwy 3) start at $65/70, with larger rooms also available.

Places to Eat

All hail to small towns with good coffee! *Jamochas Coffee House & Bagel Co* (☎ 250-423-6977, 851 7th Ave), on the west side of Hwy 3, has adopted the motto, 'Life's too short to drink bad coffee.' It's a good spot to read the paper and write postcards while you sip your tasty brew. Downtown, order a latte at *Cappuccino Corner Coffee House*, on the corner of 2nd Ave and 5th St.

For delicious breakfasts and interesting conversations, try the *Blue Toque Diner*

(☎ 250-423-4637, 500 Hwy 3). A standard full breakfast costs $6.50, but go for the feature of the day – it's likely one of the most creative meals you'll eat.

For a healthy lunch, such as a salad or wrap, try *Mug Shots Bistro* (☎ 250-423-8018, 592 3rd Ave). This casual place, with couches, a used bookstore and Internet access, also fixes yummy desserts.

The Grill Next Door (☎ 250-423-3364), in the Grand Central Hotel at 2nd Ave and 3rd St, features a large menu, including burgers ($9), pasta dishes ($12) and steak dinners ($17). *The Pub Bar & Grill* (☎ 250-423-6871, 742 Hwy 3), in the Park Place Lodge, is popular with locals and can get pretty busy after 10 pm. Earlier than that, you can order average pub food or play a game on the pool tables.

The place to go at the ski resort is *Kelsey's* (☎ 250-423-4655), in the Corner Stone Lodge. This lively place serves gooey chicken wings and palatable beer.

Getting There & Around

There is no bus depot in town, but you can book Greyhound bus services at the front desk of the Park Place Lodge, 742 Hwy 3. Two daily buses go to Vancouver ($89) and Calgary ($44). Dewdney Coach Lines (☎ 800-332-0282) offers service to and from the Cranbrook Airport for $30 one-way. It also travels to Calgary from Fernie for $50 one-way. Call for times.

Many hotels offer shuttle service to the Fernie Alpine Resort, but you can also take Kootenay Taxi (☎ 250-423-4408) for $2.50 each way. It picks up at the hostel (among other stops) at 8:40, 9:40, 10:40 and 11:40 am daily.

AROUND FERNIE

Sparwood (population 4211) lies 29km northeast of Fernie, at the junction of Hwys 3 and 43. The single town is the result of the government's attempt to join three smaller towns (Michel, Natal and Middletown) and, as such, is somewhat of a mishmash. Sparwood's big attraction is the 'World's Largest Truck,' a green Terex-Titan monster used to move coal. The Visitor Info Center (☎ 250-425-2423) is on Hwy 3 at Aspen Dr, beside the giant truck.

About 35km farther north on Hwy 43, you'll hit the coal-mining town of **Elkford** (population 3100), home to abundant wildlife and the gateway to the remote Elk Lakes Provincial Park. Look for the Visitor Info Centre (☎ 250-865-4614, 877-355-9453) at 4A Front St.

The RV-oriented *Mountain Shadows Campground* (☎ 250-425-7815), just off the highway at the south entrance to Sparwood, offers showers, flush toilets and some tenting sites for $12. In Elkford, the similarly equipped *Elkford Municipal Campground* (☎ 250-865-2650), Hwy 43 and Michael Rd, also rents sites for $12.

KIMBERLEY
• population 6700

At 1113m, Kimberley can claim to be the highest city in Canada (at 1397m, Banff in Alberta is higher, but it's technically a town, not a city), as well as one of the nicest stops in the East Kootenays.

The discovery of rich minerals in 1891 prompted the birth of the North Star Mine. The following year on the other side of Mark Creek, another claim staked out what would grow to become the largest lead and zinc mine in the world, the Sullivan Mine. Mark Creek Crossing was renamed Kimberley in 1896, after the successful South African diamond mine. In 1909, Cominco took over operations, drawing more than 162 million tons of ore out of the Sullivan, though the metal isn't worth as much as diamonds. The mine's planned closing in 2001 means that the town's focus must now shift from mineral-based industry to something that won't run out, such as tourism.

And people have known this day would come. Before 1973, Kimberley looked like what it is – a small mountain mining town. Since then it has been revamped to resemble a Bavarian alpine village. Most of the downtown section, the **Platzl**, was transformed, with city planners paying enough attention to detail to make it interesting. Kimberley's mascot, Happy Hans, lives in a huge cuckoo clock in the center of the

Platzl. Every hour on the hour, people will stand in awed anticipation for ole Hans to pop out and yodel. All of the town's fire hydrants have been hand-painted to look like little people wearing lederhosen. While slightly ridiculous, the Bavarian theme serves Kimberley well: it has prevented out-of-control sprawl and has spawned several good restaurants, jolly beer-drinking events and an overall sense of fun. Though this Bavarianism, combined with the new, rapidly growing ski resort, brings lots of camera-happy people to Kimberley, this spot still remains a quiet alpine mining town.

Information

The Visitor Info Centre (☎ 250-427-3666, fax 427-5378), 350 Ross St, is open 9 am to 7 pm daily in July and August and 9 am to 5 pm weekdays the rest of the year. Internet access is available at the library, at the east end of the Platzl. The Kimberley Book Company (☎ 250-427-7337), 180 Deer Park Ave just off the Platzl, sells travel guides and good local books.

The Kimberley & District Hospital (☎ 250-427-2215) is beside the Cominco Gardens on 4th Ave.

The Greyhound bus depot is east of Kimberley, at 1770 Warren Ave in Marysville. Buses depart daily for Banff in the east and Vancouver in the west.

Things to See & Do

Take a 9km ride on the **Bavarian City Mining Railway** (☎ 250-427-5311) as it chugs through the steep-walled Mark Creek Valley toward some incredible mountain vistas. The train operates weekends from mid-May through June and daily in July and August. Hop on at the station on Gerry Sorensen Way or on the way up to the ski hill or at the Happy Hans clock. The ride costs $6/3 for adults/children.

You can learn about mining history at the **Kimberley Heritage Museum** (☎ 250-427-7510), beside the library at the east end of the Platzl. The free museum is open 9 am to 4:30 pm Monday to Saturday (1 to 4 pm in winter).

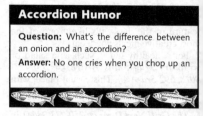

Accordion Humor

Question: What's the difference between an onion and an accordion?
Answer: No one cries when you chop up an accordion.

It costs nothing to walk around the 12-acre **Cominco Gardens**, beside the hospital above Kimberley. Full of roses, tulips and gnomes, the gardens act as testing grounds for Cominco's Elephant Brand fertilizer. On the grounds, the Greenhouse Tea Garden serves up high tea ($8) in a Victorian gazebo. If you're walking from town, take the stairway and trail at the west end of Howard St. It takes about 15 minutes.

The extensive network of trails (100km worth) of the **Kimberley Nature Park** wind around Kimberley. You can cross-country ski or walk along the well-marked trails while observing the active wildlife. Ask at the Visitor Info Centre for a copy of *Kimberley Nature Park Trail Map & Guide*.

Just west of town, in the nearby community of Marysville, take the short walk to see the **Marysville Waterfalls**. Park at the Mark Creek bridge and follow the boardwalk along the creek. It takes about 10 minutes.

Kimberley Alpine Resort

The Resorts of the Canadian Rockies have spent millions building up the Kimberley Alpine Resort (☎ 250-427-4881, fax 250-427-3927, info@skikimberley.com) with the same kind of energy and huge investment dollars that were poured into the Fernie Alpine Resort. Boasting 728 hectares of skiable terrain, mild weather and 67 runs on North Star Mountain, the resort is poised to attract lots of skiers, boarders and plenty of their tourism dollars. Lift tickets cost $43. At the resort, you'll pay $28 for skis and $30 for snowboards. To find out about conditions, call the 24-hour snow phone (☎ 250-427-7332). For more information, check out the Web site www.skikimberley.com.

Festivals

The Platzl is the perfect place to have a party, and Kimberley certainly has its share. During the winter holidays, lights decorate the snowy center. In February, the locals come out to play winter bocce, hockey and snow golf at **Winterfest**. In the second week in July, listen – or leave town – for the **Kimberley International Old Time Accordion Championships**. The following week is **Julyfest**, a week of dancing, parades and lots of beer. In early September, look out for the **International Folkdance & Octoberfest**, when there's lots of entertainment and more beer.

Places to Stay

The massive **Happy Hans Riverside RV Resort** (☎ 250-427-2929, fax 427-2917) features 142 sites, flush toilets, showers, a store and lots of room for RVs to crowd around. Tenting sites cost $16. To get there, turn off Hwy 95A in Marysville and follow the St Mary Lake Rd for 2.9km; look for signs of Happy Hans.

Right in the middle of the Platzl, above the Ozone Pub, is the **Kimberley SameSun Hostel** (☎ 250-427-7191). The excellent location and newly renovated, clean rooms make this a good place to stay, especially in the ski season. The hostel runs a shuttle to the ski hill in winter and contains ski/snowboard lockers, laundry facilities and Internet kiosks. Dorm-style beds are $15, and private rooms are $35.

Crazy Chef Bernard has his fingers in many places-to-stay strudels. He runs the **Chef Bernard's Platzl Inn** (☎ 800-905-8338), above his restaurant in the Platzl. Rooms start at $60, but prices vary wildly when demand is high or low. When the inn is full, the fine chef can supply you with accommodations at one of his condos up at the Kimberley Alpine Resort.

You can find good hotel deals if you venture off the Platzl. Two kilometers north of town on Hwy 95 is the **North Star Motel** (☎ 250-427-5633), a good value with clean rooms and a hot tub. Rooms cost $55/60 single/double.

Places to Eat

The most notable places to eat are in the Platzl. Get delicious baked goods at **Kimberley City Bakery** (☎ 250-427-2131). Though bypassing the Bavarian theme, the **Snowdrift Cafe** (☎ 250-427-2100) occupies prime real estate on the northwest side of the Platzl. The all-vegetarian menu features burritos for $6, veggie pizza slices for $3.50 and veggie burgers for $5.25.

You can't leave Kimberley without chowing on some traditional Bavarian grub. The **Gasthaus am Platzl** (☎ 250-427-4851), on the southwest side, serves schnitzel ($10) and Gasthaus burgers ($7.25). You'll hear the music and see the vast collection of trinkets spilling out the door over at **Chef Bernard's Restaurant**, where the schnitzel and bratwurst are $13 and the delicious apple strudel is $5.

On the way up to the ski resort, definitely stop for a bite at **The Old Bauernhaus** (☎ 250-427-5133, 280 Norton Ave), which offers Bavarian favorites in a 350-year-old farmhouse, moved here piece by piece from Germany in the 1980s. The stone patio enjoys pretty views. The Bauernhaus is closed on Tuesday and Wednesday.

For beers and burgers ($7), check out **Ozone Pub** (☎ 250-427-7744), below the hostel. Live bands occasionally play, and ski bums like to gather at the pool tables and the dartboards.

KIMBERLEY TO RADIUM HOT SPRINGS

Hwy 95A heads northeast out of Kimberley and connects up with Hwy 93/95. Just south of the junction on Hwy 95 is **Wasa Lake Provincial Park**, home to the warmest lake in the Kootenays. The popular campground contains 104 sites ($15), 50 of which you can reserve by calling ☎ 800-689-9025, and offers good lake access, interpretive programs and flush toilets. The park protects an increasingly rare chunk of BC's grassland, most of which has been turned into golf courses or farmland. A paved path meanders around the lake, giving you a good chance to check out this ecosystem from a bike, in-line skates or a wheelchair. For information on Wasa Lake or any of the area's provincial parks, call ☎ 250-422-4200.

After Wasa, Hwy 93/95 continues north along the scenic Kootenay River. At **Skookumchuck**, 18km north of Wasa, the Lussier and Skookumchuck Rivers join the Kootenay. You'll find little more than a gas station and coffee shop here. Continue 41km northeast to **Whiteswan Lake Provincial Park**, where the rustic **Lussier Hot Springs** lie 17km into the park. The loose-gravel road that branches off the highway is bumpy but navigable for most cars. A well-marked trailhead leads you down to the springs which, despite their remoteness, can get downright crowded in summer. Past the springs are Whiteswan and Alces Lakes, both popular with anglers. The four campgrounds in the park all contain pit toilets and good sites for $12.

To access the remote **Top of the World Provincial Park**, follow the Whiteswan Rd for 52km off Hwy 95. Once you get to the end of the bumpy road, it's an easy 6km hike or mountain-bike ride to Fish Lake, so named for its thick population of Dolly Varden and cutthroat trout. You can camp at one of the backcountry sites at Fish Lake or stay in the large rustic cabin often used by anglers.

Canal Flats
• population 500

This small lumber town sits at the southern end of 16km-long Columbia Lake, the source of the powerful Columbia River. Though it eventually heads south, the river actually flows north out of Columbia Lake to Golden, around a big bend near Revelstoke's Mica Dam, then south through the West Kootenays and through BC and Washington State before spilling into the Pacific Ocean at Astoria, Oregon in the US.

Canal Flats sits on a long narrow stretch of land; in the late 1800s, an Englishman got the bright idea to build a canal that would connect the Columbia Lake with the Kootenay River, opening up a water route from Golden in BC to Montana in the US. The canal opened in 1889, but only two boats ever squeezed through the narrow lock. A year after it opened, the canal closed for good.

North of Canal Flats, you'll suddenly come across the Dutch Creek hoodoos, a cool rock formation formed over time by wind and rain erosion.

Fairmont Hot Springs Resort

If you head north of Canal Flats on Hwy 95, you'll come to what is essentially a giant sinkhole for tourist dollars. This resort community, centered around some natural hot springs, is a place vacationing families drive into and never leave until their vacation is over. Complete with golf courses, a 311-site RV park, a private airplane landing strip, a small ski hill and plenty of shops and restaurants, the resort lacks anything low budget and definitely caters to high-end, short-term vacationers with plenty of money.

But the hot springs are open to the public, and though the super-sanitized pools lack the crude beauty and grit of natural springs, their setting in the lap of the Rockies will take your breath away. The pools are open 8 am to 10 pm daily. A single entry costs $6.50/4.50 for adults/children, and a day pass is $8.50/6.50. For more information on the resort, call ☎ 800-663-4979 or check the Web site www.fairmontresort.com.

Windermere Valley

This narrow valley between the Purcell and Rocky Mountains has long been a bountiful transportation route for the Ktunaxa and Kinbasket First Nations people. Pioneer David Thompson began his exploration of the Columbia River here in 1807. Today, the area surrounding Windermere Lake attracts both family vacationers and backcountry explorers. The towns of **Windermere** and **Invermere** are often overlooked by visitors heading to the national parks, but they are both worthwhile stops for stocking up on supplies before heading into the backcountry. The Columbia Valley Visitor Info Centre (☎ 250-342-2844, fax 342-3261), 651 Hwy 93/95 in Windermere, is open 9 am to 5 pm daily in summer and weekdays only in winter.

Panorama Mountain Village Resort

Taken over in 1993 by Intrawest, the same folks who own Whistler-Blackcomb, the Panorama Mountain Village Resort (☎ 250-342-6941, 800-663-2929) went from being an understated, local skiers' mountain to a major, full-service resort. Boasting 12,000 vertical meters of immaculately groomed runs, plus a gondola that shuttles people from the upper to lower villages and an endless array of new services and condos, Panorama is fast becoming a built-up, expensive and exclusive resort. The 18km drive up a winding road, combined with limited shuttle services from Invermere, tends to isolate the mountain. Critics of the resort's growth argue that most tourist dollars stay at the resort and don't add fuel to the region's economy. Regardless, the resort enjoys a growing popularity. For further information, visit the Web site www.panoramaresort.com.

RADIUM HOT SPRINGS

• population 600

The eighth-smallest municipality in BC, 164km north of Cranbrook on Hwy 95, lies just outside the southwest corner of Kootenay National Park. Along with Golden, 103km away, Radium Hot Springs is a major gateway to all four Rocky Mountain national parks: Kootenay, Banff, Jasper and Yoho.

The town sits in the Rocky Mountain Trench, with the spires of the Purcells to the west and the Rocky Mountains directly east. Radium was so named after a government test conducted in 1914 showed small levels of radioactivity in the nearby hot springs. The surrounding Columbia River wetlands north of Radium attract more than 100 species of birds, including migrating waterfowl traveling along the Pacific Flyway. Radium boasts a large resident population of Rocky Mountain bighorn sheep, which often wander through town during the winter.

The biggest draw in Radium, however, is the famed hot springs, which are located just inside the park's west gate (for details on the springs, see the Kootenay National Park section in the Rockies chapter).

Mountaineers come from around the world to test their skills on the sheer rock faces and 3000m-high granite pinnacles in **Bugaboo Glacier Provincial Park** (☎ 250-422-4200), a bit of a drive northwest of Radium Hot Springs. To get there, take Hwy 95 north to Brisco (27km from Radium Hot Springs) and then follow a gravel logging road for 45km. This is a backcountry park for experienced climbers and well-equipped hikers only.

The Kootenay National Park & Radium Hot Springs Visitor Info Center (☎ 250-347-9331, 800-347-9704, fax 250-347-9127, chamber@rhs.bc.ca), 7556 Main St E (Hwy 93/95), offers information about the parks. It's open 9 am to 9 pm daily in July and August and 9:30 to 5:30 pm daily the rest of the year. The town maintains a Web site at www.radiumhotsprings.com.

Places to Stay

Despite its tiny population, Radium Hot Springs contains more than 30 motels. Despite all the accommodations, though, it's a good idea to arrange accommodations ahead of time in July and August. But as soon as the madness of summer ends, you can find great deals and lots of vacancies. Prices below are peak summer rates. The best camping is in the park (see the Places to Stay section under Kootenay National Park in the Rockies chapter).

The *Misty Mountain River Lodge* (☎ 250-347-9912, 877-347-9644, fax 250-347-9397, 5036 Hwy 93) is a new hostel right outside the park gate. The homey atmosphere makes this a great place to stay over on your way into or out of the park. The dorm-style rooms are small (no more than six beds to a room), but the communal kitchen and large sunny patio (with views of the Purcells) give you space to hang out. Dorm beds cost $16/21 for members/nonmembers. Private rooms start at $42.

If you can cope with bad 1970s decor, one of the cheapest places to stay is the *Ritz Motel* (☎ 250-250-347-9644, 4883 Stanley St), which offers large rooms with kitchenettes for $50. Across the street, the more modern *Pinewood Motel* (☎ 250-347-9529, 888-557-5567, 4870 Stanley St) features clean rooms with kitchens starting at $60. Also check out the similarly priced *Sunset Motel* (☎ 250-347-9862, 800-214-7413, 4883 McKay St).

For a little more atmosphere, try the *Motel Bavaria* (☎ 250-347-9915, 888-749-1119, 4872 McKay St), with an inviting alpine theme. Each of the tidy rooms contains a small fridge and coffeemaker. Rates start at $65. The *Gables Motel* (☎ 250-347-9866, 877-387-7007, 5028 Hwy 93), distinguishable by the outside flower boxes, features rooms with mountain views, TVs and whirlpool bathtubs. Rooms start at $70/80 single/double.

Places to Eat

Though there are plenty of fast-food options, a healthy meal is hard to come by in Radium. Along the highway, *Back Country Jacks* (☎ 250-347-0097) is a dark, smoky place that serves up ribs, steak and chicken dishes starting at $9. The *Horsethief Creek Pub & Eatery* (☎ 250-347-6400) offers standard pub fare. *La Cabina Ristorante* (☎ 250-347-2340, 7493 Main St N), in the Prestige Inn, is probably your best bet for pizza, pastas and steaks. Dinners start here at $10.

For the best food in town (by far), head to the *Springs at Radium Restaurant* (☎ 250-347-9311), located at Springs Golf Course off the west side of the highway. You can sit on the deck and enjoy great views of the Bugaboo spires in the Purcell Mountains. The delicious breakfasts start at $8, while lunches cost about $10 and dinners average $15.

GOLDEN
• population 4000

Sandwiched between the Purcell and Rocky Mountains and surrounded by six national parks, Golden is the first town of any size you encounter if you're coming west from Alberta. One hundred kilometers north of Radium Hot Springs on Hwy 95 and 148km west of Revelstoke on the Trans-Canada

Hwy (Hwy 1), Golden sits near the confluence of the Columbia and Kicking Horse Rivers and lies 57km west of Field in Yoho National Park.

Cree and Stoney Natives first came west over the steep pass to travel the rivers and trade with the Kootenai Natives in the 1700s. In the 1800s, explorer David Thompson passed through the area to map the turbulent rivers. Before prospectors came rolling into the area in search of gold, the town was referred to as the 'Cache' because it was little more than a storage spot for supplies. It was later renamed Golden City (the 'City' was later dropped) to compete with Silver City, a nearby, momentary boomtown where someone had planted decoy deposits of silver ore.

Later, with the advent of tourism in the Rockies, the Canadian Pacific Railway hired Swiss guides to lure rich Europeans to explore the pristine mountain peaks. To make the guides feel at home, the CPR housed them in Swiss-style chalets just above Golden. You can still see remnants of the village.

Many guidebooks and highway tourists give Golden a bad rap. If you never venture off the Trans-Canada Hwy, it looks like an unattractive commercial strip of motels, fast-food restaurants and service stations. But once you get off the highway and discover the year-round outdoor opportunities, you might change your mind. White-water rafting is incredibly popular. The area mountains beckon skiers, boarders and hikers, while other brave souls launch hang gliders off Mt 7, so named for the way snow falls on the ridge – in the shape of a seven.

Information

The center of town lies 2km south of the highway. The Visitor Info Centre (☎ 250-344-7125, 800-622-4653, fax 250-344-6688), 500 10th Ave, is open 9 am to 5 pm daily in July and August, 9 am to 5 pm weekdays only in winter. The post office, 525 N 9th Ave, is beside the downtown fountain.

For a good selection of local books and maps, check out Food for Thought Books (☎ 250-344-5600), 407 N 9th Ave. The

The Story of the Kicking Horse

With a burning desire to 'open up the west,' the Canadian government started looking for ways to push the railway over the high, icy Rocky Mountains. In 1858, it sent a scientific and exploratory expedition out to survey the land and return with suggestions for a feasible route over the Rockies. Led by John Palliser, the expedition was accompanied by a geologist named Sir James Hector, who is credited for finding the Kicking Horse Pass, albeit by rather unfortunate circumstances.

Fatigued and cold after a long day hiking in the mountains, Hector camped with his cohorts near the Continental Divide. Just as the beginnings of sleep finally closed Sir James' eyelids, one of the packhorses escaped across the river. In fear of losing valuable gear, Sir James jumped in the chilly river waters and swam after the horse. He dragged it back to camp, tied it up next to his own horse, and before long the two horses started biting each other. (Poor James wasn't getting much sleep.) Finally he intervened, and for his troubles, his horse delivered a swift kick square to his abdomen. The kick broke three ribs and left him unconscious for so long that the Natives he was traveling with presumed he was dead.

They dragged his corpse to a gravesite in a valley away from camp. Just before they threw him into the ground, Sir James revived – apparently not dead after all. Once he healed, he set off to explore the pretty valley and stumbled onto the pass that would become the CPR's route to connecting the west.

Golden & District Hospital (☎ 250-344-5271) is at 835 S 9th Ave.

The Greyhound bus depot (☎ 250-344-6172), 1402 N Trans-Canada Hwy, sits beside the Esso gas station. Every day, four buses head west to Vancouver ($83 one-way), and four go east to Banff ($21) and Calgary ($37). There are lockers at the station.

Activities

White-Water Rafting Golden is the center for white-water rafting trips on the turbulent and chilly Kicking Horse River. Powerful Class III and IV rapids and breathtaking scenery along the sheer walls of the Kicking Horse Valley make this rafting experience one of North America's best. The fainter of heart can take a mellow but equally scenic float trip on the upper river. Many operators run the river in the busy summer season, making it sometimes resemble a traffic jam.

Strict BC rafting regulations and training ensure each company employs qualified, experienced staff. One of the first companies to start running the river in the early 1980s

was the family-run Glacier Raft Company (☎ 250-344-6521, glacierraft@redshift.bc.ca), which offers trips for $49/85 per half day/full day; day-long float trips cost $50. Another reputable company with similar trips is Wet 'n' Wild (☎ 250-344-6546, 800-668-9119, info@wetnwild.bc.ca). All gear and lunch are included in the tour price.

Kinbasket Adventures (☎ 250-344-6012) offers wildlife-observing float tours of the Columbia Valley wetlands for $40/20 for adults/children.

Mountain Biking Golden's passionately enthusiastic mountain-biking community spends a lot of time cutting and maintaining a variety of trails around town. Whether you'd rather putter around or really test your limits, there's likely a trail to suit you. For easy riding in town, you can bike along the trails following the Kicking Horse River or head across the Columbia River to the West Bench, where you can tool around on 40km worth of trails. Hard-core types with good lungs peddle the steep trails up Mt 7 and then scream down technical single track.

THE KOOTENAYS

Source for Sports (☎ 250-344-2966), 509 9th Ave N, rents full-suspension bikes for $30. Summit Cycle (☎ 250-344-6600), 1007 11th Ave S, has knowledgeable staff and a tech shop if you need your bike tuned.

Heli-Skiing & Hiking South of Golden, in the Purcell Mountains, lies a world center for helicopter skiing – in districts such as the Gothics, Caribous and, perhaps best known, the Bugaboos. The latter includes 1500 sq km of rugged, remote mountains accessible only by helicopter during the winter months.

This dangerous, thrilling sport attracts rich visitors from around the world every winter and spring.

The skiing is superb, but a portion of the appeal is the danger. Avalanches are not uncommon, and tumbling snows claim lives on a regular, though not frequent, basis – just often enough to give your run downhill that extra kick.

Canadian Mountain Holidays or CMH (☎ 403-762-7100, 800-661-0252), 217 Bear St in Banff, Alberta, specializes in four- to seven-day heli-skiing trips to some of the best and most remote areas in the BC mountain ranges. These superb trips range from $3300 to $7000. RK Heli-Ski (☎ 250-342-3889, 800-661-6060) operates out of the Panorama Ski Resort and offers one-day trips starting at $600. In Golden, Purcell Heli-Skiing (☎ 250-344-5410, 877-435-4754) features many packages, including three days of heli-skiing, starting at $2250.

During the summer months, you can helicopter into some of the area lodges and enjoy incredible alpine hiking in wildflower meadows.

Kicking Horse Mountain Resort

Big plans are underway for Golden's Whitetooth Mountain. Recently taken over by the same folks who run Vancouver's Grouse Mountain, the new resort will eventually include an eight-passenger gondola, four new chairlifts, a lodge and village plaza, all to be built by 2007. With 1,245 vertical meters and a relatively snow-heavy, wind-free position between the Rockies and Purcells, the resort is a future contender in the race for ski-resort tourist dollars. For more information, call ☎ 250-344-8626 or 888-706-1117.

Places to Stay

The *Golden Municipal Campground* (☎ 250-344-5412, 1407 9th St S) contains flush toilets, showers and 69 sites ($13) – some right beside the railway tracks and some in the woods. For less urban camping, try *Sander Lake Campground* (☎ 250-344-6517), 12km southwest of Golden off Hwy 95. There is a main building with flush toilets and showers. The 25 tent sites, which come with picnic tables and fire pits, cost $13.

The recently renamed and renovated *Kicking Horse Hostel* (☎ 250-344-5071, 518 Station Ave), formerly Station Ave Backpackers, is a casual place with a communal kitchen, living room, barbecue and deck. The hostel's downfall is its location right on the railroad tracks (across from downtown), so unless you're a heavy sleeper, bring earplugs. The small, dorm-style rooms sleep no more than six and cost $20 per bed. For additional information, check out the Web site www.kickinghorsehostel.com.

As Golden is still a developing ski town, winter is a slow time for motels, whose rates almost double in summer. Rates listed here are for summer . Of the scores of motels on Hwy 1, those with good deals include the *Sportsman Motel* (☎ 250-344-2915, 1200 12th St N), where you can swim in the outdoor pool. Rooms cost $58/63 single/double. The nearby 85-room *Ponderosa Inn* (☎ 250-344-2205, 1206 Hwy 1) offers large air-conditioned rooms for $74/82. The *Golden*

Super 8 Motel (☎ *250-344-0888, 800-800-8000, 1047 Hwy 1*) serves free breakfast and rents nice rooms starting at $90.

In town right along the river, *Mary's Motel* (☎ *250-344-7111, 603 8th Ave N*) offers indoor and outdoor pools, two hot tubs, an exercise room and views of the ski hill. Rooms are reasonably priced at $65/75.

Golden contains a good selection of mountain lodges – from rustic to lavish – that are worth checking out. The *Beaverfoot Lodge*, 42km east of Golden, offers horseback riding, snowmobiling and good hiking, with rooms starting at $90, including meals and activities. The secluded *Purcell Lodge* (☎ *250-344-2639, fax 344-5520*) is a luxurious, all-inclusive lodge only accessible by helicopter. One-night rates start at a whopping $680. More information on lodges is available at the Visitor Info Centre.

Places to Eat

Check your email and grab a coffee right in the center of town at *Jenny's Java Express/Internet Cafe* (☎ *250-344-5057, 506 N 9th Ave*). You'll find good $5 sandwiches and baked goods at the *Dogtooth Café* (☎ *250-344-3660, 1007 11th Ave*). *The Mad Trapper Pub* (☎ *250-344-6661, 1203 S 9th St*) is a popular place to watch the hockey game on TV or play pool. The food is better than average pub fare, with burgers and sandwiches going for $8. Though pricier, the refreshing menu and ivy-covered patio at *Sisters & Beans* (☎ *250-344-2443, 1122 S 10th Ave*) make it the best food stop in town.

The Rockies

The Rocky Mountains, the world's fourth-highest mountain chain, sit on the eastern-most part of the Canadian Cordillera, the name for all the mountains in western Canada. Starting as stubby knobs in central Mexico, the Rockies quickly rise into the majestic peaks that run through New Mexico, Colorado, Wyoming and Montana, before crossing the US border into Canada at Glacier National Park (in the US) and Waterton Lakes National Park (in Canada). The Canadian Rockies then act as a natural boundary between Alberta and BC, where the mountains eventually form a geographically different range north of Liard River. All told, the Canadian Rockies stretch out for almost 1500km.

Alberta's Banff and Jasper National Parks and BC's Kootenay and Yoho National Parks, together with British Columbia's Mt Robson, Mt Assiniboine and Alberta's Hamber Provincial Parks, comprise the Canadian Rocky Mountain Parks UNESCO World Heritage Site, one of the largest protected areas in the world. Banff and Jasper lie in the province of Alberta, BC's eastern neighbor.

The entire area is a place of spectacular beauty, with some of the best scenery, climbing, hiking and skiing in the world. The national parks offer jagged, snow-capped glacier-covered mountains, peaceful valleys, rushing rivers, natural hot springs and alpine forests. The opaque emerald-green or milky-turquoise color of many Rocky Mountains lakes will have you doubting your eyes. The parks also features both modern conveniences and plenty of back-country trails. Wildlife abounds, particularly in Jasper National Park.

To preserve the region, Parks Canada controls the impact of visitors by designating specific park areas for campgrounds, picnic sites, service centers and townsites. Each park's *Backcountry Visitors' Guide*, available at all park gates and at visitor centers, offers advice on how to minimize your impact on the parks' environment.

The small townsites of Banff, Lake Louise and Jasper act as service centers where you can pick up supplies and information. In summer, accommodations are expensive and hard to find, though they're a little easier to come by in Jasper than in the other two towns. It's worth booking ahead or staying in one of the towns outside the park, such as Canmore in Alberta or Golden or Radium Hot Springs in BC, and making day trips.

Highlights

- Rejuvenating your soul in Radium, Miette or Banff Hot Springs

- Wandering through the massive and elegant Banff Springs Hotel

- Driving or cycling the spectacular, glacier-filled Icefields Parkway

- Watching for bears and moose and listening for the sounds of rutting elk in Jasper National Park

- Skiing and boarding to your heart's content at postcard-perfect Lake Louise

- Hiking on the many trails surrounding the turquoise-colored Lake O'Hara in Yoho National Park

Information

You have to buy a park pass upon entry into any national park. Day passes cost $5/4/2.50 for adults/seniors/children, and they're valid in any of the parks until 4 pm the following day. If you're planning on spending more than a week in the national parks, your best bet is to buy a Great Western Annual Pass (sometimes also called the Western Canada Annual Pass), which gives you unlimited admission to all 11 national parks in western Canada for a year. The pass costs $35/27/18 for adults/seniors/children. If you've already bought a day pass, you can upgrade to an annual pass at anytime. To find out more about fees or to purchase a pass ahead of time, call ☎ 800-748-7275.

For information about other mandatory park fees (including backcountry camping fees), see National Parks in the Facts about British Columbia chapter. For information on necessary safety precautions in the parks, see the Dangers & Annoyances section of the Facts for the Visitor chapter.

On entering Banff and Jasper National Parks, you'll be given *The Mountain Guide*, an excellent booklet with information and maps about all the parks, including Mt Revelstoke and Glacier National Parks (see the Kootenays chapter).

Parks Canada offers links to all of the country's national parks from its Web site, www.parkscanada.pch.gc.ca. For more information, call or write to the parks at:

Banff National Park
(☎ 403-762-1550), Box 900, Banff, AB T0L 0C0

Jasper National Park
(☎ 780-852-6176), Box 10, Jasper, AB T0E 1E0

Kootenay National Park
(☎ 250-347-9615), Box 220, Radium Hot Springs, BC V0A 1M0

Yoho National Park
(☎ 250-343-6783), Box 99, Field, BC V0A 1G0

Books It seems like there are endless books about the Rockies, but a few stand out from the crowd. The bible for the region is the encyclopedic *Handbook of the Canadian Rockies* by Ben Gadd. For fun, scholars try

to find errors in this incredible work about the geology, history, flora and fauna in the Rockies. They rarely succeed.

Good hiking guides include the discerning *Don't Waste Your Time in the Rockies* by Kathy and Craig Copeland, with good maps and trail descriptions, and the longtime, solid guide *Classic Hikes in the Canadian Rockies* by Graeme Poole. *Canadian Rockies Access Guide* by John Dodd and Gail Helgason will also help lead you off the beaten path.

History buffs should check out *The Canadian Rockies: Early Travels & Explorations* by Esther Fraser or *A Hunter of Peace* by Mary Schaffer, about her early travels in the Malign Valley. Finally, if you're caught looking for a novel to read while you're in the Rockies, *Icefields* by Thomas Wharton is a beautifully written book that offers excellent insight into Victorian-era exploration of the vast Columbia Icefields.

Yoho National Park

Established in 1886, waterfall-filled Yoho National Park is the smallest of the four national parks in the Rockies, with an area of merely 1310 sq km. Still, with its mountain peaks, river valleys, glacial lakes and beautiful meadows, it's a truly awe-inspiring place, as befits its name (Yoho means 'awe' in Cree). The park is adjacent to the Alberta border and Banff National Park to the east and Kootenay National Park to the south. Not as busy as Banff, Yoho often has campground vacancies when Banff is full, though its position on the west side of the Rockies means that Yoho experiences more wet or cloudy days than Banff. The rushing Kicking Horse River flows through the park.

FIELD

The very small town of Field, which lies in the middle of the park along the Kicking Horse River, is the last town in BC as you head east along the Trans-Canada Hwy from Golden (see the Kootenays chapter). Many of its buildings date from the early days of the railways, when it was the Canadian

THE ROCKIES

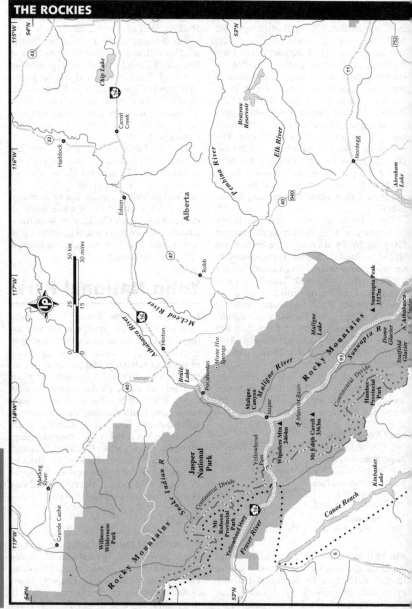

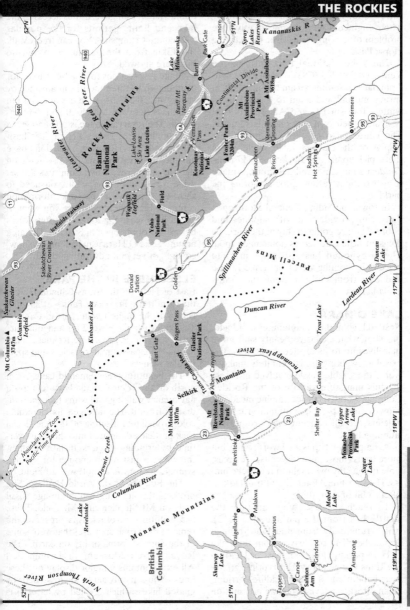

THE ROCKIES

Pacific Railway's headquarters for exploration and, later, for strategic planning when engineers were trying to solve the problem of moving trains over the Kicking Horse Pass.

The Yoho National Park Information Centre (☎ 250-343-6783) is open 8:30 am to 7 pm daily in summer, 9 am to 5 pm daily in spring and fall and 9 am to 4 pm daily in winter. Tourism BC and Alberta Tourism both staff their own desks here in summer. The center also contains an interesting display on the Burgess Shale. While you're there, pick up the free *Backcountry Visitors' Guide*; its map and trail descriptions make it an excellent resource for exploring the park.

In town, the Siding General Store, open daily, can provide you with supplies and booze if you're going to stay in the park. Its pleasant little café serves homemade food. The Greyhound bus also stops in Field twice daily, coming west from Lake Louise and east from Golden along the Trans-Canada Hwy.

LAKE O'HARA

Nestled high in the mountains east of Field, this somewhat exclusive beauty spot more than lives up to its exalted reputation. The excellent walking trails definitely make it worth the sizable hassle involved in reaching this miniature version of the Rockies. Compact wooded hillsides, alpine meadows, snow-covered passes, mountain vistas and glaciers are all concentrated around the stunning lake.

A simple day trip is well worthwhile, but more trails (most fairly rigorous) are accessible if you stay overnight in the backcountry. The very fine Alpine circuit trail (12km) offers a bit of everything.

To reach the lake, you can take the shuttle bus from the parking area ($12), which runs daily from mid-June through September. The bus leaves from the Lake O'Hara parking lot, 15km east of Field on the Trans-Canada Hwy. This is prime grizzly bear habitat and a major wildlife corridor. In an effort to alleviate human pressure on the trails, park officials have come up with a quota system that governs bus access to the lake and limits permits for the popular backcountry campsites. You can freely walk the 13km from the parking area, but no bikes are allowed.

Make reservations for the bus trip or for camping up to three months in advance by calling ☎ 250-343-6433 from 8 am to 4 pm weekdays between March 20 and September 30. The reservation fee is $10, and given the popularity of Lake O'Hara, it is basically mandatory. However, if you don't have advance reservations, six day-use seats on the bus and three to five campsites are set aside for 'standby' users, but you need to show up in person at the park information center in Field the day *before* you want to go. In high season, a long line often forms before the doors open at 8:30 am. The area around Lake O'Hara usually remains snow-covered or very muddy until mid-July.

ELSEWHERE IN THE PARK

East of Field on the Trans-Canada Hwy is the turnoff for **Takakkaw Falls** – at 254m, it is one of the highest waterfalls in Canada. Takakkaw is a Cree word for 'magnificent,' and it certainly is. From here, **Iceline**, a 20km hiking loop, passes many glaciers and spectacular scenery.

The beautiful green **Emerald Lake**, 10km north off the Trans-Canada Hwy, features a flat circular walking trail with other trails radiating from it. The lake gets its incredible color from light reflecting off the fine glacial rock particles, deposited into the lake overtime by grinding glaciers. In late summer, the water is just warm enough for a quick swim. Look for the turnoff west of Field.

The **Burgess Shale World Heritage Site** protects the amazing Cambrian-age fossil beds on Mt Stephen and Mt Field. These 515 million-year-old fossils preserve the remains of marine creatures that were some of the earliest forms of life on earth. (The Royal Tyrrell Museum in Drumheller, Alberta, contains a major display on these finds.) You can only get to the fossil beds by guided hikes, which are led by naturalists

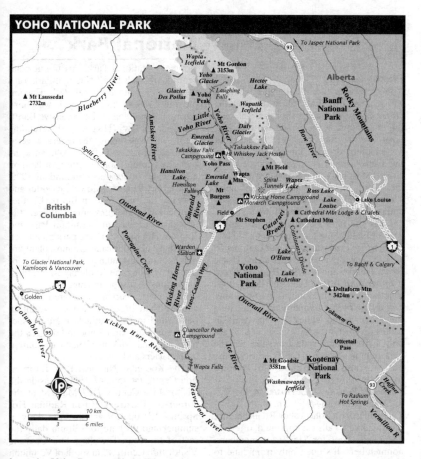

YOHO NATIONAL PARK

To Jasper National Park
93

Mt Laussedat
2732m

Blaeberry River

Split Creek

Amiskwi River

Wapta Icefield

Mt Gordon
3153m

Yoho Glacier

Glacier Des Poilus

Yoho Peak

Laughing Falls

Hector Lake

Alberta

Banff National Park

Rocky Mountains

Little Yoho River

Waputik Icefield

Emerald Glacier

Daly Glacier

Yoho River

Takakkaw Falls Campground

Takakkaw Falls

Mt Whiskey Jack Hostel

Bow River

Hamilton Lake

Yoho Pass

Hamilton Falls

Emerald Lake

Wapta Mtn

Mt Field

Spiral Tunnels

Wapta Lake

Emerald River

Mt Burgess

Kicking Horse Campground

Monarch Campground

Ross Lake

Lake Louise

Cathedral Mtn Lodge & Chalets

Lake Louise

British Columbia

Field

Mt Stephen

Cataract Brook

Cathedral Mtn

Otterhead River

1

Continental Divide

1

To Banff & Calgary

Porcupine Creek

Warden Station

Lake O'Hara

To Glacier National Park, Kamloops & Vancouver

1

Golden

Kicking Horse River

Trans-Canada Hwy

Lake McArthur

Deltaform Mtn
3424m

Columbia River

95

Kicking Horse River

Tokumm Creek

Chancellor Peak Campground

Ottertail River

Yoho National Park

Ottertail Pass

Ice River

Mt Goodsir
3581m

Kootenay National Park

Wapta Falls

Beaverfoot River

Washmawapta Icefield

93

To Radium Hot Springs

Haffner Creek

Vermillion R

0   5   10 km
0   3   6 miles

THE ROCKIES

from the Yoho-Burgess Shale Foundation. The 10-hour hike to Burgess Shale in Walcott's Quarry costs $48, and the shorter but more strenuous six-hour jaunt to Mt Stephen and the fossil beds is $26. You need to be in good shape for either, and you must call to reserve ahead of time. For more information, call ☎ 250-343-6006 or 800-343-3006 or check out the Web site at www.burgess-shale.bc.ca.

The famous **spiral tunnels** – the engineering feat that enable Canadian Pacific Railway trains to navigate the challenging Kicking Horse Pass – lie 8km east of Field along the Trans-Canada Hwy. When the railway was completed, it demanded that trains climb the steep 4.5% grade, the steepest railway pass in North America. Many accidents occurred when the trains lost control either hauling themselves up or down the tricky pass. In 1909, the spiral tunnels were carved into the mountain, bringing the grade to a more reasonable 2.2%. If you time it right, you can see trains twisting in on themselves as they wind through the spirals.

Near the south gate of the park, you can reach pretty **Wapta Falls** via a 2.4km trail. The easy walk takes about 45 minutes each direction.

Places to Stay

Yoho contains five campgrounds, all of which close in winter. Only the *Kicking Horse Campground* has showers, making it the most popular; the 86 sites cost $17. Interpretive programs run on summer nights. To get there, drive 3.2km east of Field on the Trans-Canada Hwy, then proceed 1km along the Yoho Valley Rd. Nearby, right at the turnoff to Yoho Valley Rd, the quieter *Monarch Campground* offers 46 sites ($13) and pit toilets. No fires are allowed.

Near the park's south entrance, 24km west of Field along the Trans-Canada Hwy, *Chancellor Peak Campground* features 58 sites ($13) with views of the Kicking Horse River. Nearby, the wooded *Hoodoo Creek Campground* offers 106 sites ($14), flush toilets and nighttime interpretive programs. *Takakkaw Falls Campground*, 13km along the gravel Yoho Valley Rd, has walk-in campsites for tents only. The sites ($13) are only a five-minute walk from the parking area, but the absence of cars is a rarity in the busy Rockies campgrounds – it's a nice treat.

The *HI Whiskey Jack Hostel* (☎ 403-762-4122, fax 403-762-3441), 15km off the Trans-Canada Hwy on Yoho Valley Rd just before the Takakkaw Falls Campground, offers 27 dorm-style beds for $15/19 for members/nonmembers. It's open only from June to September. The daily shuttle bus between Banff and Jasper takes a detour off the Icefields Parkway to pick up and drop off people at the hostel.

Field contains several B&Bs and a lodge; ask for details at the park information center in Field. Highly recommended and pleasantly rustic, the *Cathedral Mountain Lodge & Chalets* (☎ 250-343-6442), 4km east of Field, offers cabins at the base of Cathedral Mountain and alongside the river; rates start at $135/144 single/double. For more information, visit the Web site www.cathedralmountain.com.

Kootenay National Park

Kootenay National Park, in BC but adjacent to Alberta's Banff National Park, runs south from Yoho National Park. Encompassing 1406 sq km, the park was born during the building of the expensive Banff-Windermere Hwy (Hwy 93). When funding for the highway ran dry, the federal government stepped in and offered to finance the highway's completion in return for land on either side. It became parkland in 1920. Today, Hwy 93 travels down the center and is really the only road in the park, other than a few gravel deviants. Between the northern entrance at Vermilion Pass and Radium Hot Springs at the park's southern end, there are four campgrounds, plenty of points of interest, hiking trails and views of the valley along the Kootenay River. Most attractions lie just off the highway.

Kootenay experiences a more moderate climate than the other Rocky Mountain parks, and in the southern regions especially, summers can be hot and dry. It's the only national park in Canada to contain both glaciers and cactuses.

The Kootenay National Park Information Centre (☎ 250-347-9505) is inside the Visitor Info Centre, 7557 Main St at the corner of Redstreak Rd in Radium Hot Springs. It's open 9 am to 9 pm daily in summer and 9:30 am to 5:30 pm daily the rest of the year. The Vermilion Crossing Visitor Info Centre, 8km south of Vermilion Pass and 65km north of Radium Hot Springs, is open 10 am to 6:30 pm daily, May to mid-October. It's closed in winter. Here you can pick up the free *Backcountry Visitors' Guide*, an excellent resource with a map and trail descriptions.

Things to See & Do

The park boundary between Banff and Kootenay National Parks marks the **Continental Divide**, which runs through Yellowhead, Kicking Horse, Vermilion and Crow Nest Passes. At the Divide, rivers flow either west to the Pacific or east to the Atlantic. If you stood on the top of the Continental Divide and poured out a glass of water, the contents could, theoretically, flow west into the Pacific Ocean or east into the Atlantic.

For an adrenaline rush, head to **Marble Canyon**, where a short trail begins at the parking lot just off the highway and follows the rushing Tokumm Creek, crisscrossing it frequently on small wooden bridges. As you climb higher, the drop below gets narrower and deeper as the roaring water rages through the limestone and dolomite (not marble) canyon walls. Hang onto your camera, sunglasses and small children while looking down.

Some 2km farther south on the main road is the short, easy trail through forest to ochre pools known as the **Paint Pots**. For years, first the Kootenay people and then European settlers collected this orange- and red-colored earth. They'd shape it into patties, dry it, grind it, then mix it with fish or animal oil to make paint. Today, you can walk past the muddy red pools and read panels describing the mining history of this rusty earth.

Long gone are the days when Natives and trappers soaked in the natural hot pools, but built-up **Radium Hot Springs** (☎ 250-347-9485), 3km north of the town of Radium Hot Springs, is always worth a visit. The large pools can get very busy in summer, when they're open 9 am to 11 pm daily. It's best to go early in the morning or late at night after all the kids have gone to bed. The facilities include showers and lockers. Admission is $6. The springs are open year-round, with hours varying each season.

Places to Stay

It's a good idea to make reservations at any of Kootenay's front-country campgrounds (☎ 250-347-9615), one of which (Dolly Varden) is only open in winter. Another (**Crook's Meadow**) is only available to large groups. The **Marble Canyon Campground**, 88km from Radium Hot Springs and about 8km from the park's east gate, offers flush toilets but no showers. Its 61 sites cost $13. With similar facilities, **McLeod Meadows Campground** features good, wooded sites

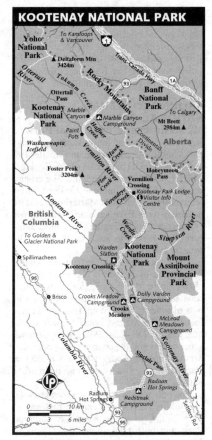

along the Kootenay River for $13. **Redstreak Campground**, near the park's west gate, contains 242 sites (154 tent sites and 88 partial and full hookup sites for RVs) and offers full services, including flush toilets, showers and nightly interpretive programs. Tent sites cost $17. It's free to camp in the wintertime at the seven-site **Dolly Varden Campground**, which has pit toilets. Ask for a list of the park's backcountry campsites at the Visitor Info Centre.

If you're looking for a roof over your head, the **Kootenay Park Lodge** (☎ 403-762-9196, fax 283-7482), at the Vermilion

Crossing, offers cozy rooms with fireplaces and puffy duvets. Rates range from $89 to $99. For more information, visit the Web site www.kootenayparklodge.com. Radium Hot Springs contains lots of motels, many in alpine style (see the Radium Hot Springs section of the Kootenays chapter).

AROUNDKOOTENAY NATIONAL PARK
Mt Assiniboine Provincial Park
Between Kootenay and Banff National Parks lies this lesser-known and smaller (39 sq km) provincial park, part of the Rockies' UNESCO World Heritage Site. The craggy summits of Mt Assiniboine (3618m), often referred to as Canada's Matterhorn, and its near neighbors have become a magnet for experienced rock climbers and mountaineers. The park also attracts lots of back-country hikers.

This park takes its name from the Assiniboine ('Ass-in-a-boyne') Natives, who are also referred to as 'Stoney' for the way they cook some foods – by putting hot stones in pots of water to warm it up. The park's main focus is Lake Magog, home to park headquarters (☎ 250-422-4200), a *campground*, some *cabins* and the commercially operated *Mt Assiniboine Lodge* (☎ 403-678-2883 in *Banff*). There's wilderness camping in other parts of the park.

The only way in is on foot. From Hwy 93, two hiking trails start near the highway at Vermilion Crossing in Kootenay National Park, and both take about three hours to Magog Lake. Another hiking trail begins at Sunshine Village ski resort in Banff National Park; allow a good eight hours to make this 27km trek to Magog Lake.

Banff National Park

Established in 1885 and named for two Canadian Pacific Railway (CPR) financiers who hailed from Banffshire in Scotland, Banff National Park became Canada's first national park, built around the thermal sulphur springs at what has become the Cave & Basin National Historic Site. Today,

it's by far the region's best known and most popular park, covering an area of 6641 sq km and containing 25 mountains of 3000m or more in height. The tall peaks here make for world-famous skiing and climbing.

BANFF TOWNSITE
• population 7000

Banff, 138km west of Calgary and 90km east of Field, is Canada's No 1 resort town in both winter and summer and as such is really the center of the Rockies. The town, built in a rustic-alpine style, is surrounded by unbeatable scenery. Despite attracting several million visitors a year, Banff is very small, consisting essentially of one main street, so it can get crowded. In July and August, the normal population swells by 25,000. Although this can cause problems, the many vacationers create a relaxed and festive atmosphere. Many of those smiling young workers in and around town were once visitors themselves, now enjoying the low pay and squalid living conditions that enable them to make their home in the Rockies.

History
Born because of the Canadian Pacific Railway company's dream to build a health spa town in the middle of the park, Banff was destined only to draw tourists from its beginnings in the 1880s. The growth happened quickly. Wealthy, well-traveled Victorian adventurers flowed into the park on the CPR trains, ready to relax in the rejuvenating hot springs or hire one of the many outfitters to take them up the mountains. In 1912, the decision to allow cars in Banff opened up the area to auto travelers. Soon, people other than rich Victorians wanted to check out the scene, and the town began pushing its boundaries. The south side of the river, with the Banff Springs Hotel, catered to the wealthy crowd. The north side of the river, however, resembled more of a prairie town, with small lots zoned in a grid system. This class-distinctive boundary is still evident today.

Banff continues to face conflicts over its growth. Many people complain that the

BANFF NATIONAL PARK

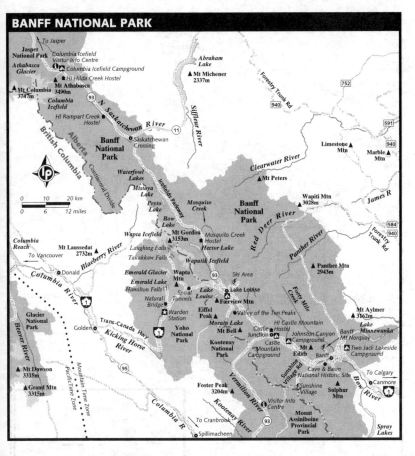

townsite is too crowded and argue that it should build more hotels and streets to accommodate all the camera-clicking tourists. But at what size does Banff start losing its charm? To control growth, the federal government has decreed that only those people who can demonstrate a valid need (such as owning a business) will be allowed to live in the town; those who can't will be taken to court and made to move. Also, there's a movement afoot to begin buying up the commercial part of town in order to tear it down to make room for government buildings. Needless to say, these proposals from

Ottawa are not popular with local business owners who thrive on tourism, nor do they help solve the problem of what to do with all of the tourists. But without protective measures from the government, Banff could become a sprawling city. With Banff's popularity continuing to grow, the debate will only intensify.

Orientation

Banff Ave, the main street, runs north-south through the whole length of town, then heads northeast to meet the Trans-Canada Hwy. The stretch of Banff Ave between

BANFF TOWNSITE

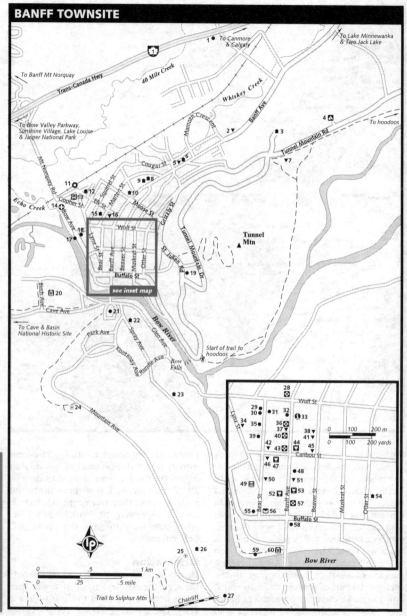

To Canmore & Calgary

To Lake Minnewanka & Two Jack Lake

To Banff Mt Norquay

Trans-Canada Hwy

40 Mile Creek

Whiskey Creek

To Bow Valley Parkway, Sunshine Village, Lake Louise & Jasper National Park

Mammoth Crescent

Banff Ave

To hoodoos

Tunnel Mountain Rd

Cougar St

Squirrel St

Marten St

Moose St

Grizzly St

Tunnel Mountain Dr

St Julien Rd

Echo Creek

Mt Norquay Rd

Gopher St

Beaver St

Elk St

Wolf St

Bear St

Lynx St

Banff Ave

Beaver St

Muskrat St

Otter St

Buffalo St

Tunnel Mtn

see inset map

Birch Ave

Cave Ave

Bow River

To Cave & Basin National Historic Site

Park Ave

Spray Ave

Glen Ave

Kootenay Ave

Rumble Ave

Bow Falls

Start of trail to hoodoos

Mountain Ave

Trail to Sulphur Mtn

Chairlift

THE ROCKIES

0   .5   1 km
0   .25   .5 mile

Inset map

Wolf St

Lynx St

Bear St

Banff Ave

Beaver St

Muskrat St

Otter St

Caribou St

Buffalo St

Bow River

0   100   200 m
0   100   200 yards

BANFF TOWNSITE KEY

PLACES TO STAY
3 HI Banff International Hostel
4 Tunnel Mountain Village
   Campground
6 Spruce Grove Motel
8 Irwin's Mountain Inn
9 Red Carpet Inn
10 Traveller's Inn
12 C Riva's Place
15 Holiday Lodge
22 YWCA;
   Y Mountain Lodge
23 Banff Springs Hotel
26 Rimrock Resort Hotel
54 Tan-Y-Bryn

PLACES TO EAT
2 Bumper's Beef House
5 The Pines
7 Cilantro Mountain Cafe
16 Safeway
34 Melissa's Restaurant
37 Grizzly House
38 Sushi House Banff
41 Bruno's Cafe & Grill
42 Coyote's Deli & Grill

45 Aardvark Pizza & Sub
46 Magpie & Stump
50 Keller Foods
51 Welch's Chocolate Shop

BARS & PUBS
44 Rose & Crown
47 Outabounds
52 Barbary Coast
53 Tommy's Neighbourhood
   Pub

OTHER
1 Banff Warden Office
11 Train Station &
   Greyhound Bus Station
13 Brewster Bus Station
14 Mineral Springs Hospital
17 Canoe Dock
18 Park n' Pedal
19 Banff Centre
20 Luxton Museum
21 Parks Administration
   Building
24 Middle Springs
25 Upper Hot Springs

27 Sulphur Mountain
   Gondola Terminal
28 Cascade Plaza
29 Backtrax/Snow Tips
30 Johnny O's Emporium
31 Mountain Magic
32 Banff Ave Mall
33 Visitor Info Centre
35 Canadian Mountain
   Holidays
36 Sundance Mall
39 Banff Adventures Unlimited
40 Park Ave Mall; Evelyn's
   Coffee Bar
43 Town Centre Mall;
   Wild Bill's
   Legendary Saloon
48 Trail Riders Store
49 Whyte Museum of the
   Canadian Rockies
55 Public Library
56 Main Post Office
57 Clock Tower Village Mall
58 Book & Art Den
59 Central Park
60 Banff Park Museum

Wolf and Buffalo Sts is lined with hotels, stores, restaurants and gift shops, many of which cater to the heavy Japanese tourist trade. Toward the south end of Banff Ave is Central Park, where you can stroll or rent canoes to paddle on the mellow Bow River. Still farther south across the Bow River Bridge is the Parks Administration Building, a good place for a view and a photo of the town. Behind the building, Cascade Gardens burst with flowers. A stream, ponds and a few benches dot the gardens.

Past the bridge, Mountain Ave leads south to Sulphur Mountain and the hot springs, while Spray Ave leads east to the Banff Springs Hotel, the townsite's most famous landmark. To the west, Cave Ave goes to the Cave & Basin National Historic Site, which contains the first hot springs found in the area.

Information
Tourist Offices Parks Canada (☎ 403-762-1550) and the Banff/Lake Louise Tourism Bureau (☎ 403-762-8421, fax 762-8163) both maintain counters inside the Visitor Info Centre, 224 Banff Ave near the corner of Wolf St, in the center of town (add the postal code T0L 0C0 to mail inquiries). Before doing any hiking, check in here; Parks Canada publishes a detailed map, and the staff will tell you about specific trail conditions and hazards. Anybody who's hiking overnight in the backcountry must sign in and buy a wilderness permit (for information on permits see National Parks in the Facts About BC chapter). Free naturalist programs and guided hikes take place regularly. The center is open 8 am to 8 pm daily from June to September and 9 am to 5 pm daily the rest of the year.

Money You can change money at the Foreign Currency Exchange (☎ 403-762-4698), 110 Banff Ave in the Clock Tower Village Mall. It's open 9 am to 11 pm daily in summer, 9 am to 9 pm daily in winter. The Custom House Currency Exchange (☎ 403-660-6630), 211 Banff Ave in the Park Ave Mall, is open 9 am to 10 pm daily.

THE ROCKIES

Post & Communications The main post office (☎ 403-762-2586), 204 Buffalo St at Bear St in the southern end of downtown, is open 9 am to 5:30 pm weekdays. To surf the Internet or check your email, go to Cyber Web (☎ 403-762-9226), 215 Banff Ave on the lower level of the Sundance Mall. This spot contains lots of terminals and plays good music. You'll pay $3 for 15 minutes or $8 per hour.

Bookstores & Libraries The excellent Book & Art Den (☎ 403-762-3919), 94 Banff Ave, features comfortable quarters and a good selection, with a wall full of books on the mountains, history and outdoor activities of the area.

The public library (☎ 403-762-2661), 101 Bear St across from the post office, has one computer terminal with limited Internet access.

Laundry Johnny O's Emporium (☎ 403-762-5111), 223 Bear St, makes doing the chore a little more agreeable, as it contains a TV lounge, bakery, Internet kiosk and pinball games. It's open 9 am to midnight daily. Cascade Coin Laundry (☎ 403-762-3444), on the lower level of Cascade Plaza (317 Banff Ave at Wolf St), has a public posting board where you can shop for used ski gear, find a ride to Jasper or, if you're lucky, locate a place to live. It's open 8 am to 11 pm daily.

Medical Services Mineral Springs Hospital (☎ 403-762-2222) is on Bow Ave near Wolf St.

Emergency For any problems in the backcountry, be it hiking accidents, avalanche scares, missing persons or grizzly sightings, call the Banff Warden Office emergency line (☎ 403-762-4506), which operates 24 hours year-round. In town, dial ☎ 911 for police, medical and fire emergencies.

Dangers & Annoyances The police are strict in Banff, and it is a very bad idea to drive after a night at the bar; not only are you putting yourself and others at risk, but after

Elk stroll the streets of Banff.

1 am, police often check cars for drunk drivers and drugs. The fines are heavy.

As for all those photogenic elk you may see wandering the streets, remember that they're wild animals and will charge you if they feel threatened. Every year people are attacked. It's advisable to stay 100m away, particularly during the autumn rutting and spring calving seasons.

Things to See & Do

Banff Park Museum The park museum (☎ 403-762-1558), 93 Banff Ave, near the Bow River Bridge at the southern end of town, sits in an old wooden building, built by the CPR in 1903 before Banff had electricity. Before trails first led curious wildlife watchers into the bush, the museum also housed a zoo and aviary, so Victorian visitors to Banff could catch a safe glimpse of the park's wildlife. The museum, declared a National Historic Site, contains a collection of animals, birds and plants found in Banff National Park, including two small stuffed grizzlies and a black bear, plus a tree carved with graffiti dating back to 1841. The museum is open 10 am to 6 pm daily in summer and 1 to 5 pm daily the rest of the year. Admission is $2.50/1.50 for adults/children. In summer, a free half-hour tour takes place at 11 am weekdays and at 3 pm weekends.

Whyte Museum of the Canadian Rockies The Whyte Museum complex (☎ 403-762-2291), at 111 Bear St between Buffalo and Caribou Sts, features an art gallery and a vast collection of photographs

Finding Work & a Place to Crash

Employment is usually easy to come by in and around Banff in the hotels, bars, restaurants and ski areas. In many ways, the employment scene is like one big international party. Most of the casual and seasonal workers are between 20 and 30 years old. Though you'll be inclined to socialize, don't forget that it is, after all, work.

Finding work without a permit has become more difficult for non-Canadians, and many establishments are asking for proper documentation. If you want to be absolutely sure of being able to earn some money, inquire about work visas at home before you start your trip.

Before you arrive in Banff, be sure to contact the Job Resource Centre (☎ 403-760-3311, banff@jobresourcecentre.com), which gives good advice and can arrange jobs for you before you even get there. When you arrive in town, stop by the center's office at 314 Marten St. You can also visit the Web site www.jobresourcecentre.com. For a listing of government jobs, check out the Web site www.banffjobs.com.

The hardest part about working in Banff is finding affordable (or any) accommodations. Some employers provide a place to live in exchange for paying not-so-great wages. At some of the hotels, accommodations may be included or offered at modest rates. In Lake Louise, all jobs come with accommodations (otherwise you'd be sleeping in the bushes).

If you're jobless and homeless upon arrival, peruse the classified advertisements in the local newspaper *Crag & Canyon* and look in store windows for 'help wanted' signs. The YWCA publishes the handy *Local Lowdown*, which offers good advice on finding work, meeting employment standards and dealing with the alcohol-consumption rigors of living in Banff.

telling the history of early explorers, artists and the Canadian Pacific Railway. The archives also contain manuscripts, oral history tapes and maps. On the property are four log cabins and two Banff heritage homes, one dating from 1907 and the other from 1931. For $5, you can go on an hour-long tour of Banff's pioneer homes or join a 90-minute guided historical walk. Call for times. The museum foundation presents films, lectures and concerts regularly. This must-see site is open 10 am to 5 pm daily. Admission is $4/2 for adults/children.

Luxton Museum This museum (☎ 403-762-2388), 1 Birch Ave, is in the fortlike wooden building to the right as you head south over the bridge. Worth your visit, it mainly explores the history of the Native Indians of the Northern Plains and the Rockies but also covers indigenous groups from all over Alberta. The museum features life-size displays, models and re-creations depicting various aspects of traditional cultures. Note the woven porcupine quills, the old photographs and the human scalp as well as the stuffed animals. You can buy some authentic and interesting knickknacks at the Indian Trading Post. The museum is open 9 am to 7 pm daily in summer and 1 to 5 pm daily the rest of the year. Admission is $6/4 for adults/children.

Natural History Museum This crammed, private museum (☎ 403-762-4652), at 110 Banff Ave on the 2nd floor of the Clock Tower Village Mall, features displays on the geological history of the area, from the formation of hoodoos to the telling tales of fossils. Another exhibit includes a model of the notorious Sasquatch, the elusive, abominable snowman of the Rockies. This character is said to be about 3m tall and to have been sighted upwards of 500 times. Of course, many of those who claim sightings also claim to have been abducted by aliens. The museum is open 1 to 5 pm daily; admission is free.

THE ROCKIES

Canadian Ski Museum West Under the guise of a shopping mall, this 'museum' in the Cascade Plaza chronicles Banff's ski history through bronze statues of skiers and panels describing the evolution of the sport and its growth in Banff. As you wander amid the boutique stores, you can learn about everyone from the charming Swiss guide Bruno Engler to modern national ski greats like Ken Read and Karen Percy.

Banff Springs Hotel Since it was completed in the 1920s, this 800-room baronial palace, on Spray Ave 2km south of downtown, has posed for thousands of postcards and millions of snapshots. The spectacular design includes towers, turrets and cornices, giving the impression that the hotel is full of hidden secrets. Within its thick granite walls are myriad public spaces, bars and restaurants. At any given time, 13 to 18 restaurants inside the hotel are busily serving guests. Even if you're not staying here, it's a fascinating place to wander around.

Banff Centre The Banff Centre (☎ 403-762-6300), on St Julien Rd east of downtown, contains one of Canada's best known art schools, complete with facilities for dance, theatre, music and the visual arts. Exhibits, concerts and various other events take place regularly. During the Festival of the Arts, which happens throughout the summer, students and internationally recognized artists present pieces in workshops and performances. Events that are open to the public take place most days from May through August, and some are free. The Visitor Info Centre can provide you with a complete schedule.

Sulphur Mountain Gondola In less than 10 minutes, the Sulphur Mountain Gondola (☎ 403-762-2523) zips you up to the summit. There you'll see spectacular views over the surrounding mountains, Bow River and Banff townsite from an altitude of 2285m. You can hike up the steep east side of the mountain in about two hours one-way. You will be aptly rewarded with great views and a free lift down; tickets are only needed

going up. The trail starts from the Upper Hot Springs parking lot.

The lower terminal is just over 3km south of Banff on Mountain Ave; it's adjacent to the Upper Hot Springs pool. You can hitch a ride from town fairly easily. You can also take the Brewster bus, though it costs $25 per person, including the gondola fare (the bus fare portion is $7 per person); if there's more than one of you, it's cheaper to take a cab, which costs about $9 for up to five people. The Brewster bus departs the depot every hour on the hour and the Banff Springs Hotel every hour on the quarter hour. The gondola runs 8 am to 8 pm daily in spring, 7:30 am to 9 pm daily from mid-June to September. Hours vary in winter months, so it's best to call first. Tickets cost $18/9 for adults/children.

Cave & Basin National Historic Site This is the birthplace of Banff. The discovery of hot sulfur springs in a cave here led to the creation of Banff National Park. The swimming pool and complex (☎ 403-762-1557), southwest of town at the end of Cave Ave, has been rebuilt in the original style of 1914, but you're not allowed to bathe at the site. Visitors can see (and smell) the cave and sulphurous waters, as well as view exhibits and a 30-minute film. It's open 9 am to 6 pm daily from mid-May to mid-September. The rest of the year, it's open 9:30 am to 5 pm on weekends and 11 am to 4 pm weekdays. Admission is $2.50/1.50 for adults/children.

You can stroll around the attractive grounds, where you'll see both natural and artificially made pools, for no charge. It's a good place for picnics, as there are tables, a fine view and a snack bar. Several pleasant short walks begin here: the 400m Discovery Trail, the 2.7km Marsh Loop and the 3.7km Sundance Trail.

Upper Hot Springs You'll find a soothing hot pool and steam room at the Upper Hot Springs spa (☎ 403-762-1515), 3km south of town near Sulphur Mountain. Besides soaking in the balmy pool (where water temperatures average 60°C), you can also indulge in a massage or aroma-therapy treatment.

Admission to the pool is $7/6 for adults/students. You can rent bathing suits ($1.50), towels ($1.25) and lockers (50¢). The busy hot springs are open 9 am to 11 pm daily in summer and 10 am to 10 pm daily the rest of the year.

Lake Minnewanka Lake Minnewanka, the largest reservoir in the national park, is 11km east of the Banff townsite. Forests and mountains surround this scenic recreational area, which features plenty of hiking, swimming, sailing, boating and fishing opportunities. Lake Minnewanka Boat Tours (☎ 403-762-3473) offers a 90-minute cruise on the lake to Devil's Gap for $26/11 for adults/children. To get to the lake from the townsite, take Banff Ave east over the Trans-Canada Hwy to Minnewanka Rd and turn right. In summer, Brewster (☎ 403-762-6767) runs a three-hour bus tour to the lake, which includes a 90-minute boat cruise, for $41/20.50 for adults/children.

Activities

Hiking You'll find many good short hikes and day walks around the Banff area. Parks Canada publishes an excellent brochure outlining hikes accessible from the townsite. For longer, more remote hiking, pick up the helpful brochure *Backcountry Visitors' Guide*, which contains a simple map showing trails throughout the whole park.

You can take a pleasant, quiet stroll by **Bow River**, just three blocks west of Banff Ave beside Bow Ave. The trail runs from the corner of Wolf St along the river under the Bow River Bridge and ends shortly after on Buffalo St. If you cross the bridge, you can continue southwest through the woods along a trail to nearby **Bow Falls**.

For a good short climb to break in your legs and to view the area, walk up stubby **Tunnel Mountain**, east of downtown. A trail leads up from St Julien Rd; you can drive here, but it's not a long walk from downtown to the start of the path. From the southern end of Buffalo St, a short interpretive trail between Bow River and Tunnel Mountain heads north and east toward the **Tunnel Mountain Hoodoos**. The term 'hoodoo' refers to the distinctive vertical pillar shapes carved into the rock face by rainfall and glacial erosion.

Just west of downtown, off Mt Norquay Rd, is the 2km **Fenland Trail** loop, which goes through marsh and forest and connects the town with First Vermilion Lake.

Some excellent hiking trails meander off the Bow Valley Parkway (Hwy 1A), northwest of Banff. The Parkway branches off from, but finally rejoins, the Trans-Canada Hwy en route to Lake Louise. Pick up the Parks Canada brochure for details on specific trails.

Canoeing You can go canoeing on **Lake Minnewanka** and nearby **Two Jack Lake**, northeast of Banff. The **Vermilion Lakes**, three shallow lakes connected by narrow waterways, attract lots of wildlife and make excellent spots for canoeing. To get to the lakes, head northwest out of town along Lynx St and follow signs toward Hwy 1. Just before the highway, turn left onto Vermilion Lakes Dr, and you'll soon come to small parking areas for the lakes.

If you're car- or canoe-less and want to stay close to town, your best bet is the **Bow River**. Bow River Canoe Rentals rents out canoes ($16/40 per hour/day) from Canoe Dock, on the corner of Bow Ave and Wolf St near the river. It's open 10:30 am to 6 pm daily.

Cycling You can cycle on the highways and on some of the trails in the park. Excursions of all varieties are possible, whether you're looking to ride for a few hours, a day or several days with overnight stops at campgrounds, hostels or lodges. Two good, short cycling routes close to Banff run along **Vermilion Lakes Dr** and **Tunnel Mountain Dr**. For a longer trip, try the popular and scenic 24km **Bow Valley Parkway**, which connects Banff and Lake Louise. Bactrax/Snow Tips (☎ 403-762-8177), 225 Bear St, runs excellent two- to four-hour mountain biking trips that cost $15 to $60. Parks Canada publishes a brochure *(Mountain Biking Banff Area)* that describes trails and regulations. (For information on renting bikes, see the Getting Around section, later.)

THE ROCKIES

Horseback Riding Horseback riding is a great way to explore the area. In Banff, the most popular routes lie south of Bow River. Holidays on Horseback (☎ 403-762-4551), which operates out of the Trail Riders Store at 132 Banff Ave, offers a variety of horse-riding trips on trails around town. An hour-long ride along Spray River costs $29; the three-hour Bow Valley Loop is $58; a full-day ride up Sulphur Mountain, including down-home barbecue, costs $115.

Rock Climbing Banff's rocky crags and limestone peaks present almost endless opportunities for good climbing. In fact, many of the world's best climbers live in nearby Canmore so that they can enjoy easy access to this mountain playground. This is not terrain for unguided novice climbers; even experienced climbers wanting to go it alone should first talk to locals, read books and get the weather lowdown before venturing out. Inexperienced climbers will find quite a few companies offering climbing courses and organized tours into the mountains. Mountain Magic (☎ 403-762-2591), 224 Bear St, holds indoor classes that'll teach you some basics for $45 per person.

In Canmore (southeast of Banff on the Trans-Canada Hwy), Yamnuska (☎ 403-678-4164), 1316 Railway Ave, offers a lengthy list of mountaineering adventures for all skill levels around Banff and throughout the Canadian Rockies. Also in Canmore, the Alpine Club of Canada (☎ 403-678-3200) can provide information and/or a guide.

Skiing & Snowboarding Three excellent mountain resorts with spectacular scenery are accessible from Banff. **Banff Mt Norquay** (☎ 403-762-4421, info@banffnorquay.com), just 10 minutes from downtown Banff on Mt Norquay Rd, is the area's oldest resort. **Sunshine Village** (☎ 403-762-6500, 800-661-1676, reservations@skibanff.com), 22km southwest of Banff, rises to 2743m and boasts 91 runs. Its high-speed quad chairlifts zip you up the mountain in no time. **Lake Louise** (☎ 403-522-3555, 800-258-7669, info@skilouise.com), near the Samson Mall, ranks among Canada's largest ski areas, boasting

28.5 sq km of terrain spread over four mountain faces.

A one-day lift ticket at each mountain is $54. A three-day pass, usable at all three resorts, is $158. Other multiday packages are also available. For more information, stop by the Ski Banff/Lake Louise office (☎ 403-762-4561), in the Banff Ave Mall, or call ☎ 800-661-1431.

Heli-Skiing Canadian Mountain Holidays (CMH; ☎ 403-762-7100, 800-661-0252), 217 Bear St, specializes in four- to 10-day heli-skiing trips to some of the best and most remote regions in the western mountain ranges. These superb trips cost around $6000. RK Heli-Ski (☎ 403-762-3771, 800-661-6060) offers one-day trips starting at $550, as well as longer packages. Both companies use ski areas in BC.

Organized Tours

Brewster Gray Line (☎ 403-762-6767) offers a three-hour Discover Banff tour for $40. The bus goes to the hoodoos, Tunnel Mountain Dr, Sulphur Mountain and Cave & Basin National Historic Site. For more information, visit the Web site www.brewster.ca.

Brewster also runs tours to Lake Louise, the Columbia Icefield and Jasper. The tour to Lake Louise goes via the Vermilion Lakes and Bow Valley Parkway, stopping at Johnston Canyon and at viewpoints for Castle Mountain. The trip takes four hours and costs $36/49 one-way/roundtrip. The tour to the Columbia Icefield takes approximately 9½ hours roundtrip and costs $89. The trip to Jasper lasts 9½ hours one-way. It stops at Lake Louise, then runs along the Icefields Parkway and stops at the Columbia Icefield, with time allowed for a ride on the Athabasca Glacier SnoCoach (not included in the price). The one-way fare is $89; a roundtrip costs $124, and you must arrange and pay for overnight accommodations in Jasper. All these rates are about 25% cheaper outside the peak season.

For a cheaper tour, contact Out of This World Adventure Tours (☎ 403-760-0999), whose two-hour Banff tour stops at all the popular spots for $29. The nine-hour Co-

The snowy summit of Kootenay Pass

A rushing river in Yoho National Park

Elk resting near Banff, Alberta

The craggy peaks of the Cassiar Mountains in northern BC

Dawson Creek from the sky

lumbia Icefield trip is $79. For more information, see www.outofthisworldadventures.com on the Web.

A couple of companies offer budget-oriented tours, with overnight stays at HI hostels along the way. These tours are generally geared for younger, backpacker types (usually age 18 to 30), but they are open to anyone. The Rocky Express (☎ 403-912-0407, 888-464-4842) runs a six-day, five-night trip starting in Banff and slowly traveling through Lake Louise, along the Icefields Parkway, up through Jasper and returning to your choice of Banff, Lake Louise or Calgary. The price, including tax and park fees, is $199 but does not cover accommodations at the hostels or food. Bigfoot Adventure Tours (☎ 604-278-8224, 888-244-6673) offers a two-day tour from Banff to Jasper and back again for $89, also not including accommodations and food. Its two-day, one-way trip from Banff to Vancouver, with an overnight stop in Squilax (near Shuswap Lake), costs $99. For more information on various tours, see the Getting Around chapter, earlier in the book.

Places to Stay

Accommodation is fairly costly and, in summer, often hard to find. The old adage of the early bird catching the worm really holds true, and booking ahead is strongly recommended. The rates listed here apply to the peak season (basically July and August); rates fall considerably at other times of the year. If you're not camping or staying at hostels, B&Bs and private tourist homes can be a reasonably priced alternative, and they're usually good sources of local information.

The Banff/Lake Louise Tourism Bureau tracks vacancies on a daily basis; check the listings at the Visitor Info Centre.

Some people stay in Canmore or Golden (in BC) just outside the park, where the rates are lower, and enter the park on a day-trip basis.

Camping

Banff National Park contains 13 campgrounds, most of which lie right around the townsite or along the Bow Valley Parkway. Most are only open between May or June and September. They are all busy in July and August, and availability is on a first-come, first-served basis, so check in by noon or you may be turned away. Campgrounds with showers always fill up first.

Tunnel Mountain Village Campground, on Tunnel Mountain Rd, actually includes three separate campgrounds: two primarily cater to RVs needing electrical hookups and one accommodates only tents, with a whopping 622 tenting sites. Close to town, Tunnel Mountain has flush toilets and even showers. Elk freely roam, and at night you may hear coyotes howling. Tenting sites cost $17 without a fire pit, or $21 with a pit and firewood. You can camp here year-round.

At Two Jack Lake there are two campgrounds. *Two Jack Lakeside Campground*, 12km northeast of Banff on Lake Minnewanka Rd, offers 80 sites ($17) and showers; it's open from mid-May to mid-September. About 1km north, *Two Jack Main Campground* features 381 sites ($13), flush toilets and running water but no showers.

Johnston Canyon Campground, about 26km along the Bow Valley Parkway west of Banff, is wooded and fairly secluded, though trains whistle by at night. Sites cost $17, which includes access to flush toilets and showers. The *Castle Mountain Campground*, 2km north of Castle Junction on the Bow Valley Parkway, is a smaller campground without showers. Sites are $13.

There are those who unfold sleeping bags in the woods surrounding Banff and think that camping anywhere in this vast wilderness should be allowed. But if the warden catches you doing so, you may have to go to court and pay fines up to $2000. If you're still not discouraged, remember: Don't *ever* light a fire and always hang your food. Hungry bears, wolves and cougars roam all spring and summer in search of food – your trail mix might tempt them.

Hostels
The *HI Banff International Hostel* (☎ 403-762-4122, fax 762-3441, banff@hostellingintl.ca), on Tunnel Mountain Rd

3km from downtown, contains 216 beds, the Alpenglow Cafe, laundry facilities, a game room and a common room with a fireplace. At this hub of activity, you can arrange everything from ski trips and tours to mountain bike rentals. Beds in dorm rooms go for $20/24 for members/nonmembers. Private rooms for two people are also available. You can reserve rooms online at www.hostellingintl.ca/alberta.

This hostel acts as the central reservations service for all the other HI hostels in the region (except the one at Lake Louise), including the seasonal hostels along the Icefields Parkway. In the summer, the hostel also operates a shuttle between hostels; it runs from Calgary and Banff to Lake Louise daily and from Lake Louise to Jasper and points between every other day. You can arrange to take bikes on the shuttle.

The rustic *HI Castle Mountain Hostel*, on the Bow Valley Parkway, holds up to 36 people and includes pit toilets and volleyball courts. Lodging will cost you $13/17 for members/nonmembers. For information, call the Banff hostel.

The centrally located *Y Mountain Lodge* (☎ 403-762-3560, fax 762-2602, 102 Spray Ave), in the YWCA building, makes a great alternative if the hostel is full. It accommodates both men and women in its 120 dorm beds and 45 private rooms. The facilities include a café and common cooking area. Dorm beds cost $21, and private rooms start at $55. Reservations are both accepted and recommended.

B&Bs & Tourist Homes The Banff/Lake Louise Tourism Bureau, in the Visitor Info Centre (see Information, above), keeps a complete list of B&Bs. To obtain information in advance, write to the bureau at PO Box 1298, Banff, Alberta T0L 0C0. Most B&Bs provide private rooms and full breakfasts, while 'tourist homes' – basically B&Bs without the breakfast – offer rooms in houses or small separate cabins.

The prices for B&Bs and tourist homes vary depending on size and facilities, your duration of stay and the season, but they generally range from $55 to $80 for a single

or double, though rates sometimes skyrocket in July and August. Call around before landing on a doorstep, because some places prefer to rent weekly and others prefer not to take young people. For a good deal, try *Tan-Y-Bryn* (☎ 403-762-3696, 118 Otter St), which has been housing tourists since 1926. Single rooms cost $40/35 in summer/winter; doubles are $50/45, including continental breakfast. All rooms share bathrooms.

You'll find several tourist homes on Marten St. *Holiday Lodge* (☎ 403-762-3648, 311 Marten St) is one of the nicest in town. Summer rooms cost $60 to $100. *C Riva's Place* (☎ 403-762-3431, 328 Elk St) rents out one regular room ($60) and one suite for up to three people ($80).

Motels & Hotels Banff has no cheap motels or hotels, especially in the busy summer months. About 20 places line Banff Ave north of Elk St; generally fairly large, they cater to tour groups and entice visitors with numerous perks like saunas and hot tubs. Many places are geared toward skiers and boarders, offering kitchens and rooms with two beds, which can be a good value for groups of four or more. Remember, the following are peak summer rates – expect lower prices at other times.

The cheapest motel in town, *Spruce Grove Motel* (☎ 403-762-2112, 545 Banff Ave)offers standard double-bed rooms for one or two people starting at $75. Guests can use the pool next door at the Voyager Inn. *Red Carpet Inn* (☎ 403-762-4184, 800-563-4609, 425 Banff Ave), close to town, charges $125 for one double bed and $150 for two double beds. Guests can use the pool next door at the High Country Inn. Nearby, *Irwin's Mountain Inn* (☎ 403-762-4566, 800-661-1721, 429 Banff Ave) offers covered parking and a hot tub, sauna and fitness center. Rooms start at $130.

The *Traveller's Inn* (☎ 403-762-4401, 800-661-0227, 401 Banff Ave) features friendly staff and a good location close to the center. The rooms come with large balconies; other amenities include an outdoor hot tub and heated underground parking. Rates start at

$180. *Rimrock Resort Hotel* (☎ 403-762-3356, 800-661-1587) is 4km outside of town on Sulphur Mountain Rd next to the Upper Hot Springs. This large resort offers a free shuttle to town, excellent mountain views and large, luxurious rooms starting at $240.

If, somewhere along the way, you win the lottery or simply want to super-splurge, the historic *Banff Springs Hotel* (☎ 403-762-2211, 800-441-1414), on Spray Ave 2km south of downtown, offers packages that include everything from meals to golf starting at – are you ready? – $930 a night.

Places to Eat

Like any resort town, Banff has plenty of restaurants. However, there are those that cater only to tourists who aren't likely to return, and there are those sought out even by discriminating locals. We've listed the latter below.

Budget You can pick up some prepared deli foods and other picnic fixings at the biggest supermarket, *Safeway* (☎ 403-723-3929, 318 Marten St), just off Banff Ave. *Keller Foods* (☎ 403-762-3663), on Bear St, also contains a deli and bakery and offers a good grocery selection.

For reasonably priced meals try *Café Alpenglow* (403-762-4122), in the HI Banff International Hostel, which even attracts longtime residents with its large portions and 'awesome' breakfasts starting at $6. Sandwiches go for a mere $4, and full dinners start at $7.

The best local coffee place, *Evelyn's Coffee Bar* (☎ 403-762-0352, 201 Banff Ave), in the Town Centre Mall, serves good sandwiches and excellent baked goods made on the premises. On the upper level of the Sundance Mall on Banff Ave, the *Fossil Face Café* (☎ 403-760-8219) offers healthy and organic soups, salads, sandwiches, hot dishes and desserts. It's a rarity in Banff: a quiet place to sit and write a postcard. Lunch costs $7.

Shiki Japanese Restaurant (☎ 403-762-0527, 110 Banff Ave), in the Clock Tower Village Mall, serves large and warming ramen soups for $7. *Aardvark Pizza & Sub*

(☎ 403-762-5500, 304A Caribou St) offers the best pizza and subs in town. You can get a medium pizza oozing with cheese for $12. This is the place to go when the bars close and you've got the munchies; it's open until 4 am daily.

Chocoholics can gorge themselves at *Welch's Chocolate Shop* (☎ 403-762-3737, 126 Banff Ave), a local institution where you can get giant slabs of chocolate and just about any kind of candy. Pick up a 'bear claw' filled with chocolate and almonds at *The Fudgery* (☎ 403-762-3003, 215 Banff Ave), where you can peer in the window and salivate while you watch gooey fudge being made. Chocolate's great for energy on the trails, and besides, you're burning off calories, right?

Mid-Range A major local favorite (especially at breakfast) is *Melissa's Restaurant* (☎ 403-762-5511, 217 Lynx St), near the corner of Caribou St. The 1928 log building looks like a wooden cabin inside and an English cottage outside. The menu includes pizza, burgers, steaks and seafood, with main dishes priced $9 to $20. Melissa's includes a bar and stays open 7 am to 10 pm daily. Don your fleece vest and blend in with the locals on Tuesday, when highball cocktails are only $1.50.

For lively atmosphere, head to the *Old Spaghetti Factory* (☎ 403-760-2779), in the Cascade Plaza, where you can carbo-load on pasta meals that include bread, salad, ice cream and coffee, starting at $8.25 – an excellent value. *Magpie & Stump* (☎ 403-762-4067, 230 Caribou St) serves up Tex-Mex lunches starting at $7 and dinners starting at $12. Its minimal windows give it a cozy, barlike atmosphere.

Bruno's Cafe & Grill (☎ 403-762-8115, 304 Caribou St) offers good vegetarian salads, burgers and wraps. Enter on Beaver St. Next door in the same building, a mini-train chugs around the sushi counter at *Sushi House Banff* (☎ 403-762-4353), and you take your pick from its cargo.

For inventive southwestern, try *Coyote's Deli & Grill* (☎ 403-762-3963, 206 Caribou St), where the open kitchen gives you a chance to see the chefs in action. For a front-row seat, hop up on a chair at the counter. The hip and lively setting is as refreshing as the menu. Main courses average about $15. Coyote's serves breakfast, lunch and dinner, when it's a good idea to book a table.

You can relax out on the patio at the **Cilantro Mountain Cafe** (☎ 403-760-3008), in the Buffalo Mountain Lodge on Tunnel Mountain Rd near the hostel. This spot specializes in fresh pastas prepared with seasonal ingredients and in gourmet pizzas that start at $13.

Top End Another local institution, **Grizzly House** (☎ 403-762-4055, 207 Banff Ave), achieves a romantic atmosphere with dark lighting and secluded booths. Adventurous eaters can sample buffalo and caribou meat. The menu centers on fondue, and you and your partner can dip away to your heart's content. For a full fondue dinner including salad, appetizer and dessert, it's $35 per person. Grizzly House stays open until midnight so you can linger over your meal.

Though **Bumper's Beef House** (☎ 403-762-2622, 603 Banff Ave) is north of downtown, it remains one of Banff's busier restaurants. Carnivores can chomp into Alberta beef steaks, prime rib and barbecued ribs, while vegetarians can enjoy the good salad bar. Main courses start at about $18.

The Pines (☎ 403-760-6690, 537 Banff Ave), also north of downtown in the Rundlestone Lodge, is probably the finest restaurant in town. Fresh Canadian ingredients such as salmon and venison get the full artistic treatment in main courses that average $17 to $25. The extensive wine list features Canadian vintners. This is another place where it's best to book a table.

Entertainment

Banff is the social and cultural center of the Rockies. You can find current entertainment listings in the 'Summit Up' section of the weekly *Banff Crag & Canyon* newspaper, or in the monthly *Wild Life*.

The **Rose & Crown** (☎ 403-762-2121, 202 Banff Ave), on the corner of Caribou St, is a British-style pub and restaurant with live

The Ultimate Mountain Man

Entering Banff, you'll see the town's signs adorned with the image of a rugged-looking man. It's Bill Peyto, a legendary character who explored much of the wilderness around Banff after his arrival from England in 1886. His exploits in the high peaks were matched by his hijinks around town: His cabin featured a set bear trap to thwart burglars, he brought a wild lynx into a bar and then sat back with a drink while chaos reigned, and so on. Generally regarded as the hardiest of the hardy breed that first settled high in the Rockies, he died in 1943 at age 75. In his honor, one of the region's most beautiful lakes is named for him. So, perhaps most appropriately, is a bar in Banff – Wild Bill's Legendary Saloon.

rock music, darts and pool. The friendly, local place **Barbary Coast** (☎ 403-762-7673, upstairs at 119 Banff Ave) features live rock and jazz. Across the street, join a local crowd at **Tommy's Neighbourhood Pub** (☎ 403-762-8888, 120 Banff Ave), which has a sunken patio – perfect for Banff Ave people-watching.

Wild Bill's Legendary Saloon (☎ 403-762-0333, upstairs at 201 Banff Ave) is dedicated to the memory of legendary Bill Peyto (see the boxed text 'The Ultimate Mountain Man'). On any night, it's crammed with folks hoping to re-create some of its namesake's wilder exploits. **Outabounds** (☎ 403-762-8434, downstairs at 137 Caribou St) is a hot dance bar. Another place to groove and sweat is **Aurora Nightclub** (☎ 403-760-3343, 110 Banff Ave), downstairs in the Clock Tower Village Mall.

Getting There & Away

Greyhound buses (☎ 403-762-1092) operate from the train station, 106 Railway Ave (it's the ochre building at the north end of Lynx St). Five buses a day travel to Calgary (1¾ hours, $20), Vancouver (14 hours, $99) and points in between. Greyhound also serves

Lake Louise ($11.50) and Canmore ($7.50); call for a schedule.

Brewster Transportation (☎ 403-762-6767) operates one express bus a day to Jasper (4½ hours, $51) from April to October. It also runs buses to Lake Louise ($11). The Brewster bus depot is at 100 Gopher Way.

It's really a crime that VIA Rail no longer serves Banff, as the line goes right through town. However, the privately owned *Rocky Mountaineer* stops at Banff on its way between Calgary and Vancouver. The basic one-way fare from Banff to Vancouver is $650 per person based on double occupancy. This price includes breakfast, lunch and an overnight stop at a hotel in Kamloops. The service runs between mid-April and mid-October, with three departures a week in June, July and August. For information, contact a travel agent or Rocky Mountaineer Rail Tours (☎ 800-665-7245).

Getting Around

To/From the Airport Sky Shuttle (☎ 403-762-1010, 888-220-7433) offers the most frequent service from Calgary International Airport to Banff. Shuttles depart every hour between 9 am and 10 pm. The fare is $34/62 one-way/roundtrip. Brewster Transportation (☎ 403-762-6767) runs four buses daily in winter, three in summer and two in fall and spring. The fare is $36/65. The Banff Airporter (☎ 403-762-3330, 888-449-2901) makes eight runs daily. Tickets cost $36/70.

Bus Banff Transportation operates the 'Happy Bus,' a fake trolley bus that travels on two routes through town. One route follows Spray and Banff Aves between the Banff Springs Hotel and the RV parking lot north of town; the other goes from the Luxton Museum along Banff Ave, Wolf St, Otter St and Tunnel Mountain Rd to the hostel and Tunnel Mountain Village Campgrounds. Both stop at Banff's Visitor Info Centre. Buses operate every 30 minutes from 7 am to midnight, mid-May to September, and from noon to midnight the rest of the year. The fare is $1.

Car All of the major car rental companies have opened branches in Banff. During summer, all the cars may be reserved in advance. If you're flying into Calgary, reserving a car from the airport (where the fleets are huge) may yield a better deal than waiting to pick up a car when you reach Banff. The agencies include:

Avis
  (☎ 403-762-3222, 800-879-2847),
  Cascade Plaza on Wolf St
Banff Rent-A-Car
  (☎ 403-762-3352), 204 Wolf St
Budget
  (☎ 403-762-4565, 800-268-8900),
  Caribou Ave at Bear St
Hertz
  (☎ 403-762-2027, 800-263-0600),
  Banff Springs Hotel on Spray Ave
National Car Rental
  (☎ 403-762-2688, 800-227-7368),
  Lynx St at Caribou Ave

Taxi Try Taxi Taxi & Tours (☎ 403-762-3111) or Mountain Taxi (☎ 403-762-3351).

Bicycle There's no shortage of bike rental places in Banff. Park n' Pedal (☎ 403-762-3191), 229 Wolf St, rents out many types of bikes. Most cost $6/24 per hour/day. Banff Adventures Unlimited (☎ 403-762-4554), 209 Bear St, rents out standard mountain bikes for $7/24 and full-suspension bikes for $12/50. Bactrax/Snow Tips (☎ 403-762-8177), 225 Bear St, also offers rentals, ranging from $6 to 10 per hour and $22 to $36 per day.

LAKE LOUISE

Lake Louise, known as the jewel of the Rockies, lies about 57km northwest of Banff, at the conjunction of Hwys 1 and 93. Before you get to the lake, you'll reach the uninspiring village of Lake Louise, which is essentially nothing more than the Samson Mall shopping center and a service station. Though small, the convenient strip of shops can provide you with everything from postal services to groceries and liquor, from restaurant meals to hiking boots (in case

THE ROCKIES

you forgot yours at home). The town is essentially a tourist attraction, few permanent residents actually live here except for those who staff the hotels.

The lake, named for Queen Victoria's daughter Louise (neither of whom ever came to the lake), is 5km uphill from the village. If you're walking, it takes about 45 minutes on the footpath. The much-visited and stunning lake sits in a small glacial valley, surrounded by tree-covered, snow-capped mountains. Come here early in the morning, when it's less crowded and your chances of seeing the classic reflection in the water increase. One of the Rockies' best known and original hotels, the Chateau Lake Louise, sits grandly at the northern end of the lake.

At 1731m above sea level, Lake Louise is high enough to escape the arctic air but still averages a chilly 4°C.

Information

Both Parks Canada and the Banff/Lake Louise Tourism Burea offer information at the Visitor Info Centre (☎ 403-522-3833, fax 522-1212), beside the Samson Mall in the village; the center also features an exhibition on the geological and natural history of the Rocky Mountains. It's open 8 am to 8 pm daily from June to September and 9 am to 5 pm daily at other times of the year.

Next door at Wilson Mountain Sports (☎ 403-522-3636), you can rent camping equipment, bikes and skis. The bookstore Woodruff & Blum (☎ 403-522-3842) carries general guides and maps to the Canadian Rockies.

Things to See & Do

The Lake Louise Chalet opened in 1890 to alleviate some of the pressure on the Banff Springs Hotel. Renamed **Chateau Lake Louise** in 1925, the hotel features 489 rooms on eight floors, six restaurants and three lounges. Though smaller than its Banff counterpart, it enjoys a lakeside setting just as grand. You can join the other millions of tourists who wander through the hotel every summer on their own, or take a tour.

The tours run in July and August and include lunch for $50. Guests staying at the hotel have priority, so call the concierge (☎ 403-522-3511) or stop in to see about availability.

Mt Whitehorn and the Lake Louise ski area lie east of the village, 4.5km along Lake Louise Dr. In summer, a **gondola** (☎ 403-522-3555) takes you to the top, where you can hike the trails and enjoy views of Lake Louise and Victoria Glacier. The gondola ride costs $11 roundtrip. If you're hungry when you get to the top, try the buffet restaurant and snack bar at the Lodge of the Ten Peaks.

Though lesser known than Lake Louise, **Moraine Lake**, may be more impressive, naturally speaking. Surrounded by peaks and a deep teal in color, it is nothing less than stunning. If you get your hands on an old $20 bill (first produced in 1969), take a look at the picture on the back , and you'll recognize the view of the lake. Look for an attractive lodge, gift shop and numerous trails. The lake sits in the gorgeous Valley of the Ten Peaks 15km (mostly uphill) from the village. To get there, take Lake Louise Dr toward the Chateau, turn left on Moraine Lake Rd and follow it to the end. If you're camping, you can also take the free shuttle from the campgrounds (see Getting There & Around, later).

Activities

Lake Louise boasts 75km of **hiking** trails, many of which lead to beautiful alpine meadows that fill up with colorful wildflowers in July and August. It is common to see pikas (plump, furry animals also called conies) and the larger, more timid marmots along these trails. You often hear ice rumbling on the slopes, too. Note that trails may be snowbound beyond the 'normal' winter season – often there are avalanche warnings well into July. The Parks Canada booth at the Visitor Info Centre gives out excellent trail information.

Many of the hiking trails become cross-country ski trails in winter. For downhill types, Lake Louise boasts the largest **skiing** area in Canada. The resort operates in conjunction with Banff Mt Norquay and Sunshine Village. See the Banff section earlier in this chapter for details on all three areas.

Wilson Mountain Sports rents out a full range of winter sports gear, including downhill ski packages starting at $30 and snowboarding packages for $40. It also offers telemark ($32) and cross-country ($20) ski packages.

Rock climbing on the Back of the Lake, a backwater crag, is popular, partly because it's easy to access. There are lots of different routes with interesting names like 'Wicked Gravity' and 'Chocolate Bunnies from Hell.' Other places to climb, of varying degrees of difficulty, include Fairview Mountain, Mt Bell and Eiffel Peak. But no one, not even very experienced climbers, should venture out to any of these spots without getting the full avalanche and trail conditions report from Parks Canada. For contact information, see the Information section at the beginning of this chapter.

Places to Stay

Parks Canada runs Lake Louise's two campgrounds (☎ 403-522-3980), both on the Trans-Canada Hwy. The *tenting campground*, off Moraine Lake Rd, contains 220 sites ($17); it's open from mid-May to October. The *RV campground*, at the south end of Fairview Rd off Lake Louise Dr, offers 189 sites ($21) year-round. Both the tenting and RV campgrounds have flush toilets and showers.

The excellent *HI Canadian Alpine Centre at Lake Louise* (☎ 403-522-2200, fax 403-522-2253, llouise@hostellingintl.ca), on Village Rd north of Samson Mall, is by far your best accommodations bet. A joint venture of Hostelling International and the Alpine Club of Canada, this giant lodge has all the charm of a mountain chalet without the big expenditure. The hostel arranges hiking trips and offers interpretive programs on summer evenings. The facilities include beds for 155 people, a kitchen, showers, Internet access, laundry, a large mountaineering library and Bill Peyto's Café. Dorm beds cost $22/26 for members/nonmembers; private rooms are $28/32.

Beware that you must reserve beds ahead of time from June through September and during winter holidays. The hostel is often booked up a year in advance.

Hotels mean serious dollars. *Paradise Lodge & Bungalows* (☎ 403-522-3595, 105 Lake Louise Dr, info@paradiselodge.com) is a good and cute choice, just a short walk from Lake Louise. Rates start at $130. *Lake Louise Inn* (☎ 403-522-3791, 800-661-9237, 210 Village Rd, llinn@telusplanet.net) offers numerous facilities, including a gym and hot tub. The 232 rooms start at $130.

The *Chateau Lake Louise* (☎ 403-522-3511, 800-441-1414), on the lake, lacks the majesty of scale of its sibling, the Banff Springs Hotel, though it doesn't lack charm. On the tip of the famous lake, it features a more scenic location and a quieter, less touristy atmosphere, especially at night after the tour buses have gone. The wide assortment of rooms range from $370 to $930 in the high summer season, though that's the 'rack rate' – there are often other deals available. During winter, prices can drop by 40%. Call the hotel to find out about various ski packages.

Places to Eat

You'll find several places to eat at all price levels in the *Chateau Lake Louise* (see Places to Stay, above). The Sunday brunch in the Poppy Room is a Bow Valley institution. Be sure to reserve and be prepared to pay about $20 per person for brunch.

Chow on some yummy eats, including a good vegetarian selection, at *Bill Peyto's Café* in the hostel (see Places to Stay). You can get a full breakfast for $6 or a burger (meat or veggie) for $6.50.

Lake Louise Station (☎ 403-522-2386), 1km from the Samson Mall on Sentinel Rd, offers you the chance to eat in a historic 1884 train station. Dinners on the broad-based menu average $14 per person. It's open daily for lunch and dinner.

Getting There & Around

Parks Canada runs the Vista, a shuttle bus that takes RVers and campers from the campgrounds up to Lake Moraine and

Lake Louise. This free service runs daily from mid-June to September. It's so popular that you might find it quicker to walk up.

The bus terminal (☎ 403-522-3870) is at Samson Mall. Both Greyhound and Brewster Transportation buses stop here en route to Banff. For bus service details, see Getting There & Away in the Banff section, earlier.

ICEFIELDS PARKWAY

Opened in 1940, this 230km road (Hwy 93) that links Lake Louise with Jasper remains one of the most spectacular stretches of asphalt in Canada. The highway follows a lake-lined valley between two chains of the Eastern Main Ranges, which make up the Continental Divide. From here, watershed rivers flow either eastward toward the Atlantic Ocean or westward toward the Pacific. The mountains here are the highest, craggiest and maybe the most scenic in all the Rockies. If you're on the bus, you'll see the best scenery if you sit on the left-hand side going from Lake Louise to Jasper. The highway is in good condition, but it's slow going nonetheless. In addition to the gawking tourists (you'll be one of them), animals (including goats, big horned sheep and elk) often linger beside the road or even on it.

You can drive the route in a couple of hours, but stopping at the many viewpoints, picnic spots and sights or hiking on one of the many trails can require a full day or

longer. You can take your time and camp along the way or stay at one of the many rustic hostels. Cycling the Icefields Parkway is so popular that often you'll see more bikes than cars on the road. Because of the terrain, it's easier to bike from Lake Louise to Jasper than vice versa.

Parks Canada publishes a useful brochure, *The Icefields Parkway*, which includes a map and describes the sights along the way.

As is so often the case, the best time to see **Peyto Lake**, one of the world's most beautiful glacial lakes, is early in the morning. Farther north, around **Waterfowl Lake**, moose are plentiful. Other points of interest include **Sunwapta Falls** and **Athabasca Falls**, 55km and 32km from Jasper. Both falls are worth a stop, though you may be appalled by the bonehead decision to put an ugly utility road bridge over the most scenic part of Athabasca Falls.

Athabasca Glacier

About halfway between Lake Louise and Jasper is the Athabasca Glacier, a fat tongue of the vast **Columbia Icefield**, itself a big frozen river whose meltwaters feed many rivers, creeks and lakes.

The Columbia Icefield Visitor Info Centre (☎ 780-852-6288), across the highway from the glacier, contains numerous well-designed displays that explain glaciers. One of the best is a time-lapse film showing a glacier in action as it alters the ground

---

Glaciers Are Cool, but Icefields Are Awesome

The Columbia Icefield contains about 30 glaciers and reaches the epic volume of 350m thick in places. This remnant of the last Ice Age covers 325 sq km – about the size of Vancouver – on the plateau between Mt Columbia (3747m) and Mt Athabasca (3491m) off the parkway connecting Lake Louise to Jasper. This mother of rivers straddling the Continental Divide is the largest icefield in the Rockies and feeds the North Saskatchewan, Columbia, Athabasca, Mackenzie and Fraser River systems with its meltwaters. They flow to three oceans: the Pacific, Atlantic and Arctic.

The mountainous sides of this vast bowl of ice rise to some of the highest heights in the Rocky Mountains, with nine peaks over 3000m. One of the icefield's largest glaciers, the Athabasca, runs almost down to the road, close enough for you to visit on foot or on specially designed bus-like vehicles. The water you see at the toe of the glacier fell as snow on the icefield about 175 years ago.

THE ROCKIES

beneath it. The Parks Canada desk offers trail details, ecology information and back-country trek planning. In addition to the obligatory gift shop, the center has several restaurants that share two unfortunate qualities: they're pricey and the food is not tasty. The complex is open 9 am to 6 pm daily from May to mid-October.

You can walk to the toe of the glacier from the visitor center, or you can save yourself from slogging across the moon-scape of gravel by driving the short distance.

For a further look, Athabasca Glacier Icewalks (☎ 780-852-5595, 800-565-7547), with an office in the visitor center, offers a three-hour trip up the glacier for $31 and a five-hour trip to various destinations in the snowfields for $32. Bring warm clothes. Crampons, boots and rain gear are provided when necessary.

You'll find it impossible to miss the hype and hard-sell for the 'Snocoach' ice tours offered by Brewster (☎ 403-762-6735, 877-423-7433). On busy days, up to 5000 people take a tour. The 90-minute trips drive out on the ice and reach the vast areas of the glacier that can't be seen from the road. The cost is $25/13 for adults/children. Bring your sunglasses, as the glare off the glacier can be intense.

Places to Stay

You will find a few Parks Canada camp-grounds along the way, all with pit toilets and no showers. *Columbia Icefield Camp-ground*, close to the Icefield Visitor Info Centre, has 33 sites ($10) with picnic tables and firewood. It's open from mid-May to the first sign of snow. Also nearby is *Wilcox Creek Campground*, with similar amenities and 46 sites ($10). It's open June through September. Remember, you're in glacier territory and it gets downright cold at night.

The Parkway is also lined with a good batch of rustic *HI hostels* that charge $11 to $13 for members and $16 to $18 for non-members. Most lie quite close to the highway in scenic locations. Though these small spots lack showers, there's usually a 'refreshing' stream nearby. Contact the HI Banff International Hostel (☎ 403-762-4122,

fax 403-762-3441, banff@hostellingintl.ca) for details on these hostels.

Choices include the excellent *HI Mosquito Creek Hostel*, on the Icefields Parkway about 27km north of Lake Louise, with cooking facilities, a fireplace and sauna. Open year-round, it contains 38 beds in four cabins. Ice and rock climbers should head to the *HI Rampart Creek Hostel*, 11km north of the Saskatchewan River Crossing, which also includes a sauna. Rampart Creek closes for part of the winter. The *HI Hilda Creek Hostel* (☎ 780-762-4122), 8.5km south of the Visitor Info Centre, offers 21 beds and a kitchen.

Also along the Icefields Parkway are *HI Beauty Creek Hostel*, 87km south of Jasper, and *HI Athabasca Falls Hostel*, 32km south of Jasper. Both can be contacted through the HI Jasper International Hostel (☎ 780-852-3215, fax 852-5560, jihostel@hostellingintl.ca).

The Columbia Icefield Visitor Info Centre (see the Athabasca Glacier section, above) contains a *hotel* (☎ 780-852-6550 in season, 403-762-6735 at other times), where rooms range from $100 to $175.

JASPER NATIONAL PARK

At 10,878 sq km, Jasper National Park is larger, wilder and less explored than Banff National Park, but like Banff, offers excellent hiking trails. Established later, in 1907, Jasper attracts fewer tourists than Banff, making it a quieter, more peaceful destination.

JASPER TOWNSITE
• population 4000

Jasper, 369km southwest of Edmonton and 376km east of Prince George, is Banff's northern counterpart and, in many ways, a much more pleasant place. The town is smaller, with fewer things to see and do, but the quieter, less tourist-oriented streets offer an excellent respite from the frenzy of Banff.

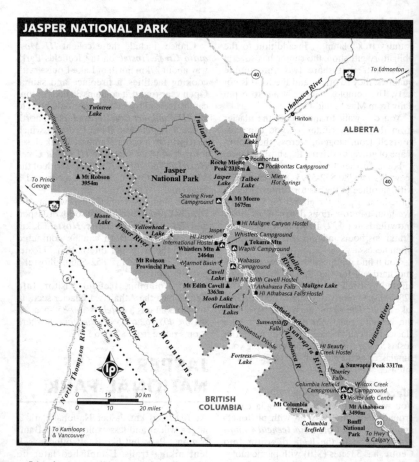

JASPER NATIONAL PARK

It's also a good connecting point. The Yellowhead Hwy (Hwy 16) and the VIA Rail line run east to Edmonton and west to Mt Robson and onto Prince George. The Icefields Parkway travels south to Lake Louise. Since Jasper is generally less expensive than Banff, it's a good place to stock up on supplies before heading into the backcountry.

Wildlife is incredibly abundant throughout Jasper National Park; you'll often see elk and black bears munching on the side of the road. In town, the most visible members of the animal population are the elk, which like to hang out downtown during the autumn rutting and spring calving seasons. Besides leaving millions of nut-size pellets of poop on almost every surface, they occasionally charge tourists and emit a haunting cry like that of a child in agony. It's best to keep your distance.

History

Archeological evidence shows that First Nations people lived here as early as 12,000 years ago. It is believed that the Natives came here seasonally, arriving with the snowmelt to gather food, then leaving again once everything iced over. Many groups used the area, including Shuswap, Sekani and Beaver from the west, Iroquois and Stoney from the east and Cree from throughout the area.

In the early 1800s, David Thompson and the North West Company established a fur-trading route into the Kootenays over Athabasca Pass. Fur traders soon intermarried with Iroquois and Cree, creating a Métis 'mixed-blood' group whose descendants shaped Jasper's history. Though the fur trade slowly died out, the steady flow of scientists and explorers did not. People were curious about the great glaciers, and soon adventurers and mountaineers were exploring the majestic peaks.

A proposal to build railway tracks over Yellowhead Pass prompted the government to protect the area as Jasper Forest Park in 1907. In 1930, the National Parks Act passed, fully protecting Jasper as a national park.

Orientation

The main street, Connaught Dr, has everything, including the bus terminal, train station, banks, restaurants and souvenir shops. Outside the toy-like train station, a 21m totem pole carved by a Haida artist from the Queen Charlotte Islands was erected in 1920. Nearby is an old CN steam engine. On Patricia St, parallel to Connaught Dr, traffic runs one-way north of Hazel Ave. And no, it's not just you – the street numbers throughout town, when posted at all, are difficult to follow.

Off the main street, the town consists of small wooden houses, many with flower gardens befitting this alpine setting.

Information

Right in the heart of town is the Parks Canada/Jasper Information Centre (☎ 780-852-6176), 500 Connaught Dr, easily one of Canada's most eye-pleasing tourist offices. Built in 1913 as the park office and superintendent's residence, the stone building is surrounded by flowers and plants. The large lawn is a popular meeting place that's often strewn with travelers and backpacks. The center is open 8 am to 7 pm daily in summer, 9 am to 5 pm daily in winter.

Jasper Tourism & Commerce (☎ 780-852-3858, fax 852-4932, jaspercc@incentre.net), 623 Patricia St, offers information on the town. It's open 9 am to 5 pm weekdays.

The main post office (☎ 780-852-3041), 502 Patricia St near the corner of Elm Ave, is open 9 am to 5 pm weekdays. The Jasper Municipal Library (☎ 780-852-3652), 500 Robson St, offers limited Internet access. More Than Mail (☎ 780-852-3151, 888-440-3151), in Connaught Square on Connaught Dr, is the place to go to surf the Web or check your email. Net access costs $1.10 for 10 minutes or $6 per hour. The store also offers postal and fax services, photocopying and baggage storage. It's open 9 am to 9 pm daily.

The community newspaper, *The Booster*, is published every Wednesday.

Clean yourself and your clothes at Coin-Op Laundry (☎ 780-852-3852), 607 Patricia St, where the showers cost $2 (you need quarters); it's open 8 am to 11 pm daily. Or try the Jasper Laundromat, between the post office and Athabasca Hotel. It's open until 10 pm daily.

For medical services, go to Seton General Hospital (☎ 780-852-3344), 518 Robson St.

Things to See & Do

A small historical society museum, the **Jasper-Yellowhead Museum & Archives** (☎ 780-852-3013), 400 Pyramid Lake Rd, contains some interesting displays on the town's development, making it a good half-hour stop. It's open 10 am to 9 pm daily in summer, 10 am to 5 pm daily in spring and fall and 10 am to 5 pm Thursday to Sunday in winter. Admission is $3.

The Den, a wildlife museum downstairs at the Whistlers Inn (see Places to Stay, later) features a rather tired collection of stuffed animals representing Jasper's wildlife. It's open 9 am to 10 pm daily; admission is $3.

The busy **Jasper Tramway** (☎ 780-852-3093) goes up Whistlers Mountain – named for the whistling marmots that live up top – in seven minutes and offers panoramic views 75km south to the Columbia Icefield

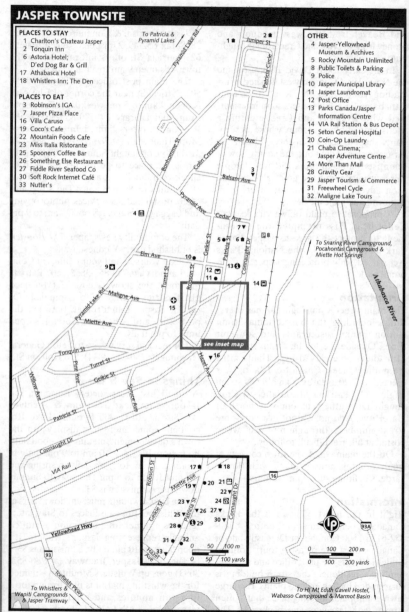

JASPER TOWNSITE

PLACES TO STAY
1 Charlton's Chateau Jasper
2 Tonquin Inn
6 Astoria Hotel;
   D'ed Dog Bar & Grill
17 Athabasca Hotel
18 Whistlers Inn; The Den

PLACES TO EAT
3 Robinson's IGA
7 Jasper Pizza Place
16 Villa Caruso
19 Coco's Cafe
22 Mountain Foods Cafe
23 Miss Italia Ristorante
25 Spooners Coffee Bar
26 Something Else Restaurant
27 Fiddle River Seafood Co
30 Soft Rock Internet Café
33 Nutter's

OTHER
4 Jasper-Yellowhead
  Museum & Archives
5 Rocky Mountain Unlimited
8 Public Toilets & Parking
9 Police
10 Jasper Municipal Library
11 Jasper Laundromat
12 Post Office
13 Parks Canada/Jasper
   Information Centre
14 VIA Rail Station & Bus Depot
15 Seton General Hospital
20 Coin-Op Laundry
21 Chaba Cinema;
   Jasper Adventure Centre
24 More Than Mail
28 Gravity Gear
29 Jasper Tourism & Commerce
31 Freewheel Cycle
32 Maligne Lake Tours

To Patricia &
Pyramid Lakes

Juniper St

Patricia Circle

To Patricia &
Pyramid Lakes

Aspen Ave

Colin Crescent

Balsam Ave

Bonhomme St

Pyramid Ave

Cedar Ave

Elm Ave

Geikie St

Patricia St

Connaught Dr

Turret St

Robson St

Maligne Ave

Pyramid Lake Rd

Miette Ave

Tonquin St

Turret St

Pine Ave

Geikie St

Spruce Ave

Willow Ave

Patricia St

Connaught Dr

VIA Rail

Yellowhead Hwy

Hazel Ave

To Snaring River Campground,
Pocahontas Campground &
Miette Hot Springs

Athabasca River

see inset map

16

93A

0   100   200 m
0   100   200 yards

Miette River

To Hi Mt Edith Cavell Hostel,
Wabasso Campground & Marmot Basin

To Whistlers &
Wapiti Campgrounds
& Jasper Tramway

Icefields Pkwy

93

Inset map:
Robson St
17
18
Miette Ave
19
20
21
22
Geikie St
23
Patricia St
26
27
24
25
28
29
30
31
32
33
Hazel Ave

0   50   100 m
0   50   100 yards

THE ROCKIES

and 100km west to Mt Robson in BC. Board the tramway gondolas at the lower terminal, about 7km south of town along Whistlers Mountain Rd off the Icefields Parkway. The upper terminal sits at the lofty height of 2277m. You'll find a restaurant and hiking trails up there. From the upper terminal, it's a 45-minute walk to the summit over the tree line, where it can be very cool. The tramway is open during daylight hours daily from April to October. The first tram runs at 8:30 am, the last one at 8:30 pm (daylight permitting). Tickets cost $17/8.50 for adults/children. Even if you tackle the two- to three-hour steep hike up, you still have to pay half-price to come down.

Lakes Annette & Edith, 3km northeast of town along Lodge Rd (off the Yellowhead Hwy), sit at about 1000m altitude and can be warm enough for a quick swim. In the wooded parks around the lakes, you'll find beaches, hiking and bike trails, picnic areas and boat rentals.

The small and relatively quiet **Patricia & Pyramid Lakes**, about 7km northwest of town along Pyramid Lake Rd, offer picnic sites, hiking and horse-riding trails, fishing and beaches; you can rent canoes, kayaks and Windsurfers. In winter, you can go cross-country skiing or ice skating. It's not uncommon to see deer, coyotes or bears nearby.

Organized Tours
A few companies in Jasper specialize in booking tickets for the various tours and activities. Jasper Travel Agency (☎ 780-852-4400), in the VIA Rail station, coordinates and sells tickets for tours, river trips, sightseeing and adventures. Three others that do the same are Maligne Lake Tours (☎ 780-852-3370), 627 Patricia St; Rocky Mountain Unlimited (☎ 780-852-4056), 406 Patricia St; and Jasper Adventure Centre (☎ 780-852-5595), 604 Connaught Dr in the Chaba Theatre.

Brewster Gray Line (☎ 780-852-3332) runs a three-hour 'Discover Jasper' trip to some of the local sights, including Jasper Tramway, Pyramid and Patricia Lakes and Maligne Canyon. The trip costs $42. The

Watching Wildlife
Nowhere else on earth can you observe the collection of critters found in the Canadian Rockies. Like most people, you're probably looking out for the big guys – black and grizzly bears, moose, bighorn sheep and elk, but keep your eyes and ears open and your senses in tune to the murmurings of nature. There's wildlife moving all around you, whether you can see it or not. Small animals such as pikas, martens, marmots and squirrels skitter by, munching on tiny insects, while 277 species of birds nest, hunt, mate, sing and squawk in the Canadian Rockies. Frogs, snakes and salamanders slither under rocks. Give yourself a couple of hours one day and just sit and wait to see what pops out and tickles your senses. But while you're at it, keep an eye out for those big bears, too.

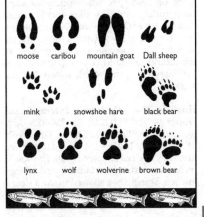

five-hour Maligne Lake trip costs $59. The company also offers 7½-hour Icefields Parkway tours to Lake Louise for $82 oneway. Prices are lower in spring and autumn.

Places to Stay
In general, prices here are lower than in Banff, though motels and hotels get pricey in the height of summer.

Camping Jasper National Park contains 10 campgrounds operated by Parks Canada

THE ROCKIES

(☎ 780-852-6176). They are generally open from May to September, although a few stay open until the first snowfall (which may not be that much later). Closest to town is **Whistlers Campground**, about 3km south of town on Whistlers Rd (off the Icefields Parkway). The good set-up here – which includes electricity, coin-operated showers and flush toilets – means that it can get crowded, despite having 781 sites. In summer, films and talks are presented nightly. Sites cost $15 to $24.

About 2km farther south on the Icefields Parkway, **Wapiti Campground**, beside the Athabasca River, is the only campground in the park that stays open during winter. Facilities include flush toilets but no showers. Sites cost $16 to $19 ($13 to $15 in winter). Two other campgrounds reasonably close to town are **Wabasso Campground**, 17km south on Hwy 93A, which offers showers, flush toilets and 228 sites for $13; and **Snaring River Campground**, 17km north on the Yellowhead Hwy, with pit toilets and 66 sites for $10. **Pocahontas Campground**, at the turnoff to the Miette Hot Springs, has 140 sites ($13) and flush toilets but no showers.

Hostels The **HI Jasper International Hostel** (☎ 780-852-3215, fax 780-852-5560, jihostel@hostellingintl.ca) lies 6.3km south of Jasper on Whistlers Rd toward the Jasper Tramway; the last 2km are uphill. The hostel includes a barbecue, a laundry and a large kitchen. You are not allowed to use a sleeping bag (they don't want bugs brought into the hostel), but they'll supply you with free linens. The hostel runs a shuttle bus into town. Rates are $16/21 for members/nonmembers.

Also south of Jasper, the **HI Mt Edith Cavell Hostel**, on Mt Edith Cavell Rd 13km from the junction with Hwy 93A, sits below the Angel Glacier. The hostel offers excellent access to hiking trails, including the gorgeous Tonquin Valley. The rustic accommodations include outhouses and creek water only, with no showers. It's open from May to October and charges $11/16. Also rustic and close to good hiking, the **HI**

Maligne Canyon Hostel, 11.5km east of town on Maligne Canyon Rd, contains 24 beds in two cabins and charges $11/16.

Tourist Homes The Visitor Info Centre and Jasper Tourism & Congress can provide you with names of more than 100 tourist homes that are usually centrally located and open all year. There are only a few B&Bs in Jasper, mostly because anyone serving food needs to jump through several hoops of approval from the local health authority before getting the go-ahead. Some places may offer you a muffin with a cup of tea.

Jasper Home Accommodations Association will send you its list of rooms so you can make reservations. Write to them at PO Box 758, Jasper, Alberta T0E 1E0. Or you could wander down the streets close to the center of town, where almost every house has a sign offering rooms. In summer, many of these places fill up early, so it's a good idea to book ahead. Rates average $60/70 single/double and drop considerably in the off-season.

Motels & Hotels The prices listed are peak summer rates, but at other times you can get significant discounts. In town, the **Athabasca Hotel** (☎ 780-852-3386, 877-542-8422, info@athabascahotel.com, 510 Patricia St) contains small but recently renovated rooms that start at $89 with a shared bath, $135 with private bath. At the **Astoria Hotel** (☎ 780-852-3351, 800-661-7343, astoria@incentre.net, 404 Connaught Dr), doubles start at $150. **Whistlers Inn** (☎ 780-852-3361, 800-282-9919), on the corner of Miette Ave and Connaught Dr, features rooms overlooking the park for $171 and up. All three hotels have a pub and restaurant.

On the north side of town, the **Tonquin Inn** (☎ 780-852-4987), on Juniper St at Connaught Dr, includes an indoor pool, two outdoor hot tubs, a sauna and restaurant; rooms start at $174. **Charlton's Chateau Jasper** (☎ 780-852-5644, 800-661-9323, 96 Geikie St), on the corner of Juniper St, is a quiet and refined motel with large rooms and a pool, hot tub, pub and gourmet restaurant. Rooms go for a steep $300.

The deluxe *Jasper Park Lodge* (☎ 780-852-3301, 800-441-1414), northeast of town, is Jasper's answer to the Banff Springs Hotel. Here the charm permeates a massive log cabin–style main building, and the resort features every possible amenity, including a world-class golf course. In winter, you can skate on the lake. If you don't want to stay in the main lodge, you can also rent one of the small cabins beside Lac Beauvert. Rates start at a whopping $459.

Numerous motels line Connaught Dr on the approaches to Jasper. Outside of town, several places offer bungalows (usually wooden cabins) that are only open in summer. Ask at the Visitor Info Centre for a list.

Places to Eat

For a wide selection of bulk and natural foods, go to *Nutter's* (622 Patricia St). The best supermarket is *Robinson's IGA* (218 Connaught Dr).

The comfortable *Coco's Café* (☎ 780-852-4550, 608 Patricia St) makes a good stop for $4 breakfasts, such as muesli or muffins. Up the street in the Patricia Centre, *Spooners Coffee Bar* (☎ 780-852-4046) serves good coffee and gigantic homemade cinnamon buns for $2. Need to surf the Net while you chow down on breakfast? Try the *Soft Rock Internet Café* (☎ 780-852-5850), on the lower level of the Connaught Square. Excellent omelets start at $6. Internet access at the eight terminals costs $2 for 10 minutes or $8.50 per hour.

Herbivores will be happy at *Mountain Foods Cafe* (☎ 780-852-4050, 606 Connaught Dr), where you can get vegetarian wraps and burgers for $6.50 or fresh bread from the bakery. Follow the scent of garlic to *Miss Italia Ristorante* (☎ 780-852-4002, 610 Patricia St). This 2nd-floor spot serves breakfast, lunch and dinner, when the great pasta specials start at $10. The friendly *Something Else Restaurant* (☎ 780-852-3850, 621 Patricia St) offers spicy Greek dishes ($12 and up), plus pastas and pizzas.

Locals love *Jasper Pizza Place* (☎ 780-852-3225, 402 Connaught Dr), where the excellent pizza feeds two people for $10 to $13. You can eat on the rooftop patio. In the

Astoria Hotel (see Places to Stay), the *De'd Dog Bar & Grill* serves up great burgers ($9) and good beer in a lively atmosphere.

For the best seafood in town, head to *Fiddle River Seafood Co* (☎ 780-852-3032, 620 Connaught Dr), which enjoys a fine view from its 2nd-floor location. The salmon and trout average about $16 and couldn't be any fresher. It's open for dinner only, from 5 to 10 pm. Another good spot for seafood and steaks is *Villa Caruso* (☎ 780-852-3920, 640 Connaught Dr), on the 2nd floor. At lunch, the fish and chips cost $9; beef sandwiches are $10. At dinner, try the garlic- and butter-soaked prawn dinner ($22) or the pork tenderloin ($18).

Entertainment

Except for the cries of rutting elk, Jasper gets quiet pretty early. Save your nighttime energy for an early morning hike.

The *Atha-B Pub* (☎ 403-852-3386), in the Athabasca Hotel, regularly features live rock bands and dancing. The *De'd Dog Bar & Grill* (see Places to Eat) is a good place to drink draught and play pool and darts with the colorful locals.

The *Chaba Cinema* (☎ 780-852-4749, 604 Connaught Dr), opposite the VIA Rail station, shows first-run movies.

Getting There & Away

Bus The bus depot (☎ 780-852-3332) is in the VIA Rail station on Connaught Dr. Brewster and Greyhound share a ticket booth. Greyhound operates four daily buses to Edmonton (five hours, $49), plus a twice-daily service to Prince George (five hours, $49), Kamloops (six hours, $57) and Vancouver (13 hours, $100).

Brewster's daily express bus to Lake Louise ($44), Banff ($51) and the Calgary Airport ($71) leaves at 1:30 pm.

Train VIA Rail (☎ 780-852-4102 or 800-561-8630) stops at Jasper three times a week en route between Vancouver and Toronto. In addition, VIA's *Skeena* runs three times a week to Prince George, where the train continues to Prince Rupert after an overnight stay. Fares vary wildly depending on when

THE ROCKIES

you go and when you book, but the one-way economy fare on the *Skeena* is around $150 in summer, not including meals or accommodations in Prince George. It's about $170 for the overnight trip to Vancouver.

After the gutting of rail funding by the Canadian government, these trains mainly cater to sightseeing tourists who are willing to pay the price for a scenic journey. Call or check at the VIA Rail station for exact schedule and fare details.

The private *Rocky Mountaineer* tour train runs between Jasper and Vancouver via Kamloops. It operates from May to mid-October, and the number of trips varies each month. Call ☎ 604-606-7245 or 800-665-7245 for details.

Getting Around

To/From the Airport Brewster (☎ 780-852-3332) runs a daily shuttle to the Calgary International Airport, leaving from the Jasper Park Lodge at 12:30 pm and from the bus depot at 1:30 pm. It arrives at the airport at 6:30 pm. The one-way fare is $71. The Jasper Express (☎ 403-762-9102, 800-661-4946) runs a daily shuttle to the Edmonton International Airport for $55. It stops at Jasper hotels between 6:30 and 7 am, arriving at the airport at 11 am. Call for specific pick-up times.

Car The car rental agencies in Jasper include the following:

Avis
(☎ 780-852-3970), Petro Canada station at 300 Connaught Dr
Budget
(☎ 780-852-3222), Shell station at 638 Connaught Dr
Hertz
(☎ 780-852-3888), 702 Connaught Dr
National
(☎ 780-852-1117), VIA Rail station

Taxi Jasper doesn't have a public transportation system. For a taxi, call Heritage Taxi (☎ 780-852-5558) or Jasper Taxi (☎ 780-852-3600).

Bicycle Freewheel Cycle (☎ 780-852-3898), 618 Patricia St, rents out front-suspension mountain bikes for $6/26 per hour/day. Full-suspension bikes are $9/36.

ELSEWHERE IN THE PARK

About 12km east of Jasper on the way to Maligne (pronounced 'ma-**leen**') Lake on Maligne Lake Rd, you'll pass **Maligne Canyon**, a limestone gorge about 50m deep, with waterfalls and interesting rock formations. You can walk from the teahouse along the floor of the canyon. Continue 21km farther up the road to **Medicine Lake**, whose level rises and falls due to the underground drainage system; sometimes the lake disappears completely.

The largest glacier-fed lake in the Rockies and the second-largest in the world, **Maligne Lake** lies 48km southeast of Jasper at the end of Maligne Lake Rd. The lake is promoted as one of the most scenic of mountain lakes, but this is perhaps unwarranted. It's a very commercial, busy destination, and the classic view with the island is only accessible by boat. You can, however, go horseback riding nearby for a good view or rent out a canoe for $10 per hour from Maligne Tours (☎ 780-852-3370). Alternatively, take the 20km, 90-minute boat tour to Spirit Island with Maligne Tours for $32. From November to May, try some of the excellent cross-country skiing in the highlands around the lake; the rest of the year, wander down some of the fine hiking trails. If you don't have a car to get to the lake, Maligne Tours runs a shuttle service from Jasper for $12 each way.

To rest your weary bones, stop at **Miette Hot Springs** (☎ 780-866-3939), 61km northeast of Jasper off the Yellowhead Hwy (Hwy 16) near the park boundary. Miette has the warmest mineral waters in the Canadian Rockies. Left alone, the springs produce a scalding 53.9°C, but the water is cooled to a more reasonable 39°C. The modern spa includes three pools (hot, warm and freezing) and incredible surrounding scenery. It's open 8:30 am to 10:30 pm daily in summer and costs $5.50; you can rent

Victorian-era bathing suits for $1.50 and towels for $1.

Activities

Hiking Fewer hikers tramp through Jasper than Banff, but more wildlife scampers through the woods, which means that you stand a good chance of spotting some. In addition to the hikes around the lakes (mentioned in Things to See & Do, above), many other paths meander through the terrain. The leaflet *Day Hikers' Guide to Jasper National Park* offers good descriptions of hikes that last anywhere from a couple of hours to all day. If the weather has been wet, you may want to avoid the lower horse trails, which can become mud baths. Topographic maps are available for all routes; buy them at the Visitor Info Centre.

If you're hiking overnight, definitely pick up a copy of the *Backcountry Visitors' Guide*, available free from Parks Canada at Visitor Info Centres. It offers overnight trail descriptions along with a map. If you're camping in the backcountry, you have to obtain a backcountry permit from Parks Canada (see National Parks in the Facts about British Columbia chapter). For detailed information and reservations for routes with capacity restrictions, call ☎ 780-852-6177.

Cycling As in Banff National Park, you can cycle on the highways and on most of the trails in the park. For more information, pick up a copy of *Trail Bicycling Guide, Jasper National Park* at the Visitor Info Centre. At Freewheel Cycle (☎ 780-852-3898), 618 Patricia St, you can ask the staff about good rides and pick up the free *Mountain Biking Trail Guide*. You also might want to ask which trails the horses are using, so you can be sure you don't go there. Freewheel also rents out bikes (see Getting Around, earlier, for rates).

Rock Climbing With all the rock around, it's no wonder climbers are in harness heaven in Jasper. Experienced climbers like to head to the popular Mt Morro, Messner Ridge, Mt Athabasca, Mt Andromeda and Mt Edith Cavell. In winter, you can ice-climb on the frozen waterfalls. Stop by Gravity Gear (☎ 780-852-3155, 888-852-3155), 618 Patricia St, where the friendly staff will tell you the best places to go while they rent you some shoes ($8) and harnesses ($5) but not ropes.

Jasper Climbing School & Mountaineering Service (☎ 780-852-3964) offers beginner to advanced climbing courses, ranging from three hours to five days. Courses run from May to September. Call for more information about the offerings.

White-Water Rafting Calm to turbulent rafting can be found on the **Sunwapta River** and the **Athabasca River** near Athabasca Falls. Recent regulations prohibit rafting (or any boat usage) on the **Maligne River**, to protect the habitat for threatened Harlequin ducks.

Numerous companies offer trips of varying lengths. Maligne River Adventures (☎ 780-852-3370) runs trips on the Athabasca for $40 and on the Sunwapta for $60. You can make reservations at Maligne Lake Tours, 627 Patricia St. Whitewater Rafting Ltd (☎ 780-852-4386), with an office at the Esso station at 702 Connaught Dr, offers 3½-hour trips to Athabasca Falls and four-hour rides on the Sunwapta River. Prices start at $40.

Skiing Jasper National Park's only ski area is **Marmot Basin** (☎ 780-852-3816), which lies 19km southwest of town off Hwy 93A. It features good downhill runs for both beginners and experts, plenty of scenic cross-country trails, seven lifts and a new chalet. Call for a snow report. A day pass costs $44. For more information, check out the mountain's Web site at www.skimarmot.com. Marmot is also home to the **Alpine Sports Training Centre** (☎ 780-852-3816), which offers ski and snowboard lessons for all levels, from beginner to expert.

Near Maligne Lake, the **Moose Lake Loop** (8km) and the trail in the **Bald Hills** (11km) are easy introductions to the 200km

THE ROCKIES

of cross-country skiing in the park. The skiing season runs from December to May.

AROUND JASPER NATIONAL PARK
Mt Robson Provincial Park

The highest peak in the Canadian Rockies is not in one of the great national parks but sits majestically in its own BC provincial park to the west of Jasper National Park. The Yellowhead Hwy (Hwy 16) and the railway link the park to Jasper. While you're on the Yellowhead, watch for roadside markers detailing the work of the interned Japanese laborers who built this stretch of road during WWII.

Ambitious climbers have been tackling Mt Robson since 1907, but the sharp-edged ice castle wasn't successfully summitted until 1913. Mountaineers from all over the world come every summer to try to repeat this feat on Robson, considered one of the world's most challenging climbs.

At the base of the mountain, the Mt Robson Visitor Info Centre (☎ 250-566-4325, fax 566-9777) offers information on the park and runs interpretive programs during summer. Ask about the popular trip to Berg Lake, a two-day hike to the base of Mt Robson. Along the way, you'll pass numerous glaciers, including the Berg Glacier, which clings to Robson's northwest face. Periodically, bits of glacier fall into the lake, filling it with icebergs. You need to register and pay the $5 camping fee at the visitor center before venturing onto the Berg Lake Trail.

The Fraser River begins its long and sometimes tumultuous journey through British Columbia at its headwaters in the southwest corner of the park. (The Fraser spills into the Pacific Ocean near Vancouver after traveling some 1280km.) In August and September, you can see salmon spawning in the river at Rearguard Falls. You also stand an excellent chance of seeing moose in the park.

Adjoining the park's western end is the tiny **Mt Terry Fox Provincial Park**, named after the runner who lost a leg to cancer, then attempted to run across the country, raising money for cancer research (see the 'Terry Fox & the Marathon of Hope' boxed text in the Vancouver chapter).

Places to Stay Accommodations include three park-run campgrounds and two private spots. Close to the Visitor Info Centre, both *Robson Meadows Campground* and *Robson River Campground* offer showers, flush toilets and firewood, with sites costing $17.50. *Lucerne Campground*, 10km west of the Alberta border on the southern shore of Yellowhead Lake, charges $12. The facilities include only pit toilets and pump water.

You can also try the commercial campgrounds. *Emperor Ridge Campground* (☎ 250-566-8438), behind the Visitor Info Centre, offers showers, flush toilets and sites for $13.50. *Robson Shadows Campground* (☎ 250-566-9190), part of the Robson Lodge, charges $14.50. Rooms at the *Robson Lodge* (☎ 250-566-4821) start at $70.

Cariboo-Chilcotin

Fewer than 100,000 people live in the vast Cariboo and Chilcotin areas, which sit like a wide cummerbund around the waist of BC. East of the Fraser River and west of the Cariboo Mountains, the Cariboo region follows the 1858 Cariboo Wagon Road (now known as the Gold Rush Trail), which starts at 'Mile 0' in Lillooet (see the Whistler & the Sunshine Coast chapter) and heads north to the historic town of Barkerville. Named for Billy Barker, who discovered the area's first gold nugget, Barkerville once had more than 10,000 residents, prospectors mostly, who dug for gold by day and chugged whiskey in shanty saloons by night. Towns named for their distance from Lillooet sprouted up along the route, which explains unlikely monikers like 100 Mile House, 108 Mile House and 150 Mile House. Today the route is called the Cariboo Hwy or Hwy 97. It passes through Williams Lake and Quesnel, two substantial forestry towns, on its way north to Prince George and, eventually, Alaska. The Cariboo takes its name from the Cariboeuf, later known as caribou, which populated the area during the gold rush.

West of the Fraser River and sprawling all the way over the Coast Mountains, the entire Chilcotin region has only one paved road – and even parts of it are gravel. From Williams Lake, Hwy 20 heads west, passing large stretches of open range and grasslands, with access points to some very remote provincial parks. The road winds through Tweedsmuir Provincial Park and finally reaches Bella Coola, a remote fishing village on BC's southwest coast, 456km later.

With boundless open range and rolling grassy hills, the southern interior makes excellent territory for cattle raising. Working ranches are tucked into many folds of the Cariboo-Chilcotin landscape. The Cariboo alone boasts 500 cattle ranches, which produce 20% of the beef for the province.

This area is also home to the waterfall-filled Wells Gray Provincial Park, in the far

Highlights

- Gazing at spectacular Helmcken Falls in Wells Gray Provincial Park
- Eating fudge and reliving the Gold Rush days in Barkerville
- Paddling the Bowron Lake canoe circuit
- Hooting and hollering at the Williams Lake Stampede
- Following Hwy 20 over 'The Hill' to the remote village of Bella Coola
- Tracing Alexander Mackenzie's route from Quesnel to the coast

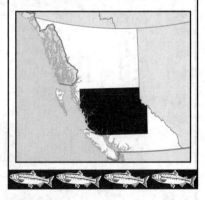

east of the region, and Bowron Lake Provincial Park, near Barkerville, where you'll find one of the best canoe circuits in the world.

The Cariboo-Chilcotin falls under the Cariboo Forest Region, comprised of five separate districts: Horsefly, Chilcotin, Quesnel, Williams Lake and 100 Mile House. For topographic maps and backcountry trail and camping information, contact the Cariboo Forest Region (☎ 250-398-4345, fax 398-4380), No 200 at 640 Borland St in Williams Lake. You can also get information from the Ministry of Forests' Web site, www.for.gov.bc.ca.

CARIBOO-CHILCOTIN

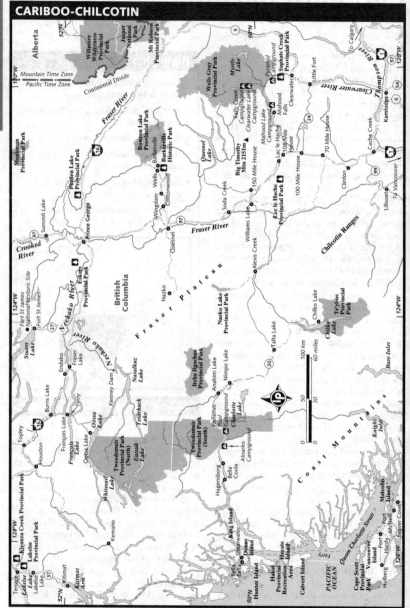

Saddle Sores & the Great Outdoors

When was the last time you sat on a horse? That long, eh? Well, here in cowboy country that just ain't good enough. So don yer chaps and cowboy hats and shuffle on up to the saddle – it's time to ride. With all the ranching going on in the Cariboo, it's no surprise to find out that hopping on a horse or rounding up some cattle is as simple as, well, hopping on a horse. Dozens of guest ranches in the Cariboo offer everything from old-fashioned trail riding and hayrides to overnight cattle drives and sing-alongs by the campfire. Whether you're looking to learn to ride or you've always wanted to wrangle with cattle, there's probably a guest ranch for you. From rustic cabin accommodations to luxurious spas, most guest ranches serve up excellent food and down-home hospitality. Find out more by contacting BC Guest Ranchers Association (☎ 250-374-6836, fax 374-6640) or by visiting the Web site www.bcguestranches.com.

WELLS GRAY PROVINCIAL PARK

In the Cariboo Mountains about halfway between Kamloops and Jasper, off the Yellowhead Hwy (Hwy 5), lies this enormous, 541,000-hectare wilderness park, a seldom-visited jewel filled with incredible waterfalls.

Wells Gray is the fourth-largest park in BC, after Tatshenshini-Alsek, Tweedsmuir and the Spatsizi Wilderness Plateau. The drainages of the Clearwater River and its tributaries define the park's boundaries and give visitors five major lakes, two large river systems and plenty of waterfalls to explore.

Though First Nations people have long lived in the area, it was a group of Overlanders who named the river for its crystal clear waters in 1862. Wells Gray almost became a rail route when the Canadian Pacific Railway (CPR) was looking for a route over the Rockies, but it was bypassed when the CPR chose the more southern, yet controversial Kicking Horse Pass. The area remained vast wilderness until various settlers started moving in. Fur trapper John Ray was the first white man to settle in the area and one of the last to leave. Remnants of his homestead, the Ray Farm, are now a park attraction. When giant waterfalls were discovered in 1913, people began making appeals to the government to protect the area as parkland. It finally happened in 1939, and the park took its name from a parks official, Arthur Wellesley Gray.

Most people enter the park through the town of Clearwater on Hwy 5, but you can also access it from 100 Mile House on Hwy 97 or from Blue River on Hwy 5 (see Getting There & Away, later). Many sights, including the absolutely incredible Helmcken Falls, where the Murtle River plunges 137m into a misty abyss, are accessible by a short road branching off the Wells Gray Corridor, which travels the 68km length of the park.

In Clearwater, the Visitor Info Centre (☎ 250-674-2646, fax 674-3693), on the corner of the Yellowhead Hwy (Hwy 5) and Clearwater Valley Rd, distributes lots of useful information and maps of the park. Pick up a copy of *Wells Gray Corridor Guide*, a brochure detailing the many sights accessible by car.

Activities

You'll find opportunities for **hiking, cross-country skiing** or **horseback riding** along more than 20 trails of varying lengths. Another great way to explore the park is by **canoeing** on Clearwater, Azure, Murtle and Mahood Lakes. Clearwater Lake lies at the north end of the Wells Gray Corridor. A narrow navigation channel from the north end of Clearwater Lake connects to the west end of Azure Lake, making these lakes form an upside-down L. You can only access the 6900-hectare Murtle Lake from the Blue River park entrance. You can reach Mahood Lake, on the southwest side of Wells Gray, from 100 Mile House (see Getting There & Away, below, for information on park entrances). Rustic backcountry campgrounds dot the area around all four lakes. To rent canoes ($35 per day), contact Clearwater Lake Tours (☎ 250-674-3052) or Helmcken Falls Lodge (☎ 250-674-3657).

The Clearwater River makes for some excellent, adrenaline-pumping **white-water rafting**. Interior Whitewater Expeditions (☎ 250-674-3727) runs the river in spring and summer. The three-hour trip costs $77.

Places to Stay

There are four campgrounds (☎ 250-587-6250) in the park, all with pit toilets but no showers; sites cost $12. *Pyramid Campground*, with 50 sites, is just 5km from the park's south entrance. At the end of the road on the southern end of the lake, *Clearwater Lake Campground* contains 80 sites and fills up the fastest. Beside it is *Falls Creek Campground*, which accommodates any overflow campers. *Mahood Lake Campground*, on the west side of Wells Gray, 86km northeast of 100 Mile House, attracts lots of anglers to its 34 sites. With the same facilities, *Saphats Creek Provincial Park* (☎ 250-587-6150) is a small 20-site park just south of Wells Gray. Sites here are also $12. A bunch of back-country marine sites surround Clearwater and Murtle Lakes. Ask for details at the Visitor Info Centre in Clearwater.

There are no commercial operations in the park, but just outside of the south gate you'll find a couple of excellent accommodations options along Clearwater Valley Rd. Rates quoted are for summer; they drop substantially in the winter. One of the best options, *Helmcken Falls Lodge* (☎ 250-674-3657, helmfall@mail.wellsgray.net) offers private rooms in cozy log cabins, with delicious meals served in the main lodge. A standard room for one or two people costs $116; the deluxe version is $143. Meals are not included. The lodge rents canoes and offers horseback riding trips. Cross-country skiers like to congregate here in winter.

Another good option with cabins that are slightly more rustic is *Wells Gray Ranch* (☎ 250-674-2774, kanata@wellsgray.net), 27km north of Hwy 5. Cabins cost $115. You can also camp in a tipi for $14. The ranch offers a good range of guided trips.

Getting There & Away

There are three access points to the park. The most popular entrance is the south gate, 36km north of Clearwater on Clearwater Valley Rd. You can also reach the park from 100 Mile House via an 86km gravel road that leads to Mahood Falls and the west end of Mahood Lake. From Blue River, north of Clearwater, a 24km gravel road and 2.5km track lead to Murtle Lake in the southeast part of the park. Greyhound buses stop in Clearwater en route to Jasper or to Kamloops, but there's no bus transportation into the park. North Thompson Taxi (☎ 250-674-0239) will shuttle you into the park for about $40 one-way.

GOLD RUSH TRAIL/ CARIBOO HIGHWAY

Following the Gold Rush Trail (Hwy 97) north of Lillooet, you'll find **Clinton**, the self-proclaimed 'Guest Ranch Capital of BC.' Its downtown streets feature western decor and some roaming dudes in cowboy boots. The service center for the southern Cariboo region, **100 Mile House** offers some excellent cross-country skiing.

Williams Lake
• population 12,500

Williams Lake makes no attempt to hide that it's in the tree-cutting business. Lumber yards, piles of logs and other evidence of the town's five mills surround the downtown area. About 65% of the population works in forestry. As such, the town is a rather charmless supply hub known mostly for the Williams Lake Stampede, BC's answer to the Calgary Stampede.

From Williams Lake, you can follow Hwy 20 west 456km to the coastal town of Bella Coola (see the Highway 20 section, later in the chapter). You can also follow the Cariboo Hwy (Hwy 97) north to McLeese Lake, a small lakeside resort with log cabins, then on to Quesnel and Prince George (see the North chapter).

Information The Visitor Info Centre (☎ 250-392-5025, fax 392-4214), 1148 Broadway S off Hwy 97, is open 9 am to 5 pm daily

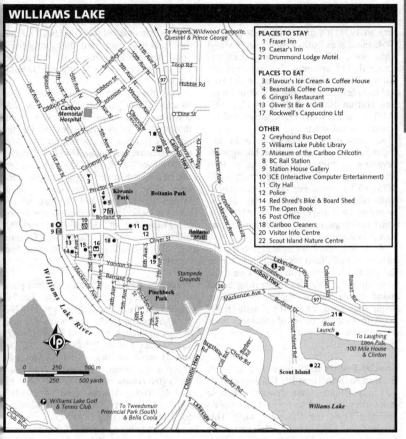

WILLIAMS LAKE

To Airport, Wildwood Campsite, Quesnel & Prince George

Toop Rd
Hubble Rd
O'Dine St

Cariboo Memorial Hospital

Kiwanis Park
Boitanio Park
Boitanio Mall

Oliver St

Yorston St

Barnard St
Stampede Grounds

Pinchbeck Park

Williams Lake River

Mackenzie Ave S
Lakeview Crescent
Broadway S
Coleman Rd
Rowat Rd

Borland Dr
Scout Island Rd

Boat Launch

To Laughing Loon Pub, 100 Mile House & Clinton

Chilcotin Hwy S
Cariboo Hwy S
Bayshore Rd
Chow Rd
Barber Rd
Bunley Rd

Scout Island

Williams Lake

0   250   500 m
0   250   500 yards

Williams Lake Golf & Tennis Club
To Tweedsmuir Provincial Park (South) & Bella Coola

PLACES TO STAY
1 Fraser Inn
19 Caesar's Inn
21 Drummond Lodge Motel

PLACES TO EAT
3 Flavour's Ice Cream & Coffee House
4 Beanstalk Coffee Company
6 Gringo's Restaurant
13 Oliver St Bar & Grill
17 Rockwell's Cappuccino Ltd

OTHER
2 Greyhound Bus Depot
5 Williams Lake Public Library
7 Museum of the Cariboo Chilcotin
8 BC Rail Station
9 Station House Gallery
10 ICE (Interactive Computer Entertainment)
11 City Hall
12 Police
14 Red Shred's Bike & Board Shed
15 The Open Book
16 Post Office
18 Cariboo Cleaners
20 Visitor Info Centre
22 Scout Island Nature Centre

in summer and 9 am to 4 pm weekdays at at other times.

The main post office (☎ 250-392-7543) is at 48 2nd Ave S. If you're looking to surf the Internet, stop by Interactive Computer Entertainment, or ICE (☎ 250-392-3269), 19 1st Ave N. This Internet café contains lots of terminals that you can use for $5 per hour.

The central Williams Lake Public Library (☎ 250-392-3630), 180 3rd Ave N, is open 10 am to 8 pm from Tuesday to Thursday and 10 am to 5 pm Friday and Saturday. The Open Book (☎ 250-392-2665), 83 2nd Ave S, features a good selection of regional titles. For information about local happenings, pick up the *Williams Lake Tribune*, which comes out three times a week.

Wash your clothes at Cariboo Cleaners, 397 Oliver St, where coin-operated laundry facilities are available 8 am to 8 pm daily. For medical care, go to the Cariboo Memorial Hospital (☎ 250-392-4411), 514 6th Ave N.

Things to See & Do The excellent Museum of the Cariboo Chilcotin (☎ 250-392-7404), at 113 4th Ave N, features a very interesting exhibit on the history and paraphernalia of the Stampede (see Special

Events, below), including photos of each 'Queen' from the annual pageant, dating back to 1933. It's interesting that prior to 1964, there was both a First Nations and white queen. After '64, only one queen was crowned. The museum also explores the history of ranching and logging in the area and includes the BC cowboy 'hall of fame.' The **Station House Gallery** (☎ 250-392-6113), at the BC Rail station, showcases different regional artists.

As usual in BC, there's lots to do outdoors. Find out about **mountain biking, river kayaking** or **hiking** in the area at Red Shred's Bike & Board Shed (☎ 250-398-7873), 95 1st Ave S. For information about **white-water rafting**, call Waterpeople Expeditions (☎ 250-392-0737, 800-908-8138), which runs trips on the Chilcotin and Fraser Rivers in summer.

While Williams Lake might not be an environmentalist's favorite destination (given the preponderance of mills in town), the town does include the interesting **Scout Island Nature Centre** (☎ 250-398-8532), on Scout Island Rd, where the marshy parklands draw varied species of migratory birds to the area, making it a popular spot for bird-watchers.

Special Events In 1919, the Pacific Great Eastern Railway (now BC Rail) pushed its way into Williams Lake. People partied so much they decided to reenact the whole shebang again the following year. This marked the birth of the **Williams Lake Stampede** (☎ 250-398-8388, 800-717-6336), an annual four-day party that happens on the town's Stampede Grounds in early July, when the town is suddenly overrun with spur-clicking cowboys and leather-clad cowgirls. It's serious business for the cowboys who come here from all over the place to compete in activities like roping, cattle penning and the always-exciting bull riding. Fringe events include the popular Stampede Queen Coronation and loggers' sports. Hotel rates go up while the stampede takes over town, and the event keeps getting bigger. One-day tickets to the festival cost around $12.

Places to Stay The only decent place to camp is **Wildwood Campsite** (☎ 250-989-4711), 13km north of town on Hwy 97. It has flush toilets, showers and laundry facilities. Tent sites are $15. During the Stampede, you can camp on the Stampede Grounds for $8.

Downtown, the large **Caesar's Inn** (☎ 250-392-7747, 800-663-6893, 55 6th St S) contains a pub, restaurant and clean rooms that start at $56/60 single/double. On the highway just east of the turnoff to downtown, **Drummond Lodge Motel** (☎ 250-392-5335, 800-667-4555, 1405 Hwy 97 S) offers one of the best values in town. Many of the large, clean rooms feature views of Scout Island. Rooms cost $65/71. Just off the highway beside the Greyhound bus depot, the **Fraser Inn** (☎ 250-398-7055, 800-452-6789, 285 Donald Rd) charges $80/90. Rates include access to the inn's hot tub, sauna and restaurant.

Places to Eat If you're looking for a place to read while you drink your coffee, head to **Beanstalk Coffee Company** (☎ 250-392-5656), attached to the library on 3rd Ave. Wraps and light lunches cost $5. **Rockwell's Cappuccino Ltd** (☎ 250-392-3633, 72C 2nd Ave S) serves sandwiches for $6. Get a fat scoop of ice cream at **Flavour's Ice Cream & Coffee House** (☎ 250-398-2275, 289 3rd Ave N). **Gringo's Restaurant** (☎ 250-392-6012, 112 2nd Ave N) features Mexican food, with dinners for $8 to $15.

Pick and choose among different sauces and noodles at the **Oliver St Bar & Grill** (☎ 250-392-5942), near the train station at Oliver St and Mackenzie Ave. Pasta dishes cost $10 at lunch and $13 at dinner; the good burgers are $8. The pool tables help to make this spot a popular place to hang out at night.

Off the highway, the excellent **Laughing Loon Pub** (☎ 250-398-5666, 1730 Broadway S) is one of the best attractions in town. Built out of materials recovered from demolished historical buildings throughout North America (from Vancouver to New York), this pub boasts an elegance – and a great patio – you don't usually find in these parts. Oh, yeah, it has good pub food, too. Dinners range from $9 to $20.

Getting There & Around The Williams Lake Airport is 13km north of town, just off Hwy 97. Air BC (☎ 888-247-2262) flies here daily from Vancouver, Prince George and Kamloops.

The Greyhound bus depot (☎ 250-398-7733), 215 Donald Rd, is just off Hwy 97. Daily buses head north to Prince George ($33.50 one-way) and south to Vancouver ($73 one-way).

The BC Rail station is on Mackenzie Ave S at the west end of Oliver St. BC Rail's *Cariboo Prospector* (☎ 800-339-8752) stops in town three times a week on its trip from Vancouver to Prince Rupert via Prince George. One-way tickets from Vancouver to Williams Lake cost around $143, including breakfast and lunch.

Car rental companies include Budget (☎ 250-398-5002), on Hwy 97.

Quesnel
• **population 11,114**

Neither Quesnel's picturesque setting at the confluence of the Fraser and Quesnel Rivers nor the carefully cultivated flowers along the riverfront trails can disguise the fact that this is first and foremost a logging town, similar to Williams Lake, 120km to the south. The pulp mills dominate Quesnel's townscape, and their plumes of smelly brown smoke permeate the air. The observation tower at the north end of town overlooks Two-Mile Flat, a large industrial area devoted to wood products. The town's welcome sign reads 'The Gold Pan City,' but the resource they're extracting is different now – perhaps a more fitting name would be the 'Fallen-Tree City,' for the massive, overwhelming pile of logs that sit around waiting to be processed.

From Quesnel, Hwy 26 leads east to the area's main attractions, Barkerville Historic Park and Bowron Lake Provincial Park (see separate headings, later).

Information It's worth stopping at the Visitor Info Centre (☎ 250-992-8716, fax 992-9606), 703 Carson Ave, on the edge of LeBourdais Park. It's open 8 am to 8 pm daily in summer and 9 am to 4 pm weekdays at other times.

Find out more about town events in the twice-weekly *Quesnel Cariboo Observer*. Do your laundry at Daisy Mae's Laundry (☎ 250-992-6770), 678 Doherty Dr, just west of downtown over the Moffat Bridge. The hospital (☎ 250-992-0600) is right in town along the highway.

Things to See & Do The excellent **Quesnel Museum**, in the same building as the Visitor Info Centre, features a quirky array of antiques from the gold rush days, a cool coin collection and other interesting displays. It's open 8 am to 6 pm daily in summer and 8:30 am to 4:30 pm Tuesday to Saturday the rest of the year.

Northwest of Quesnel, the refurbished **Alexander Mackenzie Heritage Trail** follows ancient trails from the Fraser River west to Bella Coola, on the Pacific Ocean. In 1793, Alexander Mackenzie made the first recorded crossing of continental North America in his search for a supply route to the Pacific Ocean. His carved graffiti can still be seen in a rock near Bella Coola. This 420km trail winds its way through forest and mountains and makes for a tough 16-day walk. At least one food drop is required. You can do some of the more accessible segments for a few days – for example, the section through the southern end of Tweedsmuir Provincial Park. You can also take day hikes from Quesnel. To get to the trailhead, follow the Blackwater Rd west from Quesnel. For detailed trail guides, contact the Alexander Mackenzie Trail Association, PO Box 425, Station A, Kelowna, BC V1Y 7P1. For more information, call BC Parks at ☎ 250-398-4411.

Places to Stay & Eat For a good deal, try the *Gold Pan* (☎ 250-992-2107, 885 Front St), where you can sleep in a clean room for $46/48 single/double. Nearby, the *Talisman Inn* (☎ 250-992-7242, 800-663-8090, 753 Front St) offers similar rooms for $53/63. In one of Quesnel's oldest buildings, downtown's *Cariboo Hotel* (☎ 250-992-2333, 800-665-3200, 254 Front St) overlooks the Fraser River and features a good pub. Its small rooms cost only $50/60. You can relive the prospecting days at the *Billy Barker Casino Hotel* (☎ 250-992-5533, 888-992-4255, 308 McLean St), also downtown. Rooms here start at $60.

Pick up a muffin and a good cup of coffee at *Granville's Coffee* (383 Reid St), at St Laurent Ave. In a town full of so-so restaurants, *Café Brookwood* (☎ 250-992-7338, 533 Reid St) is a real gem. Though closed on weekends and only open for dinner on Friday, the café serves up excellent lunches, including a spicy salad and sandwiches for $6. For Chinese food, try *Green Leaf* (☎ 250-992-8028, 158 Barlow St). *Murphy's Pub* (☎ 250-747-3400), on Hwy 97 at Hydraulic Rd, offers good burgers ($8) and a lively atmosphere; lots of mill workers come here for an after-work pint.

Getting There & Away The Quesnel Airport is just north of town. Look for the turnoff at the junction of Hwys 97 and 26. Air BC (☎ 888-247-2262) operates scheduled daily flights from Vancouver.

Greyhound buses operate from the downtown station (☎ 250-992-2231), 365 Kinchant St. Buses depart daily for Kamloops, Kelowna and Vancouver ($42 one-way) and for Prince George ($15 one-way). You won't find any luggage lockers in the station, but you can check your bag for $1.

BC Rail's *Cariboo Prospector* (☎ 800-339-8752) stops three times a week on its trip from Vancouver to Prince Rupert via Prince George. The one-way fare from Vancouver to Quesnel is $176, including three meals. The station is just across the street from the Visitor Info Centre.

Barkerville

Between 1858 and 1861, when the Cariboo Wagon Rd (now Hwy 97) edged north from Kamloops to Quesnel, ramshackle towns hastily built by gold prospectors from around the world sprang up along the road. In 1862, one member of this new international population hit the jackpot, making $1000 in the first two days of his claim. Despite his luck, Cornishman Billy Barker probably had no clue that more than 100,000 salivating miners would leap into his footsteps, crossing rivers, creeks and lakes to storm the Cariboo Wagon Rd in search of gold. Soon Barkerville sprang up to become, for a time, the largest city west of Chicago and north of San Francisco. In its heyday some 10,000 people resided in the muddy town, hoping to hit jackpots of their own.

If Billy was clueless about the gold rush, then he most certainly never predicted that people would still be flocking here to see Barkerville as it was, albeit with a whole lot more fudge for sale than when the miners were here.

This restored gold rush town (☎ 250-994-3332) is 89km east of Quesnel at the end of Hwy 26. More than 125 buildings have been restored to their former glory, including a hotel, stores and a saloon. People dressed in period garb roam through town, and if you can tune out the crowds, the effect is quite neat, if not all that realistic. (In the Theatre Royal, dancing shows are staged in a family friendly manner the rough-and-tumble miners would have hooted at.) The free historic walking tours relate the history of the gold rush, the

Prospectors once flocked to Barkerville.

experience of the Chinese workers who built the Cariboo Hwy and the finer details in the art of panning for gold. But don't plan on striking it rich today.

Barkerville Historic Park is open 8 am to 8 pm daily, May to September. Between mid-May and mid-June, the two-day admission is $5.25/1.40 for adults/children. After that, the admission jumps to $7.50/2. The park is open at other times of the year, but most of the attractions are closed, which may actually make for a more atmospheric visit.

Nearby **Wells**, 8km west of Barkerville, is a more authentic historic town with accommodations, restaurants and a general store. The Wells Chamber of Commerce (☎ 250-994-2323) runs an information center just off the highway.

Places to Stay BC Parks (☎ 250-398-4414) runs three campgrounds in tiny Barkerville. Closest to the townsite and mostly used by campers with tents (not RVs), *Government Hill Campground* charges $12 for its 23 sites. Facilities include pit toilets but no showers. *Lowhee Campground* is the biggest, with 87 sites ($15), flush toilets and showers. This is the only campground with reservable sites (☎ 800-689-9025). *Forest Rose Campground* contains 56 sites, used primarily for groups, which cost $15. It also has showers and toilets.

The *St George Hotel* (☎ 250-994-0008, 888-246-7690), inside the historic park, dates from the 1890s. The rooms, all filled with antiques, start at $120/134 single/double, breakfast included.

You can also stay at the popular *Wells Hotel* (☎ 250-994-3427, 800-860-2299, 2341 Pooley St) in Wells. Home to a good restaurant and pub, it's pretty much the hub of the town. Rooms with shared bath are $70; private-bath rooms cost $90. Rates include a continental breakfast.

Getting There & Away There is no public bus to Barkerville, but Gold Safari Stage Lines (☎ 250-994-3462, 888-996-4653) runs a shuttle service from Quesnel to Barkerville. Call for rates.

BOWRON LAKE PROVINCIAL PARK

Surrounded by snowy peaks, this 149,207-hectare park boasts one of the best canoe trips in the world. The 116km circular canoe route passes through 10 lakes: Bowron, Kibbee, Indianpoint, Isaac, McLeary, Lanezi, Sandy, Babcock, Skoi and Swan – and over sections of the Isaac, Cariboo and Bowron Rivers. In between are several portages, ranging from 2km to 3km over well-defined trails. The trip takes seven to 10 days. You'll find backcountry campgrounds along the way; to make sure there are sites for everyone, the park service only allows 27 canoes to start the circuit each day. You must bring your own food (or catch your own fish).

The Mowdish Range runs right through the middle of the loop, while the Cariboo Range surrounds the perimeter of the park, affording spectacular views in every direction. With all these mountains around, it's no wonder the park is often cool and wet. Wildlife abounds. You might see moose, black and grizzly bears, caribou and mountain goats. In late summer, you stand a good chance of spotting bears on the upper Bowron River, where they feed on spawning sockeye salmon.

You can paddle the circuit any time from mid-May to October. Most people do it in July and August, but September is also an excellent choice, since that's when the tree leaves change color. Mosquitoes, which thrive in the wet, relatively windless environment, are at their worst in the spring.

Before planning your trip, contact Tourism BC (☎ 800-435-5622) to request an information package and to make reservations to do the circuit; you can reserve a spot beginning in January. Once you get to the park, you must go to the Registration Centre and pay a fee of $50 per person. For more information on the park, contact the BC Parks office (☎ 250-398-4414) in Williams Lake. The lodges (see Places to Stay, below) sell a waterproof map of the circuit for $5.

You can also leave the multi-day paddle to the hard-core types and just do day trips on Bowron Lake, which require no advance registration or fee.

BOWRON LAKE PROVINCIAL PARK

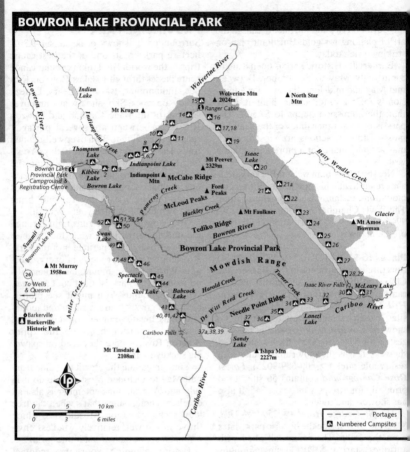

Indian Lake

Bowron River

Wolverine River

Wolverine Mtn ▲ 2024m

North Star Mtn ▲

Mt Kruger ▲

Ranger Cabin

Indianpoint Creek

Thompson Lake

Bowron Lake Provincial Park Campground & Registration Centre

Kibbee Lake

Indianpoint Lake

Indianpoint Mtn

Mt Peever 2329m

Isaac Lake

Betty Wendle Creek

McCabe Ridge

Pomeroy Creek

Ford Peaks

Bowron Lake

McLeod Peaks

Huckley Creek

Tediko Ridge

Bowron River

Mt Faulkner ▲

Glacier

Mt Amos Bowman ▲

Swan Lake

Bowron Lake Provincial Park

Mowdish Range

Summit Creek

Bowron Lake Rd

Mt Murray ▲ 1958m

To Wells & Quesnel

Anter Creek

Spectacle Lakes

Skoi Lake

Babcock Lake

Harold Creek

De Witt Reed Creek

Turner Creek

Needle Point Ridge

Isaac River Falls

McLeary Lake

Cariboo River

Barkerville
Barkerville Historic Park

Cariboo Falls

Mt Tinsdale ▲ 2108m

Sandy Lake

Lanezi Lake

Ishpa Mtn ▲ 2227m

Cariboo River

0   5   10 km
0   3   6 miles

– – – – Portages
◭ Numbered Campsites

Places to Stay

The **Bowron Lake Provincial Park Campground**, near the Registration Centre, contains 25 tent sites ($12) and pit toilets. Open from May until November, the friendly **Bowron Lakes Lodge** (☎ 250-992-2733), on the lake at the end of Bowron Lake Rd, offers cabins for two people starting at $55. You can rent canoes for $10 per hour, $40 per day or $125 and up for the circuit trip (up to 10 days). You can also camp right on the lake for $20 (for two people). Just up the road, attractive **Becker's Lodge** (☎ 250-992-8864, 800-808-4761) features a cozy restau-

rant and nice log chalets and cabins ranging from $55 to $120. Tent sites cost $18, including firewood and use of the facilities. Canoe rentals are $40 per day or $190 to $230 for the circuit. Becker's also leads an eight-day guided canoe tour. For more information visit the Web site www.beckers.bc.ca.

Getting There & Away

You can fly into Quesnel and rent a car or call Gold Safari Stage Lines (☎ 250-994-3462, 888-996-4653), which will shuttle you from Quesnel to the park. Another way to get here is by floatplane. Cariboo Mountain

Air (☎ 250-398-743) flies from Williams Lake or Quesnel. Call for current rates.

To get to the park by car, turn off Hwy 26 just before Barkerville and follow the 28km-long gravel Bowron Lake Rd.

HIGHWAY 20

Just west of Williams Lake, Hwy 20 crosses over the Fraser River, which marks the boundary between the Cariboo and the Chilcotin. This vast, scarcely inhabited land of grassland plateaus, lakes and ranches sprawls west to the Coast Mountains. Over the mountains, the landscape makes a dramatic shift to craggy bluffs and rushing rivers before dropping down into the wet, lush central coast.

The distance between Williams Lake and Bella Coola, on the coast, is a long 456km, only accessible by car on Hwy 20 or by ferry. No buses travel this route, so if you have no car your best bet is to rent one (hitchhiking would take forever).

From Hwy 20, you can take numerous side roads – most of which are gravel – to some of the province's most remote provincial parks that are still accessibly by car. Excellent canoeing on the lake chain in **Nazko Lake Provincial Park** draws adventurers to this park, 167km northwest of Williams Lake along the Alexis Lakes Rd, off Hwy 20. You can get to the north end of 233,240-hectare **Ts'yl-os Provincial Park** (pronounced '**sigh**-loss') by turning south at the town of Tatla Lake, 220km west of Williams Lake. After the turn, follow the road for 63km to the rustic campground on the north tip of Chilko Lake. Wildlife thrives here, and Chilko Lake is chock-full of fish. For information on either park, call ☎ 250-398-4414.

Hwy 20 meanders up into the mountains, passing by small towns whose services are limited. West of Anahim Lake, the road becomes gravel. It soon begins its descent into the Bella Coola Valley via the legendary 'Hill,' a winding narrow road over Heckman Pass. The road includes a stretch of steep, 18%-grade downhill that keeps you clenching the wheel the whole way down. At the bottom of the Hill is the freedom road,' built by Bella Coola residents so they could access the interior. Prior to 1955, the only way out of Bella Coola was by boat.

Tweedsmuir Provincial Park (South)

You are already in this gigantic, roughly arrowhead-shaped park when you drive the Hill. At 981,000 hectares, Tweedsmuir (☎ 250-398-4414) is the second-largest provincial park in BC (next to Tatshenshini-Alsek in the northwest corner of BC). The Dean River, roughly halfway up the park, divides Tweedsmuir into north and south. Hwy 20 is the only road through this mostly wilderness park, and it skirts the park's southern tip.

Alexander Mackenzie traveled through this area on his way to becoming the first white person to make it to the northwest coast. Long before that, Bella Coola and Chilcotin Indians thrived along the rivers full of salmon.

The park's features include the **Rainbow Range**, north of Hwy 20. The colorful dome of eroded rock and lava mountains appears, at certain lights, orange, red, yellow and purple. Most of the hiking in the park requires serious planning ahead of time. Popular treks include the 16km route to **Hunlen Falls**, which plummet 260m into the Atnarko River at the north end of Turner Lake, and some portions of the **Alexander Mackenzie Heritage Trail** (see the Quesnel section, earlier, for more information on this trail). You'll find two campgrounds along Hwy 20: *Atnarko Campground*, at the bottom of the Hill, and the *Fisheries Pool Campground*, farther west. Both offer riverside sites for $12.

Bella Coola
• population 820

The remote village of Bella Coola sits at the mouth of the Bella Coola River where it spills into the Bentinck Arm of the Pacific Ocean. This rainy community is surrounded by the sharp, spectacular Coast Mountains. More than one-third of the population is made up of First Nations people, descendents of the Nuxalk-Carriers who first blazed the trails later used by Alexander Mackenzie. The Natives were probably shocked to see Mackenzie, a white man, come down the Bella Coola River in 1793. The Nuxalk (pronounced 'new-hawk') are well known for their carvings, paintings and their trademark use of cobalt blue, which you'll see in artwork throughout the town.

Many superb hiking trails radiate out of Bella Coola, including a trail to 17th-century **petroglyphs**, carved deep into the rock. You can only explore these with a tour. To arrange a trip, contact Darren Edgar (☎ 250-799-5263), Bella Coola's self-proclaimed 'good will ambassador,' who can pass on a wealth of area information. Though it's rarely ever open, the **Bella Coola Museum** (☎ 250-799-5657), on Hwy 20 just west of

Mackenzie St, merits a visit if you can time it right. The local artifacts on display come from Native communities and early white settlements. The museum is open in summer only, with rather whimsical hours.

For information on hiking trails, the town or the ferries, contact Bella Coola Valley Tourism (☎ 250-799-5268, 888-863-1181), in Tweedsmuir Travel on Cliff St beside the liquor store.

Places to Stay & Eat Sites are $13 at *Hagar's Haven RV Park* (☎ 250-799-5659) 5km east of Bella Coola on Hwy 20, which features flush toilets, showers and laundry facilities. On Hwy 20 in Hagensborg (see Around Bella Coola, later), *Gnome's Home* (☎ 250-982-25044) charges $12 for shady

Great Bear Rainforest

Morning mist gently rises off BC's quiet central coast, revealing an emerald labyrinth of tiny islands and inlets that nudge up against the foreboding shore of the mainland. If you could soar like an eagle over this wet coastal wilderness, you could follow the long green fingers of the pristine fjords, coast high above secluded waterfalls or float along the ridges overlooking deep river valleys. On the lonely shores, you'd see timber wolves and grizzly bears, even the white Kermode bear, often referred to as the 'spirit bear.' Offshore you'd see spawning salmon searching for river mouths, sea lions playing in the lapping waves and, farther out, whales and porpoises feeding in the rich waters. You'd hear birdsong and squawks, and it might be days before you'd see a human being.

This is the Great Bear Rainforest, a vast 3,000,000-hectare area containing the largest contiguous tract of coastal temperate rain forest left on earth. This endangered forest type is distinguished by its proximity to oceans, the presence of mountains and heavy rainfall. Accessible only by boat or floatplane, the Great Bear Rainforest, dubbed such for its large grizzly bear population, follows the Inside Passage from the top edge of Vancouver Island to the Alaska border, 400km north. Short, rugged brush forests with muskeg lowlands cover its outer fringes, but along the Passage, huge granite buttresses line the deepwater fjords. These almost secret passages lead to rich valleys adorned with ancient Sitka spruce, Pacific silver fir, yellow cedar and western red cedar.

The forest industry's voracious appetite for such timber jewels – previously untouched because of their difficult access – has put the Great Bear Rainforest and all of its inhabitants seriously at risk. Forest companies try to keep up with high consumption levels and demand for BC softwoods in the USA, Europe and Japan. Meanwhile, wildlife habitat suffers the consequences. Thousands of genetically distinct races of wild Pacific salmon swim and spawn in the area waters. They provide food to bears, birds and even vegetation, with their decomposing bodies adding nutrients to the soil. Massive clear-cutting has already devastated many of the Great Bear Rainforest's productive watersheds, and the reverberation continues to wreak havoc up and down the interdependent food chain.

Coastal temperate rain forests are rare; they originally comprised only 0.5% of the world's land base. Today, almost 60% of that has disappeared, and not because of natural disturbances – forest

sites. Amenities include flush toilets, showers and a covered cooking area.

The **Bella Coola Motel** (☎ *250-799-5323*), on Burke Ave at Clayton St, includes the only campground right in town. Though uninspiring, the sites ($14) lie alongside the Bella Coola River. Motel rooms in separate cabins complete with kitchens start at $65. You can rent scooters, bikes and canoes here. The **Bella Coola Valley Inn** (☎ *250-799-5316, 888-799-5316*), at the corner of Dean St and Hwy 20, charges $80/88 single/double; the inn contains a restaurant and the Salty Dog Pub. To the east, in Hagensborg, **Bay Motor Hotel** (☎ *250-982-2212*) features a coffee shop, a restaurant and the lively Bentinck Arms Pub. The rooms cost $70/80. For a cheap meal, try the deli and bakery at the **Co-Op** (☎ *250-799-5325*), on Mackenzie St in Bella Coola.

Getting There & Away If you can't come in a car from Williams Lake, the only way to get to Bella Coola is by air or boat.

The small airport is located in Hagensborg, east of Bella Coola on Hwy 20. Pacific Coastal Air (☎ *250-982-2225*) flies daily to Bella Bella and Vancouver, but it's a pricey way to travel. The short hop to Bella Bella is about $135 (one-way), and one-way trips to Vancouver are about $240.

The scenic BC Ferries' Discovery Coast ferry runs between Bella Coola and Port Hardy three times a week in

Great Bear Rainforest

fires don't occur often in the wet coastal forests. Logging and development alone have wiped out much of the forest. North America's ancient rain forest once stretched from Alaska to Northern California. Today, no single undeveloped, unlogged coastal watershed larger than 5000 hectares exists south of the BC border. Only small pockets survive in North America, New Zealand, Tasmania, Chile and Argentina. Tiny patches also cling to life in Japan, northeastern Europe and Turkey and along the Black Sea coast in Georgia. But they are all at risk of disappearing forever.

Though some protectionist measures have preserved chunks of the Great Bear Rainforest as parkland, environmentalists say it's just not enough. Meanwhile, forestry companies are bidding top dollar to cut trees as fast as they can. Established in 1990 to combat the destruction, the Raincoast Conservation Society, a nonprofit organization based in Victoria and Bella Bella, works to protect the area by documenting bear and salmon behavior and educating the public on the area's tenuous future. For more information on the Great Bear Rainforest, contact the Raincoast Conservation Society (greatbear@raincoast.org) or check out its Web site at www.raincoast.org.

For a glimpse of this unique area, take a ride on the BC Ferries' Discovery Coast or Inside Passage ferries. But don't be surprised to see some less-than-scenic sights. For hundreds of years, the eagle's eye-view has remained unchanged. But today things look different; the eagle overhead hears machinery and watches giant barges arrive empty and leave filled with thousands of logs.

Sitka spruce

Grease Trails

Oolichan, spelled a bunch of different ways – eulachon, oulachen, even hooligan – is a small, black-and-silver smelt-fish known to many coastal First Nations groups as 'salvation' fish, since the oolichan were the first to show up in the river after the long, cold winter. Oolichan run in two- to four-year cycles. Schools are huge, and you could net millions of the tiny, oily fish with little effort. The Natives prized the oolichan for its butter-like oily fat; at the end of winter, consuming the fish must have felt like eating a hunk of chocolate after a lengthy stint adhering to an unrewarding diet.

The Natives placed the fish in pits and applied weight to squeeze out the yummy oil, which was then scooped off and placed in wooden boxes, where it could be stored for up to two years. Oolichan oil made an excellent dipping sauce for dried berries or salmon.

Inland Native groups would travel overland to the coast to vie for this delicious indulgence. They would leave a trail of oolichan drippings, and their routes effectively became 'grease trails.'

summer only. See the Ferry section of the Getting Around chapter for more details.

Around Bella Coola

Just 16km east of Bella Coola on Hwy 20 is **Hagensborg**, settled in 1895 by a hardy group of Norwegians whose hand-hewn homes were built with crude saws and axes. Attracted to the area because it resembled their homeland, the Norwegians stayed and entrenched themselves in northern BC. Today, the Scandinavian influence is still evident, and many residents still speak Norwegian. West of Bella Coola is the small coastal village of **Bella Bella**, accessible only by boat or plane.

The North

Northern BC is a vast, largely undeveloped and sparsely populated region, dominated by the Rockies and Coast Mountains and decorated with swift rivers, fish-filled lakes and lush forests. The Yellowhead Hwy (Hwy 16), coming west from Alberta, traces the southern boundary of this region; it travels through the major service city of Prince George and out to Prince Rupert, on the coast. From there, a ferry system connects the BC mainland to the Queen Charlotte Islands, a remote archipelago far off the coast. The famed Alaska Hwy (Hwy 97) runs north along the eastern side of the province, traveling from Mile 0 at Dawson Creek up to the Yukon on the 60th parallel. The Stewart-Cassiar Hwy (Hwy 37) beats a dusty path to the Yukon on the western side of the province.

An odd juxtaposition of wilderness and industry exists in the North. Timber, oil and natural gas extraction all contribute to big business, especially in the northeast. In the northwest, forestry and fisheries are major contributors to the local economy. Meanwhile, the entire area abounds with black and grizzly bears, caribou, moose and sheep. Thousands of birds migrate along the Pacific Flyway, and vast tracks of land are preserved as provincial parks. There is a fine line between resource exploitation and preservation; if you log too much, fish too much or mine too much, your economic base will be at risk. The livelihood of many northern towns rests on not crossing that line.

Though industry is relatively young – much of the region wasn't settled until the 20th century – First Nations people have long inhabited the area. To this day, especially in the northwest, they make up a considerable percentage of the permanent residents and maintain a strong presence in politics and issues of land management.

Travel in the North is pricey. Greyhound buses travel almost everywhere, but bus tickets get expensive quickly, as the distance

Highlights

- Following the scenic Alaska Highway from Dawson Creek all the way to the remote Yukon Territory

- Beachcombing on the wild, wind-swept shores of the Queen Charlotte Islands

- Dining on fresh halibut and salmon in Prince Rupert

- Challenging your travel companion to a contest: which one of you can spot the most black bears

- Following the totem pole trail through the Hazeltons

- Sipping a coffee and marveling at the mountains in Smithers

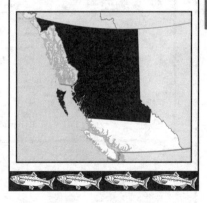

between sights is often great. If you rent a car, try to work out a deal for free kilometers, though you'll still have to pay for gas. Unless you're camping, accommodations are generally not cheap; hostels are rare and motels are often not spectacular, though they average around $60 per night. Fresh food is hard to come by, and grocery stores and restaurants often charge more than their counterparts to the south because of the added expense of transporting produce into the area.

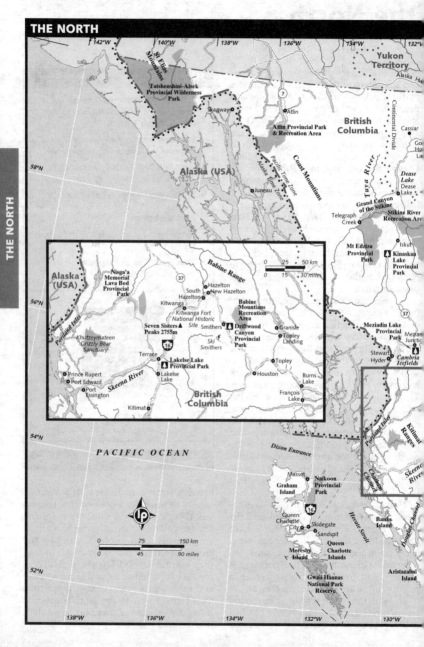

THE NORTH

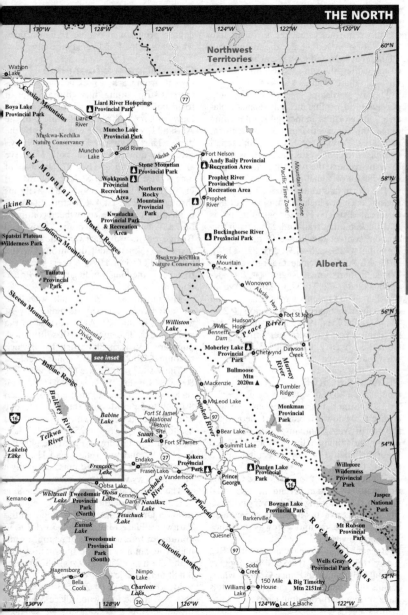

THE NORTH

Daylight seems to last forever in summer, while winter seems shrouded in darkness. In the more northerly reaches, in towns like Fort Nelson or Dease Lake, the summer sun might set at 1 am and soon rise again at 5 am. Come winter, the sun sets at 3 pm, not rising again until 10 am.

Despite hardships – harsh weather, expensive food, prolific mosquitoes and isolation – the North is an incredibly interesting place, far removed from urban cultural pressures. People are friendly, unhurried and eager to chat – plus, the North is full of majestic scenery, the type that can never be done justice on film.

The North falls under two separate forest regions, each of which contains a handful of different districts. For topographic maps and backcountry trail and camping information, contact the Prince George Forest Region (☎ 250-828-4131, fax 828-4154), 1011 4th Ave in Prince George, and the Prince Rupert Forest Region (☎ 250-847-7500, fax 847-7217), 3726 Alfred Ave in Smithers. The Queen Charlotte Islands fall under the Vancouver Forest Region (☎ 250-751-7001, fax 751-7190), 2100 Labieux Rd in Nanaimo. You can also get information from the Ministry of Forests' Web page at www.for.gov.bc.ca.

PRINCE GEORGE
• **population 80,000**

In 1807, Simon Fraser's men cut the first spruce trees down to build Fort George for the North West Company. Since then, vast cutting and milling of the tree earned Prince George the title of 'spruce capital of the world,' though most of the town's spruces sit in piles instead of forests. Prince George, dominated by pulp mills (and the associated stench), is a sprawling and not very interesting or attractive town, but it serves as a useful crossroads and gateway to other northern towns.

Because it's so close to the center of BC, many tree-planters, truckers and loggers end up killing time in Prince George, which means that bustling bars, motels and hotels have sprung up throughout town to cater to visitors' needs.

The University of Northern British Columbia, which opened in 1994, offers a degree program in Native Indian affairs, which has helped to diversify the city.

Orientation & Information

Hwy 97 from Cache Creek becomes a commercial strip cutting through the center of town before heading north on its way to Dawson Creek (406km) and Mile 0 of the Alaska Hwy. (Along the way, it goes by the names Hart Hwy and Peace River Hwy.) From the downtown area, both 15th Ave and 5th Ave lead to Hwy 97, about eight blocks west of Carney St. The Yellowhead Hwy (Hwy 16) becomes Victoria St as it runs through town. At 1st Ave, Victoria St comes to an abrupt end. The Yellowhead continues on 1st Ave and crosses over the Yellowhead Bridge on its way eastward, headed for Jasper (376km) and Edmonton. On the south end of town, Hwy 16 veers westward to become the long, winding route to Prince Rupert (724km).

The downtown area is small, with little character. The main roads running east-west are 2nd, 3rd and 4th Aves, parallel to the train tracks. The main north-south thoroughfare is Victoria St; Patricia Blvd, which becomes 15th Ave, is also a major street.

The Visitor Info Centre (☎ 250-562-3700, 800-668-7646, fax 250-563-3584), 1198 Victoria St on the corner of Patricia Blvd, is open 8:30 am to 5 pm Monday through Saturday (closed weekends in winter). A second Visitor Info Centre (☎ 250-563-5493) sits 4km southwest of downtown at the junction of Hwy 97 and the Yellowhead Hwy and operates daily during summer. The city's Web site is www.tourismpg.bc.ca.

The main post office (☎ 250-561-2568) is at 1323 5th Ave on the corner of Quebec St. London Drugs, beside the bus depot in the Parkwood Place Mall, charges $3.20 for 30 minutes of Internet access at its four terminals. You can also use the Internet for free at the library (☎ 250-563-9251), 887 Dominion St in the Civic Centre.

Mosquito Books (☎ 250-563-6495), 1600 15th Ave in the Parkwood Place Mall, and the large Books & Company (☎ 250-563-

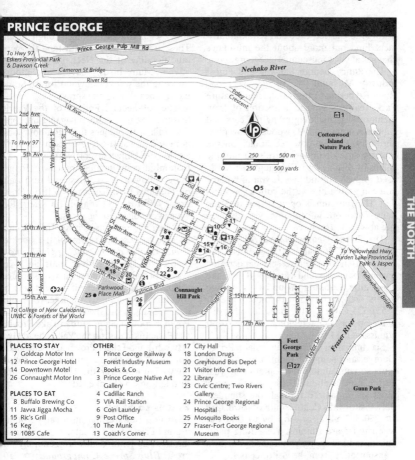

PRINCE GEORGE

PLACES TO STAY
7 Goldcap Motor Inn
12 Prince George Hotel
14 Downtown Motel
26 Connaught Motor Inn

PLACES TO EAT
8 Buffalo Brewing Co
11 Javva Jigga Mocha
15 Ric's Grill
16 Keg
19 1085 Cafe

OTHER
1 Prince George Railway &
   Forest Industry Museum
2 Books & Co
3 Prince George Native Art
   Gallery
4 Cadillac Ranch
5 VIA Rail Station
6 Coin Laundry
9 Post Office
10 The Munk
13 Coach's Corner

17 City Hall
18 London Drugs
20 Greyhound Bus Depot
21 Visitor Info Centre
22 Library
23 Civic Centre; Two Rivers
   Gallery
24 Prince George Regional
   Hospital
25 Mosquito Books
27 Fraser-Fort George Regional
   Museum

5637), 1685 3rd Ave, both carry a good selection of travel guides and maps.

The daily newspaper is the *Prince George
Citizen*. For entertainment listings, pick up
Prince George This Week. The free and colorful quarterly *Connections*, which can be
found at most cafés, covers events and activ-
ties from Prince George to Prince Rupert.

Because of all the tree-planters and
loggers passing through, Prince George has
no shortage of coin laundries, including a
nameless one downtown at 231 George St
near the corner of 2nd Ave. It's open 7 am
to 7 pm daily.

For medical services, go to the Prince
George Regional Hospital (☎ 250-565-2000),
2000 15th Ave.

Things to See & Do

The **Fraser-Fort George Regional Museum**
(☎ 250-562-1612) in Fort George Park,
southeast of the downtown area on the
corner of 20th Ave and Queensway, recently
underwent extensive renovations that resulted in a SimEx ride simulator, a public
atrium and 12,000 sq feet of exhibition
space. The renovation added more to the
interesting displays on early pioneers and

European settlement, as well as a larger area devoted to Carrier, Cree and Kwakiutl artifacts. Find out more about the museum's changes at www.museum.princegeorge.com.

The **Prince George Railway and Forest Industry Museum** (☎ 250-563-7351), 850 River Rd beside Cottonwood Island Nature Park, features a large collection of train memorabilia, including many old cars and cabooses, a unique 1903 wooden snow plow and a 1913 steam-powered crane. On the forestry side of things, there's an antique chainsaw display and a logging arch truck, used to push around logs. If you're hungry, you can grab a bite at the coffee shop and deli. The museum is open 10 am to 5 pm daily. For more information, visit its Web site at www.pgrfm.bc.ca.

The **Prince George Native Art Gallery** (☎ 250-614-7726), at 1600 3rd Ave in the Native Friendship Centre, sells handcrafted jewelry, paintings and carvings that make good gifts. Looking around is free. **Two Rivers Gallery** (☎ 250-614-7800, 888-221-1155), 725 Civic Centre Plaza, features displays on local and regional artists. Adult admission is $4.50.

Six companies operate pulp mills in Prince George, and some of them offer **forestry tours** so you can find out – literally – what all the stink is about. These free two-hour tours are organized through the summer-only Visitor Info Centre south of town. Call (☎ 250-563-5493) or stop by to find out when tours are running. Wear long pants and closed-toe shoes. You'll need your own transportation from the visitor center.

Despite all the logging happening around the town, there are 120 parks in Prince George. Right downtown, **Connaught Hill Park** sits atop the city and provides a good vantage point. This is the spot where locals probably come to 'park' on romantic summer evenings.

The 33-hectare **Cottonwood Island Nature Park**, north of downtown between the railway tracks and the river, is a protected riparian forest with a good network of trails. The park is dominated by fast-growing willow, alder and northern black cotton-

wood trees, which shed the little tufts of sticky seeds you see floating through the air. These trees are able to withstand the periodic flooding of the Nechako and Fraser Rivers. Many birds, beavers and moose thrive in the wet cottonwood forest. So do mosquitoes – bring bug spray.

The 130-hectare **Forests of the World** features 15km of easily navigable interpretive trails with plaques that tell about local flora and fauna. The forest lies at the north end of the University of Northern British Columbia campus west of town. To get there, follow 15th Ave west and turn right on Foothills Blvd. Then turn left on Cranbrook Hill Rd and left again on Kueng Rd which you follow to the forest.

When you're at the Visitor Info Centre be sure to pick up a copy of the booklet *Prince George & Area Hiking Guide* and a map of the **Heritage River Trails**, an 11km system of trails that follow the rivers around town, proving good terrain for running or walking. Around Prince George, you'll find dozens of lakes and rivers with good fishing. Popular spots include **Purden Lake Provincial Park**, 16km east on the Yellowhead Hwy (Hwy 16) and **Eskers Provincial Park**, 40km northwest of town. To get to Eskers, follow Hwy 97 north over the Hart Bridge and turn left on Chief Lake Rd.

Places to Stay

Camping Beware that most campgrounds around Prince George cater to RVs, meaning that the tenting sites are generally not great. *Blue Spruce Campground* (☎ 250-964-7272), about 5km southwest of town off the Yellowhead Hwy, offers full facilities, a store, pool and tenting sites for $15.50. *Bee Lazee Campground* (☎ 250-963-7263) 10km south on Hwy 97, features full facilities, including free hot showers, a pool and laundry machines; sites start at $14. As the name suggests, the place also includes a honey farm.

University Housing From May to mid-August, budget accommodations are available in student residences at the *College of*

New Caledonia (☎ 250-561-5849, *3330 22nd Ave*). Rooms without bedding cost $20/25 single/double. Add $5 if you need bedding. At the **University of Northern British Columbia** (*UNBC:* ☎ 250-960-6430), you can stay the night for $15 ($25 if you need bedding). Both the college and university have shared restrooms and laundry facilities. To get to UNBC, follow 15th Ave west of town. It curves south, becoming University Way, and goes to the campus.

B&Bs An association of B&B owners operates the Bed & Breakfast Hotline (☎ 250-562-2222, 977-562-2626), a free booking service that will help you arrange a B&B in your price range. The association also provides transportation from the train or bus station. For more information, visit the Web site www.princegeorgebnb.com. You can also get a listing of B&Bs from the Visitor Info Centre.

Motels & Hotels Downtown, the basic **Prince George Hotel** (☎ 250-564-7211, *487 George St*) attracts the time-biding tree planters and charges $46/60 single/double. The **Downtown Motel** (☎ 250-563-9241, *800-663-5729, 650 Dominion St*) offers basic but clean rooms for $52/56. The **Goldcap Motor Inn** (☎ 250-563-0666, *800-663-8239, 1458 7th Ave*) is very popular with business travelers. Rooms cost $60/66. Across from the Visitor Info Centre, the **Connaught Motor Inn** (☎ 250-562-4441, *800-663-6620, 1550 Victoria St*) charges $60/64 and up for its rooms.

Out on the Hwy 97 strip, **Grama's Inn** (☎ 250-563-7174, *877-563-7174, 901 Central St*) is a friendly spot (although there's no sign of Grama) with a coffee shop and rooms for $52/59. You can use the pool at nearby Esther's Inn. Behind Grama's, **Esther's Inn** (☎ 250-562-4131, *800-663-6844, 1151 Commercial Crescent*) contains a restaurant and lounge with a Polynesian theme, plus a pool and gym. Rooms cost $56/64.

Places to Eat
Despite the town's sprawling size, many of Prince George's downtown restaurants lie within easy walking distance. **Javva Jigga Mocha** (☎ 250-526-3338, *304 George St*), at 3rd Ave, serves fruit juices, coffees, soups ($4 and up) and delicious cakes and also sells second-hand books. In nice weather, eat at the outside tables or lounge around with a book in the sun.

For a healthy breakfast, lunch or light dinner, try the **1085 Cafe** (☎ 250-960-2272, *1085 Vancouver St*). This heritage-home-turned-restaurant features some reasonable prices and an outdoor patio. The **Buffalo Brewing Co** (☎ 250-564-7100, *611 Brunswick St*) is heaven for those weary of dreary Canadian lager. Good pizza and burgers average $9. You can also get steaks, salads or pasta dishes.

For dinner, try the popular **Keg** (☎ 250-563-1768, *582 George St*), at 6th Ave. Although most dinners are overpriced, with entrees starting at $17, you can get a meal-size fresh salad – a rare thing in the North – from the salad bar for $8. Across the street, similarly priced **Ric's Grill** (☎ 250-614-9096, *547 George St*) serves steaks and pasta dishes starting at $15.

Entertainment
Lots of folks congregate at the popular **Steamer's Pub** (☎ 250-562-6654), at the corner of Queensway and La Salle, south of town. It's the one with the parking lot full of pickup trucks – oh, wait, the whole town is full of pickup trucks. Anyway, you'll find it. In a town where women are vastly outnumbered, the pub **Coach's Corner** (☎ 250-563-0055, *444 George St*), in the Ramada Hotel, is a comfortable spot where single women can sip a beer without any hassles, harmless or otherwise.

For dancing, polish off your cowboy boots and swagger on over to the bustling **Cadillac Ranch** (☎ 250-563-7720, *1380 2nd Ave*), where the band or the DJ plays only country music and you can two-step to your heart's content. The younger hip-hop crowd boogies the night away at **The Munk** (☎ 250-564-3773), on the corner of 5th Ave and Dominion St. The bar doesn't get busy until after 10 pm.

THE NORTH

Getting There & Away

Air Prince George Airport (☎ 250-963-2400) is on Airport Rd off Hwy 97, 14km southeast of downtown. Several airlines fly here from Vancouver, Victoria and Calgary: Air BC, Canadian Regional (☎ 888-247-2262 for both) and WestJet (☎ 800-538-5696). Central Mountain Air (☎ 888-247-2262) also flies from Calgary. Peace Air (☎ 800-563-3060) offers scheduled trips northeast to Fort St John, Ft Nelson and Jasper (Hinton). Capital City Air (☎ 877-935-9222) serves Edmonton. For more information, visit the Web site www.airport.pg.bc.ca.

The Airporter bus (☎ 250-563-2220) will shuttle you to downtown hotels and motels for $8.

Bus The Greyhound bus depot (☎ 250-564-5454), 1566 12th Ave near the junction of Victoria St and Patricia Blvd, stays open all day, except for some afternoon closures on weekends. You can leave your stuff in the lockers here. Two buses travel daily to Jasper (five hours, $49), Dawson Creek (six hours, $51), Kamloops (eight hours, $65), Prince Rupert (12½ hours, $91), Vancouver (12½ hours, $91) and Whitehorse (28 hours, $211).

Train The VIA Rail station (☎ 800-561-8630) is at 1300 1st Ave near the top of Queensway. VIA's *Skeena* travels west three times a week to Prince Rupert ($97 one-way, 12 hours) and east another three times a week to Jasper ($76 one-way, six hours). The runs take place in daytime for maximum scenic viewing.

The BC Rail station (☎ 250-561-4033), at Terminal Blvd off Hwy 97, is southeast of town, over the Fraser River. The *Cariboo Prospector* runs south three times a week to North Vancouver ($212 one-way, 14 hours). The fare includes three meals.

Getting Around

Prince George Transit (☎ 250-563-0011) operates local buses. The one-way fare in the central zone is $1.50. Pick up a copy of the *Rider's Guide* for schedules.

The major rental companies in Prince George include Avis (☎ 250-562-2847), 1745 Victoria St; Budget (☎ 250-963-9339), 1839 1st Ave; National (☎ 250-564-4847), 1350 7th Ave; and Thrifty (☎ 250-564-3499), at 1155 1st Ave.

For taxis, try Emerald Taxi (☎ 250-563-3333) or call Prince George Taxi (☎ 250-564-4444).

PEACE RIVER & ALASKA HIGHWAY

As you travel north from Prince George, the mountains and forests give way to gentle rolling hills and farmland as Hwy 97 follows the spectacular 1923km-long Peace River. Beginning in the mid-1700s, the Cree and Beaver First Nations lived along the river and called it the 'river of beavers' for its huge populations of the thick-furred rodents. The two tribes warred periodically over the boundaries of the river, until finally coming to an agreement about 200 years ago. They renamed the river the 'Peace.' The east-flowing Peace carves the only sizeable opening through the Rockies to Alberta, making the climate in this region more similar to the prairie climate in Alberta. Unlike the rest of the province, where rain dominates, this area experiences relatively dry weather. The hot summers and fertile soil create excellent conditions for growing 90% of the province's grain. Other crops include barley, wheat, clover and alfalfa. The climate also affects the political and social slant of the northeast communities; people read Alberta newspapers, know more about Alberta politics and tend to get their city fix in Grand Prairie instead of, say, Prince George or Vancouver.

This area thrives on a natural-resource-based economy. The forestry industry fuels Mackenzie and Chetwynd, and coal extraction gave birth to the teenage town of Tumbler Ridge, while vast amounts of hydroelectricity are harnessed at the WAC Bennett and Peace River Dams, both near Hudson's Hope. Dawson Creek is an agricultural service town and the famed Mile 0 of the great Alaska Hwy, which winds through spectacular scenery as it stretches up to Fairbanks in Alaska. More wood, natural gas and oil flow out of the vast northeast, in Fort St John and Fort Nelson, where the summers are too short and the winters icy and long. Whether you're hitch-hiking, cycling, driving or watching the RVs go by, you're bound to view this area as a unique corner of the world.

PRINCE GEORGE TO DAWSON CREEK

For the first 150km north of Prince George, Hwy 97 passes Summit, Bear and MacLeod Lakes, with provincial parks and camping along the way. North of MacLeod Lake, Hwy 39 heads west for 29km to **Mackenzie** (population 5997), which sits on the southern shores of the 200km-long **Williston Lake**, the largest human-made reservoir in North America and largest lake in BC. Mackenzie's claim to tourism fame is the 'world's largest tree crusher,' a mammoth piece of machinery that sits, ironically, beside a wooded area along the town's main street. The big yellow crusher was used to clear the floodplain under what is now Williston Lake. The town's summer-only Visitor Info Centre (☎ 250-750-4497) sits on Hwy 97, where it tries to lure people into the town. Stop in at the center for regional information.

The next stop off Hwy 97, **Chetwynd** (population 3280), 300km north of Prince George, is little more than a strip of services along the highway. This industrial town contains two saw mills, a pulp mill and a gas plant; it's no surprise that such a gritty place has become known for its chainsaw art. More than 15 carvings of varying sizes are spread around town, including the bears under the 'Welcome to Chetwynd' sign. From Chetwynd, you can head south along Hwy 29 to Tumbler Ridge or north to Hudson's Hope and the WAC Bennett Dam. Halfway between Hudson's Hope and Chetwynd is **Moberley Lake Provincial Park**, a secluded park with boating and swimming on the calm lake, along with lakeside camping. To reserve the $12 sites, call BC Parks (☎ 800-689-9025).

What Time Is It Anyway?

Most of the northwestern communities share the same time zone as Alberta – Mountain Standard Time (MST) – while much of the rest of the province is on Pacific Standard Time (PST). However, the timeline does an odd little boogie through the region. Like Prince George, Mackenzie is on PST, as is Fort Nelson and all points west of it. Chetwynd, Hudson's Hope, Tumbler Ridge, Dawson Creek and Fort St John are on MST and do not observe Daylight Saving Time. This means that in winter those towns are one hour ahead of the rest of BC; in summer, everybody's on the same time.

Hudson's Hope
• population 1122

This small town, 66km north of Chetwynd on Hwy 29, overlooks the Peace River. The town's economy revolves around livestock ranching, grain and forage crops. Wildlife in the area is abundant (10 of North America's big game species live here), but the biggest draw is the WAC Bennett Dam, one of the world's largest earth-filled structures. Along with the nearby Peace River Dam, the WAC Bennett generates a significant portion of the province's hydroelectricity.

The Hudson's Hope Visitor Info Center (☎ 250-783-9154), 10507 105 Ave, is open 9 am to 5 pm daily in summer (closed on weekends the rest of the year).

The **WAC Bennett Dam** (☎ 250-783-5048), 24km west of Hudson's Hope, offers free guided tours from mid-May to mid-October. The 50-minute tour is well worth the detour. It starts with a film about constructing the land-filled dam, harnessing the Peace River's power, rerouting the river and creating BC's largest lake, the Williston Lake Reservoir. The tour takes you 150m underground to the base of the dam, where an interpreter explains how hydroelectricity works. Tours start every hour on the half-hour beginning at 9:30 am. The last tour of the day leaves at 4:30 pm. You can take a self-guided tour at the **Peace River Dam**, 6km south of Hudson's Hope on Hwy 29.

During the construction of the dams, fossils and dinosaur remains were found throughout the area. The **Hudson's Hope Museum** (☎ 250-783-5735), across from the Visitor Info Centre in town, features good fossil displays, as does the visitor center at the **Peace Canyon Dam** (☎ 250-783-9943).

Places to Stay Three municipal campgrounds lie close to town, off Hwy 29. All have free firewood and charge $7 per site. *Alwin Holland Park*, 3km southwest of town on Hwy 29, offers hiking trails, pit toilets and 12 sites. Just 4km farther is *Dinosaur Lake*, behind the Peace Canyon Dam. Here you'll find 50 sites, hiking trails, pit toilets and a boat launch. Right in town, *King Gething Park* includes flush toilets and coin-operated showers.

You can't miss either of the two hotels in town. The *Sportsman's Inn* (☎ 250-783-5523, 877-783-5520), on your left as you come into town, charges $49 and up for rooms with kitchenettes. Standard doubles at the *Peace Glen Hotel* (☎ 250-783-9966), across from the Visitor Info Centre, start at $53. Both hotels contain a restaurant and laundry facilities.

TUMBLER RIDGE
• population 2858

Mostly referred to as 'Tumbler,' this young town on Hwy 29 (94km from Chetwynd and Hwy 97) was born in the early 1980s to service the enormous Quintette Mine, the world's largest open-pit coal mine, which the mine's founders had to move a mountain to create. Despite the Quintette and newer Bullmoose Mine, the area's incredible scenery, including nearby Monkman Provincial Park, testifies that this was just woods and rivers not too long ago.

The clean, quiet newness of this town without history makes it resemble something out of the *Twilight Zone* or *X-Files*. You get the feeling that at any moment it could all just disappear, which it might. Though there's plenty of coal in the ground, slumping coal prices forced the Quintette

mine to close in early 2000. Suddenly, housing prices also plummeted, and newspapers across Canada advertised the selling of large 20-year-old houses for as little as $25,000. If the Bullmoose continues operating and coal prices take a turn for the better, the town could experience another growth spurt. Otherwise, this could be BC's newest ghost town.

For more information, stop at the Visitor Info Centre (☎ 250-242-4242) in the middle of town or visit the Web site www.district .tumbler-ridge.bc.ca. Across the street, the *Tumbler Ridge Inn* (☎ 250-242-4277), the only hotel in town, rents rooms for $55/62 single/double. The inn has its own restaurant.

Monkman Provincial Park

This park, 45km south of Tumbler Ridge on the dirt Murray River Rd, features the spectacular **Kinuseo Falls**. Just 1.5km past the park entrance is a parking lot, where a lookout lets you view the falls, which tumble down from a height of 60m – higher than Niagara Falls. You can walk along a five-minute trail to the upper lookout or carry on 20 minutes farther to the Murray River and look up at the falls. In the park, the *Kinuseo Falls Campground* (☎ 250-787-3407) offers 42 wooded campsites ($12) close to the river. From there, it's an easy 3.5km hike to the falls. To get to the park, follow Forestry Rd southwest from town to Murray River Rd. Look for the sign at the turnoff.

DAWSON CREEK
• population 11,730

Dawson Creek, 412km north of Prince George on Hwy 97, is notable as the starting point – Mile 0 – for the Alaska or Alcan (short for Alaska-Canada) Hwy. Beginning at Dawson Creek, the Alaska Hwy goes through Watson Lake and Whitehorse in the Yukon all the way to Fairbanks in Alaska.

Known only as the 'Beaver Plains,' the immediate area saw no white settlement until the turn of the 20th century. In 1879, the town's namesake, Dr. George Mercer Dawson, led a survey team through here in

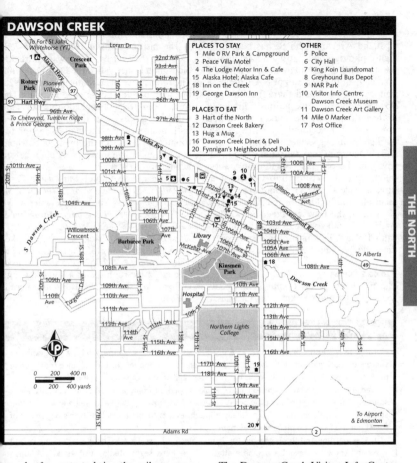

DAWSON CREEK

PLACES TO STAY
1 Mile 0 RV Park & Campground
2 Peace Villa Motel
4 The Lodge Motor Inn & Cafe
15 Alaska Hotel; Alaska Cafe
18 Inn on the Creek
19 George Dawson Inn

PLACES TO EAT
3 Hart of the North
12 Dawson Creek Bakery
13 Hug a Mug
16 Dawson Creek Diner & Deli
20 Fynnigan's Neighbourhood Pub

OTHER
5 Police
6 City Hall
7 King Koin Laundromat
8 Greyhound Bus Depot
9 NAR Park
10 Visitor Info Centre;
    Dawson Creek Museum
11 Dawson Creek Art Gallery
14 Mile 0 Marker
17 Post Office

THE NORTH

search of a route to bring the railway over the Alberta Rockies. Though the railway didn't happen until later, Dawson's studies aided settlement and prompted later exploration for oil and natural gas. Unlike many other explorers, Dawson studied Native communities and languages, which, along with his geological and botanical studies across Canada, earned him the title 'Father of Canadian Anthropology.'

When the Northern Alberta Railway (NAR) finally chugged into town in 1931, the city quickly became a thriving agricultural center.

The Dawson Creek Visitor Info Centre (☎ 250-782-9595, fax 782-9538) is in the NAR Park along the highway, which becomes Alaska Ave as it runs through town. It's open 8 am to 7 pm daily in summer, 10 am to 4 pm weekdays in winter.

The post office is at 10401 104th Ave at 10th St. The town's library (☎ 250-782-4661) is at 1001 McKellar Ave. Do your laundry at the King Koin Laundromat (☎ 250-782-2395), 1220 103rd Ave. It's open 8 am to 9 pm daily. For medical service, you can go to the Dawson Creek and District Hospital (☎ 250-782-8501), 11100 13th St.

Things to See & Do

A signpost in the middle of the intersection of 102nd Ave and 10th St has become a highly photographed post that celebrates the start of the Alaska Hwy. The real **Mile 0** is actually at the east end of NAR park – a signpost used to stand there, but the cars slowing down to look seriously hindered traffic until one day the marker got plowed down in a car accident. The site is now marked by an unspectacular cairn.

The **Dawson Creek Museum** (☎ 250-782-9595), in the old 1931 NAR train station (along with the Visitor Info Centre), features an eclectic display about area settlement and the building of the Alaska Hwy. Next door, the **Dawson Creek Art Gallery** (☎ 250-782-2601) occupies a giant grain elevator. If you're looking for some exercise, try the walking/running trails in Kinsmen Park.

Places to Stay

The *Mile 0 RV Park & Campground* (☎ 250-782-2590) is actually 2.5km along the Alaska Hwy. It offers hot showers, laundry and basic tenting sites for $10.

The historic *Alaska Hotel* (☎ 250-782-7998, 10209 10th St) is Dawson Creek's oldest hotel, once called the Dew Drop Inn. The rooms have been renovated since 1928, but the boarding-house style remains. The small rooms ($35/40 single/double) all come with a bed, desk and dresser; the shared bathroom is down the hall. Register for rooms downstairs in the lively pub, where you can enjoy live music every night before heading off to bed.

An inexpensive hotel, *Inn on the Creek* (☎ 250-782-8136, 888-782-8135, 10600 8th St, rents large rooms with a fridge, microwave and TV for $50/55. *The Lodge Motor Inn & Cafe* (☎ 250-782-4837, 800-935-3336, 1317 Alaska Ave) puts a fridge and coffeemaker in each of its rooms ($52/56). At the *Peace Villa Motel* (☎ 250-782-8175, 1641 Alaska Ave), average rooms with a TV, fridge and coffeemaker start at $59. The bonus here is the sauna.

Engineering Marvel

Northeastern British Columbia was once just a massive tract of wilderness, with a geography of squishy muskeg ground and vast prairies, so different from the rest of the province that no one really knew what to do with it. With harsh winters and short, hot summers, the massive land attracted few residents, which meant that people tapped into only a speck of its rich natural resources. While the rest of the province was settled and growing, the Peace region was just that snowy place up there somewhere. Finally, though, events totally unrelated to this big chunk of forest put the Peace on the proverbial map.

It was wartime and the US feared for its unprotected Alaska coast. There was nothing except wind and snow to prevent a Japanese attack on the long, segmented arm of Alaska's Aleutian Islands. The only way up there was by plane or by boat along the long, stormy coast. Americans needed a land route through Canada to move troops in to protect Alaska.

The engineering feat that ensued was truly incredible. With no time to waste, survey crews stormed through the vast forests, followed soon after by more than 11,000 troops, 16,000 civilian workers and 7000 pieces of equipment. From the air, it looked like a massive razor had come along and shaved a thick strip of the forest's heavy beard. More than 8000 culverts and 133 bridges closed the river gaps. A mere nine months and six days after work started, the 2453km-long route from Dawson Creek to Fairbanks, Alaska, officially opened on November 20, 1942. Though no one ever attacked Alaska, the highway was an integral part of settlement in the Peace and in the entire northern region of BC. The highway is a vital link between the US and Canada – and the scenery isn't bad either.

The *George Dawson Inn* (☎ 250-782-9151, 800-663-2745, 11705 8th St) contains a restaurant, pub and the nicest rooms in town ($70/76).

Places to Eat

Hug a Mug (☎ 250-782-6659, 1012 102nd Ave) proudly claims to serve up 'kick ass coffee.' Across the street, pick up yummy baked goods at the *Dawson Creek Bakery* (☎ 250-782-7585, 1017 102nd Ave). For breakfast or lunch, head to *Hart of the North* (☎ 250-782-7156, 1333 Alaska Hwy), where you can get a full breakfast for $5.25. The *Dawson Creek Deli & Diner* (☎ 250-782-1182), two doors down from the Alaska Hotel, offers some good lunches. The best place for dinner is the *Alaska Cafe* (☎ 250-782-7040, 10209 10th St), in the Alaska Hotel. Pasta dishes start at $8. If you're looking for a good place to sip a beer, try *Fynnigan's Neighbourhood Pub* (☎ 250-782-6462, 12121 8th St). It's a couple of kilometers south of the highway.

Getting There & Away

Air BC (☎ 888-247-2262) serves Dawson Creek Municipal Airport daily from Kelowna and Vancouver. Central Mountain Air (☎ 888-247-2262), another new affiliate of Air Canada, travels to Dawson Creek from other northern BC communities. The airport lies south of town on Hwy 2.

The Greyhound bus depot (☎ 250-782-3131) is at 1201 Alaska Ave. Buses head north daily to the Yukon, with stops at Fort St John (one hour, $13) and Fort Nelson (seven hours, $59). Buses also go south daily to Prince George (six hours, $53).

FORT ST JOHN
• population 16,448

As the Alaska Hwy heads northwest from Dawson Creek and crosses the Peace River on its way into the foothills of the Rocky Mountains, the landscape again changes, with the prairies soon left behind.

Fort St John, 75km north of Dawson Creek on Hwy 97, mainly functions as a service center for the oil and gas industries and the surrounding farms. About 18,000km of natural gas lines stretch across the province, and most of the gas comes from the area around Fort St John.

In 1794, the North West Company established the Rocky Mountain Fort at the mouth of the Moberly River, thereby creating the first non-Native settlement in BC. The fort facilitated fur trading with the Beaver and Sekani First Nations and supplied expeditions that had come to explore BC (then called New Caledonia). The fort changed locations a few times, finally settling at Fort St John. In 1851, gold brought prospectors and miners to the area, but the biggest boom came when the first oil well starting pumping in 1951.

The Visitor Info Centre (☎ 250-785-3033, fax 785-7181), 9923 96th Ave, is open 8 am to 7 pm daily in summer and 8 am to 5 pm weekdays the rest of the year.

The post office (☎ 250-785-4625) is on the corner of 101st Ave and 102nd St. The *Alaska Highway Daily News* is published in Fort St John. You'll find coin-operated laundry machines at the giant Maytag store (☎ 250-785-2920), 10703 101st Ave between 106th and 107th Sts. For medical services, go to the Fort St John General Hospital & Health Centre (☎ 250-785-6611), at 9636 100th Ave.

To learn some details of the early days, stop at the worthwhile **Fort St John-North Peace Museum** (☎ 250-787-0430), 9323 100th St, which occupies an old schoolhouse. Check out the giant stuffed polar bear, a vial filled with the first drops of oil and the 1932–48 dentist's office (and you thought going to the dentist now was bad!). It's open 9 am to 5 pm daily (closed on Sunday in winter). Admission is $2.

Places to Stay

Most of the private campgrounds along the highway are geared toward the heavy RV traffic. If you're tenting, you are much better off at one of the two excellent nearby provincial parks; you can reserve sites at both of them by calling BC Parks (☎ 800-689-9025). For local information on both parks, call ☎ 250-787-3407. You can fish or boat off the east shore of Charlie Lake when you stay at *Beatton Provincial Park*, 4km north of Fort St John and 8km off the highway on 271 Rd. *Charlie Lake Provincial Park*, about 10km north of town, contains a popular campground. Both parks offer pit toilets, walking trails, lake access and campsites for $12.

You'll find the cheapest accommodations in the center of the city at *Cedar Lodge Motor Inn* (☎ 250-250-785-8107, 800-661-2210, 9824 99th Ave). Though the name conjures up visions of a log cabin, the building looks more like an everyday motel. The clean rooms go for $45/55 single/double. Nearby, the *Four Seasons Motor Inn* (☎ 250-785-6647, 800-523-6677, 9810 100th St) offers a similar value, with rooms priced at $50/60.

Out on the highway, the *Northwoods Inn* (☎ 250-787-1616, 10627 Alaska Rd) features a restaurant, lounge, pub and live cabaret show. Rooms cost $50/55, including breakfast. The giant *Alexander Mackenzie Inn* (☎ 250-785-8364, 800-663-8313, 9223 100th St) charges $61/67 for its 113 nice rooms.

Places to Eat

Grab a coffee, a jumbo homemade muffin and lunch at *Terri's Lunch & Cappuccino Bar* (☎ 250-787-8424, 9905 100th Ave). Good sandwiches cost $4.50. The best place in town for a casual meal is *Teabag Annie's* (☎ 250-787-9444, 10615 102nd St), a ways off the highway. Wash down dinner ($9 to $20) with a margarita ($5). For average pub food but good atmosphere, try *Outriggers Pub* (☎ 250-785-6464, 10419 Alaska Rd), where the burgers will set you back $8.

Getting There & Away

The Fort St John Airport is 10km east of town. Canadian Regional (☎ 888-247-2262) flies here from Vancouver; Central Mountain Air (888-247-2262) provides service from Calgary.

The Greyhound bus depot (☎ 250-785-6695) is at 10355 101st Ave at 104th St. Two buses depart daily; one heads north to Fort Nelson (four hours, $50 one-way), and the other travels south to Prince George (7½ hours, $62 one-way).

FORT ST JOHN TO FORT NELSON

As you continue up the Alaska Hwy, you will have plenty of time to marvel at the scenery as the road gradually leaves the foothills and begins to climb up the Rocky Mountains. Most towns on the highway have only one or two service stations. The first place you'll pass is **Wonowon** or 'one-o-one,' named for its place at Mile 101 on the highway. During highway construction, soldiers were stationed here to staff the Blueberry Checkpoint, where anyone traveling the road would have to stop. The soldiers would search your car and send you back if you didn't have enough provisions (and spare auto parts) to make it through the vast wilderness that lay ahead.

Next, you will pass **Pink Mountain**, so named for the incredible pink hue the mountain takes on at sunrise. Before hitting Fort Nelson, you'll pass by a few provincial parks, all of which are nice spots to camp, with water and pit toilets. First, at Kilometer 278, is the **Buckinghorse River Provincial Park**, where you might see moose grazing alongside the river if you get up early. The 34 sites cost $12. **Prophet River Provincial Recreation Area**, at Kilometer 350, offers 12 sites ($12) and access to a section of the original Alaska Hwy. At Kilometer 430, you'll see signs to **Andy Bailey Provincial Recreation Area**, 11km off the highway on a gravel road. The park enjoys access to quiet Jackfish Lake. The fee is by donation only. For information on all three parks, call ☎ 250-787-3404.

Fort Nelson
• population 4700

The last sizeable town in BC, Fort Nelson boasts the northernmost traffic light and the northernmost golf course. Like Fort St John, Fort Nelson started as a fur-trading post, but the town didn't flourish until the Alaska Hwy came through. But 'flourish' is perhaps too grand of a word. Up here in the northeastern portion of the province, bears outnumber people 16 to 1. Only 14 cops work in the entire area, and if there's a storm, it'll be a long while until anyone gets there to help. First Nations people – mostly Dene – make up about 15% of the population.

Fort Nelson, 483km north of Dawson Creek, mainly functions as a service center and industrial town, home to Canada's largest gas processing plant and BC's largest wood products plant (which is bigger than 13 football fields). Though the winters are long, dark and cold, that's when most of the logging happens, when the muskeg freezes over and trucks can get into places not accessible in summer. Almost anyone driving the Alaska Hwy stops here, mostly because it's a long way to anywhere else. To serve this traffic, motels and restaurants have sprung up along the highway.

The Visitor Info Centre (☎ 250-774-2541) is just off the highway on the west end of town. It offers a free Welcome Visitor Program (774-2541) at 6:45 pm Monday to Thursday in June and July. Loggers, Mounties, trappers and other speakers from the community will give you great insight into life in the north.

The **Fort Nelson Heritage Museum**, also at the west end of town, shows a movie about the highway's construction. You can check out a trapper's cabin or get a close-up look at a big stuffed moose. The museum is open 8:30 am to 7:30 pm daily, mid-May to mid-September.

If your legs are cramped from sitting in the car all day, take a walk along the trails at the 400-hectare **Fort Nelson Community Forest**. Bring bug spray. To get there, turn onto Simpson Trail north of the highway, then take a left on Mountain View and follow it to the end.

Places to Stay & Eat If you want to camp close to town, go to the **Westend Campground & RV Park** (☎ 250-774-2340), two blocks west of town. The full facilities include laundry and showers. Tent sites are $13. If you're cycling, you'll definitely want to hit **Mel's Bike Repair & Bed n' Breakfast** (☎ 250-774-2254), where you can clean up and tune up for $25, including breakfast. Only cyclists can stay here. Call for directions.

The new, quiet **Almada Inn** (☎ 250-774-2844, 5035 51st Ave W) charges $49/59 single/double for nice rooms with TVs. An older but clean place, **The Pioneer Motel** offers rooms for $50/55. The bustling **Blue Bell Inn** contains a restaurant, convenience store and rooms with kitchenettes starting at $54. Avoid the large Fort Nelson Hotel. It's dirty, old and overpriced.

The most popular spot in town for a meal is **Dan's Neighbourhood Pub** (☎ 250-774-3929, 4204 50th Ave N), where you can get a meal-size salad or burger for $7. An 8oz steak is $13.

FORT NELSON TO WATSON LAKE

At Kilometer 393, past Fort Nelson, the Liard Hwy (Hwy 77) heads north to the Northwest Territories, Fort Simpson and Nahanni National Park. At Kilometer 600, 140km west of Fort Nelson, the highway passes through the north end of beautiful **Stone Mountain Provincial Park**, in the eastern Muskwa Ranges of the Rockies; the 'stone mountain' in question is Mt St Paul (2127m). The incredible vistas at the 1267m Summit Pass will leave you breathless. The park's 28-site campground ($12), open May to October, offers access to hiking trails and backcountry camping. Look for the dramatic **hoodoos** – eroded stone pillars – at Wokkpash Creek.

The **Kwadacha Wilderness Provincial Park & Recreation Area**, 160km southwest of Fort Nelson, and the **Northern Rocky Mountains Provincial Park** are primarily accessed by plane. The parks see little human traffic and mainly exist to preserve animal habitat.

At the tiny town of **Toad River**, a former hunting lodge that was opened by two brothers who worked as surveyors for the Alaska Hwy project still rents out rooms ($47/54 single/double). The lodge's restaurant ceiling is lined with hundreds of baseball caps from around the world.

Muncho Lake Provincial Park

Spruce forests, vast rolling mountains and some truly breathtaking scenery surround Muncho Lake Provincial Park (☎ 250-787-3407), located at Kilometer 650. This 88,412-hectare park lies along the emerald-green

Muncho Lake, and the highway curves along the lake's west shore. 'Muncho' means 'big lake' in the Tagish language, and at 12km long, it's one of the largest natural lakes in the Rockies. For the highway construction crews, cutting the rocky bluff along the lakeside was the most difficult and costly part of the construction. Today, it's an unforgettable piece of road. Stone sheep often gather alongside the highway to lick the artificial accumulations of salt from the stones. The mountains are part of the Terminal Range, which mark the northernmost section of the Rocky Mountains, ending at Liard River (60km northwest). The mountains extending northward into the Yukon and Alaska are the Mackenzies, which are geologically different. Muncho Lake has two camping areas: the *Strawberry Flats Campground* or the *MacDonald Campground*, 11km farther north. Each campground contains 15 sites for $12.

Liard River Hotsprings Provincial Park

This park's hot mineral springs have been used for centuries by Natives, trappers and explorers and could very well be the best natural hot springs you'll ever dip into. The underground bubbling springs create a lush boreal marsh and tropical vegetation that seems very out of place this far north. An incredible 250 species of plants, including 14 different varieties of orchids, grow in this unique ecosystem.

Just a 10-minute walk along a boardwalk from the parking lot leads to the large Alpha pool, where you can sit and soak for hours. If you get tired of that, walk around and check out some of the strikingly green ferns or colorful wildflowers that thrive in the heat and humidity. From the Alpha pool, stroll five minutes farther up the boardwalk to the deeper, slightly cooler Beta pool. Fewer people come here, so take the opportunity to jump in and swim over to the sides where it's shallower; be sure to let the warm bottom mud ooze through your toes.

The park's *campground* has 52 sites, some of which you can reserve by calling ☎ 800-689-9025. Rangers run interpretive programs throughout the summer. Visiting the pools is free, but beware that the pools can get really busy in July and August. If you can't come in the spring or fall, try coming later at night, when the families have gone to bed. The park gate closes from 10 pm to 6 am; you can still go in the springs but if you're not camping in the park, you need to leave your car outside the gate and walk in. Regardless, this is definitely a worthwhile stop.

Watson Lake, Yukon

The Alaska Hwy zigzags in and out of BC and the Yukon before leaving BC for good at Watson Lake, a service center and almost inevitable stop for people traveling through to Alaska or back down into BC. You cannot miss the **Signpost Forest** on the side of the highway. The 'signpost' was originally a directional sign put up by the army in 1942. One day a homesick soldier working on the Alaska Hwy nailed up a lone sign from his hometown of Danville, Illinois, and all hell broke loose. Suddenly, anyone stopping through town had to nail up a sign and now, at last count, 42,215 signs welcome you to Watson Lake.

In behind the 'forest,' you'll find the bustling Watson Lake Visitors Info Centre (☎ 867-536-7469), which is open 8 am to 8 pm daily throughout summer. The center has a small museum and shows an interesting 18-minute movie on the building of the highway.

YELLOWHEAD HIGHWAY

The 3185km Yellowhead Hwy (Hwy 16) actually starts on the Canadian Prairies at Winnipeg, Manitoba, climbing west through the provinces of Saskatchewan, Alberta and BC. In the North, it is the only road that connects the east and west sides of the province. VIA Rail's *Skeena* line follows the Yellowhead from Jasper to Prince Rupert.

From Prince George, the highway meanders along into the heart of the Lakes Disrict at Burns Lake, through the alpine outdoor adventure town of Smithers to the Hazeltons, an area rich in First Nations history. From there, it cuts southwest to Terrace, a service town that leads into the rich Nass Valley. The 147km drive from Terrace to Prince Rupert is consistently rated one of the most scenic in the province; the Skeena River flows along while verdant mountains and wildlife line the rolling road. From Prince Rupert, ferries cruise in every direction: north to Alaska, south to Vancouver Island or west to the Queen Charlotte Islands, where the Yellowhead Hwy begins again, the only paved road on the islands.

VANDERHOOF
• population 4470

The first settlement of any size west of Prince George (97km away), Vanderhoof is mainly a service center most noted for its annual international air show held the fourth weekend in July. Tucked in the fertile Nechako River Valley, this town, which occupies the geographical center of the province, has prime grazing lands; cattle, buffalo and dairy farming, along with forestry, provide the main sources of income here. Vanderhoof is Dutch for 'of the farm,' which is appropriate as it was the first permanent agricultural settlement in the province.

The Visitor Info Centre (☎ 250-567-2124) is at 2353 Burrard Ave. There is also a smaller, summer-only information center off the highway on the grounds of the Heritage Village. The village displays eleven heritage buildings including a museum, jailhouse and 1920s farmhouse.

Places to Stay & Eat

The *Riverside Park Campground* (☎ 250-567-4710, 3100 Burrard Ave), on the north end of town overlooking the Nechako River Migratory Bird Sanctuary, offers showers, firewood and some shady sites for $14. Though run-down, the absolutely cheapest place in town is the *Nechako River Motel* (☎ 250-567-2717, 292 Loop Rd), where riverside lodgings start at $35. On the highway, the *Siesta Inn* (☎ 250-567-2365) offers clean, basic rooms for $45/55 single/

double. The best place in town is the *North Country Inn* (☎ 250-567-3057, 2575 Burrard Ave), with a good restaurant and modern, tidy rooms with fridges for $55/62. Add $7 for a kitchen.

Get good coffee in town at *The Grind* (☎ 250-567-2253, 2448 Burrard Ave), which also offers Internet access. The *OK Café* (☎ 250-567-5252), at the historical village, serves breakfast ($8) and sandwiches ($7).

FORT ST JAMES NATIONAL HISTORIC SITE

From Vanderhoof, Hwy 27 heads 66km north to the Fort St James National Historic Site (☎ 250-996-7191), a former North West Company trading post on the southeastern shore of Stuart Lake.

Simon Fraser, searching for a navigable route to the Pacific Ocean, founded this outpost as a place to trade furs with area trappers, mostly Carrier people, who were a branch of the Dene First Nations. The Carriers got their name from the mourning ritual of widows, who carried the ashes of deceased husbands in pouches on their backs until a memorial potlatch could be held. Early French-speaking traders referred to them as 'Porteurs' (porters), which the English-speaking traders later changed to 'Carriers.'

Fraser's post became a commercial center and headquarters of the district of New Caledonia. In 1821, the fort became a Hudson's Bay Company outpost and operated until the early 20th century. Though the relationship between the fur traders and Carriers was an amicable one, it altered some of the hunter-gatherer instincts of the Carrier people and introduced a new kind of greed and materialism, all of which changed the Carriers forever.

In 1971, the fort underwent a major restoration to bring it back to its 1896 glory. After an incredible restoration job, today the site gives visitors an interesting look into recent yet pivotal history. Plus, it's free. An audio tour takes you though the fort, or you can join a guided tour from May to September. In July and August, street performers dressed in period finery pretend they are busily living in 1896. The site is open 9 am to 5 pm daily, May to September.

FRASER LAKE

West of Vanderhoof, you'll come across some small towns with the usual run of campgrounds and motels. Among them, Fraser Lake is known for a large populations of white trumpeter swans that stops by on its migratory path. The lake itself is connected to the Nechako River by the .8km-long Nautley River, touted to rank among the shortest rivers in the world. Many area residents work at the nearby Endako Mine, a large open pit mine that produces molybdenum (an active ingredient in steel hardener and lubricant). You can go on a free, two-hour **mine tour** from June through August. Call ☎ 250-699-6211 to arrange times.

BURNS LAKE

• **population 2523**

Burns Lake, 229km west of Prince George, serves as the center of the Lakes District and northern gateway to Tweedsmuir Provincial Park. It also hosts the popular **Burns Lake Bluegrass Festival**, which takes place in mid-July. Out in the middle of the lake is **Deadman's Island Provincial Park**, the province's smallest provincial park, so named after an accident killed two men working on the on the Grand Trunk Railway.

The carved trout sign that welcomes you to Burns Lake is a testimony to the serious anglers who descend upon the many area lakes in spring and in summer to catch rainbow and cutthroat trout, char, kokanee, ling cod and salmon, among other fish.

Like other towns along the Yellowhead, Burns Lake experienced its population boom during the construction of the Grand Trunk Railway. Today, it is primarily a lumber town and a worthwhile place to stock up on groceries or to sleep for a night. Like most people, you'll probably want to head to the wilderness.

For information on the best fishing holes, area fishing lodges or boat rentals, contact the Visitor Info Centre (☎ 250-692-3773), 540 Hwy 16. It's open 9 am to 5 pm daily (closed on weekends in summer).

One of the best spots for canoeing, kayaking and fishing is 177km-long **Babine Lake**, 34km north of Burns Lake on the Babine Lake Rd. The stunning lake is well worth the detour. To get there, turn off Hwy 16 across from the Husky gas station. You can also access the lake from the towns of Topley Landing and Granisle. Turn north at Topley onto the Topley Landing Rd.

Places to Stay & Eat

You cannot go wrong at the **Burns Lake Municipal Campground**, beside the lake, and the **Len Radley Memorial Park Campground**. The sites are – get this – free. Yes, free, though you can only stay for 72 hours. Turn south (left if you're coming from the east) at the carved trout sign.

The **KOA Burns Lake** (☎ 250-692-3105, 800-562-0905), 4km east of the town off Hwy 16 on Freeport Rd, offers nice tent sites away from the RVs, with picnic tables and free showers. Sites cost $12. You can also camp at two nearby provincial parks, both accessed by a gravel road just west of the town. **Ethel F. Wilson Memorial Provincial Park** (☎ 250-847-7659), 24km north of Burns Lake on Pinkut Lake, and **Pendleton Bay Provincial Park**, 10km farther, both have pit toilets but no showers; sites cost $12.

Right in the heart of town is the **Lakeland Hotel** (☎ 250-692-7771, 888-441-2999, 329 Hwy 16), with a good restaurant, bar and small but tidy rooms for $45/49 single/double.

Grab a coffee, check your email and have a light lunch at **Redfern's Coffee House** (☎ 250-692-7379, 79 3rd Ave), at Hwy 16. Just off the highway by the trout sign, Mulvaney's Pub (☎ 250-692-3078) offers burgers and other pub fare.

TWEEDSMUIR PROVINCIAL PARK (NORTH)

Encompassing more than 981,000 hectares, Tweedsmuir is the province's second-largest provincial park. On the north and northwest, the park is bordered by the Ootsa-Whitesail Lakes Reservoir, on the west and southwest by the Coast Mountains and on the east by the Interior Plateau. The park is divided into North Tweedsmuir and South Tweedsmuir by the Dean River. The only road in the park, Hwy 20, runs through the southern section near Bella Coola on the central coast (see the Cariboo-Chilcotin chapter). Otherwise, you need to boat in from the Ootsa-Whitesail Lakes Reservoir, or access the park by floatplane.

Unlike many parks named for British dignitaries, Tweedsmuir took its moniker from someone who actually saw the park. In fact, John Buchan, Baron Tweedsmuir of Elsfield and also Canada's 15th governor general, traveled extensively through the park on horseback and by floatplane before it was ever named for him.

Wildlife abounds in this remote area and includes woodland caribou, goats, moose, black and grizzly bears and wolves. Up in the air, look for willow ptarmigans, gray-crowned rosy finches and golden-crowned sparrows. In the Nechako Reservoir, look for the fish-hunting ospreys in the fallen logs.

From Burns Lake, you can access North Tweedsmuir by following Hwy 35 south and catching the free ferry across Francois Lake. Follow signs to the boat launch and park ranger station at Chikamin Bay (staffed May through October).

Most people will spend time on Eutsuk Lake, which forms a system of joining waterways with Ootsa, Whitesail and Tetachuck Lakes. Except Eutsuk, most lakes were dramatically raised in 1952 with the

Caribou call Tweedmuir home.

building of the Kenney Dam and the creation of the Nechako Reservoir. The raised waters were deemed necessary to generate enough power to serve the giant Alcan aluminum smelter in Kitimat.

Anyone venturing into wild Tweedsmuir should plan carefully and be ready to experience full wilderness camping and boating. You will need to be totally self-sufficient and prepared for any conditions.

HOUSTON
• population 3935

On your way west from Burns Lake, you'll pass through the small town of Houston, at the confluence of the Morice and Bulkley Rivers. Formerly the designated railway tie-cutting center during the building of the Grand Trunk Railway, it's become a big fly-fishing spot, as you might guess from the rather bizarre giant (18m-long) fly-fishing rod standing erect in the middle of Steelhead Park.

SMITHERS
• population 5800

In the heart of the pretty Bulkley Valley, surrounded by the stunning Hudson Bay, Bulkley and Babine Mountains, Smithers prides itself on being 'the town for all seasons' and has turned itself into a hotbed of outdoor adventure and activity.

Smithers was chosen as the divisional headquarters of the Grand Trunk Railway and was the first village to be incorporated in BC (1921). It became a town in 1967 and today is a government and administrative center with a casual alpine feel that's epitomized by Alpine Al, a wooden statue standing at the head of Main St. Al, along with his 10-foot-long alpenhorn, is the town's distinctive mascot.

The people who live here absolutely love Smithers and are protective of its bounty. The politically active, artistic community recognizes the need for tourism but yearns to maintain the town's almost secretive seclusion by vehemently resisting too much growth. If you respect the place – whether you want to kick back and sip a coffee, ski, ice-climb, hike or roar down a river –

Smithers and its people will welcome you with open arms.

Smithers and nearby Telkwa contain the area's best restaurants and accommodations.

Information

The Visitor Info Centre (☎ 250-847-5072, 800-542-6673), 1411 Court St, is across the parking lot from the Buckley Valley Museum and Central Park Building. It's open 8:30 am to 6 pm weekdays and 9 am to 5 pm weekends in July and August; 9 am to 5 pm weekdays at other times. For more information, you can also visit the town's Web site at www.bulkley.net/~smicham.

If you're looking to surf the Internet, head to the Internet Café (☎ 250-877-6228, 877-775-6227), 1188 Main St, where cyber access costs $8 per hour. It's open 10 am to 7 pm daily.

The best place in town for 'unofficial' information is Mountain Eagle Books & Bistro (☎ 250-847-5245), 3775 3rd St. Home to a great selection of regional books and a bulletin board with various postings, it's a community gathering spot where people sip lattes and discuss the news of the day.

The art, culture and outdoor quarterly *Connections* is published in Smithers. It will tell you what's happening in the area. Also look for the *Interior News*, a weekly that comes out on Wednesday. For extensive trail descriptions and topographic maps of the area, pick up a copy of *Trails to Timberline* ($17.50), an invaluable book if you're planning on spending any time hiking around.

Wash your body, your car and your clothes at Wash the Works (☎ 250-847-4177), 4148 Hwy 16, where the facilities range from coin-operated laundry machines to a car wash; showers cost $4 or $5 with a towel.

Things to See & Do

In the old courthouse now called the Central Park Building, at the top of Main St and Hwy 16, you'll find the **Bulkley Valley Museum** (☎ 250-847-5322), which features exhibits on Smithers' pioneer days. In the same building, the **Smithers Art Gallery** (☎ 250-847-3898) displays works by local and regional artists. Both are free and open

daily in July and August, with limited hours the rest of the year. If taxidermy's your thing, check out **Adam's Igloo Wilderness Museum** (☎ 250-847-3188), just west of the airport on Hwy 16, where a collection of almost 200 stuffed animals (not the cuddly kind) is on display. The museum is open 9 am to 6 pm daily. Admission is $4.

Driftwood Canyon Provincial Park, 11km northeast of Smithers, was created in 1976 to protect the rich fossil beds that were discovered around 1900 along the Driftwood Creek. Formations found in the shale indicate that plants, insects and animals lived in the area some 50 million years ago. Geologists believe the site was formerly a lake bottom that went dry through volcanic activity and ice ages. Over time, the running creek eroded through the sedimentation, finally exposing the fossil beds.

Today, you can walk to a viewing platform on the east bank of the creek, where interpretive panels describe the area's geological significance. You're not allowed to remove any fossils from the park. To get to the park, follow Hwy 16 for 3km east of Smithers, then turn onto Babine Lake Rd. From there, turn left on Telkwa High Rd, then right onto Driftwood Rd.

Five kilometers past Driftwood Canyon, you'll reach the parking lot and access point to the west end of the **Babine Mountains Recreation Area**, a 32,000-hectare park deep in the glorious backcountry wilderness of the Babine Range of the Skeena Mountains. In 1999, another 6500 hectares called the Driftwood Extension was added to the park. Trails to glacier-fed lakes and subalpine meadows provide accessible hiking and mountain biking in summer. In winter, the trails make excellent routes for snowshoeing and cross-country skiing. Look for healthy populations of moose, marmots and mountain goats. You can backcountry camp here (see Places to Stay, later, for details). Ask at the Smithers Visitor Info Centre for information on specific trails in the park.

The 1830m **Kathlyn Glacier**, left over from the Ice Age, carved a mile-wide gulch into Hudson Bay Mountain and currently recedes a bit every year. Gushing waterfalls cascade off her back, providing spectacular views in summer and world-class ice climbing in winter. From the parking lot, a short, easy trail leads to a viewing platform at the base of the glacier's **Twin Falls**. More adventurous types can do the steep three-hour climb to the toe of the glacier. Less adventurous types can view the glacier from the highway, a little farther west of town. To get there, drive 10km west of Smithers and follow signs to the parking lot on Kathlyn Glacier Rd.

Activities

Fat-tire riding is popular throughout the Bulkley Valley, and if you're interested in **mountain biking**, you'll find some excellent maintained trails for all levels of rider. Pick up a copy of the $5 *Northwest Trails: A Guide to Mountain Biking in the Bulkley Valley* or stop by McBike & Sport (☎ 250-847-5009), 1191 Main St, for trail information. The shop rents bikes for $20/30 per half day/full day and leads guided tours, including a one-hour scenic trip for all levels along the Perimeter Trail ($25). Hard-core bike riders can join like-minded types on daylong tours that start at $100.

For an injection of pure adrenaline, join a **white-water rafting** trip on the Babine River to Hazelton in the Bulkley River Canyon. Suskwa Adventure Outfitters (☎ 250-847-2885, 888-546-7238) offers full-day trips on weekends for $100, including equipment, lunch and taxes.

White-water kayaking is also popular on the Bulkley River. Rent kayaks and gear at Aquabatics (☎ 250-847-3678, 800-748-2333), 1960 Hudson Bay Mountain Rd. Prices average $25 per day for experienced paddlers. One of the best places to go is Tatlow Falls, where an annual Whitewater Rodeo takes place in late July or August, depending on water levels. Crowds gather along the riverbank to watch expert paddlers perform tricks. Even if you're not around for the rodeo, you can still watch paddlers playing in the falls throughout summer. Call Aquabatics for more information.

For **skiing**, try Ski Smithers, a low-key ski resort on Hudson Bay Mountain, with 34 mostly intermediate runs. Facilities include two lodges, a lounge and rental shop and ski school. Lift tickets cost $26/32 for a half day/full day. Ski package rentals cost $20, and snowboards with boots are $34. To get to the mountain from Hwy 16, go south on King St to Railway Ave. Turn left and follow the tracks. The road soon turns into Hudson Bay Mountain Rd, which leads to the ski hill.

Anyone interested in learning more about ice or **rock climbing** should contact Bear Mountaineering (☎ 250-847-2854, info@bearmountaineering.bc.ca). A two-day basic rock- or ice-climbing course costs $200.

Special Events

If you're around the third weekend in July, do not miss the annual **Midsummer Festival**, which features live music and good community fun. Tickets for the weekend cost $30, or you can volunteer and get in for free. Find out more at Mountain Eagle Books or at www.bvfms.org.

Places to Stay

Easy crash-for-a-night camping is available at the *Riverside Municipal Park* (☎ 250-847-1600), 2km northwest of town; the park offers unshaded sites for $12 and pit toilets but no showers. To get there, follow Victoria Dr off Frontage Rd on the north side of Hwy 16. You can also walk from downtown via the Perimeter Trail (15 minutes).

Camp in a beautiful setting at *Tyee Lake Provincial Park* (☎ 250-846-5511) in nearby Telkwa, a few kilometers east of Smithers on Hwy 16. The park contains flush toilets, showers, lake access and 55 wooded sites, 10 of which you can reserve through BC Parks. Call ☎ 800-689-9025. Sites are $17.50.

You can camp in the backcountry or use the new Joe L'Orsa backcountry cabin in the Silver King Basin for $5 per night. The cabin can sleep up to 20 people, but you must have your own gear, including a sleeping pad. Call the BC Parks office (☎ 250-847-7320) before you go so that they can monitor how many people are using the cabin at a time.

Many motels line Hwy 16, and most charge $60 to $90. *Fireweed Motor Inn* (☎ 250-847-2208, 1515 Main St N), just north of the highway beside the fire hall, offers basic but clean rooms with TVs and coffeemakers for $52/57 single/double. The popular *Hudson Bay Lodge* (☎ 250-847-4581, 800-663-5040, 3251 Hwy 16) is always a hub of activity. It contains a dining room, café, pub and lots of large rooms starting at $75 a night.

For a real treat, stay at the *Logpile Lodge* (☎ 250-847-5152, logpile@bulkley.net), a beautifully hand-constructed Swiss-style chalet overlooking the scenic mountains and valley. The private rooms, which come with balconies and private bathrooms, range from $95 to $130, including breakfast. Call ahead for reservations and directions.

Places to Eat

Get your morning cup of coffee or join the government workers for lunch at *Java's Fine Coffees* (☎ 250-847-5505, 3735 Alfred Ave). Soups cost a mere $3 or $7 with a sandwich. At the *Mountainside Cafe* (☎ 250-847-3455, 3763 4th Ave), a good sandwich costs $4.

For a lively pub atmosphere, good beer and decent food, head to the *The Alpenhorn Pub & Bistro* (☎ 250-847-5366, 1261 Main St). The fireplace in the middle of the pub makes it cozy. Try the Dog Breath Burger, which is smothered in onions, for $7.

Two of the area's best restaurants lie just east of Smithers in Telkwa. The *Crocodile Café* (☎ 250-846-9268), on Hwy 16, serves burgers and sandwiches at lunch and big portions of Mexican cuisine at dinner. Also on the highway, *Picco Bella Trattoria* (☎ 250-846-9866) serves authentic Italian food in a warm, intimate atmosphere. The eight tables are covered with traditional red-and-white checkered table clothes, and the service is excellent. Try the pasta primavera for $14 and chicken cacciatore for $15.

Getting There & Away

The Smithers Airport is 4km west of town off Hwy 16. Canadian Regional Airlines (☎ 888-247-2262) offers scheduled service from Vancouver, and Central Mountain Air (☎ 888-247-2262) flies here regularly from Prince George. Many charters also use the airport.

The Greyhound bus depot (☎ 250-847-2204), 4011 Hwy 16, is two blocks west of Main St. Daily buses head west to Terrace and Prince Rupert and east to Prince George, Jasper and Edmonton. The VIA Rail *Skeena* train stops through here on its way west to Prince Rupert and east to Jasper. The station is behind the government building at the south end of Main St.

NEW HAZELTON & AROUND

Named after the hazelnut bushes growing along the river terraces, the distinct towns of New Hazelton, Hazelton and South Hazelton sit within the walls of the rugged Rocher de Boule ('Mountain of Rolling Rock'), near the confluence of the Skeena and Bulkley Rivers.

The Skeena River, the 'River of Mist,' has long been an integral part of the area. The Gitksan and Wet'suwet-en people, who have lived in the area for more than 7000 years, first navigated cedar canoes along the treacherous Skeena all the way out to the coast. Fur trappers arrived in the area around 1866, as did workers on the Collins Overland Telegraph, which originated in San Francisco. The area fully opened up to white settlers from 1891 to 1912, when stern-wheelers braved the Skeena's rapids, bringing gold- and silver-seekers from Port Essington to the upriver terminus at Hazelton.

The town became an active and boisterous commercial center. Soon, the influx of people spread, scattering inland to find riches in the mines, to stake land claims and build farms. When the Grand Trunk Railway construction crews rolled through in 1914, they brought more people, more rowdiness and some general confusion about which Hazelton was which. Here's the deal: Hazelton (also called the Old Town) was the first settlement, established long before the train showed up. Once it did, Hazelton was slated to become a ghost town with the founding of the 'South' and 'New' Hazeltons. The new communities vied for the position of commercial center and remained in a bitter and ridiculous battle while the train went bankrupt, through WWI and the Great Depression. Today, New Hazelton (population 1169) is the commercial center; South Hazelton is essentially tacked onto it. The original Hazelton is a pioneer town with shops and the 'Ksan Historical Village. Between Hazelton and New Hazelton is Two Mile, exactly two miles from either town. Its strategic spot made it a busy brothel town, populated mostly by European women. Though a quiet spot today, the town maintains its most interesting motto: 'historically non-conforming.'

The area's Visitor Info Centre (☎ 250-842-6071) sits at the junction of Hwys 16 and 62. Upstairs is a small museum with some interesting displays on early settlers. Ask for a copy of the *Hands of History* brochure, a driving tour covering area highlights, from the Gitksan totem poles in Kispiox and Kitwanga (see the Stewart-Cassiar Hwy section, later in this chapter) to scenic Ross Lake Provincial Park. The busy visitor center is open 8 am to 7 pm daily from June through September and 9 am to 5 pm weekdays the rest of the year.

'Ksan Historical Village

This replicated Gitksan Native village (☎ 250-842-5544, 877-842-5518) may be the area's big tourist draw, but it's somewhat of a disappointment for all the hype it gets. For $2, you can walk around the totems and longhouses, one of which is a museum; another is a gift shop. In order to get anything out of the place, you really have to do the one-hour guided tour for $8. It takes you through the Frog House of the Distant Past, the Wolf House of Feasts and the Fireweed House of Masks and Robes. Along the way, you'll learn about Gitksan arts, culture and beliefs, but it's hard to shake the feeling that you're being herded through for your tourist dollars, which makes the experience lose authenticity. The tours leave every hour on the half hour. The village is open 8 am to 7 pm daily from mid-May to mid-October.

Places to Stay & Eat

The *'Ksan Campground* (☎ 250-842-5297), just outside the historical village, offers campsites for $15. You'll find some excellent sites ($12) at *Seeley Lake Provincial Park* (☎ 250-847-7320), 8km west of New Hazelton. Facilities include pit toilets but no showers. Panels at the park tell you about the unique marsh ecosystem, and most campsites lie alongside the marsh, providing easy access to the lake. From Seeley, it's a simple and worthwhile venture to nearby Ross Lake Provincial Park, a scenic day-use spot that's a perfect place for a hike and picnic lunch.

Ask at the Visitor Info Center for a list of area B&Bs.

In New Hazelton, stay at the *Robber's Roost Motel* (☎ 250-842-6916), Hwy 16 at Laurier St, where the rooms start at $40. Nearby, *28 Inn* (☎ 250-842-6006, 4545 Hwy 16) contains a restaurant, pub and rooms starting at $50.

The *New Hazelton Deli* (☎ 250-842-5622, 4361 Hwy 16) serves soups and sandwiches. Both the food and views are excellent at the *Hummingbird Restaurant* (☎ 250-842-5628), on Hwy 62 between New Hazelton and Hazelton. *The Garage Pub & Grill* (☎ 250-842-5488), in a renovated 1950 gas station in South Hazelton, features a fun atmosphere and large pub menu. Burgers are $9, and pasta dishes cost around $10.

TERRACE
• population 11,400

Surrounded by mountains in the lush Skeena Valley, 147km east of Prince Rupert, Terrace has become a logging, government, service and transportation center.

Its name comes from the natural flat benches – resembling terraces – on which the town is built. Terrace adopted the Kermode bear as its mascot, though your chances of seeing one are pretty slim. This beautiful and elusive white bear – also known as the 'spirit bear' – is a subspecies of the black bear; its unusual coloring results from a recessive gene.

The Tsimshian First Nations lived around the nearby confluence of the Kalum and

THE NORTH

Skeena Rivers long before white surveyors starting arriving in the late 1800s. Prospectors and trappers soon followed, and sternwheeler traffic along the Skeena brought people in relative droves. As usual, the railway changed the face of the town, connecting it to the rest of Canada and opening the door for exports of natural resources. The logging industry, which started with the manufacture of cedar poles and railway ties, remains the major industry today.

Despite its attractive setting, Terrace is not a pretty town, nor it is rife with things to do, but it makes a good base from which to explore the area.

Information

The Visitor Info Centre (☎ 250-635-0832, 800-499-1637), 4511 Keith Ave just southeast of downtown, is open 9 am to 8 pm daily in summer. (Hwy 16 becomes Keith Ave through town.)

For a good selection of regional books, stop by the excellent Misty River Books (☎ 250-635-4428, 800-861-9716), 4710 Lazelle Ave in the Lazelle Mini Mall. Terrace's weekly newspaper is the *Terrace Standard*, published on Wednesday.

Do laundry, have a shower or get a tan at the Coin Clean Laundry, 3223 Lazelle Ave. Showers cost $3.50 for 15 minutes, and the tanning beds are $1.10 per minute.

For medical services, go to the Mills Memorial Hospital (☎ 250-635-2211), 4720 Haugland Ave.

Things to See & Do

A worthwhile attraction, the **Heritage Park** (☎ 250-635-4546), 3215 Eby St, features a collection of log buildings that re-create different aspects of pioneer life. In summer, characters roam around in period costume and lead interesting tours through the grounds. Admission to the park is $3/2 for adults/children. It's open 10:30 am to 4:30 pm daily in summer only.

The local **farmers' market** takes place on Davis Ave behind George Little Park from 9 am to 1 pm on Saturday and 4 to 7 pm on Wednesday from May through October. You can buy fresh veggies, flowers and local crafts. If you're around the first weekend in August, join along in **Riverboat Days**, a five-day fair that includes a salmon bake, soapbox derby and parade.

Terrace contains lots of good trails for **hiking** and **mountain biking**. Ask at the Visitor Info Centre for the brochure on area hikes and stop by McBike (☎ 250-563-2453) 4710 Lazelle Ave, to find out about good mountain-biking trails.

Anyone looking to downhill ski or snowboard will want to head to the small **Shames Mountain** resort (☎ 250-635-3773), 35km west of Terrace on Hwy 16. Horizontal skiers should check out the 23km of classic and skate-skiing trails at the **Onion Lake Cross-Country Ski Trails** (☎ 250-798-2227), located halfway between Terrace and Kitimat on Hwy 37.

The mountains of the Kitimat Range surround the popular **Lakelse Lake Provincial Park**, 20km south of Terrace on Hwy 37 which sits in a 354-hectare forest of cedar, hemlock and Sitka spruce. The white sand beaches make great spots for lounging, and Lakelse Lake attracts a good number of swimmers, canoeists, windsurfers, campers and anglers. The lake's name is a Tsimshian word for 'freshwater mussel,' a bivalve mollusk found in the lake and nearby rivers.

Nisga'a Memorial Lava Bed Provincial Park

Jointly managed by the Nisga'a Nation and the government, this 18,000-hectare park in the beautiful Nass Basin, 100km north of Terrace along the Nisga'a Hwy, is one of the most unique parks in the province.

About 250 years ago, a massive volcanic eruption spilled hot, heavy lava onto the Nass floodplain. The thick molten lava spread 10km long and 3km wide, destroying entire villages, suffocating vegetation and killing more than 2000 Nisga'a ancestors. The lava rerouted the Nass River to the north edge of the valley, where it still flows today.

The lava created various formations (depending on the speed at which it flowed), including lava tubes, chunks and rope-like Paahoehoe lava. The pale gray rocks look almost furry with the hardened ash; the effect is reminiscent of a lunar landscape.

Most of the trails in the park are short and accessible from the highway. The only way to see the volcanic cone is on a three-hour guided tour given by a member of the Nisga'a Nation. The informative tour and moderate hike cost $12. Call ☎ 250-633-2150 to reserve a spot.

About 20km past the park boundary, you'll find the Visitor Interpretation Centre (☎ 250-638-9589) in a traditional Nisga'a longhouse. Here you can get information on the history of the Nisga'a and pick up the $1 *Self-Guided Auto Tour* brochure, which offers good descriptions of park highlights. A 16-site campground beside the visitor center – the only camping area in the park – has pit toilets and firewood. Sites are $12. For more information, contact the BC Parks office in Terrace (☎ 250-798-2277).

Places to Stay

East of town over the Skeena River, the *Ferry Island Municipal Park* contains 67 public campsites nestled in birch and cottonwood trees – look for the faces carved into the trees. The $12 sites, complete with picnic tables and fire pits, are surprisingly nice for a city park, though the facilities only include pit toilets (no showers). At Lakelse Lake Provincial Park, the *Furlong Bay Campground* (☎ 250-798-2466) offers interpretive programs, showers, flush toilets and 156 sites, some of which you can reserve through BC Parks by calling ☎ 800-689-9025.

The *Redsand Lake Demonstration Forest* (☎ 250-638-5100), a forest-service site 26km north of town along the West Kalum Forest Rd, charges $10 for campsites with picnic tables and fire pits. You'll find some good hiking trails in the woods here.

Budget accommodations are available downtown at the *Cedars Motel* (☎ 250-635-2258, 4030 Hwy 16 W), where the clean, newly renovated rooms include private baths and cost $35/40 single/double. Just west of downtown is the new *Evergreen Inn* (☎ 250-635-0811, 888-901-7111), where large, clean rooms go for $54/60. There's a pub next door.

Copper River Motel (☎ 250-635-6124, 888-652-7222, 4113 Hwy 16), 4km east of town, offers rooms with a microwave and fridge for $40/50 ($60 with a full kitchen). Despite the bad name, the *Costa-Lessa Motel* (☎ 250-638-1885, 3867 Hwy 16) features immaculate rooms starting at $50; for $70, you can get one with a fireplace and kitchen. Back downtown, the *Bear Country Inn* (☎ 250-635-6302, 888-226-6222, 4702 Lakelse Ave) charges $86/92 for basic rooms and operates its own restaurant.

Places to Eat

Caffeine junkies should head to *Hava Java* (☎ 250-638-7877, 4621 Lakelse Ave). Order a giant sandwich ($4) with your choice of fixings at *Bert's Deli* (☎ 250-635-5440, 4603 Park Ave).

For excellent fresh food with a Mexican slant, try *Don Diego's* (☎ 250-635-2307, 3512 Kalum St). The menu changes daily, with dinners ranging from $10 to $15. Get your pasta, steak or Cajun fix at *Zydeco Jo's* (☎ 250-638-7618, 4644 Lazelle), where dinners average $15.

Getting There & Away

The Terrace Airport is 12km south along Hwy 37. Both Canadian Regional (☎ 888-247-2262) and the lower-cost Hawk Air (☎ 250-635-4295) offer regular service to Vancouver.

The Greyhound bus depot (☎ 250-635-0683), 4621 Keith Ave, is near the Visitor Info Centre. Two buses depart daily for points east, such as Prince George (8½ hours, $75), and west, such as Prince Rupert (two hours, $22). There are no lockers at the depot.

KITIMAT
• population 12,077

Nestled in the pit of the Douglas Channel's Kitimat Arm 58km south of Terrace (at the southernmost point of Hwy 37), this town has so much natural potential – towering mountains, a deep protected port, fresh-and salt-water fishing – that it could've been a wilderness paradise. But it's not. Kitimat is like a prodigious child gone wrong. Home to Eurocan Pulp & Paper Company

THE NORTH

(a producer of craft paper) and Methanex (a petrochemical plant), Kitimat was developed in the 1950s by aluminum giant Alcan to house employees for the company's new smelter. The project included damming the Nechako River and was, at the time, Canada largest industrial endeavor. Alcan's first choice for a smelter was in Kemano, 75km southeast of Kitimat. The village proved too small for the company's operations so it became, instead, the supply center for Alcan's hydroelectricity, which is generated by the Kenney Dam on the Nechako River. The Kitimat smelter uses an astounding two million liters of water every day.

The company town is so planned it's eerie. Sidewalks bend in on themselves so you never have to walk on the road, while rows upon rows of formulaic 1950s-style houses sit slumping on the sidelines. Add a smelter that sucks up more energy than small countries, and you might think that Kitimat doesn't deserve a piece of the tourism pie. Well, hmmm….

Smelter Tours

The free tour of Alcan's Kitimat Works Facility, which employs 2200 people, offers an interesting overview of aluminum processing. First you watch a film on the building of Kemano and Kitimat, then you hop in a van for a drive around the site. You'll learn that bauxite, a red ore found close to the surface, contains lots of aluminum. Alcan buys the extracted aluminum from Australia; the metal is shipped in, processed into ingots of various sizes and then shipped back out. The smelter operates 24 hours a day, seven days a week. The two-hour tours happen at 10:30 am and 1:30 pm weekdays from June through August. To make tour reservations, call ☎ 250-639-8259.

Places to Stay & Eat

On Hwy 37 at the north end of town, the *Hirsch Creek Park* (☎ 250-632-7161) offers pit toilets and firewood, but there are only five sites ($7.50). Popular with anglers, *Radley Park* (☎ 250-632-7161) contains flush toilets, pay showers, a freezer for your fish and sites right on the river ($15).

Most of the motels in town have standard rooms. Among the better deals, *The Chalet* (☎ 250-632-4615, 852 Tsimshian Blvd) charges $45/47 per single/double. The *City Centre Motel* (☎ 250-632-4848, 800-663-3391, 480 City Centre) offers rooms with kitchenettes for $50/52.

You'll be thankful for the good coffee at *Northern Espresso* (☎ 250-632-4116), in the City Centre Mall. *The Chalet Restaurant* (☎ 250-632-2662), at the hotel, is the best place in town for a hearty meal. Lift an after-dinner stein next door at *The Ol' Keg* pub.

PRINCE RUPERT
• population 17,426

After Vancouver, 'Rupert,' as it's called, is the largest city on the mainland BC coast. The town was the brainchild of Charles Hays, the general manager of the Grand Trunk Railway who, in 1906, saw in the vast harbor the potential to build a town that would rival Vancouver. Serious financial problems plagued the railway when Hays, who was off gallivanting, unwisely booked passage on the ill-fated *Titanic*. To make matters worse, WWI came along, stripping the region of young men, and the railway eventually suffered the indignity of having its assets frozen by the courts. It ultimately became part of the Canadian National Railway system.

The town never developed into the vast metropolis Hays envisioned but instead became a fishing center for the Pacific Northwest. Its port – the world's deepest natural ice-free port – handles timber, mineral and grain shipments to Asia. The collapse of fishing in recent years and the Asian economic crisis dealt Rupert a blow it's still trying to recover from. Many fishermen who have lived and breathed by the sea for generations are now working double-time or finding new ways to earn a living.

Once known as the world's halibut capital, Prince Rupert has adopted a new title, the 'City of Rainbows,' which is one way of saying that it rains a lot. In fact, it rains 220 days a year, giving the city one of the highest precipitation rates in all of Canada. Despite this, the town's setting is

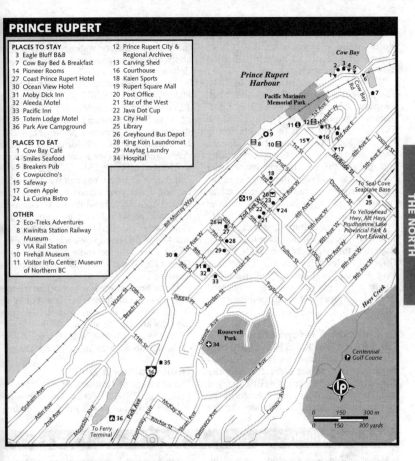

PRINCE RUPERT

PLACES TO STAY
3 Eagle Bluff B&B
7 Cow Bay Bed & Breakfast
14 Pioneer Rooms
27 Coast Prince Rupert Hotel
30 Ocean View Hotel
31 Moby Dick Inn
32 Aleeda Motel
33 Pacific Inn
35 Totem Lodge Motel
36 Park Ave Campground

PLACES TO EAT
1 Cow Bay Café
4 Smiles Seafood
5 Breakers Pub
6 Cowpuccino's
15 Safeway
17 Green Apple
24 La Cucina Bistro

OTHER
2 Eco-Treks Adventures
8 Kwinitsa Station Railway Museum
9 VIA Rail Station
10 Firehall Museum
11 Visitor Info Centre; Museum of Northern BC

12 Prince Rupert City & Regional Archives
13 Carving Shed
16 Courthouse
18 Kaien Sports
19 Rupert Square Mall
20 Post Office
21 Star of the West
22 Java Dot Cup
23 City Hall
25 Library
26 Greyhound Bus Depot
28 King Koin Laundromat
29 Maytag Laundry
34 Hospital

Prince Rupert Harbour

Cow Bay

Pacific Mariners Memorial Park

To Seal Cove Seaplane Base

To Yellowhead Hwy, Mt Hays, Prudhomme Lake Provincial Park & Port Edward

Roosevelt Park

Hays Creek

Centennial Golf Course

To Ferry Terminal

THE NORTH

magnificent, especially when it's not raining, misty, foggy or particularly cloudy. Surrounded by mountains and situated at the mouth of the Skeena River, the area displays a rugged beauty. Wind- and rain-swept houses stand high on the cliffs looking out at the fjord-like coastline, ready to accept whatever this harsh climate delivers.

Prince Rupert is a good starting point for trips to Alaska and the Queen Charlotte Islands. In 1999, the city's cruise ship terminal opened, bringing an influx of tourists. Many people, mainly young, arrive here in summer looking for work on fishing boats,

though the chances of finding it have dropped in recent years. Accommodations in July and August are sometimes difficult to find.

First Nations History

Various clans of northwest coast First Nations have inhabited the area, following oolichan and salmon runs, for almost 10,000 years. Though more than 20 distinct Native cultures lived here throughout history, the majority were (and still are) Tsimshian (pronounced 'sim-**she**-an'), as evidenced by the remains of 55 villages dotted around the harbor. Prior to the arrival of Europeans, this was one of the most populated areas in North America; archaeological digs have uncovered evidence of human habitation dating back thousands of years.

When the Europeans arrived in 1834, nearby Port Simpson (then called 'Fort' Simpson) became a Hudson's Bay Company trading post that eventually lured the Tsimshians away from their seclusion in Prince Rupert. The usual slew of disease weakened the First Nations populations, and in 1884 the government banned the Natives from holding potlatches, one of the highest forms of celebration in First Nations culture. The failing population and cultural oppression hit hard, and decades of struggle to retain land and cultural freedom ensued. Today, the Tsimshian population in Prince Rupert is thriving. Like the Haida on the Queen Charlotte Islands, the Tsimshians have a strong oral history and incredible artistic ability, both of which have allowed them to recapture and build upon their cultural past.

Orientation & Information

Prince Rupert is on Kaien Island and is connected to the mainland by a bridge. The Yellowhead Hwy passes right through the downtown area, becoming McBride St and then 2nd Ave; 2nd and 3rd Aves form the downtown core. McBride St divides the city between east and west. Cow Bay, named for a dairy farm that used to be located here, has become a historic waterfront area full of shops and restaurants sitiated just north of downtown.

The Visitor Info Centre (☎ 250-624-5637, 800-667-1994, fax 250-627-8009), 100 1st Ave W, open 9 am to 8 pm Monday to Saturday (9 am to 5 pm in winter), shares space with the impressive Museum of Northern BC. It's There's a smaller visitor center at Park Ave Campground (see Places to Stay, later).

The post office (☎ 250-627-3085) is at 417 2nd Ave W at 3rd St. You can surf the Internet and check your email at Java Dot Cup (☎ 250-622-2822), 516 3rd Ave W. For area maps and regional books, go to the bookstore Star of the West (☎ 250-624-9053), 518 3rd Ave W. To stay up on local events, pick up the *Prince Rupert Daily News* or *Prince Rupert This Week*, which features entertainment listings.

If you need to wash your clothes, try the King Koin Laundromat, 745 2nd Ave W at 7th St. Around the corner is the Maytag Laundry at 2276 7th St.

The hospital (☎ 250-624-2171) is southwest of the downtown area, in Roosevelt Park.

Things to See & Do

The **Museum of Northern BC** (☎ 250-624-3207, 800-667-1994), 100 1st Ave W, resides inside a gorgeous post-and-beam building

Watching Wildlife

Though wildlife viewing is good anytime of the year, there are certain high seasons when you'll see more of a particular animal.

animal	best viewing time
grizzly bear	mid-April through June; August and September
Kermode bear	September to mid-October
humpback whale	August through October
killer whale	May to mid-July
gray whale	mid-August through October
bald eagle	year-round (especially from mid-March to mid-April)
seal & sea lion	year-round
porpoise	year-round

styled after a First Nation longhouse. The incredible massive cedar beams exude a wonderful aroma that will chase away any moths you've picked up on your travels. The area's 10,000 years of human habitation are documented in excellent exhibits, which include a wealth of excellent Haida, Gitksan and Tsimshian art. This is definitely a must-see. It's open 9 am to 8 pm Monday to Saturday (9 am to 5 pm in winter). Admission is $5/1 for adults/children.

You'll see **totems** all around town; two flank the statue of Charlie Hays beside City Hall on 3rd Ave. Many totems are replicas of very well-known traditional works. In summer, the museum offers guided heritage and totem walking tours around town ($2/1 for adults/children). Call for tour times. To witness totem-building in action, stop by the **Carving Shed**, one block north of the Museum of Northern BC and next door to the courthouse. Often you'll see local artists there working on jewelry or cedar carvings.

The museum also arranges an Archaeological Tour to **Pike Island** (or Laxspa'aws), 13km west of Rupert in Metlakatla Pass, where remains of three ancient Tsimshian villages were discovered. Many petroglyphs trace the Native artistry back some 2000 years. The five-hour tour ($42) includes lunch. Call ☎ 250-628-9259 or the museum for details. You cannot visit the island without a guide.

The **Prince Rupert City & Regional Archives** (☎ 250-624-3326), 100 1st Ave E, contains a huge collection of photographs, nautical charts and books. It's open 10 am to 3 pm weekdays.

Fire engine buffs should check out the rebuilt 1925 REO Speedwagon fire engine at the small **Firehall Museum** (☎ 250-627-4475), beside the real fire hall on 1st Ave W. The **Kwinitsa Station Railway Museum** (☎ 250-627-1915), a few blocks south along the waterfront, features informative displays about the building of the railway and the original plans for Rupert to become a major 'super port.' Admission to both these museums is by donation.

As you head out of town, look for the **shoe tree** on the north side of Hwy 16.

Weary travelers have nailed more than a hundred shoes to the tree, making it the 'tree for lost soles.'

You can picnic, swim, fish, hike or take out a canoe at **Diana Lake Provincial Park** and **Prudhomme Lake Provincial Park**, about 16km east of town on Hwy 16.

About 20km south of Prince Rupert, **North Pacific Cannery Village Museum** (☎ 250-628-3538), 1889 Skeena Dr in the town of Port Edward, explores the history of fishing and canning along the Skeena River. The fascinating complex, built over the town, was used from 1889 to 1968. Today, exhibits document the miserable conditions of the workers, along with the workings of this industry that helped build the region. The museum should be high on your list of sights and can easily occupy half a day. Don't miss the extraordinary one-person stage show that traces the evolution of fish processing. The complex includes a café with excellent breakfasts and salmon dinners ($12 and up) and B&B accommodation (☎ 250-628-3375) inside an old bunkhouse (starting at $65 for two). The village is open 9 am to 6 pm daily from May to September, as well as many additional weekends through the year. Admission is $6/3 for adults/children. Prince Rupert Transit offers bus service to the site (see Getting Around, later).

Activities

More than 70 charter-boat operators run **fishing** trips out of Prince Rupert, some with great success; in 1997, a few happy tourists landed a 106kg (234lb) halibut. Many charter companies also offer **whale-watching** trips and various harbor tours. Contact Seashore Charters (☎ 250-624-5645, 800-667-4393) to arrange trips or ask the Visitor Info Centre for a complete list of operators.

If you're interested in **kayaking**, Eco-Treks Adventures (☎ 250-624-8311), on the Cow Bay Pier, offers a variety of guided trips, including a three-hour introductory course for $45. It also rents kayaks by the day ($35 for a single kayak, $55 for a double). Kaien Sports (☎ 250-624-3633,

Grizzlies Galore

One of the most unique pockets in BC's big purse full of parks, the 45,000-hectare Khutzeymateen Grizzly Bear Sanctuary is one of the few remaining grizzly habitats in the world. Located 45km northeast of Prince Rupert, the park sits in the remote Khutzeymateen River Valley, the traditional territory of the Gitsees people, who used the valley for fishing, hunting, trapping and growing food such as berries, crab apples and potatoes. When Europeans arrived in North America, an estimated 200,000 grizzlies lived on the continent. Today, that estimate hovers at only 25,000, and of that number, 50 live in the Khutzeymateen.

The Khutzeymateen (pronounced 'kootsama-teen') was permanently protected as parkland in 1992. In 1994, the area became officially designated as a 'grizzly bear sanctuary' to be jointly managed by the provincial government and the Tsimshian First Nations.

Because grizzlies are reclusive by nature and do better when left alone, the human presence in the park is heavily restricted, though you can join a boat tour or take a floatplane in for a peek. For more information, contact BC Parks Khutzeymateen Area (☎ 250-798-2277) or the Prince Rupert Visitor Info Centre (☎ 800-667-1994).

888-305-4400), 344 2nd Ave W, rents kayaks for the same price, though you have to transport them to the water yourself. Prince Rupert has a huge tide range, with tides rising or falling up to 4 feet an hour. Be sure to get the low-down on the tides before venturing out on the water.

Of the many **hiking** trails in and around town, one path goes up 732m Mt Hays from the Butze Rapids parking lot, east of town on Hwy 16. On a clear day, you can see local islands, the Queen Charlotte Islands and even Alaska. Beginning at a parking lot on the Yellowhead Hwy, 3km south of town just past the industrial park, trails lead to Mt

Oldfield, Tall Trees (you'll see some old cedars) and Butze Rapids. The rapids wall is a flat 4km loop to Grassy Bay; the other are more demanding. The Visitor Info Centre offers details on these and others.

Places to Stay

The municipal *Park Ave Campground* (☎ 250-624-5861, 1750 Park Ave), near the ferry terminal, contains 87 sites ($10.50), hot showers, laundry and flush toilets. Tent sites are on wooden platforms so your tent doesn't get soaked when (not *if*) it rains. In summer, on nights when the ferry arrives it's best to book ahead. You can also camp beside a lake at *Prudhomme Lake Provincial Park* (☎ 250-798-2277), 16km east of Prince Rupert on Hwy 16. Open May to September, the campground here includes 24 sites ($12) with pit toilets. Bring a tarp.

You'll find more than a dozen B&Bs in Prince Rupert. Readers rave about the *Eagle Bluff B&B* (☎ 250-627-4955, 201 Cow Bay Rd), in a heritage building right by the marina in Cow Bay. Rates for the five rooms with shared bath begin at $45/55 single/double. Nearby, the *Cow Bay Bed & Breakfast* (☎ 250-627-1804, 20 Cow Bay Rd) features cozy duvets spread on every bed in its northwest-coast theme rooms. Double rooms with a shared bath start at $75; rooms with private baths cost $95 and up.

The least expensive motel in town is *Pioneer Rooms* (☎ 250-624-2334, 167 3rd Ave E), the nearest thing in Prince Rupert to a travelers' hostel. Though the rooms are cheap, the place is a bit of a dump. You enter the rundown building through a smoky lobby, where there's a hotplate, microwave and fridge for general use. The private rooms with shared baths are tiny, and the dirty dorm rooms cry out for a coat of paint. But if you're looking for cheap digs, this is the place. You'll pay $20 for a dorm bed, $25 for a single and $40 for a double.

The friendly *Ocean View Hotel* (☎ 250-624-6259, 950 1st Ave W), in a recently renovated historic building, offers rooms with a shared bath for $40 and up. Rooms with private baths start at $50. The *Aleeda Motel*

Catching Fish

Five species of salmon – chinook, coho, chum, pink and sockeye – live in the area waters, especially at the mouth of the Skeena River and at the head of Chatham Sound. Halibut, lingcod and rockfish also show up in high numbers.

fish	best catching time
chinook salmon	May through July
coho & chum salmon	July through September
pink salmon	July through mid-September
sockeye salmon	June through August
halibut	May through September
lingcod	year-round
rockfish	year-round

THE NORTH

(☎ 250-627-1367, 900 3rd Ave W) charges $60/70 single/double for its clean rooms. Nearby, the newly renovated **Pacific Inn** (☎ 250-627-1711, 888-663-1999, 909 3rd Ave W) features a restaurant and large rooms that start at $70. The **Totem Lodge Motel** (☎ 250-624-6761, 1335 Park Ave) is a good choice, but because it's close to the ferry terminal it fills up fast; book early. Rooms cost $75/79.

The large **Moby Dick Inn** (☎ 250-624-6961, 800-663-0822, 935 2nd Ave W) boasts very nice rooms and friendly staff. Rooms with TVs and coffeemakers cost $76/86. The **Coast Prince Rupert Hotel** (☎ 250-624-6711, 800-663-1144, 118 6th St) features good views, a restaurant and comfortable rooms that start at $97/107.

Places to Eat

Stock up on food for the ferry at the **Safeway** supermarket, on McBride St between 1st and 2nd Aves.

With fishing a major local industry, it's not surprising to find seafood on just about every menu. Salmon and halibut are headliners. Top billing goes to the storied **Smiles Seafood** (☎ 250-624-3072, 113 Cow Bay Rd), on the waterfront at Cow Bay. It serves a variety of fresh ocean fare, as well as steaks and sandwiches. A salmon dinner will set you back $15. Flip over the place mat for a

look at the menu from 1945, when the same dinner could be had for 45¢.

Nearby, overlooking the marina, the **Cow Bay Café** (☎ 250-627-1212, 205 Cow Bay Rd) serves up fresh fish every night. The creative menu changes daily, so it's popular with locals as well as tourists. It's closed on Sunday. Also in Cow Bay, **Breakers Pub** (☎ 250-624-5990, 117 George Hills Way) makes a worthwhile stop for a meal and a beer. This busy place features an outdoor patio (good for the brief intervals when it stops raining) and a thick menu with tasty fresh fish specials. Try the halibut burger for $8.50.

Just around the corner, **Cowpuccino's** (☎ 250-627-1395, 25 Cow Bay Rd) is a mellow coffeehouse and travelers' hangout that maintains the neighborhood's schtick in its name – and its cow-spotted dumpsters.

Outside of Cow Bay, try the **Green Apple** (☎ 250-627-1666, 310 McBride St), on the corner of 3rd Ave E, which serves fish-and-chips and popular chowders. An authentic Italian deli, **La Cucina Bistro** (☎ 250-624-4444, 427 3rd Ave W) offers yummy sandwiches for $7 and personal-size pizzas for $6.

Getting There & Away

Air Prince Rupert Airport is on Digby Island, across the harbor from town. You must check in for your flight at your airline's downtown terminal two hours before flight time so that you can catch a shuttle bus and ferry (combined ticket $11) to the airport – no last minute showing-up here. The airport also charges a $28 departure fee. Canadian Airlines (☎ 800-247-2262) flies to Vancouver and maintains an office at the airport. Harbour Air (☎ 250-627-1341, 800-689-4234) serves small communities all over northern BC. Its planes leave from the Seal Cove Seaplane Base at the eastern end of town.

Bus The Greyhound bus depot (☎ 250-624-5090) is on 6th St between 1st and 2nd Aves. Buses depart twice daily to Prince George (10½ hours, $88). The depot contains luggage lockers if you need to dump your stuff for the day.

Train The VIA Rail station (☎ 250-627-7589, 800-561-8630) is at 1033 Waterfront St, near the harbor. This is the western terminus of the *Skeena*, the two-day daylight-only train coming from Jasper, with an overnight stop in Prince George. The three weekly trains arrive in Rupert at 8 pm on Monday, Thursday and Saturday; trains depart at 8 am on Sunday, Wednesday and Friday.

Ferry From Prince Rupert, Alaska State Ferries runs boats north through the Alaskan Panhandle. The first stop is Ketchikan, but you can go north past Wrangell, Petersburg and Juneau to Skagway.

Alaska State Ferries (☎ 250-627-1744, 800-642-0066), also called the Alaska Marine Hwy, maintains an office at the ferry terminal in Fairview Bay, 3km southwest of the center of town via Park Ave. The one-way ferry fare to Skagway (34 hours) is US$130/65 for adults/children and US$299 for a small car; a two-person cabin starts at US$93. Meals and berths are extra. If you're traveling by car or RV, you should book well ahead. You can try going standby, but you may not get on the boat.

BC Ferries (☎ 250-386-3431, ☎ 888-223-3779) sails the *Queen of the North* down the Inside Passage to Port Hardy on Vancouver Island on daytime schedules (15 hours), departing every other day from mid-May to mid-October. The spectacular cruise along the narrow Inside Passage passes small Native villages, islands and inlets. Keep your eyes peeled for the wealth of wildlife, which can include seals and killer, humpback and gray whales. The ferries feature comfortable lounge chairs and good all-you-can-eat buffet food ($12 for breakfast and lunch, $19 for dinner). To entertain yourself while you're on the boat, you can attend interpretive talks on the covered outside decks or watch movies in the forward lounge. The fare is $106/53 for adults/children (add $218 for a car). See the Getting Around chapter in this book for more information.

If you're coming from Port Hardy and you intend to continue north to Alaska by ferry, then you should note that the schedules of BC Ferries and Alaska State Ferries do not coincide; you may get the chance to spend at least one night in Prince Rupert.

BC Ferries also sails across Hecate Straight between Prince Rupert and Skidegate in the Queen Charlotte Islands (6½ hours). In summer, boats sail daily; in winter, they leave three times a week. The ferry is comfortable, with outside seats, a lounge and cafeteria. The showers on board cost $2 for 10 minutes. The one-way fare is $25/12.50 for adults/children, $93 for a car.

Getting Around

Bus Prince Rupert Transit (☎ 250-624-3343) operates buses to all ferry and seaplane terminals. For times, pick up a copy of the *Rider's Guide* from the Visitor Info Centre. The one-way fare on buses is $1; a day pass costs $2.50. The main downtown bus stop is at the Rupert Square Mall on 2nd Ave. Take No 51 east to the sea plane base, or catch the Fairview Bay bus (no number) west to the ferry terminal. The bus schedules coincide with the ferry schedules.

In summer, there is bus service to the fishing village at Port Edward. The bus stops at the Visitor Info Centre, Park Ave Campground and the main downtown bus stop. The one-way fare is $1.75.

Car For taxi service, call Skeena Taxi (☎ 250-624-5318). A one-way trip to the ferry is about $8.

For car rentals, try Budget (☎ 250-627-7400, 800-268-8900) or National (☎ 250-634-5318, 800-387-4747). Both maintain offices in the Rupert Square Mall on 2nd Ave and charge about $52 per day (plus mileage) for a compact car. Cheaper used cars (around 10 years old) are available through Car-Go Services (☎ 250-627-1525); rates start at $40 per day.

QUEEN CHARLOTTE ISLANDS

• population 6000

The Queen Charlotte Islands, sometimes known as the Canadian Galapagos, are a dagger-shaped archipelago of some 154 islands lying 80km west of the BC coast and about 50km from the southern tip of Alaska. This sparsely populated, wild, rainy and almost magical place swarms (literally) with bald eagles. Believed to be the only part of Canada that escaped the last Ice Age, the islands abound with flora and fauna that are markedly different from those of the mainland. Essentially still a wilderness area, the Queen Charlottes are warmed by an ocean current that rolls in from Japan, which means the islands get hit with 127cm of rain annually. All these factors combine to create a landscape filled with thousand-year-old spruce and cedar rainforests and waters teeming with marine life.

The islands have been inhabited continuously for 10,000 years and are the traditional homeland – Haida Gwaii – of the Haida nation, generally acknowledged as the prime culture in the country at the time the Europeans arrived. Though they were fearsome warriors who dominated BC's West Coast, they had few defenses against the diseases – primarily smallpox and tuberculosis – that were introduced by European explorers. In 1835, the Haida population was estimated at 6000 people; in 1915, that number had shrunk to only 588.

Today, the Haida are proud, politically active and defiant people who make up one-third of the Charlottes' population. In the 1980s, they led an internationally publicized fight to preserve the islands from further logging. A bitter debate raged, but finally the federal government decided to save South Moresby and create South Moresby Gwaii Haanas National Park. (Logging still goes on in other parts of the Queen Charlottes.) The arts of the Haida people – notably their totem poles and carvings in argillite (a dark, shale glass-like stone found only in southeast Alaska and on these islands) – are world renowned. You'll see evidence of the Haida's artistry throughout the islands.

Planes fly into Sandspit on Moresby Island, but the ferry dock, the three main towns and only inland road system all lie on Graham Island, where 80% of the population lives. Skidegate is a waterfront Haida community near the ferry terminal; Queen Charlotte City (QCC) is the main commercial and tourism center; and Masset, on the north coast, is a Haida community and commercial center that's also home to a closed military base. The only accessible area on the western coast is Rennell Sound, with remote wind-swept beaches and wilderness camping. From the Skidegate ferry dock, it's 4km to QCC, 135km to Masset.

Flora & Fauna

The Queen Charlotte Islands – widely assumed to have escaped the last Ice Age – boast a unique ecosystem. Poor drainage systems near the north end of Graham Island result in the growth of sphagnum moss and gentian, surrounded by lodgepole pine and yellow cedar. Elsewhere, mighty stands of western hemlock, Sitka spruce and western red cedar cover the landscape. Four unique species of moss, one liverwort and six species of flowering plants grow here. *Senecio newcombi*, a yellow flowering daisy, grows here and nowhere else.

The islands also have their own unique versions of pine marten, deer mouse, black

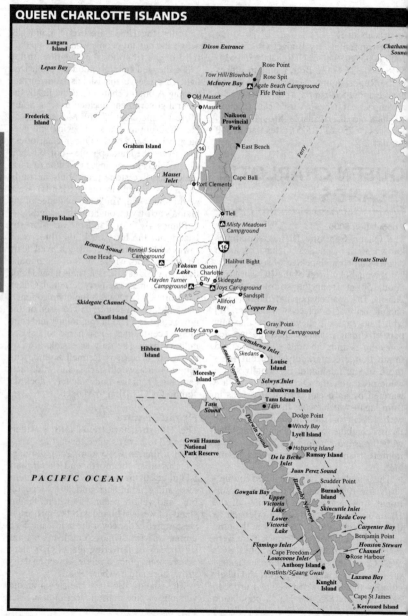

QUEEN CHARLOTTE ISLANDS

Langara Island

Lepas Bay

Dixon Entrance

Chatham Sound

Rose Point

Tow Hill/Blowhole   Rose Spit
McIntyre Bay   ⚑ Agate Beach Campground
Fife Point

● Old Masset
● Masset

Frederick Island

Naikoon Provincial Park

Graham Island

(16)

⚑ East Beach

Ferry

Masset Inlet

Cape Ball

● Port Clements

Hippa Island

● Tlell

⚑ *Misty Meadows Campground*

(16)

Rennell Sound   *Rennell Sound Campground*
Cone Head

Halibut Bight

Hecate Strait

⚑ *Yakoun Lake*   Queen Charlotte City
Hayden Turner   ● Skidegate
Campground ⚑   ⚑ Joys Campground
● Alliford   ● Sandspit
Bay

Skidegate Channel

Copper Bay

Chaatl Island

Gray Point
● Moresby Camp   ⚑ Gray Bay Campground

Hibben Island

Cumshewa Inlet

● Skedans   **Louise Island**

Louise Narrows

Moresby Island

Selwyn Inlet

Talunkwan Island

Tanu Island
● Tanu

Tasu Sound

Dodge Point

● Windy Bay
Lyell Island

Gwaii Haanas National Park Reserve

Darwin Sound

● Hotspring Island
De la Beche Inlet   **Ramsay Island**

Juan Perez Sound

PACIFIC OCEAN

Scudder Point

Gowgaia Bay   **Burnaby Island**

Upper Victoria Lake   *Skincuttle Inlet*

Burnaby Strait

Ikeda Cove

Lower Victoria Lake   *Carpenter Bay*

Benjamin Point

Houston Stewart Channel

Flamingo Inlet
Cape Freedom   ● Rose Harbour
Louscoone Inlet
Anthony Island
Ninstints/SGaang Gwaii

Luxana Bay

Kunghit Island

Cape St James

Kerouard Island

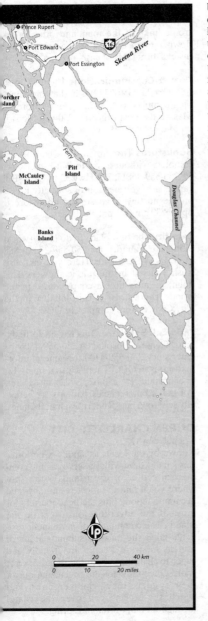

bear and short-tailed weasel. The Dawson caribou (a subspecies of the caribou) once lived here but was over-hunted to extinction. Unfortunately, introduced species have come in and wreaked havoc on the ecosystem. Though you aren't likely to see any, rats have become a big problem since their arrival (probably on the first trading ships in the mid-1700s). Raccoons and beavers, introduced for the fur trade, have also turned into a nuisance; like the rats and red squirrels, they prey on nesting shorebirds. Beavers also clog up drainages, flooding lakes and streams. Sitka blacktail deer were introduced at least five times between 1880 and 1925 as an alternate food source. Lacking natural predators, the deer became so prolific that residents are now allowed to hunt 10 deer per person per season to help control the population.

Home to 15% of all nesting seabirds in BC, the Queen Charlottes contain the only confirmed nesting site of horned puffins in Canada. A whopping 30% of the world's population of ancient murrelets nest here, as do most of the province's Peales peregrine falcons. There are no snakes on the islands.

From late April through late June, it's common to see gray whales traveling by on their 16,000km annual migration route along the West Coast. Starting in Mexico's Baja, the whales pass by California, Oregon and Washington in the US, then BC, before arriving in Alaska, their final destination before turning around and heading back down. They travel farther than any other migrating animal. The islands also include the largest sea lion rookery in BC.

Information

The islands' relative remoteness, coupled with the lure of the land and Haida culture, has put the Charlottes on the traveler's map. A number of hostels and services have sprung up to meet the needs of the intrepid, but it's still all but mandatory to make arrangements for accommodations in advance. It's also important to remember that the Queen Charlotte Islands are rural and remote. If you plan to visit the Gwaii Haanas National Park Reserve – and that's the number one reason for coming to the islands – then you should understand that a visit takes several days (see the separate heading about Gwaii Haanas, later in the chapter). Don't be one of the dullards who hop off the ferry expecting to see everything in a few hours and then depart. You won't. That said, don't be discouraged if you don't have time or money to do a long boat or kayaking trip; you can always arrange a one-day paddle or boat trip and you can actually see a lot by car or bike. Regardless, take some time to go beachcombing along the white sandy beaches, watch the sunset or chat with the locals, whose ideas and lifestyles are shaped by the salty fresh air and solitude.

The encyclopedic *Guide to the Queen Charlotte Islands* ($3.95) is updated annually. You can pick it up at many places, including on the ferry. Once you've arrived, get yourself a copy of *Islands This Week*, a free brochure detailing what's happening while you're on the islands.

Tourist Offices The Visitor Info Centre (☎ 250-559-8316, fax 559-8952) occupies a lovely building on the water on Wharf St in Queen Charlotte City (QCC) on Graham Island. It's open 10 am to 7 pm daily from mid-May to early September and 10 am to 2 pm daily for about three weeks on either side of that period. The center offers a wealth of knowledge about the islands and some good natural history displays, as well as lists of places to rent kayaks, canoes and other gear. A second Visitor Info Centre opens in summer at the airport in Sandspit. It's open 9 am to 5 pm daily from mid-May to early September and 9 am to 1 pm daily for three weeks on either side of that period.

In Masset, the Visitor Info Centre (☎ 250-626-3982), 1450 Christie St, is open 10 am to 4 pm daily in May, June and September; 9 am to 9 pm daily in July and August.

Money There are only a few ATMs on the islands. In QCC, you'll find one in the City Centre Store, another in Howler's Pub. The Northern Savings Credit Union operates ATMs in two locations: 106 Causeway in

QCC (☎ 250-559-4407) and on Main St in Masset (☎ 250-626-5231). Because the electronic links to the mainland often break down, though, don't count on using ATMs; instead, bring lots of cash.

Post & Communications The QCC post office (☎ 250-559-8349) is in the same shopping complex as the City Centre Store. In Masset, the post office (☎ 250-626-5155) is on Main St just off Collision Ave.

Bookstores No trip to the Charlottes is complete without a trip to Bill Ellis Books (☎ 250-559-4681), 720 Hwy 33 in QCC. Bill carries a huge selection of specialty books on the northwest coast. The bookstore is open 8:30 am to 4 pm weekdays.

Laundry The best place to do laundry is at Skidegate Laundry (☎ 250-559-2323), 888 Hwy 16 in Skidegate. Here you can also wash yourself in the public showers. This might be nice after a couple days in the woods. There's also a coin laundry in the City Centre Store complex in QCC.

Medical Services Queen Charlotte Islands General Hospital (☎ 250-559-4506 for emergency, 250-559-4300 for general information) is in QCC. There's also a small, 12-bed hospital (☎ 250-626-3772) in Masset. For major emergencies, patients are generally sent to Prince Rupert by air ambulance.

QUEEN CHARLOTTE CITY
• **population 1222**

Known by the locals as simply 'Charlotte,' this small fishing village serves as the commercial center of the islands – the spot where you'll find the most restaurants and accommodations, plus the headquarters for most of the adventure outfitters on the islands. The community of permanent residents takes the massive summer influx of tourists in stride. People are friendly and eager to share tips about the islands' secret spots. Once they get the socializing out of their systems, they'll hunker down and watch the storms roll over the island throughout fall, winter and spring.

Places to Stay

You can go the rustic route and camp at **Joy's Campground** (☎ 250-559-8383), halfway between Skidegate and QCC, where the only toilet is the intertidal zone. Sites cost $5 and come with picnic tables. West of QCC, follow Hwy 33 to the end, and you'll find the community-run **Hayden Turner Campground**, with pit toilets and sites for $10. The three beach sites, accessible via a short trail, cost $5.

One of the best places to stay on the islands, **Premier Creek Lodging** (☎ 250-559-8415, 888-322-3388, premier@qcislands.net, 3101 3rd Ave) offers accommodations that range from hostel-type dorms to lodge-style rooms complete with ocean views. Hostel beds cost $19, which includes the use of a communal kitchen and barbecue. You can also just stop in for a shower ($5). The lodge rooms, many of which face the ocean, range from $30 for a single bed with shared bath to $75 for a two-bedroom suite with a kitchen.

Another spot for some great views is the **Spruce Point Lodge** (☎ 250-559-8234, sprpoint@qcislands.net, 609 6th Ave), where the beachfront rooms start at $55/65 single/double, including a continental breakfast. A kitchen costs $10 extra. Ask about hostel accommodation.

At **Gracie's Place** (☎ 250-559-4262, 888-244-4262, 3113 3rd Ave), the rooms feature a nautical theme. Rooms cost $50/60 without a kitchen or $70/80 with a kitchen; a two-bedroom suite is $100/125.

The modern **Sea Raven Motel** (☎ 250-559-4423, 800-665-9606, 3301 3rd Ave) contains 29 rooms overlooking the bay. Prices for two people range from $65 to $90.

Places to Eat

Get your coffee and check out the artwork at **Hanging By a Fibre** (☎ 250-559-4463), on Wharf St right in the heart of QCC. The place for breakfast is **Lam's Cafe** (☎ 250-559-4202), just across from the Visitor Info Centre. Formerly Margaret's Cafe, most locals still call it that despite the new owners. You can get bacon, eggs, hash browns and toast for $6.50. **Howler's Bistro** (☎ 250-559-8602), at the junction of 3rd Ave and Wharf

St, features an excellent atmosphere and huge menu, including burgers, pasta and wraps. Downstairs, join others for beer and a game of pool at **Howler's Pub** (☎ 250-559-8600), the only place in town that stays open late.

The best place for fresh local seafood is the **Hummingbird Café** (☎ 250-559-8583), at the Sea Raven Motel. The smoked salmon Caesar salad is a delight ($11.95). The popular **Summerland Pizza & Steakhouse** (☎ 250-559-4588), on Hwy 33 at 3rd St, specializes in heavy meals. A steak dinner averages $13.

SKIDEGATE
• population 695

Skidegate (pronounced 'skid-a-git'), a Haida community on the shores of Rooney Bay, is a growing community dedicated to the revival of Haida culture and art. The community has big plans to build a new heritage center over the next few years. Meanwhile, the excellent **Haida Gwaii Museum at Qay'llnagaay** (☎ 250-559-4643) sits on Sealion Point, an ancient basalt outcropping that juts into Skidegate Inlet. Inside the museum, you'll find an excellent collection of Haida art, including button blankets, Brentwood boxes, silver and gold jewelry and argillite totems. Here you can learn about Bill Reid, one of the most renowned and prolific Haida artists. The good displays on the area's natural history include an extensive bird collection. The museum is open from 10 am to 5 pm daily, May to September; 10 am to 5 pm Wednesday to Saturday other times of the year. Admission is $3/1.50 for adults/children.

TLELL
• population 369

The small artsy community of Tlell, 40km north of Skidegate, is the southern gateway to Naikoon Provincial Park and home to the park headquarters (☎ 250-557-4390), which are open from late June through September. Here you can obtain information on the tides and check out the interpretive displays. Ask to watch the video describing the flora and fauna in the park.

Naikoon Provincial Park

This beautiful 72,640-hectare park on the northeast tip of Graham Island is comprised mostly of sand dunes and low sphagnum bogs surrounded by stunted and gnarled lodgepole pine and red and yellow cedar. The word 'naikoon' is a corruption of 'nai-kun,' meaning long nose – the name for the 5km-long Rose Spit that separates the stormy Hecate Straight and Dixon Entrance. The park is loosely divided into North (at Masset) and South (at Tlell). You'll find campgrounds and interesting hikes at either end.

From Tlell, take the worthwhile **Pesuta Trail** to the wreck of the *Pesuta*, a timber-hauling ship that ran aground in 1928. The trail begins at the Tlell River Picnic Area, just off Hwy 16 past the park headquarters, and follows the river to East Beach. You then follow the high tide line out to the wreck. Allow about seven hours to make the 10km roundtrip. At the north end of the park, be sure to check out **Tow Hill**, a columnar basalt outcropping an hour's hike from the parking lot. At the top, you'll enjoy incredible views. Also worth checking out is the **Blowhole**, which spurts out ocean water on incoming tides. Adventurous backpacker types should try the **Cape Fife Loop Trail**, a 21km loop that takes you over the Argonaut Plain to Fife Point and Rose Spit. To get to the north end of Naikoon, follow Tow Hill Rd northeast of Masset.

Places to Stay & Eat

Naikoon Provincial Park (☎ 250-557-4390) contains two excellent campgrounds. *Misty Meadows Campground*, just off Hwy 16 at the south end of the park, features nice, wooded sites ($12), some of which have wooden platforms so your tent doesn't get soaked. A short trail leads to the beach. See Masset & Old Masset, below, for information on Agate Beach Campground, the other park campground.

At the *Riverside B&B* (☎ 250-557-4418, 888-853-5522), all rooms come with decks overlooking the quiet Tlell River for $65/75 single/double. To get there from the highway, turn onto Wiggins Rd, then right onto Richardson Rd. The B&B is on your left.

Stay in a gorgeous beechwood house surrounded by seashells at *Cacilia's B&B* (☎ 250-557-4664, ceebysea@qcislands.net), just off the highway, with the ocean at the back door. Rooms with a shared bath start at $40/60; rooms with a private bath begin at $50/70.

The *Dress for Les* (☎ 250-557-2023) consignment store and café is the de facto community center for the area. It's usually full of people. Stop by to sip a cappuccino or find out about local events.

PORT CLEMENTS

• population 558

Locally referred to as 'Port,' this logging town lies 21km north of Tlell on Hwy 16. It's best known for the hiking trail out to the Golden Tree, a unique golden spruce tree that was cut down by a deranged forester in 1977. The story differs depending on whom you talk to, but it goes something like this: A guy was working as a surveyor in the Pemberton Valley. He had a falling out of some kind with his coworkers and thought the whole forest industry was full of hypocrites. He knew how much the forestry company (back then Macmillan Bloedel, now Weyerhaeuser) cherished its big pet tree (which he reportedly thought was silly – in his view, the company should cherish all trees, not just golden spruce), so he came on up to the Charlottes and cut the huge tree down. He was eventually charged, and, fearful that he'd take a beating on the ferry, he kayaked across Hecate Straight to attend the sentencing. He never made it to his destination. His kayak was found in the Alaska panhandle islands and – get this – his body was never found. Ask at the Port Clements Museum (☎ 250-557-4443), on Bayview Dr, for directions to the short trail, which will lead you to the golden stump on the bank of the Yakoun River.

MASSET & OLD MASSET

• population 1985

Though small and quiet, Masset is the commercial center of the north island. Old Masset, 4km down the road from Masset, is a Haida community that's home to more than 50 artists, many of whom you can visit by calling ahead. Ask at the Visitor Info Centre, 1450 Christie St, for details. A Canadian military base opened in Masset in 1971, bringing a slew of people who were supposed to integrate into the town. This never really happened, and now the base employs only 12 people instead of 300. But the base's downsizing proved to be a positive development for these Haida communities. The excessive and affordable military housing opened Masset up to investors and, interestingly, drew back some younger Haida people who had left the Charlottes. Locals believe this thrust of new energy is good for the town.

To enjoy some good bird-watching, head to the **Delkatla Wildlife Sanctuary**, off Tow Rd north of town. Masset also acts as the gateway to the north end of Naikoon Provincial Park. Along the road out to the park, you'll pass several kilometers' worth of rugged beaches – the destination for bongo drum–toting backpackers who try to set up house in little shacks made of driftwood until the cold weather and lack of services soon a their toll. If you try this, make certain your credit card has enough room left to fund your escape.

Places to Stay & Eat

The *Village of Masset Campground* (☎ 250-626-3968), 1km from Masset on Tow Hill Rd (just beyond the bridge going out to Naikoon), offers flush toilets, a coin laundry, hot showers and sites for $9. At the north end of Naikoon Provincial Park, *Agate Beach Campground* (☎ 250-557-4390) sits on the north coast, off Tow Hill Rd in the Dixon Entrance. On clear days, you can see straight through to Alaska. Named for the pretty glasslike stones found along the beaches, Agate Beach can get windy and downright cold after dark. The facilities include a shelter (if you need to get out of the wind and rain), pit toilets and sites that cost $12.

If you're looking to stay dry, the *Alaska View Lodge B&B* (☎ 250-626-3333, 800-661-0019, info@alaskaviewlodge.com) is also on the beach off Tow Hill Rd (before

the park entrance). You'll pay $50/70 single/double for an immaculate room with a shared bath, $60/80 with a private bath.

In Masset, local celebrity and chef extraordinaire David Phillips runs the *Copper Beech House* (☎ 250-626-5441, 1590 Delkatla Rd). This rambling old house whose backside faces the Masset Harbour features rooms that come complete with a teddy bear on every bed. Rates start at $50/75. Those who stay here, be forewarned: Get Phillips talking at night and you might never get to bed. Get him to cook for you and you might never leave. Ask about hostel accommodation in return for chores (like gardening or washing dishes). For more information, visit the inn's Web site www.copperbeechhouse.com.

Down the road, you'll find the pleasant *Harbourview Lodging* (☎ 250-626-5109, 800-661-3314), also on the marina. It offers clean, comfortable rooms and free juice and muffins in the morning. Rooms with a shared bath are $50. Two-bedroom suites with a deck and barbecue cost $75.

Coffee junkies should head straight to *Haida Buck* (☎ 250-626-5548), on Main St. A couple doors down, *Marj's Cafe* (☎ 250-626-9344) serves up hearty breakfasts from 7 am to 3 pm daily. The *Sandpiper Restaurant* (☎ 250-626-3672), at the corner of Orr St and Collision Ave, is the place to go for steaks and fresh seafood.

SANDSPIT
• population 568

Sandspit is just that – a long sandy spit jutting out into Hecate Straight. The only community on Moresby Island, Sandspit is home to the airport and the ferry terminal at Alliford Bay. It's also the major gateway into Gwaii Haanas, though if you're heading to the park from QCC, you will get off the ferry at Alliford Bay and bypass the town (see Getting There & Away, later, for ferry information).

Gwaii Haanas National Park Reserve

Protected since 1988, this huge, wild park encompasses Moresby and 137 smaller islands at the south end of the Queen Charlottes. This 640km-long stretch of rugged coastline is true wilderness at its best. If you take out a kayak, you can paddle for days without seeing another human being (though you'll see lots of wildlife). Recent archaeological finds have documented more than 500 ancient Haida sites, including villages and burial caves dotted throughout the islands. The most famous – and photographed – village is **Ninstints/SGaang Gwaii** (Anthony Island), where rows of totem poles stare eerily out to sea. This ancient village was declared a UNESCO World Heritage Site in 1981. (On the Charlottes, you'll notice that Ninstints is now more commonly referred to as SGaang Gwaii, pronounced 'Skung Gwhy,' which is the more traditional name.) Other major sights include **Skedans** on Louise Island and **Hotspring Island**, where you can soak away the bone-chilling cold in natural springs. These ancient sites are protected by the Haida Gwaii Watchmen, who live on the islands during summer.

Access to the park is by boat or plane only. A visit demands a decent amount of advance planning and usually requires several days. If you want to travel independently, you need to reserve in advance, as only a limited number of people can be in the park at any given time. Reservations cost $15 per person or $60 for a group. Call ☎ 250-387-1642 or 800-435-5622 to make reservations or to arrange for an information package to be sent to you. Finally, all park visitors must attend mandatory orientation sessions before entering the park. Lasting 90 minutes, these cover ecological, safety and cultural issues and take place at 8 am and 8 pm daily at the QCC Visitor Info Centre and at 11 am daily in Sandspit from May to September.

The easiest way to get into the park is with a tour company. The Visitor Info Centre in QCC can provide you with lists of operators, many of whom are located in Vancouver and Victoria. On the

islands, Queen Charlotte Adventures (☎ 250-559-8990, 800-668-4288, qciadven@qcislands.net), PO Box 196, Queen Charlotte, V0T 1S0, offers one- to 10-day trips using power boats, kayaks or sailboats. Prices start at $140 for a one-day trip to Skedans. A four-day boat trip to Ninstints/SGaang Gwaii is $860. A one-day kayak trip in the Skidegate Inlet costs $125, and the six-day paddle to Ninstints/SGaang Gwaii will set you back $1265. The owners, who maintain an office on Wharf St in QCC, take an active role in protecting the ecology of the preserve.

Another excellent company is Moresby Explorers (☎ 250-637-2215, 800-806-7633, dgmorex@mail.island.net), which operates a summer base camp so you get to the good sites faster. A kayaking trip to Ninstints/SGaang Gwaii costs $500/650 for three days/four days. Note that anyone traveling into the park must pay a park fee, which works out to $10 per day.

Getting There & Away

Canadian Regional (☎ 888-247-2262) offers daily flights to and from Vancouver, while Harbour Air (☎ 250-559-0052) operates regularly scheduled flights from Prince Rupert to Sandspit ($205) and Masset ($145). Planes land at Sandspit Airport (☎ 250-637-5313).

See the Prince Rupert section, earlier in this chapter, for information on BC Ferries service between Prince Rupert and Skidegate. Some of the sailings take place at night, others by day. As you sail between the two islands into Skidegate, you'll see a vista of rows of mountains receding into the mists; it's wild and verdant.

There are frequent daily sailings across the short distance between Graham Island, where most people live, and Moresby Island, where the Sandspit Airport is. The ferry runs between Skidegate Landing and Alliford Bay and costs $4.50/2.25 for adults/children and $16.50 for a car and driver. Kayaks or canoes cost $2, and bikes are free.

Totem pole

Historical Preservation on a Simple Cedar Log

Whether you're driving around the Hazelton area, sipping coffee in Prince Rupert or walking the windswept beaches on the Queen Charlotte Islands, you'll definitely be awed by the art around you.

Though most First Nations groups on the northwest coast lack formal written history as we know it, centuries of traditions manage to live on. Instead of communicating their rich pasts through words on a page or historical documents, the native tribes have told stories through the masterful art of carving, drawing and painting. Art has long been a method of expression, intimately linked with historical and cultural preservation, religion and social ceremony.

The artistry of northwest coast native groups – Tsimshian, Haida, Tlingit, Kwakiutl and Nuxalk tribes – is as intricate as it is simple. One of the most spectacular examples of this is the totem pole. Carved from a single cedar trunk, totems identify a household's lineage in the same way a family crest might identify a group or clan in England, although the totem pole is more of a historical pictograph depicting the entire ancestry. Like a family crest, totem poles carry a sense of prestige and prosperity.

Despite the expression 'low man on the totem pole,' the most important figures are usually at eye level; figures at the bottom usually serve an integral, grounding function that supports the rest of the pole. Totem figures can represent individuals, spirits, births, deaths, catastrophes or legends.

Unless you're an expert, it's not so easy to identify what's what on a totem. Here are a few rules of thumb: birds are always identified by their beaks. Ravens have a straight, midsize beak. Eagles feature a short, sharp, downturned beak, while hawks have a short, downturned beak that curls inward. Bears usually show large, square teeth, while beavers feature sharp incisors and a cross-stitched tail.

A few animals appear as if viewed from overhead. For example, the killer whale's fin protrudes outward from the pole as if its head faces downward. The long-snouted wolf also faces downward, as does the frog. The pointy-headed shark (or dogfish), with a grimacing mouth full of sharp teeth, faces upward, as does the humpback whale.

Though totem symbols are usually interconnected and complex, animals possess certain undeniable characteristics:

black bear – serves as a protector, guardian and spiritual link between humans and animals
beaver – symbolizes industriousness, wisdom and determined independence
eagle – signifies intelligence and power
frog – represents adaptability, the ability to live in both natural and supernatural worlds
hummingbird – embodies love, beauty and unity with nature
killer whale – symbolizes dignity and strength (often depicted as a reincarnated spirit of a great chief)
raven – signifies mischievousness and cunning
salmon – typifies dependable sustenance, longevity and perseverance
shark – exemplifies an ominous and fierce solitude
thunderbird – represents the wisdom of proud ancestors

The carving of totem poles was largely squashed after the Canadian government outlawed the potlatch ceremony in 1884. Most totems only last 60 to 80 years, though some on the Queen Charlotte Islands are more than 100 years old. When a totem falls, tradition says that it should be left there until another is erected in its place.

Today, totem carving is experiencing somewhat of a revival, though the poles are often constructed for nontraditional uses, such as public art. Modern totems commissioned for college campuses, museums and public buildings no longer recount the lineage of any one household but instead stand to honor the First Nations and their outstanding artistry.

THE NORTH

Getting Around

Harbour Air (☎ 250-559-0052) offers flight-seeing tours and charter services around the islands. South Moresby Air Charters (☎ 250-559-4222, 888-551-4222) also operates float-plane flights into Gwaii Haanas.

If you want a car, you'll have to weigh the high cost of local car rental against the cost of bringing a vehicle on the ferry. Budget (☎ 250-637-5688, 800-577-3228) and Thrifty (☎ 250-637-2299) maintain offices at the airport and in QCC. You'll find decent cars at better prices with Rustic Car Rentals (☎ 250-559-4641, 877-559-4641), located at Charlotte Island Tire, 605 Hwy 33 in QCC. Note that the many gravel roads can be dangerous. Logging trucks have the right of way in every instance, and they'll often zoom past you, kicking up gravel and dust. This can take a toll on windshields, so if you're renting, sort out breakage coverage in advance. Deer on the road also pose a distinct hazard. Your best bet is to drive slow, take in the scenery and let the loggers and deer reign.

Eagle Cabs (☎ 250-559-4461) meets all Canadian Regional flights and offers shuttle service from the Sandspit Airport to QCC for $14. Eagle Cabs also provides regular transit service from QCC to all Graham Island towns, including Skidegate ($5), Tlell ($17) and Masset ($20).

The paved roads on Graham Island are excellent for cycling. Rent bikes at Premier Creek Lodging in QCC (see Places to Stay under Queen Charlotte City, earlier) or at Moresby Island Guest House (☎ 250-637-5300), 385 Beach Rd in Sandspit.

STEWART-CASSIAR HIGHWAY

The remote Stewart-Cassiar Hwy (Hwy 37) is Canada's most westerly road system linking BC to the Yukon and Alaska. West of here, you need to take ferries to go north; east of here, it's just thick wilderness until you get to the Alaska Hwy. This raggedy route rivals the Alaska Hwy for scenery and is blissfully lacking in the RV traffic so common on the only other route north. Though the official start of Hwy 37 begins at Kitimat, most people start the journey at Kitwanga, 714km from the Yukon. The highway officially becomes the Stewart-Cassiar Hwy at Meziadin Junction.

Don't miss the chance to take the 134km side trip west to the rough-and-tumble twin border towns of Stewart, BC, and Hyder, Alaska, which sit on the coast at the head of the Portland Canal. You'll pass by glaciers, waterfalls and breathtaking scenery.

The Stewart-Cassiar is not the place for paranoid drivers. About half of the highway is still covered in only gravel or sealcoat (a veneer coating that's a precursor to pavement), making the ride often slow and bumpy. There aren't many service stations along the way, so make sure your vehicle is in good working condition. Take a spare tire, spare parts and, to be safe, some extra gasoline. Flying gravel can crack the windscreen, and headlights and dust can severely restrict your vision, so treat approaching vehicles with caution, especially the logging trucks. You'll see more bears than you can count, but remember, they are wild and surprisingly fast. Stay inside your car, keep your windows up and do not feed them. Hitchhiking is not recommended on this road; you could wait a long time between rides, and you probably don't want to get that friendly with the bears. For up-to-date road conditions, call ☎ 800-663-4997.

KITWANGA

On the Yellowhead Hwy between Terrace and New Hazelton, you'll come across the **Seven Sisters**, a beautiful mountain range on the south side of the highway. Just past that is Kitwanga, where a homemade sign at a gas station reads 'North to Alaska.' Here you start heading north on Hwy 37. Kitwanga, along with nearby Gitwangak, Kitwancool and Kispiox, is the traditional home of the Gitksan First Nations people, who traded along this section of the Skeena River for centuries. The area includes spectacular totems, as well as the **Kitwanga Fort National Historic Site** (☎ 250-559-8818). A path with interpretive signs follow a route up Battle Hill, where Canada's only Indian fort commanded the valley in pre-colonial days.

MEZIADIN JUNCTION

Meziadin Lake Provincial Park (☎ 250-847-7320), about 155km north of Kitwanga, has become a popular fishing spot and campground with pit toilets, a boat launch and 62 sites, some of which are on the lake. Don't get gas here; instead, go a little farther to Meziadin Junction, where the gas is cheaper and there is a summer Visitor Info Centre. From here, you can continue north to the Yukon or go west on Hwy 37A for 67km to Stewart. En route, watch for the stunning Bear Glacier, the largest ice tongue of the Cambria Icefields; it practically leaps onto the highway and glows a bright blue, even at night.

STEWART & HYDER

The long Portland Canal, a steep ocean fjord that extends from the coast 90km into the mountains, finally stops at Stewart, Canada's most northerly ice-free port. The fjord cuts a natural border between Canada and the US, which is why Hyder, Stewart's closest US neighbor, is only 3km away and is only connected to other parts of Alaska by water.

Stewart (population 858) was once a bustling mining town where prospectors flocked after hearing about the discovery of gold. The fierce competition increased as more people came up by steamship in search of riches. At one point, Stewart supported four newspapers, and saloons and brothels lined the busy streets. The boom, however, was short-lived, and when the riches ran dry, so did the population. Later mining efforts brought people back to the area, but that revival, too, came to an end. Today, Stewart's port shuffles logs to southerly ports and Hyder (population 90) ekes out an existence as the 'friendliest ghost town in Alaska.' Some 40,000 tourists come through every summer, and most of them get 'Hyderized' by slamming back a shot of 190-proof alcohol at the Glacier Inn,

whose walls are covered in signed dollar bills.

The towns collectively greet visitors to the area, and you wouldn't know they're in separate countries if it weren't for the small customs booth. The customs folks say they mostly check for guns (that could potentially be brought in to Hyder by boat) and booze. They say the postal code (V0T 1W0) sums it up: Very Old Town, One Way Out. You can use Canadian currency in both towns, and you can mail letters via the US Postal Service in Hyder or Canada Post in Stewart – whichever saves you more international postage.

From Hyder, take the Salmon Glacier Rd to **Fish Creek**, about 3km past Hyder, where you can stand on a viewing platform, see the salmon swimming upstream to spawn and watch bears hungrily feeding on them. The best time to do this is between late July and September. The gravel road, which runs parallel to Alaska's Tongass National Forest on the other side of the Salmon River, ultimately heads up to the spectacular Salmon Glacier. Before attempting this beautiful but bumpy drive, pick up a copy of the *Salmon Glacier Self Guided Auto Tour* from the Visitor Info Centre (☎ 250-636-9224, 888-366-5999, fax 250-636-2199) in Stewart. The center is open 9 am to 7 pm daily, June through September; 1 to 5 pm daily at other times of the year.

Places to Stay

The *Rainey Creek Municipal Campground* (☎ 250-636-2537), on 8th Ave in Stewart, offers sites for $10, showers and flush toilets. Expect a similar situation at the *Bear River Trailer Court & RV Park* (☎ 250-636-9205), just off Hwy 37A as you come into Stewart. Over in Hyder, the *Sealaska Inn* (☎ 250-636-2486, 888-393-1199) charges $32 for sleeping rooms with shared baths or $52 for rooms with private baths. The inn also rents camping sites ($10), with coin laundry and shower facilities, at the south end of town.

In Stewart, the only accommodations in town are at *King Edward Motel* and the *King Edward Hotel*. Register for both at the hotel (☎ 250-636-2244, 800-663-3126) on

5th Ave. Hotel rooms cost $60/70 single/double, but the newer rooms at the motel across the street go for $70/80.

NORTH OF MEZIADIN JUNCTION

Back on the Stewart-Cassiar Hwy, you'll come across pretty **Kinaskan Lake Provincial Park**. This park, excellent for trout fishing, offers lakeside campsites ($12) with pit toilets (but no showers) and free wood. At the Tahltan town of **Iskut**, the gateway to Spatsizi Plateau Wilderness Park, you'll find a grocery store, gas pump and two excellent places to stay. South of Iskut, the ***Red Goat Lodge*** (☎ 250-234-3261, 888-733-4628), on the shores of Eddontenajon Lake, is a haven for travelers, with hostel accommodations, a coin-op laundry and communal kitchen facilities. Beds in dorm-style rooms cost $15/18 for members/non-members. You can camp alongside the lake for $13 or stay in one of the cabins, which start at $85 (for two). The lodge rents canoes and organizes trips into the parks.

North of Iskut, the ***Bear Paw Resort*** features an alpine hotel (rooms are $95) and theme-room cabins starting at $60. The resort offers horseback riding, boating and canoeing on the river, as well as hiking trips. There's also a restaurant, saloon, hot tub and sauna.

Spatsizi Plateau Wilderness Park

This vast wilderness of more than 675,000 hectares includes the Spatsizi Uplands, the Stikine Plateau and the headwaters of the Stikine River. The park is undeveloped and isolated. From the Tatogga Junction on Hwy 16, drive north 361km on the Cassiar Hwy (Hwy 37) to Ealue Lake Rd, where you turn east and drive 22km. At this point, a rough road on an old rail track extends 114km to the park entrance. From here, access to the park is only on foot, by horse or canoe. Most people in canoes start at Tuaton Lake and paddle down the Stikine River. You can also arrive via floatplane.

In the park, Gladys Lake Ecological Reserve provides habitat for Stone sheep, mountain goats, moose, grizzly and black bears, caribou and wolves. The park's trails are often little more than vague notions across the untouched landscape. You won't find any campgrounds, although there are some primitive cabins on Cold Fish Lake for the use of people arriving by float plane. For more information, contact BC Parks in Smithers (☎ 250-847-7320) or the area supervisor in Dease Lake (☎ 250-771-4591). Mail inquiries to: BC Parks, District Manager, Bag 5000, Smithers, V0J 2N0.

Stikine River Recreation Area

This narrow park west of Dease Lake connects the Spatsizi Plateau Wilderness Park with the Mt Edziza Provincial Park and serves as the pull-out for canoe trips starting in Spatsizi. Past the bridge, the river thrusts through the spectacular **Grand Canyon of the Stikine**, an 80km stretch through a steep-walled canyon that is completely unnavigable by boat. The canyon, composed of volcanic rock carved out by eons of river erosion, is best seen from the marked viewpoints along the Telegraph Creek Rd.

Mt Edziza Provincial Park

This 230,000-hectare park protects a volcanic landscape featuring lava flows, basalt plateaus and cinder cones surrounding an extinct shield volcano. Though it's inaccessible by car, you can hike, horseback ride or fly into the park by making arrangements in Telegraph Creek or Dease Lake. Because there are no services in the park, you must be completely prepared to go it alone.

Dease Lake & Telegraph Creek

Originally inhabited by the Tahltan Natives, the area was first visited by Hudson's Bay Company traders between 1838 and 1841 and settled by Placer minors after the discovery of gold along Dease Creek in 1872. That gold rush was short-lived, but 30 years later, prospectors and miners on the Klondike Gold Rush followed the Stikine River and its tributaries north to Dawson City.

When the Canadian and US governments decided to build the Alaska Hwy, they created a demand for manpower and materials that had never been needed before. Suddenly, officials were searching for routes by which they could bring vast amounts of asphalt, gas, oil and other equipment needed to build airstrips and supply the highway construction.

The Stikine-Dease corridor, connected to the coast by Telegraph Creek, suddenly became a busy but complex transportation route. Ships carrying building supplies from Seattle hauled them all the way up to the Stikine River mouth. From there, riverboats shuttled the materials to Telegraph Creek, where they'd get loaded onto trucks and driven up the Stikine Valley to Dease Lake. From Dease, the loads would again be transferred to barges and transported down Dease Lake, then up the Dease or Liard Rivers.

Once WWII was over, the road became a transportation route to the now-defunct Cassiar asbestos mines, which operated for 40 years before finally shutting down in 1992. Interestingly, today all access to Cassiar is restricted.

Today, Dease Lake is a small stop on the highway, a supply center for people venturing into the wilderness. The couple of hotels in town include the large *Northway Motor Inn* (☎ 250-771-5341), a busy stop for truckers, with a restaurant (across the parking lot) and basic rooms for $65/70 single/double. Nicer accommodations can be found on the east side of the highway at the new *Arctic Divide Inn* (☎ 250-771-3119), where rooms in a lovely log cabin start at $65.

Take the very worthwhile 113km (one-way) side trip to Telegraph Creek by following the Telegraph Creek Rd west from Dease Lake. The mostly gravel road is steep and narrow. You'll have no problem driving in a car, but you'll definitely want to leave large trailers behind. The incredibly photogenic route follows the Stikine River as it winds its way toward the coast. In Telegraph, you can arrange river trips, eat and sleep at the *Stikine Riversong* (☎ 250-235-3196).

Boya Lake Provincial Park

This stunning little park about 100km north of Dease Lake surrounds the shock-ingly turquoise Boya Lake. Dotted with small tree-covered islets, this warm lake looks like something out of the tropics. You can camp right on the shore. The campground includes pit toilets, a boat launch and 45 sites ($12).

ATLIN

• population 480

Surrounded by the huge icefields and glaciers of the northern Coast Mountains, this small, remote town in the northwestern-most corner of BC sits alongside the 145km-long land-locked fjord known as Atlin Lake. Born in 1898 on the back of the Klondike Gold Rush, Atlin had gold of its own in nearby Pine Creek, which brought in a fast rush of prospectors. In town, colorful houses face the lake, with boats or floatplanes parked in front. Atlin served as the location for the filming of Disney's *Never Cry Wolf*, based on the book by Farley Mowat.

At the southwest corner of the lake is the imposing Llewellyn Glacier, whose meltwater carries glacial sediment to the lake, making it a fantastic hue of aquamarine. The glacier lies in the **Atlin Provincial Park & Recreation Area** – 271,134 hectares of icefields and glaciers, all of it only accessible by floatplane or boat. For any ventures into the wilderness, be it by kayak or skis, contact Backcountry Sports (☎ 250-651-2424).

The small **Atlin Museum** (☎ 250-651-7552), housed in a 1902 schoolhouse, offers area information; it's open mid-May to early September. For more information, visit the Web site www.atlin.net.

To get to Atlin, drive all the way to the end of the Stewart-Cassiar Hwy, just west of Watson Lake in the Yukon, and turn west onto the Alaska Hwy (Hwy 1). Turn south off Hwy 1 at Jake's Corner and follow Hwy 7; from there, it's 98km along a partially gravel road to the town.

Tatshenshini-Alsek Provincial Wilderness Park

Jointly managed by BC Parks and the Champagne and Aishihik First Nations, this recently designated park on the northwest tip of BC is only accessible through the

THE NORTH

Yukon or Alaska. At nearly a million hectares, the park superseded Tweedsmuir Provincial Park (981,000 hectares) as the largest park in the province. The place evokes intense historical sentiment for the Champagne and Aishihik people, who are trying to reclaim the land from the government. In 1999, remains of a man, thought to be about 500 years old, were found melting from one of the glaciers. Named 'Kwaday Dan Sinchi' (meaning 'not long ago person found'), the corpse has piqued serious inter-est, and archaeological studies are now under way to find out more.

Those who venture here often come to try river-rafting expeditions on the incredi-bly pristine Tatshenshini and Alsek Rivers. This river system passes Kluane National Park in the Yukon and Glacier Bay Na-tional Park in Alaska. As such, permits to raft the rivers are hard to come by and have lots of restrictions. For information, contact the Ministry of Environment in Victoria (☎ 604-387-4427).

LONELY PLANET

You already know that Lonely Planet produces more than this one guidebook, but you might not be aware of the other products we have on this region. Here is a selection of titles that you may want to check out as well:

Vancouver
ISBN 0 86442 659 3
US$14.95 • UK£8.99

Pacific Northwest
ISBN 0 86442 534 1
US$24.95 • UK£14.99

Alaska
ISBN 0 86442 754 9
US$18.99 • UK£12.99

Seattle
ISBN 0 86442 537 6
US$14.95 • UK£8.99

Available wherever books are sold.

Index

Abbreviations

AB - Alberta

YT - Yukon Territory

Text

A

Bold indicates maps.

Boxed Text

MAP LEGEND

ROUTES

City | Regional
...............Freeway
...............Toll Freeway
...............Primary Road
...............Secondary Road
...............Tertiary Road
...............Dirt Road
...............Pedestrian Mall
...............Steps
)=== (...............Tunnel
— — — — ....Trail
• • • • • • • •...............Walking Tour
...............Path

TRANSPORTATION

├──●──┤...............Train
──M──...............Metro
......⊟......Bus Route
— — ⊟ —...............Ferry

HYDROGRAPHY

...............River; Creek
...............Canal
...............Lake
⊙...............Spring; Rapid
◈ ≺...............Waterfall
◯ ◯ ◯...............Dry; Salt Lake

ROUTE SHIELDS

(1) Trans-Canada Highway
(95) Provincial Highway

BOUNDARIES

— • — • — ....International
— • • — • • —...............Province
— — — — ....County
— — — —...............Disputed

AREAS

↗...............Beach
...............Building
...............Campus
...............Cemetery
...............Forest
❀ ⬚...............Garden; Zoo
▣...............Golf Course
...............Park
...............Plaza
...............Reservation
...............Sports Field
⚓ ⚯...............Swamp; Mangrove

POPULATION SYMBOLS

✪ CAPITAL	National Capital	● Large City	Large City
◉ CAPITAL	Provincial Capital	● Medium City	Medium City
		● Small City	Small City
		● Town; Village	Town; Village

MAP SYMBOLS

■...............Place to Stay
▼...............Place to Eat
●...............Point of Interest

✚	Airfield	✚	Church	▥	Museum
✖	Airport	⊞	Cinema	▣	Observatory
▩	Archeological Site; Ruin	◲	Dive Site	▲	Park
⑤	Bank	◨	Embassy; Consulate	ℙ	Parking Area
◙	Baseball Diamond	⋈	Footbridge	)(	Pass
✖	Battlefield	◐	Gas Station	⊕	Picnic Area
⚲	Bike Trail	◎	Hospital	★	Police Station
◎	Border Crossing	❶	Information	▣	Pool
▲	Buddhist Temple	ⓐ	Internet Café	▣	Post Office
▣	Bus Station; Terminal	✺	Lighthouse	▣	Pub; Bar
▣	Cable Car; Chairlift	※	Lookout	⛟	RV Park
▣	Campground	✖	Mine	⊟	Shelter
▣	Castle	◧	Mission	⩗	Shipwreck
▦	Cathedral	⚘	Monument	✪	Shopping Mall
⌂	Cave	▲	Mountain	⚵	Skiing - Cross Country

⚐	Skiing - Downhill
▥	Stately Home
⚲	Surfing
✡	Synagogue
☯	Tao Temple
▣	Tax
☎	Telephone
▣	Theate
◉	Toilet - Public
■	Tomb
✦	Trailhead
▣	Tram Stop
▣	Transportation
▲	Volcano
☒	Winery

Note: not all symbols displayed above appear in this book

LONELY PLANET OFFICES

Australia
Locked Bag 1, Footscray, Victoria 3011
☎ 03 8379 8000 fax 03 8379 8111
email talk2us@lonelyplanet.com.au

UK
10a Spring Place, London NW5 3BH
☎ 020 7428 4800 fax 020 7428 4828
email go@lonelyplanet.co.uk

USA
150 Linden Street, Oakland, California 94607
☎ 510 893 8555, TOLL FREE 800 275 8555
fax 510 893 8572
email info@lonelyplanet.com

France
1 rue du Dahomey, 75011 Paris
☎ 01 55 25 33 00 fax 01 55 25 33 01
www.lonelyplanet.fr

World Wide Web: www.lonelyplanet.com or AOL keyword: lp
Lonely Planet Images: lpi@lonelyplanet.com.au